THE
AGE
OF
HAPPY
PROBLEMS

Books by HERBERT GOLD

Novels

BIRTH OF A HERO
THE PROSPECT BEFORE US
THE MAN WHO WAS NOT
   WITH IT
THE OPTIMIST
THEREFORE BE BOLD

Short Stories

LOVE AND LIKE
FICTION OF THE FIFTIES
   (*Editor*)

Essays

THE AGE OF HAPPY PROBLEMS

THE
AGE
OF
HAPPY
PROBLEMS

Herbert Gold

THE DIAL PRESS NEW YORK 1962

Library of Congress Catalog Card Number: 62-16333

ACKNOWLEDGMENTS

The essay, "A Dog in Brooklyn, a Girl in Detroit: A Life Among
the Humanities," is published for the first time in this volume.
Acknowledgment is made to the following publications in whose
pages these essays first appeared: *The Atlantic Monthly*, March
1957, for "The Age of Happy Problems;" *Mademoiselle*, February
1958, for "How to Be an Artist's Wife;" *The Atlantic Monthly*, November 1957, for "Divorce as a Moral Act;" *Charm*, October 1959,
for "The Bachelor's Dilemma;" *Partisan Review*, Summer 1957, for
"The Mystery of Personality in the Novel;" *Hudson Review*, Winter 1958, for "The Fair Apple of Progress" (originally published as
"The Purity and Cunning of Sherwood Anderson"); *Hudson Review*,
Winter 1957, for "The New Upper-Middle Soap Opera;" *Playboy*,
February 1958, for "The American as Hipster" (originally published
as "The Beat Mystique"); *The Nation*, November 17, 1957, for
"Hip, Cool, Beat, and Frantic;" *Metronome*, February 1961, for
"The Rise of the Treeniks;" *The Atlantic Monthly*, September
1960, for "Fiction of the Sixties;" *discovery*, Number 1, for "Cleveland: Inflation-on-the-Erie;" *Hudson Review*, Summer 1952, for
"Paris: Notes from *La Vie de Bohème*;" *The Yale Review*, Autumn
1954, for "Americans in the Port of Princes;" *Playboy*, June 1961,
for "The Great Divide" (originally published as "The Great American Divide"); *Playboy*, September 1960, for "The Changing Village" (originally published as "The Restless Mecca"); *The Noble
Savage*, Number 3, for "Death in Miami Beach."

DESIGNED BY ALAN M. HEICKLEN
MANUFACTURED IN THE UNITED STATES OF AMERICA
BY THE HADDON CRAFTSMEN, INC., SCRANTON, PA.

For Ann and Judy

Contents

PART II: AMERICAN PLACES

Introduction

THIS IS A REPORT about where one man stands on some matters of teaching, learning, writing, love, marriage, work, and the prospect of death, and how he came to this stand in the cities of America.

Setting out a few final, summary pages, I wish to try to call up what I have discovered in the pleasure of writing these interim communiqués, twelve years of voyages around part of the world and up certain of its dilemmas. Most of the sections of this book are aimed at specific and nonparallel subjects—Americans abroad, the hipsters, divorce, Miami Beach, Sherwood Anderson, the craft of fiction, the vocation of a teacher—and yet each seems to mark out part of the map, a place on a roadway. The map takes shape as I trace my way from one gathering of thoughts to the next. How can I total it up? What is the map of the map?

Well, to begin with, Plato was wrong. The life of contemplation is not sufficient. Neither is virtue enough. And for another thing, Plato was right. He knew that men must learn to come together in the practice of intelligence and moral privilege.

An instructive practical joke has been played on us by history since the time of Socrates. Now we know too much and we have had too much experience with evil ever to be long satisfied with the hope of ideal private purity in the quest of virtue and knowledge. To be alone in wisdom is to possess only the ghost of wisdom; it is like being a lover with no one to love. And as in love and understanding, so in the effort toward a moral life. We cannot accept the bondage of others without being ourselves enslaved. The separated soul moves inexorably from smugness to explosion. The contemporary literary parody of Diogenes is Hemingway, who turns out to be seeking good repute more than glory, formula more than wisdom, peace to his troubles and not a resolution to the challenge of mortality. Looking for an honest man in the market place, Diogenes carried a lantern, not a mirror. The autobiographical compulsion in a writer leads to a pathos which has the character of the sentences on tombstones; we do not stand moved by the stiff words—we weep to honor the body buried beneath. And when the words have been inscribed by a self-indulgent living corpse, we stand uneasy in our sympathy, we are excluded by self-pity, we have been had. The body is not even present. It is elsewhere, drafting new appeals before the mirror. Style, even the style of genius, shrivels to fashion in the paper fire of vanity. To save ourselves we must return to Aristotle's sense of the good man—the man who exercises his power of intelligence in an effort to master time and mortality through works apart from building his own person. Out of this effort come tragedy and comedy in art, comes the labor of freedom in life.

Therefore, as an American and a writer, I have aspired in these essays to an active use of my strength within the terms of those possibilities available to me. Given my failings of wisdom and virtue, there is plenty of room for future risk and maneuver under this program.

And not only do I need changing, but my friends do too, and America, and the world. Everyone knows this. Not everyone knows that there is still quite a bit of life— freedom to create—left in America and the world. I now ask myself what everyone asks upon ritual occasions: Is there a better time coming? Is final disaster just ahead?

Well, the way to know and affect the future is not through stupefied waiting, solemn assertion, or viewing with alarm. Gravity of tone and deep seriousness of manner befit television announcers more than thinking human beings. We need all our sources of energy, including appetite and play, lightness of spirit and agility of body. We need a whole list of things. Let us pin the list above the breadbox:

We need to hold the flower of feeling in our hands without crushing it. American wives need to squeeze through the narrow gates of vanity and self-loathing; American husbands the same. They both need to give up trying to solve the problems of marriage by a pious worrying about "our relationship." An active use of ourselves does not consist in panicking into fallout shelters, passive politics, make-do marriages, jobs defined by that dream world of "security." We need to give up the fashion of having "insights," which, in a society delighted by psychology because it is undelighted by most other things, has become a repulsive game of one-upmanship. I insight you; you insight me; together we know nothing of value. Instead, why don't we engage in some common labor? It is mere vanity to go about the earth listening for the rattle in the throats of the dying, and a suicidal vanity to listen for it in our own throats. Let us stop congratulating ourselves on our subjectivity, trying to find the whole number in an infinite series of fractions, and start putting two and two together. Having "Healthy Goals" is not a proper goal, either; leave that to the insurance salesmen and the educationists; for if we are alive, goals arise beautifully, like the hypotheses of a scientist or the intentions of an artist, correcting themselves through continuous activity in the continuous here and now.

Nice hobbies for the retired and planned distractions for the adolescent cannot disguise the fact that intelligent participation in community life in America is increasingly difficult. We need more civil defense against the spirit of Civil Defense. The notion of intelligent participation in one's own life also becomes a paradox when most of an intelligent adult's waking hours are spent at a make-it, make-out, make-do job. An archetypical confession begins, "I was a teen-age senior citizen." Who is old and who is young? When is motion a substitute for action, paralysis a substitute for patience? If we set out to examine the quality of American life in this time of happy problems, we must go forth knowing that every issue is in doubt. Fortunately, a fine old saying is just as true in its reversed form: *Doubt moves mountains.*

Perhaps, amid so much doubt about society and personality, we should be reminded again of the basic requirement for human life, once the primary demands of food, housing, and shelter are met. True, the Russians, the Chinese, Africa, world government, missiles, bombs, fallout, highway congestion, sex, and junk mail all present problems which fully qualify for personal reflection and action. (Mail it back! Return to Sender!) But as individuals, what we need first of all is to find a work we like; and as a nation, a future to believe in, contained within an immediate present worthy of respect, engaging our best energies. Then the problems of love and "communication," boredom and anxiety, delinquency for the young and real-estate-promotion pensionvilles for the aged can diminish into larger possibilities. When the emphasis is put where it belongs, on creative personal and national activity, not on a succession of phony goals cranked out by a succession of disposable deep thinkers, we will be equipped to respond significantly to the great social and political challenges.

These are finally all metaphysical questions, questions about the meaning of human life on earth. There is no doubt that the whole concept of man and civilization is up for grabs. Military weaponry provides a dramatic symbol and advance scout of the enemy, but it is only one manifestation of the tendency within men to seek destruction. Wide awake, we find ourselves asking a nightmare question: Is humanity possible? An impious question; we must ask it. But before we can deal effectively "in general" with the menace of race suicide, we must first in particular, as individuals, not only believe we have a right to survive but also *want* to survive.

One of the most popular poems in contemporary anthologies of verse is that which concludes: "We must love one another or die." Students and teachers enjoy this poem; it expresses a fine, elevating fantasy alternative; the proper choice can be made so nice and easy. But the poet who wrote it, overtaken by scruple, squirming, apparently an honest man, has long since revised his thought. In later editions of W. H. Auden's work, the poem has a new conclusion: "We must love one another *and* die." It remains in its lying form in the anthologies; editors have not yet corrected the soft text with the hard truth, which is so much more difficult to accept. For the sake of life we must try to love one another—moral imperative; but we shall all die—*fact*—no matter what we do. In the meantime, loving if we can, we send our lives down the roads of possibility, meeting the inevitability of final mortality when it comes and, in prospect, at every pause of joy and sorrow. And yet, despite death, despite suffering and murder, despite cruelty and vanity, despite stupidity and injustice—and perhaps, indeed, because of these natural enemies in the jungle of society which is a part of the jungle of nature—we can take joy in the power we are

given toward recognition and remedy of defeat and toward
the exercise of each possible victory of the human spirit.

This book, then, represents a going and a coming, in
and out of the cage of self and the cage of the real world.
I grant that it runs the risk of tourism; tourism, however,
is a general condition of spirit in our time. Those Southern
intellectuals who took their stand in an agrarian Dixie with
a manifesto a generation ago are mostly presently biv-
ouacked in the North. We carry as much tradition as we
can bear, but look for our truths where they may wander.
Both the world and the self are spinning in space. To find
stable balance while in rapid motion is the dangerous
modern endeavor.

An element of presumption remains. How dare we
fret from our unique privileges about our personal dilemmas
in a time of mass war, mass destruction, mass inertia, mass
everything, when the will to death seems to be on the
way to total and inane triumph? How dare anyone, how
dare I? There seems to be no other way to think about the
prime matters of life on earth than to gather the evidence
from our own particular lives. Otherwise we fall victim to
what I think of as the Uncle Distortion. "Let's talk about
things in general," asked my uncle.

"What about?"

"Things in general."

"But what *about?*"

"Things in general, didn't you hear me? You've been
to college," he said irritably. "You should be able to talk
about things in general."

But I'd rather not; and I'd better not.

Instead, through place and situation, time and event,
these essays attempt another sort of reckoning with the
voyage projected through fictions and characters in my
stories and novels. Truth is truth only by a defiant marriage of words and acts. (I mean here true statement about
how we live and how we should live and why.) How can a

conventional symbol, a word, be joined to a specific, never-to-be-repeated experience thrown up in time? That is a perpetual question in the history of thought about the act of thinking. The word, which is a distorting glass, is also the only means we have toward knowledge. Marriage, which is a distorting convention about love, wrenches two creatures out of one life and puts them together again in a new and altered one. There is an excuse for marriage. It builds as it distorts. There is an excuse for microscopes and telescopes (though they do indeed distort) and so there may also be an excuse for words in general and for these particular words, written to various ends in various places, over a dozen years, and yet coming round to some repeated general points about our lives together in America. There is a connection between a specific busted gambler in the Western Union office in Reno, writing that practical, insane, collect poem which goes RUN OF LUCK SEND MONEY QUICK, and the way we all live now, the anxious shuddering through our lives of politics, love, work, and expectations for the future.

Accidents of autobiography, observation in streets and books, generalizing theory, experimental hypothesis, the tentative and the evanescent—these are the accumulations of an effort at specific focus. I have not even excluded ideas about literature as a legitimate part of thought about the real world. Inconsistencies appear regularly; contra-dictions are a steady part of the enterprise; but I have hoped to give the evidence in experience for judgments; and in this, the habit of telling stories—the habit of the true lie —is of good service. Discreetly I warn myself, however, against the danger of seduction by what we can now recog-nize as the Nephew Distortion—an oblivious, dreamy trust in particularity and the intercourse of thought and event.

A note about the psychology of creation should be made here. Some poets commit suicide. But not in the middle of the working day. For the poet or novelist at work, even the most depressed one, a cock-crow of relish in nature sounds through the dawn air. He knows that if he tracks the cock by his call, he may find a bedraggled rooster howling from the top of a dungheap while the chicks pluck corn, the hens shuffle feathers. Which doesn't mean that the cock's song is not really triumphant. And the poet too, judging himself and the world most severely, nonetheless finds the world and himself worthy of the loud call of judgment, at least while he is at his labor of song. He keeps libidinous and happy with the hope of mastering his experience.

We have now touched upon a revelation which must seem shameful to the puritan heart. Let us give it away brazenly. The scientist, the philosopher, or the artist always takes a secret pleasure in the vividness of his feelings and the power of his invention, even if the occasions which elicit them are tragic. Trudging across the world with the common sack of morality on his back ("He still has that sack!"—Henry David Thoreau), the poet may condemn himself with the puritan's shame. What right has he to make joyous explorations in suffering? But he does. Why should Dostoevski ease his guilt for even a moment by the monuments he erects upon his dark excavations? He does anyway. This self-love and/or self-hatred may be a flaw and is certainly an injustice viewed from the traditional ideal of democracy, in which privilege is won only as a loan or a mandate. But there is a justification in history and in democratic intention (Fortunate that there is a justification; otherwise it would go unjustified!) Life in the world and the life of art are alike in this, that we are awakened to reality by tragedy, dulled by inferior imagination and a clogged, eventless passage through experience. We need a deepening of the sense of reality more than we need an inflation of moral okayness. Anxiety is caused more by boredom than by any other sort of suffering. To see clearly, playfully, with sorrow, inventively—*clearly*—must be left as an individual option even in a tragic time. The fact of death has always been democratic; the chance of sudden death has never been so impartially shared; but no two deaths are alike. To act with love upon vision is still the best aim we can give the living soul.

And who knows if that modern faith may not yet be redeemed?—that to understand and to feel can make the condition of mortality habitable. Stoicism provides a leaky roof, but the best one available to the private citizen while, chortling furiously in his kitchen, weaving his fuses and dipping his time bombs, he plots the reform of the universe. He might start by venturing out into the rain; he might start with the holes in his own roof.

HERBERT GOLD

January 1962
San Francisco

PART ONE

American Events

The Age of Happy Problems

RECENTLY I HAVE had occasion to live again near my old college campus. I went into a hole-in-the-wall bakery where the proprietor recognized me after ten years. "You haven't changed a bit, son," he said, "but can you still digest my pumpernickel? The stomach gets older, no? Maybe you want something softer now—a nice little loaf I got here."

He had worn slightly. But for me the change was from twenty-two to thirty-two, and it is this ten-year time that I want to think about—the generation which came back from the war to finish college on the GI Bill and is now deep into its career. We are the generation which knew the Depression only through the exhilaration of the burgeoning New Deal and the stunned passion of war. I remember the bank crash because my mother wept and I said, "If we're poor now, can I wear corduroy pants?" For the most part, we were taken care of and never hopelessly hunted jobs. Now some of us say we are cool, say we are beat; but most of us are allrightniks—doing okay. We are successful. In the late forties and the fifties, it was hard to know economic struggle and want—and for the most part we didn't experience these

· 3 ·

traditional elements of youth—and it was hard for the skilled and the trained not to know success. We did not doubt overmuch. We have done well. How well?

"Money money money," as Theodore Roethke says.

> I have married my hands to perpetual agitation,
> I run, I run to the whistle of money.
>
> Money money money
> Water water water

I should like to take a look at some of the college idealists. The lawyer, fascinated by "the philosophy of law," now uses his study to put a smooth surface on his cleverness. Cardozo and Holmes? Very interesting, but let's find that loophole. The doctor who sent flowers to the first mother whose baby he delivered now specializes in "real-estate medicine"—his practice gives him capital for buying apartment houses. The architect who sat up all night haranguing his friends about Lewis Mumford and Frank Lloyd Wright now works for a mass builder who uses bulldozers to level trees and slopes, then puts up tri-level, semi-detached, twenty-year-mortgaged, fundamentally identical dormitories for commuters. He admits that his designs make no decent sense, but they do have that trivial, all-important meaning: "It's what the market wants, man. You'd rather I taught city planning for six thousand a year?"

The actor becomes a disc jockey, the composer an arranger, the painter a designer; the writer does TV scripts in that new classic formula, "happy stories about happy people with happy problems." How hard it is to be used at our best! One of the moral issues of every age has been that of finding a way for men and women to test, reach, and overreach their best energies. Society has always worked to level us. Socrates has always made it hot for the citizens in the market place. But there was usually room for the heroic— hemlock not a serious deterrent—and perhaps rarely so much room on all levels as in the frontier turbulence of the nineteenth and early twentieth century in America. Hands reached out like the squirming, grasping, struggling railroad networks; the open society existed; freedom had a desperate allure for the strongly ambitious, and men stepped up to take their chances—Abraham Lincoln and William James, Mark Twain and Melville, Edison and Rockefeller and Bet-a-Million Gates.

Allowing for a glitter of nostalgia on what we imagine about the past, still something has happened to change the old, movemented, free, open American society to something persuasive, plausible, comfortable, and much less open. We are prosperous, we get what we think we want, we have a relatively stable economy without totalitarian rule. "I'm not selling out," my friend the architect says, "I'm buying in." Without attempting a simple explanation of the causes of this age of happy problems, let us look at its consequences for the new postwar young people who should be in full action toward their ambitions and the surest, sturdiest signs of a civilization's health.

What are these personal symptoms? How is the vital individual human creature doing in his staff meetings, at his family's table, over the baby's bassinet, and with that distant secret self that he may sometimes meet at the water cooler? Well, for this man it is very hard to be exceptional. Talent apart, he has too much to do, too much on his mind, to give himself over to his best energies. Think, for example, of the writers in the advertising agencies, on TV, or in the colleges. They all wanted to write great books; they tend now to prefer "competence" as an ideal to greatness. Some of them are trying, but they risk the situation of the girl in the short-story writing class: "I can't be a creative writer, I can't, because I'm still a stupid virgin." She will take up going steady, she will take up marriage; she will be mildly disappointed; she will remain as she was, but aging—"adjusted," "integrated," virgin to danger, struggle, and the main chance of love and work.

In composite, in our thirties, we of this prosperous and successful generation are still in good health and rather fast at tennis (but practicing place shots which will eliminate the need to rush the net); hair receding but still attractive to college girls, or at least recent graduates; a slight heaviness at the middle which makes us fit our jackets with especial care (sullen jowls beginning, too) or, if not that, a skinniness of anxiety (etching around the mouth, dryness of lips). We go to an athletic club. We play handball in heavy shirts "to sweat it off."

The girls we marry are beautiful in wondrous ways. Savant make-up is no longer sufficient. Blemishes are scraped until the skin is pink and new; scars are grown away by cortisone injections—what reason to be marked in this world?; noses are remade, the same for mother and daughter, just like heredity. Money is spent much more gracefully than in those fantastic times when silver coins were put in ears and jewels in navels.

The old truth—"we must all come from someplace"—is amended in 1956. We can create ourselves in our own image. And what is our own image? The buttery face in the Pond's advertisement, the epicene face in the Marlboro publicity.

The matters that we are told to worry about—and perhaps we think we worry about them—do not really trouble us. The prospect of war is like a vague headache, no worse. The memory of war is even dimmer. A depression is something which will reduce the value of our shares in the mutual fund, make us keep the old car another year. Radioactive fallout and the slow destruction of the human species through cancerous mutation—well, what is so much bother to imagine cannot really come to pass. Who lets the newspaper interfere with a good meal?

2

Still, we are not blithe spirits; birds we are not. This generation is particularly distinguished by its worry about making its wives happy, about doing right by its kids (title of a hugely popular paperbound book: *How to Play with Your Child*), about acquiring enough leisure and symbols of leisure, which it hopes to cash in for moral comfort. *Fortune* reports a method used by salesmen to get the second room air conditioner to the couple which already has one in its bedroom. "The machine operates as expected? Fine! You sleep better with it? So do I, that's just dandy. But, friends, let me tell you how I sleep so much better now that I know my kiddies are cool and comfy, too."

This capitalizes on the child-oriented anxiety which the class known commercially as Young Marrieds has been taught to feel by modern psychiatry. Advertisements for *McCall's*, "The Magazine of Togetherness," demonstrate Togetherness in a brilliant summer scene. The man, wearing a white skirtlike apron and a proud simper, is bending to serve a steak to his wife (summer frock, spike heels), who will season it for them and for their happy gamboling children. The little boy and girl are peeking and smiling. The wife is lying in a garden chair. Togetherness consists in the husband's delighting his wife and kids by doing the cooking.

Actually, of course, most American women don't want to go this far. They are already equal with men. Women are usually too wise to define "equal" as "better than." It is not momism or any such simple psychological gimmick that tells this sad tale. The consumer culture—in which leisure is a menace to be met by anxious continual consuming—devours both the masculinity of men and the femininity of women. The life of consuming requires a neuter anxiety, and the pressure to conform, to watch for our cues, to consume, makes us all the same—we are customers—only with slightly different gadgets. Women have long bought men's shirts; men are buying colognes with "that exciting musky masculine tang."

Togetherness represents a curious effort by a woman's magazine to bring men back into the American family. Togetherness does not restore to the man a part of his old-time independence. It does not even indicate that he may be the provider with an independent role defined partly by ambitions outside his family. Instead, it suggests the joys of being a helpmate, a part of the woman's full life, and battens greedily on the contemporary male's anxiety about pleasing his wife. The Togetherness theme has been a great commercial success. A full-page advertisement by that canny old American institution, the New York Stock Exchange, shows a photograph of a harried young man pleading with a young woman on a parlor couch. She remains unconvinced, pouting, hands gloved and folded together, as brutal as the shocked beauties in the classical halitosis or B.O. tragedies. The caption reads: "Is the girl you want to marry reluctant to say Yes? Do you need to build character with your wife? Then just use the magic words: I'LL START A MONTHLY IN-VESTMENT PLAN."

It used to be thought that answering economic needs was the main purpose of man's economic efforts. Now, however, an appeal to emotional insecurity about money—without crass financial trouble—can do good work for an advertiser. "Do you need to build character with your wife?" This is whimsey with a whammy in it. Money works symbolically to stimulate, then assuage male doubts.

> SHE: What can the stock do for our marriage?
> HE: It can help keep it sweet and jolly because when we own stock we are part-owners of the company.

In the image projected by this advertisement, the wife is prosecutor, judge, and jury. She may fall into a less exalted role, however, while her husband is downtown making the money which will go for food, clothing, shelter, and sound common stocks. That she too frets about keeping her marriage sweet and jolly is obvious. The popular media again point to trouble while pitching a new solution to her problems. One of the former radio soap operas is now sponsored by Sleep-eze. Apparently almost everyone uses soap these days, but not everyone has caught on to the virtues of non-habit-forming sedatives. Want your husband to love you? This pill will help or your money back. "Ladies! Fall asleep without that unsightly twisting and turning."

It's time to mention Barbara. A tough wise creature of a girl, Barbara comes to this observation out of her marriage and love life: "Men worry too much about making the girl happy. We seem to scare them out of themselves. Let them really be pleased—that's what we want most of all—and then we'll be happy. Delighted. But really."

In other words, long live primary narcissism! And secondary. And tertiary. But let us call it by an older, better name—respect for the possibilities of the self. This includes the possibility of meaningful relationships with meaningful others.

3

Our wounds as a people in this time and place are not unique in kind, but the quality of difference makes this a marvelously disturbing period. The economic problem, no longer rooted in hunger for essential goods, food, housing, clothing, is an illustration of the difference. Sure, we are still busy over food—but packaged foods, luxury foods, goodies in small cans; housing—but the right house in the right neighborhood with the right furnishings and the right mortgage; clothing—but the cap with the strap in the back, Ivy League pants, charcoal gray last year and narrow lapels this year, and male fashions changing as fast as female.

It used to be thought that, given money, relative job

security, and the short work week, culture would then bloom like the gardens in the suburbs and the individual spirit would roar with the driving power of a Thunderbird getting away after a red light.

Who could have predicted that we would have to keep pace with a cultural assembly line in the leisure-time sweatshop? At least in the older sweatshop, you sighed, packed, and left the plant at last. Now we are forever harassed to give more, more, more. We no longer have to keep up with the Joneses; we must keep up with Clifton Fadiman. He is watching *you*. The steady pressure to consume, absorb, participate, receive, by eye, ear, mouth, and mail, involves a cruelty to intestines, blood pressure, and psyche unparalleled in history. The frontiersmen could build a stockade against the Indians, but what home is safe from Gilbert Highet? We are being killed with kindness. We are being stifled with cultural and material joys. Our wardrobes are full. What we really need is a new fabric that we don't have to wrinkle, spot, wash, iron, or wear. At a beautiful moment in *Walden*, Thoreau tells how he saw a beggar walking along with all his belongings in a single sack on his back. He wanted to weep for the poor man—because he still had that sack to carry.

The old-style sweatshop crippled mainly the working people. Now there are no workers left in America; we are almost all middle class as to income and expectations. Even the cultural elite labors among the latest in hi-fi equipment, trips to Acapulco and Paris, the right books in the sewn paper editions (Elizabeth Bowen, Arnold Toynbee, Jacques Barzun—these are the cultivated ones, remember), *Fortune* and the *Reporter*, art movies and the barbecue pit and the Salzburg music festival. It is too easy to keep up with the Joneses about cars and houses, but the Robert Shaw Chorale is a *challenge*. In the meantime, the man in the sweatshop is divorced or psychoanalyzed (these are perhaps remedies in a few cases); he raises adjusted children, or kills them trying; he practices Togetherness in a home with a wife who is frantic to be a woman and a nonwoman at the same time; he broods about a job which does not ask the best that he can give. But it does give security; it is a good job. (In college this same man learned about the extreme, tragic instances of desire. Great men, great books. Now he reads Evelyn Waugh.)

In his later, philosophical transmogrification, David Reisman consoles the radar-flaunting other-directeds by holding out the reward of someday being "autonomous" if they are very, very good. Same thing, brother, same thing. When he describes the autonomous personality's "intelligent" distinctions among consumer products, exercising his creative imagination by figuring out why *High Noon* is a better western than a Gene Autry, well, then, in the words of Elvis Presley:

> Ah feel so lonely,
> Ah feel so lo-oh-oh-lonely.

We're in Heartbreak Hotel where, as another singer, Yeats, put it:

> The ceremony of innocence is drowned;
> The best lack all conviction, while the worst
> Are filled with a passionate intensity.

Refusal to share to the fullest degree in the close amity of the leisure-time sweatshop is—for Mr. Riesman—a kind of ethical bohemianism. His autonomous consumer, sociable, trained, and in the know, is a critic of the distinctions between the Book-of-the-Month Club and the Reader's Subscription, Inc., marks the really good shows in his TV guide, buys educational comic books for his children, tastes the difference in fine after-dinner coffee, knows that the novel is a dead form and why. Bumper to bumper in the traffic home from work, or jammed into the commuter train, he has plenty of time to think. And he does think (thinking means worrying) while the radio blares "The House with the Stained Glass Window" or "The Magic of Believing," a little rock-and-roll philosophical number.

Does he have a moral problem, let's say, about leaving a changing neighborhood "for the sake of the children"? He is a liberal, of course, but after all, the Negroes who are moving in come from a different world, and he should not inflict his principles on his children. Still, there is a certain discomfort. He discusses it with his analyst. *Why* does he suffer from this moral qualm? Does it have some link with the ever-ambiguous relationship with parents? *What* moral problem? They are all psychological. Anxiety can be consumed like any product. And from his new, split-level, sapling-planted housing development he speeds into the city now ten miles further out.

We are a disappointed generation. We are a discontented people. Our manner of life says it aloud even if discreetly our public faces smile. The age of happy problems has brought us confusion and anxiety amid the greatest material comfort the world has ever seen. Culture has become a consolation for the sense of individual powerlessness in politics, work, and love. With gigantic organizations determining our movements, manipulating the dominion over self which alone makes meaningful communion with others possible, we ask leisure, culture, and recreation to return to us a sense of ease and authority. But work, love, and culture need to be connected. Otherwise we carry our powerlessness with us onto the aluminum garden furniture in the back yard. Power lawn mowers we can buy, of course.

The solution in our age of happy problems is not to install (on time) a central air-conditioning system and a color TV this year because the room air conditioner and the black-and-white TV last year did not change our lives in any important respect. The solution is not in stylish religious conversions or a new political party. The answer is not even that Panglossian fantasy about "the autonomous personality" which will naturally emerge out of the fatal meeting of the other-directed consumer with a subscription to the *Saturday Review*.

The ache of unfulfilled experience throbs within us. Our eyes hurt. Vicarious pleasures buzz in our heads. Isn't there something more, something more?

There is still awareness; there is still effort. "It should be every man's ambition to be his own doctor." This doesn't mean that he should not see a dentist when his tooth hurts, perhaps a psychoanalyst when his psyche hurts; but he must hold in mind the ideal maximum of humanity—the exercise of intelligence and desire within a context of active health. The Stoic philosophers had a great, although impossible, idea for these crowding times: cultivate your own garden. We cannot retreat from the world any more—we never really could—but we can look for our best gardens within the world's trouble. There we must give ourselves silence and space; we can see what the will wants; we can make decisions. Only then—having come to terms with our own particularities—can we give the world more than a graceless, prefabricated commodity.

Hope? Some sweet Barbara is hope. And a work we love. And the strength, O Lord, not to accept the easy pleasures (easy anxieties) which have pleased us (made us anxious) so far. And the strength, O Lord, you who reign undefined above the psychoanalysts and the sociologists, the market researchers and the advertising agencies, the vice-presidents and the book clubs, to refuse the easy solutions which have becalmed us so far.

Then with good belly luck we will be able to digest strong, irregular, yeasty, black bread.

1956

How to Be an Artist's Wife

HERE IS A NORMAL CASE: a girl meets a young man at a college party. Let us say he wears a red flannel shirt, leans against the fireplace with superior ease and turns upon the girl a pair of eyes whose ferocious intensity is half ambition and half near-sightedness. At this age no special achievement or public virtue has yet graced him, but his head is a convicted one. He is a writer, a painter, a musician, some species of fanatic doodler—in short, an artist. All he wants of his future is to master the mystery of personality and communicate a sense of the glory of life on earth; he is hell-bent for immortality. And that's all he wants.

In the meantime, very young, he has only his burning with a hard, gemlike flame—a variety of pouting and sulking—to keep him company at the party. He is therefore rather lonely and, for the very good reason that this girl has slim ankles, sleek legs and excellent articulations all the way up to her scalp, he tells her about himself. Having temporarily run out of steam about his life story, he suggests that they go out for coffee. Turnabout is fair play. He now begins to tell her all about *her*self.

"I like the way you talk," she remarks speculatively.

"And your eyes remind me of . . ." he answers.

Later, after many walks, talks, long afternoons and longer evenings, the girl decides that it would be nice to join this odd creature on his voyages. That at first he was an angry mystery, like jazz, pleases her—she cracked the nut. That he has doubts and dreads and moments of terrible flagging arouses her—he will always need her. That he will be a distinguished figure amid the ruck of plump merchants, young executives and "professionals" whom her college friends marry—this tickles a fond young lady with a bit of spunk and a romantic itch to astonish the folks back home.

And with her help, she solemnly resolves, he will surely be a Great Man some day. In the meantime, even if not yet great, he is greatly skilled at coaxing and cajoling, at little flattering rhymes and sudden gifts, in short, at making her feel desired and capable of desire. He is no arty egotist, oh no, not he, like those other characters on campus. He believes that her personality is a code worth deciphering and that all individuals are magical and that each human creature testifies to the only divinity that matters.

Not just his own red-flannel and myopic soul. Hers too.

"He is a *big* person," she assures her roommate and then adds, with intense feminine realism: "Or at least I think he *can* be. I'll have to knock some of the pretentiousness out of him first. Oh, but he's wonderful!"

They commune together as two people have never before communed—kisses and hamburgers and relish and kisses.

And Time is a metaphor of change, and every event is unique, and only through art can we take a hold on this perpetual flux, and the life that risks all to attain all is the only true one, and let's run away to a justice of the peace. And so they are married.

What then?

The first thing, true for every marriage, is that neither knew what they were getting into. Marriage is always a surprise, full of risks and possibilities, a dangerous creative act. Unless mated by parents or chill calculation, they begin with the artist's defiance of history: "We will sculpt, paint, dance, compose that unique work of the imagination which we have a hunch can be made to live—The Couple!"

Of course, there are ways of putting an end to this unpredictable adventure. One partner can devour the other, as the queen wasp does so gracefully: she flies very high, chased by the drones, until she chooses one desperate love and mates with him, a mile up in the sky, then eats his head and returns to earth dangling his entrails; and fatly she remembers him by laying eggs. We all know moms like the wasp queen.

Or a man, demanding the security of easy domination, can marry a girl who is unattractive to herself and overquick to gratitude, therefore content to clean up after him and do as the Master saith.

Or there is a third, very American way of abdicating from the powers of marriage. Both partners, dreading possibility, dreading risk, dreading life, afraid to stand up on their own two legs as individuals, decide to make a steadier four-legged creature that the world cannot distress. They lean on each other to look out over the city. Like the frogs in the old story, propped like that, they see only what is behind them and cry out: "Why, there's nothing on the other side of the mountain! Why, the future is like the past!" Each plays reassuring parent to the other. Marriage for the propped ones brings kitchen warmth and no venturing outside into the snow, because it might be so cold out there.

These three marriages are fear yoked to stubbornness.

They give up the revelations of conflict and the danger of a passionate growth together. In order never to face an unknown, they are content to have very little to know.

Well, if our artist is an artist and a man despite his love of pretty words or notes, he will not marry the queen wasp, the stooping serving maid, or the shy froglet. If our girl is pretty, lusty and knows it—this is charm—she will not marry a drone, a master boor, or the amphibian without even a jewel in his forehead.

Instead, they have married each other.

One moment she is twenty-one, being courted by metaphysical verse and stammering hands; the next moment, *voilà!* She is in Paris, "the capital of misery and the paradise of hope," breathless before the elegance of the Place des Vosges, cooking rabbit and goat in liters of wine, watching her husband grow his beard, and informing him one fine evening that she is very possibly pregnant.

"I finished Chapter Seven today. This time it looks really good."

"I think I'd better see that doctor Janine told us about."

"What for?"

"Listen to me, lout. We're going to have a baby."

Cries of celebration, hoots and acrobatics, great tenderness once she gets through to him. Next morning, full of importance, he goes off to his rented room and writes Chapter Eight at a single fertile sitting. Or stretches a new canvas and gets to that tricky abstraction of a guitar on the waiting easel. Or figures out how to work an effect of honking horns in his Novum Organum for Strings and Brass without echoing Gershwin enough for *The New York Times* to notice.

American marriages being what they are, the husband in the case ultimately feels quite as pregnant as the wife. Here, as on many occasions, American artist husbands are indistinguishable from American nonartist husbands. They help with the dishes or feel guilty at not helping; they suffer everything but contractions of the uterus at childbirth; they wheel buggies built like Sherman tanks, retail the gurgles of their offspring and challenge other fathers to mortal combat by snapshot. But children, the most obvious potentiality of marriage, emphasize the special dangers that the artist's wife runs. She is most vulnerable now.

Despite his several virtues, the artist is likely to fail more than most men in living up to the standards of male husbandry current in America. Lack of money is probably not an important failure to his wife: she can follow him as he makes do with the GI Bill, the odd job, the fellowship, the prize. The important failure is that of fidelity. The artist is unfaithful to his wife with the first impudent snatch of an idea that comes along. If he is unfaithful with women, well, that's a matter of individual character; but this other sort of philandering is practically universal. In pain and awful loneliness the artist's wife learns to recognize the symptoms: a glassing of the eyes as he looks a shapely notion up and down, a tense cockiness as he draws himself up to court thought, a total withdrawal from her or a pretense at participation in family life. This is more wounding than the frankest retreat.

"Did you have a good day, dear?"

"Unh."

"Thinking, dear?"

"What? What? Unh?"

It has been established that the young wife who is being responded to at the level of a stare and a grunt is an exceptionally pretty, charming, and intelligent being. A few artists marry mousy and self-effacing women who flutter about on tiptoe in order to avoid disturbing the maestro; such women present a wholly different set of problems. For the purposes of this discussion I prefer the extraordinarily pleasant specimen supplied with such gen-

erosity by American vitamins and sports and colleges—
keen, artful, looking for that best which she surely deserves.

The hard fact about a girl of this excellent sort is that
she is accustomed, especially in America, to sustained approval. She earns it, she gets it, and she comes to require
it. Having been reared, up through her college days, in a
culture whose expectations differentiate very little between
boy and girl, she competes both emotionally and in ambitions with men. At the same time she expects to be
gratified as a woman by men. No complaint here—we
men are eager to do it.

Then one day she marries and the picture flickers.

Abruptly or, if not at once, at least when she begins
to bear children, she can no longer compete in exactly the
same way with men. Woman, wife, mother, she has somehow to reconcile these roles with her sociology or her
English lit and her ambitions for a career.

Many girls do it gracefully. Some fly very high. Some
fierce ones fly high like the queen wasp. Others, more
genial, manage to balance a husband and useful work in the
world without devouring the male.

In any case, what is common to many intelligent
young women in America is a need for attention *as women*
together with a need to compete with men *like men*. The
obvious solution is a combination of career and marriage,
and it works for some. It may work for some artist's
wives—especially since the financial need presses hard
among a group whose collective ear is bent so exclusively toward the poker-faced Muses. (A Muse is
a Greek divinity, traditionally fond of artists, traditionally depicted with no pockets in her robes and no purse
either.) Malcolm Cowley tells the story of a meeting of
poets who were asked how they survived. The answer from
the back of the room, with nervous laughter: "Our wives
teach school."

This solution, however, is not always available, as for example when the desired children appear quickly. In a world that reserves its respect for the male's capacity as breadwinner in the family, it may not even be a good idea for the wife to work while the husband stays home with his "hobby." It may be dangerous for the marriage to gratify this American girl's itch to compete with men while her husband fails to race in the workaday world. These are questions that face all working wives, and each couple solves them in their own way. If the wife is gifted enough to be successful in her job, she and her husband can probably be adult about that success. If she does not work or if she does, she should be able to show in action her respect for her husband's labor. After all, this lovely young thing is also a clever and sensible wife despite her failure to marry a nice, steady boy; this egotist about eternal Beauty and Truth is also a pretty good guy despite his reluctance to don the gray flannel uniform.

The special problem of our artist and his bride is that he is most poorly equipped to supply all the peripheral gratifications that compensate many women for being women after years of being pseudo-boys, creatures incomprehensibly endowed with nice gimmicks and yielding moods. Money, stability of job and home, respectable status, these are the least of the compensations. The chief one is the steady attendance that the typical American husband brings his wife. *She* is the charming, sensitive, tasteful one; she knows all about art and culture; she buys, outfits, equips and decorates. "Me?" says an old-style husband. "Oh, I just came along to write the check and admire the little lady." And he is present.

The artist isn't. Devoured by his steady concern with the reality of his work—call it egotism, call it the creative fire—he simply does not have the ability to compartmentalize his life in this way. He does not leave the suburb to go bully the city for eight hours, then return fortified by his gnawing at "real life" and express his sensitive, tender hungers by being a dutiful spouse. He never leaves himself except to gather himself more intensely; he lives by stripping off his skin; he finds it hard to play a mollifying role with his wife.

Maybe he is too much with her. Surely he is too much with himself. A stubborn idealist, he will settle for nothing less than the passionate best of love, a confronting of mortality in the flavor of flesh—how he needs his wife to be his true friend! And he may want to keep this wife at a letter's distance while he lowers himself into the well of his fantasy. He needs to give and take love, and he needs her, but he also needs an honorable retreat for a time, monklike, prophetlike, "lest human voices wake us and we drown."

A poet said it like that. "Good-by, honey, see you in a few days," our husband says.

Is she now supposed to cheer him off to his ease while suspending herself until he returns? What about the steady work of keeping a family going? Unless she is the angel that no man deserves, she begins to brood over her many dark moments of feeling exploited, excluded, deserted.

While not usually going so far as to be a character in a farce, the artist's wife may try to satisfy her yearnings to have a someone *there* when she needs a someone. (Remember that her husband is traveling in the empyrean, or maybe only in New York to see about a gallery.) All wives need attention from other men; no one is shocked by this. The need of the artist's wife may be greater than most. She has given up much; she is not compensated by a man who keeps regular working hours and devotes himself entirely to her on a generous schedule; she feels deprived. And she really is. The only justification is that she has a kind of spouse that most salesmen's wives do not have, a rare bird with a becoming flutter to its wings and something more for her than the privilege of cleaning up after him.

She must beware of getting her attention from other men. It will depress her husband. It will not please her very much. It carries more than the pleasant risks of adventure.

Unfaithfulness will imperil the main chance, which is to get that necessary nourishment of love from the man she most deeply has chosen. At moments he may not be a real husband to her. He may be espoused to the stanza or the keyboard; he is far gone and high as a kite. But when he comes to earth again he has a special charge and vitality for looking to his woman. If she shares his intentions she can help him to make her a delight to herself, to him, and thus to those gods who love lovers. The muscle and sinews of their bond are exercised by the rhythms of withdrawal to creative work, followed by the energetic return. If she loved him when she married him, lucky for him and lucky for her, perhaps she can wait until he comes plummeting down from the sky of his abstraction. After work well done, pleasure shakes the earth. Intimacy is a consolation and a reward—and a lasting virtue, much better than an extra arm or eye for surviving difficult times. If both husband and wife are gifted for love, they sail proudly through both the close times of intimacy and the troubled times of private wrestling.

Privacy. There again is that matter which is so hard about marriage. All right, most husbands want to give it up, or pretend to want to give it up. But here is the artist, who not only requires solitude for his work but also seems to cling to it as a second bride. He treasures it. Darkly he runs to its embrace, leaving his wife and children, with the conviction born of deep need that this lonely gathering of himself is his perfect right. It looks like childish egotism, Narcissus wanting no one to interrupt while he studies the reflection in the pool. Why then doesn't he go all the way

to self-sufficiency? Does an artist deserve a wife? What
about the constancy of feeling that is essential to the health
of marriage?

That which we call the artist's egotism, if we don't
like it, has a more sympathetic definition: his awareness
of the mystery of personality. His sense of privacy is balanced against his need to open doors to others; a jealous
integrity of the self labors toward a permanent communion
with the human race. Toward his wife at one moment
he holds up a blank *no* of secrecy—she is cruelly excluded;
then he may demand a loyalty of understanding that suf-
focates her. When he says *yes*, he demands that she be all
the way with him. Tolstoi, for example, at one period in
his life insisted, under the banner of honesty, on telling
his wife what she could not bear to hear. He kept a diary,
confessing all the trivial exasperations and judgments that
are meant to pass quickly, and he forced her to read it
every day. What a brutal intimacy! Then later he ran away
to die in a railroad station rather than remain under the
same roof with a prying and hysterically devoted woman.
Go away closer, the artist may seem to be saying, unless
his wife's movements are in profound sympathy with his.

In all of this, of course, there is something quite unexceptional. Marriage is strange and difficult for everyone,
and the elements of strain are common to all. What makes
the familiar strangeness more difficult to bear is the artist's
special heightening of it, a need for the privacy of fantasy
in addition to the other needs for privacy—and this at the
same time that, paradoxically, he demands the gift of passionate love, which can calm his awful, self-inflicted loneliness. This generous and intense dialogue can be undertaken,
of course. The artist is neither a moral idiot nor a schizo-
phrenic. The richness of his privacy and his almost religious
faith in communication are the best warranty of at least
the possibility of that warmth, concern, devotion to a com-

mon enterprise and continuing ability to surprise and charm which makes great marriages. Sometimes, of course, it's the wife who puts on the paint-stained blue jeans or the film in the eyes above a battered portable typewriter, and then it is the husband who must look resourcefully to himself and wait for the rhythm of renewal and return to carry her back to him. The structure of the marriage is similar. The mysteries of love and respect for individual personality are the great incentives.

The artist's wife has a good chance if she tries neither to judge nor reform her monstrous husband. Being a bit of a monster herself—or she would have never gotten into this fix—she may yet approach that perfect union of two separate beings which is the dream of marriage.

At bottom of all this, of course, lies the reminder that artists are merely human. The activity of art, defined as an ardent making, is not confined to artists. The doctor or lawyer, who faces risk with courage, imagination, and the ability to seize an unforeseen opportunity, needs the strength and devotion of the artist; the businessman who gives himself to his idea, making something from nothing but his avid will and intelligence, is sailing amid the reefs of creativity; even the political man, doomed to hullabaloo and intrigue, uses his professional smile and tricks of publicity to advance a vision that becomes holy as he shapes it in the dark night of calculation. An artist is an artist is an artist, but few of the rest of us are machines or brutes. Every human being in the pell-mell confusion of society pursues a lonely quest toward making his dreams coherent with what the world allows him.

The novelty of the artist's marriage can serve us as a dramatic example of the risk and glory of the ideal of marriage. Achievement in solitude nourishes fruitful union; the devoted joining of love leads to a courageous individual courting of the unsuspected possibilities of human life on earth. Therefore love him hard! Make sure he loves you hard!

Be strong enough to find security within risk, and accept loneliness as a challenge that can lead to the greatest joys. Having someone to communicate with is better— if you are a grown person—than having a loyal pet in the house.

He will learn, too, though he may not be tamed.

1958

Divorce as a Moral Act

"I DIVORCE YOU for ever and ever, and even death shall not break it."

Divorce is perhaps the extremest moral event which we can consummate on earth. It may be an evil act or it may be a good one, but it is moral all the way down—we reach it only with a rope woven of a thousand difficult decisions. Marriage, with which divorce might be compared under some of its aspects, has an older, premoral character. It usually seems to be a good thing, but it is a good act called into being without a clear sense of consequences by individuals who are led by hope, trust, and desire. Forgive them, Lord, they know not what they do. If it is good, when it is good, it begins as natural virtue, not moral virtue. It is good as growing plants are good—out of the impulse of life itself. It is good as sleep is good (sleep is a natural virtue which the divorced sacrifice) or as waking in the morning refreshed is good. Of course, the preservation of marriage depends on more than natural virtue, usually to the surprise of the married, but these later moral decisions have come unanticipated in the flesh. They are initiated after the *natural* act of marriage.

Natural virtue—doing what is right by instinct, habit, tradition, or in obedience to some great faith—is mostly past for man as a species. We are long out of the garden of innocence. The angel sent down to expel Adam and Eve was the first Reno judge, but we are conservative; despite all thunder, trouble, and waste of spirit, we failed to recognize him. Now the day of natural virtue, when divorce was almost inconceivable, is over. Decisions, decisions! To shore up a marriage, despite suffering, sinking, a reign of destruction, may be a good or an evil act—it is a moral decision; the same to enter upon this always new and strange compact, within the clutter of bitterness and mistake, among the broken furniture of intentions, in the abrupt dead silence, after much thrashing noise, of eternal acquiescence in misunderstanding—in hushed piety now: "I do divorce you and cherish you, through age and new marriages, all the way past death's vain effort to part us."

For the pulse of marriage is not broken by divorce's hemp. With children we cannot even conceive of breaking it—that eternal physical presence of the new and unending family we have created, children having children having children, long after we have died. Our being in them is never dead ("When, now you tell me *when* are you coming to live at home again, Daddy?" "Never. But I'll come to see you every day, unless, unless—" "Will I have to get a new daddy?" "I'm your daddy and you're my daughter, and we won't change that.") The state of being father and child, having children, having a parent, never changes, although the manner of that being is hurtfully altered.

Even without children, we have become ourselves only together and in our marriage, and we go toward what we are becoming only together and in our divorce. Divorce is not a dissolving fluid, although it may be a corroding acid. It is like marriage but extremer: it is to marriage as an explosion is to rust. Under certain circumstances an oily cloth may smolder and decay under slow oxidation; in a tight closet it bursts into fiery life. But all that is metaphor; marriage and divorce are kin in that we have formed ourselves together within them. We do not become innocent now. Your face is mirrored on mine; my body is written on yours. Even if we love again—and of course we will—our old marriage grows in the new love. In fact, we may only reveal the meaning of our marriage through the new love. If we are lucky and good, we will have a new marriage which is continuous with the old one. The more truly we are loved for ourselves, the more true this is. The new lover loves what we can bring; a large part of what we can bring comes from the old marriage which we created together; the old love is now a vitally changing element in our flesh and memory, fantasy and intention.

If the new love is happy, the old marriage is vindicated: *Through me you have learned to love.* Or if not so much, at least this: I left you with the strength to be happy, an ambition to know love, the suspicion that it is possible. Perhaps I have even left you with a belief and a brilliant need. Together we have put an end to the monstrous expectations of first marriage, and without cynicism we may now go on to what is possible.

How does a divorce grow into being? Or rather how is it decided into being?

It is always a question of character, not incident; personality, not anecdote. Legal briefs are notorious liars, although such phrases as "Incompatibility" or "Mental Cruelty" seem to be pathetic efforts to tell a general truth. Divorce appears as almost the absolutely free act because almost uncaused—that is, caused by anything, by any constellation of accidents. It is always caused by something but the something is never the same. Each divorce is unique. Let us dispose of some common simplisms:

The free personality married to the dependent may divorce. The dependent personality married to the dependent may divorce. And the free married to the free may divorce. In the first case the liberal, hard-loving personality feels imprisoned by a partner who feels more and more afloat, uncared for. In the second case, the two needful, lonely ones lean off balance against each other until they topple helplessly in a strident crescendo of demand for reassurance; they can no longer hear or feel each other— they have been too close. At last, in their desperation, the pain of clawing each other blindly in the dark seems less than the pain of bleeding quietly and alone in the dust. In the third and strangest case—the free and the free—it is because they are free *away* from, not toward each other.

In each case, the origin of divorce is character. The dynamics—or rather the tactics, since this becomes that worst war, civil war—are expressed in a series of incidents. However, these do not evolve in a straight line. They circle each other; they grow upon and nourish each other; is not any marriage, as Aristophanes suggests, a body? Divorce grows as the pearl grows, as the cancer grows—as the pearl in some ways, as the cancer in others. The pearl of divorce may be ejected by a powerful oyster. The malignancy, once started, is generally irreversible and proliferates with rapid fibrous insistence while the rest of the body wastes and rots.

Again: A grit of disagreement becomes, by accretion, an intolerable burden when it is not a cause of trouble but a symptom. The body of marriage is working against itself. Like the seed of the pearl, the grit torments this oyster, which increasingly busies itself with it, and so it grows; like the cancer, it steals the strength needed for health, thus mysteriously nourished through novel conduits; and like the goiter on a neck, it is soon all that you can see. This sort of grit may take years to mature within the life of its host: the marriage resists, resists, and its struggles leave sores, scars, and crippled healing.

When they can no longer bear the agonies of distrust and the weariness of effort, the couple parts, in longing and sorrow, with great staring tenderness. This false revival of the old moody courting is like the pertness of the last moments of a wasting illness. Dissolution follows fast; no longer virgin to divorce, they fly apart in a sensual rage— quarreling about money, property, those things which never troubled them before, bitter about her use of make-up and his clumsy slouch, spinning off into contempt in order to sear and so seal the wound.

True remissions sometimes occur—and false remissions. A springtime, a miraculously tender evening when desire and expectation meet—but these are reminders, depending on sentimentality, and the foreboding returns first and then the disease. The true remission of any disease, in the face of destruction, seems an almost divine intervention. With death plucking at your sleeve, the body writhes in anger and joy, "something clicks," and the course and pattern become what they have not been. Sometimes; rarely. In the face of the death of divorce— I am speaking here of people who have loved each other —at the worst and darkest moment—when they feel spiders in their ears and mice at their hearts—they may reject their monstrous denial of the past. Does it really happen? It can; at least we can imagine it, and that is enough to make it possible.

On the other hand, the healthy divorce may be the necessary radical cure of character. It is not merely surgical, although it aches as much as surgery: the divorce disentangles living flesh which has entwined and even grown together. It is systemic; and with all its pain, it may be the sign of a cure.

For example, her father was an alcoholic, say, and she never could fight him through about it. Her mother failed, naturally, but *she*. . . . So she marries an alcoholic, finds it impossible, and is freed of her father for the next marriage. Here is another trivial, overschematic example. His mother was a manager; he could not disengage himself; he crawled into another manager's pen. But lo, under threat of extinction as a man, he is *not* a child and he *can* free himself. Now having practiced successfully against his mother, he no longer needs to defeat her. He can even find, next, the yielding, giving, and responsible woman whom the glare of his mother's rage hid from him.

All examples are radically falsifying. Divorce is a fragile snowflake in the December sun. Who breathes on it decides for himself about it.

And there is something still more subtle, clever, and diseased: we may make our wife or husband into the image of the unconquered parent, just in order, later, to destroy it. This is pathetic and comic. You were chosen, but you did not know for what, and pressed into service against your will, but slowly, gradually, so that you did not know what you were doing, and then—at the moment of ripeness, when you are perfectly what your partner needs you to be —*the knife!* Perhaps the squealing cattle should organize against the slaughter, but they did not see the end, only the busy chain of events in the yard. And you were, very likely, too busy making your own effigy. This is painful. These are the very bad divorces, where there was no thou-saying ever, where human beings were used as tools. We should warm ourselves by the good divorces, rare though they are.

"Will you go to dinner with me?" he asks.

"No," she says, "I have a jealous husband." And the smile of complicity: he might find out, but if he doesn't. . . . The husband is used, rearranged, scrambled, an image formed totally of her uses for him. She does not think: I love him. Instead, she refuses the invitation with smug, mouth-narrowing thoughts of possessions: he is jealous. This woman is unfaithful even if she never enters another's bed. Her husband feels her infidelity in their own bed—in her passivity, in her absent devouring of his substance. She needs him, true; he may take that for love. She wants him perhaps. She cannot do without him.

But even in his arms she is unfaithful. She cannot love anyone but her incomplete, uncompletable self. She yearns to exist, but her yearning is a bottomless pit down which her husband and children career.

I keep promising myself not to use examples. There are too many individual members of divorce. As to incident, all marriages suggest them—money, infidelity, boredom, should we go out or should we read, in what manner shall we love, how many children do we want. Ways of being parents and friends. Taking and given ways. These matters are all symptoms of character. True, they also change character. But when they attack the marriage, it is in their role as symptoms. All married people can supply their own instances. Every marriage is a potential divorce.

So we are practical. "The children—think!" Those who for so many reasons need too much of love can do nothing to preserve a form of marriage for the sake of the children. They perpetuate their own suffering in their children, of course, but they can do nothing else.

Back for another moment to the knotty question of infidelity. Imagine this: a woman who feels wronged tells her husband of infidelities with a man now living abroad. They struggle—tears, beatings, desperate lovemaking as the husband strives to possess her for himself. At last he forgives her. When does she leave him? When does the marriage fly apart for all to see?

When the husband discovers that it is a lie, that she had been helplessly true to him, that she had fought in this hysterical way to gain ascendancy over him. Now she feels judged utterly, and with no strength to give and take from him, she gives up. She finds that last creative strength of character necessary to tear herself from him. Either that or suicide.

Rare? Mythological? Yes, but it tells how much we need infidelity, and it tells how much we can bear to suffer, and it tells what we finally cannot bear. We can suffer the hurt of strength—even the unsure, petty strength of a three-week stand, fragile and self-denying; we cannot suffer the wound administered by weakness—by weakness aware of its weakness and being nothing but weak.

It is said that the widow who was truly devoted to her husband is the one who has faith in marriage, believes in love, marries again. The unhappily married, unfulfilled man or woman, having his problem fantastically solved by a death he only dreamed of, must mourn forever—guiltily, regretfully, guiltily. He must even invent a justificatory bliss in the past. Gray-faced, always in mourning, his life is over.

No! cries the grief-stricken true lover when the time of sharpest bite is finished. This *no* is a *yes* to life. No, no, love is too important to pass out of my life by this accident. My dead lover tells me this: he wants me to have the best part of his legacy, and this is the power to give and take love. This widow or widower inspires love, deep and sensual love, at any age; and gives and takes it. A new sharing occurs on earth—the best gift which earth offers everyone in the democracy of blood.

May it not be, in the same way, that only the divorced couple who sometimes were truly happy and loving have the chance to find love again? The good divorce is that between two who have once loved each other. Justly they may pity the bad divorce—that of beings who have merely made mistakes, merely rectified mistakes, merely repeated old errors bred in the family. The bad divorce is the one of diminished decision: submission to a painful pattern, a deathly cure by living through the sins of the fathers. The good divorce dares to love again—as only the widow who was happy can dare to give up her fabricated memories.

Good luck! Let us divorce tenderly, and believe in each other forever.   1957

The Bachelor's Dilemma

THE CONFIRMED BACHELOR can be defined as the man who has the courage of his lack of convictions. Once he hasn't made his mind up, he really sticks to it. Swinging more and more wildly from his loosening trapeze, he is another reeling acrobat in the disorganized circus of American love and marriage.

Let us look at him with magical omnipresence from a privileged station in the air above a big-city party. It could be anywhere in America—New York, Cleveland, Chicago, St. Louis, Houston, Denver, San Francisco. There is a crowd—busy, talkative, curious, and anxious—of human creatures hoping for amusement. Chink of glasses, gaggle of laughter, roll of eye. The bachelor enters alone.

What does the wife see? Sometimes she sees him as a bad example for her own husband, but more often she has tender feelings for him. She sees forbidden possibility: a handsome, perfect cavalier, perhaps, mysterious and challenging—unlike her all-too-real, all-too-known, heavy, snoring husband. (The bachelor never snores in the fancy of this lady.) Or she knows he is lonely and she sees a sweet lost lad to be comforted. Or she sees a combination of challenge and need. She wants to feed him, ease him of sorrow, perhaps—she tucks a tooth into her thoughtful lip—perhaps find him someone. Or, in some cases, if she and he are crowded into a corner with their drinks in their hands, she finds herself whispering those strange, hasty words in that bizarre language of invitation: "Call me. Call me. Hang up if a man answers."

What does the husband see? He may see a lucky man who has avoided the tender trap (a trap baited only with hope and desire) or a man who has been able to undo the clamps by brute force. He claps him on the back and says, "Still got your pick of things, eh Jack?" Or he sees a poor fellow who hasn't yet tasted the joys of children, hearth, steady conjugal affection. Or a paltry jokester, still trying to make out of an evening, like a fraternity boy or a conventioneer. Or perhaps he sees a challenge and a rival. ("Funny thing keeps happening. I answer the phone and the party on the other end hangs up.")

What does the girl see? Ah, she scents rather than sees. She recognizes a possible catch. But if he carries the reputation of a confirmed bachelor, the girlish mind boggles before vague threats from Sunday supplements and ancient movies—weekends at ski lodges, abrupt petulance and shortness of mood, flowers and candy, and then echoing silence heaped up about her while she shrivels into scorned spinsterhood. . . . She blinks. He approaches. He has nice teeth. He's a pleasant chap—no spats, cane, or waxed mustache. Still, she has been told that he has run through a dozen like her, and that his gray temples may bespeak merely an ironic heart. But I am different, she decides bravely. Let's see, if I spread my net in front of the canapé table, and bait it with dimples, promises of home cooking, and—"What kind of work do you do?"

What does another bachelor see? A comrade, a rival, a friend with one button missing from his shirt, who is likely to bore him with complaints and then steal his girl.

The hostess sees the available extra man. The food table—little bits of things placed upon little bits of things —sees a gobbling mouth which has skipped dinner. And perhaps the psychiatrist sees a patient. Our individual confirmed bachelor in his J. Press suit turns out to have about as many identities as there are people in the room.

And what does *he* see when he looks into the bathroom mirror in his studio apartment while dressing for this party? Perhaps he sees a healthy young man with plenty of time, money (as much as the Bureau of Internal Revenue allows him to keep), opportunity, willingness for adventure. He is all set and the lights are winking on and the evening is before him. No wife will make demands; no child will wake him later; he can eat, drink, and wander where, when, and how he pleases; he has the initiative. He can look over the world and take his pick and accept the challenge of fighting for her, or *her*, or HER. He dwells in realms of liberal choice. He has time for everything, visions and decisions and revisions. Showered, shaved, brushed, he finds himself the freest man on earth, if only he be willing to define the world narrowly and shrewdly enough.

Or he may discover somebody else in that mirror.

He stares and sees the frazzled face of the undecided man who slides down the razor blade of time—lonely, bored, lonely, lonely, and lonely. Asked why he finally married, one ex-bachelor said, "I got sick of that same old face in the bathroom mirror." He is tormented by a twisting loneliness which, oddly enough, feels to the belly very much like the pain of jealousy. But here we find just one person involved, a straight line any way you turn him, not three people, a triangle, as in the socialized pain of jealousy. He has less to contemplate; he has only his solitary, retracted state. The bachelor often suffers from indigestion and incipient ulcers. Too much restaurant food? Pans not clean enough? Or was the restaurant good but the interior monologue accompanying dinner stewed in unfriendly juices? He knows that all the statistics give him a shorter life expectancy—practical thought—than that of married men. Despite his naps, his self-indulgence, his cheerful acceptance of the haphazard, he dies young.

There is a law that a battery must be charged or it will be exhausted. It cannot generate from itself. The bachelor is a battery trying to charge itself.

In nature there is another parallel. A certain primitive variety of one-celled creature reproduces by what is called "binary fission"—by simply splitting in two. It requires no other, no mate. There appears to be nothing like sex needed. However, scientists notice under the microscope that a culture of these paramecia soon becomes "tired," "sluggish," and inactive, reproducing more and more slowly. Unless . . . and here is the curious detail. If the creature does not occasionally swim up to another like it, move alongside and exchange nuclei for a reason which has no normal mechanical explanation, it will finally slow down absolutely, disintegrate, die. But if it *does* perform this mysteriously friendly act, it will regain strength, move and feed with healthy vigor, and renew its process of reproduction by binary fission with elegant enthusiasm.

Which leads us back to the confirmed bachelor and a delicate matter. He is not a boy. He is not a child. It is no secret: one of his major problems is sex, and this fact fills a large part of his life and has obvious repercussions on the lives of all the people around him. If he is a confirmed bachelor, the genuine article, he has no guarantees in this area. Sex produces two kinds of trouble, and accordingly two kinds of bachelor. One bachelor is the shrewd Don Juan, attractive, capable, efficient, going off into the evening of his life to do battle with little black address book in hand and perhaps a list of historical, used-up girls in a secret drawer in his heart. He gets what he wants; but the trouble is: *he doesn't want what he gets.* He is often courted by women—as in that boyish dream where the responsibilities of manhood are taken over by clairvoyant girls—and he finds himself fought for as a commodity. Especially in large cities, where there tend to be more girls than men, he has an easy time of it. Everything works in his favor, even statistics. One confirmed bachelor says, "When I want to move or furnish a new apartment for myself, I just pick a girl who knows my taste. I tell her what I want, give her as much money as I want to spend, and tell her—*go*. I don't have time. She finds me what I want."

Smug? Hard-hearted?

Perhaps, but he can point out that the girl enjoys what she is doing. She wants to oblige; she wants to be needed, even if only as an unpaid interior decorator. Unmarried, without children, she is chafing to take hold. Far from feeling exploited, she is likely to harbor a tender indulgence for the man who trusts her so. She enjoys a brief glow of maternal and wifely joy. Later he can move her out of his life—or inform her that she has never moved in. "I didn't make her do anything she didn't want to do," he says. "She could have said no. Elaine or Barbara would have been glad to do it if she hadn't."

His friend pounds him on the shoulder. "You old manipulator! Playing with fire! Just you wait!"

"Of course, she really didn't have to sew all those curtains by hand. . . ."

And then there is the meeker, milder bachelor who, in his secret reverie, imagines himself a conqueror of dames, a hero in the lists of love, a brave commissioner of apartments to be decorated. He has girls who sew curtains for him in his dreams, but not during the long waking day. What about him? He is that man who sits on the automatic washer in the basement of his apartment house, waiting for his clothes to be done—a rumble in the machine and a rumble in his heart—and trying to figure out how to pass the evening after his TV dinner and his little stint of ironing. Later, wandering, he is one of the ghost ships that cruise the great cities, watching, discouraged, gray. (If he has a sun lamp, he can cruise discouraged and tanned.) He may be lucky. Some equally saddened, equally hopeful girl may take pity. He may even find himself buying love in that most paltry way—spending a few dollars for an imitation of feeling that no paramecium would envy. More likely, he takes a couple of drinks, numbs himself, sighs, hopes for better luck another time, and tumbles into bed.

Are these two men so different—the sleek Don Juan in quest of his ideal, the meek Don Mitty unable to find anything? No, they are blood brothers under the thick or thin skin; they are both deprived. Neither can attain a state of rest; neither has been able to settle for the possible. Both are forever looking, forever disappointed. The earth spins and they spin. They may buy themselves all sorts of pleasure—hi-fi, foreign travel, sports cars, the paraphernalia of elegant consumption. They are likely to have time and money for these things—one can live cheaper than two. They pamper themselves because they have no one else to love. In the first weeks after birth, infants think of the rest of the world as extensions of their own bodies; they don't understand that mother's breast and father's arms belong to separate, other persons. Like the infant, the bachelor is in primitive contact with the world of love, knowing only his craving, and so he remains infantile—extending his solitary body with the balm of luxury and indulgence. He follows the rule of constant enticement, seduction, dissatisfaction, another girl, wandering to another town, another girl, another job, another car, another girl. And again another.

Because no one reassures him very deeply, his vanity is inflexible—it is the savage vanity of the child. In his search for "true love," he is eternally deceived and mocked. After the thrill of easy conquest, he asks himself once more, "Was it really conquest? She was, after all, so much like the others."

What does this do for the bachelor's masculine pride? It does not help it very much, any more than scratching an insect bite makes it stop itching. He itches more fiercely and knows no remedy. There are few things sadder than the success of the man who achieves all he craves, but then discovers his inmost thought: And now what? And now? And now?

The bachelor enacts an immense joke in which the leg he pulls may be his own. He searches for the "true meaning" of love, whose true meaning is that it has no single true meaning. He may finally, like the male models in certain advertisements, seem to be held together by little more than his clothes and his vanity; and if they were to let go, he would tinkle to earth in a little heap of discrete parts. His arms enfold air, his mouth kisses glass. His present is without a future or a past: it is only a place to store his tubes, drops, and pills (he grows hypochondriacal with age); with mysterious hope he takes vitamin E, which is said to be for fertility. Unless he explodes, protests, cries No! no to all that!—and thus joins the harried legions of newly-weds, forgetting his vitamins, and afterwards troubled in other ways.

Most of the time we see only the glamour of the bachelor's freedom. We find him dressed, preened, rested, at his social best. He may simply age peacefully in our sight, growing gracefully into the permanent "extra man" for hostesses. Or he may finally be more fortunate than most men and find the girl of his dreams, the girl out of whose kisses he builds—as a poet wrote—"a ladder to the stars." Equipped with experience and age, patience and determination, he wins exactly what he wants. He is then much to be envied. The prince has wandered the enchanted forest and found his heart's perfect desire—not merely fallen out of bed and awakened groping on the cold floor. What a lucky man! He lifts the wand and She speaks to him. . . .

We see him during his best moments, on the verge of that discovery, with new girls, trying.

Usually he does not find the girl of his dreams. That ladder to the stars lies folded in a closet somewhere. Another evening has been spilled away with a swell kid whose name he will soon forget.

We do not see him during those moments when he is alone in his apartment, wondering why. *Alone.* Back home alone to his cold bed, his vacant hopes, and his Dacron shirt drying in the bathroom.

1958

The Mystery of Personality in the Novel

THE NOVELIST'S BOLDEST address to himself says: "I must master the most powerful sense of human life on earth, that of individual striving in a world clotted with both trouble and joy; I mean to commit myself to love and ambition and the frustrating of mortality."

The timorous wee clerk within replies: "Who, *you?*"

"Yes," says the novelist, "and don't interrupt. I will reflect the movement of men in society in order to give an example of the glory of desire."

The inner clerk, snuffling righteously before so much rhetoric, says: "Watch out! That's very difficult."

And so it is. And so ensues a struggle. Generally the clerk wins. Often the dialogue is never quite argued through. Occasionally, a few times in each generation, the novelist wins against his other self.

In the first case there is the sleek and pure pseudo-novelist, faking passion, faking life, the opportunist of problems, the Herman Wouks and Sloan Wilsons and Cameron Hawleys, with their deep affirmations for those who admire the editorials in *Life*. In the second case there is an uneasy, unfulfilled writer, often precious, satisfied with aspects and insights and partial comfort. And in the third case, when the novelist never abandons his deepest hopes, well, there is the possibility of a masterpiece. He gives us the stories for which we hunger, rich with people we love in mortal danger; his way of telling, his angle of vision, his perspective—this is what we mean by style—give us the judgment married to perception which defines both the whole man and the artist. Sensitive and brave at the same time—what a monster!—he joins plot and perspective in a way that finally, without exhortation, suggests a vision of the good life.

This is the critical maximum which no individual can reach.

But although it is more pleasant to talk of success, I would like first to name some of the ways by which novelists evade the possibilities of their art. They construct a mannered style of arbitrary perspectives, with the intention that neither they nor their readers will be obliged to venture into the huge mystery of personality. The aim is simple: If you restrict your world, then the world is reduced in size and manageable. Hide what is difficult; trim what does not fit; make it neat. The great novelist is committed to a world without horizons, manifested first of all by a large and lyric sense for his heroes. The mediocre or tertiary writer limits and limits and limits, and so we have, sometimes overlapping, the following contemporary types:

The Forthright Brutes: Ernest Hemingway and imitators. They are bewitched boys, newly discovering verbs and nouns, physical sensation, zip-pow-wham of weather, drink, sex, war, bulls. They are too scared of what goes on inside an intelligence, inside a memory, inside a group of people to be able to face these matters except by smashing physical symbols like fists across the page. Sometimes they have sensitive nerves in their fists, but the nerve end-ings are stunned before making contact with the complex congeries of will and desire within.

Hemingway's resolution of the necessary tension of conception in fiction can be examined in the light of the traditional philosophical concept of Universals and Particulars. In one tradition "reality" is defined by abstract forms outside time, and the specific ever-changing events of our world are flickering shadows through fire on the wall of the cave, imperfect imitations of the ideal forms. In the other tradition, it is these particular events which are "real," and general statements are inaccurate, merely useful summaries of the only knowable reality—the fact in the here and now. The terms *Idealism* and *Materialism* are approximate, somewhat misleading labels for these opposing world views.

The novel as a form is obviously empirical, working toward whatever large statements it has to offer about men in society, love, death, ambition, and so on, through specific instances of *a* man, *a* love, *a* death, *an* ambition, a specific society in a specific time and place. Not merely in general approach but in method also the novelist tends to be empirical. He does not say, "She was beautiful." He describes a particular lovely creature with all her lovely attachments and gadgets, and then leaves us with one of the formal summaries which are part of the reader's active participation in a fiction: "Wow! Beautiful!" The novelist seeks what T. S. Eliot has called, in a famous phrase, the "objective correlative" of emotion.

This objectifying in Hemingway goes very far. It is as if he were a too-literal student of some early physical scientist, overskeptical about what he can learn. The abstention from analysis, deduction, conjecture, the bold hunch— these risks which are taken by the great scientist, too—in favor of a minute noting of symptoms, has a certain animal simplicity, grace, and power. But even the most graceful and powerful bull hangs from a very small head, which he uses mainly for battering, and little of what one bull learns needs to be passed on to another. He has opted for a pathetic lowering of the eyes, a doomed charge, a sword in the heart, and an occasional chance to gore before thumping in the dust with his life running out. *El pobre toro!* His head admits not enough to understanding.

A passion for objectifying emotion through physical sensation and act spins off to mania in the lesser work of Hemingway and in his fleas. The details become more and more ritual; the general emotion and sense which is supposed to emerge from the details has to be supplied entirely by the reader. In its own way, this is a highly "literary" manner, depending on knowledge of other stories, other stages in the life of the maestro, rather than on the work at hand itself: "It was hot. He took a cigarette. It was very hot. He took a drink. He went upstairs. Christ, it was hot."

This type of minimal statement in Hemingway goes very far toward forgetting that thoughts, fantasies, memories, projects, the constant inner monologue and the unspoken conversations among people are also facts in the world, facts of being human. That we think defines our humanity. We are remembering, reasoning, political creatures, constantly responding to others and constantly willing ourselves into relation with others. Eliminate these actions in the guise of objective reporting and the writer eliminates the properly human, just as at the opposite extreme, in the precious and private writer, he eliminates social meaning by signifying nothing but his own obsession. The force of an obsession cannot be communicated; the obsessed person clings to his loneliness. Hemingway's compulsion toward objectivity links him with the obsessively subjective writer: they both fail to give us sufficient criteria for judgment, sufficient material for a full participation in the life of large human beings. They bind their projections of men in action to limited conceptions of the possibilities of being human.

Obviously, however, Hemingway has found an adequate stance for expressing the sadness of the basically uncommunicative soul and for giving glory to its instants of lonely courage. When he depicts the isolated man, he knows whereof he speaks and the simplistic prose manner which he derives from Gertrude Stein serves him well. (He was a nice boy, a good pupil, she notes maliciously.) He describes a static condition, not an act of becoming. His "moments of truth" are plateaus. The consequence of revelation is a fortified stoic acceptance of mortality. He gives us a partial truth about the human condition.

Why then does so much of his work make us feel like a rainy Sunday afternoon? What depresses us finally is this vision of human possibility—one of violent compartmentalization, strict limits, and no growth possible. On the occasions when he seeks to express a sense of people coming meaningfully together, he falls into an embarrassing purple rhetoric, as in the sleeping-bag scenes of *For Whom the Bell Tolls* or in the biography of the battered old love-hungry soldier in *Across the River and into the Trees*. This is not to derogate his great achievement, the one which is responsible for his popularity and his enduring projection of an aspect of life in the twentieth century. From beginning to end, he has spun out a continuous moral romance about the lonely man striving for dignity, grace, and compassion within a world populated by real sharks and imaginary tender boys and girls.

The Cataloguers: John O'Hara is a good example. They observe. They make the discovery of the trivial—it is *most* important; in fact, even the important is merely trivial; the trivial tells us all we need to know. They soothe us with sociology. They lay us to rest with details of tailoring and brand names. Their predominant cast of mind is a sentimental passivity toward the dead weight of facts, which are seen quantitatively, and the contents of a closet are given the same loyal inventory as the two-headed contents of a bed.

The Outer-Essence Girls: Truman Capote and the chattering poets of decoration. A paragraph is a hammock in which words copulate prettily. Society is a meeting of birds on the wing. Put more formally, they do what bad poets do: They use words as if they were things and not signs representing acts and things. They drop the object of narrative prose, which is to make sense about human action, and replace it with a prettifying function. They are interior decorators for sentences. We can't all be William Faulkner, Katherine Anne Porter, or even Carson McCullers, but each and every one of us can aspire to be Speed Lamkin.

The Daintily Involved Observers of Aspects: This is *The New Yorker* fashion, although its best writers, such as John Cheever and Robert Coates, do something more. It is a variety of corporate prose less solemn-chuckly than the *Time-Life* product, but no more able to bear the full weight of experience. *The New Yorker* stylists are marvelously shy about the world. They blush before experience, but have learned graceful ways toward it, with shrewd notings of intonation and the vagaries of expression. Parts stand for wholes, although there seems to be a law of expression— the smaller the part, the larger the hole. Finally summoning up their courage before fleeing, these writers offer a pox on life in the last paragraph.

The Common-Style Fellas: Herman Wouk proudly claims to write "the common style." This cottony diction, also worked with varying degrees of efficiency by Sloan Wilson and Cameron Hawley, is the great current success. These people are the just-plain-Bills of literature, producing an upper-middle-class soap opera for the readers of Luce magazines and subscribers to the Book-of-the-Month Club's service. They love what-is, whether it be the Navy, the suburb, or the corporation, and come forward to swear their allegiance without quaver or quibble. There may be some touch of nonsense in the process, for the flesh is weak, but they rinse and bleach it all for us in the end.

It is the latter, the "common style," which enjoys the greatest success today. By the phrase "common style" is meant uninvolved, unambitious, "traditional" English diction, without excesses of feeling or rhetoric, suitable to describing the lives of people who want nothing to change, nothing to stop, just let's all pull together, hup-two-three, on to America's last frontier—Adjustment. Those who write the common style show us how to avoid adventure, giving us just enough of it along the way to keep us titillated. It is a manner of withdrawal. They use the tricks of plot to replace action, the display of hysteria to justify emotions treated by Equanil, the questioning of moral assumptions in order to tell us that these questions can be avoided. The method consists in the *ejaculatio praecox* of drama. Clear out before we feel something! The result here too, of course, is a safe but jaded withdrawal from feeling, which is seen as dangerous. (Passion builds and renews only *after* we have submitted to it utterly.)

The artisans of the common style often, like all good engineers, borrow techniques. Particularly they have mastered the cataloguing skill; occasionally they seem for paragraphs at a time almost as delicate as the *New Yorker* stylists; more rarely they imitate a Hemingway growl or a Capote fruitiness. But they turn these methods to their own ends, and go plodding on through their scenarios for adjustment. Flat-footed sentence dogs flat-footed sentence; limp paragraph folds into limp paragraph; the rhythm of phrase prepares us for the denouement, which is a calculated marriage, a comfortable job, a saving of the company.

Form follows function.

The function is to assure us that the lowest common

denominator of personality and experience is all we need. The common-style artisans give us an ideal of comfortable conforming ways. The package is all wrapped up and ready to wear, in fact, as easy as old shoes.

The mysterious longing of individuals to create and renew is excised with an almost surgical brutality and precision—although funnily enough, the American reader can teach these writers much about that of which the novelist is supposed to have special knowledge. American readers are drinkers and sometimes addicts; Americans love jazz and fast driving and secluded corners; with all the itch to conform, Americans are still trying to burst the bonds of isolation by various sorts of violent experiences, including art.

Why then do so many readers find comfort in the dry apotheosis of Marjorie Morningstar's frigidity? How can Sloan Wilson get away with a billion copies of his pettish smugness in the job, the house, the rich aunt, the old wartime affair "talked out" between husband and wife? The great novelists have always given us, before anything else, before all morality and sociology, a sense of the richness of possibility. Why do so many novelists fear the mystery of personality?

Well, first of all, they always have. Besides, life is hard enough without going out looking for challenges. In an impoverished time, palliated by plenty but worried all the same, there is a generalized loss of the sense for creative activity. Nothing more than anxiety inhibits the power to do, to make, to invent, to admit. When your belly is constricted by worry, oatmeal goes down most comfortably. Novelists are human beings more than they are anything else. The mystery of personality is a mystery: isolation, incomprehension, brusque flashes of lightning, cold and hot, danger, danger, danger. To enter into a dark place involves the risk of coming out where you won't see things as they were. In novels as in life, we cannot eliminate emotion utterly and remain human; but we can replace deep involvements by passing safely from the stage of titillation to that of being jaded without crossing through commitment. We live this way, we write these books, we read them in order to say: *I'm safe, I really am, and I'm pleased about it!* (We keep on renewing the experience because secretly we are not pleased.) Thus Sloan Wilson can declare that his novel expresses his sense for a world which has treated him "pretty well"—wars, bombs, a third of a nation watching Ed Sullivan, all of it. Better forget about adventuring, he means to say; better accept a stereotyped image of desire; better be attentive to the media and take the profit in subsidiary rights.

The novel at its best is a large perspective on life in society—large because the hero's doings are important and because the novelist is deeply concerned with the careers of his people. *Ulysses*, for example, has difficulties of manner, but is not in its conception hermetic. Leopold Bloom is a representative, poignant, and troubling instance of city-dwelling man; his fretting and wandering in Dublin bring to us the challenge and limitations of our own intelligence, ambition, and ability to love. James Joyce's personal voice here is many-focused, as true personality always is, not the pale self-contemplation, blank and onanistic, which the seventeen-year-old thinks of as the pursuit of himself; nor is it the cruelly partial view of the writer fleeing his largest intelligence. It is a lyric reverie *in the light of* the wide world of society.

What is that grit out of a unique individual which somehow provokes the novel of largest general significance? The nature of the writer's involvement with his material (which consists of all that he knows of life) suggests another clue. For complex psychological reasons, many novelists have been unavowed Platonists, philosophical idealists, possessed of a spectator theory of reality. That is, life has meaning as the shadows on Plato's cave have meaning—as flickering glimpses through fire of something beyond life, something perfect and unchanging and finally unknowable by men. Their world is a system deduced from unknown premises. *Unknown*—this paradox torments them. How can deductions be made without defined terms? Therefore they look for moral abstractions, categories, faiths, anything that can place them outside the tormenting flux of time and sensuality. Perhaps they become doctrinaire religionists or Marxists. They take their stand as viewers, as unwinders. What is the effect on their novels? Well, some of these writers are great ones, like Proust and Henry James, engaged in enterprises of passive integration in order to give some "symbolic" sense to the unruly factness of life. They shrink; still they cannot avoid rendering this dense, combative, time-ridden teeming. Despite their static position, Proust and James at their best project a moving image of desire.

But in anything less than a master, the type of self-absorption in moody fantasies is crippling. We may be hypnotized by it; we all have deep impulses to passivity before the fright of time; but an aspiration to perfection expressed as static clutching leads finally to paralysis. We stiffen; we are isolated. Platonism here parallels what the psychoanalysts call "fixation"—a retreat to impossibly perfect and unchanging gratifications or frustrations. We sneeze, we wheeze, our bodies protest.

Let us now set the empirical novelist against the deductive one. "Love" is not an abstraction to be encompassed by definition: it is this Jack and Jane, that Bud and Joy— look and see! The novelist is *not* studying shadows for some ultimate reality beyond earth; he accepts that the shadows themselves give him all that he can know; in fact, that they are enough; in fact, they are not shadows—they are thick reality itself and a marvel to behold.

There is the lesson of a Welsh phrase: "The rent that's

due to love"—you must pay and pay and pay, relentlessly
giving yourself and making others give, too. The category
"Love" does not exist; it can be merely rented, never owned;
it is unpossessable in any final way. Like the medieval cathedral, like a child, like love, the great novel gives a sense of
not yet completed life within whatever its perfections of
design. Attempting to offer the sense of life, a novel is always
in process. You can't step in the same story twice. When
the writer sits down to his desk in the morning, there is
nothing so safe and deadly as knowing exactly what comes
next. If he is a real novelist by temper of imagination, but
weakly hopes to have the security of a controlled symmetry,
he will find that his characters shake their fists into the
crooks of their elbows, set his schemes on their tails, ruth-
lessly rewrite him. All that he is makes his people all that
they are, but they are endowed with the kind of independence which defiant children have when they leave a good
home. Fortified by their parents to make their own way,
they are most loyal in being most free.

The mystery of personality can be defined again and
again, and then redefined: that's what mysteries are for. A
jittery scientist has defined personality as "the index of in-
efficiency." Machines are both efficient and free of caprice,
he assures himself; therefore personality is a negative quan-
tity with respect to intention, plan, goals; therefore the ideal
of Science must be the elimination of personality in favor
of socially governed ends. How are the ends to be determined? By what criteria are they judged? By the efficient,
impersonal needs of the smoothly running society. Needs?
Needs? Why, for Plato's sake, pal, that's more circular (in
logical terms) and hysterical (in psychological lingo) than
any aesthetic rant.

Personality is prickly against definition. Let us return
to the novel. In novels the mystery will make itself manifest
as an individual, unsocialized perception, compassion,

hatred, and love—a congeries of unique relationships with unique creatures and events. Despite the difficulties of definition, we know that the lonely, self-devouring ego is not personality and neither is the busy radar-flaunting opportunist: they are both flights from that mystery. They are willed, not willing; worked on, not working. They are not mysterious, either: they are explainable products. They can be comic and pathetic, even typical of a society—never heroic, tragic, or representative of aspiration (which is also a part of the twentieth century archetype).

However, the man moving in consciousness and contemplation of his will—really conscious and watching, really moving and committed—is the personality capable of defining freedom for all of us. His is the will which, in type, reaches to the divine maximum, where God made something from nothing, the heavens and earth popping out of his pride in six days, not seven—on the seventh day He gloated. At a slightly less monstrous level, Balzac created *Père Goriot* in fifty-eight days, complete with Vautrin swarming over Rastignac's soul. Love, ambition, power under the sun of mortality! These are the issues; the great heroes of fiction meet their risks head-on, as we all must do, but too often we do it also faces down.

The novelist must reach for the grown-up, risking, athletic personality, surely must in some way be this person, in order to find a hero who gives the sense of men at their best on earth: and catch him finally where his great gifts do not suffice: this is tragedy. American life is rich in suggestions of tragic themes: The man in politics is cracked by his ambition—but really involved, not floating above politics; the man in business fails against the fierce appetite of the devouring business world—but really struggling and pretty fierce himself while not mistaking the business world for the whole of life; the lover is lost by love, as it is perhaps still possible to be, but by a love which is health and desire for a woman worth desiring and defeated by the natural strangeness of human beings. It would not be stretching the essential definition of tragedy to show the possibilities of individual triumph in all these struggles.

Personality is a key, not a twitch.

Without personality, manifested by what is called style, there is no significant touching.

Personality in the novel leads to communion with others, a meaningful individual participation in the common career. Otherwise, despite all brilliance, emotion is reduced to the self-loathing of a Celine or the self-aggrandizement of the cripple perspectives mentioned earlier. The individual is more than the common style's stock-figure cartoon of Everyman in gray flannel. And of course the individual is more than the cracked-up romantic poet at three o'clock in the morning in the dark night of his soul.

We should expect the fragmentation of self in the modern novel, just as we expect it in the man bound to a factory or office, within a social structure which cannot use the largest capacities of millions of individuals. Writers are responsive people: the complexities of being an American in 1957 are enough to tempt all of us to turn to partial, limited, maybe soothing half-views. What a dangerous thing to be all present and awake before the front page of the daily newspaper!

Can some novelists stand up against their confusion and fright?

Yes, and even with courage, humor, and a will to do good work. Without naming specific writers, I suggest that the contemporary American novel is still the best place to look for instances of lives which seek to be whole and unafraid. Confidence and freedom of style are good signs of a writer's taking the chance. A style which attempts to use all a writer knows to tell all he can imagine involves a moral stance in favor of intelligence and liberty and risk-taking. With their varying defects and capacities, such writers have this in common: they are individuals, not products; they are making a way, not accepting a road; they do not flinch before the mystery of personality, or when they do, they give signs of knowing that there is something vital left out. Their failures are peculiarly ungracious: they intend otherwise. They will try again next time.

At its best, the art of the novel tells us more than we can find out elsewhere about love and death. We commune together before a guiding image of the always unfulfilled possibilities of life on earth. We are therefore in continual need of the dangerous, destructive moralist which the great novelist is.

1957

The Fair Apple of Progress

---

1. "A Little Worm in the Fair Apple of Progress."

HE SAID IT OF HIMSELF. He saw himself curled up, busily feeding on midwestern America, sheltered, destructive, loving his host, and needed by this age and place in order that they could get some sense of buoyancy and carry within them the richness of growth. He recognized his own childish self-absorption, great even for an artist, a breed accused by everyone of being childishly self-absorbed. Therefore he wrote about death with praise because "it will in any case give us escape from this disease of self." Self-love is surely the beginning of the love of others, but it is only the beginning. Sherwood Anderson, an old child, suffered a merely erratic love of himself, therefore writhed with a tormented love of others. All his stories are bound up in this sense of the self's isolation, seen as glory and sickness, as sickness and glory. He is one of the purest, most intense poets of loneliness—the loneliness of being an individual and of being buffeted in the current, the loneliness of isolation and that of being swallowed. One type represents the traditional retreat into the self for self-possession; the other, and its adversary at times, arises out of the angry resentment of a sensible man in an assembly-line civilization. Anderson's work is a manual of the ways in which loneliness can be used. It was his nourishment and sometimes his poison.

"I pour a dream over it. . . . I want to write beautifully, create beautifully, not outside but in this thing in which I am born, in this place where, in the midst of ugly towns, cities, Fords, moving pictures, I have always lived, must always live." Yet he fled it always. He fled in order to find himself, then prayed to flee that disease of self, to become "beautiful and clear . . . plangent and radiant." He felt that he loved only the midwestern land and people, but was still fleeing when he died—in the Panama Canal Zone.

In his photographs he often showed his hair hanging over his eyes. The affectation means a great deal: first mere arty affectation (how he loved the "free spirits" of Greenwich Village and New Orleans!), then something feminine and wanting to be pretty and lovable for prettiness, and then of course the blurring of sight when you try to see through your own hair. What do you see? A world organized by your hair. "I must snap my finger at the world. . . . I have thought of everyone and everything." His sympathy and his oceanic feelings alternate with arrogant despair in which the arrogance can deceive no one. So desperately hurt he is, trying so hard to convince the "word-fellows" he wanted to admire him. But then his nostalgia gives us the mood he sought to force: ". . . old fellows in my home town speaking feelingly of an evening spent on the big, empty plains. It has taken the shrillness out of them. They had learned the trick of quiet. It affected their whole lives. It made them significant."

We understand him at last!

And then again the helpless bombast: "At my best, brother, I am like a great mother bird. . . ." He exuded

through his pores the ferocious longing of a giant of loneliness. The typical chords from his letters sound under the
changing heroes of the stories:

> Youth not given a break—youth licked before it starts.

> Filled with sadness that you weren't there.

> I have a lot I want to tell you if I can. . . . Anyway
> you know what I mean when we talked of a man
> working in the small, trying to save a little of the
> feeling of man for man.

The romantic sentimentalist held up his mirror to look
at his world, peered deeply, saw himself instead, of course;
wrote painfully about what he saw; and it turned out that
he was writing about the world after all, squeezing it by
this palpitating midwestern honesty out of his grandiose
sorrows and longings. Sometimes, anyway. He was not a
pure man; he had a kind of farmer cunning, plus his groaning artiness and pretense, with which he hoped to convince
the "word-fellows" and the pretty girls that he was a Poet
although not a young one. What he really wanted was to
be alone in that succession of gray furnished rooms he
talked about so eloquently, making immortal the quiet
noise and gentle terror of his childhood. "I try to believe
in beauty and innocence in the midst of the most terrible
clutter." But clutter too was the truth of his life; he fed
on it; how else does a poet take the measure of his need
for "beauty and innocence"? He must have remained an
optimist, too, amidst all his disillusion. He married four
times. To the end of his life he went on believing, and
marrying.

Anderson the writer arouses a poking curiosity about
Anderson the man even in the most resolutely detached
critic. The note of confession is always with us: Here I
am, it's good that you know! he seems to be saying.

His most formal narrative paragraphs are soaked in his

own groping speech. He repeats, he cries out, he harangues, he pleads. All his work, the absymal failures and the successes which have helped to construct the vision Americans have of themselves, represents an innocent, factitious, improvised, schemed reflection and elaboration of the elements of his own life. He turns the private into the public and then back into the private again. His mystery as a man remains despite his childish longing to reveal himself—the mystery of a man who looks at a man with a beard and a scar in a conference room and sees, instead, a lover fleeing his girl's brothers through the fields. (They had knives and slashed—could this be the same man? he asks himself.) Anderson confounds us with bombast and wit, tenderness and softheadedness, rant and exquisite delicacy.

The best of his work is what matters.

Let us now look more closely at what the worm made of his apple.

2. "My Feet Are Cold and Wet."

He loved to create, he loved his fantasy as the lonely boy does. In his best work, as in some of the stories of *Winesburg, Ohio,* the fantasy is most controlled, or if not exactly controlled, simplified, given a single lyrical line. The novels had trouble passing the test of the adult imagination, being wild proliferations of daydream. The simple stories of Kate Swift ("The Teacher") or Wing Biddlebaum ("Hands") join Sherwood Anderson with the reader's sense of wonder and despair at the pathetic in his own past—childish hope of love, failed ambition, weakness and loneliness. As music can do, such stories liberate the fantasies of our secret lives. However, musicians will agree that music is for listening, not to be used as a stimulus for fantasy. We must attend to the song itself, not take advantage of it and make it the passive instrument of our dreaming. In the same way, the great writers hope to arouse and lead the reader's imagination toward a strong individual perspective on experience. Sherwood Anderson, however, was not of that vividly individualistic company, despite his personal hobby of eccentric bohemianism. Rather, he was the dreamy, sad romantic within each of us, evoking with nostalgia and grief the bitter moments of recognition which have formed him—formed all of us in our lonely America.

James Joyce used the word *epiphany*, which he took from Catholic ritual, to name that moment of revelation when words and acts come together to manifest something new, familiar, timeless, the deep summation of meaning. The experience of epiphany is characteristic of great literature, and the lyric tales of Anderson give this wonderful rapt coming-forth, time and time again.

In "The Untold Lie," for example, two men tenderly meet in order to talk about whether one, the younger, should marry the girl he has made pregnant. The older man, unhappy in his own marriage, wants to see the young man's life free and charged with powerful action as his own has never been. But it is revealed to him—revelation is almost always the climax of Anderson's stories—that life without wife and children is impossible and that one man's sorrows cannot be used by him to prevent another man from choosing the same sorrows. It would be a lie to say that the life of conjugal sorrows is merely a life of conjugal sorrows: the story finally breathes the sadness, the beauty, the necessary risks of grown-up desire. "Whatever I told him would have been a lie," he decides. Each man has to make his own decisions and live out his chosen failures of ideal freedom.

Many of Anderson's stories take for their realization objective circumstances which have a grandiose folkish quality, and many of both the most impressive and the most mawkish are concerned with an archetypical experience of civilization: the test which, successfully passed, commands manhood. Such a story as "The Man Who Became a Woman" objectifies even in its title the boy's wondering and fearful dream. The end sought is manliness, that new clean and free life; failure is seen as a process of being made effeminate, or falling into old patterns of feeling and action. At his best in these stories, there is a physical joy in triumph which is fresh, clean, genial—we think of Mark Twain, although a Twain without the robust humor; at his weak moments, we may also think of the sentimental sick Twain, and we find also the maundering moping of a prettified Thomas Wolfe.

The line between the subjects of Anderson's stories and Sherwood Anderson himself is barely drawn. His relation as artist to his material, as shaper of his material, is as intense and personal as that of any modern writer. Unlike most writing dealing with unhappy and frustrated people, Anderson's work is absolutely authentic in the double sense—not merely in communicating the feeling of these people as people, but also in giving us the conviction that the author shares both their bitter frustration and their evanescent occasional triumphs. By comparison with Sherwood Anderson, Dostoevski is a monument of cool detachment. His identification is perfect, sometimes verging on the morbid: "Everyone in the world is Christ and they are all crucified." He has a primitive idealism, a spoiled romanticism like that of Rousseau: we could be all innocent and pure in our crafts if the machines of America and the fates that bring machines did not cripple us.

This romantic idealism can be illustrated again by his treatment of another theme, marriage, in the story "Loneliness," in which he writes of Enoch Robinson: "Two children were born to the woman he married,"—just as if they did not happen to Robinson at all, which is indeed the truth about the self-isolated personality he describes. "He dismissed the essence of things," Anderson can write, "and played with realities." Again the romantic Platonist sees a conflict between the deepest meaning and the fact of our lives, between what we do and what we "really" are. With a kind of purity and cunning, Anderson seems to thrive on this curiously boyish notion the limitations of which most of us quickly learn. We work and love because we know that there is no other way to be ourselves than in relation to the rest of the world. The kind man is the man who perform kind acts; the generous man is a man who behaves generously; we distrust the "essential" generosity which is sometimes claimed for the soul of a man who selfishly watches out only for himself. And yet we can be reminded with a strange force by Anderson's conviction in his boyish dream of isolated personality that there is something totally private, untouchable, beyond appearance and action, in all of us. The observation is a familiar one, but the experience can be emotionally crucial. Cunningly Anderson makes us turn to ourselves again with some of his own purity.

The last sentence of "Departure" says of George Willard: "Winesburg had disappeared and his life there had become but a background on which to paint the dreams of his manhood." Abstracted people, playing out their time in the fragmentary society of Winesburg, these "heroes" are isolated, as Anderson himself was isolated, by art or unfulfilled love or religion—by the unsurmounted challenge of finding the self within relationship with others. It was the deep trouble of Anderson's own life that he saw his self, which could be realized only by that monstrous thing, the Life of Art, as flourishing in opposition to decent connections with others in society. Marriage, work, friendship were beautiful things; but the gray series of furnished slum rooms, in which he wrote, enough rooms to fill a city, were his real home. Writing letters and brooding behind his locked door, he idealized love, he idealized friendship. He withdrew to the company of phantom creatures. He hoped to guard his integrity. He kept himself the sort of child-man he described with such comprehending sympathy in the character of Enoch Robinson.

In many writers dealing with the grim facts of our lives, the personal sense of triumph at encompassing the material adds a note of confidence which is at variance with the story itself. Hemingway is a good example; his heroes go down to defeat, but Papa Hemingway the chronicler springs eternal. In Anderson this external note of confidence and pride in craft is lacking, except in some of the specious, overwilled novels which he wrote under political influences. Generally he does not import his poetry into the work—he allows only the poetry that is *there*—nor does his independent life as a creator come to change the tone of these sad tales. The stories of Winesburg are unselfconsciously committed to him as he is sworn true to them; the identification—a variety of loyalty—is torturingly complete; he is related to his material with a love that lacks esthetic detachment and often lacks the control which comes with that detachment. They are practically unique in this among modern storytelling, and it is partially this that gives them their sometimes embarrassing, often tormenting and unforgettable folk quality. Still they are not folk tales but, rather, pseudo folk tales. The romantic longing and grieving is not characteristic of the folk tale, despite the other elements, a direct matter-of-fact storytelling, colloquial American language (complicated by chivalry and the Bible, but at its best not "literary"), and the authority of Anderson's priestly devotion to his lives and people. Later, of course, the romantic judgment culminated in rebellion, sometimes in a kind of esthetic rant against the way things are.

In "The Strength of God," the Reverend Curtis Hartman (as in a parable, Heart-man) "wondered if the flame of the spirit really burned in him and dreamed of a day when a strong sweet current of power would come like a great wind into his voice and his soul and the people

would tremble before the spirit of God made manifest in
him. 'I am a poor stick and that will never really happen
to me,' he mused dejectedly, and then a patient smile lit
up his features. 'Oh well, I suppose I'm doing well enough,'
he added philosophically."

These, as *The New Yorker* would put it, are musings
that never got mused and philosophic additions that never
got philosophically added. They have a curious archaic
directness that amounts to a kind of stylization. The un-
analytic simplicity itself is a sophisticated manner. As the
officer of the Pharisees said, "Never man spake like this
man." It recalls to us the day of the storyteller who suggested the broad line of an action, and allowed us to give
our imaginations to it. Nowadays we demand detail upon
detail, and the phrase "I am a poor stick" would require
a chapter of exposition in the hands of a typical contemporary novelist.

The pathos of the pious man's temptation by the flesh
has a flavor beautifully evocative of adolescence. We no
longer think of "carnal temptation" as Anderson did. But
we remember our fears and guilts, and are reminded of
ourselves as great literature always reminds us. Hartman's
silent, secret battle with himself over Kate Swift is given
part of its bite by her own story—this pimply, passionate
young schoolteacher who strikes beauty without knowing
it and can find no one to speak to her. Her story is told
with a brilliant delicacy that reflects Anderson's own
reticence about women. Enoch Robinson, he says, "tried
to have an affair with a woman of the town met on the
sidewalk before his lodging house." To have an affair is
his strange idiom for a pickup! (The boy got frightened, and
ran away; the woman roared with laughter and picked up
someone else.)

Except for the poetic schoolteacher and a very few
others, women are not women in Anderson's stories. There
are the girls who suffer under the kind of sensitivity, passion,

and lonely burning which was Anderson's own lot; and then there are the Women. For Anderson women possess holy power; they are earth-mothers, ectoplasmic spirits, sometimes succubi, rarely individual living creatures. In "Hands" they are not girls but "maidens," where the word gives a quaint archaic charm to the creature who taunts poor, damned, lonely Wing Biddlebaum. The berry-picking "maidens" gambol while the boys are "boisterous," and the hero flutters in his tormented realm between the sexes.

In somewhere like Wing Biddlebaum's tormented realm, Sherwood Anderson also abode. American cities, as he wrote, are "noisy and terrible," and they fascinated him. He got much of the noise and terror into his writing about big cities, and the quiet noise and gentle terror of little towns into his stories about them. And among the fright of materialistic life, he continually rediscovered the minor beauties which made life possible for him—the moment of love, of friendship, of self-realization. That they were but moments is not entirely the fault of Anderson's own character.

3. *"The Air of a Creator."*

Anderson is shrewd, sometimes just, and has earned the right to even the unjust judgments he makes of other writers. How earned them? He was constantly fighting through both the questions of craft and the deeper risks of imagination. He has won the right to make sweeping pronouncements on his peers. Of Sinclair Lewis, for example, he offers the most damning, most apt criticism: "Wanting to see beauty descend upon our lives like a rainstorm, he has become blind to the minor beauties our lives hold." Sherwood Anderson wants the same thing, but holds to the good sense which a poet can still have in a difficult time: he clings to the minor beauties which give tenderness to his longing, a hope of something else to his despair. For this reason Anderson's critique of America finally bites more deeply than the novels of the ferocious sentimental satirist who was his contemporary.

Of Henry James, Anderson wrote that he is a man who "never found anyone to love, who did not dare love. . . . Can it be that he is the novelist of the haters? Oh, the thing infinitely refined and carried far into the field of intellectuality, as skillful haters find out how to do." The Jamesian flight from direct fleshly feeling offended Anderson. James objectified, stipulated, laid bare, and then suffused his entire yearning personality over all his work, so that Isabel Archer and Hyacinth Robinson are, really are Henry James, in all his hopeless longing, and yet spiritualized, that is, without body, epicene as James seems to have made himself in real life. George Santayana believed that by withholding love from a specific object it could be given "in general" to the whole world. This is a curiously commercial, economical notion—the idea that there is a limited amount of love and that we have the choice of spending it on a few selfishly chosen objects or distributing it generally. "In general" we know that this is nonsense; our attachments to individuals are the models for our attachments to humanity as an ideal; but like many sorts of nonsense, it worked for Henry James to the extent that he really loved some spirit of Art which his "puppets," his "fables," as he called them, served.

Is Anderson, with all his mid-American distrust of intellectualized love, really so far from Henry James? He is strikingly the perpetual adolescent in love with love rather than with a specific girl with changing flesh. One can see him dreaming after his dream-girl even as he approached old age. His romantic chivalry, his lust for the proletariat, his fantastic correspondence in which the letters seem to be written to himself, no matter how touching their apparent candor and earnest reaching out—is he perhaps the other side of the coin of his accusation against

Henry James? To be the novelist of lovers who did not dare to hate—this too is a limitation. He seems obliged to love others as a function of his own faulty self-love, and therefore his love of others seems willed, therefore incomplete, and his moments of hatred seem a guilty self-indulgence. He presents an extreme case of the imperfections of an artist just because of the disparity between his intentions and his performance. He wanted to love, he wanted to sing of love. His failures help to make still more brilliant his achievements in certain of the stories of Winesburg, in "The Egg," and in scattered paragraphs, stories, and sections of novels.

For the fault of bookish derivations for his feelings, Anderson substituted at his worst the fault of self-indulgent derivation from gratifications and dreads never altered after boyhood. He carried his childhood like a hurt warm bird held to his middle-aged breast as he walked out of his factory into the life of art. The primitive emotions of childhood are the raw material of all poetry. Sometimes the indulgence of them to the exclusion of the mature perspectives of adult life prevents Anderson from equaling his aspiration and own best work.

But this is a vain quibble. Who can do his best work always? What counts is the achievement, not the failures, however exemplary they may seem to a critic. "I have a lot I want to tell you if I can," he wrote in a letter. "I am writing short stories." The faults of unevenness, egotism, lazy acceptance of ideals, and romantic self-glorification are as nothing against the realized works of art which force their way through. Sherwood Anderson "added to the confusion of men," as he said of the great financiers and industrialists, the Morgans, Goulds, Carnegies, Vanderbilts, "by taking on the air of a creator." He has helped to create the image we have of ourselves as Americans. Curtis Hartman, George Willard, Enoch Robinson, all of the people of Winesburg, haunt us as do our neighbors, our friends, our own secret selves which we first met one springtime in childhood.   1957

The New Upper-Middle Soap Opera

(A tribute to Herman Wouk, Sloan Wilson, Cameron Hawley, and makers of fine face cream everywhere)

A NEW POPULAR NOVEL is abroad in the land. Like many a dull child, it has respectable parents: J. P. Marquand in this generation, William Dean Howells in an earlier one, and so on back. In its present best-selling incarnation, it has found a formula for success to equal Aristotle's stern definition of the nature of tragedy. No longer need a fiction lift its audience to a sense of participation in the life of a man of dignity, faced by responsibility, significant choice, and the flaws of his own humanity. Ambition and desire, the fear of passing away and the hunger for love, the use of intelligence toward a passionate growth—these strong melodies have been reorchestrated by the fabricators of the new upper-middle soap opera, just as the music is eliminated from music on Tin Pan Alley (while preserving a boom of beat) and caffeine is eliminated from coffee by the white-coated scientists (for the sake of those of us who have the jitters because we lack the ability to fulfill ambition and desire).

As we are seen in the upper-middle soap opera, Americans no longer seek the girl, the adventure, the career, or the prize of self. Now we need to get the Belongingness. Groupy man is the New American. Faith, defined as trust in a given society, becomes the prime mover. Plot, a direction of growth in time, a movement made possible by significant risks and commitments, gives way to plot defined as an anthology of cautionary anecdotes. The hero learns just how right it is to be right. Already secure in advance, a reader watches the protagonist join the company of men by the curious process of getting to be at one with the reader's own moral evasions.

In Sloan Wilson's *The Man in the Gray Flannel Suit*, for example, Tom Rath confesses that "Ralph and a good deal of the rest of the world have seemed honest to me ever since I became honest with myself. . . . I've become almost an optimist." The purging of pity and fear is replaced by contented anticipation: "Just wait till you see Gregory Peck getting honest with himself in this one!"

Was tragedy once an occasion for communion, a time for men to join their fellows in a sense of the power and glory of being human? Now a stupor of pleased submission —after a term of grief, savantly drawn out—follows the difficulties put upon this new hero in his world of real quirks and semi-real tribulations. We recognize the true enemies of success, since we have already conquered them ourselves: unfortunate accidents or temporary blindness. In this new shape of democracy, we are more than the equal of the heroes of our novels: we are the purged and cured toward whom *they* aspire. They want admittance.

Who are the fashioners of the new soap opera?

Herman Wouk, or Nobody Here But Us Career Sailors; Sloan Wilson, or Tell Your Wife the Truth, Then Wear Even Gray Flannel Lounging Pajamas; Cameron Hawley, or The Passion According to Saint Luce; and a host of less subtle apes of Marquand, or How Sad To Be Sad But How Distinguished.

From these moralists we learn that Queeg wouldn't have been so paranoid if only that bunch of anarchists and landlubbers had tried to understand Navy tradition and been more sympathetic when he clacked those queegballs. Missus Gray Flannel will understand her hubby's straying, picnicking with the grateful, pneumatic Maria, and fathering a child in Rome—just give her a few pages for being agitated in the suburban garden. The Young Designer, who really has faith in the Company, will always win out over mean, money-loving accountants, partly because he is Close to the Men and partly because his wife marches by his side some of the time. In *Executive Suite* the moment of truth is a moment of sublime obfuscation:

"As her hand touched the offered glass, Mary Walling understood, for one fleeting instant, the miracle of her husband's mind. Now it had happened to her! She knew without knowing why she knew. . . ." Even more stirring, she knows without knowing *what* she knows. But she realizes: "You'll never understand completely . . . . don't try . . . . you'll be happier if you don't . . . . he'll be happier, too." And then they go down "the dark corridor" together.

Despite mechanical construction and brazen moralizing, their thoughts about happiness separated by dot-dot-dot-dot from their thoughts about understanding, these novels are neither crude nor tasteless except in their implications. They are written by intelligent men. There is an educated restraint about their language. They are sincere writers who mean what they say: It's so hard to conform, but do it, do it, *do it*. The simplicity of the message is required by both their own lack of courage and that of the audience, but they are capable of spinning out complications, alternatives, dilemmas, and even the ambiguity of interpretation which passes for artistic quality. This high-type, college-grad, sob-and-smug story, written in the cottony "common style," has the advantage of making stops and starts without ever introducing passion or will. Perfectly planned, destined for the screen, it can be hammered into shape with a whistle and a song in the heart, five or seven or nine pages a day, without ever the terrible interruptions of doubt or drama. When it's time for a nap, the author can stop in the middle of a phrase, never breaking the easy flush and flow of his product:

"He was going to make May his wife." Willy Keith is relieved, also. May has just finished telling him that she has preserved her virginity from the importunities of an orchestra leader, she knows not why, some code or other maybe, just an old-fashioned girl who doesn't go for orchestra leaders. Everyone thinks that the musician has worked his will on May, just because she travels from hotel to hotel with him, but surprise, surprise, he has gnashed his teeth in vain. Willy "did not know what manner of life they could find together, he did not know whether they would be happy, and he did not care now. He was going to make May his wife." In *The Caine Mutiny,* as elsewhere in the woukaday world, heroes do their duty and villains merely wish they could.

The recent history of American literary vogues is an illuminating one. For a time, before World War II, there was the concern about a contracting economy and want in the midst of plenty which generated the proletarian novel. Then came the war and the war novel, in which the same quest for a better world met the rigors of regimentation and the horrors of organized destruction. In both of these periods, the writer reserved for himself the role of a moralist seeking solutions beyond immolation.

But in this new novel, built within a world of terrible beatitudes, a world of contracting freedom and organized satisfactions, the attack is concentrated on the ideals of the earlier writers. The novel of revolt has given way to the obedience novel. It is cornball to be difficult, to grope for more than a few chapters, to seek frontiers and a better life. In the new unfreedom—where all is plentiful but the chance to look and there is nearly full employment for everything but the mind and heart—the only frontier to be reached is that of Adjustment. These new agonists make it to the recruiting office, or if they don't, their authors hold them up to our contempt.

When Marjorie Morningstar attains the suburb, after passing through the crucible of a grotesque Broadway Bohemia, we are directed to cheer her luck for having found the values that the reader has already found. She is happily burned down. She is prematurely gray; presumably she has charcoal gray hair to go with her gray flannel heart. As Diderot says, commenting on the trouble we have in breaking the impulse to love: "Preparations of lead, put to use prudently, may produce good effects, being proper to stifle the venereal appetite." The leaden career of Marjorie, her single transgression justified by frigidity on the occasion, hip-heavy now, a clubwoman, keeping a kosher kitchen, is given us as an exemplary one.

What are the alternatives? The Life of Art (ingredients, in any order: Broadway, cynicism, the *rive gauche*, sex, hope, and James Joyce) vs. The Life of Life (suburb, bridge and canasta, a husband who is not very tall but very nice).

2

Probably the most respectable rationale for this new novel occurs in the work of David Riesman, who performed a brilliant metaphorical fix on the American character in *The Lonely Crowd*, and then proceeded, in the books that followed, to define the desirable "autonomous" personality as the one which is free because it accepts its society and chooses "responsibly" within the acceptable. Why persist in protest when we already have everything? Why look when we have found as much as we can consume? Why long for further goods when all the commodities needed for happiness are available to anyone whose credit is unsullied?

And don't be anxiously other-directed, either, Mr. Riesman advises, and we hear a peal from the church tower prompting him: "Think positively, dong, dong."

The autonomous personality also carries a radar which is closely tuned to others, but it makes significant and free choices anyway. They are not the compulsive, driven ones of the old inner-directed style; they are not the sheepish milling in herds of the other-directeds. Most readers of *The Lonely Crowd* felt a certain kinship with Riesman's inner-directed type, and thought that he intended it that way, despite his disavowals. Turns out that no. Further discussion laid down the line. The inner-directed man is a violent, lonely, self-seeking person, tormented by aspiration, withered of the kitchen-warm feelings, and ignorant of the common pleasures.

For Spinoza, human bondage consists in entrapment by the flesh and the material world; true freedom comes of a stoic withdrawal into these personal values which no earthly misfortune can tarnish. Riesman parodies this typically inner-directed solution to the problem of sustaining the individual spirit in troubled times. The autonomous man seeks to be a part of the leveled culture; it would be neurosis or treason to object. But the autonomous man uses his teevee in a brilliant, supple, imaginative and wide-ranging way. While mere other-directed man watches "I Love Lucy" because everyone is watching "I Love Lucy," the autonomous hero deliberates, investigates, considers, measures, and only then ventures a decision between Channel 4 and Channel 7. And of course, since we expect that he is autonomous enough to be proud of being a man of our time, in the end he will watch "I Love Lucy," too.

But there is always the subtle difference: *He really wanted to*. He drafted himself. And the possibilities of free choice unroll with dizzying challenge during the autonomous evening: beer or ginger ale, chocolate ice cream or strawberry, should I take my wife to bed or not.

Novelists are not the original seducers, then. They are accompanied by Karen Horney in psychology, David Riesman in sociology, and Batten, Barton, Durstine & Osborn in philosophy. All the current close squeezing to belong, to conform, to adjust, to sing praise to what-is in America provides the social climate of novels worthy of being serialized in *Life*. While the society reassures itself that all goes for the best, we are just busy little bees, working, leisuring, grouping, rearming, the private agony goes on. What we are and what the world seeks to make of us are continually at war. The adman knows it, the statesman knows it, even Sloan Wilson knows it, though he buzzes in the hive and says, "What a brave bee am I!" Exactly as in radio soap opera, Sloan Wilson allows us our bit of trouble to show us to what extent life can be beautiful. Later. Soon. Just pucker up, button up, and face your duty.

The sophisticates who commit the new soap opera know the people they describe, or at least know their manners, what they drink, how they joke, where they buy their clothes. These novelists have their own goals; they are relieved of the wrenching ambition of Balzac, Tolstoy, or Dostoevski—to make life large. Their task is simply to point the local personnel toward a good life waiting to receive them. You blindfold your people; you turn them around until they are dizzy; you have them stumble awhile; then—since you know where the donkey is—you let them peek under the bandage and pin on the tail. What passes for dramatic growth is the bumping against furniture which dislodges that handkerchief over the eyes. The reader is pleased that his hero has made out, but his pleasure is a smug one. How silly not to have used a finger to pry up the blindfold.

Determined to be a contented cow, such a novelist is bound to give a chalky or overbland milk. There is nothing to work toward but a job of consolidation. Social protest is an anachronism—the courts take care of injustice. The private risk and chance of trouble are mere neurosis—find yourself an analyst. Significant choice is no longer possible to individuals.

For these autonomous fabricators, everything can be reduced, encompassed, rectified. We will be teased from chapter to chapter by dread that maybe the Regular Navy breeds the wrong kind of paranoid; maybe the man in the gray flannel suit really has chosen a way of life which must leave him unfulfilled—and only Maria, the Roman fantasy-wife, can make him happy in the sack; maybe great corporations are run for profit and not for the benefit of the worker and the customer.

But all is creamy in the end. Those who rebel against Navy spirit are the selfish children of caprice, and an artist is the worst of all. Now that Tom Rath and his wife Understand, they can march on into Connecticut and the house they really want, budgeting a hundred dollars a month to help raise Tom's child in Rome and remembering now to try to Communicate while they're in bed. (Balzac said: Women, when they finally succeed in making a man into a sheep, always tell him that he is a lion with a will of iron.)

And finally, brightest faith of all, it turns out that a furniture company is really a service and chooses for its next President the man who most desires to Serve. Like Mary Walling, the Company appreciates "the miracle of her husband's mind."

3

Novels always reflect moral purpose. Every novel which takes any permanent hold differs both in goal and perspective from every other novel. We expect these differences, just as we expect each event in a life to change our view of that life. Novel-writing has always been a risky, athletic, and potentially destructive adventure, for just these reasons of uncertainty about what the work will tell us. "Pity this busy monster, manunkind, not."

These new novels also surprise us with their message. There is something new in the type, however—not merely another perspective on the meaning of human life in society. There is a new grayness and dryness, a new limit to the will and intelligence of the novelists. They reduce experience. They shrink; they join with the other shrinkers; this frightened hiving replaces the challenge of individual worth. They put alum on their lips so that they cannot even kiss properly.

A shadow of the athletic striving of the artist as moralist persists, but now the moral purpose becomes that of an exercise in submission. Faith is the famous bird flying in ever-decreasing concentric circles—faith in Faith, not in some bright tradition; the patriotism is hoarse and defensive; groupiness replaces even the bugles of glorious chauvinism. Our doubts are portrayed, sometimes vividly, in the books of Wouk, Wilson, and Hawley. They are answered at the end much in the way of the clever Italian journalists who smuggled honesty into their editorials, marshaling all the arguments against Mussolini, then concluding triumphantly: "Oh yeah? That's what our enemies think."

The journalists deceived only the censors. Not so with Sloan Wilson. He is a believer. After Tom Rath gives his wife the account of his infidelity, he is suddenly that two-headed modern fictional beast, the Honest Man. It can do anything. By the deus ex machina of this abstract, Platonic, "essential" honesty, he is saved for happy commuting despite all the evidence of his experience. Can the heavenly purity of a gray flannel career be corrupted? No! Why not? Because: "That's what our enemies think."

The commuting, business, institutionalized world— apolitical, bored and anxious, with passion the great danger

—is questioned with some skill and tension. The affirmation of allegiance to it which follows is so much more reassuring: *He knows, he knows.* Job rebelling against abomination, raises his head and cries out, "How long, O Lord?" He needs the love of God, God's justice and tenderness, but on his own most demanding terms: for what he has been, is, and can be. The three friends say *Shush!* because Job has no right to challenge the almighty Source of the universe. "Hide yourself, give up," they urge him, waving their arms and shaking their beards: "There must be a reason, and if there isn't? Be nice."

He will buy neither the comfort nor the false freedom of pretense. It is not that Job is an anarchic spoiled child. He struggles to take his place among God's children on the terms of his power and virtue as a man. There is belonging and belonging. The road by which we arrive at participation within a group cannot be separated from the quality of this participation. Community is one thing; groupiness is another. Job stands on two feet like a man, with awareness of responsibility, with a capacity to love and respect, with a sense of the value of the individual others. The temporizers band together because they cannot travel alone, and put out their hands not to pray but to lean. Job lives in both pride and piety. The three friends make a world of their fear and cunning. "Why ask for truth or justice?" they say. "Take what you can get and pretend it's what you want. After all, it's what *we* want."

The great novelists have always been Jobs; the new novelists of tremulous adjustment are the three friends: "How long, O Lord, before his wife helps him to understand?" These writers already understand, however, and here in all its simplicity is their moral message:

Virtue consists in a faithful submission, perhaps with understanding and sorrow, to the way things are. The way things are is the best way for things to be—or at least there is nothing better which we can bear to imagine. If you are still troubled, be patient. Have faith. All blessings will come to you, and in decorator colors. The path of righteousness will be made more abundantly clear in the VistaVision version.

As a television editor put it, "No more downbeat dramas! We want happy stories about happy people with happy problems." The ideal type of the happy problem is represented by the issue facing that handsome couple in the automobile advertisement, all gowned and tuxedoed, smiling at each other and wondering what kind of an evening it will be, while the baby-sitter broods benevolently in the background: "Shall we take the Cadillac tonight?"

Answer that question in 100,000 words, man.

1957

HIP, COOL, BEAT AND FRANTIC

1. The American as Hipster

In Greenwich Village a dreamy young beggar in a tattered Ivy League summer suit and a buttondown collar with both buttons missing turns on an uptown couple to ask, "Gimme a quarter for a Cadillac, hey?"

In New Orleans a pretty little department store model approaches a man at a party, takes off her sweater, then her bra, and says, "Let's ball, dig"—by which she means, Let's try a new far-out sound on the hi-fi. If he reaches out to touch anything but the tone arm, she will say, "You're through, frantic boy. You are sawed off." He disappears from future guest lists.

In Denver a gaggle of young lads, not knowing what to do on a warm spring evening, steal a car each, drive them to the other side of town, park, steal a few more, drive back to the starting point, park, and then settle down to giggle about the confusion of the owners and the police. Silence. Return of boredom. Yawn. Finally one says softly, "Pops, why didn't we think of picking up on some chicks?"

In St. Louis a girl and her friend, who used to be a drummer with a well-known quintet, both of them suffering

withdrawal symptoms—he has been working to support
their habits by pimping for the girl—beg an old pal to put
them up with bed and fridge for a few days. While the
friend is away at work, they telephone a friend in San
Francisco, give him the bit, and after gassing awhile, suggest that they both just keep the connection and leave
the telephones off the hook. Their friend won't get the bill
until they are gone, far gone. Why do this to him? "He's
square, so square, man."

In Detroit a hi-fi engineer clucks sympathetically at
the plight of a young couple in college. It's true love, but
they have no place to go. The back seat of a car is for puppy
love and sprained backs. OK, they can use his apartment.
What they don't know is that there is a microphone con-
cealed in the mattress. Their friend invites them to a
party where he plays the tape before strangers.

In San Francisco a group of young poets announces
Religious Poetry Night, attracting a hall full of the plump,
mournful ladies (purple hats, veils, heaving freckled
bosoms) who adore such things. The first poet gets up to
read. "C— S——!" he shrieks at the audience.

On State Street in Chicago a frozen-faced grifter stops
a passer-by, pushing out his hand and murmuring, "What
you say, pop? Give me a piece of skin."

"I'm sorry, I don't know you."

"I don't know you either, man, but you like to have a
party?" He slides off and away with a passive dreamy girlish
look which has nothing sweet about it: it plots impossible
meanness, anything to make him feel something. He
doesn't know anybody, and says "man" to everybody because he can't be bothered remembering names.

In midtown Manhattan a writer, Jack Kerouac, prepares for his interview on TV. "We're beat, man," he says.
"Beat means beatific, it means you get the beat, it means
something. I invented it." For the television audience he
announces, "We love everything, Billy Graham, the Big

Ten, rock and roll, Zen, apple pie, Eisenhower—we dig it all. We're in the vanguard of the new religion." Jack Kerouac likes to write of Charlie Parker as God and himself as the Prophet.

These are hipsters.

Who is the hipster, what is it? The pure beast is as hard to track as the pure "student" or "midwesterner," but let us follow the spoor of history and symptoms. We will probably find that "pure hipster" is a phrase like "100% American"—an unstable compound with an indefinite content.

Hipsterism began in a complex effort of the Negro to escape his imposed role of happy-go-lucky animal. A few highly self-conscious urban Negro men sought to imitate "white" diffidence, or coolness, or beatness. They developed a style which was both a criticism of their Bible-shouting and jazz-loving parents and a parody of the detached, uninvolved city ofays. They improvised on an unstated theme—like bop—and if you weren't with it, with it and for it, you heard nothing but jangle. The horn rims of the intellectual came to be known as bop glasses. They blew fine abstractions. The joke was a good one.

Then their white friends took up the fashion, complicating the joke by parodying a parody of themselves. Cool music was the artistic expression of this hypertensive chill. However, in order to keep from dancing, keep from shouting, keep from feeling, a further help was needed and it was found in heroin. Some of the earlier hot musicians had used marijuana, many drank; these were springs toward jumping high in a group. There was a strong prejudice against the cats who went on junk, expressed in the superstition that you might mainline a fatal bubble of air into your veins. Uh-uh, no baby, they said: and in practice they found that the junkie blew lousy drum or horn, no matter what he thought he was blowing.

The new generation preferred supercelestial private

music, however. Heroin dissolves the group and each man flies alone all the way to Barbados. And without flapping his arms.

Many other young Americans felt beat, wanted to keep cool, and so into the arms of the first hipster society, that still unravished bride of bop quietness, ran three angry herds: (1) Main-street thugs with their sideburns, their cycles, and their jeans; (2) college kids and a few literary chappies, finding in the addict's cool stance an expression of the frustration of fluid-drive lives in which the juicebox had gone dry; and (3) Upper Bohemia, tired of Van Gogh, Italian movies, charades, and sex, and so ready to try anti-art, anti-sex, anti-frantic nonmovement. These latter comprise the Madison Avenue hippies, models who strip merely to express their hatred of fashion magazines, admen and lawyers who marry call girls, a host of Ivy League symbol-manipulators, bloated with money and debt, pink with General Electric sun tans and shame, who express their benzedrine blues by wigging at night near a blasting rig. "Well, you know . . . Albert Schweitzer doesn't make me climb the wall. . . . Is it true he eloped with Kim Novak?"

"Everyone says," remarks the pretty girl who seeks to please, "that I'm exceptionally fastidious, but would you like me to do something nasty for you? I really wouldn't mind. My name is Grape-Nuts, what's yours?"

Let us now move in closer to the hipster's harried heart. When the hipster makes it with a girl, he avoids admitting that he likes her. He keeps cool. He asks her to do the work, and his ambition is to think about nothing, zero, strictly from nadaville, while she plays bouncy-bouncy on him. When the hipster makes it with boys, it's not because he's a homosexual and cares for it—it's for money, a ride home, pass the time of night while waiting for the band to come back on. When the hipster steals a car, he doesn't keep it or sell it; he hides it where the squares will have trouble finding it, and writes "Mort à Louis A" in soap on the windshield. When the hipster digs music, Proust, or religion, it's to talk over, it's to carry around in his jeans, it's to hit his buddies with; it makes no sense or feeling, and the weirder it is, the cooler the kick.

In other words, the hipster is a spectacular instance of the flight from emotion. He is like a sick refrigerator, laboring with tremendous violence, noise and heat, and all for one purpose—to keep cool. This refrigerator is powered by crime without economic need; an editor to one of the hipster writers complains, "Jeez, when I slept on park benches and boosted from the A and P, I did it because I had to. My kick was that I needed sleep and food. I didn't do it to tell people about." The refrigerator is powered by sex without passion; the sole passion is for the murder of feeling, the extinguishing of the jitters. The refrigerator is powered by religion without faith; the hipster teases himself toward the black battiness of oblivion, and all the vital refreshment which religion has given the mystics of the past is a distraction from the lovely stupor he craves. Unlike Onan, who spilled his seed upon the ground, the hipster spills his brains and calls it piety. He also wears music, art, and religion as a kind of badge for identification. Instead of the secret handshake which got him into Uncle Don's Boys' Club or the Orphan Annie Secret Society, he now says, "You dig the Bird? Proust? Zen?"

"I'm hip." says his friend. This phrase means: No need to talk. No more discussion. I'm with you. I got you. Cool. In. Bye-bye.

The language of hipsterism is a means toward non-communication, a signal for silence. The truest lingo is narcotics, because this more than anything gives Little Boy Beat what he wants—release from imagination and the body—an illusion not of omnipotence, as we are sometimes told, but of a timeless browsing in eternity. In other words, a cool simulation of death. The sentimental and sensational talk about drugs producing sex maniacs is nonsense. The man on a habit needs nothing more than his fix. Quiet, quiet. He may perform terrible violence to get the drug, but not sex: pleasure has nothing to do with the dreamy high of heroin. The pale soft face of the addict, with his smudged passive eyes and his drooping mouth, is almost ladylike in its sweetness. It has no fight or love in it.

Heroin enables the hipster to stand guard over his soul, dreaming of cool nothing, beautiful beat nothing, while his feet go ratatat and he strokes a switchblade, a hand, or a copy of *Swann's Way*. Needless to say, the proto- and quasi-hipsters do not usually go all the way to the perfection of heroin.

The current fad for the hipster—his language, manners and attitudes—indicates that he is, as that fearful phrase goes, "no isolated phenomenon." Jack Kerouac proclaimed, "Even the Ivy League is going hip." Emerging out of bop, narcotics, and the subtle rebellion of the Negro against the charge of being "happy, excitable, emotional," the hipster takes one of his chief public models from that most authentic American source, the movies. He ignores the injunction of the pious thirteenth-century moralist, John of Garland, who wrote: "Be not a fornicator, O Student! Stand and sit upright, do not scratch thyself!" The Stanislavsky hipsters scratch as if their soul's unease were actually juicy fleas, slouch as if leaning to catch Marlon's word from earth or Jimmy's from vaulted heaven. The movie shadow of Dean or the Brando of *The Wild One* is a part of the image of the hipster, whether he be the smooth pink Ivy League metahipster, staring at himself in the mirror of one of those shops where they apparently do operations to remove the bones from men's shoulders, or the long-chinned hairy protohipster with a girl jiggling on the behind seat of his Harley-Davidson "74." In many theaters where *The Wild One* played, there was a lineup afterwards in the men's room, the cyclists in their nail-studded black jackets scowling with adoration into the

mirror as they rehearsed their public roles. Each man was
Brando, distant and violent. Each man was Marlon, cool
and beat. They stood in a row without shame, almost without vanity (so pure it was), like neophytes for sacrifice in
their penitential leather, silver trim, sideburns, and duckass
haircuts. Scratch not, O Hipster!

And so the hipster's lines of communication spread
from a four-bit movie-house in a small town of the Midwest to the chic saloons of New York and the Coast. He
reminds us of the Teddy Boys of England, the breaking-
loose wild brats of defeated Japan, the existentialist *zazous*
of Paris, tootling the petrified dixie they learned from old
Beiderbecke records. His apologists, particularly the literary
hipsters of San Francisco and New York are fond of
reaching back into history to invoke the criminal gods of
French poetry—Rimbaud, who mysteriously vanished into
Africa, Villon, who ended up dancing on the gallows,
Genet, who is now a poet and playwright hero of Paris after
a career of thievery, blackmail, and male prostitution. The
very important difference between the American literary
hipster and his foreign models is that the great artist-
criminals were true outcasts from society: they did not
pick themselves up by the seat of their own pants and toss
themselves out. They were driven by class differences and
economic pressure. A few of the Americans have performed
spectacularly—mostly in the loony bin; one even played
William Tell with his wife and blew her head off—but
these are individual troubles, not the product of any vast
and windy guilt of society. Who ain't got personal troubles?
I dig yours, man; but I got mine too.

In any case, the 1958 hipster is not the bold medieval
troubadour prince of song and con, nor the romantic ad-
venturer poet of later times, nor the angry driven Depression stiff: he is the true rebel without a cause. No, of
course, he has a cause—his charred self, but a self without
connection or need. He is a reticent boyo with a yen for

thuggery, a reluctant visitor to the affairs of men, a faintly girlish loiterer near the scenes of violence. If he can't be a big boom-boom hero in a war, like Gary Cooper, at least he can take the muffler off his rod, like Marlon. Mainly he is afflicted with the great triumvirate disease of the American male—Passivity, Anxiety, Boredom. Individualists without individuality, a sleepy brawl of knowing nonthinkers, the lonely crowd at its grumbling loneliest, the hipsters fall naturally to the absolute submission of a marriage to heroin. Like the submission to boredom in television and all the other substitutes for personal creativeness in American life, narcotics involve an abdication of good sense by men deprived of the will to make their own ways.

"I dig everything, man."

"What do you want to do now?"

"I don't know, man. Get some kicks somehow."

If the description of the hipster as "passive" strikes you as harsh, look up the dictionary definition of the word: "*Med.* Pertaining to certain morbid conditions characterized by deficient vitality and reaction."

The word hipster came in with bop, which is a way of keeping cool musically, at the same time that narcotics addiction burgeoned—a way of keeping cool sexually. The drug-taking hipster is not a sexual anarchist; he is a sexual zero, and heroin is his mama, papa, and someone in bed. (The pusher in A *Hatful of Rain* is called "Mother.") Not every quasi-hipster mainlines into the tattoo on his arm, of course, but the style of life is set by those who do. The coolest boys call each other "daddy-o," as if their passivity extends to thinking of every man as a potential guardian father. Of course, the traveling musician also cannot be bothered to remember names, so everyone is "man," "pops," "daddy-o." They worship the purple fantasy of torn-tee-shirted masculinity created by Tennessee Williams, William Inge, and others who have invented a new theatrical type—the male impersonator. Adorably brutal, stripped of the prime attributes of manliness—intelligence, purpose, control—they are the curvaceous Mae Wests of popular melodrama. Having died, James Dean and Charlie Parker are defined as immortal. Living and growing up a bit, Marlon Brando is a traitor to this myth of saintly suicide by sports car or heroin. They might have forgiven his giving up the bongos, but his receding hairline is a disgrace to the cause. The strong silent hero must also be weak and pretty.

One of the curious bypaths of hipsterism leads to their far-out religious camp. Jack Kerouac says, "We're in the vanguard of the new religion," which is a little like the monk in the story who claimed that he was the world champion for humility. They picked up on St. John of the Cross for a time, Catholic ritual, St. Francis of Assisi (they were St. Frantics); then they moved on toward Byzantine, Greek, and Orthodox fantasies, with ikons and incense; they made the Dostoevski scene. In recent years some have taken to calling themselves Zen Hipsters, and Zen Buddhism has spread like the Asian flu, so that now you can open your fortune cookie in one of the real cool Chinese restaurants of San Francisco and find a slip of paper with the straight poop: "Dig that crazy Zen sukiyaki. Only a square eats Chinese food." Promiscuity in religion stands, like heroin, for despair, a feverish embracing of despair, a passive sinking into irrationality. Zen and other religions surely have their beauties, but the hipster dives through them like a sideshow acrobat through a paper hoop—into the same old icy water of self-distrust below. The religious activities of the hipsters cure their unease in the world the way dancing cheek to cheek cures halitosis.

No wonder the hipster says, "Nada, I'm beat—I'm right in there, see—I'm the most religious, the most humble —I'm swinging, man." He stammers because something is missing, a vital part, the central works. His soul, sense of meaning, individual dignity (call it how you like) has been excised as unnecessary by a civilization very often producing without good purpose. He feels that love is not love, work is not work, even protest is not protest any more. On the consumer's assembly line, in the leisure-time sweatshop, he pieceworks that worst of all products of anxiety—boredom. This is the response of retreat from the cold inanities of his time payments, luxurious discomfort, dread of the successful future. Boredom is a corollary to anxiety. As the middle-class man now buys a brick for the new church (Does God need that basement bowling alley?), so the hipster tries to find himself in intuitions of meaning through the Anchor edition of Zen tales, or through some other fashionable interior decoration. Naturally he stammers, "Cool, mon, real cool." He wants to stop moving, jittering, flittering. He displays himself as exemplary because he has no wife, children, responsibilities, politics, work. The middle-class man both has and does not have these things. Who can call moving bits of paper a job? Most Americans are paper-movers. How is love of wife and children more than a social habit when a man feels *qua* man (not as husband or father) that he has no authority except in his own home?

When a man's house is his only castle, then he has no castle.

Both smugness and ambition are characteristics of human beings, not of animals, though rats and rabbits can be taught despair by repeated electric shocks. Faced by the threat of absolute manipulation, the hipster mobilizes himself for a last stand—and hops about the cage, twitching his tail, bumping the charged wires.

The cliché which tells us that Americans love Things, Possessions, does not go far enough. Americans also demand experiences of power, one way or the other, in person or out of the picture tube. This seems normal enough to be a condition of life, but not when the starved mirage of power crowds out the quietness which gives experience meaning and organizes a man to face his private issues of working, loving, having children, dying. Certain experiences lead *away from* rather than *toward,* and faster and faster we go: the experience does not help; we try wilder experience; this does not help; still more wild, wilder. The extreme of a flatulent submission to the mass media eventually stops all experience in its tracks, in the guise of giving perfect experiences which make it possible to carry on. Television as a medium of entertainment is not the villain any more than good whiskey is a villain; they can both be good friends. It is the bleared submission by depleted souls which destroys. Relaxation is one thing—sharing experience vicariously is a great experience to which the imagination entitles us. To be stunned is another matter entirely. Despair by electronic shock.

Sensitive to all this, the hipster has decided to quit —resign—have no more of it. Instead of being part of a mass audience before the picture tubes, he becomes an audience of one before the hypo. He gives up on the issue of being human in society. He decides that the problem does not exist for him. He disaffiliates. The man who cares is now derided for being "frantic."

But of course the hipster is still a part of a bewildered America in which Tab Hunter confides to an interviewer that he can only sleep with his Teddy bear in bed with him. The hipster is victim of the most hopeless condition of slavery—the slave who does not know that he is a slave and is proud of his slavery, calling it "freedom." Incurable? Nearly. The posture of negation and passivity thinks it is religion and rebellion; instead it is a mob phenomenon. These nihilists sail dreamy down the Nile of throughway America, spending many a sleepless day figuring out something real cool to do at night, and end up trying to convince themselves, as Jack Kerouac does, that Charlie Parker is God. Kerouac's birdmen in his novel, *On the Road,* search for coolness within their beatness, hipness within their jeans-and-dirty-hair dream of quickies with marvelous girls (who also wear dirty hair and jeans). Occasionally, as in the Kerouac variety of superfrantic subhipster, sex takes the place of dope. This is a kind of sex which also takes the place of sex. The way some men gloat over possessions, he keeps score of his hero's erotic blitzes, forgetting that —if you are the trooper who uses sex as a weapon—every notch in a weapon weakens the weapon.

The hipster is a street-corner, bar, and partying phenomenon, a creature of mobs. One Rimbaud may be a genius; a crowd of them is a fad. An earlier fad for psychoanalysis has this in favor of it: Freud believed in the prime value of emotions, but in a necessary control by the intelligence. In other words, he valued society despite the discontents of civilization. The hipster gives up society, gives up intelligence, and thinks he is doing this in favor of the emotions; but he has already, without making a decision about them, let his feelings seep away through a leaky personality. What is left is a spasmodic jerk, though some of the individual spokesmen also have vivacious talent. No wonder that the madhouse is seen as the refuge of their "best minds." Catatonia, here we come.

These shrill moonbirds turn out to be rigid earth satellites, rocketed by bureaucrats beyond their ken into the air of reality, where they circle in a pattern determined without choice, give out a diminishing signal, draw to earth and burn, crumble, vanish.

When Yeats looked into the future to find a terrible savior, an evolution up from animality into something strange and wonderful:

> What rough beast, its hour come round at last,
> Slouches toward Bethelem to be born?

—he did not mean James Dean. Perhaps, as they claim, the tunneling hipster's avoidance of feeling can lead to a new honesty of emotion. Perhaps a groundhog might some day learn to fly, but man O man, that will be one strange bird.　　　　　　　　　　　　　　　　　1958

2. Hip, Cool, Beat, and Frantic

"WHOEE, I told my soul." This urgent message from Jack Kerouac to his soul contains most of the sense which emerges from his frantic tirade in the form of a novel, *On the Road*, and it is his ability to make such stuff hip, cool, beat, and frantic, all at once, which has earned him a title more valued nowadays than that of "novelist": He is a Spokesman.

For what this time? Kerouac has appointed himself prose celebrant to a pack of unleashed zazous who like to describe themselves as Zen Hipsters—poets, pushers and panhandlers, musicians, male hustlers, and a few marginal esthetes seeking new marginal distinctions. They have a center in San Francisco, another in Greenwich Village, and claim outposts in Tangiers, on merchant vessels, in Chicago, a fragment among the fragments in New Orleans, a fringe of the fringe in Mexico City. Despite all wandering, however, their loneliness for the herd sends them eagerly trumpeting back into each other's arms after brief periods of saying whoee to their souls among the outlanders. At least two of them happen to be talented—Allen Ginsberg, a poet of shock and wild wit, whose blathering *Howl* really does contain some of the liveliest epithets in contemporary verse; and Jack Kerouac, whose mammoth journal has been edited into the form of a novel by The Viking Press. One of the heroes of *On the Road*, of course, is Allen Ginsberg (under the name of Carlo Marx), just as one of the heroes of *Howl* is Jack Kerouac (under the name of Jack Kerouac).

Who are these hipsters, what are they? A distinction must be made between the authentic beast—a phenomenon of frigidity and shock—and its literary fleas, who are mainly Ivy League desperadoes, romantic dreamers fondly recalling hypes and heists that other chaps hyped or heisted. In the background of Kerouac's book glimmer the cultural signs that the people he is spokesmaning for are really here: their photographs in *Harper's Bazaar* and *Mademoiselle*; two issues of the *Evergreen Review* and *New Directions 16* largely devoted to their work; a publishing venture in San Francisco; articles on them in *The New York Times*, *The Nation*, the *New Republic*, *New World Writing*, *Dissent*, the *Chicago Review*, and elsewhere; a few books, including Clellon Holmes's *Go!*, which belongs to an earlier period (1952), although it describes many of the people implicated in *On the Road*. (Historical periods rush upon us like men's fashions: "Bop was somewhere between its Charlie Parker Ornithology period and another period which began with Miles Davis. . . .") Mr. Ginsberg and Mr. Gregory Corso recently teamed up to make an agitprop tour of New York which shook Madison Avenue real bad, though they have yet to appear on behalf of Schweppes (with beards), Hathaway (eyepatch), Marlboro (tattooed hands), or in poems by e. e. cummings (they too are free spirits, FREE, they told him).

On the Road carries the ensign of the hipster with considerable humor and vitality, much awe, and a little of the literary hipster's prevalent social disease, the faked-up pretension that these are underground intellects who know all about Zen Buddhism, St. John of the Cross, Proust, and good bad old Charlie Parker, and could tell us if they only cared to. The awe breaks to happy moments of lucidity which are those of a real writer. Kerouac then sees the hipster, agape and bedazzled, mumbling about the world-historical significance of bop—but only mumbling. What he tells, he tries to tell true enough according to his lights. At times he almost seems to understand that Charlie Parker blew fine horn, but was not God.

However, there is a structural flaw in this contemporary revival of the literary-criminal or ecstatic-delinquent underground which makes Jack Kerouac's book a proof of illness rather than a creation of art, a novel. In the first place, Villon, Rimbaud, and Jean Genet really lived by their criminal passivity and wits. They showed their rumps to society because they were caught from behind. These Americans, however, are *literary* in their coolness, hipness, beatness, and they are unauthentic exactly to the degree that they are literary. The hipster-writer is a perennial perverse bar mitzvah boy, proudly announcing: "Today I am a madman. Now give me the fountain pen." The frozen thugs gathered west of Sheridan Square or in the hopped-up cars do not bother with talk. That's why they say "man" to everyone—they can't remember anybody's name. But Ginsberg and Kerouac are *frantic*. They care too much, and they care aloud. "I'm *hungry*, I'm *starving*, let's *eat right now!*" That they care mostly for themselves is a sign of adolescence, but at least they care for something, and it's a beginning. The hipster is past caring. He is the criminal with no motivation in hunger, the delinquent with no zest, the gang follower with no love of the gang; *i.e.*, the worker without ambition or pleasure in work, the youngster with undescended passions, the organization man with sloanwilsonian gregory-peckerism in his cold, cold heart. He has entered a deep cavern where desire and art are unknown; swimming blind, scared, and silent, he eats whatever is alive—a symptom of trouble, but hardly feeling it any more.

Still, hipsterism has touched a number of writers, since the extremes always attract and the hipster fish is the coldest and clammiest and perhaps the deadliest creature of the deep seas in which we all now swim. "Nothing human is alien to me." Goethe, among others, said it. The hipster's pressured soul, squirting bile, excites the artist who, out of pity or morbidity, either saintly or slumming, dives into the world of the ice-blooded. Yes, something has made them that way. There are connections. They have carried their rebellion from society past the end: excising from their innards the cant of a mass culture, these fierce surgeons have also badly cut up their humanity. They are cool. Now they blow nothing but the miseries.

Bernard Wolfe has learned to keep a heavy leg outside, in the wide world of politics and philosophy, and therefore to make art of the hipsters' death-in-life; Norman Mailer has gone to school to them, and may yet graduate, as he has restlessly graduated from other ideologies. The poet Kenneth Rexroth is their youngish elder statesman, whose collected essays in their defense might be entitled *Zen Strikes Back*; Lawrence Lipton contributes a hairy, academic *apologia pro vita nostruomo*; the late Isaac Rosenfeld was one of their most perceptive critics. There are others whom the stoolies of criticism have fingered with deadly inaccuracy, such as Nelson Algren, Chandler Brossard, Anatole Broyard, and (may he put away his Harley-Davidson "74," nevermore to roam in nail-trimmed leather jacket and buttock-cracking jeans) Herbert Gold. But if we grant that the hipster-writer exists, the first thing to understand about him is that he is not a hipster, although he likes to play as if, any more than Nelson Algren is a Polish poker player. He is propagandist for a cause that does not ask to be preached. He is hung up on the dilemma of being cool and frantic at the same time. "Some of the best minds of our generation," chants Allen Ginsberg, "have given up thinking."

By definition an artist cannot be a hipster though he might follow the old style of dipping into forbidden waters, reminding us in various ways of Brecht, Gide, Gorki, and a number of English and Spanish philosophical picaros. Coolness can be defined as refusing-to-care—not uncaring, but refusing. The hipster steals a car with a copy of *Swann's Way* in his pocket—a book he doesn't read, a car he doesn't want. The hipster's ideal is to smoke a cigar and study the *Daily News* while having immobile sexual intercourse. He has to carry out the act in order to refuse its meaning in vitality and refreshment and to debase the girl: he cannot simply abstain. The frantic man *swings*. He may move badly; his prose may be derivative and his reactions premature; but he *moves*, man. The ash spills from his cigar. He gets more than kicks out of life.

When Kerouac wails about "many and many a lost night, singing and moaning and eating the stars and dropping the juices drop by drop on the hot tar," he is in a respectable literary tradition, and the tradition's name is Thomas Wolfe. This is not hipster talk. When he passes through Fresno, sees an Armenian, and thinks: "Yes, yes, Saroyan's town," he has some of that aging bucko's free-wheeling self-love—and just as literary. When he hints at orgy, his real daddy is the daddy of all the living boheems, Henry Miller, though he practices a conciseness of sexual rhetoric which probably derives from the publisher's timidity rather than from any cool indifference. Sometimes he writes the purest straight-and-true Hemingway, as when he meets a Mexican girl: "Her breasts stuck out straight and true." Later his friend Dean is driving a car no-hands, but "it hugged the line straight and true."

This is not beat. This is not cool. This is not hip.

This is the Columbia College boy vacationing on his GI Bill money, reading Papa. But despite all the bookish derivations, Kerouac retains a stubborn integrity: "I had nothing to offer anybody but my own confusion."

He has something more to offer. I would guess, writing before publication, that the bookselling business is not yet ready for a particular blend of nihilism and mush which might someday take its place in the gassy world of best-sellerdom.* When Kerouac mentions the Bomb, he makes us blush: he doesn't mean it, it's pure stylishness, and we resent the fact that the great disaster of contemporary history should be used in passing to let us know that a poet "cares." However, beyond the pretense, the derivations, the plotless rambling, the grate of vacant noise, Kerouac somehow achieves communication of a happy sense for the humor of car-stealing and marital confusion, for the insanity and pomp of addicts, for the joys of being tormented. And he gives us a fascinating tape recording of the skinny Bunyanesque car-thief, Dean Moriarty, craving intellect, wives, fast travel and bop, emitting fiery nonsense from the tail of his hurtling nuttiness:

> But of course, Sal, I can talk as soon as ever and have many things to say to you in fact with my own little bangtail mind I've been reading and reading this gone Proust all the way across the country and digging a great number of things I'll never have TIME to tell you about and we STILL haven't talked of Mexico and our parting there in fever—but no need to talk. Absolutely, now, yes?

He balances the crazed Dean with a certain wryness about himself, whom he calls Sal Paradise:

> She was a nice little girl, simple and true. . . .

Oh-oh, Hemingway again.

* It was.—H. G., Jan. 1962.

. . . and tremendously frightened of sex. I told her
it was beautiful. I wanted to prove this to her. She let
me prove it, but I was impatient and proved nothing.
She sighed in the dark. "What do you want out of
life?" I asked, and I used to ask that all the time of
girls.

Here he enlists both our indulgence and our sympathy
for poor impatient Sal, and does it with wit and feeling
and imaginative detachment. But at other places he is
capable of the melodrama of the pure-bred dormitory
genius:

I would be strange and ragged and like the Prophet
who has walked across the land to bring the dark
Word, and the only Word I had was "Wow."

At still another juncture he forgets that he is the Prophet
of Wow and informs us that his word is Mad. There are
other words in his sack, too.

But wha hoppin?

Nothin' hoppin, man.

Dean Moriarty is brilliantly transcribed, not rendered
as a man through time and desire, despite all his velocity.
He begins mad, he stays mad, he concludes mad: he is
a stripped, tormented, dancing celluloid doll, burning fast,
without a gesture than can surprise us. Kerouac is loyal
to him. In garlands of prose, the words *mad, madness,
madly* are the stems to which the buffeted reader can look
for a principle of organization. It is the end of the philosophy for which the hungering boy traveler yearns, the great
death-in-life to fill the boredom. He is fading away because
of boredom, since nothing can make him happy, nothing
can enlist him for more than a few spasmodic jerks, and
the mad ones seem in his eyes to have an inner purpose.
They are driven, while he is hung up. Unfortunately for
communicative purpose, after many repetitions of the
phrase, "It was *mad*," we hear not the trumpets of Blake

nor the divine flap of Antonin Artaud, but rather an interior
decorator describing last night's binge. "As in a dream,"
he adds—because he wants to make life a mad dream and
so pronounces MAD and DREAM at us over and over—"we
made the bed bounce a half hour." The precise report of
the time arouses our suspicion. *Why was he looking at his
watch?* Such modest journalism does not imply a dreamlike
transport.

Kerouac's people rarely talk, respond, exchange warmth
with each other. They split their guts to cross the continent, say "Hello, whooee, wow, Charlie Parker, soul" to
their friends, get a quick divorce, make a quick marriage,
and rush back to San Fran to a first or second or third wife,
bringing along a girl from Denver. They zoom up and
down the continent for no reason but bored impulse,
though they call it "find our souls." Then they write
eighteen thousand-word letters explaining why they never
had that good long talk. Words fly, but they cannot communicate. They "tell" each other things: "Went for a
walk in the middle of the night and came back to my
girl to tell her what I thought about during my walk. I
told her a number of things."

Even the wonderful chatter of the run-on hero, Dean
Moriarty, which is the strongest thing in the book, tells
us only one thing: He began as a psychopath and ended
as a psychotic. Though lively along the way, this is not
much of a journey, and tells little of anyone's life—including the real life of Moriarty.

On the Road asks us to judge the lives of its characters;
it requires no real-life acquaintance with them to see that
they are "true" projections—that is, the book represents
Kerouac's attempt to do justice to his friends. This is a very
different matter from the artist's attempt to project meaningful people through the medium of his imagination onto
the medium of the imaginations of readers: characters who

will be true to possibility, not necessarily to fact. *On the Road* reads right along—it contains, essentially, some lively rambling conversation about the exploits of big bad boys —but it is deeply insular in its intentions. Kerouac has not faced an important decision about whom he is writing for —his "soul" (to prove that he has one), his friends (to prove that he is worthy of them), or the public at whom his editor and publishers aim the book. He seems to be confused by the difference between writing a novel about hipsters—a legitimate stunt in an age of antiheroes—and becoming a hipster in order to leave a track of paper.

Kerouac displays some of the belly-patting in-group satisfaction which is expressed, in another arena, by another confused champion, Homer Capehart, senator from Indiana, who said, "I would rather be a friend of the President of the United States without brains than a friend of the Senator from Oklahoma with brains." Underlying Kerouac's autobiographical study of himself and his friends ("Fiction is not possible—my pals are too great—we must do justice," he seems to say) is the decision that he would rather be a friend of a mediocre poet with madness than of a good poet without madness, rather a hip madman than a nonhip sane one, rather a beat bum than anyone else in the world. The writer and the senator are equally smug.

Another example of insularity: locked in the privacy of fond illusion, Kerouac even believes in the "happy, true-hearted, ecstatic Negroes of America" with an old-fashioned heartache of nostalgia that is quite touching except for the harm and ignorance it stands for. It is my impression that such writers at Ralph Ellison and James Baldwin are responding to a different sort of experience; the evidence of Negro life shows this people moving out of the Happy, True-hearted, Ecstatic category into a more complicated set of responses to the pressures under which they live. The reader can cite his own experiences, anything from bus boycotts to cool jazz, in support of this truism. It may be cause for sighing to the sentimentalists, but like the stationary hipster, "Movement," in Bernard Wolfe's novel, *The Late-Risers*, or the unnamed hero of Ralph Ellison's *Invisible Man*, the Negro today aims to be more white than the whites.

I take the Ginsberg of *Howl* and the Kerouac of *On the Road* to be typical of their little boys' town at its rare best, serious, convinced, and trying hard. Through them, one can ask what this clan of superfrantic subhipsters wants. Are they bringing a scout's message, a Word? Do they represent a new style of American? Will they provide a bracing antidote to the chronic headache of American culture?

They seem to be more a wounded shrilling and shrinking than an angry and vital reaction. Curiously enough their command performance of ecstatic rituals has misled them; they feel no ease in the expense of impulse; puzzled, they withdraw from pleasure. Madness is the penultimate escape, which seems both to allow joy and illumination and to oil over the troubling itch of responsibility. It seems so, that is, to the broody tourist, traveling home to his mother's suburb to describe his friends to his notebook, and then justifying them to his editors. I am sure that from within madness is different, and less delightful. They are ascetics of excess. They yearn for the annihilation of sense through the abuse of the senses. They look for a society of unchanging virtue in which the risks of possibility have been removed; pure love will reign, green marijuana will be discovered in the mad glove compartments of every straight and true stolen car, Saroyan will live at peace in Fresno, souls will tell each other things. The terms of heaven have changed, but all this is very familiar. The ultimate goal is that single small step beyond madness.

What Kerouac wants is what the mystics driven by fright in all ages want, "the complete step across chrono-

logical time into timeless shadows . . . the stability of the
Intrinsic mind." Such unhappy nonsense, such droopy-
jeaned nay-saying to the blessed facts of time and change!
There are other possible mysticisms, but Kerouac models
his heaven on Marie Stopes' elegant, Swedenborgian, impossibly weary orgasm, saying "wow!" in advance just because he hopes to describe it as "MAD." No wonder all the
fireworks. The experience he craves is simple, dark, and
in any case inevitable to all of us sooner or later—immolation. He is not content to wait. Mortality terrifies him;
better death at once than the long test of life. He expresses
this fantasy with convulsive violence, trying to disguise the
truth from himself and from the reader, using breathless-
ness as a surrogate for energy. But he is compelled. The
jitters are not an active state of being. He puts to the service of his rockabye dream of oblivion all the violence, sex,
drink, dope, and the batty babbling buddies with whom
he populates his heaven, anything, every easeful and bitter
experience, even that of turning to rot in the Mexican
jungle:

> The jungle takes you over and you become it. . . . The
> dead bugs mingled with my blood; the live mosquitoes
> exchanged further portions. . . . Soft infinitesimal
> showers of microscopic bugs fanned down on my face
> as I slept, and they were extremely pleasant.

It would help Jack Kerouac if he could find within
himself the strength to stop writing about Love, Life, and
Death (with a dot dot dot between these stylish abstractions) and remember the real boy who enjoyed midget auto
races. He might then discover that he knows something
about death, life, and love. At present he is a wolf of the
hotrod age, Thomas and Virginia melted together into a
damp creature from which even Aristophanes, who loved
hybrids, would turn away. This wolf bays at the hipster
moon, but howls for the Helen of someone else's youth;

it ravens down the raw streets of America, taking gladness in the fact that the Mississippi has lived up to its advance notice in Mark Twain, describing one haunt after another as "storied," literary as literary can be, raised on the great books, as aren't we all? Where Thomas Wolfe broke his head butting against the world of New York intellectual highlife, Jack Kerouac is butting but unbroken against the world of the hipsters, a party that never quite pleases its adherents, no matter how much marvelous wild partying foreplay. Despite its drag race of words and gestures, *On the Road* does nothing, thinks nothing, acts nothing, but yet manages to be a book after all—a loving portrait of hip Dean Moriarty and his beat, cool friends as they run 110 miles an hour in order to stand still. It's a frantic book, and for that reason there is hope for Jack Kerouac.

Pseudo-Hipster, You Can't Run Further.

Meta-Hipster, You Can't Yell Louder.

Hipster, Go Home.

1957

3. The Rise of the Treeniks

A MODEST PROPOSAL: that the United States government declare the planting of trees illegal.

Result: at last the youth of America will find something new to do. Boys will sneak out in the dead of night with seedlings. The most advanced writers will discover a fresh subject matter: celebration of the gangs of roving youths, clad in torn tee shirts and blue jeans, with pockets filled with seeds and a language all their own. Defrocked tree surgeons in sordid little upstairs offices will forge prescriptions for oak, pine, and maple, for purely agricultural purposes. Teen agers, posing as landscape architects or lumber growers, will hold up nurseries and make off with truckloads of potted birch.

Naturally, there must be rigorous repression—raids of illegal plantations, destruction of smuggled saplings. Camouflaged greenhouses will spring up in every corner of the great cities. The menace of the treeniks will be explained in the popular magazines, with actual photographs of boy and girl treeniks loafing on pine needles. The fellow travelers of the treeniks, who do not actually plant trees themselves, will meet to play the bongos about it, employing with partial accuracy the language of reforestation, composing rhapsodies about the joy of the open road when you have an unplanted field before you. A few noisy tree-planters must be put in prison. Pushers, selling saplings, will go into hiding. For offering an acorn to a minor, the punishment will be twenty years. Harboring a Dangerous Vegetable will be an even greater offense.

In coffee houses all over the country, poems will be read to jazz, all about how cool it is in the shade of the willow, dig. ("This is what I mean *timber*, man.") At this point every high school boy will want to be a treenik and the price of illegal saplings to an addict who really needs his fix may go as high as a hundred dollars.

The police will be sent out on raids, burning and chopping and destroying any tree they discover. But they can never catch up with an acquiescent populace. The more they punish and destroy, the more widespread will be trees and treeniks. Certain policemen, of course, will grow wealthy. There will be mysterious traces of soil under their fingernails and in the trunks of their white Cadillacs.

Students of popular culture will attempt to define the difference between Treesters and Treeniks. (The Treester planted trees before anyone else knew that they existed. The Treenik only started when it became a federal offense, described in detail in *Life* magazine.) The metaphysical sociologists will point out that this fad represents another manifestation of what William James called the need for a "moral equivalent of war." That is, the youth of our society requires some significant action which combines violence, innovation, and rebelliousness with an outlet for creative desires, the instinct to follow fashion, and a herd obedience. The Grove Press will devote its Evergreen Review to the glorification of the New Arboreal Revolution (sex replaced by tree-watching).

And while the police raid and the non-tree un-wardens

burn and the prisons are filled with illegal tree users and the youth is corrupted and the commentators commentate, this huge America of ours will in no time at all be covered by forests, green, immense, silent, and mysteriously consoling.

1960

Fiction of the Sixties

THE PIG IS the most discreet animal; it never looks at the sky. With just this much apology for my indiscretion, let me try to anticipate the color and content of American fiction in the decade ahead. I shall first perform some harassed wigwagging before my brother novelists, stalled on our dark roadways, and then offer an optimistic view of the next place on the road, and hope that the peculiar disconnection between actual and prospective station can provide an occasion for inventory of self by both readers and writers.

The immediate decade past has not been a bad time for novelists if they did not care about getting their messages through. There have been career opportunities aplenty for bona fide, stamped and certified, government-inspected, prime tellers of stories. George P. Elliott, one of the fine writers who matured during the decade of the fifties, recently commented wryly on these fellowships and prize opportunities, academic offers, lecture offers, writers' conference offers, article-writing offers, ghost-writing offers, review offers, copy-composing offers: "Fiction writers are in short supply." Having been sponsored by United Artists and *Esquire* and sent by first-class jet on a visit to Hollywood, where he stayed at the Beverly Wilshire and had his clothes valeted by the great movie company, and having been locked in man-to-man talk with mighty agents and famous actors, all this energy spent on an article for *Esquire* about a movie producer, he returns to the little back room in New York where he does his writing. There he contemplates the enthusiastic reviews of his novel, *Parktilden Village*, which has thus far been sold to about 700 readers. Mr. Elliott has finally come into some esteem as a writer—without, however, being read.

Of course, 700 out of 180 million Americans suggests a startling number of nonreaders for a vigorous contemporary talent, but it is not a much more lugubrious percentage than 3000 out of 180 million, which is more typical of the nonbest-selling novel. The American cornucopia has enabled the American writer to keep alive, but the same embarrassment of riches which has fed his family with irregular spurts of cash has provided the prospective reader with enough distractions to avoid any imposition of books on his time. Perhaps some new foundation should give fellowships to novel-readers.

We are all aware of the peculiar inadequacy of book distribution, beginning and ending with the tic of the nervous book buyer, who asks for whatever title is floating in the air that week. The first books of Saul Bellow, Nelson Algren, and Vladimir Nabokov sell in the hundreds; in these cases, eventually something happy occurs, a peculiar combination of virtue having out and the wheel of fortune spinning. A novel like Ralph Ellison's *Invisible Man* sells poorly, receives an important prize, picks up sales, finally does okay. For the publisher, who operates by statistics and needs only one best-seller to justify ten poor sellers, the business risk is a reasonable one. But what about the forsaken novelist, who loves his book and wrote it to say something important to an audience which does not realize that it has been spoken to? Well, he either sheds a noble tear (his own view of it) or a maudlin one (everyone else's opinion). He reminds himself, if he has the required strength: "No one asked you to write stories, pal. Do you want to or don't you?"

Answer: he wants to, and wants to again; a gadfly whose victims do not know when they have been gadded.

So much for shoptalk about the writer's financial and nervous problems. But the peculiarly book-shy audience bears watching for clues about the subject matter of serious American novelists in the immediate past and in the future which we project from it.

In the thirties and the early forties, political and social ideologies preoccupied the minds of most writers, and many books ended with such rooster morals as "Strike!" or "He died for all of us" and had doctrinaire donkey titles like *Brother, the Laugh Is Bitter*. The old problems were still with us during the fifties, but the teeth of the beasts were sugared into ruin by the fact of a victorious war (however temporary), economic prosperity (however specious), and the lack of an important political ideal to set against apparent American failures. The blissful despair of the twenties had turned to the blind staggers; the great enemies of the thirties, fascism and depression, were slumbering quietly; the hopes of Marxism and Peace Through War were dead.

The coming-of-age novel, the quest novel, the novel of philosophical purpose demanded intense formal and stylistic ingenuity to fill the gaps left by diminished political passions. Novelists could not yet make their deep response to the Bomb and a lemming impulse to race suicide dramatically relevant in fiction. There was no active cause to join, no genuine war to declare (plenty of false wars and individual bandit expeditions). The simplicity and resolu-

FICTION OF THE SIXTIES

tion which even the dramatically complicated mind finds necessary were hard to discover in public life.

A characteristic expression of the period is John Cheever's uneasy exploration of middle-class decorum in *The Wapshot Chronicle* and his many stories. Truman Capote and J. D. Salinger attempted to raise elegant eccentricity and child psychology to the level of literature. Writers like Saul Bellow, Ralph Ellison, and Bernard Malamud managed to make explicit philosophical purposes relevant in fiction by the force of their personal vision.

The great fads were, first, the novel of American self-congratulation, typified by Sloan Wilson, Cameron Hawley, Herman Wouk, and other celebrants of business and obedience; and later in the decade, the so-called hipster writers, who also failed to produce a convincing voice. The trouble with both groups is a symptomatic one. They are not egotistical, but rather nonegotistical, lacking a firm sense of self, thus terribly frightened, needful, vain, demanding from a public which is itself avid for genuine personality an assurance that they really exist. The weak ego strives for strong assertion through immolation in bureaucracy or advertisements for its selfishness: Help me, tell me I am here!

Many other passive novelists settle for everybody's unhappy childhood, exposés of the already exposed, tremendously gory and horny war novels, pseudo revivals of religious conformity, imitations of Henry James and Kafka and Fitzgerald, guilt-mongering and magnolia-mongering and the moony, loony interior decoration of prose. Some of them seem to know Shelley's description of the skylark, which pours out its "full heart In profuse strains of unpremeditated art," but they forget that the sincere skylark is a mere feathered bird, not a hairy poet, and a human being's sincerity must come of more than the winds of nature blowing in his craw. The poet or the novelist sings most with his own heart when the arbiter of his intelligence has brought both his body and the rest of the world together into the room where he does his singing.

Certain ideological writers—the Freudians, the neo-religious, and the hipsters, for example—like to think of themselves as devilish chaps with probes stuck into their very depths, and so they rejoice. Milton's Satan made their point with succinct awareness and terror: "Which way I fly is Hell; my self am Hell" and thus understood that the awful privacy of the rebel must be mitigated by some meaningful communion with others. The writer needs a causal connection with his society, some sense that his work does something to make everyone's privacy a privilege rather than a burden. Else numbness, coolness, the erosion of self, and the acquiescence in self-murder around us. Without this causal connection with the wide world, the writer may issue shrill directives from his own coddled privacy; he may fidget and giggle and tell himself he is Whitman or Kafka, hip or cool, gimmicked by chic and as fashionable as a sports car; he is in hell all the same.

The categories of American virtue (material accumulation plus good intentions) and American guilt (spiritual vagueness plus nuclear derangement plus impure intentions plus a clouded future) exclude the writer who is not a compulsive joiner of causes. And yet he seeks to broaden the allegiance of his one-member team. The most serious writers of this period feel as an immediate personal deprivation the lack of an imperative politics, an enveloping and involving view of the world. And the best creation of the time has implied an effort to close this gap. Probably no imaginative writing can do the work of a society in giving a sense of public hope and purpose to a people, but awareness of the lack and the personal effort to find personal solutions constitute an essential labor in a difficult time. Literature, like politics, is an art of the possible.

A few writers have fled to traditional shelters—religious revival, political dogma, hedonism and its anemic, psychoanalytic grandchild, the pursuit of health, which provides a misunderstood parody of the classical purgation by pity and terror in order to reach order and calm. The strongest have accepted their ignorance and their doubt; they will continue, in the decade to come, perhaps learning themselves, as they note along the way what some among the world of men have learned. As Ralph Ellison's invisible man asks, "Who knows but that, on the lower frequencies, I speak for you?" The labor of opposing invisibility—to others and to ourselves—will be continued by novelists who aim not at a secondary quality of health but at the primary issue of ransoming the time by inventing a sharply personal reality.

In the decade ahead, the successors to Faulkner and Hemingway will be new novelists, striving in their little rooms and staring out the window, as writers always do; but they will be striving with issues and staring out over a world which the elder statesmen of American letters must find quite alien, slippery white, electronic, forbidding. The society celebrated by Faulkner and Hemingway, Wolfe and Fitzgerald, Dos Passos and Sherwood Anderson and Steinbeck has become a matter of history—a history of vital concern, perhaps, but history. For that essential fictional mastery of the way things are, we must now look to younger voices evaluating an altered experience of America. No one can call the roll of the strong talents of the sixties. Many of them are already at work, but some are probably still in high school. However, we can anticipate something of the kind of world out of which their stories and novels will emerge.

The environment of American writing in the sixties will provide an accelerated continuation of the postwar period, with a possibility of closer challenge and confrontation of the risks of technological explosion, of living on a shrinking globe jostled by the Soviet Union and China, and of the revolutionary reversals of the importance of work

and leisure. The bloating of cities and populations, with
resulting great shifts of power, suggests frontiers at least
as exciting as those out in space.

Many of the writers who will nominate themselves
to reckon with our world through the magical synthesis
of fiction will seem more strange than Martians to some
of us. Roosevelt, Hitler, Stalin, the Depression, and the
War will be dim history to them. My earliest "political"
memories are of a teacher weeping over the bank closings
and of the freight trains ant-heaped with men traveling
hopelessly in search of work. What political reality will
the youngest writers of the sixties carry forward from
their seventh years? A TV apology by a worried candidate?
A discussion of the effect of ileitis on the stock market?

Not many of these writers will wash dishes in diners
while going to college; scholarships even reach down to
arts students. When they rebel against their parents, suggests one psychiatrist, the mania for popular psychology
will oblige them to rebel against being understood rather
than being misunderstood. They will be richer, healthier,
groupier, more suburban, rarely driven into the early isolation of economic crisis, second-generation conflict, and
rapid changes of class.

They will nevertheless discover the eternal problems
lying in wait after their air-conditioned classrooms and
their Merit Scholarships. How to find proper work for a
man? How to find a way of living that is worthy? How
to survive in a world which is no longer addicted to necessary progress? Are we really reborn through love? If so or
if not, how to live with the cardinal fact of death?

But these new writers will have grown up among the
specters of passivity, isolation, and doubt which haunt
American political and family life. Passive self-absorption
is surely the great antagonist of the creating mind. Unless
others respond to the "moving image of desire," the writer
does not really have a command post; he is in isolation,

no matter how shrilly he raises his voice. The writer of the sixties will have to thread his way through the interlocking loneliness of contemporary America. If he accepts the ticket for the Fun House maze, where all he can make out is his own reflection in thousands of mirrors, he fails.

Dare anyone promise that fiction writers in the sixties will discover the causal connection between their work and our society, the impulse to make a self-engrossing music and the need to tell the best truth a man knows? Of course not. The first difficulty is that the imaginative writer is not that unacknowledged legislator which his dream as a young man tells him to be; he may find himself in "short supply," but the occasional accident of best-sellerdom bears little relationship to a powerfully attentive audience. He is, rather, an acknowledged nonlegislator. But more important than the personal career disconnection of the writer is the fact that he suffers like the rest of Americans, at three o'clock in the morning and all day long, individually and as a people, with the need to find a significant connection between desire and love, ambition and work, principle and actual function in the largest world. What, as a people, we lack of the large public issues of spirit and purpose, the novelists in their narrow rooms can hardly provide.

Then what will they give us in the sixties? At their strongest, they can offer relish even in trouble, freshness even in chagrin; they can tell us stories about how things are, how they might be; they can create heroes who point to better chances through being tested in extremity. They can refresh the sense of personality and remind us that the mysterious pride in self is more than the lining to our striving or cajoling public faces. If tragedy lies buried in a ruck of pathos, they can still show us where tragedy lies buried. This is familiar work for the novel, but it must be done afresh every time.

At their frazzled worst, novelists will continue to give us

the ephemera which inspire us to a constant activity of forgetting. The juvenile delinquent will remain loyally with us, as he has since Zeus made so much trouble for Kronos at dinner, but the hipster will fold his hypodermic and silently steal away; though no one can replace Jack Kerouac, the no one's name will be legion. The thick book-club novel, fashioned by steady hand and indifferent heart, and the thin interior decorator's novel, fashioned by the desire to pitch a camp in the tent of literature, will produce their accustomed results in the form of dollars and social status. The self-absorbed outpouring which sometimes precedes a controlled gift and sometimes precedes silence and oblivion will continue to find optimistic publishers and tireless but fatigued reviewers. The weekly great book about America's Mission will detonate ecstasies by the familiar missionaries.

The new serious writers will find an inadequate substitute for the moral equivalent of the traditional life-and-death struggles in the coming-of-age novel and the suburban novel and the business novel and the exposure-of-selling-out novel. The novel of political and social protest must find new energies; it is difficult to be as attentive to Margaret Mead, telling American men to unite as Men, as one was to Karl Marx, telling us to unite as Workers. Though the alarmed viewers of American family life have a pertinent "issue," "problem," "question," it does not suggest the bedrock challenge of the apparent breakdown of an economic system in the thirties. Can there be a powerful general cause for the writers of the sixties, apart from their personal need to tell a story?

The vital accommodations to reality and demands upon experience will, I think, present themselves with a force that must change our sense of the American novel. The first question is moral, philosophical, metaphysical, religious; the second, linked with it like a Siamese twin, has political roots. How does a man place himself as a *person* in the coming new world? How will Americans accommodate to this world as a *people?*

Part of the novelist's purpose has always been to present possibilities, to judge, to decide, and to give a weight, assurance, style, and energy to these decisions. In the sixties the best novelists will grapple with a problem which can be pejoratively described as "abstract" but which involves a return in extremity to the deepest poetic demand: to know.

They will ask final questions: For whom do I live? For what? They will search out examples of personal value in a massified society: What is the relationship between freedom and isolation, loneliness and independence, responsibility and that pseudo responsibility of merely following orders? Stripped down to poetry and story and the inauguration of passionate conviction, they will leave the self-conscious recording of the details of social life to the social historians; the "research team," that miniature lonely crowd, is better equipped to perform this interesting but secondary function.

Because the novelist relishes what is, he will continue to find joy in the *bizarreries* of talk and the salient observation, but he will, I believe, look for a specific coherence in much the way that philosophers and religious thinkers traditionally have done. He will do this partly because the linguistic analysis of contemporary philosophy and the sermons of contented religiosity leave the primary questions unanswered. The writer who fought in Spain did nothing more than sign a petition for Hungary, but he must find a way to translate his ardent moral judgments into literary meaning in time of shock and crisis.

And the sixties will surely be a time of shock and crisis, sensed by the artists even if the mass of Americans do not admit it. (When a body is first wounded badly, it does not feel the pain.) The novelist obliges himself to confront the individual's changed relationship toward himself and a mass society; his changed assignment of duty will also be the result of two important political facts built into the texture of American life out of which the novel of the sixties will emerge. The first fact, relatively easy to accept, is that America is neither the great villain of mass civilization nor the wistful hope of the world. American self-love and self-romanticization have jaded along with the self-hatred of the Anglophile or the Marxist myths. The second, more difficult realization has to do not with patriotic indulgence but with power. The United States is no longer the young giant (peace to Thomas Wolfe); it will be one giant among at least three, including China and Russia and perhaps India and perhaps some European complex. The drama and images of American novels will either be reconciled with these facts or unreconciled, but fiction always shows the effect of its nourishment by facts.

Let us follow this notion in one detail: If we accept the reality of Chinese power, we will begin to trade with China. If we trade with China, San Francisco will rival New York as a great port and center of cultural radiation. And when this occurs, the magnetic attraction of New York City for novelists may well be succeeded by the image of another city, in which European and Oriental influences are combined as Western and Byzantine influences were combined during the glory of Vienna. The St. Lawrence Seaway makes Cleveland, Ohio, an ocean port, with French sailors strolling up Ninth Street. Jet planes will take Huck Finn to Moscow from Hannibal, Mo., in only a few hours. The map of the world is part of every novel. Even without hydrogen explosions to break up continents, the tidal waves of transport and trade and the erupting volcanoes of national power will create a new mental geography and a new need for coherence in the sixties.

Rhetoric and the shape of speech itself must reflect these tidal changes. A small example: If Saul Bellow were writing *The Victim* now, the sentence which begins the book, in which he describes New York as "hot as Bangkok," would carry less of the fantastic *Arabian Nights* associations which it had for the writer ten years ago; he knows people who have been to Bangkok, he may go there himself, Bangkok is *there* as a part of the hard life of the times.

Fiction in the sixties will be bent to celebration of a world magnificently on edge, at the limit; while perhaps free in fact of economic crisis and war, we will remain under ultimate threat, with implications of being chastened for error by the disappearance of men from the earth. Avowing the facts of man's ambiguous destiny, the writer will try to give his private vision some viable control. He will often stumble, often settle for shrillness. Many thoughtful writers will create out of total mastery and partial awe. That is, they will know too much, or at least think too highly of their partial knowledge; brain-proud, convinced, combative, and making points, they will prune their effective awe before the brute gift of life on earth. The supple and compassionate mind is essential; knowledgeability is the enemy of awe, that sun under which the artist's wisdom turns and grows.

The best writers of the sixties, as of all periods in history, will suffer gladly under partial mastery, being gripped by strong convictions and total awe. The novelist's ideas will finally be stopped before the greatest idea of all for a writer of fiction, the fact that his people live and that what they do is important; in other words, before his awe at the spectacle of human love and sorrow, folly and dignity. Having thought, the novelist will then suspend thinking and go into the kitchens, the streets, and the dilemmas of his fictive world. Once again he will discover actions, themes, styles, and forms which enable him to do that labor which must be performed afresh for every time, finding an exemplary reality in the true lie which is a story.

1960

A Dog in Brooklyn, a Girl in Detroit:
A Life among the Humanities

WHAT BETTER CAREER for a boy who seeks to unravel the meaning of our brief span on earth than that of philosopher? We all wonder darkly, in the forbidden hours of the night, punishing our parents and building a better world, with undefined terms. Soon, however, most of us learn to sleep soundly; or we take to pills or love-making; or we call ourselves insomniacs, not philosophers. A few attempt to define the terms.

There is no code number for the career of philosophy in school, the Army, or out beyond in real life. The man with a peculiar combination of melancholic, nostalgic, and reforming instincts stands at three possibilities early in his youth. He can choose to be a hero, an artist, or a philosopher. In olden times, war, say, or the need to clean out the old West, might make up his mind for him. The old West had been pretty well cleaned up by the time I reached a man's estate, and Gary Cooper could finish the job. Heroism was an untimely option. With much bureaucratic confusion I tried a bit of heroic war, got stuck in the machine, and returned to the hectic, Quonset campus of the GI Bill, burning to Know, Understand, and Convert. After a season of ferocious burrowing in books, I was ready to be a Teacher, which seemed a stern neighbor thing to Artist and Philosopher. I took on degrees, a Fulbright fellowship, a wife, a child, a head crammed with foolish questions and dogmatic answers despite the English school of linguistic analysis. I learned to smile, pardner, when I asked questions of philosophers trained at Oxford or Cambridge, but I asked them nonetheless. I signed petitions against McCarthy, wrote a novel, went on a treasure hunt, returned to my roots in the Middle West and stood rooted there, discussed the menace of the mass media, and had another child.

By stages not important here, I found myself teaching the Humanities at Wayne University in Detroit. I am now going to report a succession of classroom events which, retrospectively, seems to have determined my abandonment of formal dealing with this subject. The evidence does not, however, render any conclusion about education in the "Humanities" logically impregnable. It stands for a state of mind and is no substitute for formal argument. However, states of mind are important in this area of experience and metaexperience. However and however: it happens that most of the misty exaltation of the blessed vocation of the teacher issues from the offices of deans, editors, and college presidents. The encounter with classroom reality has caused many teachers, like Abelard meeting the relatives of Eloise, to lose their bearings. Nevertheless this is a memoir, not a campaign, about a specific life in and out of the Humanities. Though I am not a great loss to the History of Everything in Culture, my own eagerness to teach is a loss to me.

2

News item of a few years ago. A young girl and her date are walking along a street in Brooklyn, New York. The girl notices that they are being followed by an enormous Great Dane. The dog is behaving peculiarly, showing its teeth and making restless movements. A moment later, sure enough, the dog, apparently maddened, leaps slavering upon the girl, who is borne to earth beneath its weight. With only an instant's hesitation, the boy jumps on the dog. Its fangs sunk first in one, then in the other, the dog causes the three of them to roll like beasts across the sidewalk.

A crowd gathers at a safe distance to watch. No one interferes. The becalmed curiosity of teevee viewers.

A few moments later a truckdriver, attracted by the crowd, pulls his vehicle over to the curb. This brave man is the only human being stirred personally enough to leave the role of passive spectator. Instantaneously analyzing the situation, he leaps into the struggle—*attacking and beating the boy.* He has naturally assumed that the dog must be protecting an innocent young lady from the unseemly actions of a juvenile delinquent.

I recounted this anecdote in the classroom in order to introduce a course which attempted a summary experience of Humanities 610 for a monumental nine credits. There were a number of points to be made about the passivity of the crowd ("don't get involved," "not my business") and the stereotypical reaction of the truck driver who had been raised to think of man's best friend as not another human being but a dog. In both cases, addicted to entertainment and clichés, the crowd and the trucker could not recognize what was actually happening before their eyes; they responded irrelevantly to the suffering of strangers; they were not a part of the maine. This led us to discussion of the notion of "community." In a closely knit society, the people on the street would have known the couple involved and felt a responsibility toward them. In a large city, everyone is a stranger. (Great art can give a sense of the brotherhood of men. Religion used to do this, too.) "Any questions?" I asked, expecting the authority of religion to be defended.

An eager hand shot up. Another. Another. Meditative bodies sprawled in their chairs. "Are all New Yorkers like that?" "Well, what can you do if there's a mad dog and you're not expecting it?" "Where does it say in what great book how you got to act in Brooklyn?"

I took note of humor in order to project humorousness. I found myself composing my face in the look of thought which teevee panelists use in order to project thinking. I discovered a serious point to elaborate—several. I mentioned consciousness and relevance and the undefined moral suggestion implied by the labor which produces any work of art or mind. A girl named Clotilda Adams asked me: "Why don't people try to get along better in this world?"

Somewhat digressively, we then discussed the nature of heroism, comparing the behavior of the boy and the truck driver. Both took extraordinary risks; why? We broke for cigarettes in the autumn air outside. Then, for fifty minutes more, we raised these interesting questions, referring forward to Plato, Aristotle, St. Thomas, Dostoevski, Tolstoi, William James, and De Gaulle; and then boy, dog, girl, truck driver, and crowd were left with me and the crowned ghosts of history in the deserted room while my students went on to Phys Ed, Music Appreciation, Sosh, and their other concerns. Having been the chief speaker, both dramatist and analyst, I was exalted by the lofty ideas floated up into the air around me. I was a little let down to return to our real life in which dog-eat-dog is man's closest pal. Fact. Neither glory nor pleasure nor power, and certainly not wisdom, provided the goal of my students. Not even wealth was the aim of most of them. They sought to make out, to do all right, more prideful than amorous in love, more security-hungry than covetous in status. I saw my duty as a teacher: Through the Humanities, to awaken them to the dream of mastery over the facts of our lives; I saw my duty plain: Through the Humanities, to lead them toward the exaltation of knowledge and the calm of control. I had a whole year in which to fulfill this obligation. It was a two-semester course.

Before she left the room, Clotilda Adams said, "You didn't answer my question." Fact.

Outside the university enclave of glass and grass, brick and trees, Detroit was agonizing in its last big year with the big cars. Automation, dispersion of factories, and imported automobiles were eroding a precarious confidence. Fear was spreading; soon the landlords would offer to decorate apartments and suffer the pain. Detroit remembered the war years with nostalgia. Brave days, endless hours, a three-shift clock, insufficient housing, men sleeping in the all-night, triple-feature movies on Woodward and Grand River. Though the area around the Greyhound and Trailways stations was still clotted with the hopeful out of the hill country of the midsouth and the driven from the deep South—they strolled diagonally across the boulevards, entire families holding hands—some people suspected what was already on its way down the road: twenty per cent unemployment in Detroit.

The semester continued. We churned through the great books. One could classify my students in three general groups, intelligent, mediocre, and stupid, allowing for the confusions of three general factors—background, capacity, and interest. This was how we classified the Humanities, too: ancient, medieval, and modern. It made a lot of sense, and it made me itch, scratch, and tickle. Series of three-form nice distinctions. According to Jung

and other authorities, they have certain mythic signifi-
cances. The course was for nine credits. All the arts were
touched upon. We obeyed Protagoras; man, just man, was
our study. When I cited him—"Man is the measure of all
things"—Clotilda Adams stirred uneasily in her seat: "By
which Protagoras no doubt meant Woman, too," I assured
her. She rested.

Now imagine the winter coming and enduring, with
explosions of storm and exfoliations of gray slush, an
engorged industrial sky overhead and sinus trouble all
around. The air was full of acid and a purplish, spleeny
winter mist. Most of Detroit, in Indian times before the
first French trappers arrived, had been a swamp and below
sea level. The swamp was still present, but invisible; city
stretched out in all directions, crawling along the high-
ways. Though Detroit was choked by a dense undergrowth
of streets and buildings, irrigated only by superhighways,
its work was done with frantic speed. The Rouge plant
roared, deafened. The assembly lines clanked to the limit
allowed by the UAW. The old Hudson factory lay empty,
denuded, waiting to become a parking lot. Then the new
models were being introduced! Buick! Pontiac! Dodge!
Ford and Chevrolet! Ford impudently purchased a huge
billboard faced toward the General Motors Building on
Grand Boulevard. General Motors retaliated by offering
free ginger ale to all comers, and a whole bottle of Vernor's
to take home if you would only consent to test-drive the
new Oldsmobile, the car with the. . . . I've forgotten what
it had that year. All over town the automobile companies
were holding revival meetings; hieratic salesmen preached
to the converted and the hangers-back alike; lines at the loan
companies stretched through the revolving doors and out
onto the winter pavements. But many in those lines were
trying to get additional financing on their last year's cars.
The new models were an indifferent success despite all the
uproar of display and Detroit's patriotic attention to it.

Searchlights sliced up the heavens while the city lay under flu.

Teachers at Wayne University soon learn not to tease the American Automobile. *Lèse* Chrysler was a moral offense, an attack on the livelihood and the sanctity of the American garage. Detroit was a town in which men looked at hubcaps as men elsewhere have sometimes looked at ankles. The small foreign car found itself treated with a violent Halloween kidding-on-the-square, scratched, battered, and smeared (another Jungian series of three!). A passionate and sullen town, Detroit had no doubts about its proper business. All it doubted was everything else.

I often failed at inspiring my students to do the assigned reading. Many of them had part-time jobs in the automobile industry or its annexes. Even a Philosopher found it difficult to top the argument, "I couldn't read the book this week, I have to *work*," with its implied reproach for a scholar's leisure. But alas, many of these stricken proletarians drove freshly minted automobiles. They worked in order to keep up the payments, racing like laboratory mice around the cage of depreciation. Certain faculty deep thinkers, addicted to broad understanding of the problems of others, argued that these students were so poor they *had* to buy new cars in order to restore their confidence. The finance companies seemed to hear their most creative expressions, not me. Deep in that long Detroit winter, I had the task of going from the pre-Socratic mystics all the way to Sartre, for nine credits. Like an audio-visual monkey, I leaped from movie projector to records to slides, with concurrent deep labor in book and tablet. We read *The Brothers Karamazov*, but knowing the movie did not give credit. We studied "The Waste Land," and reading the footnotes did not suffice. We listened to Wanda Landowska play the harpsichord on records. We sat in the dark before a slide of Seurat's "La Grande Jatte" while I explained the importance of the measles of pointillisme to students who only wanted to see life clear and true, see it comfortably. Clotilda Adams said that this kind of painting hurt her eyes. She said that there was too much reading for one course—"piling it on. This isn't the only course we take." She said that she liked music, though. All Moses had to do was to bring the Law down the mountain to the children of Israel; I had to bring it pleasingly.

We made exegeses. I flatly turned down the request of a dean that I take attendance. As a statesmanlike compromise, I tested regularly for content and understanding.

Then, on a certain morning, I handed back some quiz papers at the beginning of class. Out on the street, a main thoroughfare through town, it was snowing; this was one of those magical days of late winter snowfall—pale, cold, clean, and the entire city momentarily muffled by the silence of snow. The room hissed with steam heat; a smell of galoshes and mackinaws arose from the class. "Let us not discuss the test—let us rise above grades. Let us try to consider nihilism as a byproduct of the Romantic revival—" I had just begun my lecture when an odd clashing, lumping noise occurred on Cass Avenue. "Eliot's later work, including 'The Four Quartets,' which we will not discuss here. . . ."

But I was interrupted by a deep sigh from the class. A product of nihilism and the romantic revival? No. It was that strange tragic sigh of horror and satisfaction. Out in the street, beyond the window against which I stood, a skidding truck had sideswiped a taxi. The truckdriver had parked and gone into a drugstore. The cab was mashed like a cruller. From the door, the driver had emerged, stumbling drunkenly on the icy road, holding his head. There was blood on his head. There was blood on his hands. He clutched his temples. The lines of two-way traffic, moving very slowly in the snow and ice, carefully avoided hitting him. There were streaks of perforated and patterned snow, frothed up by tires. He was like an island around which the sea of traffic undulated in slow waves; but he was an island that moved in the sea and held hands to head. He slid and stumbled back and forth, around and about his cab in the middle of the wide street. He was in confusion, in shock. Even at this distance I could see blood on the new-fallen snow. Drivers turned their heads upon him like angry Halloween masks, but did not get involved. Snow spit at his feet.

No one in the class moved. The large window through which we gazed was like a screen, with the volume turned down by habit, by snow, by a faulty tube. As the teacher, my authority took precedence. I ran out to lead the cab driver into the building. An elderly couple sat huddled in the car, staring at the smashed door, afraid to come out the other. They said they were unhurt.

I laid the man down on the floor. He was bleeding from the head and his face was a peculiar purplish color, with a stubble of beard like that of a dead man. There was a neat prick in his forehead where the union button in his cap had been driven into the skin. I sent a student to call for an ambulance. The cab driver's color was like that of the bruised industrial sky. "You be okay till the ambulance——?"

Foolish question. No alternative. No answer.

We waited. The class was restless. When they weren't listening to me, or talking themselves, or smudging blue books in an exam, they did not know what to do in this room devoted to the specialized absorption of ideas. Silence. Scraping of feet, crisping of paper. We watched the slow-motion traffic on the street outside.

The cab driver moved once in a rush, turning over face down against the floor, with such force that I thought he might break his nose. Then slowly, painfully, as if in a dream, he turned back and lay staring at the ceiling. His woolen lumberjacket soaked up the blood trickling from one ear; the blood traveled up separated cilia of wool, which drew it in with a will of their own. There was a swaying, osmotic movement like love-making in the eager little wisps of wool. An astounded ring of Humanities 610 students watched, some still holding their returned quiz papers. One girl in particular, Clotilda Adams, watched him and me with her eyes brilliant, wet, and bulging, and her fist crumpling the paper. I tried by imagining it to force the ambulance through the chilled and snowfallen city. I saw it weaving around the injured who strutted with shock over ice and drift, its single red Cyclops' eye turning, the orderlies hunched over on benches, chewing gum and cursing the driver. The ambulance did not arrive. Clotilda Adams' eye had a thick, impenetrable sheen over it. She watched from the cab driver to me as if we were in some way linked. When would the authorities get there? When the medics? There must have been many accidents in town, and heart attacks, and fires with cases of smoke inhalation.

Before the ambulance arrived, the police were there. They came strolling into the classroom with their legs apart, as if they remembered ancestors who rode the plains. Their mouths were heavy in thought. They had noses like salamis, red and mottled with fat. They were angry at the weather, at the school, at the crowd, at me, and especially at the prostrate man at our feet. He gave them a means to the creative expression of pique. (Everyone needs an outlet.)

Now Clotilda Adams took a step backward, and I recall thinking this odd. She had been treading hard near the pool of blood about the cab driver, but when the cops strolled up, she drifted toward the outer edge of the group of students, with a sly look of caution in her downcast, sideways-cast eyes. Her hand still crisped at the returned exam paper. This sly, lid-fallen look did not do her justice. She was a hard little girl of the sort often thought to be passionate—skinny but well-breasted, a high hard rump with a narrow curve, a nervous mouth.

The two policemen stood over the body of the cab driver. They stared at him in the classic pose—one cop with a hand resting lightly on the butt of his gun and the other on his butt, the younger cop with lips so pouted that his breath made a snuffling sound in his nose. They both had head colds. Their Ford was pulled up on the snow-covered lawn outside, with raw muddled marks of tread in the soft dirt. When the snow melted, there would be wounded streaks in the grass. The cab driver closed his eyes under the finicking, distasteful examination. At last one spoke: "See your driver's license."

The cab driver made a clumsy gesture toward his pocket. The cop bent and went into the pocket. He flipped open the wallet, glanced briefly at the photographs and cash, glanced at me, and then began lipreading the license.

The cab driver was in a state of shock. There was a mixture of thin and thick blood on his clothes and messing the floor. "This man is badly hurt," I said. "Can't we get him to the hospital first?"

"This is only your *driver* license," the cop said slowly, having carefully read through Color of Hair: Brn, Color of Eyes: Brn, and checked each item with a stare at the man on the floor. "Let me see your chauffeur license."

"He's badly hurt," I said. "Get an ambulance."

"Teach," said the older cop, "you know your business? We know ours."

"It's on the way," said the other. "Didn't you call it yourself?"

"No, one of the students . . ." I said.

He grinned with his great victory. "So—don't you trust your pupils neither?"

Shame. I felt shame at this ridicule of my authority in the classroom. A professor is not a judge, a priest, or a sea captain; he does not have the right to perform marriages on the high seas of audio-visual aids and close reasoning. But he is more than an intercom between student and fact; he can be a stranger to love for his students, but not to a passion for his subject; he is a student himself; his pride is lively. The role partakes of a certain heft and control. There is power to make decisions, power to abstain, power to bewilder, promote, hold back, adjust, and give mercy; power, an investment of pride, a risk of shame.

Clotilda Adams, still clutching her exam, stared at me with loathing. She watched me bested by the police. She barely glanced, and only contemptuously, at the man bleeding from the head on the floor. She moved slightly forward again in order to participate fully in an action which apparently had some important meaning for her. She had lost her fear of the police when she saw how we all stood with them. The limits were established.

The police were going through the cab driver's pockets. They took out a folding pocket knife and cast significant looks at it and at each other. It had a marbled plastic hilt, like a resort souvenir. It was attached to a key ring.

"Hey!" one said to the half-conscious man. "What's this knife for?"

"Where'd you get them keys?" the other demanded, prodding the cabbie with his toe.

"A *skeleton* key. These cab companies," one of the cops decided to explain to Clotilda Adams, who was standing nearby, "they get the dregs. Hillbillies, you know?"

I said nothing, found nothing to say. I now think of Lord Acton's famous law, which is accepted as true the way it was uttered. The opposite is also true—the commoner's way: Having no power corrupts; having absolutely no power corrupts absolutely.

The bleeding seemed to have stopped. The cab driver sat up, looking no better, with his bluish, greenish, drained head hanging between his knees. His legs were crumpled stiffly. He propped himself on his hands. The police shot questions at him. He mumbled, mumbled, explained, explained.

"How long you been in Detroit? How come you come out of the mountains?"

"Why you pick up this fare?"

"What makes you think Cass is a one-way street?"

Mumbling and mumbling, explaining and explaining, the cab driver tried to satisfy them. He also said: "Hurt. Maybe you get me to the hospital, huh? Hurt real bad."

"Maybe," said one of the cops, "maybe we take you to the station house first. That boy you hit says reckless driving. I think personally you'd flunk the drunk test—what you think, Teach?"

I sent one of the students to call for an ambulance again. In the infinitesimal pause between my suggestion and his action, an attentive reluctant expectant caesura, I put a dime in his hand for the call. One of the cops gave me that long look described by silent movie critics as the slow burn. "They drive careful," he finally said. "It's snowing. They got all that expensive equipment."

The snow had started again outside the window. The skid marks on the lawn were covered. Though the sky was low and gray, the white sifting down gave a peaceful village glow to this industrial Detroit. Little gusts barely rattled the windows. With the class, the cops, and the driver, we were living deep within a snowy paperweight. I felt myself moving very slowly, swimming within thick glass, like the loosened plastic figure in a paperweight. The snow came down in large torn flakes, all over the buildings of Wayne University, grass, trees, and the pale radiance of a network of slow-motion superhighways beyond. Across the street, a modern building—glass and aluminum strips—lay unfinished in this weather. Six months ago there had been a student boarding house on that spot, filled with the artists and the beat, the guitar-wielders and the modern dancers, with a tradition going all the way back to the Korean War. Now there were wheelbarrows full of frozen cement; there were intentions to build a Japanese garden, with Japanese proportions and imported goldfish.

My student returned from the telephone. He had reached a hospital.

The cab driver was fading away. Rootlets of shock hooded his eyes: the lid was closing shut. A cop asked him another question—what the button on his cap stood for—it was a union button—and then the man just went reclining on his elbow, he slipped slowly down, he lay in the little swamp of crusted blood on the floor. You know what happens when milk is boiled? The crust broke like the crust of boiled milk when a spoon goes into coffee. The cop stood with a delicate, disgusted grimace on his face. What a business to be in, he seemed to be thinking. In approximately ten years, at age forty-two, he could re- tire and sit comfortable in an undershirt, with a nonre- turnable can of beer, before the color teevee. He could relax. He could *start* to relax. But in the meantime—nag, nag, nag. Drunk cabbies, goddamn hillbillies. The reckless driver on the floor seemed to sleep. His lips moved. He was alive.

Then a puffing intern rushed into the room. I had not heard the ambulance. The policeman gave room and the intern kneeled. He undid his bag. The orderlies glanced at the floor and went back out for their stretcher.

I stood on one side of the body, the kneeling intern with his necklace of stethescope, and the two meditative cops. On the other side was the group of students, and at their head, like a leader filled with wrath, risen in time of crisis, stood Clotilda Adams, still clutching her exam paper. There were tears in her eyes. She was in a fury. She had been thinking all this time, and now her thinking had issue: *rage*. Over the body she handed me a paper, crying out, "I don't think I deserved a D on that quiz. I answered all the questions. I can't get my credit for Philo of Ed without I get a B off you."

I must have looked at her with pure stupidity on my face. There is a Haitian proverb: *Stupidity won't kill you, but it'll make you sweat a lot.* She took the opportunity to make me sweat, took my silence for guilt, took my open-mouthed gaze for weakness. She said: "If I was a white girl, you'd grade me easier."

Guilt, a hundred years, a thousand years of it; pity for the disaster of ignorance and fear, pity for ambition rising out of ignorance; adoration of desire; trancelike response to passion—passion which justifies itself because passionate. . . . I looked at her with mixed feelings. I could not simply put her down. In order to *put down*, your own mind must be made up, put down. She had beauty and dignity, stretched tall and wrathful, with teeth for biting and eyes for striking dead.

"But I know my rights," she said, "*Mister*. My mother told me about your kind—lent my father money on his car and then hounded him out of town. He been gone since fifty-three. But you can't keep us down forever, no sir, you can't *always* keep us down—"

She was talking and I was yelling. She was talking and yelling about injustice and I, under clamps, under ice, was yelling in a whisper about the sick man. She was blaming me for all her troubles, all the troubles she had seen, and I was blaming her for not seeing what lay before her, and we were making an appointment to meet in my office and discuss this thing more calmly, Miss Adams. Okay. All right. Later.

The police, the doctor, the orderlies, and the injured cab driver were gone. The police car out front was gone and the snow was covering its traces. The janitor came in and swept up the bloodstains with green disinfectant powder. The frightened couple in the cab were released.

They all disappeared silently into the great city, into the routine of disaster and recovery of a great city. I dismissed the class until tomorrow.

The next day I tried to explain to Miss Adams what I meant about her failing to respond adequately to the facts of our life together. Her mouth quivered. Yesterday rage; today a threat of tears. What did I mean she wasn't *adequate?* What did I know about adequate anyhow? Nothing. Just a word. Agreed, Miss Adams. I was trying to say that there were two questions at issue between us —her exam grade and her choice of occasion to dispute it. I would like to discuss each matter separately. I tried to explain why putting the two events together had disturbed me. I tried to explain the notions of empirical evidence and metaphor. I recalled, without successful communication, the story of the young couple and the dog in Brooklyn.

She did not see why she shouldn't have at least a B on her quiz. Her back was strong, her head was high, she didn't need to be compared to no black dog in Brooklyn.

Finally I urged her to have her exam looked at by the head of the department, but she refused because she knew in advance that he would support me. "White is Right," she said.

"Do you want to drop out of the class?"

"No. I'll stay," she said with a sudden patient, weary acceptance of her fate. "I'll do what I can."

"I'll do what I can too," I said.

She smiled hopefully at me. She was tuckered out by the continual alert for combat everywhere. She was willing to forgive and go easy. When she left my office, this smile, shy, pretty, and conventional, tried to tell me that she could be generous—a friend.

We had come to Thomas Hobbes and John Locke in our tour through time and the river of humanities. I pointed out that the English philosophers were noted for

clarity and eloquence of style. I answered this question:
The French? Isn't French noted for clarity? Yes, they too,
but they are more abstract. On the whole. In general.

The class took notes on the truths we unfolded together. Spring came and the snow melted. There was that
brief Detroit flowering of the new season—jasmine and
dogwood—which, something like it, must have captivated
the Frenchman, Antoine de la Mothe Cadillac, when he
paused on the straits of Detroit in 1701. University gar-
deners planted grass seed where the patrol car had parked
on the lawn. The new models, all except the Cadillac, were
going at mean discounts.

"The 'Humanities,'" wrote Clotilda Adams in her
final essay, "are a necessary additive to any teacher's development worth her 'salt' in the perilous times of today.
The West and the 'Free World' must stand up to the war
of ideas against the 'Iron' Curtain." This was in answer
to a question about Beethoven, Goethe, and German
romanticism. She did not pass the course, but she was
nevertheless admitted on probation to the student-teacher
program because of the teacher shortage and the great need
to educate our children in these perilous times. Of today.

3

Humanities 610 provided ballast for the ship of culture as it pitched and reeled in the heavy seas of real life;
I lashed myself to the mast, but after hearing the siren
song of grand course outlines, I cut myself free and leaned
over the rail with the inside of my lip showing.

It would be oversimplifying to say that I left off
teaching Humanities merely because of an experience.
Such an argument is fit to be published under the title
"I Was a Teen-Age Humanities Professor." I also left for
fitter jobs, more money, a different life. Still, what I remember of the formal study of Truth and Beauty, for advanced

credit in education, is a great confusion of generalities, committees, conferences, audio-visual importunities, and poor contact. "Contact!" cried the desperate deans and chairmen, like radio operators in ancient war movies. And much, much discussion of how to get through to the students. How to get through? Miss Adams and Mr. Gold, cab driver and Thomas Hobbes, policemen and the faceless student who paused an instant for a dime for the telephone—we all have to discover how relevant we are to each other. Or do we *have* to? No, we can merely perish, shot down like mad dogs or diminished into time with no more than a glimpse of the light.

Words fade; our experience does not touch; we make do with babble and time-serving. We need to learn the meaning of words, the meaning of the reality those words refer to; we must clasp reality close. We cannot flirt forever, brown-nosing or brow-beating. We must act and build out of our own spirits. How? How? We continually need a new politics, new cities, new marriages and families, new ways of work and leisure. We also need the fine old ways. For me, the primitive appeal to pleasure and pain of writing stories is a possible action, is the way in and out again, as teaching was not. As a teacher, I caught my students too late and only at the top of their heads, at the raw point of pride and ambition, and I had not enough love and pressure as a teacher to open the way through their intentions to the common humanity which remains locked within. As a writer, I could hope to hit them in their bodies and needs, where lusts and ideals were murkily nurtured together, calling to the prime fears and joys directly, rising with them from the truths of innocence into the truths of experience.

The peculiar combination of ignorance and jadedness built into most institutions is a desperate parody of personal innocence, personal experience. Nevertheless, education, which means a drawing out—even formal education, a formal drawing out—is a variety of experience, and experience is the only evidence we have. After evidence comes our thinking upon it. Do the scientists, secreting their honey in distant hives, hear the barking of the black dog which follows them? Will the politicians accept the lead of life, or will they insist on a grade of B in Power and Dominion over a doomed race? We need to give proper answers to the proper questions. I would like for myself and everyone else to have more experience of the humanities.

Particular life is still the best map to truth. When we search our hearts and strip our pretenses, we all know this. Particular life—we know only what we *know*. Therefore the policemen stay with me: I have learned to despise most authority. The cab driver remains in his sick bleeding: pity for the fallen and helpless. And I think of Clotilda Adams in her power and weakness; like the cops, she has an authority of stupidity; like the victim of an accident, she is fallen and helpless. But someplace, since we persist in our cold joke against the ideal of democracy, the cops still have the right to push people around, Clotilda is leading children in the Pledge of Allegiance. We must find a way to teach better and to learn.

1962

PART TWO

American Places

Paris: Notes from La Vie de Bohème
(Avec Tout Conforts)

THE FAMILIAR PARTAKES of revelation in a foreign place. The traveler peeps with astounded eyes at *Lobster à l'Américaine* and at the sum of his check in the land of cheap living. The aggressive humility of the men taking sun in a square, their necks as busy as those of birds in their collars: these are the lunch-hour heliotropes of Columbus Circle or the Cleveland Public Square, but in Paris they are *French*. That a sign asks the tourist not to throw flowers in the toilet: even this is Parisian charm. That the performers at a private *spectacle* of sexual acrobatics afterwards dress and shake hands with each of the American connoisseurs of such chamber music: this is *politesse*, for the French never leave a room without taking each right hand in individual farewell. ("They say they're good friends," whispers a Marshall Plan secretary at the departing backs of the performing couple, "in real life.")

The old streets of an old city remind him of age, and he returns to his hotel to dream again the nightmares of childhood. The tourist, helpless and blind, returns to his

American infancy because he does not share that of those about him; he goes to bed with mouth nibbling over guidebook and phrasebook. Painfully awake during the first months, used and played on, he is syncopated through cunning variations into new rhythms and a questioning of all habit. Bread, words, gestures, staircases, windows, noises, the touch of linen, the smell of dust, the movement of mouths and the muscles which come of new vowels, the new laughter, the new anger, the new children and the very new old people: these summon up once more the dreams of fire, thickened air, and locked rooms mastered by the young American bent on growing up.

A discovery: the possibility of movements of love and hate from which merely his clothes, the little leap of an American step, and the Maine-to-California smile on a people who live in a morality of Happiness are enough to exclude him. This protection weighs heavy on pride. (An acquaintance at the Café Voltaire has offered three thousand dollars for his passport.)

The months pass, and he learns to sleep again. For the French he will always be *le petit Américain,* but the risks of being a tourist are met. He has his habits again. If he still moves crabwise, and his eyes on stalks, through a world whose meanings are lost to him, at least he has enough money and a large enough amiability to be forgiven his sins, *le pauvre petit, il vient d'arriver de l'Amérique, ah, oui alors. You are from New-York, le Theque-sas, or Ollywood? Est-ce vrai que le Coca-Cola donne le cancer?* He is likely to join the American Legion (Paris Post), the Chamber of Commerce, the American Students and Artists Club ("The Center"), buy a season's ticket to the American Theatre, and search out the company of the retired fullback who has lived in Montparnasse for three years while writing the biography of his football coach. Naturally they discuss France, their remarks presaged by a certain conceit: "I have a French friend, and he says. . . ."

The American notion about hospitality often disengages the first sociological bludgeon for a hurt belaboring of the French. After his initial enthusiasm about the café as institution, annex to the family, the university, the market place, and the bed, the American lonely for a home begins to wonder why his new acquaintance always proposes Les Oases or Chez Machin for their meetings instead of inviting him to his apartment. He blames the Parisian for a coldness and abstraction; he seems to seek partitions, sparing himself the surrender of reserve implied by the presence of the furniture of a life, which remind him of his lies and sit in judgment on his off-hour dreams. Leaving his new acquaintance, the American strolls the streets at nightfall and listens to the definitive clacking of shutters; one stretch and lean of those inside, and then silence—the family life of these others is blacked out by a long habit of mistrust. Alone, he knows that in a similar situation he would have invited the visitor home.

If he remains in Paris long enough for only four or five meetings among the romantic nervosities of café life, this is the judgment he will carry away: the Frenchman is stifled in armor despite his talk and his insistence on another drink, he lives behind locks, he is afraid of intimacy. *"Le domicile est sacré"*—this phrase brings a pious policeman glare to all faces. Despite its smell of food and aperitifs, its benevolent ease of smoke and gossip, its wickery luxury and its quick confidentiality, the deepest sense of a café is discretion. For the discreet ones, café life is the trapping on the armor, that tassel which distracts an eye from the blade only if it has never seen one before.

After a time, however, his friend will send him a note suggesting dinner for Saturday evening—not at his home, but at a restaurant. And then, finally, having accomplished the ceremonials of late afternoon drinks and a long meal, he will invite him—apologetically—to dine with his family.

"Is it true," asks the astounded Parisian, "that in America you can invite casual acquaintances to eat with you at your own table, and then never see them again?"— a shudder at taking *le domicile* in vain. To him this ease has the relation to responsible hospitality that the whine and the sentiment of an American soldier's harmonica has to real music. "Here," he will explain, "an invitation to my home for an evening meal means that you are becoming a part of my family, and if I fail to see you for a week I will worry that you might be ill and come to ask after you." He sees any intersecting of the circles of career, pleasure, and the family as a bravado in a history hostile to extravagant moral completions; a fatal and complicated Eden is a joke in these times, yet French irony is such as to play this joke at last as a fatality of remaining human. With a self-conscious will that *this must be*—and with that smile playing on the nervy nodules of muscle of his language made flesh—the host offers you his home and his friendship. If he rises from the table now and the shutters clack to, it is to shut the others out.

A constant in the reluctance of a Frenchman to let you see his home is the economic X; almost all families are aware of decline within their lifetimes, and the process of gradual impoverishment has been a condition of bourgeois life. Most Parisians live in shabbiness or real poverty though they may perform work of skill and power. Doomed to this, but not accepting it as have the Italians, who live within the void of their public future and have given up the justifications of power, there is the shame of those recently fallen. They dwell in urban responsibilities without the use of urban pride. There is an impulse to conceal the pulpy cushions and the children in clumsy shoes.

But this only contributes to a cultural fact which is

consistent with the Parisian's life at every turn—his separation of family life from the life connected with his work *en ville*, his impulse to keep his wife unsullied by contact with his friends, his desire to master his family and to guard its purity while he takes the risks of the wide wide world. (Though his wife may have an *ami* whom she meets in a café "from five to seven," he is likely to know outrage only if this appointment interferes with his dinner: he never keeps his wife waiting while he returns from his own *petite amie*.) The marriage of convenience, retaining its propriety at least up until the last war, is still frequent; the two categories of women—wife-mothers and *petites-amies*—are accepted by most Frenchmen, who attend all-male schools from earliest childhood. The attempt to assimilate women to "masculine" life provides one of the clichés of French burlesque of America. Skepticism about the possibility of monogamy associates itself with an assumption all the more stern concerning the sanctity of the home. Divorce is difficult and relatively rare, but the back booths of the cafés are crowded in the late afternoon with couples of all ages busy in their *cinq-à-sept*.

What Bergson called *morsellisation*—an anatomizing of living event into affairs to be filed in compartments—has triumphed in Paris as it does in all commercial cultures. False separations head off real susceptibilities. Everything has its role, its proper moment, in the life of a free citizen; the good life consists in turning up these proprieties—a mistress who knows her place, a moneychanger with sensibilities and wit about his trade, a way of saving on taxes and investing the gain abroad which does not interfere with the important business of life at home on the rue du Faubourg St.-Honoré. What are these important matters? An economy of spirit is not everything, true; but a man must recognize what is possible—a recognition usually associated with the *proper*. Is there someone who disagrees?

"Mais la vie est comme ça, mon vieux. On a vécu, quoi."
This, the voice of the bourgeois, is the voice of the guardian
of all great capitals. He gives us the way of life which we
think of as enduring, the one which preserves values.
Naturally, the word *value* is understood ostensibly, doing
the service of the geographer's baton to point to something
outside time and men.

Morsellisation offers a sort of security, a logic and a
material which is acquiescent to planning and clever book-
keeping. This is a function—the ransom of security and
dignity—partially accomplished by money in America,
but in Paris even the metaphysical uses of money are
enfeebled by inflation. You can't save for a rainy day
when the concierge tells you that all umbrellas so far
known have snapped, rotted, leaked, or skittered off in the
first high wind. The French have lived for a long time with
governments that don't govern, with money that will not
buy tomorrow what it buys today, and in a place where
war may soon make human life worth even less than
money. The habits of dignity, which include the keeping
of secrets, help preserve the sense of dignity. The terrace
of an anonymous café near one of the many railway stations
can be—under the April sun, under the September sun—
the final home of all your uneconomical dreams. And
you can still offer yourself a rich-as-blood *coup de rouge*
for five or six cents.

Coy about it, hesitant and afraid, giving this gesture
of hospitality more weight than is necessary, the man to
whom the tourist has presented a letter of introduction
at last says: "So come at eight, can you? Will you?"

When a Parisian admits a friend to his home, some
of the charm of a café acquaintanceship passes; he is introduced to the pleasures of a family, and to its troubles.
He has mounted the hierarchy of a culture built upon
class, tradition, and old troubled moralities, to a special
level of privilege and responsibility.

Most Americans in Europe prefer the frank generosity offered by Italians. Few stay long enough to see France, which displays the Louvre and Versailles, her splendid false teeth rinsing in glass, because, not only a flirt, she doesn't like to be looked at.

Nevertheless thousands of Americans remain in Paris. Apart from those who come because of a job with the government, private business, or one of the international organizations—for most of these Paris is an appendage to the working day—the largest group is still that of the Bohemes, the experts on eternal truth and irregular hours. The great run of American Bohemia is on the Left Bank, its moral politics swinging from the conservative devotion of the graduate students bent on tenure to the rabid wobblyhood of the beboppers.

Samples: The student of dress designing (GI Bill) whose mother sends him comic strips by airmail; the plump damp timid Francophile all hot for the Life of Art as a college French teacher, who earned the money for his trip to Europe by selling pornographic postcards obtained in Paris during the war; the six-foot-high graduate of Radcliffe who comes to Paris to write a dissertation on John Donne and takes a Boul' Mich' poet as lover —he tries to jump out the window when she first catches him alone in his room, but is trapped in the scaffolding; the litterateur who uses his wife's mother's money to court poets and critics, fancying himself the poor student of Flaubert and Mallarmé but hiring a cook with a high cauliflower hat when he invites his esthetic friends to dinner. This one, having been an American in Paris for four years, lives in a world of abstractions and gossip, culture and fierce incestuous rivalries with his local compatriots. He ambiguously trots between the ambition to be accepted as court American in an "aristocratic" French world and the sense of his ambition, which is to be invited to the country house of Mme. X so that he can wear his pride like a ribbon on his suede vest among his country-men.

A once-successful radio writer decides that his money will go farther among the expatriates of Paris. He has been blacklisted and can no longer find work in New York, but discovers a pleasant home and status among the American political (not "cultural" or "racial") exiles. He listens to recordings of Josh White and recalls his activist past with a group of disconsolate entertainers and pouting journalists with ambitions to eat magnificently and be in-the-know. There is a comic opera pretense of plotting and "biding our time"—like Lenin in Switzerland—but a secret con-viction that the "working class" shares nothing of his ideas, not even his opinions on jazz, and that his exile is a matter of personal comfort.

The first four of this cast represent the Americans-in-Paris of old. The cheap-livers, the lovers of Gaul, the romantic and the social climbers, the refined amorists: they were already here to greet Henry James, although the institution has since been fecundated by a spill of American public wealth in the form of fellowships, the GI Bill, and so forth. French snobbery for *la vie Américaine* (*le Coca-Cola, le Betty-Grable, le jazz-hot*) has reached the level where an American student can support himself by selling hashish under the name of marijuana.

You still find at the Dôme, the café in which Heming-way is said to have written some of the first Hemingway, the bearded American artist—he is for the ages—who suffers the audible anemia of a man who lives alone, that clacking feebleness of the heart as he enters a room where no one cares about him. Watch him mooch out the good life, which is a tingle something like the sensation the hand of the Luxembourg Gardens puppeteer must enjoy under the skirt of Becassine. The serious drama of his month is the exercise of dialectical skill with a Montparnasse whore, one of those singing mathematicians of love. The next evening, playing the role of cynical grief before her jiggle and her large-pursed bounce, he lights her a Gauloise and leans away from the flame to take the most dramatic light. He moves on, our artist who resists parody like the tubercular, as if he has some creative other thought in his mind, but only *as if*; like the chronically ill, he has precisely nothing in constant and dutiful attendance through the soft yellow-gray afternoons and the chocolate evenings of the Left Bank. He may finally assuage his solitude with some cute American girl barely over the habit of circling her *i*'s and *j*'s, having fled the textbook think-traps for the museum culture-traps. Drink up, girls, for both love and wine will become more expensive: and tomorrow you may be a teacher, or in nine months a mother.

The love-wine-and-beauty bohemes, talking art and abortion in Ivy League blue jeans—"St. Francis is a darling saint, so existentialist, I mean Freudianismly speaking"—still crowd the cafés but in a withering flock. The new model has a research grant, a wife, a beret made of the finest felt, and a vocabulary constructed of the guaranteed latest cultural truths. His eyes run with the yellow crud of scholarship and his pockets rustle with the brittle lint of moving money. Far from Mimi and Rodolphe, he accepts the responsibilities of success and the American Century; he tries to cultivate his colleagues at the Sorbonne and the Collège de France but finds them politically immature, gives a frightened *paterfamilias* sniff at the zazous of the Dupont Quartier Latin, and hurries back to America so that his friends will not scramble past him on the treadmill of university promotion. "They're hard to get to know," he says of the French; which is, besides, true.

The White Russians who trot after tourists to hiss invitations to "an interesting scientific experience, Sir" shake their heads over the last instance, the colony of American political refugees. This group bring a new form to American life abroad despite its links with the past: those who settle in a foreign land because their politics prevent their finding work and because they fear political persecution. That, as individuals, they are mostly unclear about what the heavy words *political persecution* can mean does not lighten their fears. Their situation is complicated by the efficiencies of modern politics. Some Americans are refused passports to leave the States; others, once here, have had their passports confiscated and have been sent back by State Department, Embassy, or FBI order. An indiscreet word in a café can travel far. "The American passport is a privilege, not a right." There follow lyric cries about a break for freedom in Czechoslovakia, but they dutifully embark for their Manhattan apartments which they have sublet for six months at a reasonable profit.

Of the two most impressive of the younger French writers, Jean Genet and Raymond Queneau, the first is an orphan outlaw, a prudish homosexual thief and blackmailer singing a moral invocation to what he is pleased to call Evil; the second is a metaphysician of language finding his sources in popular speech, a witty Pythagorean hoaxer dead-earnest about his jokes, an inspired grammarian. Both are intensely self-conscious artists, Genet descending willy or nilly from a French literary tradition including François Villon and Balzac's Vautrin, Queneau an erudite working at the lessons of Joyce; neither began by fitting the French cultural ideal of the *homme de lettres.* Yet both are fluttering through the wind tunnel of publicity and coterie-thinking, those special obligations which have the effect of shoving them past the matter of their effort into the category of performing celebrities. This drafty passage shimmers like the land of milk, honey, and tender justice for visiting Americans. It's worth a look at least, leaving

Jean Genet and Raymond Queneau to their proper reward, which is to be read and not gossiped about.[1]

What could be more luxurious than the ripe French assimilation of the esthetic vocations to other professions? Art is located in a world with structure and depth, like the snail expertly buttered, spiced, and replaced in its shell; competent writers are more important in Parisian life than good cooks or even *escargots de Bourgogne*. This status gives the quiet dignity of the Maison de la Société des Gens de Lettres (grass on the grounds, beards on the Gens) the relation to American literary groups that the New York Athletic Club has to an armpit-haunted Belleville public bath. While in America, poetry (for example) is almost always a solitary vice, clucked over in a family and a poor recommendation to a landlord, in Paris the tradition can make the writer as imposing a personage as Bing Crosby in America or Princess Elizabeth in England. The Academie Française, the Academie Goncourt, and lesser corporations; the circles revolving about certain cafés, philosophies, reviews, publishing houses, and commanding individuals; the prestige accorded a number of annual literary prizes greater than the number of variations on the theme of the Rose Bowl; a public interest in writers unfettered by a reading of their works; such a social texture in which is embedded the lonely joy of putting one word after the next gives meaning to the designation *homme de lettres*. It is more than a *metier* like another; it corresponds in the popular imagination to the film and sport-

[1] Queneau: *Loin de Reuil, Pierrot Mon Ami, Les Exercises de Style,* etc. *Loin de Reuil* has been published as *The Skin of Dreams* by New Directions in an excellent translation by H. J. Kaplan.

Genet: *Le Journal du Voleur, Notre-Dame-des-Fleurs, Miracle de la Rose,* etc. Bernard Frechtman's translation of *Our Lady of the Flowers* has been banned in the United States by the Douane Quixotes charged with inspecting baggage and public virtue, but can be bought at exorbitant prices from the usual bootleggers.

1962: Genet is now well-known as a playwright.

ing aristocracy in America, the royal family in England, and the bureaucratic demiurges of the Soviet Union.

In Paris culture is high on the heap. The politicians and generals having defaulted, the champion cyclists turning out to be steady and Swiss or Italian and spectacular up hills, the millionaires laying low or taking their money on the lam into Argentina or the Chase Bank, the descendants of Bourbon or Napoleonic royalty eking out a frugal living by marrying Americans, the boxers KO'd in Detroit and the *chanteurs de charme* senile or touring South America, the *gang-stairs* finding nothing left to rob but Egyptians, Americans, and each other, it has come the turn of immortal beauty & truth. Its practitioners hug the top of the hierarchy; they wiggle often enough to merit the attention of those below. Every culture needs a hero, and we select our heroes in varied modes but worship them similarly. The clothes, travels, witticisms, diseases, feuds, birthdays, and amorous fortunes of such as Sartre, Cocteau, Gide, Mauriac, Colette, Montherlant, Claudel, and the latest "Goncourt" are discussed with the same loving attention in the French press as those of Joan Crawford in a hieratic fan magazine. The tucking of a napkin under the laureate's chin at a prize dinner can be an event as crucial as the gestures of some darling Broadway character. Everyone recognizes the effigies among the wax figures of Joan of Arc and the two Napoleons at the Musée Grevin. The light reading of a Parisian office worker on the *metro* is likely to be his weekly *Figaro Littéraire*, *Opera*, or *Les Nouvelles Littéraires*— three of a selection of artistic *patisserie* in comparison to which the *Saturday Review of Literature* is weighty fodder. Between the launching of an American battleship and a parade in Red Square, the newsreels report Sartre lighting his pipe in front of the Rose Rouge or Picasso throwing sand at his wife on the beach at Antibes. (How anguished is the flame! how masterful the sidearm sweep!)

Not a day passes without radio interviews of living

writers or an "evocation" of a dead one. The interviews
are recorded and economically stored for later use, in
combination with "original music," as evocations. Death
masks, souvenir tag-ends of clothing or hair, and tender
anecdotes provide a living for the ghoul-critics and a thrill
for the rest of us, who thus partake of glory and buy the
memorial edition which includes Z's only unpublished
letter, in which he returned the unused portion of a round-
trip ticket to Lyon. Exhibitions in his honor will include,
besides the usual manuscripts, photographs, and letters,
household objects, baby shoes, and his hearing aid if possible.

When Gide died, reporters pursued Jean-Louis
Barrault, wearing a mussed toupee and carrying a bouquet
of violets, into the room where the body lay. So many
photographs of the master appeared that it seemed incredible that Gide, taken up by his duties as a model, could
ever have found time to write. The producer of a film
about him announced that he would not profiteer on the
publicity surrounding the death of his old friend and would
wait several weeks before releasing it. Besides, the editing
was not yet finished. One of the epidemic of tributes to
Gide—everyone wrote one, and those who didn't were
approached for comment by Inquiring Reporters—began:
"My intimate friend André Gide, whom I last saw in the
summer of 1937 . . ." François Mauriac, after a lifelong
struggle against Gide's skepticism, sent him to purgatory
in his column in the Figaro, sparing him the expected
eternity of burning with a remark that, where he is now,
he is busy repenting of his errors. He justifies this lenient
sentence by invoking the religiosity to be found in Gide's
great joy in a solitary making of his world.

Writers and painters are news; they have status; it's
comfortable. There is no doubt about the diffusion of interest in Picasso or Sartre in the newsreel theater, and some
of it may eventually be directed toward their work. Their

antics are enjoyed by others than their fraternity brothers. Behind this popular interest in the arts, of course, lie complex and serious justifications. The "classic" character of the language and education, the continuity of a tradition, the values and tensions created in the middle and upper classes, the ambiguous relationship to the state and the Church, and the special history and situation of a capital such as Paris: these suggest some of the sources. There are rewards for those who offer to fill the social function. But there is a price for being institutionalized.

The price is paid in a danger of abdication of the two great moral roles of the poet: the apocalyptic, which is the will to possession by prophecy—the divine afflatus—and the analytic, the examination of perspectives for a vision of social texture. (Of course there are also other and less moral reasons for any great poet's work.) The prophetic calisthenics are flabbily performed by a man who, listed in the business section of the telephone directory under "Hommes de Lettres," awaits a call from a morning paper to give his opinion on the latest cabinet crisis. The argument that, by becoming *qua* poet a respectable part of the social structure, the man of letters gains a dramatic depth of view is more seductive. The worm in this cheese is that the job of a poet remains all the same a lonely one, one not a corporate endeavor, self-separated from union, club, and class, and only partaking of these respectabilities in its most trivial aspects. The first work of creation does not change essentially under the pressures of machine culture, and the homme de lettres who feels that his craft can be compared to the daily effort of a mason or a lawyer is living a lie which will prevent his ever coming to a valid perspective on the lives of lawyers or masons. Literature is not a career like another, despite the successful effort of some writers toward comfort and a place; specialization here makes experts but involves a subtle moral disqualification. (Rimbaud foundered before a problem which in-

cludes this one.) Even a weekly book review should be a task essentially different from masonry.

Yet a poet cannot parade his exclusion as a private right. Suffering (O! le pauvre) is no longer the high privilege of his cunning. Fifty years ago, when the issues of life and death, love and power, were not yet identified with work, mass populations, total governments, and total war, it was still possible to sing songs of the greatest loneliness and the greatest truth. That the reveries of a Sade, a Kafka, or a Jarry now prove prophetic, demands of their heirs a more responsible sharing in the dirty work of being human. These others, thinking to speak for themselves or for tragic ideals, were social historians of the highest order: often— a tribute to genius but worse luck for us—in advance of their society. Reading Alfred Jarry today we hear a rustle of the ashes from the crematoriums, we watch a shift of the frozen chemical shadows of Hiroshima, we fall among the groans of the bodies in forced labor as these destroyed creatures, who are only as guilty of being human as the rest of us, join to cry out, "Vive Ubu!"—this, being no longer merely a great joke, has a tendency forever to alter the lonely estate of poetry. If Ubu Roi remains a burlesque and a happy trick, well, that's a tribute to the will to life in those left alive.

This is what we have given up for what we have learned; it's a trick in which we no longer presume to use masks. We must recognize ourselves among the actors; we should still laugh. Here is the theater-in-the-round we must dare to play in.

The dilemma for those who presume to speak for the time left us is compounded by knowledge that participation must imply a partial acquiescence in horrors, and yet only in this hard yielding can disapproval have meaning. Neither our disapproval nor any other judgment can annul our participation. (I mean by "participation" a state of causal involvement.) We're up to our necks. Not even Dante had it that hard during the most responsible literary voyage yet recorded. At least—*and from the beginning*—he had a good chance to attain the third part of the trilogy, although in our recollections of his tour he is mostly seen fixed, and Virgil too, deep in the inferno and far from divinity. *Terza rima* serves the technical uses of his language better than it does the symbolic use predicted.

Still, by his deeds and by grace, he is confident of being guided finally upward. Our world is busy telling us that this is, alas, the life of Jewish vision: salvation, if at all, here below.

In the end, because each demands a further responsibility, either the isolation or the assimilation to other work of the American writer (states having much in common) seems preferable to the moral *tout confort* of Parisian literary life. Isolated, the caustic of a man comes into full play, despite the danger of an arty frothing, and one essential characteristic of creative effort can be faced in its extreme condition: its willed loneliness. Or, for a farmer like Faulkner, a businessman like Wallace Stevens, or a teacher like everyone else, the soreness of divided attention acts against the knowledgeability of a conditional running with the pack to make possible the flight of passion off experienced fact which seems the only valid one—the one to which we still have a right.

Any remarks on this subject, however hortatory in tone, can only work as a way of judging—although they may be stated as prescriptions. What *la vie de bohème* and its partner in incest, the life of official art, imply is that the writer's self-consciousness is enough. Such artists may grant research its uses, a deliberate "experiencing"; they remain incapable of the sort of responsible participation in society which creates both persons and individuals. What the writer writes about has to be something which he knows *not* as an artist in addition to the special perspectives which he always brings to the matter of his life. Without this causal involvement in some way as a nonartist, the special consciousness of self suspended, he forfeits the possibility of his eye-and-heart's ever having anything important but itself to work on. This self-consciousness alone is important; it is no longer sufficient, nor ever really was.

Everyone whimpers about the risks and obstacles to life in America for the artist. There is no point in beating the dead horse of American cultural immaturity; it will stay as dead as usual. I want to suggest that, in a world like ours, the risks of that cultural privilege which we like to imagine for a golden age are greater and more grave than the risks of faulty connections. That is, more grave for what is essential to the artist: his first demand on himself to know and to make. The golden age returns for but an instant among the aroma of the madeleines while chatting of Proust with a Gallimard editor at one of the afternoon teas.

On the Boulevard St. Germain, near the Odéon, there is a plaque indicating "The League for the Defense Against the Enemies of Culture—Second floor to the left."

Ne pas jeter des fleurs dans les aisances, S.V.P.

1951

Cleveland: Inflation-on-the-Erie

"O CLEVELAND, the Forest City! The Fountain City! O, la Belle City!" cried a nineteenth-century newspaper editor, visiting from Wisconsin with his French phrasebook and his head full of wind. "Cleveland doesn't put enough garlic in its cooking; it's no friend to food," complained the twentieth-century wife of a professor at Western Reserve University. "I like Cleveland because it's so nice to me," said a lovely young visitor with a New York road company (waist 23, bust 34, hips 35), "with all its theaters and goodwill and its new teevee channels opening up."

The subject of these diverse meditations is the sixth largest community in the nation, a metropolitan area of about a million and a half, representing just one per cent of the total population of the United States. It is the world's center of paint manufacturing, and is said to contain the largest Hungarian settlement outside the city limits of Budapest, but is chiefly remarkable for its wealth and its stability. Newspapers estimate that Cleveland had among the largest average family incomes of the great American cities last year—about six thousand dollars. One of its suburbs, Cleveland Heights, a community of sixty thousand souls whose men coast eagerly downhill into the city each morning and rise profitably amid a bumper-to-bumper irritation each evening, boasts an average annual income of about nine thousand dollars per family.

What does Cleveland do with its money?

It worries about it, as does everyone else. It wonders whether the party will go on and it wonders why it isn't having such a good time as it expected. There is a sense of dream, as if one were to wander loose in a studio making gen-u-ine counterfeit dollars. Some of the fantasts fresh to the hiring of tax lawyers do not yet feel secure in this materialized dream. Most of us, however, are doing quite well, thank you, from the art lover who recently settled between one and two million dollars on an actress once the favorite of Pirandello, to the lowliest policeman with a bingo parlor or a bookie on his beat and an occasional all-expenses-paid trip to Miami Beach.

Spread out strategically along Lake Erie between Detroit and Buffalo, Cleveland sometimes refers to itself in magazine advertisements as "the Best Location in the Nation," with good rail, truck, and water communications, a central position among raw materials and markets, and a climate humid enough to spur on the inhabitants to energetic activity in order to forget the nasal drip with which a good proportion of us are inflicted. The members of Moses Cleaveland's party who surveyed this territory in 1796, ate delicious broiled rattlesnake and found both commercial and esthetic delights in barter with the Indians, but worried about "the subtil, baneful wind" off Lake Erie, which led straight to death if breathed through the mouth. Despite their fears, there has not been an epidemic, flood, earthquake, volcanic eruption, or other serious act of God except for the purchase by Bill Veeck of the Cleveland Indians. Mr. Veeck has since moved on.

The water on a first-baseman's knee, the laryngitis of

a disc jockey, or another policeman surprised in an act of burglary or venery while on duty provide the staple diet of newspapers in quest of local catastrophe. Cleveland policemen obey the Philosopher's great doctrine of the Golden Mean between penuriousness (Atlantic City) and profligacy (Beverly Hills), accepting just the amount required in favor and shakedown to send these commissioned Aristotelians to Miami Beach, Coral Gables, and a proper dignity in the sunset of their days. They are sometimes punished for the excessive taking of bribes by a lonely duty on the East Ninth Street pier, jutting onto Lake Erie, where they are told to watch out for invaders from Canada. Any time the Canadians want to take over, the Force can be counted upon to turn its back if the fix be put in with a minimal delicacy.

Cleveland is secure in steady employment, diversified industry, and a profitable balance between war and civilian production. Everything from television sets and chlorophyll pills to gold bricks and honorary degrees has a good market here. Racial and class tensions are relatively low, the Nationality Gardens in Rockefeller Park a symbol of the way Polish, German, Czech, Italian, Jewish, Hungarian, Russian, English, Serbian, and Greek vegetables can grow together in harmony. As long as business continues good, the antagonism among groups which is one of America's sadnesses everywhere can probably be confined to the level of personal bitterness. There may be ill feeling over the movement of neighborhoods, but no race riots for this year or next. The current controversy over slum clearance, which involves resettlement of a large area, will probably be resolved by bureaucratic rather than Klan methods. Thus far, the local officials, the Negro population, and the city as a whole have held firm against a few hysterics made at the inevitable. A fine residential community of prosperous Negroes has developed among the mansions near Western Reserve University. As to others of the oppressed proletariat, a typical real-estate item in one of the newspapers tells of the sale to a machinist of a "ranch-type" in Shaker Heights. Price: "About $45,000."

The city has expanded beyond the dreams of John D. Rockefeller, whose home on Euclid Avenue was razed to make room for a parking lot, and even now approaches the fantasies of the Van Sweringen brothers, those heroes of our mythology who lived together in one room of their castle near Cleveland and provide perhaps the most dramatic of the local success stories. (They died owing between ten and twenty million dollars.) The rapid spread of the city has created transportation difficulties, housing difficulties, and political difficulties, with slow money to be made in solving these problems and fast money to be made in compounding them. Clevelanders have not proved reluctant to accept either variety of cash. The fifty-two-floor Terminal Tower, built by the authority of Van Sweringen paper, looks out with commercial pride over the movements of money in a land once wasted by Indians, its flag far up aflutter to indicate a ball game today and its spire imperceptibly in motion against the forces of wind and gravity.

Culture is not neglected amid such prosperity. Cleveland's little-theater groups, symphony orchestra, chamber-music societies, art museum, zoo, and sandlot baseball leagues are known throughout our commuting world, from Painesville on the east to Lorain on the west, and—in justice it must be added—even beyond. Ballet, opera, and stag movies all have their enthusiasts. The Health Museum, first in America, houses "Juno, the Transparent Lady," whose inner organs light up when a button is pressed. Particularly among the "nationality" groups, traditional crafts enjoy a continued practice—ceramics, stained-glass windows, organ-building, weaving, and so on. Cleveland's sense of being a patron of the arts is fortified by such local events as the annual visits of the New York Metro-

politan Opera, the Ballet Russe, and Bennett Cerf; Hart
Crane once lived here, and *Time* was once edited in Cleveland by that young man Luce and friends. The Mad Killer
of Kingsbury Run—here reverently given his complete
title—whose capture has been announced and then retracted to the accompaniment of scandals in the sheriff's
office and accusations of police brutality, is occasionally
resurrected by the newspapers during slow days in the
cold war. (Their most generous theory: that he represents
a latter-day marriage of Malthus and Robin Hood, ridding
the community of undesirables. An estimated score thus
far: twenty-six dismemberments.)

Another burgeoning garden of culture is the local television industry. It hopes to contribute to the national glory
of Cleveland by eventually housing network shows. Western Reserve University has pioneered in teaching logic,
psychology, and literature to thousands of television viewers, morning meditations on Pavlov's dog being brought
to Mrs. Northeastern Ohio by a sixteen-inch-high homun-
culus in a Muntz or General Electric tube. These are
credit courses. Cleveland College, the downtown branch
of Western Reserve, has developed an extensive program
of evening adult classes, offering capsule courses in everything from Hats & Bonnets to Mann & Gide, with the
clatter of sewing machines sometimes interrupting the discussion which attempts to measure in pounds and ounces
just *how much madness* is proper to the most efficient
functioning of an artist. We have enough local "creative
people," painters, musicians, sculptors, writers, and disc
jockeys, to satisfy the need of the women's clubs for free
luncheon speakers. One novelist claims to have been introduced to an important lady as "a big man in the Insight
business."

But perhaps the most ambitious of the dreams in our
community is the city planner reported to be devoting
himself to a modern reconstruction of "the Best Location

in the Nation" after its helter-skelter growth will have been corrected by an atom bomb. As a more immediate concern, the planners are attempting to reform the lakefront and the Cuyahoga River, that freckled, odorous, precociously senile stream which led W. K. Kelsey, the great journalistic advantage which Detroit holds over Cleveland, to wonder if perhaps the Cuyahoga does not "begin somewhere as a limpid brooklet wandering between lush banks overhung with asphodel and floating with those nenuphars that the French poets love so well, and if along the line it loses its virginity, so that by the time it reaches Cleveland, it's just an old trot." The industries and the suburbs which use her, however, love her for what she is, a receptacle so unprepossessing that even the suicides of Cleveland are driven to the drugstore, the locked garage, or other waters.

Of the seven institutions of higher learning located in or near Cleveland, the chief is Western Reserve University, which sponsored a musical comedy two summers ago in order to celebrate a hundred years of progress. Known as "The Yale of the Middle West"—this slogan is applied chiefly during the continuous campaign for endowment— it can perhaps most fairly be stated of Western Reserve that Yale must bow to it in the financing of musical comedies. In return, Cleveland's great university should be gracious enough to concede the palm to Yale in the area of intellectual vivacity. Several of the graduate schools, those of medicine and others, deserve their respectable national reputations.

Case Institute, Western Reserve's most steadfast rival in football and fund-raising, has celebrated the victories of abstraction and officially recognized theoretical physics by changing its name from "—of Applied Science" to the luxurious "—of Technology." Dancing academies, charm schools, Diesel institutes, and evanescent colleges offering degrees in Your Memory, How to Build It, or Success the

Himalayan Way all find a clientele hot for inward betterment.

The revival meeting is cultivated with a success which depends on the preacher's satisfying the critical standards of Cleveland's sophistication in theology. At Lenten time last year, a newspaper printed a series of personal credos, fine publicity for God, by prominent leaders of business, finance, the professions, government, and the long con; the tone was one of easy social familiarity—they know whose side He is on—and they developed an image of the Almighty as the benevolent cartelist, hedging against inflation but content with nonvoting share in numerous healthy American enterprises. Some splendid local examples attest to the earthly reward of piety.

In an effort to relieve us of some of the money with which the pockets of Cleveland are heavy, the banks swollen, and the mattresses lumpy, a number of industries have undergone rapid expansion during the past ten years. (At income-tax time in town each winter, premium prices are paid for high-grade woolen socks of the sort with reinforced toe and heel in which a roll of fifties can safely be tucked, protected by mothball and prayer from the assaults of time, beast, conscience, or federal treasury agent. A light sleeper is kept awake during the March nights by the steady chuck-chuck of his neighbors' spades in their back yards.) Clevelanders have tried sex and drink and found that, although activities to be recommended in their places, they do not spend money fast enough. They have tried speculation in real estate and discovered, to their dismay, that no matter how risky the speculation, they have almost invariably suffered a profit during the past fifteen years. The distraught philanthropist who tried scattering bills of medium denomination from his office window was arrested by alert policemen and released to the custody of his heirs. Therefore, in response to great civic need, the existing brokerage firms have expanded their staffs, opened new offices, and invited aid from New York to accommodate the waiting hordes of stock-buyers who seek to regain the unencumbered agility of the fine careless days of 1932.

A more general attempt to spend money is represented by a proliferation of night clubs which astonishes lifetime residents, who remember Cleveland's café society as a choice between a Saturday night with goulash and wine or the band concerts at the shell in Edgewater Park, the lovers' sticky hands united in a box of crackerjack. The first settlers of the city converted their grain into liquid form for greater profit in the journey eastward. Their insight and ingenuity was reflected during the era of the Volstead Amendment by many contemporary settlers, now gone legit, mellowed by age and gain. Instead of bucking motor launches across Lake Erie to Canada, some of them have now flowered into a homely maturity and useful contribution to community recreation through their association with the entertainment business, importing everything from trapeze acts to "risky songs direct from New York and Miami Beach."

Not long ago, a small west-side bar, far from downtown, hired Rudy Vallee for a week of the "Whiffenpoof Song" and nostalgia about old Yale for the pleasure of the neighborhood loungers. "Big names" visit supper clubs which used to be satisfied with high-school bands. The kids who once made out with a soda and a few nickels for the juke box are now in the habit of parking their convertibles at Moe's Main Street and investing respectable sums in an evening with Johnny Ray ("Mr. Emotion in Person now"), as he puts his head against the piano, sobs briefly, and sings, "Tell the Lady I Said Good-bye." Cleveland bobby-soxers, acting under orders from the local deejays, mouths agape, deeply moved, marched among the first in Johnny Ray's crusade to carry his message to the Paramount in faraway and infidel New York. At any rate, with tin whistles passé and crackerjack prizes made of paper, the band concert has fallen into obsolesence.

The gentleness and moderation typical of Cleveland can be illustrated by a recent incident. The manager of one of the night spots, a distinguished bootlegger, racketeer, and gambler, was having a heart-to-heart talk with his parking-lot attendant. In the course of their negotiations, which were chiefly devoted to reprimands for joy-riding in the automobiles of customers, he expressed himself with an eloquence which knocked several teeth through the employee's cheek. The latter, perhaps encouraged by job mobility in a time of intense business activity, retorted by stabbing his ex-boss, who by this time had accepted his resignation. Interviewed at the police station, the parking-lot attendant, now out of work but not embittered, issued the following statement: "I used my little knife because I didn't want to cut him bad."

One of the scenic paths recommended to the tourist follows along the Cuyahoga River in the industrial flats. By day this area is covered with an acrid pall. By night the sky is violet, throbbing and flaring with the reflection from the blast furnaces. In this oldest corner of the city, from which the nutritive rattlesnake has long since fled, some of Cleveland's few poor people cower in shame for their lack of initiative and patriotism toward "The Forest City," "The Convention City," "Where Coal and Ore Meet." Nearby streets, named by the first settlers, may startle the visitor who finds rusty plaques identifying them as Literary Road or College Avenue or Professor Street or Shakespeare Avenue. Farther along, at the shoreline of Lake Erie, he can look east to the municipal rubbish dump, which smolders constantly, and admire the tranquil hobbyists who stand studying it and competing to club the rats which occasionally emerge.

On Sunday, however, the stroller will discover in this

area a calm tribute to America's industrial might. Overhead, the traffic sings across a great bridge, and at his feet,
in the shadows of the bridge, a maze of streets, paths, and
alleys leads to docks, warehouses, and small machine shops.
The stain of smoke fades briefly from the urban clouds.

If he makes his way to the bank of the Cuyahoga,
which has kept its Indian name, he can find wild sunflowers
which come six feet out of the muck in September. He
may even, as did one *flâneur*, chance upon a lovely young
artist rapidly sketching the city's skyline, her mouth in a
pout, her golden hair shining in the autumn sun, her eyes
awash with the contemplation of beauty.

To the sightseer this unexpected vision in a beige
cashmere sweater came as a wondrous example of an area
of experience still open to private enterprise. He made his
way through the brush to surprise her, coming around a
heap of tin cans and decaying tires with an inquiry which
united a theme of respectful gallantry to the grace of
esthetic sensibility: "Excuse me, Miss, are you from the
Cleveland Institute of Art? The Museum classes, maybe?"

She was reluctant to discuss her work. In fact, she fled
with wild shrieks, having been convinced by the newspapers
that he must have intended assault, purse-snatching, or at
least what is called "exposing his person."

He was left with her sketch of the Terminal Tower.
She seemed to have talent. Like the spirit of Cleveland,
her talent might develop with greater richness if she were
more confident of her power, less speedy in the flight with
money, and yet more adventurous in the exposing of her
person to the risks of love.

                                                            1951

Haiti: Americans in the Port of Princes

The little fellow does what he can;
the big fellow does what he wants.
                              —Haitian proverb

YOU CAN ENTER BY TWO ROUTES. By ship you look away from the luxury of a Caribbean cruise to the city spread out in a yellow-gray haze along the wide, wide bay—a low jumble of buildings and the guttering poverty of La Saline and the lovely blue mountains rising through the town. The first Haitians you meet are elite doctors and port officials, sweating primly and stubbornly in clothes made for another climate, and the naked boys diving for coins from their burned-out log canoes.

Or you may step from an air-conditioned airplane onto a road where the donkeys and peasant women are carrying their loads of vegetables or coffee into the market, and there you hear the insinuating greeting the mass of Haitians offer the tourist: "Geev-me-fiave-cents-Meester." If you hold your hand out right back at her, she may laugh and join you in the joke. Her mood changing, she prefers the conspiracy of shared laughter to an easy nickel. Beggars here are rarely insistent.

Haiti is surely one of the queerest places on earth. The American has little to sustain him at first except a taste for exotism. The traditional joys of tourism—swimming, sunning, running, wenching, and writing letters home— are required because they at least make contact with a familiar world.

Otherwise it is exile in a Garden of Eden fallen into permanent depression. The Republic of Haiti, a small island state in the Caribbean Sea, is tropical, mountainous, sea-bordered except for the frontier shared with the Dominican Republic, and so densely populated that the traveler finds it difficut to relieve himself by the side of the road without a crowd of peasants materializing out of the brush to observe and applaud him. Born of a slave revolt unique in history, the chief characteristic of Haiti's career has been a nervous alternation between occasional reformers and ephemeral tyrants who have used the state as the means to personal fortune. While Haiti has succeeded in producing a number of extraordinary men, it has never succeeded in developing a stable government serious about educating the illiterate masses and consistent in attempting to raise the standard of living of a people that is one of the poorest and most long-suffering in the world.

In principle, Haiti is a Negro nation, French in language, Catholic in religion, democratic in government. In practice, Haiti is a collection of almost four million Negroes ruled by a largely mulatto upper class; its business is controlled by this so-called elite and by foreigners; the people speak Creole and except for about eight per cent of the population do not understand, read, or write French; Catholicism has an ambiguous position among a people profoundly rooted in the celebrations of the *voudou* pantheon; the government, under elegantly written laws and a model constitution, is democratic in form and a military dictatorship in fact.

Some of the first leaders of the Haitian slaves against their French masters fought earlier at Savannah in the

American Revolution. The chief motive for rebellion in Haiti was the misery of the slaves. However, the genius of Toussaint and of the other slave leaders in Port-au-Prince was kindled by the same ideas of the Rights of Man that illumined the disorders in Paris and Boston in that epoch.

Despite a common parenthood of ideas—this can be seen in the declarations of independence for the United States and Haiti—official American policy, often instigated by slave-holders, remained for a long time deeply hostile to the new black nation which had won its liberty by its own efforts against a Napoleon at the height of his power. Thomas Jefferson even expressed the fear that the Haitians might invade the United States in order to free the slaves. Throughout the first hundred years of Haitian independence, the United States stayed mainly aloof from the affairs of Haiti, which was treated as an untouchable among the nations, except to warn away any Europeans who seemed to be looking for naval bases in the Caribbean Sea. The chief part of Haiti's commerce and international intercourse was carried on with France, with which the Haitian ruling class preserved sentimental ties despite the bitterness of slavery and the bloodbaths of the war for freedom. The sons of rich Haitians, perhaps bearing the blood of both Norman nobility and Guinean princes in their veins, went to school at the Lycée Stanislas and the Sorbonne in Paris.

Then, in 1915, the integration of Haiti into American hemispheric affairs began with the military occupation of Haiti by American Marines. The public explanation for the Occupation involved the revolutionary disorders in Port-au-Prince. The Haitian President, Vilbrun Guillaume Sam, following a massacre of his political opponents in prison, had just been torn to bits by a mob in the street; presidents before him had come and gone like the wind, poisoned, blown up in their palaces, and regularly removed from office by irregular means. The more compelling reason for the American Navy's steaming into the harbor concerned a debt which the National City Bank of New York wanted to make sure would be collected and which was, in fact, paid out of the customs receipts.

A just appraisal of the Occupation, which continued until implementation of the Hull-Roosevelt "Good Neighbor" policy, is not easy to make. Progress, profitable both to Haitians and Americans, was achieved in several areas, including public health, road-building, fiscal organization, etc. At the same time, the fierce individualism of the Haitian spirit was affronted by the ineptitudes (and sometimes worse) of an occupying force which, at least at first, chose Southern Marines for duty in Haiti because "they know how to deal with darkies." The sophisticated Paris-educated elite, accustomed to being the master in its own house, suffered emotional slights; the peasantry suffered from the forced labor gangs organized by the Americans to build roads—this seemed close to the dreaded slavery which Haitians have never forgotten. Military force is a poor teacher of the democratic process. The Occupation closed gracefully, however, and the general Haitian feeling toward the American colossus was not an unfriendly one.

Now, after years of sporadic sentimental efforts to relate the Haitian to the French economy, Haiti is permanently fixed as an economic pendant to the United States. Its coffee, for example, the chief money crop, is finally finding its natural market. Some light on the new role of Americans in world affairs may be generated by rubbing against some of the questions that occur to an American resident in Port-au-Prince:

How comfortable is Haiti in this necessary joining of its own national destiny with a culture which is so profoundly different from its own?

Where is the place in Haitian life of the Americans residing in Haiti?

What is it like to be an American in this "tropical paradise" which is one of the poorest, most overpopulated, most underdeveloped, most primitive nations in the world?

Every creature in the sea eats people; it is the shark which bears the bad name.
                                                    —Haitian proverb

The shadow of the United States over Haiti is a long one. It is a protective mantle for the American visitor; he feels it the first time he makes a traffic error and is whistled down by a cop who then, seeing that he is American, waves him on if his victim can walk away. The Haitian government charged the United Nations $150 for a baby run over and killed by a careless chauffeur. This seemed a fortune to the bereaved parents, but to most Americans would seem to be really a rather inexpensive baby. The famous and immensely moving Haitian hospitality—almost any peasant will offer coffee to a stranger, and if he needs a place for the night, the peasant will put his family outdoors and give the traveler his hut—is especially tender toward Americans. The desire to please can be embarrassing. If asked for a direction, the average poor Haitian will always answer, even if he does not know the answer. This may cause the traveler some confusion, but at least it attests to an eagerness to make the American happy. Most Haitians will never say *no* to an American. If an American asks a question involving a yes or no answer, he should be prepared to figure out from the way the Haitian says *yes* whether he means *yes* or *no*.

On another social level, invitations to the exclusive clubs are readily available to the visitor, while *nouveaux riches* Haitians, who may have every personal merit imaginable, are kept waiting until their children make a brilliant marriage into a "right" family or otherwise prove themselves with the elite. It is relatively easy for an American to be promoted to the highest society, there to play tennis or canasta with names that date back to Dessalines' generals; a Haitian whose wealth is new, whose skin is dark, and whose family is unknown may still be voted down by the admission committee of the Cercle Bellevue. (The question of skin color is a complicated one which it is not my purpose to discuss here. Some upper-class Haitians have dark skins; some lower-class Haitians have light skins; but nevertheless the chief criteria of class distinction are color of skin, slope of nose, twist of hair, and other tests of Caucasian blood, despite the fact that everyone is proud of his slave ancestors who won freedom from the French.)

Another sign to the visitor of the special status of the United States is the profound impregnation of the Creole and French languages of Haiti with Americanisms that set on edge the teeth of visiting Frenchmen. The policeman yells, "Faites back!" (pronounced "bock") when he means "En arrière." The verb for spraying a room with insecticide is "flitter," derived from a popular product of Standard Oil. The grammar of Creole, modeled on various African languages, is more like that of English than like French, although most of its vocabulary comes from French. High-status words and phrases, such as "Dry Cleaning" and "Air Conditioning," are often spoken and written in English rather than in their French equivalents.

The Port-au-Prince radio broadcasts singing commercials for American toothpastes and breakfast cereals in Creole; offices, parties, dances, and dinners require clothes which are a real burden in the tropics—but which give the sufferer the badge of French or American culture that separates him so visibly from the peasant or laborer; to drink *visky* instead of the excellent native rum is the pinnacle of chic; a common reading of *Time* or a common appreciation of Bing Crosby offers an occasion for communion with the forces of great power. This respect for American achievement is genuine and extends to all domains. One of the great primitive painters of Haiti, a man of enormous individuality and self-respect, has decorated his house with his own drawings, with paintings and sculpture by his friends, with relics of Catholic and *voudou* religious art, with flowers and plants from his neighborhood—and, in the place of honor on the wall, a full-page photograph of Harold Stassen. He had clipped it from *Life*. The fact that he doesn't know who Harold Stassen is makes the tribute still more touching.

Despite the evidence of favor, the deep ambivalence of attitude toward Americans expresses itself in many domains. An American has little chance against a Haitian in a court of law. The American who seeks to start a business in Haiti without Haitian partners will suffer such strange misfortunes as to make him wish he had stood in Delaware. An American who makes any slight error, such as slipping in the street, will find a crowd enormously entertained by his bad luck. They will help him up and dust him off if necessary, but their pleasure in the fall from dignity of the *blanc* is unmistakable. Incidentally, the word *blanc* has come to mean simply "foreigner," so that even an American Negro has been referred to as a *blanc*.

The world-wide stereotype of the American as a crude but efficient engineer is echoed in Haiti, where an educator will say that Haiti must import its automobiles and tractors from the States but its textbooks and "culture" from France. Only a younger generation of thoughtful Haitians has begun to point out that realities must be faced in a society that still allows students to spend their evenings outdoors memorizing Racine under streetlamps because they do not yet have electricity in their houses. For many years French law, art, and manners were painted over the realities of Haitian life: America is the turpentine which is dissolving this pleasant surface. (Some upper-class Haitians have asked the police to chase away the students working under streetlamps. They say that it makes a bad impression on the tourists.) Many Haitians can compare the styles of Bossuet and Racine; not enough can set up an electrical circuit. In part, at least, this emphasis on classical intellectual training, along with a persistent disdain of technical skills, is an inheritance from the master-slave society of the colonial epoch. "You Americans tell us to work," the Haitian seems to be declaring, "but we are masters now." And the master is a cultured gentleman for whom others do the work. "Sweating is a sign of ignorance," the Haitian says.

As the result, even the servants have servants, and a houseboy will use his own money to hire a shoeshine boy to clean his employer's shoes. To be a houseboy is to have a job of higher status than to be a shoeshine boy. A worker promoted to foreman of a gang will not deign to show the men under him how to perform a task which he used to do every day. The American drive to get the job done is foreign to the Haitian way. It is a trait of the American character that is both admired and feared.

Of course, national habit is one matter and individual personality another. Every American in Port-au-Prince knows a few angry Haitians who defy climate, custom, and public pressure in order to arrive at work promptly, become emotionally involved with their jobs, and take pleasure in accomplishment. But they have a hard time.

Haitians who are being sent in increasing numbers to the States to study often find a wall of prejudice against them when they return. The engineers have to open shops, the educators work as clerks because they no longer fit into the "Haitian way." Columbia and Carnegie Tech may replace the Sorbonne in time, but it is the graduate of the French schools who wins the respect shown a scholar. One agronomist who defended his American hosts was admonished with the peasant saying: "The fish trusts the water, and it is in the water that it is cooked." For many Haitians, aware of a history of spite and exploitation and a continuing race prejudice, the years of suspicion are not over. Charlemagne Peralte, who led a rebellion against the American Marines and was crucified against a door, is a popular hero.

A striking illustration of the overestimation of American power comes in politics, which is the chief concern of life in Port-au-Prince, even more important than love-making, except perhaps on Saturday nights. It is generally assumed that an American resident is an FBI spy, a journalist ready to imagine calumnies about zombies and black magic, or an agent sent to do in the current government. The most trivial remark of an American resident can have political repercussions as it is transmitted by that most rapid means of communication, the *telejiol* or *telemouth*. It is automatically assumed that the American Embassy is a control, for bad or for good, on Haitian affairs. The opposition to the present one-party government, which of necessity must be a revolutionary opposition, is emotionally rooted in the hope of American approval; it therefore appeals to American democratic processes against the present (and traditional) military dictatorship. During the absence of an American ambassador, no opposition newspaper was allowed to function. When the Honorable Roy Tasco Davis was appointed, two newspapers took courage again, and lo! their presses were not burned and their editors not beaten or imprisoned. (This situation has been modified. On January 8, 1954, the police broke up and carried away the printing press and type of *Haiti-Democratique*. A few days later, the editor, the deputy Daniel Fignole, together with his printers, associates, and friends, was arrested. Last July the other independent newspaper, *Le Constitutionel*, was shut down after the chief of police threatened its editor with "bodily harm.")

If you tell a Haitian in opposition to the regime of General Magloire that the American government is probably not interested in encouraging any movement that upsets the relative stability of Haitian politics, even though it is a one-party stability, you will probably not be believed. "What! But what about democracy?" The notion that the United States Embassy will exert pressure against an undemocratic government is one that does not die despite the evidence of contemporary history. In the hopeless morass of Haitian politics, many otherwise intelligent people cling to the dream of magical American intervention: those who hope for it and those who fear it both believe in it.

An example of the exaggerated esteem in which the American is held can be taken from a personal experience. As recipient of a fellowship in order to study Haitian institutions, I was interviewed by a number of journalists in Port-au-Prince. In one newspaper I was quoted as having cited Montaigne's remark that "all culture comes from the people." A-ha! It was immediately "telemouthed" that the visitor had put himself on the side of "the people" against "the regime," that he represented official American policy, and that he was a paid "fomenter." I was warned that further statements of this sort would result in my being expelled from Haiti.

A curious sidelight is that, while the citation from Montaigne is an unexceptional remark with which I can agree, it was never spoken during the interview. The journalist, playing on the exacerbated subtlety of the readers of a subsidized press, put the phrase in my mouth for reasons of his own.

Another American resident, writing in a local newspaper that fear is an obstacle to human progress, created a sensation among Haitians who took this to mean that they should not be afraid of trying to overthrow the government. The process of logic is impressive: Fear makes us obey. An American says that fear is bad. *Ergo*, the secret policy of the State Department is to help us overthrow the government of Haiti.

In a culture which Edith Efron Bogat, an American journalist resident in Haiti, has described as suspicious almost to the point of paranoia, the American is now perched among the heroes of the national fantasy life. He represents wealth, beauty, power over God's atomic earth, and the mobility of achievement. He may be loved; he may be feared; he may be loved and feared at the same time. He is never ignored. As the Haitians say, "All that you do not know is greater than you."

During my first days in Haiti, I got lost in the maze of unmarked streets near my house. I stopped and asked for my street by name. No one knew it. Then I asked where the new white man in the neighborhood lived, and I was led home immediately by people who had, apparently, never seen me before.

> *You cannot sleep on a mat and then*
> *speak evil of it.*
> 						—Haitian proverb

Americans in Haiti are not just individual human beings; they are even more than "ambassadors." They are a focus for envy, aspiration, and the mysteries of power. A Miami floozy can turn the heads of men married to the most charming Haitian beauties. A state senator down for a quick suntan becames a representative of American authority, deserving receptions, dinners, and an exchange of fountain pens with the President. A buyer for the notion counter of a department store is a *gros commerçant* and the pale literary cowboy who turns out Western stories at two cents a word is feared and buttered up as a *grand écrivain de notre amical voisin nord-américain.*

How do Americans function in this tender situation?

The thousand or so American residents, mostly located in the capital, fall into several fairly distinct categories.

First, there are the commercial and diplomatic residents who, in general, lead the familiar life of American officialdom abroad. They are assigned to a job; they do it; then they go home. Their contact with Haiti is kept to a minimum. The American country club has recently admitted its first Haitian members, but the usual social life of these Americans is one of ping pong and poker, sewing bees and bazaars, and as little contact with Haitians outside the work day as possible. Of course, the avoidance of relationship is a kind of relationship. Haitians suspect race prejudice as the reason for this isolation, and it surely does nothing to improve feeling between the two peoples, but it can be said in defense of these Americans that their behavior is not exceptional: American businessmen and diplomats live like this all over the world. Their children may learn Creole from the servants, but the mysteries of Haiti—*voudou*, the rich folk culture, the complex meeting of French and African ways of life, the bitter fret of Haitian aspiration and Haitian misery—are foreign to them. They solve the problems of living in Haiti by not really living there.

Then there is a small number of former Marines and American Navy men who stayed on to settle after the Occupation. These men, usually marrying on the island and otherwise "Haitianizing" themselves, are perhaps the most secure of the foreigners. One, the former medic who now calls himself "Doctor" Reiser, is a muscular and energetic grandfather with a career as drummer, painter, leaf doctor, and *voudou* initiate; for a time he directed the local insane asylum; he has exhibited considerable histrionic skill and attained some financial success in nursing his legend, a variation on the white-voodoo-doctor theme. Others, less spactacular than Doc Reiser, have found their levels in Haitian society and are living out their lives and rearing their children as the Haitians do.

Another curious group includes the American women who have married Haitians. Living in a Negro republic does not solve the problem of high feeling against inter-marriage. These women have families, friends, and their own pasts abroad: they cannot sever all contact. Besides, Haiti has its own home-grown variety of race prejudice. What can the American woman say when her husband forbids their coffee-colored children to play with the black children next door? Rearing children with a Haitian partner creates problems which marrying an American Negro does not involve: in Haiti the American is marrying into a culture which is deeply alien to American ways. Because of all the obstacles, most of the American women who marry Haitians are iconoclastic characters with powerful urges towards individual assertions of personality. They are also often the envy of their American friends, as they generally find husbands with special attributes of capacity, handsomeness, and fortune. The Haitian upper class which is interested in whitening its children's skins is an elite of considerable charm and drive.

A small group of Americans, living in a no-man's-land between Haitian and American life in Haiti, includes the bohemians attracted by the sun, sea, glamour, and cheap rum. They generally do not stay long. The complexities of life in a culture which is African and French at the same time, and difficult to penetrate, usually send them back to the more familiar climes of Mexico or Paris. Haiti is weird and magical and very primitive; these attributes, while potential tourist attractions, are not yet ready to be assimilated by the typical American cheap-liver abroad. The artists of Haiti do not have a tradition of discourse; they are not great café talkers. An obstacle to the male in search of passing adventure is the rigid upper-class moral code. The Creole maidens are lovely, but their fathers are all crack shots. Gossip is rapid and lethal.

More than in most places in the world, the American in Haiti is held off from sharing the life of the people. He is isolated by color, language, religion, habits, and standards, and by the economic prodigy which puts almost any American automatically in a lonely eminence at the top of a feudal structure. Poverty is bad for the rich, too. But sustained good will is rewarded by good friends, and even power has its compensations. The prestige of America focuses an exaggerated attention, sometimes hopeful, sometimes suspicious, on the actions of individual Americans. The American lives in Haiti as an honored guest, a too-much-honored guest whose slightest mistake can be disillusioning to his hosts. It is in many ways a high and intense way to live.

The problem of the American separated from his own culture is similar all over the world. Of course, he forgets about Arthur Godfrey and loses track of Walter Winchell; he takes his ease from television and the New York Yankees. Haitian art, literature, music, and dance are based on rich traditions and can show the interested outsider some luminous modern developments. The experience of living in Haiti, while exotic, is one with the life of human beings everywhere. The specific emphases of Haitian ways provide a sharp perspective on American experience.

However, the long-time American resident also runs the risk of reducing the possibility of a meaningful involvement in the life of his own society, of moving off, of becoming distant from himself. An air of inefficacy and vagueness in the expatriate is familiar to travelers everywhere.

The accusation of authority may make a mediocre man strive to live up to the expectations that surround him: dignity is contagious. Or he may take a peculiar pleasure in selling his clothes and being picked up drunk and naked in a gutter: responsibility is threatening. Both types of behavior occur. For Americans, life in tropical Port-au-Prince seems to produce an accelerated development of character in the direction of either the sick softness of a fallen mango or of a firm and sunny self-realization. Haiti is difficult for foreigners. Each difficulty presents an option. These options seem to be put forward more strictly than elsewhere in the streets, offices, homes, plantations, and social occasions of Haiti.

Nevertheless, the brilliant contrasts and powerful feelings animating Haitian life suggest the possibility of a healthful stimulus. It should be easy to keep the emotions awake—and not just at the level of a dilettante in exotism. The proud individuality of all Haitians is a lesson in human dignity amid conditions of material misery. While the average per capita income is estimated at less than thirty-five dollars a year, the Haitian remains a lively and sympathetic person, despite the occasion for deceit and craft which must also be assimilated by the stranger. The Haitian's fears are enormous and his problems intense; his urge to life is joyful, angry, and energetic. His energy is expressed more creatively at play and at talk than at work in a society in which the conventional rewards of work are difficult to attain. The possibilities of men cooperating in order both to fulfill some common design and to gain individual benefits await the evolution of a society which can properly assimilate intelligent labor. Try to build a house in Haiti, for example. Men who live in mud huts, and who live without the hope of ever having anything but a mud hut, cannot be expected to make doors fit and walls perpendicular. Why should they be interested? Children who grow up without machines or mechanical construction of any sort in the household will never develop the concept of the straight line or the right angle.

> *The stick that beats the black dog*
> *can beat the white dog too.*
> —Haitian proverb

France and Italy have had a society which rewarded labor and, at least temporarily, find their world unhappily diminished; Haiti has never had this level of civilization. The situation for the American visitor in all these places is similar, but with important differences in esteem and expectation. Being rich in population and resources, relatively immune to inflation and foreign manipulation, less scarred by war or internal conflict, and blessed by a continuity of government, America still offers a personal future to work done by the individual. This gift has been lost in many advanced societies; it has not been achieved in Haiti. The Haitian knows it; the American knows it. Their knowledge is a continual unspoken communication between them. It makes for a sort of hope and understanding: and it makes for a bitterness and unease. The troubles of pride are the most dangerous ones.

Both stubborn and yielding, tense and sleepy, heavy with pride and drenched in shame, the paradoxical Haitian character is a challenge to the American willing to participate in Haitian life. The fact of his being overvalued as an American may give him a special resonance of sense for others and of responsibility to his own capacity. As long as he remains in Haiti, he is addressed by martial music: *Be as important as Haitians want and fear you to be!* It is an expectation from others and from himself which may urge him to return to the possibilities of American life with a new awareness.

Finally, because of the special sin of American history, it is instructive for Americans to live in a culture in which the statesmen and diplomats, the brilliant educators and the artists, the agronomists and the engineers, and most of the rich businessmen are colored. The white man is the stranger, the interloper. He may be an honored guest, but he is only a tolerated guest all the same. He will see in action the liberal truism that, despite differences in condition, all peoples face similar problems with the same resources in character.

1954

Reno: The Great Divide

WOMEN ARE PURPOSEFUL IN RENO. The lovely blonde critter strolling the lobby of the Hotel Mapes, with a mole on her cheek accented by make-up as if she were Alice Faye miraculously preserved into 1961, did not come all the way to Reno in order to stake out uranium claims. She did not pack her kit bag to examine the pelicans and fossils of Pyramid Lake, where, during more idyllic days, Arthur Miller and Marilyn Monroe quietly strolled and waited for legal technicalities to be arranged. Nor is she a cultural anthropologist studying the Paiute Indians or the sheepherding Basques who gather at the Santa Fe Hotel in downtown Reno to eat and drink in French, Spanish, and Basque. She may sample all these incidental lures, but primarily she has come to Reno for one of two purposes: either to gamble (and also to find a man) or to shed a man (and also to gamble). When she pauses in her slow amble across the lobby, straightening her stocking—she bends and *harken!*—we have time to examine her third finger, left hand.

We find the circle of the abandoned wedding ring,

sunburned a bright red. She is a member of the Six Week Club. She is a joyous Jill, with her tanned face hit by a vision of the good life, her rump constricted by her new magenta Western pants and poutingly pressing for freedom. She wears heavy Indian jewelry and the stunned, goofy look of imminent divorce. She is in the molting phase, resentful but cute, ready for fun and making with rotating eyes. There are lots of women. They are waiting and bored, waiting and anxious, waiting and numerous.

Perhaps she is even one of the ladies who follow the apocryphal tradition of dropping her wedding band into the Truckee River near the Washoe County Courthouse, but more likely, our friend in the lobby of the Mapes has pawned her slender gold band in order to increase her capital at the gaming tables. Reno visitors are idealists—and practical; people of action—and people who wait. They have come to Reno after much deep thought, quiet analysis, and broken crockery. Now they busy themselves with making the most of their decision.

Helping them in this task is a permanent cadre composed of several types of specialized workers, including lawyers, gamblers, and a local brand of cowboy who is not often home, home on the range. There are other classical Reno types, including the obedient judges (trained to say "Granted" without hesitation), landladies, and ranch proprietors (trained to bear witness to the continuous residence of the plaintiffs in divorce actions), laborers all in the vineyard of marital afterthought.

Reno, "The Biggest Little City in the World," has constituted itself the Great American Divide—a man from his money, a wife from her husband. Lady Luck and Legal Liberty. There is also sex. In Reno, this is slightly more complicated than buying a drink in a saloon, but if you wait about five minutes, and smile, or scowl, or do something, *anything*, someone will surely come along.

A few years ago, they closed the Stockade, Reno's alley of legalized prostitution, but that was not a very lively place anyway. It was guarded by a policeman and the girls behaved as dully as minor bureaucrats. You transacted your business without shilly-shallying and then skedaddled, making room for the next in line—a little like getting a haircut or paying a parking ticket. Other towns in Nevada still exercise local option on the matter of commercial sack-play, and in Reno many fine citizens fought the passing of the Stockade. They felt that this was a step away from the right to free assembly guaranteed by the Constitution. It also put their innercent dotters in terrible danger from desert rats and those crazed tourists from San Francisco and the East. It abolished a reliable money-making and tax-paying business. But what with a steady influx of divorce-seekers, plus the legion of cooperative ladies who patrol the lobbies of the hotels, the passing of the old Stockade deprived only the most boorishly impatient and the most stubborn admirers of Nevada frontier tradition.

In all fairness to Reno's hospitality, it must be insisted that divorce, gambling, drinking and sex do not provide a complete summary of its services to the visitor. There is also marriage. Five times as many marriages as divorces are performed along the banks of the Truckee. Of course, these marriages have a tendency to return to Reno a few years later in the form of divorces; but still, the Park Wedding Chapel, festooned in neon ("Ring Bell for Service at Any Hour"), is the scene of a rapid marital drone and congratulation. The children of such marriages turn out to be complex creatures, often with curiously interrelated parents. ("My previous stepfather's brother was the uncle of my present stepfather's second wife . . .")

"We're not backward," declared one proud Reno cosmopolite, "we've got our Beat Generation, too, and it's doing a production of *Guys and Dolls*." The cast meets after rehearsals at *The in*, spelled with a lower-case (or hungry) "i," where a little group discusses Samuel Beckett and Sam Cooke; Kafka and Sinatra. Reno is perhaps the unhippest and zippiest town in all the fifty states. The women, clicked silly by the keno tabulator, puffy from grief and alcohol, play *femme fatale* in the gambling clubs, with shades jutting out over their sunglasses. This is the promissory land where the oppressed are liberated and the hopeful stream by on South Virginia Street. The chippies compete with the divorcettes in all the clubs, casinos, and hotel lobbies.

Our lady of the Mapes is called a divorcette in Reno. She is a prospective divorcee. She is still legally bound to a man hereinafter referred to as Defendant. Defendant has a job someplace and sends her money. She is a Permanent Resident, which is not to be confused with an Old Inhabitant. A Permanent Resident is someone in the final convulsions of marriage who plans to stay for six weeks and a day, and can prove it with witnesses. (Appropriately enough, Reno was named after a General Reno, killed in the Civil War back East, who never once set foot in Nevada. The founding fathers were looking for a convenient short name and drew the General's out of a Stetson. A practical, unsentimental people.)

Mrs. Permanent Resident may pass her six weeks weeping her eyes out, or she may spend her time in a patio discussing philosophy with other Permanent Residents. ("Beneath that rough exterior, girls, beats the heart of a wife-beater"), or she may hit the slots or the tables or the bars, or she may shyly peek around for a cowboy or a fresh future Defendant. Itchily she seeks to revenge herself on the flunkout back home in Chicago or New York. She is the made-to-order prey for the opportunists, con men, and brutal rancheros who hang around Reno. She blinks her eyes into cool desert space as they park the Hertz car off one of the roads winding into the vacant hills. Sliding across the seat, she murmurs, "Oh, Mr. What's-Your-Name, he was so mean to me." Bright desert stars wink above them.

"Call me Slim," says the wrangler, and takes a firm hold. A new groom sweeps clean.

The specialized Reno cowboy is a local representative of one of the most curious professions in contemporary America. He is known in all the great centers; his granddaddy, the gigolo, wore evening attire and a silken mustache; his unacknowledged ancestor was the simpering Greek Ganymede. Now, in New York and other urban centers, he may occupy himself with tennis or modeling or claim to be an actor while he waits to be chosen by some joy-hunting, moneyed lady. In Reno he manifests himself as a dude cowboy, based on a ranch, watching the air terminal, scouting in the better bars and gambling clubs.

Slim is a subtle, part-male creature who probably has not wrangled a four-legged cow since Reno last housed a WCTU convention. He is a shill of love, faking high stakes of passion for a small profit, just as a gambling shill pretends to gamble in order to make the house look sharp and busy. A skinny chap in chaps and a duckass haircut, he keeps busy holding hands with the blue-haired, fifty-year-old lady in the TV room of the Holiday Motel; the Trap has gleaming white teeth and the Victim has a subscription to *The Wall Street Journal*; they will make beautiful moolah together, he hopes.

Like other professional dude cowhands, Slim dwells in a series of six-week liaisons, looking always for the Big Strike—the woman who will either take him home in order to goad Defendant or perhaps will move her bank account to sunny, tax-free Nevada. When he uses rodeo language, he is thinking of stock on the wobbly high heel. A "rerun" is a cow that has been tuckered out by much use, "generally easier to wrestle and tie." "Snuffy" describes stock that is wild, ready to go. A "twister" is himself—a cow twister, suffering from scaly elbows and nocturnal premonitions.

In sad fact, he is not a happy wrangler. He sits with his aging broad, his water-slicked hair growing low down his neck, his creased, tended tan, his bland, pleased, angry, hurt, princely, bored clasp of lips; he turns his ankle anxiously in its fancy-worked Western boot. It is costly after all, making out this way. Hard to give up joy in sex and work; it's hard to give up being human. "But what is man," his neurotic ankle seems to ask, quoting Scripture in its dismay of soul, "that thou art mindful of him?"

"Nothing doing," answers the silence between his ears, the creak of his leather.

Cool, professional, a freckled desert hipster, he is tired and wants to go to bed, but there is no mama to cradle him, only this rich bitch whose particular mattress needs he tries to predict as they watch the Jack Paar show together. Well, maybe he is neither man nor woman, but our bored buckaroo with his corseted prey is in business, and doing pretty well.

There are fine hotels in Reno, the Riverside, the Mapes, and the usual glorious motels with swimming pools and round-the-clock boozing. There are also the guest "ranches" (a horse or two) or houses that cater to economical divorcettes. "Bonny Bode Inn—Divorcees Welcome," hints the newspaper advertisement; "Join the Happy Crowd at Harmony House," another chimes in winsomely; "Liberty Rooms—Free Coffee At Any Hour—Make Your Stay a Memorable One."

The proprietors of these permanent residences for permanent six-week residents also serve as cheer-mongers to the sad, introducers for the solitary, and witnesses in court to swear that the plaintiff was really there for six weeks. (Efforts to shorten the time of legal residence are met by the practical objection that Reno needs the money spent here in ransom after matrimonial jags; conversely, greedy ideas about lengthening the stay are met by prudent commercial warnings of the threat from sordid, rapid Alabama and immoral, speedy Mexico.)

Life in these guest houses generally follows a simple, healthful routine. The marital convalescents share place at table, space in the laundry room, and stories about the rat, jackal, hoot owl, dog, porcupine, hyena, or stercoricolous beetle in Washington, D.C., or San Francisco, Dallas, Bangor, or wherever. Nevada law in its majesty almost always agrees that the One Back Home is some sort of jungle beastie; those in Reno, men and women, are wronged angels. Many a joyous conversation in a Guest House patio, concerns ways to settle his/her hash, which badly needs settling. For current news of what he/she is up to, you can always get word from detective agencies or crystal ball snoops who do a thriving business:

PHYCHIC RUTH—*Card Reader and Counselor 17th Successful Year in Reno. $3.00.* "Phychic" is probably a combination word, meaning fidgety and fishy, and it characterizes the stories to which poor, long-suffering, three-dollar Ruth has had to lend an ear. "My husband, listen, he used to . . ." "That wife of mine, by God, I wanted to . . ."

Some, of course, have untraceable spouses who, for all they know, might be working for the Post Office; she lies dead in a schoolteacher's closet in Tulsa; he is producing a movie entitled *Teenagers at the SEATO Conference*; Phychic Ruth cannot see him clear. He has disappeared from the ken of mortal and gypsy, and will be symbolically reached only by that final invocation published in a legal advertisement:

The State of Nevada sends you greetings! Not having cohabited with the plaintiff . . .

And he'll never know what was said about him before the Reno judge. The judge probably won't know, either. He has heard too many stories that all have the same ending. He turns off the hearing aid and pores over his copy of *Poker—a Gentleman's Pastime.*

The garrulous camaraderie of the boarding house gives wounds a chance to heal under the gentle urging of that famous law—misery loves company of the opposite sex. One should always describe one's trouble to those who cannot check for accuracy; sympathy begets sympathy in return; and listen, pal, it sure is good to get away after what I been through. "I know, I know, and how about making a tour of the clubs?"

There are plenty of shaky stomachs and trembling lower lips, plenty of secret tears in narrow beds, but there is also the lovely resilient chick who comments, "I learned a great deal from my marriage. I don't regret anything. I learned how to give big parties and how to keep the maid from stealing."

Most things that you do furtively in other places you can do without shame in Reno. This is to Reno's credit; honesty is one of the good policies. The popular acceptance of gambling is indicated by a recent debate in the City Council. Should the city get out of the slot machine business at the Municipal Airport? Of course. Why? Declared the mayor: "We don't want to compete with private enterprise."

The private enterprise includes Harold's Club (in addition to The Nevada, The Golden, Harrah's Club, and other secondary institutions), a giant seven-floor department store of luck, with blackjack, craps, roulette and eight hundred slot machines grinding up money twenty-four hours a day. The customers pull, wait, and stare like the distraught heroes of horror movies who look at their monster and say, "I think it's trying to tell us something." (It is trying to tell them: "The grind is against you, buddy— bell, cherry, and orange.") Some slots are "humanized," being built into gorgeous female bodies, with the coins, when you hit, emerging from a dismally appropriate place.

"We build slot machines," stated one manufacturer, "but we don't build machines to force people to play." Nevertheless, the mechanism seems to be built into most of us. Jean-Paul Sartre once committed a famous remark: "Hell is other people." This is an easy epigram, since any definition of hell with such an outrageous and dogmatic format will take us by surprise and sound briefly, pretentiously true. For example: Hell is oneself; Hell is nobody. But those hip-to-hip rows of cattle before the slot machines, blind to anything but the rolling fruit, suggest some particular dramatic sense to the French philosopher's remark. Hell is other people playing slot machines.

This repetitive, ritualistic, manual game recalls fantasies in which the child defies logic—he is all-powerful; he controls his fate simply by force of will. (Dylan Thomas made fun of this primitive dream when he wrote about a rocky transatlantic flight, "Only my iron will will keep the great bird aloft.") The gambler's iron will commands a jackpot when he wants it—*right now*—and refuses to admit failure until he wakes from his dreams of omnipotence to find his pockets empty. Perhaps—while we are walking on these psychological waters—there is another factor at work: in his heart of hearts the gambler wants to lose, a stubborn guilty child asking to be punished for trying to stand outside the laws of chance.

One of the saddest, most instructive sights in the world is that of a gambling creep shuffling out of a room on South Virginia Street and over to the Western Union office on Center Street, there to mouth his stub of pencil and try to transform himself into a poet with a new way of saying SEND MONEY QUICK. Going from club to club you see the System Players, clutching their notebooks, grinning hard, with harassed eyes and chewed lips, sure that next time the laws of statistics, which they have invented, will take hold. Next time.

The Smith family, owners of Harold's Club, are respected leaders of community life in Reno. They endow concerts and the Harold's Club Scholarships at the University of Nevada. (One condition: The Scholar must not cross the threshold of Harold's Club during his college enrollment.) Legalized gambling is an important industry. The high desert skies are clear of industrial smoke; the fume and fuss of gambling leave little mark on the Nevada landscape.

Reno and environs display a distinct physical charm and diversity of terrain. Besides the gambling/divorcing Reno, there is also the typical Western town in which people live much as they do in a thousand similar places, blessed by lovely homes and mortgages, spacious lawns and chickweed, happy youngsters thronging to school, church, and dragstrip. This ignored Reno boasts magnificent surrounding mountains, the snow-fed Truckee making green the center of the city, skiing in winter and healthful dry desert air in summer—plus the University of Nevada, "finest institution of higher learning in the state." (It is also the only institution of higher learning in the state.) But it is not for these advantages in culture and climate that Reno is so much better known than, say, Ottumwa, Iowa, or Bellingham, Washington, both towns of comparable size. Reno is a rambunctious, brawling Mickey Rooney among cities. The workaday Reno grudgingly harbors its wild, permissive twin, without which, of course, any renowned Reno at all would be impossible. The two Renos are joined by common elements of the picturesque and the bizarre: the traditional rodeo, the splendors of desert sage and mountain pine, the romantic outcroppings of silver-bearing rock in nearby, antique Virginia City, where ragtime is the rule, the hot mineral springs for swimming, the general morality of No Speed Limit in Nevada.

The true churchly, cultural Reno, of which some old residents defensively prattle, also has some basis in fact, once you leave Virginia Street (the major casinos), Commercial Row (pawn shops, Indian bars, prodding policemen), and Lake Street (Chinese and Negro gambling clubs—Reno is covertly Jim Crow). But it's hard to keep the wistful visitor in church once he has found the Mint Club, where Rosemarie has been Held Over by Popular Demand—and by popular demand she holds it over the drinkers at the bar on which she prances. The place of the great rose window of the cathedral of Notre Dame is taken by the grandiose outdoor mural of an Indian massacre which is the entrance to Harold's Club, the dominating structure in town.

Over this cathedral of chance shines a beacon; within it the multitude throngs. The slot machines whir, the process servers knock, the courts do their work. A woman sniffles, a woman laughs, a dude moves in. Someone asks for change of a paper twenty in silver dollars. A spur jangles. Six weeks begin for someone; six weeks are over for another.

1959

Greenwich Village:
The Changing Village

ON A DUSTY TABLE in the back room of a Greenwich Village antique shop lies an etching that pictures a mighty stand of oak being cleared to make way for the construction of a cabin. A few disconsolate figures, their heads bowed, mourn the vile encroachment of the metropolis. The title of the etching is *The End of Greenwich Village* and the date on it is 1859.

Greenwich Village ended, then, more than a hundred years ago. The crooked lanes of "Grenege," the Green Village, where small landholders grew tobacco and whence large landholders fled to avoid creditors, were being joined to the busy geometrical grid of Manhattan. "This pleasant and salubrious corner," this ancient Dutch settlement of Greenwijk which had appeared on maps as early as 1645, was dying.

It has been "dying" ever since, regularly. Each generation, the Village has had its Cassandras to cry its coming doom, and the present generation is no exception. The truth, of course, is that Greenwich Village is no longer as it was *and never has been.* A living organism, not a fossil, its restless change is the constant proof of its vitality. Today the Village remains an essential element not merely of the New York scene but of America's long love affair with the twin mistresses Freedom and Rebellion.

The importance of the Village as actual place and symbol of change and experiment in America is demonstrated by the pathetic letter sent off by a Village wife, Mrs. Melville, to her mother: "Herman has taken to writing poetry. You need not tell anyone, for you know how such things get around."

The rumor did get around, alas for Herman, whose spouse passionately desired that he spend his time gainfully writing serial stories about whaling; Mrs. Melville bowed her head with oh! the shame of it, that her beloved Herman lay on his couch all morning, deceiving her with a muse; eventually Herman hired himself out as a salaried employee. But there has always been this small throbbing ventricle in the busy heart of New York where the poet might know honor and where the real shame for a wife would come if Herman *stopped* writing poetry. For all these years now, the inventors, composers, painters, poets, playwrights, and the various would-be and might-be geniuses have eventually floated upstream until they came to rest, at least briefly, in Greenwich Village, U.S.A.

They have sometimes been as respectable as Henry James, who later turned into a wooden-nosed Englishman, and sometimes as disreputable as Joe Gould, the shaggy Harvard-graduate hobo, author of the endless and unpublished *Oral History of the World,* a grinning gnome who lived on free cafeteria ketchup and national publicity, both of which are packed with vitamins and minerals. The geniuses have found inspiration in a certain lounging ease of life among an all-American stew of Italians, Irish, Chinese, and Jews who lived in and around the Village simply because it was their neighborhood. As dogs have

fleas, so the geniuses also found comfort in the hectoring
company of the gaffers, cadgers, sexual experimenters, political evangels, and the doddering remnants of elegance near
Washington Square and Fifth Avenue.

At its earliest beginnings, the Village was a trading
post where Canarsie Indians bargained over hides with the
Dutch settlers; there were springs of fresh water on Spring
Street, and Minetta Brook wound along Minetta Lane, and
wolves, panthers, moose, wild turkeys, and heath hens
inaugurated a tradition of good hunting which is carried on
now only by the Continental-clad wolves who prowl the
still-crooked streets of Minetta and Spring and the rest
of the drained, lit, built-up and leveled-down Village of
today. In those antique times, besides the Dutch and
Indians, there came some English, some French Walloons,
some Jews (a tiny pre-Revolutionary Portuguese Hebrew
cemetery still slices into the barrage of real estate on
Eleventh Street near Sixth Avenue); a number of Negro
freedmen and escaped slaves took their best hold on liberty
in the Village, and according to some authorities, a few
Spanish pirates dropped their eye patches into the bound-
ing main and retired to Perry Street. (Do they now model
Hathaway Shirts? And is there really any buried treasure?
Might be, beneath the pipes and cables and sewers and
foundations upon foundations.)

All this began when the Green Village was a tidy little
settlement insulated from the Manhattan colony, thanks
to swamp, salt marsh, forest, and cripple bush. Gradually
the wild berries and nuts disappeared (later to reappear
in health stores on Eighth Street, along with queen bee
jelly and wheat germ); the English installed tobacco
plantations; Sir Peter Warren owned almost the whole
caboodle. He died in 1752, "removed by the Almighty from
a place of Honour to an eternity of Happiness," and his
various heirs began the continuous process of bickering
and speculating, dividing and subdividing. On rainy nights

bearded duffers warmed their backsides by the fire and grieved over the good old days of the Village.

Soon the skirmishes of 1776 came close; Aaron Burr galloped through the meadow where the Fifth Avenue bus turns around; history advanced. But advance as history must, New York City could never quite digest this winding knot of exception on its favorite island; Manhattan swallowed it down, it swallowed it up, but Greenwich Village would not be dissolved, straightened, tamed, numbed, or numbered. And when it allowed itself partly to be numbered, it produced such examples of arithmetical chaos as an intersection of Fourth and Tenth Streets—a tribute to the old times of Indian trails, when "parallel" and "perpendicular" meant as little as "pension" and "job security" to the true Villager of today. The surveyors who laid out the map of Greenwich Village had irrigated their wits with birchbark wine.

That allegedly parallel streets should meet and cross perhaps helps to explain why Washington Irving, James Fenimore Cooper, and Edgar Allan Poe came to the Village in the early and middle nineteenth century; West Tenth Street and West Fourth Street persisted in meeting and crossing, an assignation which must be a love match since it is the despair of logical minds, and so Ada Clare (author of "the most beautiful poems in the language," according to the *New York Atlas*), also came to smoke (!), drink (!), and talk impertinently with men neither her father, brother, nor husband (!). Artistic types like dear Ada, who somehow had a child without being married (due to too much smoking, drinking, and conversation), and Henry Clapp, who found in Greenwich Village the gabled houses and the charm of Paris, began to gather the noise of nineteenth-century art about their organizing spirits. Walt Whitman toured the streets with crumbs for the birds on his shoulders ("All the critters come to me," he said); Mark Twain, rescued from bankruptcy by a lecture tour, lived at 14 West Tenth Street and then, perhaps trying to escape that maddening intersection with Fourth Street, moved to 21 Fifth Avenue. Here he took the courage to write blasphemous books which were published only after his death.

There were the famous from all over the world, like John Masefield, or later, like Maxim Gorki, who had a secretary with whom he was not allowed to register in his hotel because he admitted freely that they took dictation together. There were also the generous, like Luke O'Connor, in whose tavern almost anyone could cash a check. Luke's place came to be known as "The Working Girl's Home" because a girl could enjoy a quiet glass under the amiable protection of Luke without being disturbed by the police. When Luke's place closed, the old times were over once again.

Now, of course, time really is moving fast; the 1960 "End of Greenwich Village" tramples down that Greenwich Village which subverts the Greenwich Village which preceded it; and again change destroys its "essential character." New high-rise apartment houses, replacing the handsomely decrepit fretwork tenements, give sign of the alteration in olde New York wrought by cold cash and hot mortgage. The restless spirit of consumership has discovered the charm of nonconformity, along with coffee houses, hi-fi, and girls in tight pants; but the new, prosperous, intelligent, gifted wageslaves who seek to recapture their perhaps never-was youth by moving to the Village want to nonconform in comfort, like everyone else, with built-in air conditioners, speedy silent elevators, and a rent they are not ashamed to murmur aloud.

In the process, some of the traditional Village landmarks—the old Brevoort Hotel, the gingerbread apartment houses, and the Waldorf Cafeteria, where Maxwell Bodenheim came to make fun of the junkies, and stayed and stayed—have disappeared. Many fine blocks full of wood-

burning fireplaces have fallen under the builder's heartless
ax, making way for central heating, low ceilings, and high
rent. The Village is very much a state of mind, usually
centered at such landmarks as Washington Square, Sheridan Square, and a shifting few favorite restaurants, streets,
places, and events; unofficially—there can hardly be an
official map for a tradition—the outlines of the Village
begin to manifest themselves at Fourteenth Street on the
north, the Hudson River on the west, Canal Street to the
south, and Broadway on the east. But these are not firm
outlines, merely hints and histories. Since there are Villagers living on Fifteenth Street, is this not the Village?
And what about Sixteenth Street? And Seventeenth? And
Eighteenth? No, Eighteenth Street is certainly lost to another style, but still, how many hairs make a beard and
what does a neighbor street need in order to join the
Village?

Now the traditional locus of the Village is being
bulged outward by an American need to build a bigger,
better headquarters for nonconformity: There is the chic
Fifth Avenue Village, extended up East Eighth Street;
there is the clean, new, monumental and boring Washington Square Village development, which replaced an old
slum just south of Washington Square with a huge tenement cake of glass and aluminum (abstract expressionist
paintings in the lobby); there are the rehabilitated Italian
and Irish slums adjoining, and the refurbished dockside
tenements, and a general groaning and heaving of the
land as real-estate developers rush in to discover "the
charm of Village living." Some brilliant mice seem to have
discovered a deep truth: Build a better people trap and the
world will beat a path to your door. All you have to do is
stand in front of a building in a suit with wide lapels and
the crusted bricks come slipping down, thinking they recognize a builder.

The Village's first stock-brokerage office has opened on

Sixth Avenue, around the corner from the offices of *The Village Voice*, on ground hallowed by the tread of patrolling actors, artists, technocrats, ancient crones, homosexuals; it lies catty-corner across from the Women's House of Detention, a dismal warehouse in which prostitutes, shoplifters, junkies, molls, accessories-after-the-fact are kept in inventory. Occasionally the girls stored in their coolers grow restive, as growing girls will do; they lean against the bars and holler at each other, or bang their eating tools, screaming curses or impractical invitations into the street. Now the stroller below, wild with desire, can shout back up at them the bid and asked price on General Electric or A.T.&T., fresh off the tape.

Today the Village seems, to those for whom it was a part of their youth, like one of those jigsaw puzzles in which you put together the two hundred pieces and are rewarded with a vision of a sylvan glen and a perfect beauty dawdling from a rope swing, dressed only in her smile. Under "B" in the index of a book on the post-World War I Village, we find these entries: Babbittry; Basement tenements; Birth control clinics; Block, the, as a unit; Bodenheim, Maxwell; Bohemianism, pseudo; Bohemians, out-and-out; Bookbinding; Bourgeois morality; Bourgeois-romantic family; Bricklayers; Broccoli; Butchers' shops.

The non-"B" pieces of the puzzle, for those now suddenly middle-aged, also include the speakeasies, the old Nick's, Dixieland jazz, the anarchists and Communists and Martha Graham, the Waldorf Cafeteria, rent parties, the *Masses*, Howard Scott (founder of Technocracy), Floyd Dell and Joe Gould (founders of Floyd Dell and Joe Gould), Eugene O'Neill and a few dozen other of the dear departed, and the ageless troglodyte on every block who lived for some harmless madness of dress or manner or erotic preference. Gone, all gone; or if still there, so changed as to be occasion of deep deception to our nostalgia-bound visitor.

And yet, each piece in the eternal jigsaw game has its equivalent today, right now: the White Horse Tavern, the Five Spot for progressive jazz, the cooperative galleries on East Tenth Street which represent the avant-garde of the abstract expressionist habit, the beatniks and the hipsters and the dance students and the Actors Studio gangs, Jim Atkins' glassed-around short-order place on Sheridan Square, the Rienzi and the Figaro coffee houses, a host of vocal painters and sculptors, like Larry Rivers and Ibram Lassaw, and the poets a-reading of the jagged truth in the jazz-and-poetry emporiums like the Bizarre on West Third Street. And so our middle-aged visitor reconstructs the puzzle, every piece falling neatly into place. And yet the vision of a sylvan glen and ardent promise may elude his critical eye, for the crucial elements which give it all its excitement—the eye and hand and moiling heart of the puzzle-fitter—are irrevocably altered. The puzzle needs an organizing principle for its message to be unscrambled, and this principle seems to come from the hot blood within, that first sweet youthful discovery of freedom, passion and rebellion. And thus the word: "The Village isn't what it used to be."

But if those who came to the Village during the Depression utter this mournful complaint, so now do those who traveled toward Charles Street on or off the GI Bill after the war. They too, settled into the second marriage and third child, or into some combination of those elements, having taken on a permanent job and the habit of having habits, must mutter to their wives on their Saturday-night tour: "Ah, the San Remo is spoiled. Ah, what's happened to the old White Horse?"

"Yes, honey, and a bunch of lousy dykes has taken the place of those divine lesbians."

"Yes, darling, and where is *Death* (the magazine which answered *Life*), and where, O where is *Neurotica* (the analysts have their journals, now it's time for the patients to have one)?"

Answer: the Village has always moved fast. A generation lasts only a few seasons. *Death* has died, honey, and the editor of *Neurotica* has moved to St. Louis.

But if these visitors look at the girls down from Sarah Lawrence, searching for the ghost of poor Dylan (whom they could have saved by pure love, of course) or the shadow of Jack Kerouac (who *needs* them, dig?), squired by boys remembering that they were Holden Caulfield in some other, better life, these veterans of old Village campaigns must see familiar faces—their own. The Village jumps tirelessly to its eternal role as the objective expression of an urge to rebel, strike out anew, break the barriers of convention and (very important) have something to shock the old folks about. And in one case out of ten thousand, of course, this *"crise d'originalité juvénile,"* as a French psychologist named it, leads to that essential human crisis of discovery and creation. The habit and trapping of rebellion may involve rebellion in fact, and the destruction of worn-out ways of thinking, and the creation of works of mind and art.

For the remaining 9999, they have at least had a fling, some art movies and some pizza late at night, something to be nostalgic about in ten years, when "the Village has really changed, pal—we didn't used to have bomb shelters on Sullivan Street."

Like the mating salmon swarming up the Columbia River, the girls seeking freedom and "self-expression" rush down from the smart women's colleges; they head eastward from the big state institutions, their fins ajiggle and their gill slits pulsing; they forgather for adventure and true love in Manhattan, and a high percentage naturally finds its way to Greenwich Village. The result is a highly abnormal situation in many of the professions: an oversupply of lovely ladies. In the theatre, for example, there are more women than men to begin with; then if you subtract from the pool of available manpower—doing service at dinner and bed—those men who are contentedly married, those who are already engrossed by one girl, and those who prefer non-girls, you have remaining a lovely turmoil of lovely lost ladies, wishing they knew somebody. Because they work hard, they know few people outside the theatre. They spend many an evening walking the dog up and down Tenth Street, dreaming that somewhere in God's Green Village there must be a foot-loose heterosexual. Probably the loneliest girls in the world are theatrical beauties, alien as this idea is to the American fantasy of the wild life of actresses.

In days gone by, men went to the Village to hunt women. Now they go to be hunted; there is a remarkable contemporary tendency of the prey to track down the hunter.

A special example of Village devotion to Thespis is a girl we shall call Norma, a long-legged, creamy-skinned brunette with crisp dramatic gifts and a stubborn crush on Shakespeare and Shaw. Most actors, no matter what their preferences, take the jobs offered them. Norma, who has a degree in theatre from Carnegie Tech, fanatically refuses roles in musicals and contemporary plays because she doesn't want to risk a threat to her classic style. Therefore she makes her living, between productions of A *Midsummer Night's Dream* and *Caesar and Cleopatra*, by working as a skilled, albeit slightly sullen call girl. This she does not consider corruption because only the theatre really matters and the particular act she puts on for certain out-of-town buyers does not affect her diction. Also she plies her trade in the midtown expense-account belt which she holds in contempt; "real life" for her is located on Charles Street, where she remains a svelte young actress, taking her breakfast at lunch time in blue jeans in a drug store while she reads Eric Bentley on the theatre of Bertolt Brecht. She is considering broadening her repertoire.

Norma feels only contempt for the commercial actresses, call them Marge and Jo, who live together in precarious amity. Marge makes a steady living doing all the baby voices for one of the radio networks while she awaits an appropriate Broadway part. Jo, less successful, wrote a book about Marge between jobs and sold it to a paperback publisher. Since it exposed baby-voiced Marge's love life in adult, adulterous, and unadulterated detail, there was a strain between the two roomies which lasted almost a week. They took their meals in separate rooms. Marge calls Jo a fake because she had her nose bobbed *twice*. Once is enough for an honest girl.

"But it wasn't short enough," wails Jo. "And it hung a little to one side."

"So does your bosom, sweets," says her dear friend.

At the traditional street fairs—the big Italian ones and the smaller Spanish one just north of the Village— the aging Village-lover can still find, almost unchanged, the elements which bewitched his youth: fat, savory sausages, fried crustaceans of mysterious varieties, sold cheaply on the street, brilliant colors, gambling and drinking and the penny-toss, Sicilian street singers crying in their broken tenors of lost, lost love, thick-ankled, thick-waisted beauties, with unbobbed noses, leaving streaks of lipstick on bar glasses. On these saints' days, no injection of tourists from uptown can dilute the amiable, loud, distracted calliope pleasure of carnival nights. The parrot tells your fortune for twenty cents, plucking a piece of paper in its horny bill: and what care you if the somber slender gentleman awaiting his future in line behind you is Montgomery Clift, and if the excited lady is Shelley Winters? The Village has room for disconsolate movie actors, too.

The Village, while still a place for the young and

the undecided, is inhabited by Villagers—that is, people of all ages and conditions. The contrast between the Village and its recent rival for the hand of Youth—the North Beach area of San Francisco—tells the story clearly. The barefoot beatniks of North Beach make the staid diners at Chumley's on Bedford Street ("Patronized by Writers and Artists") look like elder statesmen. When the North Beach is invaded by middle-aged nostalgists, and the morose beatniks settle down to raising square babies, and there are memories and histories of "the way it was," and novelists, playwrights, poets and painters have fixed the scene in their work, then the North Beach will be on its way toward becoming another Greenwich Village.

In the meantime, the Village still provides the American "capital of hope and paradise of misery." The more the Village changes, settles down, rebuilds, the more it remains the same thing. And perhaps its lack of respect for Village tradition is a sign of its continuing vitality as a reflection of the realities of American life. While the Village changes under pressure, it changes in directions molded not merely by pressure from the outside. The quintessential rebellious Village strikes back, and the rest of the world falters. An example of this lively, restless, spirited Village playfulness can be found in and around *The Village Voice*, a weekly newspaper which is less a newspaper than a cause to its editors and subscribers. Hip, unbeat, irreverent and comical, the newspaper has also sharpened and led a drive against Tammany Hall; with another head it has garrulously and energetically hollered on behalf of off-Broadway theatre; it has led a victorious and well-organized battle against New York City's all-powerful Commissioner of Parks, Robert Moses. This symbolic battle can very well stand for the low-level and personal and heartening struggle of the Village against the rampant force of commercialism.

Stately Washington Square, with its Frenchified Arch

and charm one of the historical landmarks of the Village, had been under attack from several sides. New York University had spread around it, cracking up some fine old Georgian houses in its educational cobra's embrace; the police were shoving away the girls, the dogs, the hippies, the hobos, and the babies who played in the grass. Heavy traffic through the little stretch of park was poisoning the green. And then along came Moses. Unlike the Biblical Moses, who wanted to cross the desert, this bureaucratic Moses wanted to produce a desert by widening the roadway through the Square, increasing traffic, renaming and widening a narrow Village street at the opposite end. In order to create "Lower Fifth Avenue," an address which would presumably suggest an increment of verbal prestige, he was willing to destroy the park. Apparently the developers of Washington Square Village, to the south of the Square, had been promised the Fifth Avenue label through some mysterious political process.

Here was a clear issue. It was historical tradition versus real estate speculation, lovers versus automobiles, folk singers versus trucks, green versus asphalt, the people of the Village against the arrogance of New York politicians. With great relish, *The Village Voice* led its tattered batallions into action. Mothers with baby carriages filled with gallant sucklings, united legions of liberal Democrats and progressive Republicans, students and artists and hip kids and off-Broadway geniuses and crones from Washington Mews whose cronish aunts remembered Henry James— all united behind a banner decorated by Jules Feiffer and the impassioned, sometimes grammatical rhetoricians of the *Voice*.

And lo, David slew Goliath. Not only did the Village win its battle to keep the Square undiminished, but then it also attacked and eliminated *all* traffic through Washington Square. The park was preserved for its stoic pursuits —chess on the permanent concrete-and-tile chessboards

(where bundled and huffing old men study the board even
through the long winter), love, philosophy, the tranquil
digestive functioning of dogs, bongo artistry, and all the
etceteras of a city park. Robert Moses beat a sullen, screaming retreat; Tammany Hall, responsive to the pressure of
bona fide, licensed, curried and voting voters, even joined
The Village Voice in its campaign, once victory seemed
inevitable.

A small victory? Perhaps. But important as a gesture
of defiance against the march of the superhighway and the
developer. It gave courage to the Save-the-Village movement a-borning. And on Washington Square the bongos
and the guitars, their friends and their fellow travelers,
can still idle away a summer evening.

Partly as result of the Save-Washington-Square, Save-
the-Village, Save-Our-Geniuses campaign, mostly for its
five-year-old championing of the new hip Village, *The
Village Voice* has taken the title of Spokesman for the
Village away from the experimental little magazines of
an earlier period. It is in the pages of the *Voice* that the
various states of mind of Village youth find their public
masks. In a time of consumership, the Village way is very
much, at its most banal, a way of dressing. Village Ivy,
typified by Casual-aire, is the absolute iviest—no shoulders
at all, just a slight thickening at the base of the neck, and
pants so tight that they drive a man's dangling participles
someplace up near his belt, and the tie stuck to the Adam's
apple with a small, invisible thumbtack, Village jeans are
either the Actors Studio variety, white at the knees from
praying for failure in deep Tennessee Williams scenes, or
stained like an unsigned Jackson Pollock canvas. Subsidiary
Village costumes include the students' heavy-knit sweaters
and corduroy, the bull-dykey or rough trade's black-leather
jackets, studded with nails, and the sailor suits wandering
down Fourth Street, looking for professional company on

strip row. *The Village Voice* appeals to these costumes and
to the occasional human beings within, giving special
emphasis to the hipsters and their faded, anemic cousins,
the beatniks. It also parodies itself, as in this want
ad: "RENT A BEATNIK FOR YOUR PARTY. REASONABLE RATES."

The flavor of *The Village Voice*, and through it, of
the changing Village of the Sixties, can be indicated by a
quick review of one issue taken at random. On the front
page there are photographs showing the actors and actresses
of the Circle in the Square moving to a new theatre on
Bleecker Street. Reason: a new apartment development
will replace the theatre, Louis' Tavern and other historic
monuments on Sheridan Square. There is also a news
story about a quarrel between Tammany Hall and Greenwich Village Democrats. On page two there is a feature
story about a Villager who once walked a few blocks east
of the Village to make a famous documentary film, *On
the Bowery*, and then went several thousand miles away to
make a film about apartheid in South Africa. Also a cartoon
by Jules Feiffer, an advertisement for a lecture on "Love,
Justice and Adultery" at the Village Liberal Church, an
advertisement inviting us to "CONSULT FAMED HINDU"
("Astrologer and Teacher of Yoga"), and offers of jobs
to mandolin players, and an invitation to tour Scandinavia
by motorcycle. Sometimes in this section young men,
"handsome, intelligent, strong," offer to show lonely
women the Village for a moderate fee. Page three contains
the news flash that Allen Ginsberg, author of *Howl*, has
gone to the University of Conception, Chile, to represent
the United States at a writers' conference. He is quoted
as saying that there is a difference between the Chilean
university and a beatnik Hilton coffee shop in Dallas, to
which he had refused an invitation. On page four there is
another Feiffer cartoon about a man who suffers all sorts of
ailments, and therefore thinks he has become dangerously
neurotic; turns out that he has a cold. A long article mourns

the death of Albert Camus. On page five, with more about Camus, there are also advertisements for a lecture on James Joyce (Headline: JAMES JOYCE!), an advertisement for burlap to decorate your pad, and a clothing store cutely advertising a cloth called LAD CLAD, which you just paint on like aftershave, it's the iviest, mon. "But in the meantime, we are also putting out all our cloth suits at special prices . . ." On page six, we find a review of a beat magazine called *Exodus*, announcement of a lecture on "HITLER! The Artist As Fiend. . . . The Nazi Movement as Beat Generation," to be given at the New School. Then follow a couple of pages of theatre reviews, a page of sports car and hi-fi poop, an advt for the New York Telephone Company, headed WE WERE TRAPPED IN THE WILDERNESS 70 MILES FROM TIMES SQUARE. The last pages are devoted to miscellaneous material and the classified advertisements which provide the *Voice*'s most imaginative prose; they offer opportunities for folk singers, male models, female models, and pretty girls who "wish to sink teeth into non run of the mill job." Also motor scooters, guitar lessons, used men's clothes. Also acting lessons, escort services, books by Henry Miller. Also ski equipment, detective services, and free cats for cat lovers.

The Village Voice specializes in exploration of the new mental and physical geography of the Village. It provided one of the first boosts given *The Connection*, a "jazz play" written by twenty-seven-year-old Jack Gelber and performed by the Living Theatre, a group of living actors over on the north end of the Village at living Fourteenth Street. The play has no conventional plot; it includes, among its actors, an instrumental group which occasionally takes time out from the diddling movement of the play to make a bit of dawdling jazz; the situation is that of a group of junkies waiting, just waiting for its fix. When Cowboy, the connection, finally arrives, and gives an injection of heroin on stage, strong men blanch—or so the publicity says—and strong girls want to run up on stage to help. "That's the way it is, that's the way it really is, man," intones a sepulchral voice at intervals during the evening.

Heroin seems to replace politics as subject for talk in the Village of 1960, though just as there were always more fellow travelers than Communists, so there are more beatniks than genuine, hypo-carrying hipsters. (Colonel Rudolph Abel, who eked out his living as a Russian spy, was eccentric even for the Village, and his paintings were objective, square.) Like the gossipaceous politics of the Thirties, the hipnik movement provides something to talk about for a large group of bored Villagers. Most are too cool to fall up to the Cafe Bizarre, where the poetry is read to the jazz, mon, and too bored by teenage chicks to go to the Figaro on Bleecker, where the floorshow seems to consist of interracial checker playing; but espresso-shop society has proliferated rapidly south along MacDougal Street, penetrating even the Italian south Village, where the strolling amorist has his choice of many plain and fancy mausoleums—Le Petit Coin, the Couch, etc.—where to sit with a girl for a long slow evening. At the Cafe Rienzi, for example, there are French, Italian, German and Swiss newspapers available for free browsing with your java, and if you are really far out, equipped with the lingo of finance, they also carry copies of *The Wall Street Journal*. The Rienzi is split-leveled, split-sexed, and carries a bulletin board and exhibitions of photographs.

MacDougal Street is the hub of life for the couples known as Bronx Bagel Babies and A-Trainers—the home-based kids who come down for excitement in the Village and the Harlem tourists who help to give it to them. The latter are called A-Trainers because they take the Independent subway back at the end of the day.

If you invade the scene on foot and wander down Waverly Place of a soft spring evening, the following acts

might succeed each other in rapid succession on the stage
of the Village: there is that solemn, sallow, cinematogra-
phically evil chap who perpetually waits in a doorway,
selling what? numbers or ponies or marijuana; a man
ambles by wearing one earring—two would be square; a
male begger asks, "Gimme a quarter, mister, so my wife
can buy a Dior dress"; a load of abstract expressionist
paintings is being carried into the Manufacturers Trust
bank, where they will be exhibited along with naturalistic
dollars; one of the moving men has a copy of André Gide's
Theseus in his back pocket—moving men are among the
intellectual aristocrats of the Village, and it's a chic way
for a muscular actor or writer to supplement his income
and also keep in condition; a model walks toward Washington Square, where she has a date to meet under
the Arch—so skinny she looks as if she has been stretched
on a rack; and there is ubiquitous, bearded Sam Kramer
again, the psychoanalytic jewelry maker, buying cream
cheese, and a certain practicing psychologist, the rack himself, walking to meet the model.

Then if you happen to have reason for ducking down
the subway entrance and emerging in midtown Manhattan,
all is hurry, hurry, hurry, and you see why people love to
dwell near where Sam Kramer buys his cream cheese and
that psychologist does his best to fatten up skinny models.

All these varied societies—hipters, beatniks, Harlem,
Bronx and Brooklyn adolescents, Madison Avenue middle-
classniks, artists and actors, jowly rakes, Italian old-timers,
sailors, college students, cream cheese buyers—meet and
mill about together on the crowded weekend streets of the
Village. If we walk into the Cock and Bull, we may almost
think ourselves in an old-fashioned ice cream parlor. It
is a large barnlike room which used to be a book-store and
now sells sundaes with fancy names like "Orgy," costing
as much as $2.50 for enough ice cream to choke your maw
for keeps. But unlike the old-fashioned ice cream parlor,

the jukebox blares far-out numbers by the Coasters and the walls are decorated with posters from off-Broadway plays and the kids wear faces of premature cunning and boredom. The girls are mostly jailbait chicks, radically underage and looking it in their baby fat, pedal pushers, unskillful mascara, and ponytails. The men are hungry chaps who may be as old as forty. The Cock and Bull seems to specialize in men who like girls who like ice cream. On the bulletin board in back there are notices about sharing apartments, buying Vespas, providing secretarial services. One poetry-loving chick offered to type poetry free, a small charge for prose.

The great current intellectual fad, all over the Village, is the beatnik convulsion. The beatniks have been described by an acute English observer, Malcolm Bradbury, as "Nihilism's Organization Men," since like all corporate types, they tend to convene and stratify. The Village is their Eastern headquarters, just as the North Beach area in San Francisco houses the main Western office. There has been much confusion about hip and beat; this confusion can be examined in objective detail on the streets of Greenwich Village at night.

The hipster was a man who fled emotion through the use of narcotics, keeping cool, floating in his high; the beatnik is an imitation hipster, wearing the clothes and loitering at the door of the club. Allen Ginsberg and Kenneth Rexroth, the most original of the hip writers, generated a small literary following, including Jack Kerouac, Gregory Corso, and Norman Mailer, and attracted admirers among those who looked at jeans and fast driving and said, "Here is Real Life! Wow!" Alternating between San Francisco and New York, the hip and beat publicists recruit the kids into wearing free-form jewelry and saying "man" to each other. While the Village has its marvelous charm of irregularity, this should not be confused with the sort of passionate independence which provides the seedbed of genius. An avant-garde is always egotistical, self-devoted, convinced; it raises its voice, angrily and even shrilly, in order to be sure that it is heard. The pseudo avant-garde, like the hipster writers, has a distracted self-regard, troubled to be alone, weak-egoed rather than egotistical, and raises its voice desperately, like a deaf man, in order to make sure it has a voice. Not to be heard, but to be reassured.

As the naturalist Fabre wrote of the Sacred Beetle, it is sometimes worshiped by the easily awed, "a veritable living gem, shining like polished metal," but nevertheless its main activity consists in collecting great balls of dung, rolling them about, occasionally stealing from a friend, and finally, in some dark hideaway, proudly dining. These stercoriculous beasties clear the fields and serve good purpose; perhaps we praise them so exotically because they destroy their handiwork by eating it—unlike the beat rhapsodists, they are satisfied to hide it from our exploring nostrils.

Perhaps the most successful work of art produced by the hipsters, after Allen Ginsberg's exciting vaudeville *Howl*, is the campy movie *Pull My Daisy*, which stars Ginsberg (playing a beat poet), Gregory Corso (playing a beat poet), and Peter Orlovsky (playing a beat poet), plus the painter Larry Rivers and others, with a narration spoken (gargled, mumbled, yawped) and written (improvised, he says) by Jack Kerouac, the beat prose writer. A distinctly Village product, it was photographed in the lower Village by Robert Frank and Alfred Leslie, beat photographer and beat painter, respectively; and it shows the whole beat crew just goofing in a cold-water flat among all kinds of cockroaches—"sugar cockaroaches," intones Kerouac, "bread cockaroaches . . . peanut butter cockaroaches"— while various human accidents occur, such as the arrival of a "Zen bishop" with his mother who carries an American flag between her legs, a bit of wrestling among the poets, and a fight between a man and his wife, who objects to the poets just fagging around underfoot all the time. Whether intentionally or not, the film is funny and has an in-group charm.

Despite their futile gab, or perhaps because of it, the hipsters and their fleas give a strong flavor to the Village, like their allies, the homosexuals. Something relatively new in America, there is now open professional solicitation of men in the area around the corner of Sixth Avenue and Eighth Street, with a full assortment of blondined boys and leather-jacketed rough trade. Very late at night, when the hazard of true love seems to give way to the certainties of cash money, the male prostitutes stand waiting in the doorways, like chippies everywhere, gossiping with each other, falling silent when a possible mark strolls by. They murmur Rodgers-and-Hart show tunes, substituting the pronoun "he" for "she"; they lift their delicate heads; they stroke their cheeks and stand very close to their pants; they push forward their bellies in a parody of the model's pelvic pout.

Then in the morning, at Pam-Pam or Jim Atkins', they take long leisurely breakfasts, standing like Air Force officers in a hundred familiar movies, discussing their missions of the night before, the successful raid and the downed flight, checking with the queens from friendly squadrons, loitering over the third cup of coffee and blinking in the smile of sun through the window. Occasionally, confusingly, a beautiful girl joins them for breakfast, an actress or a model, secure in the sanitary devotion of men who want nothing from a woman but praise.

And sometimes at breakfast a tender mixed couple, man and woman, rising late after the night before, holding hands at the counter.

And sometimes a handsome Village mother, wheeling her baby carriage, doing the shopping after sending her husband off to paint in his studio, or write, or sell space.

The Village has set sail for the future, like all of unanchored America, set sail or set adrift, take your choice. A visit to the Village always provokes a crisis of nostalgia in those who have moved on but do not want the Village to move on. The lovely, long-legged blonde girl who used to be seen strolling with Sam Kramer, the bearded jewelry maker—gone. The Waldorf Cafeteria, where the bums and the junkies and Maxwell Bodenheim convened all night over moldy prunes and coffee—gone, replaced by a bank. Roman Marie, who used to feed the wild and the artistic— very quiet. Djuna Barnes and e e cummings—in seclusion. (It is said that a group of beat poets made a pilgrimage one night to cummings' house on Patchin Place. "We're *poets!* We're *poets!*" they shouted, and a ghostly voice issued from a window: "Go away.") And Bodenheim him- self, poet of delicate wit and ribald enthusiasm: he went down to drink and died of blows on the head, strokes with a knife, administered by the crazy thug with whom he shared —it seems—both bottle and wife. The Brevoort Hotel, home of elegant artists in moments of triumph—gone, re- placed by a boring luxury apartment house. The Rhine- lander Gardens—also raped by an apartment house. Joe Gould—dead. Max Eastman—rich. The Group Theatre— disappeared.

And yet . . .

Young Boris, proprietor of the old Borsch Bowl, dis- penser of philosophy and black bread, is gone. But long live Boris! Grayer, plumper, presiding over a new Borsch Bowl, Boris lives on, garrulously, offering black bread.

Edna St. Vincent Millay, who once inhabited the narrowest house in New York, at 73 Bedford Street, has finished burning her candle at both ends, but next door another artist works late into the night. This new poet of Bedford Street inhabits a book-lined study; his lovely slim wife stands by with coffee as he works; they can both be seen from the street, bending over his desk, he fretting, she peacefully confident, watching with a halfsmile on her face, until she taps him gently on the shoulder: "It's very late, dear." (It turns out, alas, that this nocturnal creator is the author of one of the important comic strips.)

And there is another long-legged blonde who can be seen strolling with Sam Kramer, the still-bearded jewelry maker—the same beard, a similar blonde.

And there are coffee houses which have Sunday-afternoon chamber-music recitals. And some eccentric ones which merely serve coffee.

And Charlie Van Doren, the defrocked quiz star, quietly writing a novel (a play?) which everyone supposes will deal with a simple, true-hearted, slightly greedy young quiz star who, nearly corrupted by the mass media, receives a letter from a little old lady named Checkers, just in time to keep him from perjuring himself before a Congressional committee . . . In Jim Atkins' eatery the odds are against his starring in the movie version.

And the lovely fashion model who transmitted a small crablike infestation to a whole group of poets—"like that's her protest against the whole sex-oriented system, dig," explained one of them, scratching. And the eager virgin who makes a hobby of suggesting that she and her date go back to his place so that she can take a shower—and then she takes a shower. And carries a switch-blade to make sure that her date keeps the peace. And the girls who live by remittances from home while they find their souls, and seem to find them, for they usually disappear into social work after a year or two. And the girls, girls, girls. Italo Calvino, a distinguished Italian novelist, declared that the most monumental, splendid, and architecturally efficient structure he found in America was not a skyscraper but a small flexible device; it was first modeled for him in Greenwich Village: "Change my whole life! the dee-ah-fragum!"

There are no more rent parties, at which you paid a small admission to dance the Charleston, eat cheap spa-

ghetti and drink bathtub gin so that your host could keep
body, soul, and furniture off the street, but there are shin-
digs like the STOMP OUT BOBBY BREEN PARTY (at Madame
Irma's Dancehall on Second Avenue) to which you are
asked to bring your own booze, although the mimeographed
invitation assures you that "BEER, MUSIC, ICE CUBES, PAPER
CUPS, THE HALL, MOXIE and GENERAL FUNKINESS are provided by the Management." You are also warned: "This
party is by private invitation only . . . don't bring your
friends . . . don't bring good old Harry who lives in Queens
but is a nice guy . . . nor your Aunt Lucy who has always
wanted to go to a Real Village Party . . . don't hip the
Bronx . . . if your girl is the kind who locks herself in the
can at parties to weep, don't bring her . . . if you insist on
singing, forget it . . . if your idea of a good time is charades,
we don't want you . . . no marrieds except the unhappily
. . . don't tell *Life* magazine . . . wear a funny hat if you
like, but no costumes!" There are other parties for little
companies of off-Broadway players, who offer Gallo wine
and corrosive martinis in the hope that you may write a
check to help support their production of a symbolic drama
by Ionesco, Adamov, Ghelderode, or the omnipresent revival of *Winterset*. The actors now have pads (or live with
their hip parents in Forest Hills), and worry about unpaid
parking tickets rather than the grocery bill, but the theatre
needs a stage, brother, and the union gives us lip. Those
uptown bankrollers who used to say "nix" to the avant-garde
have now learned to say "Bug off, Buster." It turns out that
many of us need our daily dose of anxiety. If we can't
worry about our own landlord, we'll fret about the bourgeois
proscenium type who holds the keys to the Circle in the
Square.

And so it goes in the eternal Village—that impossible,
actual American dream of freedom through bohemia. Amid
all the open possibilities of American life, which permits
a young man to select any variety of togetherness he
chooses, there are many who feel constricted. They ask,

Why this? Why not that? And perhaps even, Why not the other thing? Why not try my impulse, try my luck, try my talent, try my skills at loafing and self-generating labor? They are squeezed in the direction of declared rebellion, abstention, disaffiliation.

These patient and impatient yearners after truth, beauty and easy living will always float toward the Village —the artists and the art-lovers, the worshipers of sex, the sick and the spoiled, the young and the special and the adventurous, all making common cause in the pleasure of their differences. In 1960, when the pressure to do like others is high in America, the Village takes a new shape, molded by money. It is becoming an elegant bohemia in which radical politics are replaced by the hip and the beat; the bearded poets are crowded to one side by the bearded advertising men with sports cars sold them by bearded salesmen. Though it changes as it mirrors the times, the Village is still necessary. It is that bottle in which Americans put whatever the suburbs and the colleges and the middle-class family cannot happily contain.

So listen, Herman, tell Mrs. Melville to get in line. Come back to the Village and write poetry if you like. Open the bottle and free the djinn—yourself—into the carrousel whirl of Greenwich Village, where change is ever-lasting and the permanent never remains the same. There's a fellow over on Cornelia Street who looks like a homesick Canarsie ghost returned to sell wolf pelts and otter meat on his ancient lands. In fact, of course, he is a peaceable, poetry-loving Arab weaver, a frequent tea drinker, who grows irate if you call him beat. "I'm a member of the *Post* Beat Generation," he says with quiet dignity, shuckling his hands in his embroidery. "The difference between us and the beats, man, is . . . Well, like we're different. Like we *affirm*, man. I mean, like we protest."

Apparently, affirmative protest is here to stay. Green-wich Village may have ended at twelve o'clock this evening, but it has begun again at midnight.   1960

Death in Miami Beach

THE STATE OF MADNESS can be defined partly as an extreme of isolation of one human being from everyone else. It provides a model for dying. Only an intermittent and fragmentary awareness of others interrupts the black folding of the layers of self upon each other—this also defines the state of that dilemma known as "mental health."

There is a false madness induced by the accidents of isolation which prisoners, travelers, and the very ill may sometimes experience without giving up their return ticket. Surely you out there all know what I mean from your own troubles and painful decisions. To say that it is false madness does not soften its extremity. The mask of existence fits harshly on your skin, but it is in fact your only skin; and when harshly your skin is peeled off—beneath it you are naked and your naked isolation is no joy to you.

During a period of work on a long job of writing in the winter of 1958, I deliberately withdrew myself from all those who knew my name and traveled by automobile in slow stages through the deep South to Miami Beach, Key West, Havana, and finally back up toward Detroit. No one asked me to write a novel, no one asked me to go away; but I did anyway. I was tempted by the prospect of dreaming through my story amid a pleasant chaos of sun and sea, all other responsibilities suspended, and so I arranged it for myself.

Work is very fine, but after the day's work, isolation, silence, and death seemed to follow me through the zazzy carnival of Miami, the casual resort indolence of Key West, and the smoky, blistered elegance of a tourist's Havana. In Havana, from the rooftop of the Ambos Mundos Hotel, I could see Batista's police loafing with their weapons in front of public buildings; occasionally there were bombs; once a body happened to be left in the street and people hurried by as if they knew nothing, nothing, nothing at all but the next step before them.

At Key West, a few days before Christmas, I visited the turtle slaughterhouse. It is one of the few tourist attractions on this spot of island, "North Havana," raised far out into the sea off the coast of Florida. Visitors take their kiddies by the hand and lead them to see the nice turtles.

Before being killed and canned, the turtles swim in dense kraals, bumping each other in the murky water, armor clashing, dully lurching against the high pens. Later, trussed on a plank dock, they lie unblinking in the sun, their flippers pierced and tied. The tough leather of their skin does not disguise their present helplessness and pain. They wear thick, sun-hardened accumulations of blood at their wounds. Barbados turtles, as large as children, they belong to a species which has been eliminated locally by ardent harvesting of the waters near Key West, but the commercial tradition still brings them here to be slaughtered. Crucified like thieves, they breathe in little sighs, they gulp, they wait.

At a further stage, in the room where the actual slaughtering occurs, the butchers stride through gore in heavy boots. The visitor must proceed on a catwalk; a misstep will plunge him into a slow river of entrails and blood.

Because it was near Christmastime, the owners of the
plant had installed a speaker system for musical divertisse-
ment of the butchers, and while the turtles dried under the
sun or lay exposed to the butchers' knives, Christmas bells
tolled out, electronically amplified, "God Rest Ye Merry,
Gentlemen," or the Bing Crosby recording of "*Adeste
Fideles.*"

These commercial details are not intended to support
a special plea on behalf of the humane harvesting of Barbados turtles. In fact, let me grant that I sought out this
scene and visited the abattoir without having any proper
business there at all: merely curiosity and the need to confirm my imagination about it. I should be judged for
vulgarity by the man who chooses out of purity not to
follow me, not by the man I saw lurking outside, with a
face ravaged by the horrified fascination which makes it
impossible for him to visit his dreams. What had I done
which he could not permit himself? Was I filthied, was I
weakened by pleasure but obscurely nourished, was I fed
on coveted turtle joys after trampling in turtle blood? Had
I asked permission from the butcher and plied a knife
with my own hands on the belly of one of the slow, unblinking, dragon-headed, ancient sea-beasts? And did it
arch its graceful dragon neck in reproach as I stabbed? He
stared at me like a jealous lover, imagining my wickedness,
rabid and hopeless, wanting to bury his head in the reek
on my hands.

Most of us turn from the vision of death only out of
weakness, and this is no turning from death. Serve up your
turtle steak, gourmet friend, with no protest from me;
I'll eat at your table. ("A nice rendition," one gentleman
said of Bing Crosby to his wife. Turtle is tasty, somewhat
gamy meat. Protein nourishes the brain—brings oxygen
and freedom.)

A few days later, in Miami Beach, I participated in
two trivial accidents. My hotel was in one of the oldest,

therefore least expensive, parts of the town, only a short block from the sea and a short block from restaurants and therefore very convenient to my casual schedule: breakfast at Whelan's, a stretch of writing, a long swim, lunch, a pleasant bit of loafing on the beach, then perhaps some sunbaked work at my typewriter on the tar roof ("solarium"), and another swim before dinner. I had the habit in the morning of disregarding the elevator, hurrying down a back stairway of the Webster Hotel, through an alley, and so shortcutting to the drugstore. One day, wearing tennis shoes, I felt an evil slide and crunch underfoot, and knew first by the shrinking in my heart and then by simple inspection that I had stepped on a small animal.

It seemed to be a variety of tropical cockroach. It had been perhaps an inch and a half long, longer with its wings spread, and it had strayed from the raised platform nearby where the hotel stored its rubbish. Now it lay twitching, legs scrambling in the air without moving, and a yellow ooze seeped from its body within the crushed carapace. I suppose it was already dead despite all this nervous movement. I went for a walk, told myself that this was a silly matter to be fretful about (I was merely isolated), and finally took my habitual breakfast: orange juice, scrambled eggs, toast, coffee.

An hour later the dead beast was glued by its own innards to the paving of the alley; the Florida sun was moving through the sky above it. But now there was also a row of ants leading to it, another leading away, like twin caterpillars dissembling their unity of purpose. They were not merely eating, of course, they were carrying off the meat to their hill someplace. But the dead roach still twitched, and when the tickling jaws struck, it fluttered, squeezed, blindly pushed in its place. The ants went scrambling away, each carrying its minuscule steak.

All afternoon the shell of the roach lay there. Its row of legs no longer waved of their own power, but there were still tremors as the eating ants tugged at it. Unfatigued and busy, they were determined to wipe this slate clean.

Shortly before dark I again came down the back stairway. Now the familiar arena had changed. Another foot had struck, more strange and haphazard than my own. The shell of the roach was destroyed; there were also dead ants freckling the stone; stillness and death. The ants were suddenly individual in death; the undulating columns were erased. And the work of eating was permanently interrupted for both eaters and eaten.

The next morning when I walked through the alley no sign remained. A sweeper had done her work; there were straight, mechanical striations—a friendly broom. Good. But I bent to look for some sign or memorial to the departed beast on this stretch of alley which I now knew very well. There was none. Marks of broom; new arrangements of pebbles and dust; history here had entered upon an epoch which was strange to me.

Then finally a homely death entered what might pass for society in my isolated Miami Beach—the world of the soda fountain at Whelan's, where strollers came into an air-conditioned place to shake off the sand of the beach, sip a Coke, buy lotions and plastic sunglasses, and sometimes order a quick meal.

I was taking my breakfast, according to my habit, on a stool at the counter. By this time I was acquainted with Frank, the short-order cook, who had emigrated from Second Avenue in New York twenty years ago for his health and, for sweet health's sake, still managed to cover the leathery pouched skin of age with a fierce Miami tan, despite his long hours in Whelan's service. It relieved the silence to exchange a few morning words with a man who by now knew my face: "Two scrambled light."

"Same as yesterday, Mister."

"Yes, like yesterday." (Triumph in my voice: He

remembers me!) "Whole-wheat toast. You got marmalade today?"

"Marmalade." Frank knew my face and my eggs.

Other eaters, like me, were forking up eggs and grits and sipping their Cokes or coffee when the woman entered. She was blotched with sunburn, had a swollen nose, and a mouth open so wide for noise that all her features were distorted. Emitting emergency alarm signals, turning her head and staring, demanding passage, demanding attention, a shouting vehicle, she pushed a stumbling old man along with her. "Ohh," she screamed, "a Bromo! For God's sake a Bromo! My husband is dying, a Bromo, for God's sake!"

The man's face was blue and he seemed barely conscious. He swayed stiffly as she steered him toward a stool near me.

"Oh, a Bromo right now, please!" she wailed.

Frank, behind the counter, looked sideways at her, pretended the impossible—that he did not hear her—and went on making a bacon-lettuce-and-tomato sandwich on whole-wheat toast, light on the mayonnaise.

Two or three of us jumped up to support the old man. His skin had a thick purple glow that said death to all our eyes.

"Oh, have mercy, a Bromo for my poor husband!" the woman screamed. "He didn't do nothing to you! For God's sake why don't you give it to him?"

Floundering, I watched Frank finish the bee-ell-tee, slide it onto a plate, and hand it to his customer. The hot-rodder bent his head to the spilling sandwich and ate as if his life depended on it, thrustingly. In the meantime, the pharmacist, a short man in a white coat, sweating profusely despite the air conditioning, came bustling from his cubicle and said, "Heart attack? You want I should call a doctor, Missus?"

"Ohh, please, dear God, a Bromo!" she shouted.

"I'll call a doctor, he'll be right over."

"Bromo for a dying man! Why don't you give it to him? Mercy, mercy!"

The pharmacist was on the telephone and the howling woman subsided in shrill spasms. Her husband swayed on the stool, his eyes shut, while his wife leaned sobbing against his back to keep him from toppling onto the ground. She refused to let anyone touch him in order to lay him out on the floor—someone's idea—as if this ministry would commit him once and for all to the hands of death. Naturally, my innards shrank from this; the layers of the self closed tight; the flower of feeling was shut, sealed. I wanted to rush in some place, rush away; strike, destroy, *run*; kill Frank, kill the hotrodder, because a man was dying and nobody could do anything. Thus righteousness substitutes for being straight with the world. I was sly and scared. Thus I occupied myself with rage at my friend Frank, who pretended to hear nothing and stubbornly refused to make the glass of Bromo Seltzer.

During the five minutes before the doctor arrived, the scene altered rapidly and tensely. Of course, all the break-fasters but the determined hotrodder stopped their eating. The kid in the leather jacket asked for pretzels with his Coke for sustained strength behind the wheel. The rest of us drifted, lurking behind the sick man on his stool. His wife wept and cursed and heaved out her sobs because no one would supply a Bromo.

Then abruptly the man shook himself and opened his eyes and tried to stand up. He stumbled; his wife pushed him back onto the stool. He shook his head and mumbled. Then rapidly the purple color diminished; his eyes stopped their blind rolling; he began to talk with his wife. He was returning to the living. He and his wife had a whispered consultation. She nodded rapidly at him, like a bird.

Suddenly she alighted and flew out the door. The man, left behind on the stool, said hoarsely, "Lemme have a glass of water, will you, pal?"

Frank gave him the water.

Now the doctor entered, rolling his sleeves down and carrying his black bag open. He had apparently run a block in the tropical morning heat.

"Haha!" said the formerly dying man. Just like that: "Hahaha! Hi, Doc!"

"You're the sick man?" said the doctor. "Let's see now—"

"Hahaha! Don't touch me, Doc," said the old man, leaning away. "Listen, Doc, it's a funny thing. My wife gets herself all excited—aggravated."

"You mean you're all right?" the doctor said.

"Just like a little attack was all I had, hahaha," said the old man.

"You're okay?"

"Look, Doc, I ain't been eating right, you know, enjoying myself, hahaha. A little attack. I get them sometimes. Like a little attack is all."

"Okay," said the doctor firmly, "you don't want me to look at you? Okay." He nodded briskly to the pharmacist, said, "I've got a patient in my office," and trotted off again into the heat.

The old man smiled and gazed without malice at Frank, who had refused him the Bromo. Instead of leaving a tip he left him one word of explanation before he headed off after his wife. The word was deposited on the counter behind him with an apologetic smile: "Constipation."

Eggs in the plates of all the late breakfasters were left cold and shiny. The hotrodder alone had finished his sandwich, Coke, and pretzels, and left whistling. Angry at last, I discharged an unformulated hostility on Frank: "Why the devil didn't you give the man his Bromo?"

His reply seems an obvious bit of logical disquisition at this remove, but there in the shadow of panic and crisis it struck me with the force of revelation. Rubbing a dirty cloth on the counter—formulating and reformulating a smear of grease before me—he said, "If he was dying of a heart attack, what good would a Bromo do him? And if he was not dying, what good is a Bromo?"

"Yes, but."

"So I have to do my job, but I don't have to listen to nuts."

"But you didn't say anything! That woman was hysterical."

He looked at me with undisguised pity for my ignorance. "That's why I didn't say anything. I been in trouble for saying things before, I learned."

He went back to work; the pharmacist was back in his cubicle, counting pills into a bottle; the doctor had returned to his office. It was eleven o'clock and Frank took down the sign about the breakfast special. A man came in frightened to ask for the special, and Frank pointed to the sign, which was upside down on the counter, and said, "It's five minutes after eleven already. But I'll give it to you." The look of despair faded from the man's face.

In a few days I finished my own job and began the long drive out of the false Florida summer into the northern winter, my heels passing over all sorts of unfelt beasties, my gullet accepting steaks and chops, my heart leaping with no better welcome to death than before. In Detroit my daughter asked me, "What's God's last name? How big is the whole world? Where do you go when you die?"

The foregoing inconclusive words were written two years ago. Now I have seen fit to return to my cafeteria-and-old-folks slum on lower Collins Avenue, and ostensibly for the same lure of cheap sun, sky, water, beach, boredom. I write, I swim. I stroll on Lincoln Road, I eat steaks and pizza, I sniff the sea with my sunburnt beak, I suck in my belly and run barefoot on the sand, I sleep, I write. In front of one of the new hotels I found a nude in plaster, beckoning, with her hand lifted as if hitching a

ride. All aboard, you masturbators. Some of the fruit juice
and hamburger stands have disappeared; new ones have
opened. The Ellis Department Store, Here Since 1919, is
closed, looks ransacked, has a box of Fruit of the Loom
T-shirts spilled in the window and a U.S. Federal Court
bankruptcy notice affixed to its sealed door.

I met a waitress in a restaurant which advertises nine-
course dollar dinners. She has a pretty, lively, thirty-five-
year-old girl's face, with all the black brightness of eye a
man could want; she turns out to be Corsican and we
speak French; an artillery sergeant brought her to Florida
and apparently tired of her brightness of eye. She has a
rattling Corsican accent, likes Edith Piaf records, and
gives me extra shrimp bits in my shrimp bits salad. So
some things change. Last time I heard no Edith Piaf and
earned no extra forkfuls of shrimp. The sirloin steak she
brings me spreads its wings and seems ready to flop off
the plate. My gut talks French and I take ease in the flattery
of food. I wait and at last she slips into my booth with me
and sighs. It is eleven o'clock, time to begin real life. Her
history is sad. I feel obliged to offer some recompense for
the evil done her by men and luck, and so I listen, wondering how her eyes can remain so bright as the disasters
and disillusionments unroll.

When I said good night, she replied with a funny,
rapidly fiddling, diddling, twenty-one-fingered gesture at
her mouth. I asked what it meant. "Fun and glee!" she
said, "fun and glee! *Maintenant je suis une vraie Américaine.*" Her eyes burn like stars, but like the stars, she has
darkness between them.

A day and a night and another day. The first week
passes.

I eat salty bagels in the sun, I listen to the teenage
girls after school with their curious mixture of Florida
cracker and Bronx accents. I go back into the damp of
my room—the peculiar dank assault of cheap tropical bed-

rooms—and think my novel through once again, examining the pile of manuscript with my intentions in motion like a column of ants working over the struggling body of an insect. And when the life seems to weaken, I leave it and go out onto the beach or into the street.

Madness consists partly in an extreme of isolation? Partly. But the demented tumble down from their associations and memories into other associations and memories; they are sent away into the future with a map of the past which conforms to no agreed past and to no other map—and yet it is their only chart, their history and route, their needs which are unfailingly present. The lonely traveler also brutally inflicts absolute possession of his movements upon the endless day, and the novelty of what he sees joins him in yet another way to his deepest desires and dreads. He returns, he never lets go. There is no escape even in isolation; there is no isolation, merely interrupted and distorted association, until death claims us. Then every man is an island entire of itself.

In love, we seek freedom and purity even more than the comfort of diminished isolation. Those few fortunate ones who have the talent can bear the paradox of love. The rest of us are harassed by our contradictory demands —*join me, make me free*. With age and aging, the model of all voyages (learn and grow, diminish and weary), comes final approach to the ultimate simplicity which love seeks to confound—death. A paradox forever out of balance to answer a grave black simplicity: *we are ill used*. The facts we make for ourselves disappoint the intentions with which we make them. The opposable thumb, which is said to be responsible for civilization and history, give us no answers here, though with it we can grasp our pens and break insects in our hands. Finally we die, opposable thumbs and all.

In the meantime, I visit my story. We exchange visits. I laugh over it, frown and worry over it, and urge it for-

ward. Then I leave it for the Miami streets. The book
follows me; it does not let me visit unaccompanied; it
enters me instead and I try to shake it off as an adept at
voodoo fights against possession by the importunate god.
The opposable thumb is of no use in this contest; both
the prize and the weapons have reached beyond tools, even
tools of thinking; I am the quadruple god's horse—dream
of love, hope of meaning, joy of power, relish in being.
Too much burden on one soul. Who asked me to feel
sorry or glad for others? They were merely pious who asked
me. Why follow their orders? I decide: I *won't*. But I
cannot escape my self, which also gives orders. The flower
of feeling opens; the flower shuts; it obeys the freshness of
weather. All emotion flowing from health or illness partakes of the pathetic fallacy, identifying moral value with
the gifts of nature. My feet want to run; I am wearing
Keds, and feel light on the foam rubber soles; but the heat
of the sun holds me to earth.

There is a hotel on Washington Boulevard which
specializes in "economical, comfortable living for the retired." It is a huge dark building like the Women's House
of Detention in Greenwich Village, but without the bars
on the rooms, and there are purple lights playing on the
palm trees outside, soft music piped throughout the
grounds, and the frequent blare of a loudspeaker: "Missus
Goldberg to the telephone! Missus Goldberg! *Sadie, answer
the phone!*" when the children call from New York. The
streets of the neighborhood are filled with chattering of
mournful elder statesmen, mostly losers after sixty years of
continual negotiation, men with chagrined pouches slipping
sideways beneath their eyes, women with hair bursting onto
their cheeks and upper lips, as if all at once, near the end,
they have decided to make a final try at being better men
than their husbands.

To walk through the crowd during the hour following
their afternoon naps is to wade in senility. There is a

deep-sea lack of light despite all the sun and brisk resort clatter; you gasp for life and run to look in a dusty window. Narcissus wants to be just thirty-five, *"nel mezzo del cammin di nostra vita,"* and not seventy, not seventy! The crowd flutters by. "She thought she could be my daughter-in-law! A girl like that! To be my daughter-in-law! And you know what? Now she is." "I used to be in business. I had a good business. It was a nice store, good location. Furniture. I should have kept my location." "What does the weather report say? Does the weather report ever say anything but the weather?" "Moishe died. He had an attack. Well, we all got to go."

Is it the same voice, the same rhythm? It is the same crowd—grief, isolation, death. There almost always seems to be an ambulance pulling up or pulling away.

It is fine to tell a story, which feels like affirmation, but afterwards, after the morning's writing, then what? Writing is an expression of affirmation, power, longing, but not a proper cause of these emotions in the writer. He is a guide into delight and dread because he can escape victimization (he thinks); he has left a little trail of paper behind him as he threads his way into the maze, and can find his way back (he believes—though the roar of the maze sets up a disarray in anything as fragmentary as his intentions about return). He tracks the minotaur with an open mind. "Maybe I'll like it," he says, "and maybe I won't. At least I'll see." He initiates passion only because he has it—otherwise self-delusion and covetous self-therapy. And so it is not good to be alone for long, entirely alone.

But at least for a time, until they dim out, loneliness sharpens the eyes. I feel like a safecracker; loneliness has also sharpened my fingertips, and my entire body throughout feels the clicking tumblers as I yearn toward the combination. I come to focus, I work. But afterwards, then what? I have retreated from the distractions of Manhattan.

There are no telephone calls. No friendship, no duties, no hazards of pique or pleasure. I shall work till the battery runs down, frozen and stilled by this busy emptiness under the sun. I ask myself: Can the silent column of ants reconstruct the living roach at its leisure underground? No, only a tree can make a tree, only a winged roach can make a winged roach. A column of ants works by an invisible will which resides in no one of its jointed parts, but only a swollen green ant can breed an urgent ant.

As I walk on Lincoln Road, the smart shopping area of "the Beach," I ogle the oglers, the sunburned sun-worshipers basted with oil, cream, tonic, and lotion—the touts, boxers, fairies, grandmothers, exiled Cubans, local hotrodders and their gumchewing molls, sportsmen, natty invalids in gabardine, drunks, stockbrokers, antique collectors, Semites and anti-Semites all taking the air together on Lincoln Road. Hill people, swamp people, and ex-pugs sell newspapers flown in from all over—New York, Chicago, Los Angeles ("Smogsville!" cackles a refugee). And New York is harried by flu and Chicago is black with coal and damp. And here we all are on Lincoln Road, with a delicious breeze, courtesy of the steakhouse pumping cool air into the street. So let's buy the hometown paper to see how miserable we might have been, for others are.

On Lincoln Road, fair Lincoln Road in Miami Beach, the Negroes have been freed; freed of existence, that is; only a few black ghosts slip discreetly by. Even if they were not so discreet, they would be invisible, though for a new reason: they are going someplace, namely, to work, or at another hour, home. For them, Lincoln Road is a mere artery for transit, while for the others, Lincoln Road is parlor, sunroom, promontory into health and beauty. For the visitors, Lincoln Road is a slow matter, a recipe for yearned-for slowness, sloth, strolling ease, delicacy of control. The cocky Broadway chapparoonies are wearing their new pleatless "Miami-Tailored Daks." Their bellies do the work of belts, hiding the place where belts would be. Now I'm so slow I don't need a belt, the pants proudly announce; I'm just walkin' along, just struttin' down the avenue, just here and pleasant with myself, and when I take a breath, the expandable elastic waistband expands with me. In the men's room of a bar off Lincoln Road, hung with photographs of wrestlers, there is a curious vending machine which is decorated with a crown and raised scepter and submits a product called DE-LA: "Say Delay, a light lubricating ointment designed to aid in the prevention of premature climax. Odorless. Safe. Stainless. Easy to apply. Directions on package. 50¢ coins only. Machine does not give change."

Machine makes comment, however. Machine is trying to tell us something.

The Negro girl who cleans my room gets yelled at, screamed at, all morning. "Stupid, stupid, stupid! A single room only gets two towels, one face, one bath!" She smiles slyly to herself as if she knows where the manager's DE-LA is hidden. This is the southland, I am reminded, where we have grits for breakfast. But it is not quite dat ole Dixie, boss, which changeth not, nor can age alter it. It is Miami Beach. The Sholem Aleichem Literary Society ("Managed by Tourists—Managed for Tourists") has a For Rent sign on it. "Owner Will Remodel for Any Business."

I decide as I walk: I'll write my book till the battery runs down, though distraction seems necessary; other duties, friends, "real life."

The sirens of the police ambulances work up and down the Beach all day and night, announcing the news as they carry away the attacked, the fallen, the stroked, the perished. A population of the aged sheds its members at the merest trifle of an excuse—a bottle of cold pop in the sun, a skipped nap, somebody raising his voice suddenly—or no excuse at all. It touches life and someone dies. It treads carelessly and someone dies. The sirens

whir and howl and Negroes courteously open the back door
for the corpse. For some reason people smile at the ambulance as they stroll, sucking ice cream. Perhaps they
dream of an accident, a distraction: *Siren meets white
Thunderbird, boy of forty cut off in his prime, had a girl
in there with him, not his wife.* Perhaps thinking: *Not me
this time.*

One of those impossible coincidences. Today I met
Dr. Meyer leading his blind wife. He was our family doctor
in Cleveland, addicted to practical jokes, who always said
he wanted to do research, and in fact he had some sort
of connection with one of the important drug laboratories.
When he retired from practice, he announced to my
parents over a bottle of wine that now he would begin his
true life's work. I had decided that his practical jokes,
bought in Jean's Fun House on East 9th Street—buzzers,
false flies, stomach noises, leaky cups—were a symptom of
childish anger at adult responsibility. But now that he could
retire from practice and try his hand at research. . . . It
turned out that his wife had inoperable cataracts; she went
blind fast, and he went sour, quiet, mean; and they left
Cleveland for Miami Beach, where I saw him leading her,
walking with the stiff, frightened step of the unaccustomed
blind. He is shrunken; only today do I notice that he is a
small man—when I was a boy, he was immense. At present,
and forever until the very end, his life's work is to steer his
wife to the beach in the morning and sit with her to
describe what he sees. He has replaced both practical jokes
and dreams of a laboratory with loyalty to his wife, but virtue has made him a furious runt.

Fantasies of thighs, breasts, bellies as I nap on the
beach. I awaken, sticky with salt. My nose is peeling. Shall
I visit the Corsican waitress again tonight? Shall I ask the
Meyers to dinner? But I have made this disappearance into
Miami Beach in order to avoid the troubles of others and
of myself. I swim again. I doze again. I dream of sex with a

woman I overheard describing the proper way to kill a chicken "so it don't suffer. You ask anyone, they'll tell you. And there's nothing like fresh-killed chicken. You can't trust the butchers."

A man in the coffee shop later said to the cashier: "I been sick, that's why you ain't seen me. Doctor said coronary thrombosis. You ever heard of that?"

"Naw. Lots of people got coronaries, but that thrombosis, that's a new thing. The docs keep finding new things so they can charge us."

"Well, I'll tell you, it left me feeling pretty weak."

I went one night to see a road company version of *My Fair Lady* at the Miami Beach Auditorium, which more frequently provides hospitality for wrestling or boxing matches. A maggoty, bored imitation of Rex Harrison, a thick Eliza without any bounce. The audience is quietly taking in the famous sight. They write on their postcards home: Tonight we saw a Broadway show, but the girl was fat.

Crazy Louie on the beach—a frantic grandfather with Latin records, maracas, castanets, silk Cuban shirts, feathers, straw skirt, rubber Halloween masks, a huge earring loosely hooked to his ear by a bent hairpin, thick glasses sliding down his nose, leathery withered legs, dancing and dancing, all sinews and grins and shakes to some inner song while the portable phonograph goes rattle-and-scrape, screech, rattle, and scrape. Amazingly, the crowd which regularly gathers on the sand nearby seems to enjoy his music; some of them shake, too, dreaming of the days when they had lust to squander on their legs. Dr. Meyer's wife smiles as he describes the scene. "Are you smiling, Meyer?" she asks. He says yes, but is lying. Crazy Louie bangs his castanet under her nose and screams *"Ole!"* and she jumps. At last Dr. Meyer smiles.

Then he tells her that sometimes the beginnings of arteriosclerosis can be detected at age twenty-five. "Cuts off the blood supply to the brain. The psychiatrists think they're smart, but they can't do anything about the histological system. The brain dries up like a scab."

"Meyer, you shouldn't use such language."

"You mean histology?"

"I mean scab, Meyer."

Crazy Louie is dancing and cackling, kicking sand. The old ladies in their bathing skirts fan themselves contentedly as he enters his Afro-Cuban apocalypse. On the beach there is a rural, village tolerance of madness. Louie doesn't do any harm. His children sent him down. He is new since my last visit.

And where are my old friends?

The cockroach in the alley is long gone, of course, and its grandchildren unto many generations. But I have found cheap sun again for my sinus, and white ocean breaking against the distractions of Manhattan in winter, spring, summer, fall. I think of a friend, a Jewish chauvinist, arguing with his girl: "When your people were still living in trees and hitting each other with sticks, my people already had sinus trouble."

The Spinoza Forum is gone, replaced by a motel. Dr. Wolfson still goes to the beach every afternoon. But the neighborhood is changed. He has nothing to say to me except that raw beets, honey, and tangerines keep a man virtuous and healthy, no matter what his age.

The woman who knew Thomas Wolfe—did I forget to mention that last time?—and swam as if she wanted to die, and worked as a B-girl . . . gone. She wanted to reconstruct some cabin-in-the-woods dream of perfection, but she could never find the missing pieces. Life is not a jigsaw puzzle; once it has been scrambled, the old picture is gone.

The racing-car driver with whom I chatted a couple of times at breakfast—gone.

The column of ants at the cockroach—gone.

The drummed-up acquaintances—even their names forgotten.

The hotel clerk who wanted to explore in Guatemala —perhaps he is exploring in Guatemala. The new manager of the hotel has never even heard of him.

And the man who died—dead.

I know this for certain, for I have finally discovered an old friend. Frank, the gray bozo behind the counter at Whelan's, is still there. I had taken up new eating habits and did not return to Whelan's during my first week in Miami Beach, but then I did and found him, still building hamburger platters and scrambling eggs. At first he did not remember me. He never knew my name. When I reminded him of the incident about the man who died, and of our long breakfast friendship, a look of irritation captured his face—demands were being made on him— but then his cross mug creased into a smile. He did remember me! He only needed to be reminded!

"You know that old fool," he said. "Later really did die. He's dead. Later died."

There was a new cat in the store. A new special on toothbrushes. A new pharmacist.

I had a hamburger on our old friendship, and Frank put an extra slice of tomato on the side to *prove* that he remembered me. But why should he? He had been an experience for me—the same now, with balder eyebrows— but what was I to him? For me he existed as an example of something, a moment of frightening history, a troubled memory which I had set down in words. I had needed a friend then, but he did not. I was frightened by death then, and worse, by a way of receiving death, but he was not and perhaps never admits that he might be.

Why does he stay in Miami Beach?

Yes, for a job. Yes, for the sun. But why there?

All right, then why not there?

Why do I go back?

Why did I go back? What happened to those dead and dying ones? They died and were dead; they were swept away. I thought, the first time I went to Miami Beach, that I had made a free choice to be isolated, but I discovered that everyone comes to the state of isolation in time—though not freely. What I did out of apparent health and youth, in the pleasure of work, those others did in sickness and age, in the anxiety of boredom. But eventually work is done, health turns to decay, youth turns to ripeness turns to age; feebleness and dying must precede death except for fighter pilots, who are anachronisms. Miami Beach is an extension, adult education course in how to die, pursued with great seriousness by the enrollees. The old folks work at it with deliberate and modest intensity, in group sessions, complimenting each other on their tans, their sport shirts, their postgraduate skill at finding a proper weather. The young vacationers flush in on packaged tours, immerse themselves in the ceremonial indulgences of resort hotels, eat, swim, and enjoy their honeymoon wrestling, take in Eartha Kitt or Leo de Lion, sigh with boredom and excess, buy bottles of Man Tan at the air terminal ("Arrive With Fresh Sun On Your Cheeks!"), and flee back to real life with a secret conviction that this is leisure? Strictly for the birds, brother.

That first time in Miami Beach, I was a curious observer, obscurely moved, with the face of a man who fearfully unwinds a rope as he visits his dream of the turtle slaughterhouse. The second time (the last time!), two years' change had begun to discover my implication to me; I broke the rope; the model of death is real; the dream of dying is real. The tanned, reduced, heliotropic Doctor Meyer recognized me despite his wife's blindness ("Hannah! Look who's here!"), and when I spoke to her, she gropingly embraced me. This was why I went back—to feel Mrs. Meyer's arms hotly convulsed about my neck, as if I were still a boy in Cleveland, and to know that I was not a young man from Cleveland visiting Miami Beach as he had toured carnivals, the war, the Caribbean, Europe, and taken the boat ride around Manhattan. I was a winter visitor, tired of town, come for the sun, who had been there before.

Am I now satisfied with what I found? Which is: "Later really did die. Later died." Just as in the alley two years ago, in that swept space where there was no longer any roach and no column of ants, history enters upon new epochs which begin to grow familiar to me.

LIKE YOUNG

ALSO BY FRANCIS DAVIS

Jazz
and
Pop,
Youth
and
Middle Age

LIKE YOUNG

Francis Davis

DA CAPO PRESS

Designed by Jeffrey P. Williams
Set in 11 point Electra by Perseus Publishing Services

Cataloging-in-Publication data for this book is available from the Library of Congress.

First Da Capo Press edition 2001
ISBN 0–306–81056–5

Published by Da Capo Press
A Member of the Perseus Books Group
http://www.dacapopress.com

Da Capo Press books are available at special discounts for bulk purchases in the U.S. by
corporations, institutions, and other organizations. For more information, please contact the Special Markets Department at the Perseus Books Group, 11 Cambridge
Center, Cambridge, MA 02142, or call (617) 252-5298.

1 2 3 4 5 6 7 8 9—05 04 03 02 01

For our mothers,

DOROTHY DAVIS

(1923–2001)

AND

ANNE GROSS

(1918–2001)

and in memory of

RICHARD HOGAN

(1947–1999)

AND

SUSANNAH MCCORKLE

(1946–2001)

Contents

Jazz
and
Pop,
Youth
and
Middle Age

LIKE YOUNG

Advertisements for Myself

M iles Davis detested liner notes, regarding them almost as a form of insult. Though less vehemently opposed to them than Davis was, John Coltrane also failed to see their point. Like Davis, he believed that technical analysis was superfluous, and that an annotator's subjective descriptions were likely to inhibit a listener from forming his own impressions. I think pride entered into it as well. For a musician to bother to *explain* himself—to discuss his aims with a hired expert, who would then pass the information along to record buyers—was a tacit admission of failure. Never mind what you were *trying* to do. Music ought not just be allowed to speak for itself, but *forced* to—to Davis and Coltrane's way of thinking, this was the only true measure of its success.

I am of a different mind on the value of liner notes—not surprisingly, you might be thinking, given that I've earned a buck or two signing my name to them. But trust me, it often wasn't much more than a buck or two, and besides, I have been reading liner notes a lot longer than I have been writing them. I started listening to jazz in earnest—that is to say, buying albums—in 1964, midway through my senior year in high school. One difference between pop albums and jazz LPs that I spotted immediately was that the essays on the back covers of the latter were far more substantive, comparable in their offhand way to the introductory essays in the Signet Mentor editions of Hawthorne and Melville that I was reading for class. Months before I stumbled on Martin Williams's monthly column in *Saturday Review*, liner notes were my introduction to jazz criticism. Unless written by a disc jockey, in which case they tended to be pseudo-hip blather on the order of *So sit back . . . Relax . . . And dig!*, they provided an intellectual framework for the music. They were piecemeal jazz history. Along with valuable biographical information, they supplied newcomers like me with an idea of where individual performers fit into the contemporary zeitgeist and the evolutionary continuum. What I liked best about them, though, and maybe why I'm sentimental about them now, is that they gave me something to read on the bus ride home from the record store.

To record companies, liner notes are a form of advertising. In accepting an assignment to write a liner, I see it as an opportunity to weigh in with the first review (detailed and unapologetically enthusiastic) of a recording I greatly admire. I admit to addressing my fellow critics as well as potential record buyers: My goal is to influence the opinion of the opinion makers by suggesting the terms according to which the recording in question ought to be listened to and discussed. If my colleagues think less of the recording than I do, so be it; I have at least given them something to argue with.

There are obvious similarities between liner notes and the preface to a collection such as this one. This is where I am supposed to alert readers, beginning with reviewers, to the larger themes that drift through these pieces on music. In a way, this is just one more liner note, an advertisement for myself.

So why do I this once find myself siding with Miles and Coltrane, reluctant to reveal my intentions for fear that to do so will be proof I haven't fulfilled them? Part of it, I guess, is that despite my liberal use of the first person, I am more comfortable discussing someone else's work than my own. The contradiction is that my *subject* per se—this particular musician or that particular recording—has increasingly become merely my starting point. At a recent panel, I heard a musician say that the role of the critic was to "translate" music into another medium. The way I see it, the job only begins there. Describing music, which I think I do reasonably well, isn't as important to me at this point as describing my reactions to it, which calls for equal parts detachment and self-examination (this might be what lures certain writers into criticism in the first place: the luxury of being introspective without being particularly revealing). As analytical as I can be about music, my approach to writing about it is largely intuitive. I don't have a formula for judging music: 30 points for technical competence, 25 for innovation, 20 for sheer pleasure, and so on. Something either gets to me or it doesn't, and I don't have to like something for it to provoke a strong response—quite the contrary, as you will see from a few of the pieces here. Music criticism is a form of cultural criticism, if one goes about it the right way. For me, it also seems to have become autobiography by other means.

Like Young is the most personal of my collections and, perhaps for that reason, the most difficult for me to talk about in broad, sweeping terms. In addition to jazz, *In the Moment* (1986) was about money and race, *Outcats* (1990) about alienation, and *Bebop and Nothingness* (1996) about all of those things plus my love of mischief. What else, besides music, is the present collection about? The realization that modern jazz, what used to be called rock 'n' roll, and I myself are sinking deeper into middle age at a time when popular culture has become synonymous with youth. But this wasn't a "theme" I began with, then sought subjects to illustrate. It's something I noticed only as I reread these previously published pieces, expanding or condensing them as seemed necessary for inclusion here (no piece appears exactly as first published).

INSOFAR AS INTRODUCTIONS TO WORKS OF NONFICTION SERVE AS USERS' guides, I should say a few things about *Like Young*'s format. Though my primary identity is that of jazz critic, I occasionally write about other kinds of music and about other cultural phenomena. *In the Moment* was the only one of my three previous collections devoted exclusively to jazz, and even it offered a thought or two about classical music, opera, and funk. Bobby Darin and the comedian Mort Sahl found their way into *Outcats*, as did John Zorn. Along with Zorn, *Bebop and Nothingness* offered my reflections on Prince and Michael Jackson, rap, Don Byron's klezmer, Barbra Streisand, Stephen Sondheim, and *Guys and Dolls*.

Like Young opens the floodgates, with an entire section on pop. The last piece in the book is also the earliest—"The Moral of the Story from the Guy Who Knows," on Dion DiMucci, of Dion and the Belmonts, is from 1989. It would have appeared in *Bebop and Nothingness*, but my former publisher worried that jazz readers would be leery of buying a book that gave too much space to rock. It all worked out for the best, I think; this piece and a few others of similar vintage make more sense here, given their subtext of asking whether music you grew up with and once thought of as *yours* gains meaning as the years go by or loses it, becoming hollow memory. My thanks to Andrea Schulz, of Da Capo Press, for backing my bet that most jazz fans aren't as parochial as their reputation suggests. Nobody I know under the age of sixty grew up listening only to jazz; the younger jazz musicians I admire tend to listen to all sorts of things—why should someone who writes about them be any different?

In the introduction of my first book, which was published when I was working as a stringer for a daily newspaper, I described myself as a beat reporter—though maybe what I really meant was a beat cop. Back then, I made a conscientious effort to hear at least a few tracks of every new album that arrived in the mail, and to review as many of them as possible, all the while hearing as much live music as I could. No one can keep up that pace for very long, nor should anyone want to. Cops can become desensitized not just to violence but to the suffering of innocent victims. I'm not saying it's a good comparison, but the rigor of turning out copy on recordings and live performances about which you have no strong opinion (and therefore have nothing very interesting to say) can be deadening for a critic. You even begin to despise that unobjectionable but uninspired new recording you're forcing yourself to listen to strictly out of duty; it's keeping you from playing Duke Ellington or Charlie Parker or early Ornette Coleman. My solution has been to bump myself up to investigator, taking on fewer subjects but examining them at greater length and in greater depth. In that sense, my writing on pop is my version of going undercover. Although these pieces are similar to my jazz pieces in voice and sensibility, I judge pop by a very different set of standards. I don't think that anyone reading me on pop would "make" me for a jazz critic.

SOME ARE GOING TO COMPLAIN THAT *LIKE YOUNG* IS TWO DIFFERENT BOOKS, which I say is precisely the point. Anybody remember those Ace paperbacks of the 1950s, which offered readers two complete mysteries for the price of one, with a different cover for each? You finished the first novel, then turned the book upside down and started reading the second from the back. Minus the handguns and cleavage, that's what I wish the design for this book could be.

The pieces on jazz at the front of the book are themselves divided into two sections. Singers (I count Hoagy Carmichael and Dave Frishberg here) get a section to themselves, because their art has evolved differently from that of jazz instrumentalists; besides, does someone like Carmichael or Sinatra belong in jazz or pop? The pieces on instrumentalists and composers are sequenced to suggest the enduring impact of the major movements of the second half of the last century—bebop, modal jazz, Ornette Coleman's free jazz and John Coltrane's messianic variation on it, and the sort of mix-and-match postmodernism exemplified by Dave Douglas. A few of the musicians here, including Sun Ra and Rashaan Roland Kirk, defy such neat categorization; indeed, this is a large part of their appeal. I put them where they seem to fit least uncomfortably. The chapter on Sun Ra—a partial transcript of a baffling interview he gave me in 1990, portions of which I drew on for a piece on him that was collected in *Bebop and Nothingness*—is here by popular demand, as it were. I've honored so many requests for tapes from authors of books and dissertations on Ra that it seemed only fair to make the best stuff available to everyone. The reason I interject so little is that very little of what he said was in direct response to my questions, and not even I pretend to be able to make sense of all of it—and I was sitting just a few feet away, flushed with warm feeling for him. I'm told that this was the fullest account he ever gave of his alien abduction. (*Taken: The True Story of an Alien Abduction* is the name of a novel from the "slush pile" in David Leavitt's *Martin Bauman: Or, A Sure Thing*.) The piece on Walt Dickerson was a liner note; its ability to withstand scrutiny as a combination profile and critical essay is testimony to the free hand and virtually unlimited space that Verve Records allows annotators. Like nearly every jazz critic I know, I think that some of my clearest thinking and most persuasive writing occurs in record reviews of moderate length; accordingly, I have included a miscellany of them in a separate section. The chapter that ends the section combines a stage review, a movie review, and a television review in an attempt to examine how the world at large perceives jazz, when it happens to throw a glance that way.

WITH THE EXCEPTION OF THE SUN RA INTERVIEW, ALL OF THE PIECES IN THE section subtitled "Change of the Century" were written during the last five years—a trying time for jazz. The period began with the major record companies having decided that an effective way of expanding the market for jazz might be to present listeners in their twenties with a host of instrumentalists their own age, with whom they would presumably be

able to identify—a decision eagerly endorsed by others in the jazz industry, including concert promoters and festival organizers, magazine editors, and the bureaucrats at the jazz nonprofits. It didn't seem to occur to
any of these people that the problem might be with jazz itself, not the
way it was presented. They crossed their fingers and prayed for another
Wynton Marsalis—better yet, three or four per instrument. Everyone
now concedes that this strategy has been a failure, just as I predicted it
would be in an essay I wrote for *The Atlantic Monthly* in 1996 (the piece
that gives this collection its name). Jazz's market share has actually
decreased since then, and the average age of its audience has continued
to creep upward. ("The audience for straight jazz is made up of aging
white males," a record company executive recently told Richard B.
Woodward, in *The Village Voice*. "In 10 years, after they've all had heart
attacks, it'll be left with no audience.") Columbia and RCA Victor have
virtually dismantled their jazz divisions, and who knows how long Blue
Note and Verve will stay the course? The biggest fear of all is that ambitious reissue programs are forcing jazz to compete with its own past, a
game it just can't win. The small number of young people who have
begun listening to jazz in the last few years are more likely to spend their
dollars on acknowledged classics by Miles and Coltrane and Thelonious
Monk than they are to gamble on someone new.

But who can blame them? Don't Mozart, Beethoven, and Bach outsell John Adams, Christopher Rouse, and Aaron Jay Kernis? This particular dilemma is one that any art form durable enough to have accumulated a surplus of masterpieces has to face sooner or later. What
makes facing it especially difficult for jazz right now, however, is that
the recent Ken Burns documentary series, although it resulted in
increased public appreciation for jazz, as many hoped it would, aggravated the problem by mythologizing the music's past at the expense of
its present. (Or maybe I mean anthologizing the jazz past: The last
time I looked, thirteen of *Billboard*'s twenty-five top-selling jazz CDs
were reissues tied to the Burns series.) As for the rest of it—the dwindling overall numbers for jazz, its aging demographics, its inability to
compete with pop in the marketplace—I have no ready answers here or
in any of what follows, except to point out that jazz fans have to stop
trying to have it both ways: They (rightly) speak of jazz as an incredibly
sophisticated form of modern music requiring from its listeners an

intellectual as well as emotional commitment, then in the next breath question why the audience for jazz is so small. I say they've unwittingly supplied their own answer.

I also find it significant (not merely amusing or ironic) that the only style of jazz to become a youthful fetish in the last few years has been one that almost nobody in the jazz establishment likes—latter-day free improvisation at its most fevered and squalling. In a roundabout way, this raises the (inexhaustible) subject of Wynton Marsalis, who, despite his scorn for free jazz along with many other revolutionary winds of the 1960s, seems to me very much a child of that decade in his pedagogy and rhetoric. In the 1960s, it was accepted as a given that improvisation without boundaries was a cry for other sorts of freedom, an assertion of black autonomy. For Marsalis, the equation is slightly different: Jazz remains expressive of black consciousness, but its root feeling is one of bourgeois savoir faire. Marsalis's agenda in his own music, and in his programming for Lincoln Center, seems to be to allow Americans of all races to take pride in black achievement without having to endure the demagoguery and the twenty-minute saxophone spasms of an Archie Shepp. This isn't necessarily a bad thing, but what's missing is the illusion jazz once offered of providing young whites with a way into black culture at its most esoteric and oppositional. Rap now fills that role, and except for the youthful fringe devoted to free jazz, jazz has relinquished an audience it once took for granted.

(A necessary aside: If I often seem to be debating Marsalis and his associate Stanley Crouch, even in pieces where they figure only tangentially, be advised it's nothing personal. Stanley is a friend, and Marsalis has been unfailingly gracious to me on the few occasions we've spoken. My readiness to argue with these men should be taken as a sign of my esteem for them.)

AS A SEGUE BETWEEN THE SECTIONS ON JAZZ AND POP, I'VE INCLUDED TWO travel pieces. The first is an example of a type of writing about jazz that I'd like to see more of, even if I have to do it myself—a piece on an overseas jazz festival that goes beyond the usual account of who played well and who played badly to say something about what different audiences bring to music. And the piece on Santa Cruz is here because it matches many of my recent pieces on music in theme and mood, and is the only article in which I've had much to say about recent pop. At this point in my life, my relationship to pop is like that of the narrator in Theodore Roethke's "Elegy for Jane" to the young woman thrown by a horse: neither father nor lover, with no rights in the matter. (I don't have a kid to keep me up to date, and I don't have the time or inclination to make the effort myself.) The frustrating thing about popular culture is that there's so much of it: It now has the capacity to make you feel as guilty as you once felt for not being able to tell Chopin from Liszt or not having finished *War and Peace*. Friends think I'm joking when I say that I once thought Britney Spears was a porn star and Daisy Fuentes one of those female Third World novelists I really ought to try reading. Santa Cruz is where I play catch-up, during my August vacations there, but it no longer bothers me that I'll probably never catch up completely.

The other night on *The Simpsons*, Bart and a few of his buddies formed a boy band called Party Posse. Getting ready to perform at their school assembly, they accuse Principal Skinner of trying to suppress their music. "Nonsense," he replies. "I'm a fan of your innocuous brand of pop music." "Screw you, man," Bart sneers. "We're gonna do our music anyway." That's right on the money. Since the 1950s, pop music has divided its stars into good kids and bad kids. These days, even the good kids try their best to act like hoodlums and hookers. But the genuine bad boys—Eminem, Kid Rock, Jay-Z, et cetera—strike me as far more juvenile than Britney and 'N Sync. I have adult responsibilities and adult concerns, and I don't hear them addressed in much of today's pop music.

To my great surprise, I do hear them addressed in many of the songs I identified with as a kid. An encoded message in some of the most urgent pop hits of the chaste 1950s and early 1960s was that there's nothing sadder than teenage sweethearts living with their parents and having to spend their nights apart. As I write, my wife and I have been sleeping apart for what feels like forever but has really been only ten days—she in Florida at her dying mother's bedside, I at home with my mother as she recovers from a stroke. I catch meanings I never heard before in those old songs, and it practically goes without saying that these are meanings neither their performers nor composers ever intended. Pop begs you to put yourself into it; this is what gives pop its power, and what these pieces on older pop are finally about.

Only two of the pieces in "Undercover" require explanation. My piece on Bob Dylan was written during the thick of the impeachment crisis, several thoughts on which wound up in my original manuscript. Faced with a three-month lead time, my editors at *The Atlantic Monthly* and I thought it best to excise these comments for fear of appearing to be behind the news instead of on top of it. I've restored them here, because they once again seemed relevant in light of Republican trickery in the 2000 presidential election. (Those parents who worried so publicly about how to explain to their kids Bill Clinton's predilection for oral sex now ought to be worrying how to explain the actions of a man who pledged to restore honor and integrity to the Oval Office, then bent every rule to get there. Am I bothered by Clinton's pardons of Marc Rich and Carlos Vignali? Yes, but not as bothered as I am by George W. Bush's appointment of John Ashcroft — or, for that matter, Antonin Scalia's appointment of George W. Bush.) The piece on Dion DiMucci was assigned by Robert Gottlieb at *The New Yorker* but wound up running in *The Village Voice* Rock & Roll Quarterly. Pauline Kael and Doug Simmons assured me the rejected manuscript was salvageable, and R. J. Smith read through it and found a logical ending I might never have spotted. It seemed a logical place to end this book, too.

MY LIST OF PEOPLE TO THANK BEGINS WITH BILL WHITWORTH, WHO BROUGHT me to *The Atlantic Monthly* in 1984, and whose notion of journalistic ethics extends to treating writers fairly. Every writer should be lucky enough to work with Bill at least once; I had the privilege of working with him for fifteen years. Thanks also to the magazine's other editors and fact-checkers, including Corby Kummer, Cullen Murphy, Barbara Walraff, Amy Meeker, Avril Cornell, Jack Beatty, Martha Spaulding, Jessica Murphy, Joshua Friedman, and Daniel Smith. And my gratitude to Michael Kelly, Bill's successor, for realizing that we thought of ourselves not just as colleagues but as a family, and for so self-effacingly making himself a part of it.

For their able work on these pieces, I also give thanks to Fletcher Roberts, John Rockwell, and Ann Kolson of *The New York Times*, David Remnick, Charles Michener, William Cohen, Gita Daneshjoo, and Nandi Rodrigo of *The New Yorker*, Fred Kaplan of *Fi*, Avery Rome of *The Philadelphia Inquirer*, Chuck Eddy and Gary Giddins of *The Village*

Voice, Mark Smirnoff of *The Oxford American*, Ken Richardson of *Stereo Review's Sound & Vision*, Lee Mergner and Mike Joyce of *JazzTimes*, and Peter Keepnews of Verve Records. Karen Bennett, Henry Braun, Robert Buttel, Beth Case, Bill Crow, Bob Dickie, Harris Eisenstadt, Nathaniel Friedman, Sydney Goldstein, Robert Gottlieb, Pauline Kael, Bryan Koniarz, Allen Lowe, Milo Miles, Dan Miller, Leslie Saunders, David Schiff, John F. Szwed, Quincy Troupe, Spencer Weston, Ben Young, and the gang at Philadelphia Record Exchange assisted in the preparation of these pieces, often without realizing it. And I owe more than I find it easy to express here to my editor Andrea Schulz, my agent Mark Kelley, my mother Dorothy Davis, my father-in-law Irving Gross, and Terry Gross—my wife, my moral center, my heart.

FRANCIS DAVIS
Philadelphia
March 2001

part one

VOICES

Swing and Sensibility

When anyone asks did I see Sinatra, I answer yes: I saw him in Philadelphia in 1991, on his "Diamond Jubilee" tour (given that he joined Harry James in 1939 and left Tommy Dorsey to go out on his own in 1942, what fiftieth anniversary he was celebrating was vague). Really, though, all I saw from my seat in the press box in the Spectrum—a basketball arena suitable for the inflated theatrics of a Garth Brooks or Bruce Springsteen, but all wrong for a self-professed "saloon singer" a month away from his seventy-sixth birthday—was a tuxedoed snowcap who looked a little bit like Casey Stengel and occasionally sounded like him, too. I wound up watching Sinatra on a color monitor suspended from the scoreboard, feeling no closer to him than if I were at home, watching him on video. What I most noticed were his hands—translucent, veined, and, to judge from his weak grip on the microphone, arthritic—and the poor fit of his Roman-senator toupee, which was absurdly iridescent under the harsh lights.

Almost forty years before, on his first collaboration with the arranger Nelson Riddle, in 1953, when Sinatra sang of having the world on a string, he might as well have really had it dangling. He spent the next fifteen or so years taking songs off the market. Who wanted to hear anyone else do "Angel Eyes" or "I've Got You Under My Skin"? His interpretations were unquestionably definitive. During these years, with assistance from Riddle, Gordon Jenkins, and Billy May, among other arrangers, Sinatra originated what is generally defined as the concept album,

3

though in his case I prefer to think of it as the LP of sensibility. Many performers, including Sinatra, had released collections of songs that were related in some way as far back as the 1940s, before the long-playing album was even invented. Sinatra's innovation, on a series of albums initiated by *Songs for Young Lovers*, was to make a concept out of mood. Unlike Ella Fitzgerald, whose albums for Verve in the late 1950s combined with Sinatra's for Capitol to define an adult market for pop standards at a time when teenagers were beginning to dominate the singles charts, Sinatra never recorded composer songbooks—he didn't share billing. The unifying theme of his classic albums was either that he was feeling dreamy and sad (as on *In the Wee Small Hours* and *Only the Lonely*) or that he was feeling too marvelous for words (as on *Come Dance with Me* and *Songs for Swingin' Lovers*). Eventually he himself became the concept; by 1964, when he recorded *Frank Sinatra Sings Days of Wine and Roses, Moon River, and Other Academy Award Winners*, the selling point wasn't that all of the songs were Oscar winners but that Sinatra had deigned to perform them.

Who remembers now—or cared then—that "It Was a Very Good Year" was first recorded by the Kingston Trio, in 1961, four years before Sinatra? In terms of what we were invited to read into them, the numbers with which Sinatra became most associated were like chapters in an ongoing autobiography. A large part of his appeal, like that of any iconic performer, was in permitting his male fans, in particular, to believe that his life and theirs were inextricably linked. This was true not only for men of Sinatra's own generation, but for many of their sons—baby boomers who, as they grew older, found themselves identifying more with their fathers than with their own contemporaries. In his liner essay for the four-disc *Frank Sinatra: The Reprise Collection*, the novelist William Kennedy, who describes himself as the "Methuselah" of his "set" of Sinatra admirers, writes of watching Sinatra exit the stage: "He fades down the stairs and out, and you follow him with your eyes because he is carrying the sound of your youth, the songs of your middle age. And then you think, the song is you, pal, the song is you."

Sinatra apparently brings out the Hemingway in Kennedy:

In the 1950's there came *In the Wee Small Hours*, which conditioned your life, especially with a young woman with lush blonde hair who used to put the record down and pray to Frank for a lover. . . . [B]ut it remained for another album, *Swing Easy*, to teach you how to play a record twelve times in one night, which was merely a warm-up for 1983, when you listened to "New York, New York" for the first time seriously and then played it sixty times until 5 A.M., also calling your friends in New York and San Juan and Aspen and permitting them to stop sleeping and get out of bed and listen along.

The author of *Ironweed* tells us that when he listened to Sinatra uninterruptedly for too long a time, his wife, "a tepid Sinatra fan" at the start of their marriage, would fix him with a stare and cry "Overdose." Where is she when he starts speaking about himself in the second person?

An example of the extremes to which younger writers can go in their idolatry of Sinatra is Bill Zehme's recent *The Way You Wear Your Hat: Frank Sinatra and the Lost Art of Livin'*, a Little Red Book for middle-aged men that a reviewer for *The New York Times* beat me to the punch in renaming *The Sayings of Chairman Frank*. Zehme, a senior writer for *Esquire* whose dust-jacket author's bio informs us that "Men had gone soft and needed help, needed a Leader, needed Frank Sinatra," passes along Sinatra's wisdom on matters ranging from picking the right barber ("When you leave the shop and no one hands you a hat, you're okay") to what never to do on a date ("Yawn").

I tell ya, chum, it's time to come blow your horn. One reason so many men turn to Sinatra for help in weathering their midlife crises might be that he weathered his so gracefully. Despite early fame as the best of the "boy" singers of the early 1940s, and also as the cutest in the eyes of that era's hysterical teenage girls, Sinatra didn't hit his stride as a singer or actor until the early 1950s, when he was pushing forty and starting to lose his hair. Part of the Sinatra legend is that he was destined for oblivion until he switched labels, from Columbia to Capitol, in 1953. But Sinatra wasn't really washed-up; he was just no longer a craze. His recording of "Mam'selle," a keepsake from the movie *The Razor's Edge* that reached the top of *Billboard*'s chart in 1947, would be his last No. 1 single until "Learnin' the Blues," in 1955. But he put a whopping forty-three songs on the Top 40 between "Mam'selle" and the expiration of his Columbia contract, including nine in the Top 10. These were mostly covers of other singers' hits, including Nat Cole's "Nature Boy" and the Weavers' "Goodnight, Irene," or novelty tunes, such as "One Finger Melody" and "Don't Cry, Joe (Let Her Go, Let Her Go, Let Her Go)," for which

Sinatra hardly bothered to conceal his contempt. But also among his chart entries in these years were "Almost Like Being in Love," "What'll I Do?," "But Beautiful," "I've Got a Crush on You," and the haunted "I'm a Fool to Want You"—which, legend has it, Sinatra, still licking his wounds after being dumped by Ava Gardner, completed in one take before fleeing into the night. Sinatra's dip in popularity, his romantic misadventures, his quick temper, and the rumors that began to surface about his mob connections—all the things that supposedly put his career in jeopardy—ultimately worked to his advantage. They shifted his appeal from women to men, giving him credibility as the guy on the next barstool, a singing Bogart, a graduate of the School of Hard Knocks. At least two generations of American men came to love him not just for his singing but for having met middle age head-on, with a combination of style and swagger they hoped might also do the trick for them. He was them with talent and the privilege it can buy.

F. SCOTT FITZGERALD TO THE CONTRARY, AMERICAN LIFE IS SWIMMING WITH second acts, the longest of them interminable. Performers who die young, in full possession of their gifts, are remembered mostly for dying. Those who survive to old age—as Sinatra somehow did despite those unfiltered Camels and sips of Jack Daniels that were never just bits of stage business—suffer a perhaps greater indignity: They become living reminders of their audience's mortality. In the final gasp of his career, Sinatra had the aura of a fallen god. If age could so humble him, what hope was there for the rest of us? Maybe it was time for us not just to put our dreams away for another day (as he advised in one of his earliest hits) but to put them away for good.

Writing about Sinatra in 1965—the year he turned fifty and introduced "The September of My Years," the first of several songs he recorded on the subject of growing older—Gay Talese marveled that "[h]e is a piece of our past, but only we have aged, he hasn't." The Sinatra I saw inspired no such poetic license. He was on stage about ninety minutes that night in Philadelphia—a good night's work for anyone. But he spent a good deal of that time resting on a stool while being serenaded with a medley of his greatest hits by the unctuous Steve Lawrence and Eydie Gorme (the image that popped to mind was one from the 1990 movie *Misery*, of a psychotic Kathy Bates reading to the novelist played by James Caan from his own work, after breaking his legs to make sure he wouldn't be going anywhere). The most alarming sign of his diminished capacity was the TelePrompTer he apparently needed to recall lyrics he'd been singing from the heart for decades.

Am I making too much of Sinatra's electronic crib sheet? A friend who saw him on the same tour points out that photographs of Sinatra in the recording studio in the 1950s and 1960s show him looking at scores, even though he was unable to read music. I doubt that this proves that Sinatra never bothered to memorize lyrics. I see it as evidence of his intuitive musicianship, his way of keeping an eye open for dynamic markings and the vertical movement of notes. Regardless of his arranger or conductor, or who was listed as producer, Sinatra was the arbiter of how the final take should sound. Jimmy Van Heusen and Sammy Cahn's "Only the Lonely" is familiar as the title track of a 1958 album that Sinatra often named as one of his personal favorites. On the three-disc *Frank Sinatra/The Capitol Years* this art song disguised as a ballad—which Sinatra seems never to have performed in concert, presumably because of the difficulty that certain of its intervals would have presented to a road-show orchestra—begins with Sinatra's spoken instructions, and he could be Martin Scorsese telling his cinematographer what he wants in the next shot. "The whole orchestra should be fairly light from the beginning of the vocal," Sinatra says, presumably to the violinist and concertmaster Felix Slatkin. "From bar eleven . . . to the beginning of the crescendo."

One gathers that Sinatra's studio associates followed his orders not because he was a star and a mobbed-up tough guy but because his suggestions invariably worked like a charm. (He is said to have given Gordon Jenkins the idea for the out-of-the-mist solo French horn that precedes the full orchestra on their 1957 recording of Leonard Bernstein's "Lonely Town.") By 1993, when he began to record the material for *Duets* and *Duets II* (dreadful albums that proved to be his all-time best sellers, and also his recording swan song), he wasn't even in the studio at the same time as his duet partners, an assembly of rock-and-pop-glitterati many of whom Sinatra had probably never even heard of. He simply laid down his vocals, then (in effect) told his producers to send in the clowns. (The worst offender was the singer Bono, from the ponderous Irish band U2, whose wormy falsetto on "I've Got You Under My Skin" would have been better suited to a dramatic reading of a Clive Barker novel than to a lyric by Cole Porter.)

The night I saw Sinatra, it took all of his concentration just to get the words right. He seemed never to glance at the prompter, but there were times when he probably should have. He was a brilliant ad-libber to the end: On "Mack the Knife," as on the 1984 recording, his Macheath spent not "just like a sailor" but like a "pimp," which is probably closer to what Bertolt Brecht had in mind than anyone else has come up with. But on "Luck Be a Lady," instead of asking Lady Luck not to "blow on some other guy's dice," he twice asked her not to "spit."

Sinatra's failing memory, rumored to be a symptom of Alzheimer's and to be compounded by failing eyesight, was hardly the only problem on his final tours. The sheer size of the venues he played (the 18,000-seater in Philadelphia where I saw him was among the smallest) precluded the intimacy he needed to put across his ballads. His claim to be a glorified saloon singer was a showman's conceit; he was a big-band singer who had outlived his era's ballrooms, movie palaces, and music fairs. As a singer whose pipes gave out on him before his desire to perform did, he might have found his natural habitat in cabaret—if only he could have followed the example of many of the singers he most admired, including Mabel Mercer and Sylvia Syms, and fallen back on his phrasing, limiting his accompaniment to his longtime pianist Bill Miller. But what room could have accommodated the throngs who would have wanted to hear him, no matter how many sets a night he pushed himself to perform?

IN HIS PRIME, SINATRA WROTE THE BOOK ON PHRASING. NO POPULAR SINGER ever knew better the combined value of precise diction and conversational delivery, and no other has ever been more aware that the beat shouldn't necessarily fall where the rhyme does. (One of a lyricist's jobs is to make the words rhyme; one of a singer's is to deliver them in such a way that nobody much notices they do.) Sinatra may have been an intuitive musician, but he was an analytical singer. He knew that to inflect a word or a syllable that seems not to call for it can shift the rhythm and increase the sincerity of a lyric by making it more like speech; it also serves the purpose of lavishing attention on an especially attractive melodic phrase. If this sounds arcane, just listen to Sinatra sing "*Don't* change a hair for me" on his 1953 recording of "My Funny Valentine." Most singers stress "change" or "hair," passing up the opportunity to plumb the lowest, most unexpected, and loveliest note in

Richard Rodgers's melody. In Sinatra's case the usual stress would also have meant passing up an opportunity to show off his bottom range, which he tended to use sparingly but always to gorgeous effect.

The strings and horns on Sinatra's greatest Capitol and Reprise recordings weren't there for protective coloration, even though some of Sinatra's staunchest champions have questioned his pitch. I side with Henry Pleasants, who argued, in *The Great American Popular Singers* (1974), that because the trombonist Tommy Dorsey and the violinist Jascha Heifetz, both of whom Sinatra frequently cited as influences, played instruments of unfixed pitch, Sinatra emulated their "ambiguity of intonation," along with what he once referred to as the "flowing, unbroken quality" of their phrasing.

A taste for Heifetz would explain Sinatra's flair for *portamento*—the ease with which he glided from note to note without taking an audible breath. The tips on breath control that he picked up from watching Dorsey (it boils down, I think, to what wind players call "circular breathing," the trick of taking in air even while exhaling) enabled the young Sinatra to hold a note practically forever, as we hear him doing to climax "Ol' Man River," in the 1946 film biography of Jerome Kern, *Till the Clouds Roll By*. But I think Pleasants would say that the technique served a greater musical purpose. It allowed Sinatra to deliver lyrics in phrases longer and more irregular than the standard four or eight bars, thus liberating him from the sing-songy delivery of most of his generation's white pop singers. And it allowed him, while holding a note, to move it up or (more often) down the scale without disrupting the melodic flow.

This last trait would also help to explain why Sinatra was drawn to songs liberally spiked with chromatics, including Harold Arlen's "One for My Baby," though Sinatra may initially have been drawn to the message of barroom camaraderie in Johnny Mercer's lyrics. The several recordings of this tune that Sinatra made with just Bill Miller on piano (including one from 1993, to close *Duets*, on which Sinatra exploits his aged vulnerability to great interpretive effect) give a hint of the pleasures he might have offered toward the end of his life had he been able to perform in small rooms.

BUT INTIMACY WAS SOMETHING HE ALLOWED HIMSELF ONLY ON RECORDINGS. His legend demanded bigness. The night I heard him, a thirty-one piece orchestra conducted by Frank Jr. pushed the beat too hard on the uptempo numbers and forgot about it altogether on the ballads, generally forcing Sinatra to forego the seductive legato swing that had once been his trademark. To make matters worse, a few loudmouths in the cheaper seats up top, apparently mistaking the distant figure on stage for a jukebox, yelled out requests for "Summer Wind" whenever there was a quiet moment, even during the verse to "Luck Be a Lady." Growing more desperate as the evening wore on, and possibly sensing that this might be their last opportunity to hear Sinatra live, they attempted to bully him into singing their favorite of his songs. He scored points with me by *not* singing it: a bully who refused to be bullied.

Despite it all, Sinatra was occasionally Sinatra. The spotlights surrounding him with a four-leaf clover of shadow Sinatras, he cocked an elbow and lit a smoke and delivered an "Angel Eyes" that briefly transformed the packed-to-capacity arena into a half-empty tavern, and himself into a guy alone at the bar—his cigarette in the ashtray, along with his hopes. And at the end of "Luck Be a Lady," despite no longer being able to hold each of the song's final two syllables smoothly and without cheating (they came out *"TOOO-nayayayt"*), he was the ultimate high-roller, compulsively blowing on his dice and willing to leave his fate to chance.

Sinatra saved these numbers with a gift that never deserted him—his showmanship or what, taking a cue from something I heard Will Friedwald say on television the night Sinatra died, I am tempted to call his acting. Friedwald, the author of *The Song Is You*, a chatty and informative book on Sinatra's recordings, called Sinatra "the greatest American actor," adding that he gave his best performances in concert and on records, not necessarily in his movies.

The explanation usually given for Sinatra's spotty track record on screen is that he didn't take acting as seriously as he did singing. The way I see it, anyone capable of giving performances as nuanced and immensely watchable as Sinatra's in *From Here to Eternity*, *The Man with the Golden Arm*, *Some Came Running*, and *The Manchurian Candidate* has nothing to apologize for on balance. Hollywood misused him, first by remaining skeptical of his sex appeal despite the quakes he set off at the Brooklyn Paramount, and later by giving him carte blanche to run wild with his Rat Pack in vanity productions like *Robin and the Seven Hoods* and *Sergeants Three* (a remake of *Gunga Din* notable only for the preposterous sight of Dean Martin, Joey Bishop, and Sammy Davis, Jr. on horseback).

The young Sinatra was not conventionally handsome; with his looping forelock, hooked eyebrows, facial concaves, and oversized ears and Adam's apple, he looked like Hirschfeld's caricature of him, instead of the other way around. His visible ethnicity—though it would be no roadblock to movie stardom today, in the aftermath of Al Pacino, Robert De Niro, and Sylvester Stallone—worked against Sinatra at a time when Italy was an Axis power (and only a few years after *Life* magazine sought to assure its readers that Joe DiMaggio, a native Californian, "speaks English without an accent" and "never reeks of garlic"). So skinny that not even superpatriots questioned his 4-F, Sinatra spent the Second World War in uniform only on screen, where he always seemed to be on leave or having just been discharged (as if no one could imagine him hitting the beach at Iwo Jima). He was rarely the leading man; even his role as Maggio, sidekick to Montgomery Clift's Prewitt in *From Here to Eternity*, was a hung-over mutation of his roles as Gene Kelly's sidekick in *Anchors Aweigh* and *On the Town*.

By the mid-1950s, when he was no longer young or dreamy-looking enough to be cast as a singing male ingenue, neither he nor the directors of some of the light comedies he starred in ever seemed certain whether he was playing the character named in the script or Frank Sinatra. In *The Tender Trap* (1955), for example, he plays a Broadway agent stuck on his newest client, played by Debbie Reynolds. She lands a role in a new show in which her big number is Jimmy Van Heusen and Sammy Cahn's title song—not coincidentally a hit record by Sinatra that same year. At one of her rehearsals Sinatra tells her she's doing the song all wrong. He takes her to the piano and sings it himself, showing her how it might sound with a little bit of relaxed swing in place of her nervous syncopation. You expect the producers of Reynolds's show to show her the door and write a new one starring him. But nobody seems to notice Sinatra's great singing. We next see him leaning forward in his seat in the empty theater, swept away by Reynolds as she delivers "(Love Is) The Tender Trap" with only slightly more snap than she did before.

My favorites of Sinatra's star vehicles tend to be those in which his acting and singing are indivisible. *Young at Heart* (1954) is one of Sinatra's best pictures for the same reason that *Viva Las Vegas* is one of Elvis Presley's: As Ann Margaret was to Presley, Doris Day was to Sinatra—the female co-star who came closest to matching him in screen presence, singing ability, and androgynous erotic force. (Sinatra also has great chemistry with Ethel Barrymore, who plays Day's aunt, and with whom he flirts shamelessly.) *Young at Heart* is a remake of *Four Daughters*, the 1938 movie that made John Garfield a star. Sinatra inherits Garfield's role as a Gloomy Gus songwriter who turns up on the doorstep of a cheery, small-town family whose eligible daughters are all in love with another composer—a happier, better-adjusted fellow played by Gig Young.

For once, Sinatra's ethnicity goes unalluded to, though his being cast as an embittered loner, in a role originated by Garfield, who was Jewish, suggests that Hollywood once automatically saw what sociologists today call "difference" as chronic alienation or just a stubborn refusal to fit in. To make ends meet while he helps Young orchestrate his magnum opus, Sinatra takes a job singing and playing piano in a noisy local pub. In a virtual dramatization of his postwar skid he sings "Someone to Watch Over Me" beautifully—shiveringly—but almost to himself, amid the clatter of dinner dishes and the conversation of people doing a fine job of entertaining themselves. The only one paying any attention to him is Day, who realizes there's more to him than meets the eye. She's as transfixed by his interpretation of Ira Gershwin's lyric as if it were a mating call.

This was Sinatra's rite of passage as a leading man, in real life as well as in the movies. He may no longer have had bobbysoxers swooning in the aisles, but his turn opposite Day suggested that he was capable of turning grown-up women to mush with the bottomless emotion he conveyed in song. Acting was extra.

A QUESTION REPEATEDLY ASKED ON TV FOLLOWING SINATRA'S DEATH WAS whether he was different in private from the way he was in public. My guess would be that, for better or worse, he was no different at all. "Sinatra singing a hymn of loneliness could very well be the real Frank Sinatra," Jimmy Van Heusen and Sammy Cahn, who probably knew him better than anyone else, once wrote. Wouldn't it be nice to think so? From the very beginning the source of tension was between Sinatra's image and the slightly different story told by his voice. His initial appeal to teenage girls of the 1940s was comparable to that of Leonardo Di Caprio to pre-teen girls in our quicker, more jaded day. The young Sinatra came across as a boy who might try to sweet-talk a girl into going all the way, but wasn't going to be insistent—unlike the boys his fans knew in real life, most of whom were desperate not to march off to war still virgins. Indulgent parents perceived Sinatra as safe, and so did many of their daughters. Often what young girls want in a boy is another girl, and the girls who swooned to Sinatra pressed him to their hearts as a young man who was as sensitive and, on some level, as self-conscious as they were.

But listen today to Sinatra's recordings with Dorsey and you hear something else—something of which his female fans may have been subliminally aware as they pressed themselves in other places. You hear a singer whose control of every aspect of his delivery hints at other kinds of expertise, including sexual.

Sinatra's technique and almost literary insight into lyrics gave him greater staying power than any of his rivals singing with big bands. The other quality that separated him from them was the subtlety of his rhythm, which was superior to that of most of the Dorsey band's instrumental soloists and arrangers—even though swinging wasn't necessarily part of a band singer's job description.

IN THE LATE 1960S AND EARLY 1970S SINATRA RECORDED HIS OWN INTERPRE-tations of songs by Stevie Wonder, George Harrison, Paul Simon, and Jim Croce, among others, in a bid to stay current. He sounded absurd, and not just because the lyrics held no meaning for him. Whatever its virtues, rock 'n' roll doesn't swing, and Sinatra couldn't bring himself not to. Yet neither the implied condescension of these performances nor Sinatra's earlier antipathy toward rock and everything he took it to stand for ("the martial music of every sideburned delinquent on the face of the earth," he called it in 1957) has prevented today's middle-aged rockers from claiming him as a father figure, in what one could interpret as an attempt to make peace with their actual fathers.

During a televised salute to Sinatra on his eightieth birthday, in 1995, Bruce Springsteen told of first hearing Sinatra on a jukebox in New Jersey one night as Springsteen and his mother searched the taverns for his father. "It was a voice filled with bad attitude, life, beauty, excitement, a nasty sense of freedom, sex, and a sad knowledge of the ways of the world. Every song seemed to end with the same postscript: 'And if you don't like it, here's a punch in the kisser.'"

Springsteen wasn't hearing things; nor was Bono, who, in presenting Sinatra with a Grammy Legends award in 1994, waxed poetic: "Rock and roll people love Frank Sinatra because Frank Sinatra has got what we want—swagger and attitude." But this is something that fans project onto Sinatra's music based on what they know about him as a person. Sinatra singing a ballad could be courtly and compassionate, and much of what Bono and Springsteen, too, applaud as swagger in his uptempo performances was actually swing—the *je ne sais quoi* of jazz but a commodity foreign to most of today's rock and pop.

On an episode of A&E's *Biography* that was shown a few weeks after Sinatra's death, Camille Paglia said, "Sinatra belongs to a period where men were men and women were women." What seems more important is that he also "belonged" to the swing era, a period when pop and jazz were more or less the same thing. Sinatra considered himself a jazz singer, and I fear that the fewer Americans there are who know anything about jazz, the harder this aspect of his style is to grasp.

The jazz instrumentalist of whom Sinatra has always most reminded me is the tenor saxophonist Lester Young—perhaps the most innovative soloist to come along in jazz between Louis Armstrong and Charlie Parker. Young first announced his individuality by foregoing the rococo sound projection and slow vibrato favored by his day's reigning tenor star, Coleman Hawkins, in favor of a leaner, more quicksilver tone with almost no vibrato. Hawkins was to Young, who in the 1930s used his bottom register only strategically, as Bing Crosby was to Sinatra, who may have been the first pop baritone not to try to make his voice sound deeper. Young's most vital contribution to jazz, however, was the slipperiness of his rhythm—an area in which Sinatra also excelled. Sinatra often swung by postponing or displacing the beat rather than by emphasizing it. On records when we hear Sinatra snapping his fingers, it's usually to acknowledge that he and the beat are a few degrees apart, though destined for an eventual rendezvous.

Young, like many jazz greats, adored Sinatra; legend has him sitting in his hotel room across the street from Birdland, alcoholic and near death, playing Sinatra records over and over, perhaps recognizing something of himself in them. Miles Davis also loved Sinatra, and his LP collaborations with the arranger Gil Evans, beginning with *Miles Ahead* (1957), may have been inspired by Sinatra's with Riddle (like Evans, Riddle was a genius at isolating fragments of melody and highlighting specific instruments, especially woodwinds). One of Sinatra and Riddle's models, I think, was the great Count Basie Orchestra of the mid-1950s—a powerhouse noted for its biting brass. References to Basie, both musical and lyrical, abound on Sinatra's Capitol recordings (on "Come Dance with Me," for example, Sinatra sings "Hey there, Cutes, put on your Basie boots"), and it seems like more than coincidence that the two men experienced career renewals around the same time. One of my unsubstantiated beliefs is that Sinatra's chief goal in forming his own label in 1959 was to sign Basie and be able to record with him whenever he desired.

A few nights after Sinatra's death, Nick at Nite rebroadcast a grainy black-and-white film of a 1965 St. Louis benefit concert featuring Sinatra and Basie on the same bill with Dean Martin and Sammy Davis, Jr. The show was promoted as a Rat Pack spectacular, and anybody who tuned in hoping to see the three singers getting juiced together and cracking wise about it would not have been disappointed. But Sinatra is all business during his own uptempo set with Basie, even while being heckled from the wings by Davis and Martin, both of whom are armed with hand mikes. Martin attempts to throw off Sinatra's timing by singing along with him on "Please Be Kind." At one point Martin, after correctly observing a rest, moos the title phrase dead on the beat, a split second ahead of Sinatra. "You got a beat like a cop," Sinatra deadpans, while the Basie band soars behind him. And it's true: Compared with Sinatra, most pop singers of his day were flatfoots.

SINATRA'S DEATH IN THE WEE SMALL HOURS OF THE MORNING ON MAY 15, 1998, banished *Godzilla*, Suharto, Kenneth Starr, and the final episode of *Seinfeld* to the inside pages of the daily tabloids for a few days. CNN and MSNBC gave the event round-the-clock coverage, the way they do with breaking stories of national importance, though this was a story in which there could be no sudden developments. On "The House I Live In," Sinatra sang "all races and religions, that's America to me." All weekend long we were told that *he* was America by a parade of celebrities, music critics, and social commentators. Pete Hamill likened the elderly Sinatra to a "magnificent ruin." But ruins inspire awe not just because they were there long before us but because they will be there long after we are gone. The most astute comment I heard regarding Sinatra's immortality came from a used-record store owner in South Philadelphia (a Sinatra stronghold) who told me his phone had been ringing all day with people asking if their Sinatra albums had increased in value on account of his death. The answer was no: "Whether he went to heaven or hell, he didn't take his records with him." Sinatra's recordings with Dorsey may evoke sweet memories of the 1940s for people who remember the decade first-hand, but those Capitol albums he made as he neared middle age belong to no one's youth, including Sinatra's. They are timeless.

Sinatra was all over television and radio the weekend following his death. American Movie Classics and Turner Classic Movies each showed an entire day of his movies, and my local PBS affiliate broadcast two of his concerts from the 1980s. As I switched from channel to channel, from movies to concerts to news and back again at random, there he was as a young sailor singing "I Fall in Love Too Easily" in *Anchors Aweigh*; there he was on television in 1951, with a poor excuse for a mustache (you weren't sure at first if he was Sinatra and apparently neither was he); there he was as an old man belching "My Way," his pitch so bad and his diction so careless that you wondered if he was going deaf.

All sorts of things turned up. On Sunday TMC showed a 1943 Warner Bros. cartoon called "The Swooner Crooner," in which Porky Pig, to assist the war effort, starts an egg farm. His only problem is a singing rooster who distracts the hens from laying eggs. The rooster is named "Frankie," but he sounds more like Russ Columbo, the most flatulent of the Bing Crosby–influenced baritones. Through middle age Sinatra was inimitable. Not so the blustering old man who, already a self-parody, presented impressionists like Joe Piscopo and the late Phil Hartman such an easy target—the Sinatra whose anthem became "My Way," a tuneless bolero of self-seduction, less a song than an epitaph inscribed on the tombstone he dragged on stage with him toward the end.

This Sinatra was the one I saw most often on television in the days after he died, and before the weekend was over, I wanted to grab a shovel and bury him myself. I hope this doesn't sound like I resented Sinatra for getting old, or for not calling it quits when he probably should have. It's just that I fear this is the only Sinatra younger people know, and therefore the Sinatra who will live the longest in our national memory. I don't want to remember him singing "My Way," a lyric that spoke to something crude and self-delusional in contemporary American life and in Sinatra himself. It's practically a musicalization of Las Vegas, the alternative universe Sinatra created for himself in the desert when rock and roll proved not to be a passing craze. Besides, if he always did it his way, why did he record songs for which he is said to have had little respect, like "My Way" and "Strangers in the Night"? Sinatra's evolution from Roosevelt liberal to Reagan conservative is chalked up by some people to his having been shunned by JFK after the president's advisors decided that a celebrity with ties to organized crime was more trouble than he was worth. Isn't it more likely that having hits with songs he knew to be second-rate combined with rock 'n' roll to undermine Sinatra's faith in the public's taste, fostering in him a bilious cynicism that played as great a role as age in his decline? My notes, from the night I saw him, say of "My Way" that he "ate it up and spit it out," which is about all he or any-one could have done with those crude lyrics. But except for "Angel Eyes," this was how Sinatra sang everything that night.

I PREFER TO REMEMBER THE SINATRA WHO SANG ANY NUMBER OF HYMNS TO romantic love as absolute as any Christian prayer, beginning (when you think about it) with his 1939 recording of "All or Nothing at All" with Harry James. Even more I prefer to remember the Sinatra I saw with Count Basie on Nick at Nite. That Sinatra was irresistible, not just for his singing but for the cocksure way he moved his shoulders in time with the rhythm section and even for the way he looked in what I have come to think of as his Yves Montand period—fifty years old and no longer pretty, but the perfect embodiment of a uniquely American type, the swinger existentialist, right down to the cigarette and booze and the slight indention in his right cheek (said to be from the forceps that were used to deliver him) that made him ruggedly handsome as his face started to crease.

In 1965, the same year that Sinatra and Basie did the St. Louis bene-fit concert that was rebroadcast on Nick at Nite, they also performed together at the Newport Jazz Festival. Among those in attendance in a crowd of perhaps 15,000 was the photographer Burt Goldblatt, who years later wrote about the event in his book *Newport Jazz Festival: The Illustrated History*:

> Looking around me I saw hardened booking agents, artists and repertoire men, record-company presidents, musicians, and people who had been there alongside me for years, listening quietly in awe. He sounded great. As good as he ever sounded on record. Better, as a matter of fact. All the magic was still there, and he glided through his program of twenty songs.

Sinatra left the stage by helicopter, already airborne as the applause for him crescendoed:

The audience responded with a genuine outpouring of warmth in return. His impeccable phrasing, his way with a lyric—that night he had it all— and if he had the greatest public-relations firm working out a dramatic departure, they couldn't have come up with a more effective answer than that slowly ascending helicopter blinking its lights good-bye. When the crowd finally drifted off, something seemed to be missing that night. I think it was the opportunity to tell him in person how great he had sounded to us all.

I wasn't there to see it, but this is the Sinatra I want to remember.

The Atlantic Monthly, September 1998

The Great Hoagy

oagy Carmichael, the composer of "Star Dust," "Skylark," "Georgia on My Mind," "Heart and Soul," and "Two Sleepy People," among dozens of imperishable songs, was born in Bloomington, Indiana, on November 22, 1899—a hundred years ago tomorrow. If his centennial passes by relatively unnoticed, as I fear it might, the only good explanation will be that there have already been so many centennial celebrations this year, beginning with Duke Ellington's and Ernest Hemingway's, that a predictable element of fatigue has set in. Carmichael wasn't the greatest of the songwriters born around the turn of the century, nor was he the most prolific—not with such contemporaries as George Gershwin, Richard Rodgers, and Harold Arlen. But Carmichael was arguably the one whose melodies best captured the moods of this country from the 1920s to the 1940s, a time of enormous change in America.

"Star Dust," Carmichael's most famous song, which he first recorded as an instrumental in 1927 and to which Mitchell Parish added lyrics four years later, has endured for so many generations (I first heard it done by Billy Ward and the Dominoes, on the near-operatic doo wop version they recorded in 1957) that its specificity to its own time is often overlooked. It is to popular song what *The Great Gatsby* is to the novel, a distillation of romantic wanderlust that seems at once quintessentially American and specifically Midwestern. Quite apart from Parish's lyrics, Carmichael's melody is as evocative of sophistication paid for with the loss of innocence as the Fitzgerald character Nick Carraway's memories of the chatter of frozen breath on Chicago train station platforms and small towns whose houses were identified by the names of the families who lived in them for generations.

Carmichael was a product of his time, which, given the accelerated pace of American life after the First World War, often meant being slightly ahead of it. Discussion of his music inevitably seems to begin with mention of the inspiration he found in jazz in the early 1920s; the melody of "Star Dust," in particular, is often said—and quite correctly—to be an idealization of a typical solo by Bix Beiderbecke, the doomed, Iowa-born cornetist who was his era's James Dean and the first great white jazz musician. Carmichael never made a secret of his admiration for Beiderbecke, who was his best friend and also his idol; *The Stardust Road*, the first of Carmichael's two autobiographies, begins with his being told of Beiderbecke's death in 1931, and he named his first son Hoagy Bix.

Contrary to popular wisdom, however, Carmichael wasn't the only songwriter of the 1920s whose melodies captured something of Beiderbecke's impromptu lyricism; the melody of Cole Porter's "Looking at You," from 1929, is more or less a paraphrase of Beiderbecke's famous solo on his 1927 recording of "Singin' the Blues" with the saxophonist Frankie Trumbauer. Rather, it was Carmichael's understanding of the rhythms of black jazz that put him in front of the pack; in 1924, the year that Gershwin exoticized jazz for concert audiences with *Rhapsody in Blue* (a masterpiece, but also a pastiche), the Wolverines recorded Carmichael's "Riverboat Shuffle," an example of "hot" jazz at its most genuine and freewheeling ("Freewheeling" was its original title, in fact). Three years later, Jerome Kern's *Show Boat* included "Can't Help Lovin' That Man of Mine," a song notable for reintroducing Broadway to the cakewalk, a black dance style going back to the turn of the century; Carmichael was already writing popular songs that were rhythmically right up to the minute, including "Star Dust."

Carmichael was unlike other songwriters of his generation in also being famous as a performer (Ellington and Gershwin each being sui generis). If only in this sense he had more in common with such contemporary singer-songwriters as Randy Newman and Tom Waits than with Porter or Rodgers, who, whatever name recognition they enjoyed, were faceless craftsmen who did their work behind the scenes. "Hoagy" was a diminutive of Hoagland, and this given name hints at something else different about Carmichael. In common with only Ellington and

Porter, Carmichael wasn't Jewish. For someone like Irving Berlin, a first-generation American of Eastern European extraction and a New Yorker, Broadway was a staging ground for assimilation. Unlike Porter (a fellow Indianan), Carmichael seems to have had little interest in writing for the theater, apart from one unsuccessful stab at Broadway in 1940 — a collaboration with the lyricist Johnny Mercer called *Walk with Music*. Growing up in Bloomington and Indianapolis, he was drawn instead to recordings, radio, and film — the mass media that brought an emerging popular culture into every living room affluent enough to afford electricity and every hamlet large enough to accommodate a movie house. The son of a woman who played piano for silent films, he was especially drawn to the movies, eventually becoming a staff songwriter at Paramount in the late 1930s.

For a period beginning in the 1940s, Carmichael also became a familiar face on screen, and his movie appearances became more than incidental to his career as a songwriter. He had made his film debut in 1937, leading Cary Grant and Constance Bennett in a tipsy singalong in *Topper*, but this was essentially a cameo. Of the films in which he actually played a role, Carmichael always named as his favorite *Young Man with a Horn*, perhaps because his role as a journeyman pianist and nursemaid to the self-destructive trumpeter played by Kirk Douglas allowed him to act out his youthful fantasy of hitting the road with Beiderbecke. But the movie that established Carmichael as a reliable character type — a chain-smoking, piano-playing citizen of the barroom who's seen it all but isn't tattling — was *To Have and Have Not* (1943), which was also the film in which Lauren Bacall introduced Carmichael and Johnny Mercer's "How Little We Know," a nifty little number with special appeal to anyone who enjoys a good mystery as much as a pretty melody.

FOR FILM BUFFS THE QUESTIONS SURROUNDING *TO HAVE AND HAVE NOT* HAVE always been whether Howard Hawks really bet Ernest Hemingway he could make an enjoyable film out of Hemingway's worst novel (*Across the River and Into the Trees* was still a few years off) and whether Bacall's singing voice was dubbed by the teenaged Andy Williams (unlikely, given that the grown-up Williams has never sounded so butch).

For Carmichael fans, "How Little We Know" is a source of greater fascination, beginning with the question of which time signature it's in —

though a waltz in the movie, it was published in four-quarter time and recorded that way by Benny Goodman in 1945 (somebody probably worried that the era's jitterbugs would sneer at a waltz). There is also the matter of the alternate lyric to the bridge that Carmichael fetchingly sings to Bacall several scenes earlier, in his role as Cricket—the droopy-lidded but watchful piano player in Frenchy's, the Martinique cafe in which *To Have and Have Not*'s various romantic and political intrigues unfold.

Bacall is lingering over her morning coffee, after presumably having spent her first night with Humphrey Bogart, and Carmichael is musing at the piano, playing a fast waltz that Ms. Bacall says is pretty and asks what it's called. It doesn't have a name yet, Carmichael tells her, because he's unhappy with the lyrics. Then—smiling after each line and lowering his eyes without averting them, as if emulating Bacall's flirtatious manner around Bogart—Carmichael sings her all he's been able to come up with so far:

> *I run to the telephone,*
> *Whenever it rings.*
> *I can't be alone.*
> *It's one of those things.*
> *I tell a star*
> *My little woe*
> *Hang around at a bar,*
> *'Til it's ready to close.*

"And so it goes," he says. "And that's about as far as it goes."

These lyrics are exquisite, but whose are they? They're more wistful than Johnny Mercer's published lyrics—quasi-philosophical ones about "an April breeze" and "stars in the trees" that Bacall sings not twenty minutes later. And the climactic near-rhyme of "woe" and "close" seems awfully uncharacteristic of Mercer.

Could they be Carmichael's? He supplied lyrics to several of his own tunes, including "Hong Kong Blues," the other song he performs in *To Have and Have Not*. According to his son, Carmichael always had suggestions for the lyricists he worked with. "It didn't matter if it was someone as good as Johnny Mercer or Frank Loesser," says Hoagy Bix, a former stockbroker and jazz drummer who now administers his father's song catalog. "Dad was usually able to convince them, by use of whatever tactics, that he had a better idea."

Though "How Little We Know" never caught on, Carmichael did, stealing nearly every scene he's in with a matchstick dangling from his mouth (an actorly bit of business comparable to Bogart's trick of constantly hitching up his trousers). Because of his exposure on recordings and live radio, by the time audiences saw Carmichael in *To Have and Have Not*, they were already familiar with his uninflected and somewhat nasal twang. But *To Have and Have Not* put a face to that voice, establishing Carmichael as the first of a new breed—a multimedia, songwriting star.

In the late 1950s, rock 'n' roll put an end to the demand for new songs by Carmichael, even though pop performers continued to have hits with his older songs well into the next decade. (In addition to Ward's "Star Dust," there was Ray Charles's definitive "Georgia on My Mind," the Cleftones' "Heart and Soul," Aretha Franklin's "Skylark," and Bobby Darin's "Up a Lazy River.") By that point, Carmichael had become as well known as an actor as he was as a songwriter. With the movie *Timberjack* (1955) and the TV series *Laramie* (1959), Hollywood even figured out a way to remove him from the piano bench and put him in a saddle, without risking incredulity. (Try to imagine Irving Berlin on horseback. Or Cole Porter, without jodhpurs.)

In *Sometimes I Wonder*, his second autobiography, Carmichael called himself "a folk artist," presumably referring to his success with self-consciously rural material like "Ol' Buttermilk Sky," his best-selling record of 1946. This description was clearly disingenuous; no folk performer could have written harmonic sequences as elegant and sophisticated as those in "Star Dust," and Carmichael's son points out that he prided himself on being "a songwriter for hire," a professional confident of his ability to supply any manner of song demanded of him.

Yet there was a strong element of regionalism to Carmichael's melodies, specifically Midwestern in character, although often mistaken for Southern when the lyrics were by the Savannah-born Johnny Mercer, or for Southwestern if the song in question was written for a cowboy movie.

THE EARLY DECADES OF THIS CENTURY WERE A TIME OF ARTISTIC FERMENT IN the Midwest, even if that became fully apparent only after many of the artists who were responsible for it migrated to New York or Paris. This was especially true in literature, although it is significant that Thomas Hart Benton, the most famous American painter of the 1930s, was from Missouri. F. Scott Fitzgerald will forever be associated with the Ivy League, but he grew up in Minnesota. Though imported from France, naturalism as it was practiced by the American novelists Theodore Dreiser and Upton Sinclair was almost entirely a by-product of Chicago's stockyards and meat-packing plants.

Writing in 1951, the editor and literary critic Malcolm Cowley pointed to "the creation of a rich and flexible prose style based on Midwestern rather than New England speech" as one of the most significant developments in American literature over the previous fifty years. By Cowley's reckoning, this Midwestern prose style was derived from Mark Twain but also owed much to Sherwood Anderson and Gertrude Stein; it had entered the mainstream through Hemingway, whose early novels were so influential that "soon the Midwestern style was affecting the popular speech from which it had developed, so that a whole generation of young Americans learned to talk like Hemingway's heroes."

In music, ragtime was a product of St. Louis, and even the early styles of jazz said to have originated in New Orleans around the turn of the century entered public consciousness by way of Chicago speakeasies and the riverboats that sailed up the Mississippi.

There are echoes of all of this—Hemingway and Fitzgerald no less than ragtime and jazz—in Carmichael's melodies, even when the lyrics seem as far removed from Indiana as those to "Georgia on My Mind" or "Memphis in June." Listening now to "Star Dust"—a song whose lyrics might as well be Fitzgerald's reflections about boats against the current, borne back ceaselessly into the past—we hear yearning not just for a lost love but for a way of life that was becoming a thing of the past even when the song was new. The mass media that brought popular culture to the hinterlands did so at a price, absorbing regional culture to the point where it quickly became unrecognizable as such. Carmichael doesn't sound Midwestern to us now, just American. But it pretty much amounts to the same thing, thanks to him no less than to Twain or Hemingway.

THOUGH HE DEFERS TO HIS FATHER'S BIOGRAPHER, RICHARD M. SUDHALTER, ON factual matters, no one knows more about Hoagy Carmichael than Hoagy Bix Carmichael, whose view of his father is loving but unsentimental. A story he tells illustrates Carmichael's unrest beginning in the late 1950s, when rock 'n' roll threatened to make him a forgotten man.

On arriving at a party or Hollywood restaurant, Carmichael would shoo the pianist and take the bench himself. "It was his way of preserving his ego, of saying 'I'm Hoagy Carmichael and you're not,'" the younger Carmichael remembers. "He wasn't an obsessed pianist who, if we were home, would bang at the piano all night. He just enjoyed entertaining people and being the center of attention. That's who he was.

"At one point, around the time that Hawaii became a state, he went there and wrote a bunch of Hawaiian songs, which was about as far from his roots as he could get. Then, when I was running a brokerage firm here in New York, on his regular visits to see me, he found a public piano in a bank at 48th and Madison. He'd get a drink, sit down, and play for the lunchtime crowd. The people there got to know him, and inevitably, someone would request 'Star Dust.'

"Well—how many times can you play 'Star Dust' without getting a little sick of it, even if you're the guy that wrote it? To keep it interesting for himself, he would take such liberties with it that he sounded like Hampton Hawes or some other bebop pianist playing an original based on 'Star Dust,' much to the chagrin of whoever requested it."

One of Carmichael's current activities on behalf of his father's music is commissioning new orchestrations for pops orchestras. "The orchestrations that exist are forty or fifty years old and sound like it," he says. In addition to working with the playwright Peter Nichols on a musical that will incorporate many of Hoagy Carmichael's best-known tunes "without forcing them to tell a story they were never intended to tell," Carmichael also hopes to convince an unspecified ballet company to choreograph *The Johnny Appleseed Suite*, a work from the late 1950s that was one of his father's few attempts at extended composition.

The Carmichael centennial has inspired a rash of product, some of it not due in stores until early next year, including Sudhalter's biography, which promises to be definitive. In the meantime, Da Capo Press has released a volume combining both of Carmichael's biographies: the rambling but enjoyable *The Stardust Road* (1946), which Carmichael wrote without a ghost, and the more straightforward *Sometimes I Wonder* (1965).

Carmichael's songs are being interpreted by the unlikeliest of performers, including the country singer Crystal Gayle, who has just released an entire album of them—*Crystal Gayle Sings the Heart and*

Soul of Hoagy Carmichael (Platinum 9362). Blue Note has again issued *Hoagy Sings Carmichael*, recorded in 1956 with a stellar group of West Coast jazz musicians, including the alto saxophonist Art Pepper, and featuring some of the loveliest and most effortlessly expressive singing that Carmichael ever did in a recording studio.

Some of the best Carmichael items predate the centennial. *The Classic Hoagy Carmichael*, an indispensable collection of his songs by performers ranging from Mildred Bailey to Wynton Marsalis (and including Carmichael himself), was issued in 1988 as a joint venture between the Indiana Historical Society and the Smithsonian Collection of Recordings; this collection, three CDs or four cassettes, is available only by mail order. A curiosity well worth hunting for in used-record shops—though it figures to be pricey—is *Jazz Canto* (World Pacific WP-1244), on which Carmichael delivers crusty recitations of two poems in the American grain by William Carlos Williams, accompanied by period-sounding cool jazz.

The New York Times
November 21, 1999
(with added material)

Not Singing Too Much

Three cheers for the champs of yesterday!
Jack Dempsey, John McGraw,
Joe Louis, Sammy Baugh
The movers and the shakers
Here's to the teams that moved away
from disenfranchised towns,
the old St. Louis Browns,
the Minneapolis Lakers
That's when basketballs had laces
and halfbacks played safety on defense.
That's when there were parking places.
Hot dog for a dime,
White Castle seven cents
And here's to White Castles by the sack.
I heard somebody say
they're still around today,
but they wouldn't taste the same now. . . .

The pianist and singer Dave Frishberg once introduced his song "The Dear Departed Past" by explaining that it was written from the point of view of "a guy very much like myself, very much hung up on the old ways and the old days—pathologically hung up, I guess—[who] also happens to be, like myself, a sports-trivia enthusiast." In the lyrics Frishberg wonders, "Can one feel a real nostalgia for a time and place one never even knew?" For the sixty-four-year-old Frishberg, who writes both words and

27

music (usually in that order, although he has written just lyrics to melodies by Johnny Mandel and others), the answer is yes. Many of his lyrics satirize contemporary foibles, including the propensity of many successful people to take themselves far too seriously ("I'm impressed with my attorney Bernie," begins a Frishberg song that marvels at the aplomb of a fellow who is obviously quite impressed with himself). But in one song Frishberg offers cautionary advice to the dissolute cornetist Bix Beiderbecke, who died of infirmities brought on by alcoholism in 1931, two years before Frishberg's birth; in another he raises a cheer for the deadball-era pitcher Christy Mathewson, who hung up his glove in 1916.

A throwback to the days when most jazz instrumentalists who wrote music were songwriters rather than composers, Frishberg is also something of a throwback as a pianist, without being a musical revivalist. Although his ambition as a teenager in St. Paul, Minnesota, was to go to New York or Los Angeles and become "a bebop pianist," his formative influences included such blues and boogie-woogie men as Jay McShann and Albert Ammons. And despite cracking one of modern jazz's many inner circles by becoming the pianist in a quintet under the joint leadership of the tenor saxophonists Al Cohn and Zoot Sims in 1963, a few years after arriving in New York in the early 1960s, Frishberg also found himself in demand among swing musicians—if for no other reason than that he was one of few younger pianists familiar with the swing repertoire.

As a singer, Frishberg is an acquired taste, which is to say that his voice takes some getting used to. A typical Frishberg vocal is a series of witty asides, delivered in a small, reedy tenor at once tenacious and unassuming—not a singer's voice, as Frishberg cheerfully admits, but that of a songwriter and pianist overcoming his inhibitions and giving a lyric his best shot. Less certain of his larynx than of his fingers, he took up singing nearly thirty years ago, when the Paul Ankas and Steve Lawrences for whom he imagined he was writing hits refused to give him a nibble. Blossom Dearie, also a songwriter, a pianist, and a conversational singer, was the first to recognize the potential of Frishberg's songs. In recent years his tunes have been performed by many jazz and cabaret singers, including Rosemary Clooney, who dedicated Frishberg's road-weary lament "Sweet Kentucky Ham" to President Clinton when she sang it at a jazz festival on the White House lawn in 1993. Frishberg affectionately refers to most of the others who have recorded his songs (and, by extension, to himself) as "cult" singers—"'cult' being an accounting term, I guess."

He says that when he listens to other singers performing his songs, he sometimes thinks, "I wish they wouldn't sing so much." This is a wish unlikely ever to be made about Frishberg. An arranger hoping to orchestrate one of his songs once accused him of writing in too "confidential" a key. "Singers like to hear their voices," Frishberg says, "and they get caught up in the sounds they're making, bending notes and all of that. But because I'm usually writing for myself, I very seldom write anything that's vocally challenging. A lot of them I like to deliver out of tempo, as conversation. And when I hear them stretched out into long, songy lines . . . it works, I guess, but I get impatient, because I want people to be able to concentrate on the words. Somebody once asked me if I wanted to submit some songs to a certain singer, a big Broadway star, and I answered, without trying to be funny, that I didn't think I had anything that loud."

FRISHBERG'S MOST POPULAR SONG, IF MEASURED BY THE NUMBER OF recorded versions, is a ballad called "Heart's Desire," for which he wrote only the lyrics. (The melody, which has a musing quality that makes it ideal for a pianist, is by Alan Broadbent, a former Woody Herman sideman and arranger who is now the pianist in Charlie Haden's Quartet West.) The song that has earned Frishberg the most in royalties over the years, however, is one that neither he nor any of his usual interpreters has ever recorded. Written in 1974 on assignment for the Saturday-morning TV series *Schoolhouse Rock*, and still in the show's rotation, sung by Frishberg's friend Jack Sheldon, "I'm Just a Bill" follows a bill through Congress on its way to becoming a piece of legislation. In addition to easing some of Frishberg's financial anxieties, the ditty has made him a hero to his sons, Harry and Max, twelve and ten.

"In my kids' world, my credential is that I wrote 'I'm Just a Bill,'" Frishberg said when I called on him at home in the hills of Portland, Oregon, last year. The song has given his sons, who live not far away with their mother, Frishberg's ex-wife, something to boast about to their schoolmates, the more doubtful of whom have been dragged to Frishberg's living room for an in-person performance. According to Frishberg, even his boys' teachers are impressed. This could be because Frishberg's song is one of only a few from the series that fulfills its educational mission (Strunk and White might have had trouble following Bob Dorough's "Busy Prepositions" and "Conjunction Junction"), though a likelier explanation is that plenty of today's younger teachers grew up with it. It's their generation's musical comfort food—the song that their contemporary Winona Ryder in effect pigs out on after breaking up with her boyfriend in the pandering 1994 movie *Reality Bites*.

Frishberg has accurately described the rest of his songs as being "for adults, or at least for people who wouldn't mind growing up." "Heart's Desire" is more typical of his work, though it, too, is a kind of children's song; Frishberg wrote it soon after his divorce, in an attempt to pass along some fatherly wisdom to his boys. At face value, Frishberg's lyric is about the importance of heeding what you perceive to be your calling—your heart's desire. As he sings it, however, the focus of the lyric shifts from the words of wisdom to their giver, a man whose own heart's desire is the future happiness of the person or people he's addressing. As featured on his album *Where You At* (Sterling S1005-2), "Heart's Desire" is one of very few songs on which Frishberg, who usually has just as much voice as he needs, gives evidence of straining, perhaps because Broadbent's melody goes a little high for him—or perhaps because a degree of strain is called for in a song that is ultimately about a divorced father's worry that he will play a diminished role in his children's lives.

In his stage banter and private conversation as well as in his lyrics, Frishberg has a way with a quip that is often the public face of mild depression. I once heard him tell an audience that Minnesota Public Radio had asked him during the 1992 presidential elections to write a song about the ailing economy. At first he had refused, he explained, not thinking of himself as a topical songwriter. But when the network said that it was really after a song about "hopelessness and despair," Frishberg said, "You've come to the right guy." He then wrote a dystopian anthem called "My Country Used to Be."

Frishberg is usually the butt of his own jokes. He still occasionally performs a lovely early song of his in a semi-country vein called "Cornflower Lonely, Wallflower Blue," which he likes to tell audiences he wrote for Johnny Tillotson, a long-forgotten teen idol of the Fabian era for whom Frishberg briefly served as conductor. Tillotson, whose hits included "Poetry in Motion" and "Send Me the Pillow That You Dream On," never got around to doing the song, so Frishberg found himself auditioning it for a song publisher. "He stopped me on the bridge, when I played the chord behind the word 'sunflower,' which was a B-7th," Frishberg says. "'That's not a cowboy chord,' he told me." In real life the audition ended there, but in telling the story, Frishberg gives himself the last word. "I asked him, 'You mean I'll lose the audience if I play a B-7th?' 'That's right,' he said. And I said, 'Jeez, I didn't know it was that easy.'" (Thanks to its offending jazz chords, the song would be perfect for Willie Nelson.) About an early effort called "Another Song About Paris," Frishberg once commented in a liner note: "I wrote it for a specific character to sing—a dyspeptic, bad-tempered American. Imagine my surprise when, with the passing of years, the character turned out to be me."

IF NOT FOR THE CD-ROM SPEAKERS UNDER HIS WORKTABLE AND THE VIEW OF A forest over his piano, the main room of Frishberg's home could be a stage set for "The Dear Departed Past." In addition to a random selection of baseball and football annuals from the 1930s and 1940s, his sports memorabilia include an autographed copy of a Christy Mathewson baseball novel for boys that Frishberg believes once belonged to Hal Chase, a first baseman of Mathewson's era who left the major leagues under suspicion of throwing games. (Frishberg says he began to lose interest in baseball around the time of Mickey Mantle, when major-league rosters suddenly became full of players his own age or younger.) Frishberg also owns first editions of Robert Benchley and Ring Lardner, and a wall of cassettes and framed photographs is practically a shrine to Al Cohn and Zoot Sims. In a shed just off the main room, there are framed photos of Frishberg with some of the legendary figures he accompanied in the 1950s and 1960s, including the tenor saxophonist Ben Webster, whose reputation as a ballad player was exceeded only by his reputation as a brawler. "I think I would have found Ben intimidating even if he hadn't been a great musician, because he was a loose cannon," Frishberg said, as he gave me a tour. "He once came over to my place for dinner before a gig, and phoned Coleman Hawkins. They planned to meet after the gig that night, and Ben hung up, saying, 'We'll have a pajama party, then— ta, ta.' I have no idea what that was supposed to mean, but I've never forgotten it."

My visit to Frishberg's home was more on the order of a continuing conversation than an interview. I had first met him about eight years earlier, in a used-record store in London, where we chatted over coffee after I beat him to a used copy of Cohn's *Mr. Music* (the British audience at Pizza on the Park was thrown by the many baseball allusions in his songs). I think we next talked in New York a few years later, between his sets in a jazz club on Union Square; the maitre d' interrupted us at one point to tell Frishberg that "Vegas is calling, Dave." "About time," Frishberg replied, without missing a beat. (The call turned out to be from the wife of a musician he once knew; she wanted Frishberg's help in lining up gigs for her son, a trombonist determined to try his luck in New York.) Frishberg and I also once talked after his show at a midtown-Manhattan cabaret, around the same time that he made an appearance on the radio program A *Prairie Home Companion*. Seeing the nostalgic faces of the locals all around me as he sang his evocative "Do You Miss New York?," written several years after he switched coasts in 1971, I realized that New York had become a city one no longer needed to leave in order to miss—as imaginary a place as Garrison Keillor's Lake Woebegone.

No doubt thinking of this song's passing reference to *Annie Hall*, and Frishberg's passing resemblance to its star and director (beaky, bespectacled, and balding), a British journalist once proclaimed him "a Woody Allen of song." This quotation still shows up in Frishberg's press releases, but it doesn't faithfully describe him. For one thing, Frishberg's background is closer to that of Diane Keaton's title character than to that of Allen's Alvy Singer. Culturally, he seems more Midwestern than Jewish. When explaining to audiences the sort of man who is singing "The Dear Departed Past," he pronounces "enthusiast" with the stress on the final syllable, and he may be the only person I know who, when receiving a bit of incredible information, responds with a comic-book exclamation very much like "Pshew!" His singing, too, is Midwestern in character, and this could be what people have in mind when they liken him to the Indiana-born songwriter Hoagy Carmichael. But even Carmichael had greater vocal range.

"Singer-songwriter" is a designation more common in pop than in jazz, and because so many of today's pop songwriters refer to their own experiences in their songs, people assume that Frishberg must be speaking personally, too. But he often writes in character—or as he puts it, "Every song I write seems to have a little character in my head singing it, and it's often not me. And this to me is an aid in writing. I can give myself a point of view that isn't always the same nagging, neurotic point of view. Or if it is, at least it's somebody else talking."

More than Frishberg himself, the characters to whom he sometimes yields the floor are familiar types from Allen's films. One of his cleverest uptempo patter songs, in the same vein as "My Attorney Bernie," is "Quality Time," in which a yuppie dealmaker proposes a romantic idyll to his fast-track wife, though he is apparently unable to imagine even an amorous getaway without power lunches and access to a laptop fax:

> *I know a small hotel, remote and quiet.*
> *If they decide to sell, my firm could buy it.*
> *Then we'd develop it and gentrify it.*
> *We're talking quality time. . . .*

One of Frishberg's heroes was Frank Loessor, whose scores include *Guys and Dolls* and *How to Succeed in Business Without Really Trying*, and who once advised Frishberg that song lyrics were not poetry but a form of journalism. This must have come as good news, given that Frishberg had majored in journalism at the University of Minnesota and contributed first-person-plural "Talk of the Town"–like pieces to a campus literary magazine. Frishberg likes to say that as a lyricist he is still a kind of journalist. But because he writes in so many different voices, his modus operandi is more like that of a novelist or playwright. ("Quality Time" was, in fact, pressed into service as the title number of a Frishberg revue presented by the Milwaukee Repertory Theater, in 1995. The show also recycled numbers from *The Catbird Seat*, an earlier unproduced Frishberg musical. Frishberg's dissatisfaction with his own book for the show *Quality Time* caused him to put the project on hold.) As he wrote "Quality Time," he once told an audience, "I kept asking myself, 'Who *is* this jerk?' Then I realized—it's Bernie."

WHEN I VISITED FRISHBERG, BOTH HE AND HIS CURRENT HOUSEMATE WERE trying to quit smoking. Neither of them had gotten past the bumming-but-not-buying stage. "Break out the ashtrays," he told her, on spotting my Marlboro Lights. "This is a smoking house again."

"I heard something funny the other day," he said after lighting up, in response to a question about his affinity for times gone by. "Somebody asks a guy, 'Where are you living these days?' And he says, 'In the past.' At times I wonder if we don't subconsciously borrow our parents' expectations about life and refer back to the things that touched them when they were young." Gesturing toward his books, he added, "Because that's what I sometimes refer back to, a period when I wasn't even alive."

Frishberg "borrowed" from his two older brothers, as well as from his parents. "My brothers were jitterbugs," he told me, laughing at his memory of them "in their saddle shoes, twirling their keychains as they listened to their Benny Goodman records. Mort, who was the closest to me in age, was seven years older than I, so that when I was, say, eight, he was already fifteen. He had very refined taste in music and literature, and whatever he was reading, I was reading. I thought Benchley was the greatest, James Thurber, too. Reading stuff like that was a big part of my life as a kid."

Nostalgia isn't what it used to be, as the cliché goes; it has become politically incorrect. Once regarded as a harmless expression of alienation or an inevitable side effect of growing older, a belief that life was once better is now frequently taken to be a rejection of the creed of multiculturalism—a pacified form of white male rage. Frishberg leaves himself open to such charges. The book he was reading when I visited was Nelson George's *Elevating the Game*, whose subject is the way in which black athletes have altered the nature of professional basketball. Frishberg seemed irked by a passage in which George argued that a "black" approach to basketball involved not just defeating your opponents but showing them up. "I mean, poor sportsmanship is poor sportsmanship, right?" Frishberg asked. In the inverted world of jazz, white musicians are often the ones nursing racial grievances, and Frishberg remembers getting the cold shoulder from some black musicians in New York in the 1960s, during the height of the black power movement.

"Archie Shepp was, I think, the first guy to challenge me directly about being white, and I was taken completely unawares by this. My feelings were hurt from that standpoint, because I thought that the fact that we both knew how to play 'Groovin' High' was enough to make us some sort of brothers. And at the same time this was going on, I was losing interest in jazz as a genre, maybe because I felt excluded in a way that seemed kind of arbitrary. The music was changing in character, and I didn't really feel comfortable affecting a menacing posture as a jazz musician. And yet that's what seemed to be happening all around me. I kind of enjoyed, at arm's length, the funk movement—Bobby Timmons and Cannonball Adderley. But I never felt like I was entitled to play that way. I would have been posing. I also felt that part of what was so great about being a jazz musician was interpreting material by Irving Berlin and Cole Porter and George Gershwin. I loved songs. I loved songs! And they were becoming unfashionable."

In his defense, Frishberg's nostalgia isn't based on an unconscious desire to return to a time when a woman's place was in the kitchen or the maternity ward, homosexuals expressed affection only in private, and the onus was on blacks to get along with whites. His is a nostalgia largely without memory, and it is becoming a universal condition. In 1947 the poet Parker Tyler, who was both his era's most probing film critic and its most Freudian, wrote that the "psychoanalytic trend in movies," as represented by dream sequences in such films as *Spellbound* and *Lady in the Dark*, had the potential to transform the unconscious into *"a place."* Along with television and photographs, movies have similarly transformed the past, making it a visible part of the present that is different from the rest of our world only in not including us. Just as Frishberg isn't alone — or necessarily mistaken — in believing that yesterday was more civil, he isn't unique in lamenting that time enjoys too great a head start on him. This is what collecting tends to be all about, and it is also the *raison d'être* for American Movie Classics and Nick at Nite. It's what makes "The Dear Departed Past" a song about looking back in longing, not in anger, and what accounts for its unexpected power.

PORTLAND SEEMS LIKE THE PERFECT HEADQUARTERS FOR A MAN AWASH IN memories real and imagined. Its downtown looks stylish rather than derelict because of the many older buildings still in use, including a restored 1920s movie palace that now houses the symphony, and a luxury hotel known as the Heathman. Until last year Frishberg accompanied the singer Rebecca Kilgore in the hotel bar three nights a week. Frishberg moved here from Los Angeles in 1986, thinking that Portland would be a better place to raise his boys, and stayed on to be near them after his divorce. His reason for going to the West Coast in the first place was to take a job as a songwriter for a TV comedy hour called *The Funny Side*, a vehicle for Gene Kelly that was canceled after half a season in 1971. Frishberg recalls that the first song he wrote for Kelly — "Save Us from Sundays," about the things that can go wrong when one attempts to take a day off — gave Kelly problems, because it required him to begin singing between beats. "Jack Elliott, the music director, says to me, 'You gotta learn to write simpler.' I said, 'Simpler? What could be simpler than an eighth-note rest? I thought Gene Kelly was musical.' And Jack said, 'He is, from the ankles down.'"

Luckily for Frishberg, Portland brought the unaffected Kilgore his way. Her taste in songs, like his, runs to worthy items from the 1930s and 1940s that haven't already been done to death (such as Cole Porter's "Looking at You," which is on Kilgore and Frishberg's album *Looking at You*, PHD Music PHD 1004-CD, and Hugh Martin and Ralph Blane's "An Occasional Man," which she recorded for the more recent *Not a Care in the World*, Arbors Jazz ARCD–19169). A surprise for me, when I heard the two on their final night at the Heathman, before the hotel switched to a rock band, was that Kilgore didn't sing any of Frishberg's songs, and he didn't sing at all. Nor, he told me, would he be singing or featuring any of his own numbers while subbing that weekend for another pianist in the bar of a hotel closer to the waterfront. "I need a place to be a pianist," he explained. "If you start to sing here, especially your own songs, right away you're an 'act,' and you don't get called for other gigs. That's what had started to happen in L.A., and I couldn't afford to let it happen in Portland."

The thin line that separates jazz and cabaret can be an abyss for a performer who's caught in the middle, as Frishberg is. The cost he's paid for his small bit of renown as a songwriter who performs his own songs is that even fellow musicians frequently overlook his facility as a pianist. The song that Frishberg was writing when I visited him is called "I Want to Be a Sideman," and this time the identity of the "little character" with a claim to Frishberg's ear is no mystery. Frishberg also told me that when not performing his own songs, he not only doesn't mind a noisy room like the Heathman bar but actually prefers one. "Sometimes it's good to feel that you're not under a microscope, with everyone waiting for your next note. Several musicians I know have said that to me, and we've agreed, 'Gee, I wish they'd talk among themselves so that I could loosen up a little bit.'"

It's another story when Frishberg sings. "I want their attention so bad," he said. "I don't want them to miss a single word." This reminded me of something he had said earlier, in talking about the advice he received from Frank Loessor. "I remember him going over one of my lyrics and telling me, 'Now, there's a colorful word, but do you really want it where it'll get lost in that jumble of notes? Put it near a rest.' He cautioned me against using what he called 'colorful' words where they might draw so much attention to themselves that they would prevent the listener from absorbing what was coming next."

Frishberg seems to have taken Loessor's words to heart, not just as a lyricist but as a self-accompanist. "I think I play a lot less for myself than I do behind other singers," he told me. "I sometimes fear that I can be a rather intrusive accompanist. I tend to play too much, to try to inject my own personality, because I'm basically a piano stylist, as opposed to an all-arounder. I know I'm a better accompanist for myself than I am for anybody else, because I know where in the lyric it's better for me to let my hands be quiet, to draw attention to the words."

Frishberg is correct in thinking of himself as two different pianists. One is the unencumbered orchestra-in-miniature who can be heard to ideal advantage on Frishberg's 1989 recording of Duke Ellington's "The Mooche," from *Let's Eat Home* (Concord Jazz CCD–4402). This is also the pianist who demonstrates his bebop expertise in a series of duets with the Portland area–based alto saxophonist Warren Rand on *Dameron II-V* (Aspen Grove AC CD 001). (Frishberg's rhythmic displacements are those of a modernist, though not usually as percussive as those of pianists who have been directly influenced by Bud Powell. His voicings are full and orchestral, but devoid of Bill Evans's or McCoy Tyner's impressionistic shimmer.) The other pianist lurking in Frishberg is the epigrammatist who takes over the bench behind Frishberg's vocals. The album on which these two creatures most happily coexist is *Where You At?*, recorded in Paris in 1991. This is an atypical effort for Frishberg in that it features him singing a few songs he did not write, and he does a very likable job of phrasing them. They include Johnny Mercer's "Harlem Butterfly" and "I'm an Old Cowhand," and Walter Bullock and Allie Wrubell's "The You and Me That Used to Be," a wonderful song from the 1930s about the old days that was the title track of a classic LP that Frishberg arranged for Jimmy Rushing in 1971. *Where You At?* also has going for it the definitive reading of Frishberg and Broadbent's "Heart's Desire," featuring an exquisitely wounded-sounding solo by the expatriate trombonist Glenn Ferris. The best recorded version of "The Dear Departed Past" is the one on Frishberg's 1984 solo album *Live at Vine Street* (Fantasy OJCCD–832–2). A more recent version is on *Quality Time* (Sterling S1006–2), from 1993, but here Frishberg, in his capacity as producer, undermines himself by adding a rhythm section and horns. "The

Dear Departed Past" is a song about a man alone with his own thoughts, and it should sound that way.

EVEN SO, *QUALITY TIME* IS WORTH SEEKING OUT FOR A BLISSFUL AND FAIRLY new Frishberg song called "Snowbound" and for the devastatingly funny title tune. A good selection of Frishberg's earlier numbers, including "Sweet Kentucky Ham," "Do You Miss New York?," and "My Attorney Bernie," can be found on *Classics* (Concord Jazz CCD–4462), a reissue of recordings from the early 1980s. "I Want to Be a Sideman" is one of four vocal performances on the new *Dave Frishberg by Himself* (Arbors Jazz ARCD–19185), an album featuring Frishberg the expansive solo pianist.

The reason that Frishberg has never gotten around to recording "I'm Just a Bill" could be that he's content to let everyone else sing it. He performs the song in concert upon request, but requests for it aren't all that common. Few people in Frishberg's age group have ever paid attention to "I'm Just a Bill," much less associate it with him. But the song does have a way of following him around, as he told my wife Terry Gross, of the National Public Radio program *Fresh Air*, in a story about visiting a friend in the hospital.

"I went to his room and he was sharing it with somebody else who must have been really sick, because there was this big screen. Behind the screen this other patient was ghostly pale and he had tubes sticking out of every orifice. Looked like he was on his way out. So, I was talking to my friend and my friend said, 'What have you been doing?' I said, 'Well, I'm working for *Schoolhouse Rock* again.' He said, 'Gee, that thing you wrote years ago, "I'm Just a Bill"—I still hear that. And from behind the screen came the voice of this other patient. He said, 'Did you write "I'm Just a Bill?"' . . . And then from behind the screen he began to sing it. The dying man singing my song with what sounded like his last breath: '*I'm just a bill, from Capitol Hill. . . .* ' I kept saying, 'You're singing too much,'" Frishberg said, embellishing a little. "'Do it conversationally.'"

Billie Holiday, Cover Artist

F ew people alive today, even among her most ardent fans, have heard
Billie Holiday other than on recordings or seen her other than in photographs and random film clips. Holiday was eighteen years old and a
worldly former prostitute when she recorded "Your Mother's Son-in-
Law" with Benny Goodman in 1933; she died from the cumulative
effects of heroin and alcohol in 1959, a ravaged forty-four. Yet with the
obvious exception of Frank Sinatra, who was born in the same year as
Holiday but outlived her by almost four decades (during which he was a
constant presence in movies and on television), no other recording artist
from the first half of the last century seems more real to us—more like
our contemporary.

Dating back to the 1940s, when schoolkids fought over whose big band
was better, Goodman's or Artie Shaw's, jazz aficionados have enjoyed
nothing more than debating the relative merits of different performers.
But when conversation turns to Billie Holiday, the only way to start a fight
is to state a preference for early, middle, or late—her jaunty recordings of
the 1930s, her diva-like ballads of the 1940s, or her work from the 1950s,
when she had almost nothing left but compensated for her husk of a voice
with the intimacy of her phrasing (by that point, closer to speech than
song). That Holiday was the greatest woman jazz singer ever is accepted
as incontestable fact, no matter how fond you or the person you're talking
to might be of Mildred Bailey, Ella Fitzgerald, or Sarah Vaughan.

But Holiday has never appealed exclusively to jazz listeners, nor has
her appeal ever depended solely on her vocal artistry. As was true in

1939, when she first sang the anti-lynching song "Strange Fruit" to an audience consisting mostly of bohemian artists and left-wing intellectuals at Café Society (a Greenwich Village nightclub whose owner, Barney Josephson, and his regular patrons were as committed to racial integration as they were to hedonistic pleasure), many people today are unable to listen to Holiday without projecting into whatever lyric she happens to be singing their sense of her as a martyr to an uncaring world and to her own bad judgment.

Holiday, born Eleanora Fagan, was black, the child of an unwed mother. Rumored to be bisexual, she was drawn to abusive men; on her recordings of the song "My Man" the lines "He beats me too/What can I do?" are disturbing less for the sentiment than for the near-ecstasy with which she delivers them. Raised as a Catholic, Holiday, according to at least one biography, may have seen her inability to conceive when she was married as divine retribution for having aborted an unwed teenage pregnancy by sitting in a bathtub full of hot water and mustard. She was a substance abuser whose name recognition made her an easy target for publicity-hunting police departments; during her final hospitalization, she was arrested for illegal possession of heroin, fingerprinted, and photographed for mug shots on her deathbed. As a convicted user, she was prohibited by law from performing in New York City nightclubs for the last twelve years of her life.

Singing should have been her salvation, and perhaps it was. But there is a widespread belief that she was discriminated against even as an artist, especially toward the beginning of her career, when, according to a dubious bit of folklore, white performers fed off Tin Pan Alley's choice cuts and black performers like her were forced to make do with the musical equivalent of intestines and jowls—not just leftovers, but leavings. Although famous, Holiday never achieved the mass popularity of some white big-band singers, possibly because the liberties she took with melody and rhythm required of listeners a sharper ear than most of them had. Or was it, as she may have believed, simply because she was black?

Holiday was, I think, a victim of both injustice and her own vices—a week's worth of *Oprah*, with the requisite confessional streak. She may have sung that what she did was nobody's business (on a fiercely independent number she borrowed from her girlhood idol Bessie Smith), but she made it everybody's business with the publication of her "frank," if not always factual, autobiography *Lady Sings the Blues* (1956), actually written by the journalist William Dufty. (Winfrey would probably tell Holiday she suffered from low self-esteem, nothing that couldn't be cured by daily self-affirmations and a big hug.)

All of us identify, to an extent, with the music we are most fond of; it defines us, in some vague way. But we also define *it*, in keeping with our own needs and desires. A prior knowledge of Holiday's hard knocks darkens some listeners' perception of even her earliest recordings, which were ebullient more often than not. The singer nicknamed "Lady Day" or just "Lady" has become an all-purpose Our Lady of Sorrow—embraced by many of her black listeners (and by many women and gay men) not just as a favorite performer but as a kind of patron saint. She touches such fans where they hurt, soothing their rage even while delivering a reminder of past humiliations and the potential for more. Especially since the 1972 Diana Ross movie loosely based on Holiday's loose-to-begin-with autobiography (and perversely enjoyable as a color-conscious variation on an old Lana Turner or Susan Hayward tearjerker), only part of Holiday's allure has come from her intuitive swing and the interpretive depth she acquired with maturity—qualities matched by no other woman singer, and among male singers only by Louis Armstrong (in headlong swing) and Frank Sinatra (in depth of interpretation).

EVEN LEAVING ASIDE THE MORASS OF RACE AND SEX, HOLIDAY IS A GIANT subject for a biographer. A friend of mine, a fellow music critic, gave up on the idea of writing a book about her when he realized that each photograph taken of her seemed to show an equally beautiful but otherwise entirely different woman—a phenomenon not fully explained, he thought, by her mounting drug habit and evident fluctuations in weight. There are at least four full-length biographies of Holiday; the one that achieves the best balance of empathy and detachment is Donald Clarke's *Wishing on the Moon* (1994), but we come away even from it convinced that Holiday and her different moods were finally unknowable.

In the new *Strange Fruit*, a slim volume expanded from a 1998 article in *Vanity Fair*, David Margolick approaches Holiday sideways, examining her relationship to a single song. The lyrics of "Strange Fruit" are from a poem written by Abel Meeropol, a Jewish schoolteacher from New York, who, following the execution of Julius and Ethel Rosenberg in 1953, adopted and raised as his own the Rosenbergs' two sons.

Southern trees bear a strange fruit,
Blood on the leaves and blood at the root,
Black body swinging in the Southern breeze,
Strange fruit hanging from the poplar trees.

In her autobiography Holiday recounted how she and the pianist Sonny White, working closely with Meeropol (who wrote under the pseudonym Lewis Allan), came up with a melody for "Strange Fruit." Reference books, however, list Lewis Allan as the sole composer, and Margolick offers evidence to substantiate that Meeropol wrote the melody as well as the words. At only 152 double-spaced pages, Margolick's book feels padded, with one person after another telling essentially the same story of having been chilled to the bone on first being exposed to Meeropol's disturbing imagery ("The bulging eyes and the twisted mouth") and Holiday's restrained, almost-serene delivery, whether in performance or on recordings (the assembled witnesses include Tori Amos, Cassandra Wilson, and a member of the lesbian a cappella group Amasong, all of whom have recorded their own versions of "Strange Fruit"). Along with its readability, the book's virtue is in shoehorning into a brief text so much useful anecdotal information—about Holiday, Meeropol, Café Society, and the mixture of rapture and disdain with which "Strange Fruit" was originally greeted.

Margolick shows how "Strange Fruit" became identified with "Strange Fruit," and because he is a scrupulous reporter, he also questions to what extent and on what terms Holiday identified with it. (He wisely dismisses persistent speculation that the poorly educated singer was only dimly aware of what the song's lyrics were about.) In Holiday's own book she told of once refusing to honor a request for "Strange Fruit" from a "bitch" who called it "that sexy song [about] the naked bodies swinging in the trees." Margolick repeats the story, but earlier offers this surprising observation from a black woman named Evelyn Cunningham, a former reporter for the *Pittsburgh Courier*: "The song did not disturb me because I never had the feeling that this was something [Holiday] was very, very serious about. . . . Many times in nightclubs when I heard her sing the song it was not a sadness I sensed as much as there was something else; it's got to do with sexuality." Cunningham saw couples moving closer and holding hands as they listened. Holiday usually performed "Strange Fruit" as an encore, rightly convinced that nothing could follow it. But the late Jimmy Rowles, once Holiday's accompanist, told of a night in a Los Angeles club when she opened with it, after a beating from her husband and a shouting match with a customer at the bar.

According to Rowles, Holiday stormed offstage after that one number. If the story suggests that "Strange Fruit" ultimately became a way for her to release her anger, it also suggests that her anger could be unfocused, her racial indignation mixed up with her resentment at her mistreatment by the men in her life, her persecution by the law, and the mass public's preference for blander (and paler) female singers. Though I hear nothing sexual in her recordings of "Strange Fruit" (including the original 1939 recording, which was reissued earlier this year on the CD *The Commodore Master Takes*, Commodore 314 543 272-2), I think I understand how Holiday herself and those couples Cunningham noticed might have. Once Holiday added "Strange Fruit" to her repertoire, Margolick tells us, "some of its sadness seemed to cling to her." And some of the carefree sexuality she projected on her earliest recordings possibly rubbed off even on "Strange Fruit."

Though "Strange Fruit" was unofficially banned from radio, and the label to which Holiday was then under contract refused to let her record it for them (she took it to Milt Gabler, who ran a jazz specialty label out of his New York record store), the song had unexpected commercial benefits; in addition to establishing her credentials as a "race woman" (her own term for a woman committed to the cause of racial equality), it transformed the public's perception of her from jazz singer to cabaret artist. As Margolick points out, however, "Strange Fruit" is unlike anything else she ever recorded. The only numbers even close to it, in terms of having lyrics that could be heard as pertinent to Holiday's being a black woman, are "God Bless the Child," about knowing what it's like to be poor and hungry, and "Don't Explain," about forgiving a cheating husband or lover to whom the singer is in sexual thrall. Holiday is officially credited as having written the melodies and words to both songs in collaboration with Arthur Herzog, Jr., though many believe that Herzog alone wrote them, using Holiday's anecdotes as a starting point and cutting her in on the credit as a reward to her for recording them.

Except for coming up with a few impromptu blues lyrics at recording sessions, Holiday was certainly no songwriter. Yet we listen to her sing "Strange Fruit" and "God Bless the Child" and "Don't Explain" and imagine that the lyrics represent her innermost thoughts. And we think we hear her keeping an ironic distance from the fluffier numbers that first earned her a following, in the late 1930s—improving them by virtually rewriting their melodies on the spot, and implicitly offering a critique of the dreamy sentiments expressed by their lyrics, which were presumably of no relevance to a black woman with her knowledge of the seamier side of life.

I USUALLY BEGIN MY DEFENSE OF SONGS LIKE "SAY IT WITH A KISS" AND "THE Moon Looks Down and Laughs" with an analogy (Holiday's interpretation of them needs no defense). The tenor saxophonist John Coltrane, whose biography I am writing, was a 1943 graduate of the all-black William Penn High School, in High Point, North Carolina. Though William Penn closed years ago ("a casualty of integration," in the words of a black High Point businessman who saw its closing as symbolic of the local black community's loss of autonomy), its graduates maintain an active alumni association. They believe their school was academically one of the best in the state, black or white. Their only complaint is that they were never given new textbooks, which they perceive to have been a racial slight. But in *my* twelve years of public school in Philadelphia, I never saw a new textbook either; nor did anybody else I know who attended public school. The only way to get new books was to go to private school, where you were expected to purchase your own.

Still, it's easy to understand why black students at a segregated Southern high school would feel singled out. It's just as easy to see how the idea got started that Holiday and other black recording artists were denied access to the best material of the late 1930s and early 1940s. From 1933 to 1942 Holiday, on her own or as a featured vocalist with all-star groups led by Teddy Wilson, recorded 153 numbers for Columbia, Brunswick, Vocalion, and OKeh (this material is chronologically assembled on the nine volumes of Columbia's series *The Quintessential Billie Holiday*). Although she had the honor of being the first non-operatic singer to release a version of "Summertime" and was given a shot at "Solitude," "You Go to My Head," "Easy Living," and "These Foolish Things" when they were brand new, nobody would remember many of the other songs she recorded as a young singer— including "Me, Myself, and I," "Foolin' Myself," and "What a Little Moonlight Can Do"—if not for the alchemy she performed on them. But did Holiday think of these songs as shabby goods? Did Wilson and her black sidemen? Did the record-buying public, including Holiday's black fans?

The evidence overwhelmingly suggests not. According to Teddy Wilson, before each of their recording sessions he and Holiday would go through the new songs submitted to their record company by music publishers, and she would pick out the ones she liked best. Often, "they were pretty good songs," Wilson once said, by which he may have meant that many of them became hits, either for Holiday or other performers.

In the 1930s Holiday started her career as what would today be called a "cover" artist—frequently recording her own versions of current songs originated by other performers. The term seems not to have come into widespread use in the recording industry until the mid-1950s, when Pat Boone and other white teen idols began "covering" rhythm 'n' blues hits by Fats Domino and Little Richard, in direct competition with them for a place on the charts and with a distinct advantage in being white. But the practice is as old as the record business itself. Black performers have covered whites, and also one another. The aim of Holiday's first recording sessions with Wilson, starting in 1935, was to stock juke boxes in black neighborhoods with cover versions of songs her record company reckoned might soon become hits by white singers. In one sense almost everybody making pop records in those years was a cover artist: A song would be introduced by Fred Astaire or Alice Faye in a major motion picture, and the race would be on to see who could get a version into the stores first. Two or more versions of the same song, recorded within days of one another, might become best sellers simultaneously, sometimes appealing to slightly different markets. Most consumers didn't particularly care whose version was the original—only which version they happened to like best.

In 1937 Holiday recorded "A Sailboat in the Moonlight," one of her most thrilling performances with the tenor saxophonist Lester Young. This is often cited as the most obvious instance of her transforming the dross available to her into gold. But as Holiday entered the studio, Guy Lombardo's version of the song (written by his brother, Carmen) was already on its way to the charts, eventually to become No. 1. It wasn't necessarily a good song, but it was a hot property.

Among the famous composers or lyricists whose work Holiday recorded during the late 1930s and early 1940s—when, myth has it, she was limited to songs beneath the contempt of white performers—were Cole

Porter, Irving Berlin, Jerome Kern, George and Ira Gershwin, Harry Warren and Al Dubin, and Jimmy McHugh and Dorothy Fields. The list of performers Holiday covered, or with whom she shared a hit song, includes many of the favorite white popular singers of those decades, some of whom were featured with the leading society orchestras and swing bands: Bob Eberle, Skinnay Ennis, Charles Chester, Bea Wain, Helen Ward, Helen Forrest, Edythe Wright, Jack Leonard (Frank Sinatra's predecessor with Tommy Dorsey), and Harriet Hilliard (Ozzie Nelson's wife and Ricky Nelson's mother). The performer she covered most frequently—no fewer than nine times, beginning with "I Wished on the Moon" (lyrics by Dorothy Parker), in 1936—was Bing Crosby, who had his pick of new songs, even though he didn't always choose well. (Does anyone remember "One, Two, Button Your Shoe," which he introduced in the 1936 movie *Pennies from Heaven*, and which Holiday covered that same year?) The runner-up was Fred Astaire, from whom she borrowed seven of the songs he introduced in *The Gay Divorcee*, *Swing Time*, *Shall We Dance?*, and *A Damsel in Distress*. So much for the notion that the best popular songs of the late 1930s and early 1940s were, symbolically, cordoned off behind a sign that read FOR WHITES ONLY.

Not every song Holiday sang in the late 1930s and early 1940s had a pedigree; some of them, including "Eeny, Meeny, Miney, Mo," an early effort by Johnny Mercer, really were mutts. But it's wise to remember that many songs that strike us as nonsensical today were intended by their composers as "rhythm" songs; Holiday had fun with them, and so did her listeners. Did she find anything relevant to her own experience in the lyrics that movie stars like Astaire and Crosby sang to court their virginal leading ladies? Anyone reflexively answering no should be informed that the former Eleanora Fagan read romance magazines, longed for the day when she could record with strings, and adopted the name "Billie" from the fluttery silent-movie star Billie Dove.

Many 1930s leftists, disdainful of the pleasures to be gained from movies and popular music unless they delivered a forthright message along with the he-loves and she-loves, would have been appalled at such middle-class inclinations. In the view of many white intellectuals of the 1930s, Holiday was a standard-bearer for the downtrodden who had more in common with the Scottsboro Boys or the kitchen help at Café Society than with white performers like Crosby or Mildred Bailey. I fear that this is the view of Holiday that has prevailed, even among some black intellectuals.

A PRINTED SIGN OVER A DISPLAY OF CDS BY MACY GRAY IN THE VIRGIN Megastore in Times Square: BILLIE HOLIDAY = NINA SIMONE = MACY GRAY: THE BEST ARGUMENT FOR REINCARNATION. Or the worst argument for evolution. Gray is a young neo-soul singer whose voice is like an elderly woman's death rattle. She presumably reminds people of Billie Holiday at the end of her life. A few years ago, it was Erykah Badu who was supposed to be the new Billie Holiday. I frankly don't know what people are hearing when they listen to Holiday. Today's listeners have a tendency to make of her whatever they want her to be. It's as though Holiday is still a cover artist, only now she's "covering" us—expressing our need and our hurt, or so we like to think.

Even some jazz singers, who should know better, attempt to demonstrate her influence by scatting—something she never did. Listening to her, I sometimes wonder if I and others are hearing the same singer. She herself added to the confusion in *Lady Sings the Blues*, misleading her readers (and possibly herself) about her early influences. She said she admired Bessie Smith for her big voice (this was somewhat ironic, because her own voice was rather small) and Louis Armstrong for his feeling (no argument there). But she omitted Ethel Waters, the great black star of vaudeville and Broadway, whose influence Holiday may have been reluctant to admit because of a long-standing animosity between them (Waters was territorial about her songs, and the younger Holiday had made the mistake of singing one of them right in front of her). Holiday also said that her voice and Lester Young's tenor saxophone were so similar in timbre that when they practiced together, her own mother couldn't tell them apart from the next room. Soulmates they were, but Holiday's phrasing and beat were closer to Armstrong's than Young's. (Unlike the similarly doomed Young, an introverted alcoholic who also died at an early age, just a few months before her, Holiday wasn't a prototypical jazz modernist—a harbinger of bebop. What they did have in common was being among the first jazz performers to be viewed by audiences not as happy-go-lucky Negro entertainers but as alienated black artists. Given her greater fame, she anticipated even more than Young the romance of self-destruction that supplied a grim counterpoint to bebop's narrative of artistic progress in jazz.)

From time to time early in her recording career, Holiday would revive an older song closely associated with another performer. She did her own versions of numbers first made popular by Waters ("Sugar," "Trav'lin All

Alone," and "Am I Blue?"), Armstrong ("All of Me" and "When You're Smiling"), and Bessie Smith ("St. Louis Blues"). But as if giving her audience a clue to her larger ambitions, she more often revisited songs first sung by and still closely associated with the most flamboyant white torch singers of the 1920s and early 1930s—Ruth Etting ("Mean to Me," "More Than You Know," and "I'll Never Be the Same"), Marion Harris ("The Man I Love"), Helen Morgan ("Why Was I Born?"), Libby Holman ("Body and Soul" and "Moanin' Low"), and Fanny Brice ("My Man"). At that point Holiday was arguably better suited to upbeat love songs with a hint of self-mockery—among them Jimmy McHugh and Dorothy Fields's "I Must Have That Man," whose clever lyrics ("I need that person much worse'n/just bad!/I'm half alive and it's drivin' me mad") let her indulge her rhythm playfulness and a boundless joie de vivre we tend not to associate with Billie Holiday, though we should. It was a few years later, eerily coinciding with her first recording of "Strange Fruit," that Holiday acquired the maturity a singer needs to make her listeners feel as though they're the ones carrying a torch. (*The Commodore Recordings* includes a haunting version of Jerome Kern and Otto Harbach's "Yesterdays," also from 1939, which seems to have marked a turning point.)

What part heroin or brutal men or racial oppression played in Holiday's gaining greater depth we should be hesitant to speculate. Not everyone who suffers becomes a great artist. Heroin bespeaks a death wish, but to the user it must also seem, if only at first, a life force—a source of defiant pleasure, like risky sexual encounters or an adolescent's first cigarette or drink. This self-abandonment is the animating quality I hear in Billie Holiday's early recordings, when she was defying social convention and her threatened marginalization as a black woman—and in her later recordings, when she was defying not only all of that but also the damage she had inflicted on herself. In fighting to become her own woman she also became her own victim—nobody else's.

The Atlantic Monthly. November 2000

Betty Carter, For Example

Some arts are best defined by example, and there were few better examples of jazz singing than Betty Carter. Few singers proved so conclusively that vocal jazz need not be tainted by commercialism or histrionics, and even fewer were as willing to take risks in the name of improvisation. Carter, who died in September of pancreatic cancer, at the age of sixty-nine, confronted both pop standards and songs indigenous to jazz with a musing skepticism worthy of Charlie Parker or Sonny Rollins—swooping down on a melody and lifting it to a crescendo, subjecting it to abrupt shifts in tempo and dynamics, occasionally abandoning it altogether for a bold, Parker-like harmonic paraphrase. Carter phrased like a horn player because she thought like one; especially on uptempos, but even on ballads, a rhythm section wasn't there just to accompany her, but for her to spar with.

"I remember one time I was playing some of the obvious changes, and she was like 'uh, uh, uh, uh,'" Jacky Terrasson, who was Carter's pianist for a year beginning in 1993, told *The New York Times* shortly after her death. "She wanted to make sure that we stayed in the area where we weren't very sure where we were going to go and where it kept the spontaneity going."

Carter was also a consummate actress. She knew that a singer is a musician, that the voice is an instrument subject to the same demands as a trumpet or tenor saxophone. But she also understood that no improviser bears a greater burden (or, the way she looked at it, enjoys a greater advantage) than the improvising singer, who must do justice to words as

well as music. "Words are one of the options a singer has that instrumentalists don't have," she told me in 1984. "That's why we last so long."

Though she was justly celebrated for her scatting and all that went
into it—her rhythm punch, her crisp syllabification, and a sense of pitch
that gave some critics problems but was as unerring as it was idiosyncratic—her forte was her distended ballad interpretations, beginning
with her 1964 recording of Tom Wolf and Fran Landesman's "Spring
Can Really Hang You Up the Most," a song as quirky as "Lush Life" that
owes its niche in the standard jazz repertoire to Carter, rather than to
Ella Fitzgerald or Carmen McRae, each of whom also recorded it that
year. "Spring," as musicians generally refer to it, was Carter's first masterpiece, not counting her 1961 duets with Ray Charles. She made it so
much her own that perhaps only obscurants familiar with Jeri Winters's
original 1959 recording of the song realize what enormous liberties
Carter took with it—strategically lagging so far behind the beat that it
ceased to be one, then double-timing the occasional telling phrase for
great dramatic as well as musical effect, almost as if italicizing key words
and phrases in keeping with the ironic emotions they were meant to con-
vey. Like all great jazz and pop singers, but especially Frank Sinatra,
whose insights into the relationship between music and lyrics were analytical, and Billie Holiday, whose were largely intuitive, Carter gave the
impression of making up both melody and story as she went along; she
interpreted Wolf and Landesman from the point of view of a loser at love
who has resolved to quit moping—though maybe not just yet.

When Carter isolated a melody's more unusual intervals, it also
allowed her to test the sentiments of its lyrics. She had the range of a
great instrumentalist, but she used the tug of words and the scrape of the
human voice to achieve emotional shadings that are off-limits to instrumentalists. Like Sinatra and Holiday she wrung a bit of truth from the
very words we tarnish daily with lies, making them words she could stand
proudly beside, not cower behind. Once, when I asked her which typically drew her to a number—its words or its music—she unhesitatingly
answered "Both!"

I WAS WILD ABOUT HER THE FIRST TIME I HEARD HER, IN THE SUMMER OF 1964,
when the disc jockeys on my local jazz station seemed to be playing her
just-released *Inside Betty Carter* day and night—if it wasn't "Spring Can
Really Hang You Up the Most," it was her fierce, pouncing "My Favorite

Things," which owed as little to John Coltrane as it did to Julie Andrews. I went on to hear her perform live on countless occasions and to interview her by phone for various publications three or four times. On learning of her death I realized with a shock that I had never spoken with her face to face. Her frankness during our phone conversations made it feel as if I had.

I remember thinking each time she picked up the phone that I must have dialed a wrong number. Her speaking voice could be surprisingly phlegmy; then again, singers often sound a little wounded when caught unawares. I knew going into that first phone interview that she could be a difficult subject. I'd once heard her upbraid a deejay who clearly adored her for playing too much commercial jazz and not enough Coltrane or Miles—he was almost in tears when she finished with him. She was more patient with me, but mocked me for responding to some point she made with an astonished "gee" (I must have sounded like Archie Andrews), and took genuine offense at one of my questions. I'd recently seen a video of Nat Cole and—noticing that he smiled all the way through his songs, never opening his mouth very wide even on high notes—I couldn't help thinking of Carter as his exact opposite. Instead of primly folding her hands she would jerk to her own angular rhythms ("as if she were dodging her own notes," Whitney Balliett, the jazz critic for *The New Yorker,* nicely put it). Instead of fixing audiences with twinkling eyes she threw back her head and contorted her entire face into a mouth. Knowing that she'd started singing professionally with Lionel Hampton's band in the late 1940s, when the role of a "girl" singer with a big band could be partly decorative, I asked if anyone had ever advised her to knock it off—to stand still and try to look pretty.

"Don't say it was 'decorative,'" she scolded me on behalf of all women singers. "Sure, you had to wear a pretty dress. You still have to wear a pretty dress. But what's wrong with that, if the men are wearing suits? We weren't decorative. We had to do the shows and ride the buses, just like the men. Our role was much harder than theirs because we had to put up with them and look good besides, while doing everything they were expected to do."

Fair enough. In point of fact, Jimmy Scott was the ballad singer with Hampton; Lorene Carter, as she was known then, sang the swing tunes. (Born Ellie May Jones in Flint, Michigan, in 1929, she became "Betty" when the peevish Hampton, who had trouble pronouncing "Lorene," started introducing her as "Betty Bebop," half in admiration of her scat singing, and half in retaliation for her not keeping it a secret that she would have preferred to be singing with Dizzy Gillespie's big band.)

Even while scolding me, Carter referred to me as "sweetie" or "dear"—reverting, I guessed, to her offstage role as the single mother of two grown sons. "It's what I have to do to sing a song," she explained once I rephrased the question. "I mean, I'm not a classical singer. They stand straight and tall, and sing. A lot of popular singers, too, including Nat and Frank. So did I, in the beginning of my career. But I realized that if I was going to improvise, I had to move in order to communicate with my musicians. Plus, I think audiences like to see a singer giving off that kind of energy. As for what happens to my face when I sing, there's nothing I can do about it. Look at Leontyne Price—she opens her mouth and you can practically see her tonsils. Singers do what they have to do to get the notes out."

Another time, she offered a critique of modern jazz I found surprising, given her image as the quintessential hard bop singer. "The intellectual thing took hold of jazz in the late 1950s and jazz lost contact with the public. Lost 'em completely—black people and women, especially. No matter what crisis occurs in life, women always seem to want to love, or be loved, or be in love. That makes us more sensitive to music, you know, and many women are repelled by the harshness and bitterness they hear being expressed in jazz. Sometimes you like to light the candles and gaze across the table at someone, and jazz should express that mood too. As for black people, take away the beat and they don't want to know about it, and neither do I."

As she spoke I had a memory of her wearing a stylish canary pants suit for a show I'd seen her give in a funky church basement on a college campus, where audiences and performers alike generally wore denim or kinte cloth. It was her stage—the rest of us had underdressed.

THE FOCUS OF THAT POSTHUMOUS FEATURE ON HER IN THE *TIMES* WAS THE guiding hand that Carter lent her young accompanists, including Terrasson, Benny Green, Cyrus Chestnut, and Javon Jackson. This was also something we usually wound up talking about. "I may sometimes be harsh with them," she once admitted, justly proud of her dual reputation as a great entertainer and an Art Blakey in gold lamé. "But young musicians need that. They'll thank me for it down the road, because they're going to learn secrets they would never learn working behind a horn player. With me, there are going to be all sorts of subtleties to pay attention to—key changes, changes in tempo, attention to texture and dynamics—everything they need to put a tune across to the people sitting out there, instead of just going for themselves. It's a dying art."

Along with her scatting, so much was made of Carter's role as a mentor that several of her other talents were generally overlooked. Not content to limit herself to "Lover Man" and "'Round Midnight," she was a dedicated songfinder. Who else would have revived "What's the Use of Wond'rin,'" Rodgers and Hammerstein's stand-by-your-man song from *Carousel*, as Carter did for her 1991 album *Dropping Things?* "Oh, but it's such a pretty song and nobody ever does it," she protested when I questioned her about the dated lyrics. "Let the men feel good for one number. So what?"

The men in Carter's audience may have felt entitled after enduring "30 Years," a Carter original from *Dropping Things* on which she expresses the scorn of a woman whose husband is leaving her for someone younger after three decades of marriage. "30 Years" could have been an unbearable weeper but it wasn't. Carter—an underrated composer and lyricist who seasoned every kernel of truth with a grain of salt—saw to that by taking the song at a medium-tempo bounce instead of the funereal pace the lyrics might have suggested. And because of its unusual structure—no verses are repeated and Carter sings the title phrase only once, at the end—the song draws you in the way a good short story does, gradually telling you so much about the valiant woman who's singing and the fool she's singing to that you feel you could recognize both of them on sight.

"I wrote it years ago when that seemed to be happening to every woman I knew, and I played with the tempo until it became fun to sing," Carter told me. "It was originally called 'Somebody Else Will Soon Grow Old, Too,' but that was too long for my musicians to remember. They started calling it '30 Years,' and I liked that as a title. So I learn from them too."

EARLIER IN THIS DECADE, WHEN SARAH VAUGHAN, CARMEN MCRAE, AND ELLA Fitzgerald died in what seemed like rapid succession, newspaper obituary writers mourned that all the great ones were gone. They forgot about Betty Carter, who belonged in the same breath but who—along with

Sheila Jordan, Abbey Lincoln, Shirley Horn, Jeanne Lee, and Helen Merrill—was from a generation of women singers who fell into an abyss in the 1960s, when jazz and pop parted ways once and for all. At last year's Jazz Awards ceremony in New York, Cassandra Wilson, whose gifts have always seemed more dramatic than musical, lifted her trophy as Best Female Singer and told the audience, "This has been fifteen years in coming," or words to that effect. Jordan and Lincoln each once went more than fifteen years between *records* (and might have gone longer were it not for Europeans and the Japanese). Betty Carter might have suffered a similar fate had she not taken matters into her own hands and started her own label, BetCar, in 1969.

Though my favorite of Carter's albums is always going to be *Inside Betty Carter*—the one that got to me first—the pick of her BetCar LPs, all of which (like *Inside*) were eventually reissued as Verve CDs, is *The Audience with Betty Carter*, a 1979 concert recording with electrifying remakes of "Spring Can Really Hang You Up the Most" and "My Favorite Things," along with the explosive "Sounds (Moving On)," a nearly twenty-minute-long joust between Carter and her rhythm section. In addition to *Dropping Things* the best of Carter's albums from the 1990s was *I'm Yours, You're Mine* (1996), which found her extending her noblesse oblige to the young trombonist Andre Hayward and the tenor saxophonist Mark Shin. And no connubial home should be without *Ray Charles and Betty Carter*, from 1961 and now available as a Rhino CD; their version of "Baby, It's Cold Outside" almost makes flirting seem more gratifying than sex. But it's tough to think of a Betty Carter album that isn't essential, in some way, to an understanding of the vanishing art of jazz singing.

Fi, January 1999

part two

CHANGE OF
THE CENTURY

Bud's Bubble

S peed in music can be a form of abstraction. About fifteen or twenty years ago the vibraphonist Milt Jackson, traveling as a single while on temporary leave from the Modern Jazz Quartet, played an engagement at a Philadelphia neighborhood lounge, accompanied by a trio of uninspired local musicians. Visibly unhappy, Jackson sleepwalked through the first few numbers, sinking to the level of the house trio. To make matters worse, a patron at the bar, who was either drunk or eager to show the rest of us how down with bebop he was, acted as if Jackson were taking requests.

The man wanted to hear a certain Charlie Parker tune. "How 'bout some 'Scrapple from the Apple,' brother?" he whined before every number, disrupting the band's concentration as Jackson counted off tempos.

After enduring this several times, Jackson fixed the man with a contemptuous stare. Without a word of warning to his sidemen, he tossed off the opening bars of "Scrapple from the Apple" at a tempo about twice as fast as Parker's moderate gallop. Racing to keep up after joining him on the bridge, the local musicians were soon playing way over their heads. The tempo kept accelerating, with Jackson's hands and mallets disappearing into twin blurs. Small talk at the tables came to a stop, and there was an extra split second of silence at the end, before we could bring our hands together to applaud. It lasted just long enough for Jackson's final note to echo gracefully, and for a familiar voice to plead, "'Scrapple from the Apple,' huh, Milt. Do it for me?"

I DOUBT THE BARFLY WOULD RECOGNIZE "TEA FOR TWO" EITHER AT THE DIABOLICAL tempo the pianist Bud Powell chose for the ten consecutive versions he recorded, one right after the other, at a 1950 recording session with the bassist Ray Brown and the drummer Buddy Rich. Some of these may have been false starts or incomplete takes; only the fifth, sixth, and tenth have ever been released. These three turned up again last year on *The Complete Bud Powell on Verve* (Verve 314 521 669-2), a five-disc set of Powell's recordings from 1949 to 1955 for Norman Granz's various labels (Mercury, Norgran, and Clef, as well as Verve).

Take ten is the killer. Powell begins slowly, as he does on the earlier takes, with an arioso statement of the seldom-performed verse, all the while half-humming and half-grunting an eerie countersong (a tic he shared with Glenn Gould, although the ghost "voice" here could actually be Brown bowing his string bass). After you've heard Powell play "Tea for Two" and know what's coming next, your pulse begins to race in anticipation. A pianist I know says this performance is in "one," by which he means that no bandleader could count off four beats that fast without getting tongue-tied. Powell's improvised choruses hurry along at 336 quarter notes a minute, though a metronome would be useless in clocking his accelerating parade of sixteenths. This is not a tempo you could tap your foot to—who can tap his foot that fast?

Recognized by fellow musicians as the seminal bebop pianist almost from the moment in 1943 when, as a teenager, he made his professional debut as a sideman with the trumpeter Cootie Williams's big band, Powell is usually spoken of today not as an innovator but as a carrier of innovation. That is, he is credited with "translating" Charlie Parker's harmonic ideas to piano, much as J.J. Johnson is credited with translating them to trombone and Milt Jackson to vibraphone. This is meant figuratively—a way of saying that Parker showed the way and others including Powell soon followed. But the guitarist Bill De Arango tells an anecdote that puts a literal spin on the idea. Powell could be obnoxious as a young man, and De Arango once heard him bedevil Parker at a jam session by echoing each of Parker's phrases on piano a split second after Parker delivered it on his horn.

Some performances of Powell's sound like direct replies to Parker's. A good example is "Bud's Bubble," from Powell's daredevil first session as a leader, in 1947. It's included on *The Complete Blue Note and Roost Recordings* (Blue Note CDP 7243 6 30083 2 2), a four-disc set that arrived in stores almost simultaneously with *The Complete Bud Powell on Verve* and overlaps with it chronologically, beginning in 1947 and ending with a track recorded in Paris in 1963, three years before Powell's death from tuberculosis, malnutrition, and the effects of alcoholism. Nearly all of the important recordings he made as a leader in the late 1940s and very early 1950s are on one or the other of these two sets, together with hours of performances from 1953 onward that trace his irreversible decline.

"Bud's Bubble" is Powell at the top of his game. The tune itself—the "line," as musicians say—is essentially a speeded-up, more percussive version of Parker and Little Benny Harris's "Crazeology," which was itself based on the chord changes of George and Ira Gershwin's "I Got Rhythm." The specific Parker performance that Powell is chasing is probably the warp-speed "Koko," which Parker had recorded just two years earlier, with Curly Russell on bass and Max Roach on drums—the same rhythm team as on "Bud's Bubble." The tempo here might actually be a hair faster than on the tenth take of "Tea for Two," and given that horn-like lines delivered with such velocity on piano require that each note be struck with even pressure and achieve equal duration, Powell's effortless articulation becomes even more impressive than his speed. But the most impressive aspect of all might be his ability to phrase coherently at such a daunting tempo—to think that fast and to translate his thoughts into action.

Powell was no match for Parker on ballads or blues. All too typical of his ballad interpretations, the Blue Note set's "I Should Care," from 1947, and the Verve set's "You Go to My Head," from 1955, are somber and without lilt, full of puddled arpeggios and sub-Lisztian block chords worthier of the average cocktail pianist than of one of the finest improvisers in the history of jazz. (In contrast, Powell's 1949 "Celia" and his 1951 "The Fruit," both on the Verve set, are among the most winning of bebop ballads, once you accept the premise that ballads don't have to be slow.) Powell's blues, though crisp and delivered with élan, lacked the sensuality of Parker's. But on uptempo tunes of the sort at which both men excelled, Powell enjoyed one advantage over Parker: He didn't occasionally have to pause for breath. If only in that sense, his style wasn't hornlike at all.

Besides, to emphasize Powell's conceptual debt to Parker risks overlooking Powell's considerable influence on several generations of pianists, beginning with George Wallington, Walter Bishop, Jr., and others of Powell's contemporaries whose solos often anthologized his. Hank Jones and Tommy Flanagan softened Powell's attack with generous amounts of Teddy Wilson and Nat Cole. Bill Evans's inner voicings originated in Powell's 1951 Verve recording of "Oblivion," and the beginnings of both McCoy Tyner and Cecil Taylor are discernible in the skeletal harmonic structure and implied double meter of Powell's 1951 Blue Note recording of "Un Poco Loco."

THE QUESTION OF HOW MUCH POWELL OWED PARKER ALSO IGNORES HIS arguably greater debt to two fellow pianists, Art Tatum and Thelonious Monk. Powell's senior by fifteen years and the reigning virtuoso among jazz pianists when Powell burst on the scene in the late 1940s, Tatum once dismissed him as "just a right-handed piano player," supplying a corollary of sorts to the notion that what Powell played with his right hand was merely transposed Charlie Parker. Powell ultimately gained Tatum's approval by sitting down at Birdland, the famous New York nightclub, and playing a song at lightning speed with his left hand alone.

Or so the story goes, but it misses the point—or Tatum did, if the story's true. In effect, Powell reconfigured the keyboard to the specifications of bebop, not just spinning out fleet successions of single notes with his right hand but also sounding broken chords and off-the-beat accents with his left. His left hand catapulted his right. The best way to explain its often misunderstood function in Powell's music might be to say that he drummed with it, instead of playing stride bass with it in the manner of Tatum and most other earlier jazz pianists.

Powell's left hand was so effective in this role that even as resourceful a drummer as the young Max Roach seems to be there mainly to supply texture on "Bud's Bubble" and his numerous other early recordings with Powell. You certainly don't miss drums or bass on the eight performances from Powell's 1951 solo session for Verve. (These include his first recording of the Gershwin-like "Parisian Thoroughfare," the one tune of Powell's to enter the standard repertoire, largely thanks to a later recording by Roach and the trumpeter Clifford Brown, with Powell's younger brother, Richie, on piano.)

In keeping tempo with bass and drums on "Tea for Two," Powell's left hand underlines just how impossibly fast his right hand is moving. The specter of Tatum hovers over all three of Powell's surviving takes of the song, from Vincent Youmans's 1925 Broadway musical *No, No, Nanette*. The song was already known as a Tatum tour de force, a showcase for his harmonic daring as well as for his nimble fingers. (Hearing Tatum play "Tea for Two" in a nightclub, Timmie Rosenkranz, a jazz writer and hanger-on, once marveled, "It sounded like 'Tea for Two Thousand.'") That Powell bothered to record ten takes of a number deemed good enough for release on the fifth could be interpreted as an attempt to beat Tatum at his own game, just as Powell frequently attempted to beat Parker at his.

Playing the verse, or introduction, at an exaggeratedly slow tempo was Powell's idea (Tatum also began out of tempo, but with several bars from the end of the song, the part that goes "We could raise a family"); he may have gotten the idea from Monk, a connoisseur of American popular song who also led with the verse when he finally got around to recording "Tea for Two," in 1956. (Whereas Powell seemed intent on demonstrating that he could play the song faster than anybody else, Monk seemed determined to prove he could play it slower.) Verse aside, what most distinguishes Powell's "Tea for Two" from Tatum's is his abrupt bebop cadences and the modernist gambit of reharmonizing the melody into ascending chromatics—as much a form of disguise as the whirlwind tempo. Whitney Balliett, in one of his periodic forays into literary criticism, once characterized the novelist Alice McDermott as "Henry James without the furbelows, bibelots, and antimacassars." This was Powell's relationship to Tatum: He retained few of Tatum's neo-Victorian frills.

Another modern element in Powell's "Tea for Two" is the suggestion of dissonance in his jabbing right hand—not as pronounced as on some of his recordings of his own material, but there all the same. This, too, would seem to reflect the influence of Monk, of whom Powell was simultaneously champion and disciple (he was the first to record Monk's "Off Minor," and it was almost certainly he who persuaded Cootie Williams to debut Monk's "'Round Midnight," in 1944). At a time when Monk was still being dismissed as irrelevant, Powell's liberal use of dissonance provided a blueprint for jazz after Parker. "[It] is vintage bebop to be sure, yet there's something else present, something suggestive of jazz in the fifties," the late David Rosenberg wrote of Powell's 1949 Verve recording of "Tempis Fugit," in *Hard Bop* (1992):

The minor mode in itself makes the piece somewhat unusual in bebop and accounts in part for the tune's dark mood. This quality, however, derives mainly from Bud's solo. Equally far from the exuberance we hear in Parker and [Dizzy] Gillespie and from [Tadd] Dameron's lush romanticism, Bud's playing is full of seething intensity, and it is this brooding, obsessive side of Powell that leads into [the late fifties style of] hard bop.

IN OTHER WORDS, POWELL'S INFLUENCE (AND MONK'S) ON NON-PIANISTS fully asserted itself only after Parker's death, in 1955—by which time Powell himself was no longer the pianist he had once been, and no longer quite a person. Bebop's wanton speed and abstraction—its affronts to melody and its harmonic and rhythmic cubism—still account for a large part of its appeal. But at least as much of its lingering mystique depends on our perception of many of its originators as self-destructive black outlaws who conducted themselves as though they believed that dying young was the best revenge against the philistines and racists who denied them recognition as artists and their rights as men.

It is frequently suggested in the literature on Powell that he acted *un poco loco*, as it were, because Monk or Parker or the pianist Elmo Hope or somebody in a position to know convinced him that it was the only sane way of dealing with an insane world (early bop seemed precariously balanced on the thin line between madness and black rage). But Powell was crazy by any standard, from the outset of his career.

"Bud was always . . . a little on the borderline," the tenor saxophonist Dexter Gordon once told the critic Ira Gitler. "Because he'd go off into things—expressions, telltale things that would let you know he was off." Powell was first institutionalized in 1945, following his arrest for being drunk and disorderly in a Philadelphia train station, while on the road with Cootie Williams. He is believed to have been clubbed repeatedly about the head by the arresting officers and, consequently, to have suffered dementia pugilistica and other lifelong neurological problems.

He suffered his first nervous breakdown in November 1947, ten months after recording "Bud's Bubble," and was committed to a Long Island sanitarium for almost a year. There he was first given shock treatments—possibly electroconvulsive therapy, which can induce seizure (because drowsiness is one of its side effects, ECT was once a common way of ensuring tranquillity in public mental hospitals). Powell's 1951 arrest for possession of a small amount of marijuana resulted in another extended period of confinement and (some of his friends believed) enough electroconvulsive therapy to short-circuit him for good.

Powell has been undervalued as a composer, a point driven home in listening to the Verve and Blue Note sets in tandem. His most ambitious piece was "Glass Enclosure," which he recorded for Blue Note in 1953, with George Duvivier on bass and Art Taylor on drums. There's a story attached to the title. Powell had been released from a mental institution only six months before. Oscar Goodstein, the manager of Birdland, had been appointed Powell's legal guardian, and he kept Powell under what amounted to house arrest in an East Side high-rise. "They wanted to be sure he'd appear [at the club], so they took complete control of his life," Alfred Lion, of Blue Note Records, recalled years later. "One day, Oscar gave me the key and I went up. There was a piano there and [Powell] played me some new things. One piece really stood out. I asked him what he called it. He looked around the apartment and said 'Glass Enclosure.'"

Worlds away in mood from the effervescent "Bud's Bubble," despite the grim similarity of the two titles, "Glass Enclosure" juxtaposes to harrowing effect an agitated blues riff and a ten-bar fanfare fit for a king. It includes no improvisation; Duvivier probably deserves credit for the arrangement, as well as the steel-ribbed bass lines. This piece has to be played Powell's way or not at all, which explains why it's so rarely performed. But Powell also composed any number of conventional bop lines that might serve as excellent blowing vehicles—for example, the breezy "Celia" or, better still, "Dance of the Infidels," with its flatted and slightly demented bugle-call introduction, from Powell's 1949 Blue Note date with Fats Navarro on trumpet and a very young Sonny Rollins on tenor saxophone. Powell's introductions and bridges were often wonderful little songs in themselves—perhaps another beneficial effect of his friendship with Monk.

It's possible that the reason so few musicians played Powell's compositions along with the usual ones by Monk and Parker and Dizzy Gillespie is that Powell's tunes are perceived as inextricable from his virtuosity as a pianist. But there might be another reason. A first step for a composer who wants to make a number a jazz standard is to perform it in concert night after night. Powell didn't do this, at least not to judge from recorded air checks of his 1950s nightclub performances, which typically feature him playing pop standards and such familiar bebop anthems as

Gillespie's "Salt Peanuts" and "A Night in Tunisia." Powell either couldn't remember his own tunes by that point, or was in no shape to teach them to his sidemen.

It's also worth wondering why, given the success of the 1949 session with Navarro and Rollins, neither Blue Note nor Verve seemed eager to record Powell with horns again. An answer is suggested by three tracks from 1957 on the Blue Note set, where Powell seems oblivious to the trombonist Curtis Fuller; he and Fuller are rarely in the same key.

A FEW MONTHS AFTER RECORDING HIS FINAL BLUE NOTE ALBUM AS A LEADER, IN the closing days of 1958, Powell emigrated to Paris for five years, where he was eventually cared for by the graphic artist Françis Paudras (their friendship was the inspiration for the 1986 movie 'Round Midnight, though the character played by Dexter Gordon had more in common with Lester Young). Paudras nursed Powell back to partial health, with the emphasis on "partial."

"He was overweight, sullen, and unapproachable, given to staring silently at the wall, twiddling his fingers when not playing," Alan Groves writes of seeing Powell in Paris, in 1961, in The Glass Enclosure, a slim but informative volume on Powell's life and career written with Alyn Shipton and published in England in 1993. "He sat virtually motionless, and it was only his hands that moved when he did play. He appeared to have no interest in his surroundings, and little interest in his music."

Powell displayed symptoms that may have been related to schizophrenia or head trauma. He was said to alarm people by grinning or grimacing for no apparent reason, to look out at audiences with a blank stare, and to hold his breath almost to the point of asphyxiation during some of his solos. According to Groves and Shipton, Paudras once "listened in on a long and sympathetic interview with Bud [by a French doctor], at which Powell admitted to dreaming at night that he was constantly playing the piano, and that, even when awake, he was prone to the same dreams." The Complete Blue Note and Roost Recordings ends, in 1963, with a version of "Like Someone in Love" that was recorded during a lull in a Dexter Gordon session. Powell might as well be playing that dream piano—he doesn't sound much interested in the one in front of him. The track is as much an afterthought as Powell's death in New York three years later. It's difficult to believe that this is the same man who, at his first recording session only sixteen years earlier, confidently tossed off eight numbers in the time allotted for four, with no need for retakes. The only hitch occurred when Max Roach asked Teddy Reig, the date's producer, if he and Curly Russell would be paid double for recording twice as many titles as called for in their contracts. "What are you complaining about?" Powell asked Roach, displaying an arrogance that may have been a warning sign of trouble ahead. "I'm doin' all the work—you're just keeping time."

Powell never lost his velocity—just his intensity, his sense of continuity, his rhythmic spring. The most alarming evidence on his American recordings of his decline after 1953 was the decreased activity of his left hand. He continued to drum with it, but almost absent-mindedly, not to such furious purpose as before—this was more like a man at a bar, vacantly drumming his fingers between drinks. The later material on *The Complete Bud Powell on Verve* and *The Complete Blue Note and Roost Recordings* isn't appalling, just uneven. He would recapture his form and then lose it again, often within one recording session, or one number. Performances like "Blue Pearl" and the two takes of "Comin' Up," from his very last Blue Note session as a leader, suffer only by comparison with his earlier work. To ask which pianist's recordings don't suffer by comparison to Powell's early ones misses the point. Less than a decade separates early Powell from late. A foreknowledge of this shadows even his early masterpieces in tragedy.

The Atlantic Monthly, January 1996

The Sound of
One Finger Snapping

B rowsing in a Tower Records about a dozen years ago, I heard a piece of music I knew but couldn't immediately place. It wasn't a ballad, exactly; the tempo wasn't slow so much as *suspended*. Over a two-note figure, repeated ad infinitum by bass and piano, a tenor saxophonist with a prayerful tone like John Coltrane's worried the notes of a scale as though they were beads on a rosary. There was a noticeable echo to the sound of his horn, and though it was clearly intended to lend his playing greater presence, it had the opposite effect of drawing the ear to the surrounding hush—even the drummer sounded contemplative, no more than hinting at a beat with wire brushes on his cymbals. My first guess was that this had to be something on ECM, a label that once advertised its releases as presenting "the most beautiful sound except for silence" and whose recording technique left so much space between instruments that you felt invited to make your own comparison. I almost smacked myself when it dawned on me that the saxophonist sounded so much like Coltrane because it was Coltrane. The piece was "Flamenço Sketches," from the best-selling jazz album of all time, Miles Davis's *Kind of Blue*— a recording I had prided myself on knowing note for note.

What fooled me was that echo, which is present on no other edition of the album. Its appearance on this, the first digitally remastered CD of *Kind of Blue*, was, I suppose, a bid to put a contemporary gloss on a classic from another era. Befitting an album that not only elicits a subjective response from each listener but practically demands one, no two editions of *Kind of Blue* have sounded exactly the same. Beginning with the original 1959 LP, each has left something to be desired. The poet Michael S. Harper once told a story that I wouldn't be so quick to dismiss as apocryphal, about a man from Iowa who became so transfixed by the three numbers on Side One of *Kind of Blue*—"So What," "Freddie Freeloader," and "Blue in Green"—that he never got around to flipping the record over to hear "All Blues" and "Flamenço Sketches." He told Harper that Side One was so profound that he was afraid Side Two would be a letdown. I wonder if this Midwestern mystic ever noticed anything awry about those three tracks as he listened to them over and over. They were made at the first of two recording sessions, during which an undetected problem with the speed of one of the tape recorders resulted in a quarter-tone sharpness in pitch. For decades this mistake bedeviled inexperienced musicians who tried to play along with the tracks, sheepishly blaming themselves when they ended up in another key. For the rest of us, this tonal ambiguity actually worked in the album's favor, creating the seductive illusion of music that inhabited its own dreamlike space (nothing on *Kind of Blue* is taken very fast, and even the medium-tempo numbers seem to be floating by in slow motion). No engineer seems to have identified the error until 1992, when someone at Columbia Records who was preparing an audiophile edition bothered to listen to a safety copy that had been recorded at the correct speed (for many of us this new, improved *Kind of Blue* took some getting used to). The most recent reissue of *Kind of Blue*, which appeared in 1997, uses the correct pitch for the first three tracks and drops the echo effect on "Flamenço Sketches," but it features a new distortion—an occasional tape hiss that is possibly intended to assure listeners that the producers have left well enough alone (that is, no filtering has been done, for fear of eliminating the music's high end, along with extraneous tape noise.)

Inattention to sound wasn't the only problem with earlier generations of the album. On the disc labels and jacket sleeves of the initial release, "All Blues" was misidentified as "Flamenço Sketches" and vice-versa, which created confusion for people hoping to share their impressions of the album with others. On all editions before the most recent, the alto saxophonist Cannonball Adderley's last name was misspelled, and the pianist Wynton Kelly and the drummer Jimmy Cobb were listed as Wyn Kelly and James Cobb. When the album made its debut on CD, nobody but me seemed bothered by the period echo; what did bother some people was the photograph of Davis that had been chosen for the cover, which showed him wearing his freaky-deaky duds of the 1970s (in 1959 he was still wearing Brooks Brothers and fine Italian silk) and gave the false impression that he played trumpet left-handed.

None of this has prevented *Kind of Blue* from selling more than two million copies over the years—a remarkable figure for such uncompromising jazz. More than four decades after its first appearance, it routinely sells between four and six thousand copies a week in the United States alone. Although many of these buyers may be people who are otherwise disinclined to take a chance on jazz, there is no telling how many copies a week are sold to repeat customers—longtime owners of *Kind of Blue* replacing worn-out LPs, hoping for improved sound, or in the market for déjà vu.

In the history of jazz, *Kind of Blue* is famous as the album that popularized modal improvisation—it alerted musicians to the lyrical potential of riffing on simple modes and scales, in repudiation of bebop's augmented chords and quick-change harmonics. But this hardly explains why generations of listeners whose knowledge of scales might be limited to hearing Julie Andrews sing "Doe, a deer . . . " (and who think you're getting too technical if you tell them to visualize five or more consecutive white keys on a piano) identify so intensely with the album. *Kind of Blue*'s fortieth anniversary last year generated as much press coverage and inspired as many commemorative concerts as Duke Ellington's centennial. It is the only album ever to have a ghost band (with the trumpeter Wallace Roney and other ringers joining Cobb, the only surviving musician from the original cast). Recordings are valued as the "textbooks" of jazz, as the drummer Max Roach once put it. But *Kind of Blue* is frequently spoken of in language more befitting a sacred text. In *Kind of Blue: The Making of the Miles Davis Masterpiece*, Ashley Kahn says that "in the church of jazz, it is one of the holy relics." And in another new book on the same subject, the similarly titled *The Making of Kind of Blue*, Eric Nisenson, Kahn's more hyperbolic competitor, tells us that the album was for him "a gateway to the world of adult emotions," and "one of the stepping stones toward adult maturity."

WITH THE EXCEPTION OF *SGT. PEPPER'S LONELY HEARTS CLUB BAND*, HAS ANY pop album ever been the subject of two full-length books? The names of the musicians who were involved in *Kind of Blue* provide the most obvious clue to the album's enduring mystique. Besides Davis, Coltrane, Adderley, Kelly, and Cobb, they included the pianist Bill Evans and the bassist Paul Chambers—a post-bop summit. But this was no ad hoc gathering put together by a record producer oblivious to the question of musical compatibility. All seven musicians were current members of Davis's band, except Evans, who was a recent alumnus (Kelly, his replacement, plays only on "Freddie Freeloader," the album's closest thing to an uptempo number). In its own day *Kind of Blue* appealed to listeners as an informal symposium on the various directions jazz might pursue in the 1960s. Part of what fascinates us now is that the recording sessions took place in the nick of time: It's virtually impossible to imagine Davis, Evans, Adderley, and Coltrane getting together two or three years later, by which point each had become not just the leader of his own band but of his own school.

Davis was an unorthodox bandleader, if hardly as laissez-faire as his reputation might suggest. He occasionally relied on traditional means of ensuring contrast and variety—including gradual or sudden shifts in rhythm or texture and dynamics (it's taken me all these years to notice that the drums are silent during Davis's opening solo on "Flamenço Sketches," finally coming in under Coltrane). But his typical strategy was to bring together sidemen who were radically different from himself and one another, both in temperament and musical inclination, and wait for the friction to produce heat and light. On *Kind of Blue* he and Coltrane were the most opposite polarities: Davis's solos, spare and confidential, drawing you in by holding something back; Coltrane's confrontational and densely packed, aiming for musical and spiritual transcendence with a downpour of notes. The two men were philosophical opposites as well: Davis, who was admired for the stylish lines of his suits and sports cars and women, and whom Ornette Coleman once described as "a black man who lives like a white man," was a materialist, not a mystic. Adderley and Evans sounded exactly the way they looked, which almost conformed to stereotype: Adderley was fleshy and jovial, a motivating force in the "soul jazz" movement of the 1950s (even his ballad solos danced the hucklebuck, tacitly inviting listeners to do likewise); and Evans, the band's only white face, was shy and intellectual (he wore glasses and sat hunched over the keyboard as though trying to make himself invisible). His friend the composer and modal guru George Russell tells Eric Nisenson that Evans looked like a "nonperson."

Last year during a joint interview he and I did with Scott Simon of National Public Radio, on the occasion of *Kind of Blue*'s fortieth birthday, Jimmy Cobb said that to him the music on the album sounds as characteristic of Evans as of Davis. Certainly, Evans seems as much responsible for the distinctive melancholy that has long been *Kind of Blue*'s strongest lure, notwithstanding its formal innovations. There is evidence to suggest that he co-wrote "Flamenço Sketches" and "Blue in Green," although Davis was given sole credit. ("Flamenço Sketches" sprang from Evans's "Peace Piece," which was itself based on the intervals of Leonard Bernstein's "Some Other Time," from the show *On the Town*. Kahn, who is a good tune detective, finds the roots of "Blue in Green" in Evans's introduction to "Alone Together," on a recording of that standard he made with the trumpeter Chet Baker a few months before *Kind of Blue*. Nisenson has it that Davis claimed only co-composer credit for "Blue in Green"—a factual error in a book riddled with them.) Evans also wrote the album notes, and the generations of listeners who have cherished *Kind of Blue* as an unrivaled exercise in spontaneity have been taking their cue from him. Evans compares what happened at the sessions to "a Japanese visual art" in which "an unnatural or interrupted stroke will destroy the line or break through the parchment," and in which "erasures or changes" are therefore impossible—Kahn identifies it as *suibokuga*, a form of black-ink painting introduced to Japan by Buddhist monks toward the close of the fourteenth century. Overlooking his own compositional contributions, Evans writes, "Miles conceived these settings only hours before the recording dates . . . and I think without exception the first complete performance of each was a 'take.'" In fact, the complete session tapes, which have been circulating among historians and collectors for years— despite Kahn's naive belief that being allowed to hear them was a rare privilege—tell a different story. There were two complete takes of "Flamenço Sketches" (the earlier one is now a CD bonus track), along with a lot more stopping and starting than Evans's notes would have us believe. And contrary to what he implies, it has always been common for jazz musicians to be asked to sight-read new pieces at recording sessions. There have been many bandleaders for whom this was a deliberate strategy, including Duke Ellington. (The composer Maria Schneider recently told me that, in occasionally springing new pieces on her musicians during record sessions, she hopes "they'll sound like they're discovering each note, even if this risks making the performance sound a little uncertain.")

The difference on *Kind of Blue* was that the musicians were required not just to interpret new compositions but also to improvise according to unfamiliar procedures. Evans identifies what was musically visionary about the album in the final paragraph of his notes when he refers to one of the pieces as "modal"—a word that few listeners were familiar with in 1959, although they would soon be hearing it plenty. (Jazz musicians tend to use the word loosely, referring to any piece built on scales as "modal," but the term properly refers to music built—as both "So What" and "Flamenço Sketches" were—on one or more of the archaic "church" scales, or modes, that were the basis for most European composition before Bach.) *Kind of Blue* is frequently hailed for having introduced modes to jazz, but this distinction seems to belong to George Russell's "Cubano Be" and "Cubano Bop," a two-part work recorded by Dizzy Gillespie's big band in 1947. There were numerous other precedents for *Kind of Blue*. A 1956 album by the clarinetist Tony Scott (with Evans on piano) had featured a tune called "Aeolian Drinking Song," named for the mode on which it was based. Davis himself had already recorded a bona fide modal piece called "Milestones," and a few other pieces— including a handful of stark themes for the soundtrack of Louis Malle's *Ascenseur pour L'Échafaud* and his version of "Summertime" with the arranger Gil Evans (no relation to Bill)—whose use of a minimum of slow-moving chords at least hinted at modality.

But modes and scales were tricky business for most musicians in 1959. Among the never-before-published session photographs in Kahn's book is one of Cannonball Adderley's well-fortified music stand. It shows Adderley's mouthpiece, a box of reeds, a pack of Newports, a sugar substitute, a diabetes medication, a bottle of Bufferin, and a lead sheet for "Flamenço Sketches" outlining its five modes. Adderley suffered from migraines, but he might have needed the Bufferin in any case. Like Coltrane, he was venturing into unfamiliar territory, and there are moments when both men sound as though they're treading cautiously. This wasn't entirely to either player's disadvantage: Coltrane benefited from a little slowing down at that point in his career, and Adderley needed a safeguard against glibness. Indeed, *Kind of Blue* presents the antithesis of spontaneity. One hears a good bit of tentativeness on the part of everyone but Davis and Evans, and it probably tells us something

that when Davis added "So What" and "All Blues" to his concert repertoire, both tunes gradually became a lot faster. This element of caution
is one of the album's most compelling aspects; it comes across as passionate deliberation—an antidote to the unmediated virtuosity of so
much modern jazz.

Evans, with his analogy to *suibokuga*, captures the music's peculiar
Zen. "So What," for example, begins with a questioning, out-of-tempo,
piano-and-bass introduction that later musicians have tended to skip in
favor of going straight to the main theme. (Both Kahn and Nisenson write
that the introduction may have been composed and arranged by Gil
Evans, in his uncredited role as a troubleshooter.) "So What" eventually
becomes a bouncy semi-blues, an orchestrated fingersnap, with the horns
and bass doing a catchy, Baptist-style call and response not much different
from dozens of other numbers of the period, including Nat Adderley's
"Work Song," Bobby Timmons's "Moanin'," and even "Freddie Freeloader," the very next track. But the memory of that austere opening
lingers, and "So What" could be the sound of one finger snapping.

NISENSON, THE AUTHOR OF PREVIOUS BOOKS ON DAVIS, COLTRANE, AND SONNY
Rollins, tells us early on that he hopes to do with *Kind of Blue* what Greil
Marcus did with Bob Dylan's *Basement Tapes* in *Invisible Republic*—that
is, to examine the album as an unofficial history of its era. His idea of
doing this is to paraphrase Dylan every now and then: *Kind of Blue*
offered proof that "the times, they were a'changin'," but Nisenson never
clearly establishes what these changes were or exactly how *Kind of Blue*
anticipated them. He can't even keep his clichés straight: "Rear vision is
20/20," he observes at one point, meaning hindsight (and Kurosawa's
Rashamon, with which he compares *Kind of Blue*, tells the same story
from four different points of view, not five). Instead of digging for information about the origins of *Kind of Blue*, Nisenson is content to sit back
and dig the sounds, occasionally delivering Big Thoughts about "the
desire for authentic personal identity and expression" and "the search for
freedom" implicit in jazz.

Modes are something that the average listener can choose to think
about or not in responding to *Kind of Blue*, but the author of a book
about the album does not have that liberty. In an appendix Nisenson lets
George Russell, whose modal theories influenced both Davis and
Evans, expound on the subject for several pages, as if this will suffice to

clarify any confusion a reader might still have. The problem is that Russell uses standard musical terminology rather idiosyncratically, and not even a trained musicologist can be expected to understand everything he says. Why doesn't Nisenson step in to translate from time to time? Probably because he doesn't always have a clue what Russell is talking about either, to judge from the shortage of informed musical analysis in the main text. Russell is an engaging anecdotalist, and *The Making of Kind of Blue* comes alive only in a chapter devoted to him, where he relates interesting stories about Evans, Charlie Parker, and such minor figures as Sylvia Goldberg, a bebop pianist of the 1940s who moonlighted as a prostitute. But Nisenson seems to have talked to almost no one else.

Kahn's book is far more valuable. A former music editor for VH1, he has done a good deal of research, and his book is a small treasure. Among other things, we learn how many microphones and what brand of tape were used for the recording, the distinct acoustics produced by the high ceilings at Columbia's Thirtieth Street Studio, and how much each musician was paid. These are the sorts of things that I find weirdly valuable to know as I listen to *Kind of Blue*, though others might be inclined to dismiss them as fodder for obsessives.

Kahn examines the roles played in Davis's career by various Columbia Records' personnel (including George Avakian, who signed him to the label, and who tells Kahn that the head of the publicity department could hardly wait to approach the magazines on behalf of Davis, "with his Italian suits and Cole Porter mute"), and he follows *Kind of Blue* into the marketplace. An incident that took place a week after the album's release gave it an unforeseen splash of publicity. Davis was playing at Birdland and, after stepping outside to hail a cab for a white woman who was a friend of his, stood outside the club smoking a cigarette. A white cop who had seen him with the woman told him to move along, and when Davis refused, he was clubbed. His beating and arrest made front-page news. Kahn refrains from making too much of the incident, but takes notice of it all the same. His book also includes such intriguing memorabilia as a facsimile of the handwritten manuscript for Evans's notes; it reveals that the pianist's penmanship was as tidy and as precise as his playing.

Kahn solicits the opinions of numerous musicians who were not directly involved in the album, and they turn out to be fans like the rest of us. The pianist and composer Herbie Hancock, who was a sideman with Davis in the 1960s, marvels at Davis's boldness in assigning the melody of "So What" to bass. The trumpeter Hugh Masekela and the arranger Quincy Jones are more subjective. "Miles juxtaposed the modern, fantastically, against something very primitive on *Kind of Blue*," Masekela says. "It had very deep Congolese overtones for me." Referring to the music's slow-moving cadences, Jones says, "You know what it is? It's a junkie tempo."

It's no fault of Kahn's that his book includes little comment on *Kind of Blue* by the musicians involved in making it. To them, the two recording sessions seem to have been merely two more days on the job. Davis, in his autobiography, published in 1989, said that with *Kind of Blue* he was trying to evoke the sound of a gospel choir he had once heard on a dark road in Arkansas and the sound of an African thumb piano he had heard during a performance by an African ballet troupe. Like Nisenson, Kahn gives these remarks more credence than I think they deserve: Davis may have been engaging in revisionism, in an attempt to make the album seem "blacker" than it really was. Although Nisenson suggests that *Kind of Blue* was Davis's effort to divert jazz from conventional Western tonality, the modes he and Evans employed *were* Western; it was Coltrane who, a few years later, popularized the use of non-Western scales. Nisenson seems on safer ground when he describes *Kind of Blue* as "the jazz equivalent of the impressionism of Debussy, Ravel, and Scriabin"; he quotes Davis as having said, around the time of the sessions, that some European composers had "been writing this way for years." People listen to *Kind of Blue* just, I think, as concert audiences have traditionally listened to a disphonous Debussy work like "La Mer." They may sense that something unusual is being ventured, but their emotional response is triggered by the music's mood, not by its modus operandi.

KAHN'S CRITICAL INSIGHTS ARE SHARPER THAN NISENSON'S, THOUGH HE slightly exaggerates the album's radical effect on the very framework of jazz. "So What" may be modal, but it is still structured according to the standard length of thirty-two bars, with an eight-bar bridge; "All Blues" is indeed a twelve-bar blues, even though it is in triple meter. Davis and the other soloists observed these structures in their improvisations, blowing for only a few choruses each. But as Kahn points out, in antic-ipation of Coltrane's epic modal solos of the early 1960s, not having to deal with a new set of chord changes every few measures soon enough resulted in players feeling free "to invent and reinvent as long as nec-essary to tell a story."

This hardly seems to have been what Davis had in mind. Early in his career Davis had rid his trumpet style of gratuitous technical flourishes; by 1959 modern jazz had become congested with chords, and for Davis, embracing modes and scales was another attempt to streamline. Modal jazz eventually brought its own abuses: An uninspired soloist diligently racing through a set of chord changes can sound like he's caught in a maze; scales release the soloist from the maze, but glue his ass to a see-saw. Unlike bebop and the style of free improvisation that Ornette Coleman introduced the same year that Davis recorded *Kind of Blue*, modal jazz never became a widespread movement—though once Davis showed the way, it was a style that nearly every jazz musician felt he had to try, if only to keep up (I remember a veteran pianist whose allegiance was to the swing era proudly telling me that he was taking "modal les-sons" from a younger saxophonist). Always something of a chameleon, Davis quickly moved on. Not even Coltrane, the soloist who became most identified with modes, ever committed himself to them exclusively.

A question that neither book addresses is whether any jazz album recorded today could have anything approaching *Kind of Blue*'s impact. Sadly, the answer is no. Nisenson tells us that in the 1950s jazz was still "somewhat isolated, alienated from American society at large," but this observation seems more accurate about jazz today. Kahn is more on tar-get in implying that Davis's celebrity in the 1950s owed a great deal to Columbia's practice of marketing and promoting jazz LPs through its pop division. Davis's records weren't pop by any means, but they often reached as large an audience. Davis is often said to have anticipated almost every new direction in jazz from cool in the late 1940s to fusion in the early 1970s, but he also had an uncanny knack for being at the center of cultural trends. (In Kahn's book, the novelist Dan Wakefield reminds us that Davis's next landmark album, *Sketches of Spain*, was released in 1961, when everyone Wakefield knew was listening to Flamenço guitar and had a bullfighting poster on the wall.) On *Kind of Blue*, with help from Evans, Davis captured the mood of uncertainty that

prevailed in bohemian and intellectual circles at the end of the 1950s—
a time when the artists and audiences who were most committed to the
modernist ideal of ongoing progress in the arts were also reading the
Beats and J.D. Salinger and pondering Zen Buddhism's riddles of blissful acceptance of things as they are. Something of a riddle itself, *Kind of
Blue* continues to speak to us so clearly today because it seems so much
a creation of its own time.

The New Yorker, December 4, 2000

Aftershocks

$\overline{\overline{}}$

O bserving the scene around McCoy Tyner at Penn's Landing this summer, a stranger to Philadelphia might have thought that being a jazz
fan there was a patronage job. Everybody lining up to shake the pianist's
hand as he made his way from his trailer to the stage seemed to be related
to a jazz giant by blood or marriage, or to have taken auto shop with one
in high school. It was as though *not* to pay respects to Tyner would have
been a serious breech of protocol that could have resulted in immediate
dismissal from the local jazz community.

Things are different in New York, where the fifty-eight-year-old Tyner
lives now and where audiences seem more aware that giants need their
space. A few years ago, when Tyner was performing with his trio in
Greenwich Village, the latecomers to his final set one evening included
Reggie Workman, a bassist who played alongside him in John Coltrane's
rhythm section in the early 1960s, but whose relationship with Tyner
went back even further, to when both were growing up in Philadelphia.
(Workman often traveled from his parents' home in the Germantown
section to Tyner's mother's beauty shop, on the corner of May and
Fairmount Streets, in North Philadelphia, for late-night jam sessions.)
Workman hoped to touch base with Tyner after the set—as did a writer
working on a Coltrane biography, who was sitting at the same table.

What proved to be the final tune ended with a long, sliding bass solo
by Avery Sharpe, accompanied by only an occasional cymbal tap by the
drummer Aaron Scott. Surprisingly, Tyner never returned to the bandstand to take the tune out. As Sharpe zipped up his bass and Scott tight-

ened his drums, Workman and I looked for Tyner at the bar and on the
street, but were told that he had last been seen fleeing into a taxi.

His job completed for the night, Tyner had retreated back into private
life—which he seems to protect more zealously now, since entering middle age.

Every summer the Mellon PSFS Jazz Festival honors an internation-
ally prominent musician born in Philadelphia; this year was Tyner's turn.
Wearing a stylish mustard-colored jacket over black slacks, his eyes con-
cealed behind dark shades and his thinning hair ending in a rattail,
Tyner responded vacantly to the people grabbing his elbow or draping an
arm around his shoulder. It would have been impossible for an onlooker
to guess which of these people Tyner actually remembered and which he
was merely indulging. He addressed everyone in a rumbling baritone,
giving the impression that his mind had arrived on stage a good five minutes before his body.

Across the Delaware River, in Camden, New Jersey, in line of sight of
the large audience, stood the old RCA Building, which was scheduled to
be imploded the following morning—part of a haunted complex that seventy years ago hosted recording sessions by Jelly Roll Morton and His
Red Hot Peppers. That night, however, with Tyner being joined by Ravi
Coltrane (John Coltrane's saxophonist son) and a variety of former associates, including Workman and the violinist John Blake, the agenda
called for an explosion—the kind of liquid and fiery music Tyner made
with Coltrane and in the early 1970s with his own bands.

The following morning the Camden implosion went off without a
hitch, shaking the earth for miles on both sides of the river. As for Tyner,
what he delivered was more like a series of aftershocks from earlier in his
career.

"YOU'D WALK INTO A CLUB LIKE THE HALF NOTE [IN NEW YORK CITY] AND JOHN
would be playing with McCoy and Jimmy [Garrison] and Elvin [Jones],
and John's solo would go on for, like, forty-five minutes and you'd think
it was the most exciting music you had ever heard," Paul Bley, a pianist
and Tyner's contemporary, recently recalled. "Then, McCoy and
Jimmy would drop out and the *real* set would begin, with just John and
Elvin. And it would turn out that everything leading up to that was just
a prelude."

Coltrane so stretched the limits of conventional harmony that Tyner's piano often seemed vestigial—a dimly audible reminder of the bonds the saxophonist had broken. Yet in listening to the many recordings Tyner made with Coltrane, one recognizes Tyner's mastery. Not just a dazzling improviser in his own right, he was also Coltrane's ideal accompanist.

"He gave me a lot of room, and I tried to do the same for him," Tyner now says matter-of-factly. "It was almost like mental telepathy. I could almost visualize where he was going harmonically, and he used to tell me he liked the way I moved the chords behind him. He liked my chordal suspensions and harmonic substitutions, because of the freedom they gave him. They didn't lock him up, the way another approach to piano might have."

Bley, whose lean style is the antithesis of Tyner's rhapsodies, recalls the one occasion he sat in: "It was as though John took me by one arm and Elvin by the other, and within a few bars, I was playing exactly like McCoy Tyner did with that group. There was no other way to play with them."

Along with the course of jazz improvisation, John Coltrane altered the public image of jazz musicians. Charlie Parker was the hipster's hipster, a pied piper for heroin as well as for bebop. Coltrane, after kicking his own habit, became the mystic's mystic—a man whose music was regarded as a ritual of self-purification. After Coltrane, a jazz musician was more likely to be a vegetarian than a junkie, and more likely to wear a kufi than a beret. The new jazz musician was a man with his nose buried in books on Eastern religions and Nicholas Slonimsky's *Thesaurus of Chords*. Musicians and professional athletes have traded roles today: Prizefighters and power forwards attract notoriety with their flamboyant wardrobes, crude behavior toward women, and dependence on controlled substances, whereas pianists and tenor saxophonists are celebrated for their modesty, mental and physical preparedness, and belief in a power greater than themselves.

The first of the new models was McCoy Tyner, a man exactly like Coltrane, only more so. A story illustrates what kindred spirits they were. Coltrane's quartet, early in its existence, would frequently travel by station wagon from its headquarters in New York to engagements as far away as San Francisco (the cost of air travel was prohibitive in those days, and Tyner reckons that Coltrane "wasn't too comfortable with flying any-

way"). Jones, a voluble sort, as drummers tend to be, remembers hours
drifting by with neither Coltrane nor Tyner saying a single word. Yet
from Tyner's point of view these long journeys were rewarding: "They
gave us so much chance to talk." Maybe he and Coltrane practiced mental telepathy off the bandstand as well.

Coltrane and Jones would share the driving on these trips, because
nobody trusted Jimmy Garrison to drive (he liked a good time too much)
and because Tyner, then in his early twenties, didn't know how—presumably having spent every spare moment as a teenager at the piano.

SO MUCH HAS BEEN MADE OF THE CULTURAL SIGNIFICANCE OF THE NEIGHBOR-
hood barber shop to African-American men that the importance of the
beauty shop to black women risks going overlooked. The beauty shop
owned and operated by Tyner's mother may have been the only one in
Philadelphia with a piano—"a console spinnet, it was called, halfway
between a spinnet and an upright in size," says Tyner, who was the oldest of three children. "We lived upstairs but the piano was in the shop
because that was the only place it would fit. Even after we moved to West
Philly, my mother's shop in Fairmount was where I practiced. My friends
and I would play between her appointments, and occasionally even
when she had someone in the chair."

Tyner, whose teenage friends included such names-to-be as Workman,
Lee Morgan, and Archie Shepp, wasn't the only pianist who worked on
his intervals and block chords in the shop. In 1953, when Tyner was fifteen, it happened that Bud Powell, the closest thing to Charlie Parker on
piano and one of Tyner's idols (the other was Thelonious Monk), briefly
lived around the corner. Powell was convalescing following his confinement in a sanitarium.

"One of my mother's clients was the wife of the apartment building's
superintendent, and she mentioned to my mother that a guy was staying
there who was supposed to be a great pianist, but didn't have an instrument to practice on. Of course, as soon as she said his name, I told her
to tell him to come right over. He only came around that one time to
practice, but sometimes after that, I would be practicing and look up,
and there he would be outside the door to the shop, watching me and, I
guess, listening. It was intimidating, but it was also encouraging."

Within a year or so Tyner was playing club dates around Philadelphia
with veteran musicians, one of whom influenced his life in a couple of

ways. Calvin Massey was a trumpeter whose drug habit and dental problems hampered him as a soloist, but he enjoyed some renown as the
composer of "Fiesta," a tune recorded by Charlie Parker. The singer in
Massey's band introduced Tyner to her sister, whom Tyner ultimately
married. And Massey introduced Tyner to his friend, John Coltrane.

IT IS IMPOSSIBLE TO SPEAK OF THE 1960S, THE DECADE OF TYNER'S ASCEN-
dancy, without acknowledging its political turmoil. In Coltrane's case,
what some heard as a quest for spiritual enlightenment, others insisted
was a cry for black freedom. Yet Tyner—whose younger brother, Jarvis,
ran for vice-president on the Communist Party ticket in 1972 and 1976—
says that both he and Coltrane were essentially apolitical: "I mean, we
would talk about political issues, as everybody did back then," Tyner
reveals. "It was impossible not to be caught up in what was happening,
seeing the sit-ins and the riots and the Vietnam war and the student
protests on television every night. But nothing that anyone in that band
ever said that I happened to hear would have labeled us as revolutionar-
ies, or even as a politically conscious group of men. John did write a
beautiful tune called 'Alabama' for the little girls killed in the church
bombing [in Birmingham, in 1963], but that was about it."

Even Jarvis Tyner concurs with this view. Still, as Jarvis points out, the
band's music "projected anger, it projected dignity and determination,
and it projected a rebellious spirit that was very much in keeping with
what was going on in America's cities in the 1960s."

It isn't just that times change. So do people. To hear McCoy Tyner
talk about his current life, his middle years are shaping up as extremely
mellow. Divorced now, his three sons grown up and on their own,
Tyner has sold his house in Connecticut and moved back to
Manhattan. "It's the best place in the world for a single guy, which I am
again," he says. Years ago, a jazz fan could show he was in the know by
referring to Tyner as Sulaimon Saud, the name he took on becoming a
Muslim but never used professionally. "Spirituality is one thing and
religion is another," Tyner says now, responding to a question about
whether it bothers him as a Muslim to play in nightclubs, where people are drinking. "At this point in my life, I am no longer a member of
any organized religion." On the subject of politics, he and his brother
long ago agreed to disagree. "Jarvis sees the world through his particular ideology," Tyner observes. "But I've been to some of the former

Communist countries, and the quality of life in them didn't look so ideal to me."

Tyner is one of a handful of jazz musicians able to work as much as he wishes, not just in Europe and Japan, but also in this country. Being a little road weary isn't the only downside to all of this activity. "I just heard McCoy Tyner at a festival here," a friend from Portugal recently wrote. "More of the same."

Whitney Balliett, the poet laureate of jazz critics, once described jazz as "the sound of surprise." What happens when a musician's revolutionary style becomes so integral to the canon that it ceases to deliver surprise? This is the dilemma now facing McCoy Tyner, whose vast influence on younger pianists has had the paradoxical effect of making his original article sound overly familiar.

Tyner himself does not feel he's in a rut. He tries to ensure variety by presenting himself in different contexts. In addition to his trio and his solo concerts, he leads an all-star big band that has won two Grammys; it remains a part-time outfit, by Tyner's choice. He freely admits that his latest album *What the World Needs Now Is . . . the Music of Burt Bacharach*, which swamps his trio with a string orchestra, is a bid for a larger audience. Bacharach's music represents a change of pace, Tyner says—an attempt to introduce some fresh songs into the nearly depleted jazz repertoire. Next up for him is a Latin album, his first since *La Leyenda de la Hora*, in 1981.

"I ALWAYS LOOK FORWARD TO COMING BACK TO PHILADELPHIA," TYNER SAID before his show on Penn's Landing. "I need to come back some time just to visit. I still have relatives here, you know, and it would be fun to visit my old haunts."

Oh, well, maybe next time—Tyner had to rush to the airport for a concert in Maine the following evening. Time might be gaining on him, as it does on all artists, but he's giving it a merry chase. Whatever his music has lost in intensity, it's gained in elegance, and at his very best—when he dispenses with horns and rhythm accompaniment to examine a great old ballad, each variation shining like a diamond—he convinces you that elegance is enough.

The Philadelphia Inquirer Magazine, October 5, 1997

Taken: The True Story of an Alien Abduction
(A Conversation with Sun Ra)

'**ve** been in different time frames, [outside] the division of time that man has. He lives in a time zone. I've been outside of a time zone. That makes a difference, because, outside, you don't pay any attention to what's happening, because you know it doesn't matter.

But you occasionally step inside?
Yes, and you have to adjust yourself to the fact that you're in a time zone.

When did you first become aware that you had a special destiny?
I always knew I was different. I came from somewhere else. It took me a long time to figure this world out because I was thinking about where I came from.

How old were you when you realized all of this?
About seven years old. They kept talking about God. In the churches, my grandmother. But I never could understand if Jesus died to save people, why people still have to die. That seemed ignorant to me. That's how I felt as a child, and I never changed.

My mother didn't go to church. She said you make your own heaven and hell. She was opposed to my grandmother, who was very strict, you know—very religious. She didn't like me to play nothing but church songs.

When I came home from school one day, my mother had a so-called birthday present for me. A piano. I never wanted to be a musician, because I heard that musicians died young. I sat down and played it. I didn't have a teacher. The boy next door played violin. He said I was playing by ear. I didn't have to buy any music for about a year, because every day he brought over a piece of music for me and I played it. Difficult classical compositions. I played everything. I was just a natural.

Then I went through high school, in the school band, and I still didn't want to be a musician. They gave me a scholarship to college to lead the band. I was stuck with leading the band.

That was in Alabama. How did you wind up in Chicago?
I went to Nashville first; with Wynonie Harris, the blues singer. He wanted me to play with his band.

I believe you also played for a singer who performed in top hat and tails?
JoJo Adams. Imagine that. Singin' the blues and wearin' tails. He had this knock-kneed dance he would do. I think of him when I see Chuck Berry. He was sort of that type. "12 O'Clock Blues": X-rated. His stage presentation was spectacular. He was very slender, too.

In Chicago, I played with different musicians. I was playing different. They knew I was playing different. They didn't understand what I was doing, but they were fascinated by it. So I never had to worry about working. I was talking about space and everything—shocking musicians. I told them things that were going to happen. I predicted synthesizers. I told them they would have electric instruments that you could blow; and they told me your saliva gets down in there, you'll be electrocuted—you couldn't do that. But they do have them now. Then I was talking about sending men to the moon. They called me "the moon man" then.

Then I decided to try to reach God. What they were teachin' in churches—was it true? What did He want? He told me He wanted to find one pure-hearted person on this planet. Just one.

And that was you?

Must have been. I had it all written down. I used to keep a diary, until one day the students found it on my bed. Everybody in the band was on my bed readin' my diary. They were havin' a good time. So I abolished the diary. But I still retain the memory.

Then, these space mens contacted me. They wanted me to go to outer space with them. They were looking for somebody who had that type of mind. They said it was quite dangerous because you had to have perfect discipline. When I went up, I'd have to go up like this [*elbows pointing in, fingers touching shoulders*] because [they said] don't let no parts of my body touch outside of the ship. Because if I did, going through different time zones, I wouldn't be able to come back. So that's what I did.

It looked like a giant spotlight [was] shining down on me. I call it transmolecularization: My whole body was changed into something I could see for myself. And I went up. Then I landed on a planet that I identified as Saturn. First thing I saw was something like the monorail of a railroad track comin' down out of the sky. Now when this picture came out, *Space Odyssey* or something like that—they had it right.

Then I found myself in a strange stadium, sittin' in the last row, in the dark. I knew I was alone. They were down there, on the stage, [in] something like a big boxing ring. They called my name and I didn't know it. They called my name again and I still didn't answer. Then all at once they teleported me, and I was down there on that stage with them. They had one little antenna on each ear. A little antenna over each eye. They talked to me. I was takin' teachers' training in college. They told me to stop that, because there was going to be great trouble from teenagers in the schools. There was going to be trouble in every walk of life. That's why they wanted to talk to me. "Don't have anything to do with it. Don't continue." When it looked like the world was going into complete chaos, then I could speak, but not until then. I would speak, and the world would listen. That's what they told me.

Next thing, I found myself back on earth in a room with them. It was the backroom of an apartment, and there was a courtyard. They was all with me. I was in Chicago. I was laying down on a stone park bench. Some park, near a river. There was a bridge. The sky was purple and dark red, and through it I could see the space ships. I heard a voice say, "You can order us to land, but the space ships can't land unless you say so." I think I said yes—they started to land. And there were people running to [see] the landing, and they shot something like bullets. But they weren't bullets. They were something that, when they hit the ground, they were like chewing gum. . . .

[Years later] when I found myself in New York City, and I was near Columbia University, I saw the bench. I saw the bridge. So those things have been indelibly printed on my brain. I couldn't get 'em out if I tried.

The aliens told you that the world would soon be in chaos?
They said when it was in chaos—when the teenagers would not listen to *anybody*, neither mother nor father nor church nor school nor nobody—that I would clarify the issue.

And people would listen?
And people would listen.

Has that moment arrived yet?
Well, I just came back from Russia, and they gave a toast to me as a world citizen. They said I represented friendship.

You once said that knowledge is laughable when attributed to a human being.
It is, because they're into something they shouldn't be into. Sickness and death and slavery—all these things that happen. It's a scenario—they have to follow it. Lack of choice.

[Man has] symbols, but I'm talkin' equations. The symbols written up on the cross: "NRI" [or "IHS," for "I have suffered"]. That's "SHIT" backwards. That ain't too good. See, the cross is the "T." Because all these religions came from the east, and in the east they read right to left. Japanese do it too. So therefore—"SHIT." They can be intelligent and still not see this simple symbol. You have to go by the symbols. It's there: "INRI—T."

They say the first shall be last, the last shall be first. That's an equation. Therefore, "a" equals "z." If that is true, you don't have a creator no more. You take the "a" away for a "z," you got a "creztor." But they have to be careful because you got that "or" there, so that doesn't mean anybody created something. A creator would be "c-r-e-a-t-e-r"—he created something. But "c-r-e-a-t-o-r" is just a position, like Governor, [with] "or" on the end. Like mayor. You see? Doctor, too. These are just positions. Therefore, anybody can be a creator. I mean, they got authority, [but] that doesn't necessarily mean they created anything. They could, because they have the authority. But they might destroy, too. They might be Hitler. Or they might be Stalin.

Do you consider yourself a human being?

No. Too many things have happened. As a man thinketh, so *is* he. And these things that have happened to me, they haven't happened to everybody. That makes my mind totally different. . . .

A fellow who was sort of managing me, he went down the subway in New York City—14th Street. The police came down, said he jumped the turnstile. He said, "I didn't, I paid." So they took him back up to the booth. The woman said, "Oh, no, that was two white fellows jumped the turnstile—it wasn't him." So he said to the police, "See, you embarrassed me and I haven't done anything. You see how you all do things if someone's a black man?"

So one of the police got behind him, on his knees; the other, like little boys, pushed him over. They did that, and somehow the nightstick hit the pavement. So here come the other police. They didn't ask no questions. They formed a ring around him and tried to hit him with their sticks, but they couldn't hit him. He moved his head about, and moved his head about. They surrounded him and all at once, he said "Creator, help me." And then, this voice came out of nowhere and said "LEAVE THE MOTHERFUCKER ALONE."

So they stopped and looked around. They didn't see nothing, but they didn't continue. So [James] Jackson, our conga player, was telling them in Philadelphia about that incident. He said, "The Creator talks like that. He talks my language." The other fellow said, "Yeah, He talks whatever language that you understand. He won't tell you something that you don't understand, 'cause you won't get the message."

Do you have earthly needs?

I have to eat properly, though I forget about eating quite often. I have to cook for myself, because I have to have food a certain way. I always like for my foods to be real done—almost black. Bread and everything. I don't like no wishy-washy stuff. Sometimes, I have to cook me a moon stew—a moon soup. Everybody likes that. You have to choose the vegetables just right, they have to be fresh, and they have to be of a certain quality.

You have to know which ones to pick, [or] it's not going to taste right. You pick the tomatoes, you pick the okra, you pick the corn, and you cook it [at] just the right temperature. You can taste each vegetable individually. It doesn't just become a soup where you taste nothing.

I have to take care of everything myself. Nobody help me. Got to take care of the bookings, their health—see that they eat properly. It's more than one man can do. But the Bible say death came in through one man. It has to be done away with by one man. And that book is the law right now, because King James put his stamp on it. So it's the truth. We just a suburb of England, anyway. And all England and the rest of the world is just a suburb of the Roman Empire.

Why are you here, on earth?
Because people need me. There is a God, you know. He just let [people] go on and on and on, so he can teach them something. Because they got their own minds. They free to think what they want. But they don't ask no questions. They accept this as the norm. I don't.

About two months ago I asked the minister "How's your boss?" Nobody ever asks God how's He doin'. They never ask Him nothin'. So, the minister said, "Oh, He's doin' all right." I said, "That's nice, but a lot of bad things happen on this planet. What about that?" He said, "Oh, He knows about it." I said, "People are dyin' and gettin' killed and all that. What is He gonna do?" He said, "He's not gonna do anything." I said, "Why not?" He say, "He's tryin' to get their attention. He did all kinds of nice things for them, they didn't see that. So now He's doin' these other things to get their attention." That's what the minister told me.

Does that make sense to you?
Yeah, it makes sense. If you a teacher and the students are all out of order, you have to do something. You can't let the tail wag the dog. You have to be able to take control. . . .

You got brother against brother in every country. I'm of a scientific mind, so I want to know why. It's Jesus they worshipping. He told them, "I came not to bring peace; I came to bring a sword." So you got war on this planet, brother against brother, son against father—you got that. You have to deal with it. Why are these folks using dope and everything? I [say] well, they gave God's son some dope on the cross. What's sauce for the goose is sauce for the gander. I think they should wake up and see, they should stop teaching that that was Good Friday.

They gave dope to Jesus. That's in the Bible. They gave Him some stuff to ease the pain. So now, their teenagers using dope. And even down to the subteenagers. That's God doing that, who they say is love, but actually it's reap what you sow. But you have to spell [it] "s-o." And not "sow." That means what you say is true—that's what you get. So what we're doin' here is reapin' the fruit of some lies people told about God. Like, you know, [that] he forgives sins. He don't forgive nobody. He doesn't have to.

What about the Nation of Islam?
They're very devious. They tell lies all the time. [One told me] "I'm a Muslim, I been a Muslim my whole life"—but his people weren't Muslims. So then he [said], "I got a piano here"—he's in St. Louis—"and this piano's really worth money, because it's from France, and I know if you play it, it'll be worth millions. I'm gonna bring it to Philadelphia for you." I haven't heard any more from him. Then he said, "I'm gonna send a thousand dollars to you, put out some records." No money. So they [tell] lies—tell you what you want to hear and don't intend to do none of it, and that's what's wrong with this planet. Stop telling these lies. They think they free. And that's the trick that God got. Make them think they're free.

He don't care what you worship. It's all a part of Him. Anything you [can] make is made out of some material because of him. Man doesn't make nothin'. Except plastic and stuff like that. But you do have to use the stuff that's here. You can't create somethin' out of nothin'.

What about music? Doesn't man make music?
Well, he get inspired. It's as difficult for a musician as it is for a scientist. You can't do anything unless you sacrifice. You have to give up some time. And you have to rehearse, because in America, they can build you up like you're a genius, the people believe what they [hear] on TV and what they read in the papers. They easily brainwashed in America. But in Europe, it's not like that. They go by what you doin'. You can't fool them neither, because they got the classics—they can compare. If you come up with somethin' them classical composers didn't do and nobody else is doin', they want to hear [it]. That's why they're interested in me.

I'm gettin' ready to go to Sicily. They want me to teach their musicians over there. That'll be the first time I stepped outside of this band to teach the musicians. But they need the teaching because they're [blocked]. The potential for creativity is vaster than it's ever been, because of the electronics, but I have to show them how to use them. The band that I'll be teaching already has a bandleader—but he wants me to come over there and write for them, so they can understand a little bit more about what I'm talkin' about.

Does it ever bother you that you're not more popular here in the United States?

I didn't make any moves here. The main problem in America is black folks worshippin' the wrong thing. You can't get them to change. . . .

The black races were in touch with the real creators of the universe at one time—in perfect communication with them. They lost it, and ever since then, they be lonely—tryin' to reach a state of the same ecstasy or whatever you want to call it that they had at one time. So they go to church, and they do all kinds of things trying to reach that state because they had it. The white race never had it. He never sent them a prophet. He always sent them to black folks. But then, they went the wrong way so the communication was broken, and that meant that the white race couldn't get the real truth.

James Baldwin said in *The Fire Next Time:* Man only knows one truth, and that is death. In Spain, when they kill the bull, what do they call that? The moment of truth.

When I hear folks singin' "Joy to the world, the Lord has come," it kind of upsets me. Because they talkin' about death.

I've written some things I've held back. I don't know if the world is ready for them. I gave an interview to the Kansas City *Star*. They took my picture, put it up above the name of the paper. Under my name it said "Revolutionary." Inside they had something about "Beyond Infinity." The first thing I [was quoted as saying] was "Death is the God of this planet, and the ruler of it." It says that in the Bible. Moses: "Death reigns." I said, "It's almost over for the reign of death, and it's gonna get a lot of people—hundreds of thousands at once—before its rule on this planet is over." That's what their Jesus said: "I came to cast fire on the earth." It's happening every day. Atomic bombs—fire, that's what it is. They don't believe nice, beautiful Jesus would do that. But he is.

In Rome, I got a book. On the cover, Jesus was givin' a man a karate chop. That's in Italy, though—they got a different mindset there. You know, when he went in there where the merchants were? You know, people don't run from their money. They love their money. But he came in there and people fled for their lives. What was they runnin' from? So we have to take a good look at Jesus.

Judas didn't really intend for Him to get hurt. Judas thought he would demonstrate his powers and take the whole world over. But when he didn't and meekly went to his death, Judas was astounded.

Did you ever meet Elijah Muhammad?

Before he got his temple, I went to see him at a Baptist Church. And I realized there was some things he didn't know because right before him was a Christian sign—SHIT. So, that was that. I knew [the Nation of Islam would] go so far and not be able to go no farther, 'cause that's the way it is with Islam. They was on top of the world at one time, and they just stopped. They haven't been able to get it together since. It's up to the so-called Christians to tell the truth, and the main one they have to tell is that black folks in America can change the world. But they have to be their real selves. They can't be pretendin' they're slaves, that white people got control over them. They have to stand on their feet and say what they know and they will be respected.

Sometimes when I be talkin' to a black person, they go to sleep. They just go [*he demonstrates, closing his eyes and laying his head on his steepled hands*]. I can talk so much and their eyes close. All the time. Sometimes, it happen to people in this band. I be talkin', and after a while their eyes get heavy.

What makes a musician right for the Arkestra?

The Creator sends them. If they do not belong in this band, they won't stay here.

A lot of black people scared of me. For instance, in Philadelphia, they say I got a statue of Satan in this room here, that I makes the band bow down to it—if they don't, I beat 'em with a whip. They're made to crawl like the snakes of Satan. You tell them, well, "Why don't you go over there and see?" They say, "I'm not goin' in that house!"

What brought you to Philadelphia [in 1969], *and why have you stayed here?*

I had to change the planet, so I had to find the worst spot on Planet Earth, and that was Philadelphia. That's where liberty started. The bell cracked on 'em, so [liberty] ain't what it's cracked up to be, and now folks are using crack. Crack goes with liberty.

[Philadelphia is] the murder capital of the U.S. right now. Tyrone [Hill, a trombonist with Sun Ra's Arkestra] was in the subway, and some black teenagers were shootin' at one another from opposite ends of the platform, and he had to jump down on the track. Fifteen other black people jumped down there with him. They didn't think about the danger of the third rail. They had to get out the way of those teenagers.

It's dangerous. But it can change, the music has to do it.

A teenager told me last month, "I heard a piece you did. It was sixth-grade jazz." I said, "Sixth-grade jazz?" He said, "Yeah, because the average person in America has a sixth-grade education. You brought it down where the average person can hear." I said, "You mean I came down to earth." He said, "Yeah—I love you to death." In Philadelphia, that means they really love you.

[The tenor saxophonist] John Gilmore once told me, "I would like to travel." We been travelin' ever since. I would like a young Egyptian to come up, fall in love with me, fall in love with my music, say "I would do anything for you," and offer me so much money I would never have to worry about it again. But you have to be careful what you wish for—you might get it.

I have to be like a little child. I have to be totally sincere—to put my music out there and say take it or leave it. I can't be like other earth people.

Why is this planet called "earth"? Because earth should be spelled "E-R-T-H." If you turn it backwards, it's number three from the sun. In ancient days, people knew something. They had "g" as the third letter of the alphabet. Gamma. And since "g" is the name of this planet—you can prove it by the word "geography"—it should be put back there where it belongs. Now it's number seven. That's Uranus. Seventh Heaven. This is the third heaven. It ain't good when you say that when you die you want to go to heaven. They put you in the earth—underground.

You talk about "equations." Is music an equation?

They have to put a certain number of notes in a measure. That's an equation right there.

[A medical student once told me] "Don't do that. Stop playing that mad music." [It touched] every nerve in his body. Everything else has reached it. But I might as well. The military use their nerve gas. I'm gonna use my music. I'm playin' nerve music.

Why do you call your band "the Arkestra."

It's a play on words. "A covenant of Arkestra." It's like a selective service of God.

You once complained that black people were too materialistic.

Black people, they been into sex and drugs and religion. I like the word "dark" better than I do "black." Black folks used to be darkies. "That's Why Darkies Were Born." "Without a Song." I take that as my song. God didn't give black folks nothin' except music. Black folks too close to slavery. They worked four hundred years, don't have nothin'. They tryin' to make up for that. It's about money, money, money. It's about power. Pride. Black and proud. They don't realize it say pride goeth before the fall. Black is beautiful. You just can't say things. You have to know the equations. . . .

I read the Bible like it was a textbook, with my red pencil, and I have found astounding things. I haven't put out my version yet.

Philadelphia, January 14, 1990

Rashaan, Rashaan

It figures, I suppose, that the first jazz musician I got to know offstage was one who was larger than life there too. I met Rashaan Roland Kirk in 1971 . . . no, I *inherited* him, when I was hired as record buyer for Radio 437, a Philadelphia audio store whose selection of jazz imports put to shame any in New York, at least according to Rashaan. I remember him telling me that what had first lured him into the store was our voluminous stock of Folkways African LPs. He had no way of knowing that these very albums had hastened my predecessor's departure. African field recordings must have seemed like a good idea in those days of nascent cultural nationalism, when even our older black customers were starting to wear dashikis and grow naturals. But Rashaan was practically our only customer for them, and in desperation, my bosses slashed prices on our Folkways stock and hung a large banner announcing RADIO 437 IS RE-TURNING TO THE ROOTS! Which prompted one of my colleagues in the record department to quip, "Sure, all the way back to Moloch, the first thief in the Old Testament." A friend of mine, a native New Yorker, who wandered in during a heated argument between one of my bosses and me, described 437 as Philadelphia's only "Brooklyn" store. Conversations there tended to be shouting matches and if no Yiddish word existed for something, my bosses would make one up (crappy equipment bought cheap and sold at a high markup was a "klomus"). Every day at 437 was an object lesson in the tensions that can result when one ethnic group is doing the selling and another is doing the buying. To our audio salesmen the adage that the customer is always right meant telling *schwartzes* with money to spend whatever would close the sale. One day as I slouched against the 8-tracks yawning away a hangover, I heard the owner's brother tell a black couple that Panasonic was the brand all the "brothers" were buying, on account of what he described as the company's "enlightened" hiring policy. The next day, his pigeon was a turbaned Indian. "Panasonic," he rasped, "it's the brand the Pakistanis swear by."

Into this madness entered Rashaan Roland Kirk, whose sightlessness must have given him the look of an easy mark. I don't know exactly what happened on his first trip in. The story had it that he paid cash for an armload of records and accused the cashier (the owner's brother again) of shortchanging him. The upshot was that Rashaan insisted on writing a check on subsequent visits, only to be informed that no check could be accepted without a driver's license. Intervening on his behalf, I would be required to initial his check—the implication being that the amount of his purchase would be deducted from my pay if his check bounced. Then, as a standard courtesy to the blind, I would slit open the shrink-wrap on his albums. The whole time this was going on, my bosses would smile blandly at Rashaan, as if to say, it's store policy, babe—nothing personal. Rashaan, meanwhile, would scowl at them and glare, his eyeballs (when not hidden behind dark glasses) jumping every which way, though his head never moved and his expression never changed.

THIS HAPPENED ONCE A MONTH OR SO, UNTIL RASHAAN UNDERSTANDABLY TOOK his business elsewhere. What I wondered about then, and still do, is why someone so quick to take offense—someone whose race and physical disability gave him a chip on either shoulder—put up with such disgraceful treatment for so long. I guess it was because European labels were then beginning to fill the gap left by Blue Note and Prestige, and Rashaan just had to have all those Sabas and BYG Actuels that apparently only 437 could supply. In a 1974 *Down Beat* interview he complained that very few musicians knew his recent tunes, whereas he could "tell them about all their records, including the latest ones." I don't doubt it. Unlike most of the musicians I've met since, Rashaan was a record collector. And to judge from his purchases and our conversations about them, he went out of his way to hear every new jazz release—not necessarily expecting to like everything he heard, but curious about what this cat or that cat might be up to, and willing to spend money to find out.

Joel Dorn, the producer of a dozen or so of his releases for Atlantic and Warner Bros. in the decade before Kirk's death in 1977, asks us, in effect, to grant similar leeway to Kirk. Dorn's recent efforts on Kirk's behalf have included anthologies, facsimile reissues, and never-before-released location recordings that serve as reminders of how electrifying Kirk could be in concert, but also of how uneven and, occasionally, how tedious he could be too. The latest Kirk from Dorn is *Aces Back to Back* (32 Jazz 32060), a four-CD set of exactly that number of Kirk's Atlantic albums from the late 1960s and early 1970s. Also new in the stores, and produced by Dorn for Rhino in conjunction with Atlantic's fiftieth anniversary, is a lavishly packaged, quasi-audiophile edition of *The Inflated Tear*, a 1967 album that many point to as Kirk's best (Rhino R2 75207).

If all schoolkids learned something about jazz, what facts would they be able to rattle off about Rashaan Roland Kirk? First and foremost that he often played as many as three horns at once, including such curios of the reed family as manzello and stritch. (Extra credit would go to the child aware that Kirk eventually trained himself to play two melodies simultaneously, in counterpoint.) Also, that as a flutist, his signature was to growl or hum one series of notes while fingering another, a technique since adopted by nearly every jazz flutist (to say nothing of Ian Anderson, of Jethro Tull, who, in shameless emulation of Kirk, fashioned an entire career out of it).

But all of this merely describes Kirk as a multi-instrumentalist; it doesn't define him as an improviser and composer, which was something no one was able to do while he was alive either. The most idiosyncratic reed soloist since Sidney Bechet, with whom he shared a tendency toward operatic excess, Kirk fits easily into no school. In a 1965 article on the "New Thing" for *Esquire*, Leonard Feather named him as one of that era's most intrepid explorers, along with Ornette Coleman, John Coltrane, Cecil Taylor, and Archie Shepp. On the other hand, Amiri Baraka — that decade's ultimate arbiter of out — dismissed Kirk as a novelty act, after seeing him play a tenor solo while spinning a bass on his head.

Baraka probably thought he was hitting Kirk where it hurt; writers friendly to Kirk went to great lengths to disassociate him from carny performers with a similar bag of tricks. But I think Kirk's genius was in having it both ways—in knowingly exploiting the sideshow aspects of his act in the cause of musical advancement. Peter Townsend once dubbed Kirk an honorary rock musician—a bit of praise that, however self-serving, seems to me to be right on target. Rock 'n' roll is a form of music in which no clear line exists between novelty and innovation, and Kirk demanded the same privilege for jazz.

My favorite of Kirk's albums—my choice as his most consistent—is *Rip, Rig & Panic* (1965), an encounter with Elvin Jones, Jaki Byard, and Richard Davis that marked one of few occasions on which Kirk, as a bandleader, entered a recording studio with sidemen of equal stature. But I can easily comprehend the preference of others for *The Inflated Tear*, the most personal of Kirk's recordings and perhaps the most revealing. The title track, with Kirk producing hair-on-edge overtones on three horns, is essentially an *étude*—a study in multiphonics. But it beautifully demonstrates that even Kirk's most abstract musical gambits were rooted in physiological sensation. Art Tatum's musing touch and incredible keyboard wingspan are often assumed to have been tactile compensation for his blindness. Kirk's compensation was auditory, and "The Inflated Tear" offers evidence of his willingness to surrender himself to pure sound. A crusader for jazz tradition long before it became fashionable, Kirk also turns in an idiomatically perfect rendition of Ellington's "Creole Love Call" and leads his own New Orleans funeral parade on a hallucinogenic piece called "The Black and Crazy Blues." The CD's one bonus track is an uptempo romp on the standard "I'm Glad There Is You."

Of the four albums joined together as *Aces Back to Back* the most consistently rewarding is *Left & Right*, from 1968, a "with orchestra and strings" extravaganza that deftly avoids the genre's usual languors. The showstopper is Kirk's "Expansions," a twenty-minute suite enlivened by his rustic string writing and successful evocations of Ellington and Charles Mingus (his onetime employer). Kirk's relaxed interpretations of six Gil Fuller–arranged ballads, including Mingus's "I X Love," Billy Strayhorn's "A Flower Is a Lovesome Thing," and Fuller's own "I Waited for You," are also choice.

Rashaan Rashaan, from 1969 (and not to be confused with *Rachelle, Rachelle*, the story of a young girl's strange, erotic journey from Milan to Minsk), is mostly live, and shows Kirk succumbing to a self-indulgence characteristic of both him and jazz in the decade to come. Lecturing a Village Vanguard audience on their ignorance of John Coltrane and Charlie Parker is an example of chastising the converted, a reminder of how long-winded and dour Kirk could be when expounding on "black classical music." And a long studio performance that fails to tap the potential of an ensemble boasting the likes of Leroy Jenkins and Howard Johnson is annoyingly childlike in its rhythmic infrastructure. On the plus side we do get to hear Kirk play "Sentimental Journey" and Dvořák's *New World Symphony* simultaneously.

The title tune and centerpiece of *Prepare Thyself to Deal with a Miracle* (1973) is a Kirk "breathathon," a tenor solo of some twenty minutes' duration with not a single pause for air. At the time, I recall thinking this a rather tedious gimmick; now I find it astonishing. As a saxophone technique, circular breathing isn't all it's cracked up to be. Scattered throughout *Aces Back to Back* are Kirk solos that sound overcrowded—solos that could have benefited from air. By contrast, "Prepare Thyself" is filled with light and shade, much of it supplied by the ever-changing orchestral colors underneath Kirk, but just as much of it supplied by his own darting phrases. On this album, Kirk also puts to good use the voices of Jeanne Lee and Dee Dee Bridgewater, the latter of whom captures more of Ella Fitzgerald's élan here than she did on her recent Ella tribute.

Though it opens with a set piece dedicated to Paul Robeson and featuring Kirk on harmonica (of all things), *Other Folks' Music* (1976)—with numbers by Charlie Parker and Frank Foster, and by Kirk and his sidemen—is as close as he ever came to presiding over a studio blowing session. Kirk improvises with zest on all of his horns, and there are also tasty spots by the trumpeter Richard Williams and the then very young pianist Hilton Ruiz.

Excerpted for highlights, shorn of their bullshit, these four CDs would have supplied the material for a terrific double. I'm glad, though, that Dorn has reissued them in their entirety, because Rashaan Roland Kirk wasn't about good taste. His frequent misses somehow counted as much as his bull's eyes in making him one of a kind. Or put it this way: Any musician as eager as he was to hear everything, good and bad, deserves the same courtesy.

Inward

That was a very monumental time. The issue that we were dealing with, that A Patch of Blue *was addressing, was interracial relationships: a very sensitive, important issue—how America was viewing those relationships, what solutions were being put forth. Looking back, with all of the good intentions, we find ourselves approaching the new millennium with the same problems. They haven't been resolved.*

A Patch of Blue *was addressing racism through the metaphor of being without sight—being without sight. Then, in society, we find those who are blinded by sight. Because what they see is so important. It's what they base their decisions on. They either accept or don't accept on the basis of what they see. Minus the sight, it would be a different story. Different perception, a different view.*

—WALT DICKERSON

I remember the date as quite a challenge. I don't think there was any music there to refer to. Or if there was, we didn't necessarily follow it. There was an understanding who would begin each piece and who would solo on it, and so forth. But that was it. The album was called Impressions of "A Patch of Blue," *and that's what they were—improvisational impressions.*

—BOB CUNNINGHAM

Overlooked at the time of its release, the vibraphonist Walt Dickerson's *Impressions of "A Patch of Blue"* has become a pricey collector's item because it features Sun Ra in one of his few appearances as a sideman. But there's more to the story than Ra.

Written and directed by Guy Green and starring Sidney Poitier, the film *A Patch of Blue* opened in theaters at the end of December 1965, just under the wire for Academy Award consideration. Poitier, an Oscar winner two years earlier for *Lilies of the Field*, is, as usual, unindividualized except for his race and limitless bonhomie. His character befriends and becomes a sort of mentor to a blind young white girl, played by Elizabeth Hartman, in her film debut, whose sightlessness is the least of her problems. She's white trash: the daughter of a bullying middle-aged prostitute who is also a bigot (a typecast Shelley Winters, earlier Lolita's mom as well as Anne Frank's, and *A Patch of Blue*'s only Oscar winner, for one of those extended shrieks of a performance Academy voters often mistake for great acting). By the time Hartman learns that Poitier is "colored," she's fallen in love with him. Their relationship is a prescription for a color-blind society—salve for the liberal conscience just in time for the 1965 holiday season.

Like most movies of its day concerning "the race question," *A Patch of Blue* seems hopelessly dated now—another of those talky melodramas starring Poitier as (in effect) the Lone Negro, an unimpeachable black man whose lessons in racial tolerance serve the double purpose of teaching troubled white people something about themselves. Examples of what the writer Albert Murray once described as "social-science science fiction," such movies are watchable today only for Poitier, whose ingratiating screen presence makes do-gooderism sexy. *A Patch of Blue* has one flash of originality. Unless there is a comedy I'm forgetting, it's the only movie in which a black character introduces someone white to the customs and comforts of the middle class ("You sound like the radio," Hartman tells Poitier early on, meaning that she's never heard proper English spoken in real life—at least not so clearly enunciated). But even in 1965, against the backdrop of an emerging black cultural nationalism, the idea that race was only skin-deep must have seemed like the most nostalgic of liberal pieties.

BUOYED BY POITIER'S STAR POWER, *A PATCH OF BLUE* BECAME THE TENTH-best-grossing movie of 1966, the only "serious" drama (other than *Who's*

Afraid of Virginia Woolf?, which had already enjoyed success on Broadway) to win mass favor in a year dominated by James Bond and costume epics like *Dr. Zhivago*. Presumably among the moviegoers touched by *A Patch of Blue*'s good intentions was the late Tom Wilson, a Harvard graduate then with M-G-M Records after having operated his own Transition label, served as head of jazz A&R for Audio Fidelity, and broken the color bar as the first black staff producer at Columbia (this may have given him good reason to identify with Poitier).

Wilson, whom Walt Dickerson remembers as "a man on the rise, a man on the go," was the first to record Cecil Taylor and the mastermind behind the controversial pianist's only studio encounter with John Coltrane. Other than Sun Ra himself, he was the first to record Ra's Arkestra. At Columbia he supervised Bob Dylan's earliest electric sessions (including "Like a Rolling Stone") and overdubbed drums and amplified guitars to Simon & Garfunkel's "The Sounds of Silence," giving the song a beat and rescuing it from folkie oblivion. Wilson's projects at M-G-M's Verve subsidiary included the Velvet Underground and the Mothers of Invention. He was a visionary producer, but in the parlance of the trade, he was also a Record Man—a pro ever on the lookout for exploitable trends. (For Audio Fidelity he produced Bill Barron's *West Side Story Bossa Nova* and—following the success of Ray Charles's "I Can't Stop Loving You"—an unlikely album of country-and-western favorites by the pianists Steve Kuhn and Toshiko Akiyoshi.) At a time when both jazz and the pop record business were changing too quickly for even Wilson to keep up, *A Patch of Blue*'s healthy box-office receipts gave him what might have been a surefire commercial idea just a few years before: an album of jazz interpretations of themes from Jerry Goldsmith's score.

The sales of Shelly Manne's 1957 album of songs from the Broadway hit *My Fair Lady* had made film scores as well as Broadway shows fair game for jazz, even though the typical film score presents an obstacle to reinterpretation by its very nature. A dramatic film score consists largely of *underscore*—of mood-setting but fragmentary themes, as opposed to a Broadway musical's bona fide *songs*. Goldsmith has written some great scores, including one for *Chinatown* (1974). *A Patch of Blue* isn't among them. Its greatest virtue as a movie score is its unobtrusiveness; it did what needed to be done in terms of revealing the lead characters' few unspoken thoughts.

By subjecting Goldsmith's score to jazz interpretation, Wilson was aiming for the sort of casual record buyer who claims to like jazz but prefers hearing songs with which he is already at least vaguely familiar. Such listeners were a vanishing breed by 1965, and no one had left a movie theater humming the music from A *Patch of Blue* anyway. Not surprisingly, *Impressions of "A Patch of Blue"* stiffed, becoming an instant cut-out even though the Walt Dickerson Quartet went on a brief promotional tour in support of it. (I even remember seeing the band on a Philadelphia afternoon talkshow, with Sun Ra on piano, but with a different bassist and drummer. In case you're wondering, Ra wore the sort of conservative dark suit that was de rigueur for "progressive" jazz musicians at the time, but topped it off with a tinfoil headpiece.) Going unreviewed in *Down Beat* (probably because M-G-M, in the middle of a decade-long identity crisis, neglected to send out review copies), the album also failed to reach hard-core jazz listeners. Jazz fans noticing the album in stores may have passed it by, believing it was the original soundtrack; the album cover featured a title graphic identical to the one used for the movie in lobby posters and newspaper ads.

But none of this matters now. What does is that Wilson assigned the task of reinterpreting Goldsmith's delicate, essentially functional themes to Walt Dickerson, who had recorded a similar project for Wilson a few years earlier—an album of variations on Maurice Jarre's themes for *Lawrence of Arabia*, on Audio Fidelity. Dickerson's high-minded approach to Goldsmith's music transformed a potential novelty item into compelling chamber jazz.

ARRIVING ON THE NATIONAL SCENE IN THE VERY EARLY 1960S—HALF A BEAT ahead of Gary Burton and Bobby Hutcherson—the Philadelphia-born Dickerson was the first post-bop vibraphonist to escape the direct influence of Milt Jackson. Although Dickerson, during a recent conversation, prefaced his litany of role models with an ode to Lionel Hampton and Red Norvo, the grand old men of the vibes, his primary influences were saxophonists and pianists—Charlie Parker, Art Tatum, Bud Powell, Thelonious Monk, and the fellow Philadelphians Dickerson affectionately refers to as "John and John": John Coltrane and John Dennis, an obscure pianist whom Dickerson describes as "a genius" and whose only recordings as a leader were the sides he made for Charles Mingus's Debut label in 1955.

Dickerson was in his early thirties when he started recording, and his style—less percussive than rhythmically daring, and pianistic only in its shadings—was already fully formed. Consciously or otherwise, the physical aspects of that style seemed chosen to ensure that Dickerson would sound like no one else who ever played his instrument.

Dickerson's first step on buying a new pair of mallets is strip away their fur; he then soaks the exposed rubber tips in a mineral solution to get a sound he describes as "plush"—though, paradoxically, it is also very hard. His use of smaller mallets, gripped closer to the tip than is the custom for vibraphonists, allows Dickerson extraordinary speed on the bars, and because he uses his motor and damping bar so sparingly (if tellingly), he *vibrates* less than any other vibraphonist. The tradeoff is a commensurate lack of volume, and this is surely one of the reasons he steadfastly refuses offers to work as a sideman, why he has never featured a horn in his own groups (despite having played alongside plenty of them as a teenager in Jimmy Heath's Philadelphia-based big band in the late 1940s), and why he now mostly plays solo on his frequent trips to Europe and Japan. He is one of a handful of improvisers whose instrumental style amounts to a free-standing musical conception.

Dickerson has always been a figure of some mystery, and not having performed in New York or recorded for close to twenty years has compounded his elusiveness. He lives in the leafy town of Willow Grove, Pennsylvania, about thirty miles north of Philadelphia, in a home on the same block where Bud Powell recuperated after being clubbed on the head by a Philadelphia policeman in 1945. Dickerson's living room is immaculate, with every sofa cushion and candy dish in place—a tribute to the housekeeping skills of his wife, Elizabeth (to whom he dedicated the title track of his 1962 album *To My Queen*), but also evidence that the Man of the House spends too much of the day practicing or wrapped up in his own thoughts to leave newspapers and empty beer cans lying about. Dickerson's end of a conversation resembles one of his solos: He will repeat words or entire clauses for emphasis (achieving rhythmic variety in the bargain), and the silence between words often lasts long enough to seem ominous. He didn't seem fully comfortable talking until we walked down to his basement, where he keeps his vibes. "It's all inward," he said, hunched over the instrument with arms akimbo and mallets flying; he was referring to his unusual attack, but he could have been talking about his introspective approach to music.

TO JUDGE FROM THE LINER NOTES OF DICKERSON'S EARLY ALBUMS FOR Prestige/New Jazz, his own compositions and even his interpretations of standards usually have a philosophical element as their starting point (this is a man to whom Irving Berlin's "How Deep Is the Ocean" wasn't just a song title or a rhetorical question). Along with Dickerson's genuine admiration for the movie, the philosophical underpinning of *Impressions of "A Patch of Blue"* was provided by his lengthy discussions about race and other matters with Sun Ra. "Our conversations were not the norm," Dickerson told me. "Sometimes it was a conversation without periods or commas, and we would extend that into the musical realm, with no musical composition as such. Music was a part of our extended conversation."

To those of us who were lucky enough to hear *Impressions of "A Patch of Blue"* in 1966, the album was a revelation largely on account of Sun Ra's puckish piano solos. By that point Ra had already released a solo piano album on his own Saturn label, but almost no one had heard it (including me). Those of us who admired Ra as a bandleader and composer knew that he played piano, but we didn't necessarily think of him as a pianist. His work on *Impressions of "A Patch of Blue"* was, for most of us, the first indication of his talent as a soloist.

"Cecil [Taylor] can be a blur, but Sun Ra's piano playing always has a serious beat to it," says Bob Cunningham, who has accompanied both of them, and whose masterful plucking and bowing supplies backbone to the music. Indeed, Ra's beat is the first thing you notice, along with his splintered, dissonant rhythmic accents; behind Dickerson on "Bacon and Eggs," he sounds almost like a second drummer.

"Bacon and Eggs" is Ra's finest moment here, essentially a showcase for him. The piece itself, though written by Goldsmith, could pass for a Dickerson original—a close cousin to the similarly funky "Sugar Lump," from his Prestige/New Jazz LP *Relativity*. Ra's solo shows that he knew how to use even silence rhythmically; building on the figures with which he answers Dickerson, it's a series of well-timed explosions, a virtuoso turn all the more remarkable for eschewing virtuoso flash. Elsewhere, Ra is identifiably Ra on both piano and an aviary-like celeste, though there are ensemble passages where a listener who was none the wiser might guess the pianist to be John Lewis (except that no one would mistake Dickerson for Milt Jackson). The drummer Roger Blank functions much as he did with Ra's Arkestra—more as a sensitive colorist than as a timekeeper.

As for Dickerson, the clearest demonstration of his originality and finesse is his solo on "Selina's Fantasy," on which he follows his characteristic strategy of tossing off runs against the beat and at twice the song's tempo. (These runs are like Coltrane's "sheets of sound," though given the intrinsic properties of the vibraphone, they're more like sheet metal.) It's an example of the quiet intensity that makes Dickerson a major figure in jazz despite his current low profile, and an example of the forceful improvisation that makes this album infinitely more than the discographical curiosity it might have been.

Liner notes, August 1999

A to Z

A given in much of the literature on jazz is that a player's sound on his instrument is an extension of his speaking voice—a clue to his personality. The pianist Paul Bley is an exception to this rule. In the 1960s, on albums like *Footloose*, with the bassist Steve Swallow and the drummer Pete LaRoca, and *Closer*, with Swallow and the drummer Barry Altschul, Bley trimmed the outsized emotions of that decade's jazz avant-garde to fit the more intimate setting of the piano trio—a major contribution to jazz, though one initially drowned out by the angry rant of many of Bley's saxophonist contemporaries. At the piano, Bley gives the impression of weighing each note before delivering it, even when phrasing at a rapid clip. He will often repeat a phrase, giving it greater emphasis the second time, like someone mulling over what he has just said and deciding it bears immediate repeating, with verbal italics to underscore its significance. Unafraid of silence, Bley makes it swing.

He is just the opposite in conversation: a non-stop anecdotalist with the booming voice and affable manner of a morning disc jockey and with an inveterate outsider's eye for comic detail. I first spoke with him at a Portuguese jazz festival in 1997; as the only American journalist at the festival, I was enlisted by my Portuguese colleagues to approach Bley on their behalf (they were hoping to interview him but hesitant to approach him themselves on account of their limited English). I called Bley in his hotel room, he came right down, he did the interview with me helping the Portuguese over a few linguistic rough spots, and four hours later we were still talking—and not just about music. He even passed along a few travel tips: "If there's a problem with your hotel bill, don't argue with them," he warned. "Just pay it. You have to realize you don't have the same rights in Europe that you have in the United States, including the presumption of innocence. The next time you come here, they'll detain you at customs over a difference of a few dollars they say you owe." Bley travels so much that one country must look like another: The next time we ran into each other, in New York a few months later, he remembered meeting me but was confused about where. "That was nice the last time we talked," he said. "Surrounded by all those Italians, who treated us so well."

Bley was in the crowd the night in 1959 that Ornette Coleman, playing an unusual looking plastic alto saxophone, made his East Coast debut opposite the Art Farmer–Benny Golson Jazztet at the Five Spot in Greenwich Village—the opening volley in the first revolution to shake jazz since bebop in the 1940s. "Everybody was there, including Miles Davis, who stood talking to the bartender with his back to the stage, as though he was thirsty and just happened to stop in for a drink," Bley recalled during a recent chat from his home in Cherry Valley, New York, just north of Woodstock.

Seemingly everybody who was anybody in the world of jazz at that time was there, but Bley was one of very few who knew what to expect from Coleman and the trumpeter Don Cherry, having played with them regularly in Los Angeles the year before. (They had been members of Bley's band, along with Charlie Haden and Billy Higgins, the bassist and drummer Coleman brought to New York.) "When Ornette finished and the Jazztet came on, I turned to the bartender and asked him to dance," Bley said. "Because after Ornette, this band that had sounded top-of-the-line just a week before suddenly sounded like the society orchestra at the Hotel Taft."

At a time when most musicians were basing their compositions and their improvised solos on the 32-bar, A-A-B-A popular song format, with its recurring chord changes and clearly delineated choruses and bridge, "Ornette was going straight from A to Z, and nobody knew what hit them," Bley said. "They felt threatened. For weeks afterwards I couldn't walk down Broadway or my street in the Village without some musician I knew grabbing me by the elbow and asking me to explain what Ornette was doing."

Bley was a good person to ask, because he and the trumpeter Herbie Spanier had, at Bley's instigation, been playing long, completely improvised duets without chord changes or set tempos in Los Angeles in 1957, a year before Bley's first brush with Coleman. But despite this head start, Bley once seemed a somewhat peripheral figure in free jazz, the movement that Coleman spawned. By the end of the 1960s, Bley had become the revolution's odd man out—second in influence only to Cecil Taylor among free pianists, but by an absurdly wide margin. As a very young man in his native Montreal, Bley (who was born in 1932) had played with Charlie Parker and Lester Young, and joining Sonny Rollins's band in 1963 further enhanced his credibility with critics and musicians who deplored most free jazz as the raving of rank amateurs. ("I came to New York in 1950, so I was pre-Ornette, pre–Bill Evans, pre-Coltrane, pre-everybody," Bley points out.) To Bley's disadvantage, however, his music was uncommonly quiet for free jazz, and being white put him at risk of being drummed out of a movement whose black majority was becoming increasingly separatist.

NOW THAT THE SMOKE OF THE 1960S HAS CLEARED, THERE HAS BEEN A LONG overdue shift of opinion in Bley's favor. "Cecil Taylor is an extraordinary virtuoso who figured out for himself the way that he wanted to play, but Paul Bley is to Ornette Coleman what Bud Powell was to Charlie Parker," the influential black critic Stanley Crouch said recently, voicing what is becoming a common opinion. "He was the one who understood what Ornette was doing, and who brought that kind of tonal mobility and melodic freedom to the piano."

Crouch is an advisor to Jazz at Lincoln Center, a program notoriously dedicated to upholding the verities Coleman dispensed with. Yet Wynton Marsalis, Jazz at Lincoln Center's artistic director, has long expressed admiration for Coleman's early music, even while condemning most of what has followed in its wake. Marsalis and Crouch are usually on the same wavelength, and Crouch's favorable appraisal of Bley surely goes a long way toward explaining Bley's participation in Jazz at Lincoln Center's "Duets on the Hudson" series. (Bley will be reunited with Haden, on a bill that also featured duets by the pianist Kenny Barron and the alto saxophonist Gary Bartz.)

Reconfiguring Ornette Coleman for piano was no mean feat, because it was accomplished largely in absentia and against formidable odds:

Coleman's own early groups were pianoless, and his unnotatable sharps and flats were supposedly antithetical to tempered instruments. "How do you deal with that, playing a pitched instrument?" Bley asked, anticipating my question. "By playing microtones, for one thing. Playing with Ornette in California, there was a gap for me to fill even before it was my turn to solo, because he didn't write out a piano part. It was like solving a problem. The piano is not a piano. It's a piano only if I say it is. To acknowledge that it's a piano is to acknowledge that it's an instrument suitable for playing Mozart. Well, it can be, but that's not the way I look at it. As far as I've been concerned, it's an instrument that allows you to delve into sound. So that was the challenge of that gig.

"I think one of Stanley's fantasies is to reunite me with Charlie Haden and Billy Higgins. But a lot of other things have happened for me musically since then."

ONE OF THE MANY MUSICIANS LURED BY THE POTENTIAL OF SYNTHESIZERS AND stacked keyboards in the late 1960s and early 1970s, Bley was one of the few to use them for more than whooshing sound effects and cheery funk grooves. And his plugging in had unexpected long-term benefits, both for Bley and for improvised music in general. While recording the solo album *Open, To Love* for the German label ECM in 1972, in an effort to replicate the longer sustain he liked on synthesizer, Bley requested closer miking and special attention to timbre in recording his piano—recording techniques that became ECM trademarks, though they have generally been more associated with Keith Jarrett than with Bley.

Bley has recently published a memoir in which he proves to be a perceptive jazz critic as well as an engaging storyteller. In *Stopping Time* (Véhicule Press), written with David Lee, Bley remembers that when he first arrived in New York in the early 1950s, a handful of composers, including George Russell and John Carisi, were challenging bebop orthodoxy by writing scores that made use of atonality and free meter. Change was in the wind, but it was revolution from the top down— doomed to failure, Bley says, because after reading the scores, musicians would revert to familiar bebop licks in their improvised solos. Coleman was a revelation when Bley first heard him, because he was exploring the same areas as those New York composers but doing it on the spot, in a decisive victory for improvisation.

"But he was still using steady tempo, and I thought that was a step back, though a necessary step back," Bley said, expanding on his observations in *Stopping Time*. The breakthrough that he had been waiting for finally came in 1964, when the bassist Gary Peacock called him for a job in Greenwich Village with the tenor saxophonist Albert Ayler and the drummer Sunny Murray. Murray's anarchic drumming amounted to free counterpoint, and this was confirmation to Bley that the last shackles had been thrown off—rhythm instruments had finally been liberated from their traditional supporting roles.

This hints at Bley's real contribution to jazz: the rhythmic and harmonic license he allowed his various bassists and drummers beginning in the 1960s. Miles Davis's group of the mid-1960s, with Herbie Hancock, Ron Carter, and Tony Williams, is rightly credited with opening up the field for rhythm sections behind horns. But it was Bley who brought the same freedom to the piano trio, with bass and drums as full melodic partners.

What made this remarkable was the constant turnover among Bley's sidemen. In *Stopping Time* he says that musicians who play together regularly might as well be "married." By this standard, Bley has made a career of promiscuity, working with a variety of different partners. ("That's the nicest thing anyone's ever said to me," he said, laughing, when I put it that way to him.) In the 1960s Bley's playing seemed indivisible from the writing of his first wife, Carla Bley, a fellow pianist who began to establish an identity as more than her husband's compositional Adam's rib only toward the end of the decade.

Following their divorce, Bley teamed up with Annette Peacock, the former wife of Gary Peacock, who, though she was a non-musician who had never previously written a note of music, blossomed as a composer after marrying Bley, almost as if in fulfillment of her husband's needs. (Carla Bley once advised a fellow musician who complained that *his* wife couldn't write a lick of music to "give her to Paul Bley for a couple of weeks." Ouch.) For a time, Bley played new compositions by both women, and Gary Peacock was frequently his bassist. "The music was easy," Bley said. "The relationships, though. . . . "

MARRIED FOR CLOSE TO TWENTY YEARS NOW TO THE VIDEO ARTIST CAROL Goss, his partner in an independent record label and video production company in the 1970s, Bley prefers to dispense with written music alto-gether. "Or what I might use is so infinitesimal that it might as well be totally improvised. When I play a concert in Madrid, and I hear the women in the street snapping their fingers and clicking their castanets a couple of hours before the gig, the memory of that rushes in to fill the void left by the absence of written music when I go on stage.

"That's the problem with written music. You're trying to predict how you'll feel tomorrow by writing it down today. That's fear. I have a theory that you can tell who the fearful piano players are. They can't go on stage without written music and thirteen or fourteen players. They're nervous pianists. That includes Ellington and Basie and Kenton."

Commenting on the records that Bley made with Sonny Rollins in the 1960s but also speaking from personal experience, the alto saxophonist Lee Konitz once said, "Paul Bley can play one cluster, or just one note, and if you're in any sense willing, it can take you right outside." Mr. Bley still occasionally plays standards. His style is intensely rhythmic without being percussive; unlike many avant-garde pianists, he rarely feels a need to hammer. Even when he is working with skeletal or non-existent chord structures, his angled phrases are full of unexpected blues and Latin accents—in keeping with his belief that "the nice thing about free music is that it reflects back on the music that came before it, so you can keep the character of different kinds of music that have influenced jazz over the years, but without the form. I'd much rather hear free music being played by a master of all forms of jazz than by somebody who jumped headfirst into free."

At a certain point in their careers, jazz musicians tend to keep making the same record over and over. Bley, who records prolifically for a variety of European labels, keeps making the same two. His ECM releases tend to be speculative and impressionistic: *Not Two, Not One* (ECM 1670), the most recent of these, begins with "Not Zero, In Three Parts," on which Bley plays inside the piano, plucking its strings and using his hands to deaden the sound of the hammers in a manner that recalls his work of the early 1960s with the Jimmy Giuffre 3—a band that pro-foundly influenced Anthony Braxton and a host of European free impro-visers a decade later, though its immediate impact was slight. Once Gary Peacock joins in with his snarling bass, and then Paul Motian with his slow-moving and echoing cymbals, the performance becomes almost menacing—like an improvised, acoustic version of industrial rock. Elsewhere on *Not Two, Not One*, Bley demonstrates his knack for phrasing against tempo, even when tempo is merely implied. His releases for the Danish-based SteepleChase label are generally more straightforward and openly lyrical, sometimes even including jazz or pop standards. The recent *Notes on Ornette* (SteepleChase SCCD 314377), with the bassist Jay Anderson and the drummer Jeff Hirschfield, is a buoyant program of vintage Ornette Coleman that brings Bley full circle.

Since 1993 Bley has taught two days a month at the New England Conservatory of Music, in Boston. He encourages his students to try their hand at unaccompanied performance, which is the area he himself is most interested in now. "You think of something in your hotel room in the afternoon, and you get a chance to try it out that night," he said, describing the advantages for him of playing alone. "After playing for more than forty years, you know how to listen to an audience breathe. You've made a lot of records, so they know more or less what to expect from you. You know when they're ready for a left turn or a right turn. You get good at it, even if you weren't very good at it to start. But I'm not really concerned with the audience, although I know that sounds selfish. The purpose of playing a concert should be to know something at the end of it that you didn't know at the beginning."

The New York Times, February 13, 2000

BLEY ON HIMSELF AND OTHERS:

On being likened to Ran Blake, another quiet white pianist: "Ran hardly ever plays with drummers, whereas I've collected them like a gunslinger putting notches on his belt. Starting with Art Blakey and Roy Haynes in the 1950s, it was my goal to play with every great drummer there was, including some that only other musicians knew about, like Willie Jones."

On the politics of jazz: "You've got to have a sponsor to be accepted by critics and other musicians. If you have the right sponsor, everyone will embrace you. If you have no sponsor at all, you'll be a source of amusement—people will joke about you. I was very lucky, because [Charles] Mingus and Art Blakey were on my first record, on Mingus's label; and even before that, Oscar Pettiford and Kenny Clarke, on a record I made for Stinson, that never came out."

On joining Sonny Rollins's band, rather than Miles Davis's, in 1963: "My accountant has never forgiven me, because if you played with Miles for even five minutes, your future was financially secure. Sonny had just broken up the band he had with Don Cherry, which I thought was a failure. I thought Sonny was making a mistake by trying to play totally free, like Ornette, which by then had become fashionable, because Sonny was a master in the Coleman Hawkins tradition who could have injected new life into the standard A-A-B-A form. The whole year I was with him, he never played as well as he did at Birdland the night I auditioned, and I was kind of disappointed, because that's why I had taken the job.

"I thought that with Sonny, we could look at standard tunes freshly again—improvise on them so that nothing was repeated from chorus to chorus. That record he made with Coleman Hawkins [*Sonny Meets Hawk*, in 1963]—to me that was Sonny's last great creative statement. I remember Sonny started playing overtones, and Hawk was so thrown he looked at me and said, 'Please, when it's my turn to play, just give me a nod.'"

On producing two albums by Sun Ra in the late 1970s (*St. Louis Blues* and *Solo Piano*, on Bley's Improvising Artists Incorporated label): "The thing that no one mentions about him is that he could play cakewalks, and that was a style I had only read about. I mean, there are piano styles that predate jazz and what they sounded like is guesswork, because they weren't recorded. Sunny knew how to play cakewalks, and his approach to them was amazing."

On suggesting to Carla Bley that she start her own band: "That was a mistake, because she became involved with Michael Mantler, her trumpet player, and three weeks later—whoosh, she was out the door. I woke up in the middle of the night and she was putting her clothes on. She told me she was leaving; I thought she meant she was going to the corner store for cigarettes.

"She became a star overnight. I remember, at her first recording session with her own band, she turned to me and said, 'This isn't what I wrote.' I told her, 'Shut up! It's the best thing since Duke Ellington! It sounds like a Sicilian funeral band. Everybody's out of tune. It's perfect!' Because a great band is when everybody with a different sound is playing together, as opposed to a band like Tommy Dorsey's, where the problem was that everybody had the same sound."

On race in jazz: "There's a point in every revolution where you have to say 'no' to outside help. That happened in the Civil Rights movement around '63 or '64; the whole business of telling the white people who were helping with things like voter registration in the South 'we don't need you anymore,' not because you haven't done good, but because we need to develop more black leaders. The fact that all of the black leaders, like Martin Luther King, were clergymen exposed the lack of leadership in the rank and file, and this was something that people like Cecil Taylor and LeRoi Jones [the poet and critic later known as Amiri Baraka] were acutely conscious of. . . .

"That was the beginning of the problems between black and white musicians. It became easier for black musicians to work together in their groups, and easier for white musicians to work together in their groups. My joining Sonny Rollins in 1963 was the turning point. It couldn't have happened after that. The opportunity to have a career in a mixed band was pretty much over.

"Earlier I never felt a draft, because when I played with Al Collins's Tramp Band in Canada, those guys treated me like a member of the family, not just a member of the band. When I played with Ben Webster in New York in the 1950s, we would go get beans and ham hocks together. I was the mascot—the minority mascot.

"But the majority and the minority have become reversed now. Because now the majority of people playing this music are white. They've mastered the language. What was the domain of few has become the domain of many.

"The saving grace in all of this—black/white, American/European and so on—is that jazz so easily absorbs the music of other cultures. And that's part of what keeps it interesting for the players."

On the cultural differences that can make this sort of cultural synthesis difficult, at least initially: "I once rehearsed with an Indian musician. I put a piece of music in front on him. He said, 'This is evening music. I can't play this until it's dark.'"

On why he records as much as he does: "I don't practice and I won't play a concert unless it's being taped. If it's totally improvised or mostly improvised, it's an opus number, and you don't want an opus number to just go up in smoke."

On the influence of Bud Powell and bebop: "Bud Powell was a relatively late influence on me, because I started out playing with swing bands. In the bebop period, we didn't know that Charlie Parker would become the dominant influence and Lennie Tristano and Lee Konitz and Warne Marsh would be considered peripheral. Because when I got to New York, Charlie Parker and Lennie Tristano were playing in clubs on the opposite side of the street, and their accomplishments seemed equal. When I was younger, I stopped taking piano lessons because I didn't want to be influenced by my teacher. My goal was to avoid influences, whether it was Bud Powell playing bebop or Lennie Tristano playing an early version of free jazz."

On possibly having influenced Keith Jarrett: "Keith Who?" [Laughter.] "Any piano player who makes $50,000 a night is doing something right."

On being his own influence: "The name of the game is to make professional recordings and to listen to them carefully for things that you did that you like, so that you wind up playing more of those and less of the things that you don't like. Over time, that means that you're finding new material by listening to the material that you've already recorded. So you become influenced by a certain record that you made or by a concert that you recorded.

"When I recorded *Footloose*, the choice before me was to repeat the stuff I had played in the '50s or to push forward. I was nervous at the recording date and I remember asking Pete LaRoca what he thought I should do—stick with what I knew or take a blind leap into something I might mess up. He handed me a fat joint and said, 'Smoke this, and the answer will reveal itself.'"

Interview transcripts, 1997/2000

Charlie Haden, Bass

A 1999 issue of the magazine *Jazziz* featured on its cover a black and white photograph of the bass player Charlie Haden cropped so that the fingerboard and tuning pegs and scroll of his string bass occupied center page, and only the left side of Haden's face, the fingers of his left hand, and his left shoulder were visible. Haden was one of the sidemen with whom the alto saxophonist Ornette Coleman turned jazz upside down at the end of the 1950s. He was a member of the Coleman-alumni band Old and New Dreams from its formation in 1976 (by which point Coleman himself was playing an idiosyncratic brand of funk, in an amplified setting) until its demise, a few years ago. Whenever Coleman unplugs, Haden is still the bass player he is likely to call. But Haden also enjoys a sovereign identity as the leader of two ensembles that are as different from each other as they are from Coleman's bands or anyone else's: the *engagé* Liberation Music Orchestra, for which Haden and the arranger Carla Bley have written music in solidarity with revolutionary movements, often using actual field recordings as a springboard; and the in-search-of-lost-time Quartet West, whose evocations of *film noir* and the detective fiction and torch songs of the 1940s and early 1950s heighten nostalgia from the cheapest of emotions into one of the most powerful. (Haden's best-known composition for the LMO is "Song for Ché," an anthem dedicated to a figure who called for a worldwide people's revolution. As if to show that the difference between the bands isn't merely one of size, with Quartet West he has recorded "Lady in the Lake" and "The Long Goodbye," moody numbers written by the band's pianist,

Alan Broadbent, and named for Raymond Chandler novels featuring the gumshoe Philip Marlowe, who was committed to not taking sides.)

Haden, who is conscious of his rank in jazz and proud of it—he has won numerous readers' and critics' polls on bass, and five of his albums, including one with Old and New Dreams, have been voted best of their year in *Down Beat* magazine's International Critics Poll—was said to have taken offense at being crowded off the magazine's cover. Yet the unusual angle actually represented him better than a smiling headshot would have, because no bass player since Charles Mingus has seemed so thoroughly joined to the instrument. Mingus, who had a beat like a wrecking ball and a temperament to match, bent the instrument to his will, but Haden has bent his will to its (Mingus, who was bad with names, called him "Bass," which Haden took as an honorific).

Like the saxophone, though older by some three hundred years (a prototype has been traced to the mid-sixteenth century), the double bass—or contrabass or bass violin—has become more closely identified with jazz than with the symphonic literature for which it was intended. In classical music the string bass—nicknamed "Bach's foot" because it was originally designed as a stand-in for the organ's foot peddle—is usually limited to shadowing the cellos at the bottom of the octave or (in this century) to occasionally delivering a series of arhythmic pizzicato thumps to signal that a piece is atonal or otherwise "modern." In jazz, no other instrument is more essential. A common misconception about jazz is that drummers keep time, like conductors with two sticks instead of one. Drummers do control tempo, which is quite a different matter from time, and they supply color and momentum with their accents and punctuations. But the job of actually keeping a beat (or implying one, as the case may be) ordinarily falls to a group's string-bass player, and the group isn't going to swing unless his notes suggest a heartbeat, rather than a metronome. The "walking" bass line—four equal beats to the measure, in steplike motion, as perfected by Walter Page with the Count Basie Orchestra in the late 1930s—has become a trademark of modern jazz: what people are tapping a foot to when they think they're tapping it to the drums. But a bass line of whatever sort—walking in time or running free of it—serves a second vital purpose in jazz. Since the 1930s, and especially since bebop in the late 1940s, much jazz improvisation has been guided (though not necessarily dictated) by harmonic progressions, or what musicians call chord changes. Spelling out the chords is the bass player's other responsibility, and his choice of notes and accuracy of pitch are thus as important to a band's well-being as his ability to lay down a flowing beat. The bass line is the thread that connects improvised solos to an underlying harmonic framework—a backbone as well as a heartbeat.

Bebop relieved drummers and pianists from any semblance of regular timekeeping—but only because bass players continued to tend the beat, their job becoming more demanding then because of bebop's increased harmonic complexity. The first radical departure after bebop was free jazz, a movement that became recognizable as such with the arrival in New York of the Ornette Coleman Quartet for a highly publicized extended engagement at a club called the Five Spot in the late fall of 1959. Coleman frequently dispensed with chord changes and regular meter altogether; if this sounds like a day at the races for a bass player, quite the opposite was true: Harmony still mattered in Coleman's music, even though it no longer took the form of set patterns, and a good beat mattered more than ever, even though it might not always be where the foot expected it to be. Fortunately for Coleman—and for jazz as it has evolved in the forty years since—he found in Haden a bass player who intuitively realized that the only thing worse than falling back on the old rules would be to assume that all rules were out.

"With Ornette, there was no piano, but I became the piano," Haden told me last fall over a leisurely breakfast in the dining room of his New York hotel.

"I had to learn right away how to improvise behind Ornette, which not only meant following him from one key to another and recognizing the different keys, but also modulating in a way that the keys flowed in and out of each other and the new harmonies sounded right. Ornette sometimes wrote bass lines or chord symbols, but what usually happened is we would play a tune he wrote and I would figure out a bass line that complimented it harmonically, but also one that new chords could be built on. You could hear the harmony notes that *weren't* being played, from the bass part.

"I really welcomed the challenge, because it meant using my ear, like when I was singing country music with my family on the radio as a child in the Midwest, and had to know all the harmony parts—mine and everybody else's—if we were going to blend. There was no such thing as 'I don't know them.' You had to know them."

HADEN'S BACKGROUND IS AN UNUSUAL ONE FOR A JAZZ MUSICIAN, MUCH LESS a political radical. In the late 1930s the Hadens were a country music act like their friends the Carter Family, but famous only within reach of the 50,000-watt radio station in Shenendoah, Iowa, that carried their live broadcasts twice daily. According to a family legend, the youngest of the Hadens' four children was musical practically from the cradle. He made his debut on the program in 1939, when he was twenty-two months old, after his mother heard him humming along with her lullabies and harmonizing with his sister and brothers as they practiced their hymns and folk songs for the radio. Haden has a cassette of one of his early broadcasts, which he copied for me. Between songs and spiels for All State Insurance (the show's sponsor), Carl Haden, Charlie's father, offers listeners a Haden Family Songbook for fifty cents plus a two-cent stamp, and a 5-by-7 inch photograph of the Haden children, including "Charles Edward, the little two-year-old yodeling cowboy" for a dime. The baby who does the best he can with the hymn "This World Is Not My Home Anymore" doesn't much sound like the adult Charlie Haden—at two years old, he doesn't sound like he's anyone yet.

The family made personal apppearances at revival meetings and county fairs, but they were hardly in show business. "We'd wake up at 4 A.M., milk the cows, and then do the show," Haden recalled, describing the family's daily routine after starting a farm near Springfield, Missouri, and beginning a program for a station there. "The station put all the equipment we needed in our living room, including this little crank thing," Haden told me. "You'd ring the studio, they'd ring back, and we'd be on the air."

Haden remained on the program until he was fifteen, when he contracted polio, which weakened nerves in his face and throat and put an end to his singing career. (Even today, there are people who know nothing of Haden's career in jazz for whom his name rings a bell as that of a child who once sang on the radio.) In 1955, about a year after he stopped singing with his family on the radio, he was hired as the house bass player on *Ozark Jubilee*, a network television program produced in Springfield and hosted by the country singer Red Foley. Musicians frequently choose instruments similar in character to their speaking voices, but Haden speaks in a light, melodic tenor with sudden increases of vibrato that one writer (the novelist Rafi Zabor, who used Haden as a character in *The Bear Comes Home*) has attributed to the polio.

The bass violin comes in various sizes, with the most common ones being three-quarters and seven-eights (of full size); Haden has one of each, and the larger of the two—one of a small number of basses made in the nineteenth century, before the sizes were standardized, by a French luthier named Jean-Baptiste Vuillaume—is his prize possession. He plays it only on recording sessions and jobs close to home, for fear of damaging it in transit. "Vuillaume was one of the only luthiers elsewhere in Europe to come close to the Italian varnish," he explained. "The varnish, that's the secret, along with the wood and the artistry of the instrument maker."

Bass players themselves tend to come in two sizes: tall and lean, with long arms that entwine the instrument; or built close to the ground, with enough belly in their sound to make up for what they might lack in reach. Haden is exceptional for being of average height and weight, especially since losing twenty excess pounds following the removal of his gall bladder, in 1998. (He went into the hospital for back surgery, contracted pneumonia while healing, and was eventually diagnosed with pancreatitus. Not realizing he had been ill, I made the mistake of complimenting him on having shed some weight.) Unassuming despite his designer eyeglasses and stylishly short hair and dark clothing, he has the settled look of an intense man whom middle age has gradually persuaded to relax. The only hipsterism in his speech is his habit of ending nearly every sentence with "man." The singer Sheila Jordan, who has known Haden for years, once remarked, "Charlie even calls *me* 'Man.'"

Musicians can be at their most talkative and reflective in the morning—nightworkers at ease while the rest of the world hurries about its business. Over a leisurely breakfast Haden, who lives in Santa Monica, California, with his wife, the singer Ruth Cameron, talked about suffering from tinnitus (a persistent ringing in the ears, which he attributes to having played an especially tumultuous style of free jazz with the tenor saxophonist Archie Shepp and the trombonist Roswell Rudd in the late 1960s—"Music doesn't have to be amplified to be too loud") and hyperacousis (extreme sensitivity to loud noises). This second condition obliges him to position himself behind Plexiglas baffles when playing with a drummer, as in Quartet West. "We need a stage at least fifteen feet wide and fifteen feet deep, which rules out most clubs. At first, it was very cumbersome. Now, it's no big deal. It actually improves the on-stage acoustics." He talked about having started the Jazz Studies program at the California Institute of the Arts in 1982, where his students have included such up-and-coming musicians as the tenor saxophonist Ravi Coltrane, the trumpeter Ralph Alessi, and the bass player Scott Colley. He spoke with pride about his four children, three of whom have made a splash in pop music: his son Josh, with the group Spain (his singing voice is remarkably similar to his father's speaking voice), and his daughters Rachel and Petra, with the group That Dog (the daughters are triplets, with their sister, Tanya, a cellist). According to Haden, when That Dog opened for Johnny Cash at Carnegie Hall a few years ago, June Carter Cash (whose family used to stay with the Hadens when they were in Missouri to appear on *Corn's A-Crackin'*, a radio barn dance broadcast nationally from Springfield) spotted Petra on an elevator and said, "I heard that Little Cowboy Charlie is your daddy. Isn't that something!"

OUR CONVERSATION KEPT RETURNING TO HADEN'S CHILDHOOD. "'AIR CONDI-tioning needs hundreds of men—*thousands* of men—right now,'" Haden said, affectionately mimicking his father's sales pitch on behalf of one of the Haden Family's sponsors, a training program for air-conditioning repairmen. To hear Haden reminisce, one might think that he was motivated to play bass by a boyhood crush on one of the Carter sisters and by an element of rivalry with his late brother, Jim. "I was about nine and Anita, who was the youngest of the three Carter girls, after Helen and June, was about fifteen," he told me. "She played bass on their radio shows, and she was so beautiful, man. I fell in love with her, but of course I never told her." Jim Haden was an avid bebop fan who also eventually became a professional musician, working mostly in the casinos in Lake Tahoe.

"Jim was in high school when we moved back off the farm and into Springfield, and he listened to a lot of Dizzy Gillespie and Charlie Parker. He sent for these stock arrangements of some of the early bebop tunes, like 'Anthropology' and 'Ornithology,' and he and his friends would get together and play them after school, while I sat right next to him and listened. I wasn't allowed to play his records—but I would, the minute he left the house. He didn't want me to touch his bass, either, but I would play it when he left. I loved the depth of the instrument, and how it made everything sound richer."

What also seems to have drawn Haden to the instrument, to judge from what else he told me, was his keen ear for harmony and his fascination with singing voices deeper than his. "I used to listen to a lot of

Bach on the radio," he said, "and when the basses started to sing, it made everything *complete*—it made it all make sense."

When Haden was about fifteen, his father took him and a friend to hear the Stan Kenton Orchestra. After the show, Haden went backstage to talk with the band's bass player, Don Bagley, who invited him back to the band's hotel. "I'll never forget it, man," he recalled. "It was the Colonial Hotel, in Springfield. I knocked on the door and it opened and smoke billowed out and I smelled something I had never smelled before. There was a gin bottle over here and a whiskey bottle over there, and all these guys in their undershirts surrounded by women." Laughing at the memory, Haden imitated the hoarse voice and stoned cadence of one of Kenton's men. "'So you wanna be a jazz musician? Look around this room, kid. You wanna end up like this?' And I said, '*Yeah!*'"

Even though jazz mystified them, Haden's parents never opposed his desire to become a jazz musician: "My father went along with whatever I wanted, and my mother strongly encouraged me because she was happy that at least one of her children was going to college." A member of his high school orchestra, Haden was offered a full scholarship to Oberlin College but turned it down and worked as a shoe salesman for a year to pay his own way at Westlake College of Music, in Los Angeles, a school that offered a jazz program. He dropped out of Westlake after one semester, by which point he had achieved his real goal of playing with some of the musicians whose recordings had inspired him—most notably, the pianist Hampton Hawes. Haden soon found work with the pianist Paul Bley, who was leading a quartet featuring the vibraphonist Dave Pike at a club called the Hillcrest. Perhaps exaggerating a little, for the sake of a good story, Bley says of the young Haden, "He was a country boy who used to come to rehearsals without shoes and chose all the wrong notes—but he had good time, from the very beginning. I figured I could teach another bass player the right notes, but good time is something that somebody has or doesn't have—you can't teach it."

HADEN'S GRANDMOTHER USED TO TELL HIM SHE SAW WILD BILL HICKOK SHOOT a man dead for stealing his watch. In another family story, Haden's grandfather once got into an argument with a professional gunslinger. Armed with only a knife, Haden's grandfather drew a line in the dirt with his boot and dared the gunslinger to cross it. Just then, Haden's grandmother came riding by on her horse and told her husband to stop this madness instantly or they were through. He jumped up with her on the horse, and they never looked back.

Haden's own story of first laying eyes on Ornette Coleman, in a Los Angeles nightclub in 1957, though historical fact, also has the air of legend. "I think Gerry Mulligan was playing at the Haig, and it was my night off from my gig at the Hillcrest with Paul Bley, so I went over there," he told me.

"The place was packed, and this guy with long hair like nobody wore it in those days asked if he could sit in. He took out this plastic alto saxophone and started playing and the whole room lit up for me. See, I loved playing chord changes, but sometimes when I took a solo, there would be parts of the melody that we were playing that were so beautiful I wanted to stay there for the rest of the song. Or I might be inspired to create a new chord structure on the spot. The guys leading the jam sessions would get dragged and ask me what the fuck I thought I was doing. I would have to play the original melody to let everyone know where I was and give them a cue to come back in. So here was Ornette, who was playing what I was hearing. But as soon as he started to play, they made him stop. He put his horn back in his case and left. I tried to run after him through the mob of people, but when I got to the door, he had disappeared. I ran into the street, but I didn't see him."

Some musicians were leery of Coleman even before hearing him play that plastic saxophone, which must have looked like a toy compared with the metal ones they were used to. But Haden was from the Ozarks, where nobody thought it particularly odd for a left-hander like Haden's father to play guitar wrong side up, or for Haden's grandfather to bow a fiddle while holding it against his chest. Asking around, he learned Coleman's identity from Lennie McBrowne, the drummer in Bley's band at the Hillcrest. "At my request, Lennie brought Ornette to the club for one of our Sunday morning jam sessions—one of those things where you play your gig until two in the morning, then take a break, then play again until nine, with different guys sitting in," Haden recalled.

"Ornette was sitting at one of the tables, and I told him I had heard him the other night and how beautiful I thought he sounded. He thanked me and said that not many people told him that, and asked if I wanted to hang out and play. We walked out the door together, and the sunlight came rushing in and everybody was on their way to church. I put my bass in Ornette's old Studebaker, and we went to this little room he had. He had just broken up with his wife, and there was music all over the place, all over the dressers and all over the floor. He picked some music off the floor and said, 'Let's play this'—one of his tunes; I don't remember which one. He said, 'There are changes underneath the melody that I was hearing when I wrote this, but you should listen to what I'm doing and make up your own.' I was scared to death of him and scared that I wouldn't play right, but he loved what I was doing and we played all day, then took a break for some hamburgers and went back to his place and played all night."

In a sense country music had prepared Haden for Coleman; in country music, harmonies are at their most exact when they sound most out of control. Coleman and another acolyte, the trumpeter Don Cherry, wound up joining Haden in Bley's band at the Hillcrest. The club was a musicians' hangout, and Bley, who had been experimenting with free form even before hearing Coleman, once joked that you could tell when the band was playing a set, because most of the audience would be standing outside the club with their drinks, waiting for it to end. This negative response puzzled Haden: "Only the improvisations were new—the way we improvised, on the melody or the rhythm or the shape of the tune, and not necessarily on the chord changes. But Ornette's tunes, and our arrangements of them, were so precise they stopped on a dime. It was amazing to me that more musicians didn't respond to that immediately."

Artists in other disciplines soon did, however. When Coleman opened at the Five Spot with Haden, Cherry, and the drummer Billy Higgins, "it was packed every night, not just with musicians trying to figure it out, like in L.A., but with painters and writers and poets." On any given night, the audience might include Willem de Kooning, Larry Rivers, James Baldwin, or Norman Mailer. Around this time Haden began playing with his eyes shut, a habit he says helps him to rid his mind of passing thoughts and concentrate on music—although his original motive was that he was intimidated by looking out and seeing "every great bass player in New York, including Mingus, Percy Heath, Wilbur Ware, Paul Chambers, and Henry Grimes, staring me right in the face." Once, he opened his eyes and there was Leonard Bernstein practically on the bandstand, with his ear an inch away from the f-hole of Haden's bass. Bernstein was no dummy: He sensed that contrary to what people were saying, Coleman's music wasn't atonal or even bitonal. He knew where to listen for its tonal center.

HADEN ONCE TOLD THE WRITER JOSEF WOODARD THAT PLAYING MUSIC WAS "almost a religious ritual," like "walking into a holy place." Beginning with his use of heroin when he was in his twenties, and continuing with his involvement in political causes and his readiness to surrender himself to art forms other than his own, Haden's life has been a search for a way to stay in that holy place when the music ends. In Los Angeles in the late 1950s, he roomed with Scott LaFaro, the other leading young bass player of the period, whose lifestyle was the antithesis of Haden's. "I admired him for doing push-ups out in the yard and practicing all day, while I would be out copping drugs," Haden told me. The last time he saw LaFaro was in New York a few days before Christmas in 1960, after playing with him on the recording session for Coleman's *Free Jazz*. "I was outside with my bass on Seventh Avenue in a snowstorm, looking for a taxi to go uptown so I could cop. I asked Scotty for twenty dollars, and he got angry, because he had just seen me bum twenty dollars from someone else upstairs. He said, 'Charlie, I love you and I'm not going to let you kill yourself, man.' I said 'OK, man,' and we hugged, and a few weeks later, he died in a car accident." It still amazes Haden that he wasn't the one who died young.

One of the friends Haden made while with Coleman at the Five Spot was Bob Thompson, a black figurist painter who used color expressionistically and a fellow junkie who died of an overdose in 1966, at the age of twenty-nine. Thompson then lived as a squatter in a Greenwich Village loft without electricity or running water. "I used to go over there and watch him paint," Haden recalled. "He would be up on a ladder, working on these big canvases, and we would have some heavy conversations about improvisation in music and in painting. One night, he called me and said, 'Come down here quick.' I thought he was looking to score from me, but he said, 'I'm putting you in a painting.'" The painting was "Garden of Music"; roughly six by twelve feet and a centerpiece of the Whitney Museum of American Art's 1998 Thompson retrospective, it shows figures representing Haden, Coleman, Sonny Rollins, John Coltrane, and Ed Blackwell surrounded by male and female nudes in a primordial forest. Haden is in the background, facing away from the viewer and holding his bass aloft by the stem, as though trying to keep it from sailing out of his grip; his body is the painting's only splotch of white.

In New York in the late 1960s Haden was frequently the only white musician on the bandstand, as the avant-garde movement that had been

given impetus by Coleman at the Five Spot became increasingly identified with black separatism. Amid much militant rhetoric and posturing
before sympathetic mixed audiences, Haden was practically alone in
voicing his political beliefs within earshot of authorities who could punish him. During a tour of Europe with Coleman in 1971, he was
detained by police at the Lisbon airport and questioned for more than
five hours about having dedicated—before an audience of ten thousand
people—a performance of "Song for Ché" to independence movements
in the Portuguese colonies of Mozambique, Angola, and Guinea. (To
this day, he is regarded as something of a folk hero in Portugal.) Haden
got no argument about his politics from his parents back in Missouri,
who were lifelong Democrats. Surprisingly, the strongest objection came
from a fellow musician. Haden and the pianist Bill Evans would "argue
about Vietnam for hours," Haden told me. "He was adamant that we
should be there, which amazed me, because his music was so sensitive."

One suspects that Haden's politics are more intuitive than ideological,
born out of an identification with the underdog that began when he saw
the raw deal given tenant farmers—black and white alike—in the country near Springfield. He told me about the connection he sees between
country music and jazz: "One is the music of poor whites, and the other
grew out of the struggle for freedom by black former slaves." Haden's
mother used to take him to hear black church choirs when he was a child,
and he remembers going to segregated movie houses and gazing at the
balcony and being curious about what the screen looked like from up
there. He has a touch of Tom Joad. "Whenever there's a fight so hungry
people can eat, I'll be there," Joad, played by Henry Fonda, says toward
the end of John Ford's movie of Steinbeck's *The Grapes of Wrath* (1940).
"Whenever there's a cop beating up a guy, I'll be there." These could be
the Liberation Music Orchestra's mottoes. In addition to his song for
Guevara, Haden's four LMO albums have included numbers written by
him in tribute to, or adopted from folk songs associated with, the Chilean
resistance, the Salvadoran rebels, the African National Congress, and the
Abraham Lincoln Brigade (the American volunteers who fought against
Franco on the side of the Republic in the Spanish Civil War).

Yet the mood of these albums has been lyrical and jubilant rather than
strident. Along with Carla Bley's independent projects of the same
period, the first LMO album was historically significant for bringing the
most daring improvisational aspects of free jazz into an orchestral frame-

work at a time when the new style was thought to be suitable only for small groups. Haden is fond of pointing out that each of the orchestra's albums was recorded, as if by necessity, during a Republican administration. Owing to the staggering costs of maintaining a big band, the LMO has been on hold since 1992, and Haden doesn't know if he will reconvene the band for another album anytime soon. "If Bush gets elected, I'll have to," he said, not wholly joking.*

NO BAND IN JAZZ HAS A STRONGER SENSE OF PLACE THAN QUARTET WEST. THE place is Los Angeles in the period immediately after the Second World War—the city that Haden just missed on arriving there in 1957, though traces of it remain. "My kids were in L.A., and I wanted to be near them while they were growing up," Haden told me about his decision to move back to California in 1984. "Los Angeles has many qualities that are attractive to me, beginning with the sun. You can see it in the work of some of the painters who live here, including David Hockney. They have an energy and a sense of light in their work that's indigenous to this part of the country. Then, there's the whole history of the city and its place as a melting pot of so many different cultures. You also have the movie industry and everything that came from it, including the art deco of the 1930s and 1940s."

Formed by Haden in 1984, Quartet West found its identity with *Haunted Heart*, its third album, recorded in 1991. The title tune is a gorgeous ballad from the 1940s, written by Arthur Schwartz and Howard Dietz and rarely played by jazz musicians, despite a memorable recording by Bill Evans in 1961. Just as the track seems about to fade out, following the tenor saxophonist Ernie Watts's glowing recapitualtion of the theme, a twinkle of strings introduces Jo Stafford's 1947 recording of the song, which is heard in its entirety, slight surface noise and all.

Deliberately evocative of Hollywood movies of the 1940s (it even begins with Max Steiner's Warner Bros. fanfare), *Haunted Heart* reminds me of a line spoken by Humphrey Bogart as Sam Spade at the end of John Huston's *The Maltese Falcon* (1941), when a cop asks him what's so special about the jeweled bird that everyone's been scheming to get hold of. It's "the stuff that dreams are made of," Bogart wisecracks,

*"I've already put a call into Carla," he told me the morning after Gore conceded and Bush was declared the victor of the 2000 presidential election.

referring to the falcon and also thinking of the double-crossing woman he loves—and whom he has just handed over to the police. Written by Huston and nowhere to be found in Dashiell Hammet's novel, the line also tacitly refers to that era's movies, the best of which were like dreams to begin with.

Given Haden's leftist convictions and his founding role in the jazz avant-garde, the last thing anyone expected of him was a love of vintage Hollywood and of singers and songs often dismissed as exemplars of middle-of-the-road escapism. Inevitably, there was speculation among jazz fans that this new direction reflected Haden's more relaxed lifestyle in Malibu, where he and his wife live in a rented house with an expansive view of the Pacific Ocean. (Malibu isn't far from Santa Monica, where Haden weaned himself from heroin in the mid-1960s, as a live-in member of the controversial self-help group Synanon, and where Philip Marlowe had his office.) But Haden brought his usual passion to Quartet West, even if the recordings he used on *Haunted Heart*—by Stafford, Jeri Southern, and Billie Holiday—called on emotions more refined than those triggered by the field recordings from Cuba and South Africa that he occasionally used with the Liberation Music Orchestra.

Haden's vision of the 1940s recognizes the beginnings of modernism in jazz. Along with lush 1940s ballads and lilting originals by Haden or Alan Broadbent in the same mood, the band has tackled some of the trickiest of uptempo early-bebop numbers by Charlie Parker, Bud Powell, and Lennie Tristano, among others. And Quartet West is one of only a few contemporary jazz bands to capture early bop's angular geometrics and dark emotional undercurrents, along with its stylish drum accents and rhythmic lickity-split. Parker and Dizzy Gillespie gave Los Angeles its first taste of bebop when they played a club called Billy Berg's at the end of 1945. Around the same time, Bogart was preparing to play Philip Marlowe in *The Big Sleep*, a movie that Haden says he tries to watch at least once a month; when he plays with Quartet West, it's as though Haden were imagining Parker and Marlowe prowling the Hollywood streets with himself there beside them. Unlike those pop stars who fashion a new identity for each album and tour, Haden wasn't trying on a new persona with Quartet West—he was revealing an unsuspected inner life.

HADEN SUMMONED SOUTHERN, CHET BAKER, COLEMAN HAWKINS, DJANGO
Reinhardt, and the Duke Ellington Orchestra for cameos on *Always Say
Goodbye*, recorded in 1993. It's almost impossible to describe this album
and *Haunted Heart* without giving a misleading impression of what
Haden was up to on them. Haden doesn't "sample" in the manner of a
Sean "Puff Daddy" Combs, and his encounters with the dead haven't
been presumptuous, technological duets, like Natalie Cole's duet with
her father on "Unforgettable," or Celine Dion's with Frank Sinatra on
"All the Way"—the older recordings and Quartet West's interpretations
of the same songs are discreet events. Haden isn't a postmodernist: He
doesn't treat the older recordings he uses ironically and he isn't out to
"valorize" anything. Despite his romance with the 1940s, a Quartet West
concert isn't a revue" like the shows put on by those neo-swing bands that
have convinced themselves and their audiences that it's hip to be hep.
Haden doesn't twirl his bass or jitterbug or dress himself and his sidemen
in period finery. In fact, with Haden protecting himself from the drummer Larance Marable's cymbals behind Plexiglas, there's almost nothing
to watch. Ernie Watts paces as he solos, and Broadbent hunches at the
piano, the way that Bill Evans used to (a lyrical and introspective soloist,
he has an Evans-like hunch in his playing, too). The man up front is the
slumped and implacable Marable, the unflashiest of drummers, if also
one of the most resourceful. The only concession to the eye when I heard
Quartet West in San Francisco a few years ago was a night-time cityscape
of Los Angeles from a rear projector.

Though similar in mood to *Haunted Heart* and *Always Say Goodbye*,
Now Is the Hour (1995) avoided what might have become a formula by
featuring Quartet West with strings and no appended vocals. The recent
The Art of the Song, recorded in 1999, keeps the strings and adds the live
vocalists Bill Henderson and Shirley Horn. Sounding much more ani-
mated than she has singing with her own trio in recent years, Horn is
wonderful on Cy Coleman's "I'm Gonna Laugh You Right Out of My
Life." Henderson also performs capably, even if his slower-than-molasses
rendition of "You, My Love," from the 1954 movie *Young at Heart*, is
unlikely to make anyone forget Frank Sinatra. But without some
uptempo bebop as a change of pace, and without the voices from the past
and the explicit dialogue they encouraged between past and present on
the earlier albums, the only frisson on *The Art of the Song* comes at the

end, when Haden steps out of character to sing "Wayfaring Stranger" —
a folk song his mother occasionally sang and one whose grim lyrics,
promising heaven as a reward for a hard life on earth, and accepting
death as a form of deliverance, are typical of the songs Haden performed
on the radio as a child.

The Hadens' theme song was the Carter Family favorite "Keep on the
Sunny Side of Life," but hardly anything else they sang was as cheery.
One song that Haden especially remembers, and that he says gave him a
chill when he was old enough to understand what the lyrics meant, was
called "Mama's Not Dead, She's Just Asleepin'" — the next line went
"waiting patiently for sweet Jesus to come." On "Wayfaring Stranger,"
Broadbent scores the strings in intervals of fifths, which give the impression of being much wider, on account of Haden's uncertainty as a singer.
Sounding as if he is walking through the shadow of the valley of death,
he never seems as sure of himself as he would if he were playing the
same notes on bass. But all of the notes land exactly where they belong,
in perfect relationship to one another harmonically. Baring his soul,
Haden also displays his innate musicality.

THE NUTS AND BOLTS OF WHAT REMAINS THEIR PRIMARY JOB—MINDING BOTH
pulse and chord changes—keep bass players relatively unpretentious, even
when, like Haden, they enjoy respect as soloists and bandleaders (in all my
years of listening to jazz, I have never heard one call himself a "bassist,"
even though this is how they are usually referred to in print). Some older
bass players who lead their own bands like to introduce numbers featuring
themselves with a little joke at their own expense. The joke is from the days
when bass was strictly a supporting instrument and Africa meant ooga-
booga even to many blacks. I heard it from Milt Hinton; a friend of mine
says he heard it from Ray Brown. A hunter goes on an African safari. He's
bagging plenty of wild game, but the drumming he hears day and night is
driving him nuts. Asking the natives when it will stop, he's told he should
hope it doesn't, because that would mean something "bad, bad—very
bad." One morning he wakes from the first good sleep he's had in weeks
and—no drums! Just a distant rumble. Stepping outside his hut, he sees
what looks like the entire village running in terror. Has a volcano erupted?
No, he's told—worse than that. "Bass solo! Bass solo!"

Along with political correctness, what would prevent a bass player
Haden's age or younger from telling such a joke is that bass solos are no

longer a novelty requiring advance explanation. Everyone has some vanity, and for the typical modern bass player it is believing that he is entitled to a solo on every number, just as if he were playing piano or a horn. (Decades of prattle about jazz as an example of democracy in action have taken their toll.) Jimmy Blanton was the first to suggest the instrument's solo potential, with Duke Ellington's band in the early 1940s. Two decades later Scott LaFaro added a few twists as a member of the Bill Evans Trio. And the most compelling of all bass soloists was Charles Mingus, who had the facility of a Casals or Segovia, and a dramatic presence unlike anyone else's. But in most hands, bass solos are a recipe for boredom, if only because of the instrument's pinched dynamics. After a succession of horn solos, even the fleetest and most artfully conceived bass solo risks being anticlimatic.

Haden is a glorious exception: a bass soloist with a recognizable sensibility as well as technical range. His most celebrated recorded solo—among the most celebrated by any bass player—is the one he played on "Ramblin'," with Ornette Coleman in 1959. Fingering the instrument briskly but spacing his musical lines so that the silences between them carried as much meaning as the notes, Haden drew on his own background and underlined the country flavor of Coleman's tune by quoting snatches of folk songs he remembered from Missouri, including "Old Joe Clark," "Ft. Worth Jailhouse," and "Jesse James." But Haden usually favors a more deliberate pace, and he rarely quotes. Jazz musicians know, even if many in their audience do not, that slow tempos can be more demanding than breakneck ones; Haden has what I've heard musicians praise as a "long" beat, meaning the ability to sustain rhythmic vitality at a relative crawl. Artists whose deviations from the norm initially shock others in their discipline often turn out to be traditionalists of a sort. This was true of Coleman, who restored a primal cry to jazz and rid it of bebop's harmonic clutter, and it was true of Haden, who has gone on insisting that a bass is a bass even as other bass players have tried to convince themselves that it can be a horn or an oversized cello or guitar.

In a bid for greater velocity and carrying power, most bass players long ago switched from gut strings to steel; Haden still uses gut strings, which are more difficult to manipulate and don't accept a bow as easily, but which vibrate more deeply, if not as loudly. (Mingus was another proud throwback. "You must go back to gut," he once advised his fellow bass players in a symposium on the instrument published in *Down Beat*. "Ask

132

that little kid who was with Ornette Coleman, what's his name?") In another effort to help bass players achieve greater facility, manufacturers years ago began producing models with a lowered bridge, which brings the strings closer to the fingerboard and makes for a faster action on the strings, especially in the upper end. Haden prefers a high bridge, "because I like a deeper sound, and the closer the strings are to the fingerboard, the thinner the sound is going to be." Half the battle for any bass player is being heard over horns and drums, and this is why so many of them now attach electric pickups to their instruments. After years of experimentation, Haden now uses a custom pickup he says "amplifies the sound of the bass—not the sound of the amplifier it's plugged into, which usually has its own personality." He wishes he could forego amplification altogether, but with the sound levels turned up unreasonably high in clubs and concert halls today, the price would be not being able to hear himself, much less be heard.

When I spoke with Haden, he was in New York to mix a new album by his wife and to play duets with the pianist Kenny Barron at a garish midtown club called The Iridium. Duets once were blue-moon occurrences in jazz, but they have been a Haden specialty since the late 1970s, when he released two albums of them with different partners, including Coleman, the pianist Keith Jarrett, and the drummer Paul Motian. "There's a vulnerability to duets, because you're so exposed," Haden told me. "You can hear the musicians' fingerprints." With Barron, the most impressive aspect of Haden's solos was his sense of continuity in moving back and forth from traditional accompaniment to freestanding improvisation. Tempos never stopped dead during his solos, the way they often do when bass players have the floor to themselves. The most handsomely carved of his solos were on the neglected standard "For Heaven's Sake" and his own "Our Spanish Love Song," a lilting melody one suspects was not written from the bottom up, with the chords coming first—the method employed by many bass players out of sheer habit. Though Haden draws on a vocabulary of slides and drones and double stops common to all modern jazz bass players, what sets him apart is the deep penetration of his notes, his flair for melody, and his gravitas. As on his vocal recording of "Wayfaring Stranger," there is more shadow than sunshine in Haden's bass solos—a tacit acknowledgment of the impermanence in the way he will sometimes let a note resonate and then decay, without rushing to fill the silence with another one.

Watching Haden play, one might think that he and his bass were engaged in a life-and-death struggle—a danse macabre. Most bass players lean the instrument against a shoulder to relieve the stress of holding it upright with one hand for as much as an hour at a time, or they turn it toward them at an angle of approximately forty-five degrees, for better reach. Haden starts off with the bass turned toward him, but moves around so much as he plays that he often winds up doubled over, with his neck bent, or holding the bass an arm's length away and looking in the opposite direction—a position that requires a long reach and puts a strain on both shoulders. He and the bass often seem to be dancing, with the bass rocking wildly on its stem and Haden holding on for dear life (or "holding on like death," to quote a line from Theodore Roethke's "My Father's Waltz" that jumped to mind as I watched him, not knowing that Roethke was also one of his favorite poets). Between sets at The Iridium, he handed me what I at first thought was a teabag or a stash of marijuana. It was a handwarmer like the ones skiers wear inside their gloves. Haden said he needs a handwarmer to ward off the effects of air-conditioning in clubs, but my guess is that the occasional numbness he suffers in the hands might be the result of continually pressing the strings of his bass with the fingers of his left hand and plucking them with the index and middle fingers of his right, while leaving his other two right fingers tensely bent. Though he often speaks of improvisation as if it were an out-of-body experience, his body has paid a price; he has had recurring back problems, and various doctors and chiropractors have suggested that he try sitting down, or at least keeping still, when he plays. "When you're involved in a creative process, unless you're a dancer, you lose contact with your physical being," he told me, before returning to the bandstand. "But after all these years of standing the way I stand and moving the way I move, it's too late for me to change. One of the things you can't do when you're playing is think, because once the thought process starts, the spontaneity begins to suffer." At the end of his last number with Barron, Haden and his bass wound up turned the same way and were some distance apart—facing the audience and leaning slightly forward, as if bowing in acknowledgment of applause meant for both of them equally.

The Atlantic Monthly, August 2000

?Ornette

Jazz fans are frequently at odds not just with one another (you say Marsalis, I say Masada) but with themselves. After crowding themselves out of their apartments with albums and CDs, they'll claim that jazz, as a largely improvised art form, defies technological representation. I don't say they're wrong, just that they talk as if theirs were the only music whose nuances depend on being there in the flesh. If this were so, what need would there now be for live performances of Beethoven or Mozart, especially given the superiority of the best home sound-systems to the acoustics in modern concert halls? If recordings matter very little in jazz, they matter even less in cabaret and what Will Friedwald calls "adult" pop—genres in which an icon like Julie Wilson or a has-been like Vic Damone goes on drawing audiences year after year without benefit of a new release.

The relationship of recordings to live performances is more complementary than acknowledged by the typical jazz fan, who dismisses the former as a necessary evil. It's often also far more problematical. Most of us, for example, have heard Charlie Parker and Lester Young only on records; without this audible evidence of their genius, would we be inclined to assume their legends were exaggerated, like Buddy Bolden's? On the other hand, I for one sometimes resent mediocre live jazz because it's keeping me from my Parker records. We haul our collections with us into a concert or a club, and when we go home and pop a disc into the changer, our idealized memories of how the performer in question sounded in concert also receive a spin.

THE ABOVE MIGHT BE AN ATTEMPT TO RATIONALIZE COMMENTING AT LENGTH ON a series of concerts in a magazine primarily devoted to recordings. Ornette Coleman's *Colors* (Harmolodic/Verve 314 537 789-2), a live album of duets from Leipzig with the German pianist Joachim Kuhn, and Geri Allen's *Eyes . . . in the Back of Your Head* (Blue Note CDP 7243 8 38297 2), with Coleman making a rare appearance as a sideman, were released within days of one another last summer, along with a reissue of Coleman's 1987 *In All Languages* (Harmolodic/Verve 314 531 915–2). All three discs pale in comparison with an ambitious Coleman retrospective staged over four nights at Avery Fisher Hall, around the same time the discs showed up in my mailbox. "?Civilization," as the series was called, was presented by Lincoln Center, as part of its interdisciplinary Festival 97—*not* as part of Jazz at Lincoln Center, even though Wynton Marsalis and Stanley Crouch have expressed admiration for Coleman's early work. The series opened with Kurt Mazur and the New York Philharmonic joining Coleman and his amplified octet Prime Time for two performances of *Skies of America*, his rarely performed concerto grosso from 1972 and a key work in the formulation of the arcane theory of rhythm and harmonic unison that the alto saxophonist (and occasional trumpeter and violinist) ultimately christened "harmolodics." On the third night Coleman was reunited with Charlie Haden and Billy Higgins, the bassist and drummer in the pianoless quartet with which Coleman shook the world of jazz in 1959. After intermission the trio was joined not only by the trumpeter Wallace Roney and the pianist Kenny Barron (stand-ins for Marsalis and Cecil Taylor, if you can believe the scuttlebutt) but also by Lauren Kinhan and Chris Walker, a pair of ersatz soul singers. The singers were a preview of things to come on closing night. Against a jittery backdrop of video images displaying world leaders and victims of imperialism—it had me waiting for the Smothers Brothers and the drum solo from "Innagadadavida"—Coleman and Prime Time brought the mini-festival to an end by playing harmolodic houseband to Lou Reed and Laurie Anderson (both of whom seemed to be hearing echoes of Coleman's early recordings, and both of whose tunes suited Coleman surprisingly well), a female rapper lacking in both inflection and beat, two female contortionists in studded leather and fishnets who began their act by crushing out cigarettes on each other's tongue (shades of San Francisco, where Coleman subjected an audience to a stomach-turning body-piercing exhibition by Fakir Mustafah, in 1994), and three "interpretive" dancers, one male and two female, who stabilized tempos that weren't meant to be stabilized and who escaped untwisted, unburned, and unpierced—although they might not have, if I had been allowed a say.

They would have been better off dancing in their heads. I mean, even Sinatra drew the line at Corbett Monica and Steve & Eydie. But I shouldn't be emphasizing what were only distractions. Ornette's has been the music to which my heart beats most naturally since I started listening to jazz some thirty years ago, and he himself was brilliant even on closing night. His tendency to drift in and out of public view (these were his first New York performances since 1991, even though he lives there) has obscured Coleman's great consistency as an improviser. Back in the late 1960s, when Miles Davis first went electric, apologists ignored his cracked tone and overdependence on his wah-wah to claim that only his context had changed—Miles himself, supposedly, was playing as lyrically as always. In Ornette's case, such a claim would be true. The question of good or bad finally boils down to the telepathy of his accompanists. I heard the second night of *Skies of America*, a performance occasionally compromised by Mazur's foolhardy attempt to achieve through cacophony the kind of levitational release that Coleman, in his performances with smaller ensembles, routinely achieves through his use of sprung rhythms and intervals more like those in traditional ethnic musics than those in jazz. ("The boppers flat their fifths; we drink ours," Eddie Condon is supposed to have said. Coleman sharps his.) Even so, the episodic work took wing whenever both bands played simultaneously, allowing Coleman to weave his supple lines between Prime Time's guitars and the Philharmonic's massed strings and horns.

The series' *pièce de résistance*, however, was Coleman's only reunion since *In All Languages* with the bassist and drummer who first showed the wonderful possibilities that could result from cordial disagreements over where "one" was. Too much has generally been made of Coleman's affront to the harmonic conventions of bebop. His most radical departure from convention was rhythmic, and both Haden and Higgins (and then Ed Blackwell) were intuitive enough to realize that the drumlike nature of Coleman's written lines and improvised phrases demanded a kind of melodic counterpoint from them. At Avery Fisher it was obvious from

Haden's first slide and the first tap of Higgins's cymbals that the magic was still there.

STILL, OUR EARS OBEY THEIR OWN LOGIC, AND MINE LISTENED SIMULTANE-ously to the musicians on stage and to those nearly forty-year-old Atlantics, mentally filling in Don Cherry's missing unisons on the heads. Maybe that's why I felt a twinge of satisfaction when Roney joined Coleman on the front line, even though as a soloist he made the same miscalculation that Freddie Hubbard did in 1961 on Coleman's *Free Jazz*, mistaking a paucity of chords for an invitation to run scales.

The afternoon of the final concert I was on a symposium moderated by Gary Giddins, whose reasonable question of why the music of the night before no longer seemed as shocking as it must have in 1959 caught me by surprise. My immediate response was to mumble something about Coleman's acoustic music still sounding fresh, shocking or not. But I found myself returning to the question during the final night's circus, and deciding that neither of the two most obvious answers (continued progress or *après Coleman, la deluge*) made complete sense. The only conclusion I reached was that the music of a man in his sixties is inevitably going to sound less intense than the music he made when he was in his late twenties. Swing musicians had it easy; bebop allowed them to age gracefully, on their own timetables. Those boppers who failed to live up to their image by not dying young have enjoyed no such luxury, and the tattered survivors of the revolution that Coleman announced in 1959 will probably be expected to go on delivering jolts until they drop. At this point in his career Ornette's only possible shock value is the company he keeps, which may explain why he willingly shares the stage with amateurs and exhibitionists. Coleman has always been the jazz musician most implicitly in tune with interdisciplinary avant-garde trends, but this is becoming a problem as he seeks to make the connection explicit. For John F. Szwed, in *The Village Voice*, the high-jinks at Avery Fisher signified either Coleman's desire "to return us to the functional music of another era, and like Sun Ra [to] immerse us in the logic of black cabaret" or "a tactile expression of a new age of race-, gender-, and shape-changing which is the visual equivalent of note changing, [and which brings] the music back to its corporeal base in dancing, procession, and ecstatic release." Body mega, in other words. Or it could be that Ornette now confines his reading to REsearch publications (which tend to have titles like *Incredibly Strange Sado-Masochists Who Have Been Funded by the National Endowment for the Arts*), or that his generosity compels him to give the benefit of the doubt to people who think that being an artist is simply a matter of saying that you are. All I know is that I liked it better when female contortionists were grifters who made a few extra bucks taking on all comers after the sideshow — they were more honest with themselves, and there was some payoff for the audience in their kink. As for the singers, I don't know what it says about Coleman that he's able to write a piece for a symphony orchestra without overreaching, but not a credible pop tune — unless it says that a credible pop tune is more difficult to pull off. (Both singers preened and flirted with the audience as though they thought Ornette called his music "harmolodix," with a smiley face over the "i.")

ON A BRIGHTER NOTE, THE COMPANY ORNETTE KEEPS HAS INCREASINGLY COME to include pianists, a breed he once banished, presumably on account of the unwanted element of tonal hegemony their instrument might have lent to his bands' untransposed unisons. In performance with Coleman at Lincoln Center, Kenny Barron soloed with such abandon on Coleman's themes, while adhering so carefully to their melodic and rhythmic outlines, that at first I hardly noticed he mostly laid out behind Ornette's alto solos — an option unavailable to Joachim Kuhn in his duets with Coleman on *Colors*. A fact generally ignored in all the wonderment over Coleman's sudden embrace of pianists is that David Bryant has played keyboards in Prime Time for going on seven years. In light of Bryant's weakness for pastels and Coleman's collaboration with Pat Metheny a decade ago, instead of wondering why he suddenly has an urge to record with pianists, maybe we should be wondering what draws him to partners who mistake his rural edge for proof that he's a pastoralist like themselves. Despite a penchant for full-keyboard body slams, *à la* Cecil Taylor, Kuhn has quite a bit of Keith Jarrett in him, and I doubt it's a coincidence that the only three performances on *Colors* that fail to jell — "Hymn of Stained Glass," "Story Writing," and "Night Plans" — all begin with soft-focus piano introductions and wind up with Coleman orbiting the tempered scale. Surprisingly, it's often Coleman (to whom all eight of the album's compositions are credited) who adjusts to Kuhn, rather than the other way around. Yet on the other five duets, Coleman — who has more pet phrases than any improviser since Charlie

Parker—plays what might be described as "typical" solos for him, and my pleasure in his improvised Mozart is such that *Colors* will probably wind up making my year-end Top 10, regardless of my arguments with Kuhn. In fairness to the pianist, on the exciting "Three Ways to One," he beautifully anticipates each of Coleman's spontaneous accelerations. And the work of both men is extraordinary on "Passion Cultures," the latest of Coleman's keening dirges.

On last year's *Three Women* and *Hidden Man*, Geri Allen's quick reactions to Coleman helped her over the hurdle of playing a concert-instrument in a setting alien to it. Coleman joins her for two relatively unstructured and disappointingly inconclusive duets on her *Eyes . . . in the Back of Your Head*, an uneven album whose tracks without Coleman somehow reveal more about his influence on contemporary jazz. Miles Davis may have denounced Ornette as a man whose music suggested that he was "sick inside," but this didn't stop Miles and his quintet of the mid-1960s, with Tony Williams on drums, from emulating the Coleman Quartet's daring in setting one tempo or one time signature against another. This is the tradition that spawned Allen, and the most satisfying music on *Eye . . .* comes when she bounces crooked lines off Cyro Baptista's already asymmetrical percussion. Wallace Roney appears on four tracks and his playing, though Miles-like as usual, is uncharacteristically dark. But he and Allen, who are husband and wife, share a weakness for watercolors, and two or three too many of them considerably weaken the album's impact.

That leaves *In All Languages*, Ornette's 1987 harmolodic convergence, with ten short tracks featuring his original quintet and thirteen even shorter ones featuring Prime Time. The quartet performances sounded like instant classics ten years ago, and the passage of a decade hasn't robbed such tunes as "Peace Warriors" and "Latin Genetics" of their power or charm. Unfortunately, the same can't be said for Prime Time's contributions—which sounded a little dated to me even then, owing in part to Denardo Coleman's obtrusive, pop-influenced production techniques (including what sounds like mechanized drumbeats on a few tracks). Even so, this edition of Prime Time, which still featured such assistant tone scientists and harmolodicians-in-training as Bern Nix, Charles Ellerbee, and Jamaaladeen Tacuma, outkicks the current edition, whose members (with the significant exception of Coleman's son on drums) are more like employees. The band's lackluster showing at

Lincoln Center makes me think the time has come for downsizing, or pulling the plug once and for all.

As long as I'm offering recommendations, and given Ornette's current yen for pianists, why not an album of duets with Paul Bley, the pianist who introduced him to California audiences in the late 1950s and remains perhaps his finest reinterpreter? One's favorite records inevitably include a few that no one has gotten around to making, and one of mine would team Coleman with Sonny Rollins and Lee Konitz, his nearest matches in their mastery of theme and variations. Or what about Bill Frisell, another pastoralist but an uncommonly tough-minded one? And while I'm wishing, a reissue of the incomplete 1972 *Skies of America* would be nice,* but even nicer (despite my already stated caveats) would be a complete studio recording, with Mazur conducting. *Skies of America* is unthinkable without Coleman's active participation, and he isn't going to be around to perform it forever. Future generations shouldn't have to take the word of those of us who were on hand to hear it this summer at Avery Fisher Hall.

Fi, November 1997

---

*It was in fact reissued in 2000: Columbia/Legacy CK63568.

The 1970s, Religious and Circus

Julius Hemphill's *Blue Boyé* (Screwgun SCREWU 70008), Arthur Blythe's *Lenox Avenue Breakdown* (Koch Jazz KOC-CD-7871) and *Illusions* (Koch Jazz KOC-CD-7869), and the anthology *Jazz Loft Sessions* (Douglas Music ADC-3) are recent reissues from the late 1970s—a period I look back on as a fertile time for jazz, though not many other people do. Nobody argued with the writer and photographer William P. Gottlieb when he gave the name *The Golden Age of Jazz* to a 1979 collection of pictures he had taken of musicians in nightclubs and other natural habitats over a ten-year period beginning in 1939. The 1940s, after all, were a decade in which, as Gottlieb reminisced in his foreword, "big band jazz—mostly under the name *swing*—reached its peak," "bop and other modern forms developed," and audiences were still able to hear the earliest forms of jazz "played by legendary musicians who had started blowing way back when jazz first began." To top it off, jazz was truly popular in the 1940s, even if Gottlieb was exaggerating slightly in calling this "the only time when popularity and quality have coincided; when, for once, the most widely acclaimed music was the best music."

Like Gottlieb's memories, his assembled photographs were especially beguiling at a time when jazz was slowly rebounding from its various setbacks in the late 1960s and early 1970s (though it seemed unlikely, one could fantasize that Gottlieb had shot Duke Ellington and Charlie Parker—Chronos and Zeus, respectively—in New York on the same night, perhaps in adjoining clubs along the block-long Mount Olympus

141

on Fifty-second Street between Fifth and Sixth). Being a young jazz fan had begun to feel awfully lonely; I speak from experience, having started listening to jazz in 1964, as a high school senior. The writing was on the wall as early as 1957, in the Elvis Presley movie *Jailhouse Rock*. In one scene, Presley's girlfriend (and business partner) brings him home to meet her upper-crust parents, who are gathered around the hi-fi with their other guests, listening to far-out jazz and debating how much atonality is too much. Asked his opinion as a professional musician, Presley sneers that he doesn't know what they're talking about, and storms out the door.

In the mid-1950s a taste for "progressive" jazz, as exemplified by Stan Kenton and Dave Brubeck, or "cool" jazz, like that played by *Jailhouse Rock*'s fictional Stubby Wrightmeyer (a stand-in for Shorty Rogers?), was virtually a rite of passage for a certain type of male college student with horn-rimmed glasses and intellectual aspirations. After the arrival of the Beatles that niche was filled by progressive rock. By the mid-1960s, even if jazz was no longer a music of youthful rebellion, the jazz avant-garde could loudly claim to be the musical wing of a black political revolution. In his 1989 autobiography the trumpeter Miles Davis blamed the avant-garde's excesses for the exodus of listeners from jazz—a common opinion, though Davis alone, from his position at the center of the universe, viewed what was variously called "avant-garde," "free jazz," "the new thing," and "the new black music" as an attempt by white critics to detour audiences from *him*.

I remember thinking even then that the avant-garde was merely a scapegoat. Its squalling improvisations undeniably presented difficulty for many listeners, as did its equation with black power in the minds of many of its leading figures and their champions in the jazz press (the most demagogic of whom were black, despite what Davis asked readers to believe). But avant-gardes are *supposed* to rub people the wrong way; this is what makes them avant-garde. Ornette Coleman and others presented jazz with exciting tonal and rhythmic possibilities; the jazz rank and file rejected these in favor of the avant-garde's skeletal harmonic framework and a depoliticized version of its nationalistic message—almost as if to ensure boredom and white alienation. Too much jazz of the early 1970s consisted of what sounded like instrumental yodeling over a two-chord vamp, frequently accompanied by a lecture on the natural wonders of blackness, the confusing gist of which was likely to be that only blacks were culturally equipped to understand jazz and white people ought to be ashamed of themselves for not supporting it in greater numbers.

In emulation of John Coltrane, whose death, in 1967, had robbed jazz of the one figure respected by both the mainstream and the avant-garde, improvised solos became too long for even the most knowledgeable jazz fan to follow. Coltrane was an obsessive whose solos (unlike Louis Armstrong's and Charlie Parker's, or even Coleman's) were measured by the clock rather than by the chorus, sometimes running to forty minutes or longer. But enough seemed at stake for him in them, both musically and emotionally, that listeners felt they had something at stake too. There was little possibility of a similar vicarious involvement in the colorless droning of the many horn players who followed Coltrane's example but lacked his vast knowledge of harmony—and his charisma.

The real reason for the dwindling audience, it seemed to me, was that mainstream jazz, by then called hard bop, borrowed unwisely from both free jazz and rock 'n' roll. Envious of rock's greater popularity, many jazz musicians naively assumed that the way to compete with rock was to use its hardware. The most annoying thing about the electric keyboards and basses on so many jazz albums of the early 1970s is that they hardly ever serve an organic purpose; they are there because they were briefly fashionable, like the floppy hats and bushy sideburns the musicians are shown wearing on the covers.

THE GRAVEST PROBLEM FACING JAZZ WAS AN UNAVOIDABLE CONSEQUENCE OF its rapid evolution, which paralleled that of European concert music but at several times the pace. In his 1955 book *The Agony of Modern Music* the critic Henry Pleasants had outraged the classical-music establishment by siding with concert audiences that shied away from serialism and the like. As Pleasants saw it, these presumed philistines exhibited good taste in rejecting a European art-music tradition that had reached a dead end with Schoenberg. The truly creative music of the twentieth century was jazz, which to Pleasants meant the songs of Irving Berlin and George Gershwin as well the improvised solos of such early jazz musicians as Louis Armstrong and Sidney Bechet. By 1969, when he published his next broadside, *Serious Music—and All That Jazz!*, Pleasants had heard enough modern jazz, bebop and free, to know that jazz was experiencing its own agonies, largely as a consequence of severing its ties with pop.

Pleasants exaggerated the complexity of modern jazz and failed to take into account that by then pop meant rock 'n' roll—a form of music that had little in common rhythmically with jazz (a reason for the awkwardness of most "fusion," a hybrid of jazz and rock introduced by Miles Davis and others in the late 1960s). Even so, Pleasants was correct to accuse jazz of compounding the mistakes of "serious" music in endeavoring to be taken seriously. Jazz had begun to ask much of its audience without promising much in return. Bebop increasingly offered pleasure only in the virtuosity (or, usually, subvirtuosity) of its leading players; free jazz sometimes perversely denied audiences even that, substituting first its energy and then a quasi-spiritual vibe that epitomized another questionable trend.

Worse than overserious, jazz was becoming pious. Jazz can amount to a religion for those fans whose dedication to it becomes a ruling passion in their lives, often to the amusement of their unconverted family and friends. But that isn't what I mean. An oppressive solemnity descended on the music itself, as musicians who embraced Islam or various alternative religions dragged their beliefs on stage with them, defining their music as simultaneously a manifestation of and a tribute to some higher power. Even fusion—a style that in its studied resemblance to rock and roll might have been expected to prize irreverence—suffered from this tendency. Except for Miles Davis, who was regarded as a deity unto himself, every star of fusion seemed to give credit for his inspiration to one avatar of consciousness or another, whether it was the pianist Chick Corea with his L. Ron Hubbard, or the guitarist Mahavishnu John McLaughlin with his Sri Chimoy.

THINGS BEGAN LOOKING UP EVER SO SLIGHTLY AROUND THE BICENTENNIAL, and this upward trend—perhaps identifiable as such only in retrospect—lasted well into the 1980s. Jazz remained commercially marginal; the signs of hope were in the music, not in its record sales or box-office receipts. No one burst onto the scene to alter the course of jazz almost single-handedly, as Louis Armstrong had in 1927, Charlie Parker in 1945, and Ornette Coleman in 1959, and the evidence began to suggest that no one ever would. In the absence of a new messiah the guiding principle became diversity—always a sign of well-being in the arts, if perplexing to those conditioned to measure progress in jazz in terms of seismic disruptions.

The members of the Chicago-based Association for the Advancement of Creative Musicians (AACM) drifted almost en masse to New York, bringing with them radical notions about the relationship between sound and silence which reanimated a moribund avant-garde. Forming Prime Time, Ornette Coleman combined loopy funk polyrhythms with an arcane theory he called "harmoldics," arriving at a synthesis of jazz and rock that didn't smack of middle-age panic or an attempt to make a quick buck. Dexter Gordon's triumphant return from Europe and Art Blakey's tireless leadership of the Jazz Messengers sparked a hard bop revival, ultimately setting the stage for Wynton Marsalis. Art Pepper, released from prison in 1966, published *Straight Life* (1979), a scorching autobiography that drew attention to him as an unfairly neglected figure and to West Coast jazz of the 1950s as an unfairly maligned bebop subgenre. Small-group swing, which had been swept aside for most of the 1960s and early 1970s, made an encouraging comeback—or, to be more accurate, labels such as Pablo, Chiaroscuro, and Concord Jazz began recording it, filling a gap created by the major companies.

Amid fears that young musicians were bypassing jazz for rock, there was an influx of fresh new faces, including some (the trumpeter Warren Vaché and the tenor saxophonist Scott Hamilton, for example) whose arrival made it clear that not even styles of jazz perfected as long ago as the 1930s and early 1940s were in danger of extinction. The era's most provocative newcomers, though, were second-wave avant-gardists, including the trombonist George Lewis, the flutist James Newton, the pianist Anthony Davis, and the tenor saxophonists David Murray and Chico Freeman, for whom free jazz was merely a starting point—a part of jazz history subject to revision and elaboration but no longer open to dispute.

As if to underscore the lack of a single discernible musical trend, newspapers and magazines began to alert their readers to something called "loft jazz"—the first time an adjective had been pressed into service to describe a venue for jazz, as opposed to a way of playing it. *The New Grove Encyclopedia of Jazz* defines loft jazz as "a term sometimes applied to the styles of free jazz which were performed in lofts in New York [City] in the mid-1970s." Yes and no. A modified version of free jazz was the music most frequently performed in the lofts, which were exclusively a New York phenomenon—a creation of that city's highly speculative real-estate market, and then a casualty of it (most of the lofts were in former warehouse districts on the verge of gentrification, and many doubled as the living quarters of musicians who were eventually priced out of them). But among the performers I heard in the lofts during my frequent trips to New York in the late 1970s were Chet Baker and Lee Konitz, both typecast as "cool" (if to varying degrees) rather than avant-garde.

For avant-gardists shut out of New York's front-line clubs and forced to conduct their experiments in joyless church basements and the dankest of watering holes, lofts were a step up in more ways than one. They were also far more pleasant for audiences, who instead of being crowded together at tables or seated in uncomfortable folding chairs were permitted to stretch out on sofas and loveseats or, when there was an overflow crowd, to sit on the floor in front of the makeshift stage. There was rarely a minimum, which kept the price of going out to hear music within reason, and often no liquor was served at all, which greatly pleased the growing number of musicians who objected to their music being used to sell drinks but felt that they played best with an audience in closer proximity than was possible in concert halls.

The lofts were a genuine phenomenon of the late 1970s, yet so much attention was paid to them that sometimes the exact nature of the music being played in them escaped notice. This was the period during which "tradition" first became a jazz buzzword, largely as a result of the avant-garde's determination to establish its lineage from earlier forms of jazz. Sun Ra and his Arkestra began to feature numbers that Fletcher Henderson and others had written for Henderson's band in the 1930s, and the alto saxophonist Henry Threadgill and his group Air reached all the way back to Scott Joplin and Jelly Roll Morton. At a time when it was practically a given that creativity entailed playing only original compositions, Archie Shepp, Anthony Braxton, and Arthur Blythe confounded expectations with relatively straightforward interpretations of bebop and popular standards. The message seemed to be that any tradition broad enough to encompass both ragtime and bebop was broad enough to encompass free jazz as well.

THE MOST SURPRISING DEVELOPMENT OF ALL WAS A SHIFT IN EMPHASIS ONLY somewhat presaged by these excursions into the jazz past. "Jazz is by its very nature a music of improvisation . . . Therefore of innovation . . . Therefore of ongoing change," Ross Firestone, a writer better known for a biography of Benny Goodman, fingersnapped in the opening paragraph of his blanket liner notes to all five volumes of *Wildflowers*, a series of five LPs recorded amid much fanfare in the summer of 1976 at Studio Rivbea (not a "studio" at all but a performance space run by the tenor saxophonist Sam Rivers and his wife, Bea, in their lower-Manhattan loft). The notes for *Jazz Loft Sessions*, a single CD culled from those five LPs, omit Firestone's opening paragraph and begin instead with his reasonable observation that Studio Rivbea and other New York lofts afforded musicians of the late 1970s an opportunity to try new things in public, free from the pressures of nightclubs and concert halls. Though the probable explanation for this omission is lack of space, it would be nice to think that someone realized that Firestone's generic ode to improvisation missed the point. Improvisatory freedom was a given for the musicians on *Jazz Loft Sessions*, their birthright as children of Coltrane and Coleman. Their search was for expanded improvisational contexts—that is, new ways of approaching the question of composition in jazz.

For all its sound and fury, the avant-garde of the 1960s had left the structure of jazz fundamentally unchanged. In free jazz as in bebop, a "tune" was something played at the beginning and repeated at the end, generally little more than harmonic scaffolding for improvised solos (and frequently not even that in free jazz, where reference to the tune's chord changes was optional). Beginning around 1976, in the work of the alto saxophonist Julius Hemphill and numerous others, including many of the players on *Jazz Loft Sessions*, composition and improvisation started to overlap—the way they had, perhaps not coincidentally, on Jelly Roll Morton's recordings in the 1920s with his Red Hot Peppers and in Fletcher Henderson and Duke Ellington's scores for their big bands.

For someone like Hemphill or Henry Threadgill, a "composition" could be a piece written out from beginning to end, with multiple themes and a limited amount of improvisation, or it could be nothing more than a riff. When it was only a riff, the riff was likely to turn up anywhere—between solos and underneath them, but not necessarily at the beginning and end.

Every period of jazz has its excesses and one of this period's was the solo-saxophone concert, an exercise in self-indulgence that ultimately convinced players and audiences alike that no further advances were forthcoming in terms of individual expression. The unaccompanied saxophone recital was something the period's more adventurous players needed to get out of their systems before embracing the greater challenge of extending their individual concepts to their ensembles. In so doing they wound up bringing something of the levity of early jazz to the music's more advanced forms, where levity of some sort was badly needed. Much of this seemed to be a natural consequence of reinterpreting jazz of the 1920s and 1930s, but some of it had been implicit in free jazz from the beginning—in Ornette Coleman's rambling Texas blues, in Albert Ayler's Salvation Army–like dirges and skewered national anthems, and in Archie Shepp's periodic evocations of James Brown and John Philip Sousa. The turning point seemed to come with the release of Anthony Braxton's *Creative Orchestra Music 1976*. Unlike most of his peers in the jazz avant-garde, who recorded for a variety of domestic and European labels with limited studio budgets, Braxton was under contract to Arista, a mid-major (in the language of that day's record business) with the resources to indulge his grandest ambitions. Arista failed in its attempt to position Braxton as the most significant new voice in jazz since Coleman; not even the most intrepid record buyers knew what to make of a saxophonist who gave his compositions diagrammatic titles and whose newest release might well be an album of Stockhausen-like pieces for solo piano on which Braxton himself did not play a note.

But Braxton's affiliation with Arista enabled him to write for and perform with large ensembles, and he caught his most ardent admirers by surprise with two numbers on *Creative Orchestra Music 1976*—both saddled with titles that looked like the doodles of a daydreaming physicist. One, described by Braxton in his notes as an exercise in "repetition structure" and as having been inspired by Duke Ellington, borrowed Ellington's harmonic tapestry to make a ballad inlaid with countermelodies more dissonant than his, but not by much. Less than two years after Ellington's death, when tributes to him abounded, this one did more than echo his orchestra's sound; it demonstrated his continued relevance to composers working in idioms far removed from the dance band.

The album's other winner was a Midwestern circus march—authentic three-ring music replete with tuba, glockenspiel, bass drum, and improvised solos that sounded as though they were being executed by acrobats atop the high wire. In the movie *My Left Foot*, Daniel Day-Lewis, as the Irish writer and painter Christy Brown, tells a questioner, "There are only two kinds of painting—religious and the circus." The same goes for art in general, including jazz. Having reached a dead end with religion in the early part of the decade, the jazz avant-garde of the late 1970s gave itself and its listeners a break by unexpectedly opting for the circus.

SOME MIGHT ARGUE, AND I WOULDN'T NECESSARILY DISAGREE, THAT BRAXTON and others tried nothing in the late 1970s that Charles Mingus hadn't already done twenty years earlier, including the Ellington and the Ringling Bros. But Mingus was one man, not a movement. *Creative Orchestra Music 1976* is out of print, but you can hear the avant-garde's spirit lifting—its music becoming more robust and communicative—on a variety of albums of the same vintage, including Hemphill's *Blue Boyé*, a solo-saxophone recording from 1977 that was originally released by Hemphill on his private label (another period trend, reflecting both a desire for self-determination on the part of musicians and a lack of inter-est on the part of established record companies). *Blue Boyé*, restored to circulation as a two-disc set on the private label of the alto saxophonist Tim Berne, a Hemphill protégé, is an exception among solo-saxophone recordings in being only sporadically solipsistic. Hemphill "cheats"—and more power to him—by overdubbing one or two additional horn parts on half of the set's eight performances, including the opening "Countryside," in which his slowly intersecting lines on flute and soprano and alto saxo-phones create a haunting pastorale. With the notable exception of "Kansas City Line"—nine thrilling minutes of bebop stripped to its essen-tials—the tracks on which Hemphill eschews overdubbing are interesting mainly as inventories of the advanced or "extended" saxophone and flute techniques favored in the lofts during this period, such as the use of growl-ing or humming to give the illusion of producing two or more notes simultaneously on instruments theoretically incapable of doing so. These performances are never as dry as they might be, because Hemphill—a Texan, like Ornette Coleman—packs even the most abstract of them with blues fervor. The tracks I remember returning to most often in the late 1970s, and that hold up best now, are those featuring Hemphill in dupli-cate or triplicate. These predicted the voicings he would use in his writ-ing for World Saxophone Quartet—the rhythm section-less co-operative ensemble he formed with Hamiet Bluiett, Oliver Lake, and David Murray the year before he recorded *Blue Boyé*.

Essentially a chamber group—but one capable of delivering the knockout punch of a big band—WSQ brought to fruition many of the ideas formulated in the lofts. It became the benchmark jazz ensemble of the 1980s, then seemed to lose much of its original character following Hemphill's departure, in 1990. WSQ's most imaginative and prolific composer, Hemphill was also the bandmember most adamant about letting the four saxophones stand alone. For the remainder of his life (he died in 1995) Hemphill's primary vehicle was an all-saxophone sextet that frequently sounded more like WSQ than WSQ did in its subsequent encounters with rhythm sections and African drummers.

The four original members of World Saxophone Quartet are present on *Jazz Loft Sessions*, three of them leading their own bands (Lake performs as a sideman with the guitarist Michael Jackson, adding a nervous edge to what might otherwise sound like an early example of New Age). At under three minutes—atypically short for Murray, who was then just twenty-one and profligate—"Shout Song" is a frustrating snippet, very possibly a set opener intended to establish a mood for a series of longer pieces featuring extended solos by Murray and the cornetist Olu Dara; when Murray recorded the number again two years later with just bass and drums, on a live album from Switzerland, his performance lasted close to twenty-five minutes. (The drummer on this 1976 version of "Shout Song," by the way, is Stanley Crouch, today a respected essayist and spokesman for the jazz establishment as an artistic consultant to Jazz at Lincoln Center, but then a ubiquitous presence on the avant-garde jazz scene as a booker for at least one of the lofts, a reviewer for the *Village Voice* and the *Soho Weekly News*, and an occasional performer. Whether Crouch could keep a beat is impossible to say from the evidence here, because he is called on merely to supply color on his cymbals.) To understand why Murray was the source of so much excitement during this period, you need to hear *Ming* (Black Saint 120045-2), a 1980 octet album that struck a workable balance between ambitious writing and riotous improvisation, and captured its moment in jazz as vividly as Miles Davis's *Kind of Blue* had twenty-one years earlier.

Unlike Murray and Lake, Bluiett and Hemphill are represented by performances typical of their best work. Bluiett's "Tranquil Beauty" is a plangent and rather traditional blues and also a springboard for liberated simultaneous improvisation between Bluiett (on clarinet and baritone saxophone) and Dara, whose puckish wit was one of the era's frequent pleasures. Hemphill's "Pensive" is reflective in all but its tempo, never quite settling into a ballad. The four-man rhythm section, featuring the cellist Abdul Wadud, the guitarist Bern Nix, and two percussionists, functions more like an orchestra behind Hemphill's agile, voicelike alto-saxophone lead. The result is a minor, spur-of-the-moment masterpiece.

The rest of *Jazz Loft Sessions* is uneven, though at least one perform-ance has dated better than I would have expected. On the strength of his work with Cecil Taylor and Albert Ayler in the 1960s, Sunny Murray was once regarded as the most innovative drummer in jazz after Elvin Jones. By 1976 he had entered the journeyman phase of his career. Byard Lancaster, the featured soloist in Murray's group, the Untouchable Factor, was another veteran of free jazz then at loose ends. Murray and Lancaster's fluttering interpretation of "Over the Rainbow"—emotion-ally, as well as tonally, high-pitched—initially seemed interesting only for demonstrating Albert Ayler's lingering influence on jazz. Now it just seems a moving ballad for which no historical context is needed; it's the only version of "Over the Rainbow" I know that sounds like the musi-cians playing it have already gotten there.

Braxton's "73°-S Kelvin," though one of his exercises in long division, zigzags as contagiously as his marches, with Braxton and George Lewis mewling on contrabass clarinet and trombone, respectively, and the pianist Anthony Davis (uncredited both here and on the original LP) upping the intensity a notch with a technically impressive and logically constructed solo. The tenor saxophonist Kalaparusha, formerly known as Maurice McIntyre, sounds caught in an early-1970s time warp, noodling on one chord for six minutes on a piece called "Jays" (Chris White's thwacking electric bass doesn't help). The unrelated Ken McIntyre's "Naomi," featuring the unsung multi-instrumentalist on flute (not his best horn), sounds like it's here only because the reissue producer Guy M. Manganiello felt another ballad was called for. For much of the 1960s, following the debut of Ornette Coleman's pianoless quartet and his abandonment of just intonation, avant-garde pianists seemed a van-ishing species. In the 1970s I attended concerts for which there would be a piano on stage but no one seated at it, unless one of the saxophonists felt a sudden urge to tinker. Perhaps because so few of the groups that were recorded at Studio Rivbea included a pianist, tuning the loft's old upright apparently wasn't a top priority. The instrument defeats Dave Burrell's attempts at whimsy and rhythmic displacement on "Black Robert"—a shame because Burrell was ahead of the crowd in incorpo-rating elements of ragtime and stride into a stark, modernist setting. On the captivating "Portrait of Frank Edward Weston," Randy Weston—the collection's odd man out: a pianist active since the early 1950s whose solos are rife with allusions to Duke Ellington and Thelonious Monk, and unclassifiable as hard bop or avant-garde or anything else—almost seems to be playing a different instrument from Burrell. Not exactly a mambo and not exactly a waltz, the piece finds Weston hinting at both in his playful exchanges with the conga player Azzedin Weston.

THE ORIGINAL *WILDFLOWERS* LPS ARE WORTH SEARCHING FOR, BECAUSE IN reducing them to one CD, Manganiello or whoever was responsible for the selections has made some questionable choices.* Air's "USO Dance" should be here, as should the alto saxophonist Roscoe Mitchell's "Chant," despite its twenty-five-minute length. And the omission of Sam Rivers is unforgivable, given his importance as landlord and pater familias to the original project. *Jazz Loft Sessions* is the best one-disc survey we have of the avant-garde at a crucial stage in its evolution, but too many of the era's pacesetters are missing for it to be considered definitive.

One of these pacesetters was the alto saxophonist Arthur Blythe, a ubiquitous presence in the lofts who somehow wasn't included on the original LPs. Like Braxton, Blythe was once the beneficiary of a major-label push; though his music was more accessible than Braxton's, he too proved to be a hard sell, and Columbia Records eventually forgot all about him in its rush to coronate Wynton Marsalis as the new king of jazz. I contributed in a small way to the hype surrounding Blythe, writing a cover story about him for *JazzTimes* and conducting a "Blindfold Test" with him for *Down Beat*. The point of a Blindfold Test is for a musician to comment on and grade recordings about which he has been given no information beforehand, hopefully telling *Down Beat*'s readers something about his own musical values in the process. One of the recordings I played for Blythe was a "live" duet between Byard Lancaster and the cellist David Eyges, which Blythe said sounded more like a "tape" than a commercial recording. I assumed he was commenting on the indifferent sound quality, but listening again to *Lenox Avenue Breakdown*—Blythe's 1979 Columbia debut, reissued last year by Koch Jazz—I now think he meant that making a recording involves more than

---

*The contents of all five LPs are included on *Wildflowers: The New York Loft Sessions* (Knit Classics KCR–3037), released several months after this piece was published.

blowing while the tapes roll. *Lenox Avenue Breakdown* has a cohesiveness missing from even the best of the live performances on *Jazz Loft Sessions*, perhaps owing to its balance of instruments—something crucial to the success of music dependent on spontaneous interplay, but hardly possible when recording on the fly.

Blythe seems to have been determined to put his best foot forward on record, and on *Lenox Avenue Breakdown* he succeeded in channeling his natural exuberance as a soloist into the writing of themes and backgrounds for a small group. His septet's unusual instrumentation remains part of the album's charm. James Newton's flute is voiced in such a way that it often sounds like a shadow falsetto to Blythe's alto, and Bob Stewart's mobile tuba is sometimes a string bass and sometimes a one-man brass section. James "Blood" Ulmer's guitar rumbles menacingly with its dual suggestions of heavy metal and backwoods blues, and the percussionist Guillermo Franco adds a touch of Carnival with his woodblocks and whistles. Cecil McBee and Jack DeJohnette are the sort of bassist and drummer who can light a fire under a soloist; here it is Blythe who lights a fire under them. Blythe likes to riff on simple chord patterns—a common practice in jazz since Coltrane, and one that can land a soloist in quicksand. Blythe's salvation is his patience, his mastery of tension and release: You can hear him thinking ahead several choruses on his lengthier solos. His themes are deceptively simple and full of piquant details. The most attractive cuts on *Lenox Avenue Breakdown* are "Odessa," a lilting melody with a slightly Moorish cast, and the title track, a fast quasi-bebop line minus the customary bridge.

Illusions, from two years later, showcases Blythe with the two different groups he led at that time—a quartet with a conventional rhythm section, and a colorful quintet with tuba, guitar, cello, and drums. The mere presence of a cello in a band led by a saxophonist who had once called himself "Black Arthur" was a clue that change was in the air; instruments associated with longhair music had as much to do as skin color in earning 1950s West Coast jazz a reputation as white. Blythe's most potent solos here are with the quintet; "Carespin' with Mamie," a shuffle, is a fine example of his wisdom in framing his most ambitious improvisations with his catchiest themes.

WHY DOES NO ONE, INCLUDING ME, REMEMBER THE PERIOD REPRESENTED BY these reissues as a golden age? In my case, the answer could be that I was thirty years old in 1976 and had already been listening to jazz for more than a decade. In his introduction to Gottlieb's *The Golden Age of Jazz* the critic John S. Wilson observed, "For most of us, the Golden Age of Jazz turns out to be the time when we first discovered the music." This may be true, but by the time people my age began listening to jazz, a lengthy history, available through recordings, had become a considerable part of the music's lure.

A problem with recordings, however, as with other means of reproduction, is that they permit nostalgia without memory. Starting with those fans of the 1940s who believed that the only jazz worthy of the name was the freewheeling style played in New Orleans before 1927 or so, there have always been jazz-record collectors obsessed with memories they feel cheated out of by having been born too late. This tendency is most pronounced among listeners who fell in love with jazz in the same bleak period I did—a time darkened by Coltrane's death, Miles Davis's defection to fusion (followed by that of his star sidemen), and the inactivity, for a few years each, of Davis, Sonny Rollins, Charles Mingus, Ornette Coleman, and Thelonious Monk—not just marquee names, but musicians to whom others looked for direction. We and the listeners who discovered jazz ten years later listened to the 1970s avant-garde with our minds already made up that things would never again be as good as they once were.

Another problem is that almost nobody remembers anything about the 1970s very fondly, partly because the 1960s were a tough act to follow. Yet the 1970s were a time of great artistic ferment, especially in the popular arts. The collapse of the Hollywood studio system enabled directors such as Martin Scorsese and Francis Ford Coppola to bring their movies to the screen with minimum commercial interference (test screenings and the millions made by *Star Wars* and its sequels soon put an end to that). The original cast of *Saturday Night Live* broadened the parameters of television sketch comedy. In classical music the composers Steve Reich and Philip Glass made tonality and rhythm and a large vision of the world acceptable again, after several decades of composers who made minute adjustments to the twelve-tone scale. (That Reich and Glass were supposed to be "minimalists" was one of the decade's delicious ironies.) In pop, disco sparked what may prove to have been the last national dance craze, and punk and New Wave set the tone for most of today's alternative rock. Yet all that anyone seems to remember about the 1970s is the sexual promiscuity and the polyester (it was the decade that fashion forgot, which was just as well, considering all the time we spent naked).

Beginning in the late 1980s, jazz has supposedly experienced a commercial renaissance, but that isn't necessarily the same thing as an artistic rebirth. Blythe and most of the performers on *Jazz Loft Sessions* are still active, working along the same lines they pursued in the 1970s. Their influence is apparent in the music of John Zorn, Dave Douglas, Bobby Previte, and others associated with New York's downtown avant-garde scene. But the avant-garde has become marginalized again, and everyone on the business end of jazz seems happier with them safely out of earshot. In keeping with what seems to be the spirit of the times, *Billboard* now features two jazz sales charts: "jazz/contemporary" for smooth jazz and fusion, and "jazz" for more traditional forms—an arrangement that doesn't leave much room for experimentation. To me, this doesn't seem to be an especially exciting time for jazz, though there may be young people just now discovering it, and going to hear it in out-of-the-way places, who will one day look back on this as its golden age. I hope so; I just find it difficult to believe.

The Atlantic Monthly. February 2000

Like Young

Youth has become the most frequent topic of conversation in jazz. The talk concerns a crop of instrumentalists in their twenties and very early thirties, including the tenor saxophonists Joshua Redman and James Carter, the trumpeters Roy Hargrove and Nicholas Payton, the pianists Cyrus Chestnut and Jacky Terrasson, and the bassist Christian McBride, who are supposedly luring audiences their own age and younger to jazz.

This accent on youth could be interpreted as an effort to shake the blues of just a few years ago, when all anybody seemed to talk about was death. Sarah Vaughan died early in 1990, followed in less than three years by Art Blakey, Stan Getz, Miles Davis, and Dizzy Gillespie. Along with grief, these deaths triggered panic that time might also be running out on jazz as a commercially viable form of music. It didn't matter that there were still plenty of great musicians in or near their prime, because only a relative handful of people knew who they were. The core audience for jazz (let's define it, only somewhat facetiously, as those people able to name their *second* favorite bass player) is small in number, disputatious, and scattered over several continents. The sort of casual fan on whom the jazz box office ultimately depends might recognize Vaughan or Davis by name, but is unlikely to be familiar with Abbey Lincoln or Joe Henderson. Jazz was already short of marquee names when the 1990s began; the loss of five more left what threatened to become a permanent void at the top of the bill.

Some New York–based critics blamed their city's club owners and the producers of the annual JVC Jazz Festival for having failed to groom successors to bebop's aging stars. JVC, in particular, was in danger of becoming an annual series of memorial concerts. Even so, the assumption that presenters of live music still turn the crank of the starmaking machinery strikes me as naive.

Duke Ellington used to say that he was born in Newport, Rhode Island, in 1956. He meant reborn at that summer's Newport Jazz Festival, when an outbreak of dancing in the aisles during his band's performance of "Diminuendo and Crescendo in Blue" helped to land him on the cover of *Time*. But that was forty years ago. Journalists, booking agents, and record company executives still flock to the major summer festivals, the grounds of which often resemble trade shows. But most of today's biggest festivals are in Europe, and there are far too many of them for any single one to matter in quite the same way that Newport used to.

An increasing number of festivals defray their costs by subletting their stages to record companies for "An Afternoon with Blue Note" or "An Evening with Columbia." Nobody seems to mind this egregious conflict of interest, because it's too late to mind; in most cases, the entire festival might as well be programmed by record companies, because only performers who have a major label's publicity campaign behind them draw big crowds today.* Word of mouth about a newcomer or resurgent veteran can still begin at an overseas festival, in a New York nightclub, or occasionally in a favorable notice by an influential critic. But only the major labels have the juice to amplify such word of mouth into what broadcasters and newspaper and magazine editors traditionally unrecep-

---

*The largest festival in North America is the Montreal International Jazz Festival, where the young musicians Joshua Redman, James Carter, and Jacky Terrasson were among the featured performers in 1995—their shows were among only ten sold out in advance of opening day. I caught only portions of their sets, because there was so much else I wanted to hear. A certain New York critic is notorious among his colleagues for never sticking around one club long enough to hear a complete set. Fearful that he might be missing history in the making a few doors away, he lives in a perpetual state of "fifteen minutes to McCoy Tyner," as I once heard him rationalize walking out on Illinois Jacquet. With tickets to as many as a dozen overlapping shows a night free for the asking to anyone with press credentials, all of us found ourselves practicing this peculiar form of math in Montreal, whose annual festival not only puts to shame any in the United States,

tive to jazz might recognize as a buzz. Once a buzz gets started, the role of everyone who hopes to win bigger numbers for jazz—including compliant critics—becomes to keep it going.

THE LOUDEST BUZZ RIGHT NOW IS ABOUT THOSE ABOVE-NAMED YOUNGER musicians, who are credited with bringing jazz back to life or—what might amount to the same thing—putting more warm bodies into the seats. It should come as no surprise that the most talked-about of them happen to record for the big labels. Joshua Redman may prove to be the most talented in the group; at twenty-seven, he's already far and away the most successful, with sales of each of his first three Warner Bros. albums having topped 100,000. Last fall DKNY Menswear (the designer Donna Karan's line of casual wear for "the urban guy who lives for the risk") outfitted Redman and his sidemen for their fifty-city tour to promote *Spirit of the Moment* (Warner Bros. 9 45923-2), Redman's fourth release. This was hailed as a breakthrough: Pop stars who go on the road to promote their new albums can usually count on corporate sponsorship to offset the costs of their tours, but jazz performers are rarely so blessed. On the eve of the tour, DKNY and Warner Bros. threw a party for Redman at the Fashion Café, a New York City theme restaurant whose investors include the supermodels Elle MacPherson and Naomi Campbell. After playing a brief set that was broadcast on the Internet, Redman presented his horn and his DKNY sportscoat to MacPherson, to be put on permanent display in the café, joining a gown worn by Madonna, a pants suit worn by Jodie Foster, and napkins smeared with the lipsticks of Lauren Bacall, Tatum O'Neal, and RuPaul. "What [do] fashion and jazz have in common?" MacPherson mused in accepting Redman's gifts. "I think it's sex. They're both so sexy."

---

but rivals those in Umbria, Montreux, San Sebastian, and the North Sea in quality and size—and without completely relinquishing programming responsibility to record companies (language aside, its festival might be the only way in which Montreal lives up to its billing as the most "European" of American cities). All of the main concert halls were downtown, within what would normally be a five-minute walk. But the mobs that gathered for another dozen or so free outdoor concerts nightly (counting them, total attendance for the festival was 1.6 million) meant that anyone trying to hotfoot it between halls was forced underground, through a labyrinth of subway concourses, hotel garages, and indoor shopping malls. Your odds of getting anywhere in time for the opening announcements depended on your intimacy with subterranean Montreal, or your luck in bumping into a resident willing to speak English.

I could make fun of this; in fact, by quoting it I already have. But with corporate underwriting taking the place of federal arts funding, we may soon see a new form of Social Darwinism: survival of the cutest. In addition to being photogenic, Redman is good copy twice over—as a biracial, second-generation jazz musician (his father is the black tenor saxophonist Dewey Redman, formerly a sideman with Ornette Coleman and a member of Old and New Dreams), and even more so as a Harvard summa cum laude who passed up Yale Law for a career in jazz ("He gave up Yale for a career in music, and now he's working in basements," reads an ad for *The Spirit of the Moment*, a double CD recorded in performance at the Village Vanguard, New York's most venerable cellar).

You could call it the Wynton Marsalis factor. Every ten years or so, for a different set of reasons each time, cultural trendsetters rally behind one musician with whom they sense a bond and who then comes to symbolize jazz to the mass media. Before Marsalis, it happened in turn to Dave Brubeck, Miles Davis, John Coltrane, and Keith Jarrett (an unlikely candidate in that his lengthy solo improvisations would seem to epitomize everything the general public distrusts about jazz—but then, little about the 1970s made sense). When Marsalis exploded on the scene fifteen years ago, the proof of his commitment to jazz was supposed to be that although he also played classical music, he clearly regarded jazz as a higher calling. Marsalis improbably combined youthful arrogance with an obeisance to tradition that bordered on ancestor worship; Columbia's success in marketing him convinced the other majors that the trick to selling jazz was to play up its genealogy and long history of esoteric appeal even while attempting to demystify it by means of trim young figures in designer suits. This is now the strategy being employed on behalf of musicians as much as a decade younger than Marsalis who have begun not only to outsell him but to collectively displace him as jazzman of the hour. Though unprecedented in recent memory, the election of a *type* of musician to carry the banner for jazz was probably inevitable, given the difficulty of finding another individual as charismatic as Marsalis and given the long-standing preference of magazine editors for "trend" pieces on jazz, as opposed to pieces on individual musicians (when Marsalis made the cover of *The New York Times Magazine* last year, the novelist Frank Conroy's smoochy story on him was part of a larger package explaining how "by returning to its roots, jazz has found its future"; no record company press release ever put it better).

At thirty-four, Marsalis is more visible than ever, what with his recent books and radio and television programs. But he no longer sells as many albums as he used to, and tempting as it is to blame this on a combination of overexposure and the ill will he has aroused as the artistic director of Jazz at Lincoln Center (he's been accused of cronyism, ageism, reverse racism, and narrow-mindedness in closing the doors of that establishment to reputed avant-gardists), I think there's another explanation— one entirely to Marsalis's credit as an artist unwilling to let his audience tell him who he is.

Marsalis initially won mass acceptance as a kind of substitute Miles Davis, and many of his fans were taken by surprise when his efforts to define himself as a composer led him to embrace New Orleans polyphony and Duke Ellington's talking horns. Marsalis's dance suites and extended compositions have been extremely uneven, but the problem with them from the standpoint of units sold may be that dance suites and extended compositions simply aren't what his fans expect from him or want from jazz. Besides giving him something in common with those postmodernists who are unlikely to receive commissions from Lincoln Center as long as *he* has anything to say about it, Marsalis's emphasis on composition has created an opening for Redman and the others—none of whom has demonstrated much interest in larger forms, though many have inherited some of Marsalis's other traits, including his attitude toward tradition and innovation.

The animosity with which many jazz critics regard Marsalis owes something to his having usurped their authority. His pronouncements on jazz in interviews and in occasional bylined articles carry more weight with readers than do those of any of us who regularly write about jazz (including even Albert Murray and Stanley Crouch, Marsalis's associates at Lincoln Center). And in turning thumbs down on most of the innovations in jazz since 1960—in vehemently insisting that it can't be jazz if it doesn't swing from beginning to end and explicitly refer to the blues— Marsalis has been telling many disgruntled listeners exactly what they were waiting to hear.

He has delivered the same message to a much larger audience of people curious about jazz but afraid of being left behind before they even begin. I used to believe that what scared most people away from jazz was their suspicion that they would be bored by it. In the case of much latter-day bebop, with its lineup of soloists running down the chords to no apparent purpose after stating a sketchy theme not to be heard again until the end, boredom is a reasonable response. The solution, I always thought, was to expose people to kinds of jazz in which composition and improvisation overlap, and in which something is going on in every measure. It wouldn't have to be Muhal Richard Abrams or Sun Ra or anything too far-out; it could be Ellington or Charles Mingus or even Marsalis's score for the 1990 movie *Tune In Tomorrow*. But if new audiences are flocking to jazz on the heels of a generation of musicians who were themselves receptive to Marsalis's ideology at an impressionable age, I must be wrong. People who have never really listened to jazz want it to go on sounding the way they've been led to believe it should, so that they'll be able to recognize it in case they ever chance to hear any.

Longtime jazz listeners, for their part, want jazz to be as it was in the 1950s and the early 1960s, when a devotion to jazz was still a sign of being hip. Iridium, a fairly new Manhattan club, features on its menu mixed drinks described as "retro cocktails." The adjective also applies to most of the music now heard in New York's front-line clubs—especially when the players on the bandstand are roughly the age now that Miles Davis and John Coltrane are in those vintage black-and-whites on the walls of the Village Vanguard.

THE MOST EVOCATIVE OF ALL JAZZ PHOTOGRAPHS MIGHT BE ONE TAKEN BY ART Kane for a 1959 issue of *Esquire*, showing fifty-seven musicians, famous and obscure, posed outside a brownstone on East 126th Street in Harlem. Inspired by the success of Jean Bach's lovely 1994 film *A Great Day in Harlem*, which examined both Kane's photograph and what else went on among the musicians that day, *Life* magazine last fall assembled ten of the twelve survivors to have their picture taken again, outside the same brownstone (now gutted and missing its cornice). By coincidence, it was the day of the Million Man March, when there was much talk on radio and television about the shortage of positive male role models in black communities (O.J. Simpson and Mike Tyson were frequently mentioned as fallen idols; maybe they should have been cited as examples of the folly of pinning too much hope on jocks). There were exemplary role models on the steps in Harlem that day: dedicated artists and family men such as the tenor saxophonist Benny Golson, the trumpeter Art Farmer, the bassist Milt Hinton, and the pianist Hank Jones. Jazz could also offer inspiration in the stories of those musicians who reclaimed their lives from drugs (for every Charlie Parker, there's a Sonny Rollins). That jazz goes virtually unmentioned in the national discourse on race underlines its diminished relevance to everyday African-American life.

If this helps to explain why the emergence of talented young instrumentalists not much older than the members of Boyz II Men answers a prayer, it also raises the question of whether a player's race much matters at this point. All but a few of the younger musicians being pushed by major labels are black; this has created a backlash of sorts among white musicians, who feel left out. The harshest critics of today's newcomers, however, are musicians over forty, including black musicians, who lament that they themselves were young too soon—a decade or so before Marsalis, when an unspoken grandfather clause was in effect at record companies and only acknowledged old masters whose careers predated rock and roll were eligible for jazz stardom. "The young lions," as everyone seems to call today's young musicians, are an easy sell to longtime jazz fans who recall the 1970s and the early 1980s with a shudder. Unlike their immediate elders, these newcomers don't have synthesizers in their closets to apologize for. Nor are they asked to atone for the excesses of the period, not so long ago, when cutting-edge jazz was associated with a black-separatist agenda. However much they revere the past, they're not tainted by its compromises, as musicians who actually lived through it tend to be.

Nobody resents these recent arrivals for making a splash; they're resented for *not* making waves the way that Charlie Parker and Dizzy Gillespie did in the 1940s and young players have been counted on to do periodically ever since. (Even Marsalis stirred things up, in his own way.) There are no Thelonious Monks or Ornette Colemans in this bunch— no innovators or woolly eccentrics among those we've heard from so far. In setting craftsmanship as their highest goal these neophytes remind me of such second-tier stars of the 1950s and 1960s as Blue Mitchell and Wynton Kelly—players whose modesty and good taste made them ideal sidemen but whose own record dates invariably lacked the dark corners and disfigurements of character that separate great music from the merely good.

SOMETHING FURTHER INHIBITING THIS LATEST GENERATION IS THE IMPLICATION that the future of their art form, as well as their own careers, rides on the commercial success of their CDs. In concert, Roy Hargrove can be positively fiery, but his albums—including the recent *Parker's Mood* (Verve 314 527 907-2), a collection of tunes written by or associated with Charlie Parker which also features Christian McBride and the pianist Stephen Scott—have been cautious and bland. The same is true of Nicholas Payton, a gifted trumpeter barely out of his teens whose work on *From This Moment* ... (Verve 314 527 073-2) comes across as "mature" in all the wrong ways, owing to an overabundance of medium tempos and minor keys, plus the restraining effect of no fewer than three chording instruments (Mulgrew Miller's piano, Mark Whitfield's guitar, and Monty Croft's vibes).

Blandness and premature solemnity aren't among James Carter's worries. If anything, he would do well to calm down. Carter's main horn is tenor, but he's also proficient on a variety of other reeds and woodwinds, including soprano, alto, and baritone saxophones. He's the only one of the major-label bonus babies with avant-garde credentials, having worked with Lester Bowie and the late Julius Hemphill, among others, before starting his own quartet. Because of this, he's regarded by many as a kind of gap sealer—a figure who deserves praise for drawing on both "inside" and "outside" approaches to improvisation. Carter might erupt in screams even on a ballad or a medium-tempo groove tune, his rhythm section suspending the beat as it pummels its instruments into cacophony. This lends an element of unpredictability to Carter's solos, but the problem is that his solos are always unpredictable in exactly the same way. You know the fireworks are coming, and after a few numbers, you can almost predict when. Carter's screams and lower-register blasts are his way of signaling to his audiences that he's reached such a level of inspiration that the bonds of propriety and just intonation no longer apply. But I suspect that the reason even those listeners who normally shun what used to be called "free" jazz in fear of just such episodes willingly go along with Carter is that they know his paroxysms will be short-lived. Minus the sort of thematic development that is as possible in free improvisation as in any other kind, his farrago-like solos reduce thirty years of sonic exploration to a handy vocabulary of stock effects not much different from the honks and screams of the average rhythm-and-blues saxophonist of the 1950s.

Even so, Carter's virtues almost outweigh his faults. Though primarily influenced by John Coltrane, Wayne Shorter, and Sonny Rollins, today's young tenor saxophonists have begun to investigate the work of a host of muscular and once overlooked players of the 1950s and 1960s, typified by the late Gene Ammons. Not for nothing were Ammons and others of this school (whose own role models were Arnett Cobb, Illinois Jacquet, and Ben Webster) frequently referred to as "tough" tenors. They turned uptempo numbers into bloody brawls and more or less shadowed the melody on ballads, like a pulp detective tailing a beautiful woman he thinks he's falling in love with but doesn't quite trust. The style calls for a lot of swagger, and Carter might be the only young saxophonist who has the size for it. His best recorded performances in this vein, in which he displays an effortless swing rare for an improviser of any age, are his two versions of Duke Ellington's "The Stevedore's Serenade," one on *The Real Quietstorm* (Atlantic Jazz 82742-2) and the other on a promotional CD of duets with Cyrus Chestnut from early last year which was distributed to journalists and radio stations but not released commercially.*

The Real Quietstorm—not a make-out album, despite its title and cover shot of Carter with his fiancée draped all over him—opens and closes with examples of Carter's graceful control of his baritone saxophone's upper register. He's such a talented musician that it becomes all the more frustrating when he screams gratuitously, when he taps his saxophone's keys while breathing into it to produce a sound like that of a rusty pipe, when he slurps up to a note or holds one for several measures—these are devices that can be put to imaginative use, but twenty-seven is awfully young for a musician to be falling back on them on nearly every number. Carter's most questionable trait may be his habit of interpolating familiar licks from Ellington, Gershwin, and Charlie Parker into solos in which they simply don't belong. Quoting can be an art; Dexter Gordon was a master at jimmying a song's chords to fit the chords of another. His quotations could be delightful for seeming so off-the-wall. Carter's are merely patterns that fall easily under his fingers and

---

*Chestnut, a gospel-influenced pianist who shows a surprisingly light touch even when he's pouncing on the beat, tends to be glib and anonymous as a sideman with horn players. But he can be heard to good advantage both here and with his own trio on *Revelation*, Atlantic Jazz 82518–2.

help to kill time: musical equivalents of "To be or not to be" or "All the world's a stage." The one he ought to try is "To thine own self be true."

WHEN I SAW CARTER PERFORM AT THE MONTREAL INTERNATIONAL JAZZ Festival last summer, he strutted across the stage as if he was already a star, displaying an abundance of what a rock or hip-hop audience might call "attitude." His playing was loopy, even by his own standards. My notes don't mention what he was wearing, but if I close my eyes and recall the spin and pop of his phrases, I can see him dressed-to-kill in a long-tailed yellow zoot suit and a feathered fedora, like Jim Carrey in *The Mask*. I kept expecting him to roll himself into a bouncing rubber ball, or to hiss with satisfaction, "Sssomebody ssstop me!" Carter seems that intent on turning himself into a special effect—though so much sanctimony now surrounds jazz that his insincerity is refreshing, in a curious sort of way. Carter's most recent release, *Conversing with the Elders* (Atlantic ATL 82908), which features numbers by Coltrane, Parker, and Lester Young, and guest appearances by the tenor saxophonist and clarinetist Buddy Tate and the trumpeters Lester Bowie and Harry "Sweets" Edison, among others, casts Carter in a reverential role to which he doesn't seem very well suited.

Joshua Redman was another of the festival's headliners. I thought I sensed an element of rivalry between him and Carter even before hearing them go head to head on the soundtrack of Robert Altman's *Kansas City* (Verve 314 529 554-2) and reading an article on Carter in *New York*, in which he boasted of having taken Redman's measure in a bandstand showdown (and of having caught the eye of Redman's girlfriend). With Carter stealing some of his ink, Redman seems to be favoring a broader style of playing than he did just a few years ago. He, too, risks overdoing a few pet devices, the most annoying of which is the comic, upper-register burp that he uses to end far too many of his lines—to the apparent delight of audiences, who are doing him no favor by encouraging this sort of thing.

On *Spirit of the Moment*, which was recorded last March, Redman sounds much as he did in Montreal. The average new jazz CD is too long; though consumers seem to like the idea of an hour or more of music at a single pop, the playing time practically ensures inconsistency—especially on the part of younger performers who haven't yet learned to pace themselves. *Spirit of the Moment*'s two discs clock in at almost two and a half hours, and this is more than enough time to showcase Redman's obvious gifts. The most notable of these might be his admirable sense of uptempo melodic continuity ("Slapstick" is the best of several examples), his success at forming a band in his own image (the drummer Brian Blade is especially tuned in to him), and his increasing maturity as a balladeer (though I do wonder if it's wise for him to end almost every ballad with an unaccompanied cadenza that inevitably begs comparison with Sonny Rollins). Such a generous helping of Redman also serves to expose the formulaic and derivative nature of many of his solos. His debt to Rollins is as evident on Jule Styne's "Just in Time," from *Bells Are Ringing*, as it is on Rollins's "St. Thomas." When Rollins recorded the song from *Bells Are Ringing*, he was having fun with a show tune; Redman is playing Rollins and setting the bar far too high for either him or us to have much fun. Critics used to chide Branford Marsalis for mimicking a different tenor player on every number; his Zelig-like approach is now standard for younger players. I don't remember Redman ever sounding as much like Coltrane as he does on "Lyric" and "Second Snow" (the latter is in triple-meter and features him on soprano). Yet oddly enough, it's on *Spirit of the Moment*'s most Coltrane-influenced performance— "Dialogue," a modal, folksong-like dirge similar to Coltrane's "Alabama"—that Redman gives promise of finding his own voice, in his elegant and suspenseful shadowplay with the rhythm section (the performance demonstrates that Redman knows that going "outside" isn't simply a matter of getting "hot"—a lesson it might profit the combustible Carter to learn).

"Dialogue" first appeared on Redman's 1994 studio album *MoodSwing*, which also featured a tune called "Chill," a syncopated finger-snapper that drew a cheer of recognition from Redman's audience in Montreal. "Chill" is a cleverly constructed tune, funky and relaxed, much like something Horace Silver or Bobby Timmons might have written in the early 1960s, but with a bridge that goes all the way back to Lionel Hampton's swing-era anthem "Flying Home" (Hampton borrowed the riff from Charlie Christian). On first hearing "Chill," I thought the bridge was the reason Redman's melody struck me as familiar, but in Montreal, I realized how similar the tune's cadences are to those of an obscure pop song I doubt Redman has ever heard.

THAT SONG IS ANDRÉ PREVIN AND PAUL FRANCIS WEBSTER'S "LIKE YOUNG." A
track from Perry Como's 1961 album *Young at Heart* that resurfaced a
few years ago on Rhino/Word Beat's *The Beat Generation*, a likably goofy
multidisc set aimed at people whose serious interest in Allen Ginsberg
and *On the Road* doesn't preclude an affection for Maynard G. Krebs
and *Route 66*. Webster's lyrics have the clueless, middle-aged Como flipping for a kooky beatnik chick who "goes where all the angry young men
go," "recites poetry," and "drinks coffee with café espresso." She's got
Como feeling "like young," but he's really just showing his age.

Jazz is showing its age, too, or else why would there now be such a
preoccupation with youth? Charlie Parker was twenty-five when he
recorded "Koko" and "Now's the Time"; he was dead at thirty-four,
Wynton Marsalis's age now. Ornette Coleman was twenty-nine and not
considered especially young when he caught the world by surprise with
The Shape of Jazz to Come, in 1959. There have always been young jazz
musicians, but only lately has anyone made a fuss over them just for
being young—instead of for auguring change.

The major labels have convinced themselves (and the press) that the
survival of jazz depends on selling youth to the young. *Are* more young
people listening to jazz by virtue of being able to identify with Redman
and the others? From what I've noticed, the answer is yes only if you
count as "young" dating couples in their late twenties and early thirties.
I've been to shows where the youngest people in the house were on the
bandstand. In allowing itself to become so identified with its past, jazz
may be bargaining away its future. Positioning jazz as a sane acoustic
alternative to raucous, mechanized pop might be an effective short-term
sales strategy, but doesn't all this sanctimony about "tradition" and the
emphasis on boilerplate bebop send a message to teenagers and college
students that jazz offers absolutely nothing of interest to them? And isn't
the form of music that rings someone's bells at eighteen or nineteen
likely to remain his music of choice for life?

Something else to worry about is whether all this publicity about
today's young musicians is creating unrealistic sales expectations.
Another of the young headliners in Montreal was Jacky Terrasson, who
gave a solo recital. On his 1994 album *Jacky Terrasson* (Blue Note CDP
7243 8 29351 2 4), the bassist Ugonna Okegwo and the drummer Leon
Parker at least supplied Terrasson with a semblance of rhythmic momen-

tum. Playing by himself he drifted, turning even "Just One of Those Things" into a reverie and coming across like a better-behaved Keith Jarrett. Unlike Jarrett, Terrasson didn't hump the piano or squeal along with his solos—he doesn't have that much passion in him. His music offers very little for an audience to latch onto. Yet Blue Note is rumored to have signed him for $100,000. What happens if he and others fail to sell albums in numbers sufficient to justify these generous advances? The majors are likely to take this as evidence that jazz just doesn't sell. It wouldn't be the first time they've arrived at this conclusion and then turned it into a self-fulfilling prophecy.

The Atlantic Monthly, July 1996

In His Father's House

It's possible that Ravi Coltrane, clutching his tenor saxophone as he passed through the living room to the makeshift bandstand in the back yard, didn't give a second thought to being in his father's house. If he noticed the upright piano at which John Coltrane spent hours writing music or just puzzling over chords—visualizing the fingerings that would enable him to sound two or three tones at once—it was probably out of the corner of his eye, the way someone half-sees the furniture in a room he's been in countless times before.

For the second of John Coltrane's three sons, now thirty-one and a musician himself, this probably applied even to the framed, faux-Bachrach photograph of John Coltrane in his Navy uniform, and to the two watercolors painted by the man whose death from liver cancer at the age of forty, in 1967, curiously only strengthened his claim to immortality.

Mementos such as these attract pilgrims from as far away as Europe and Japan to this house in Strawberry Mansion, across from the Fairmont Park driving range. Decaying and jittery with crime, this block must have been beautiful and serene when Coltrane moved here from South Philadelphia, with his mother, Alice, and his cousin Mary Lyerly, in 1952. Coltrane's cousin—the "Cousin Mary" for whom he named one of his most upbeat and enduring numbers—still lives here. Only she's Mary Alexander now, a recent widow who just last year resumed her leadership of the John W. Coltrane Cultural Society, whose fund-raising concert brought Ravi Coltrane to town.

John Coltrane was gone from this house by 1959, having moved to New York with his first wife, Naima, around the time he left Miles Davis to start his own band. But the strangers who ring Cousin Mary's doorbell, even though the house isn't officially open to the public, know that this was where Coltrane, in 1957, sweated alcohol and heroin out of his system—where he hallucinated a visitation from God, an experience he later described in the prayer he wrote for the liner notes to his watershed album A Love Supreme (1964). The faithful stare at that piano and imagine they hear Coltrane picking out the chords to "Blue Trane" or one of the other tunes he is believed to have written at it. They sense his earthly presence here.

Ravi Coltrane isn't saying he doesn't, but these four walls hold actual memories for him, not just emanations. The backyard roses, vivid with color on this afternoon in late July, remind him of the woman who planted them. "I knew my father once lived there, but I always thought of it as my grandmother's house" where he'd visit in the summer. "And now I tend to think of it as the place I go to visit my cousin."

Besides, the house in Philadelphia is just one of a number of shrines to John Coltrane around the country. In San Francisco there is even a church devoted to John Coltrane (he was demoted from deity to saint a few years ago, when the ministry became affiliated with the apostolic African Orthodox Church). Even though Ravi has become friends with the son of the church's founder—an aspiring tenor saxophonist who seeks his advice on mouthpieces and reeds, much as an earlier generation of players once sought John Coltrane's advice—he has never set foot in St. John's. For one thing, his mother surely would disapprove: Alice Coltrane was one of the church's early funders, but withdrew her support when the congregation redefined its mission from meditation to community service.

"In addition to which," Ravi Coltrane explains, "it would feel a little odd for me to be there, because the man they think of as some kind of divine messenger was my father."

JOHN COLTRANE'S MUSIC EVOLVED SO QUICKLY IN THE TWELVE YEARS AFTER HE shook listeners to their foundations with his solo on Miles Davis's 1955 recording of "'Round Midnight" that he left some of his fervent admirers behind. Some fans talk as though there were two John Coltranes: one admired for his questing spirit, and one who ultimately went too far, tempting musical chaos in the last two years of his life, after A Love

Supreme. Ravi Coltrane, who diplomatically refuses to state a preference, even though his own music suggests an affinity with early Coltrane, recognizes a different split. On the one hand, there is "John Coltrane," the father who died when Ravi was not yet two years old and whom he barely remembers. Then there is "Trane," almost a creature of myth—a father figure to nearly every saxophonist of Ravi's generation.

"I try to keep my thoughts of them separate," he explained a few days after the backyard concert, back home in the apartment he shares with his girlfriend, Kathleen Hennessy, atop an OTB on a busy avenue in Queens, New York. Even without John Coltrane gazing down at him from a framed print, Ravi Coltrane would bear a striking resemblance to his father, albeit looking more bookish in his round, half-rim glasses. He has his father's broad shoulders and long, curving fingers.

"I mean, I'm not playing saxophone because my father was John Coltrane, any more than I might play certain tunes because they were associated with him. If I happen to play something he did, or even if I sometimes approach a tune the way he did, it's because it's music I love and want to be a part of—the same way I feel about Charlie Parker or Sonny Rollins."

Record companies, whose job it is to sell musicians along with their music, view the situation somewhat differently, which is why Ravi Coltrane—despite growing acclaim for his work as a sideman with Elvin Jones, Wallace Roney, and Steve Coleman—has so far rejected their offers.

"I won't mention the label," he says, "but I was told by another musician that an executive there said he would sign me right this minute on the basis of my name—period. The offers that I've had have been based on that kind of thinking. Even if nothing was said, you could hear the wheels turning.

"Frankly, the other reason I've turned them down is that I don't feel that I have any kind of personal statement I need to put on record yet. I'm not saying that I feel I would have to come up with something completely new that nobody's ever heard before. I just feel that I still have more to do in terms of my playing, and maybe especially in terms of my writing.

"You know, most of the records that are coming out today don't really need to be coming out. We don't need two dozen young tenor players making records as leaders of their own bands. And we don't need another recording of guys my age playing older tunes like 'Autumn Leaves.'"

RAVI, HIS TWO BROTHERS, AND A HALF-SISTER FROM ALICE COLTRANE'S FIRST marriage (to Kenny "Pancho" Hagood, a singer who recorded with Miles Davis, Dizzy Gillespie, and Thelonious Monk in the late 1940s) enjoyed what in Ravi's telling emerges as a typical suburban childhood, first in Dix Hills, Long Island, and then in Woodlawn Hills, near Los Angeles. One imagines the Coltrane home overflowing with music, the scene of regular encounters between Alice—a pianist and composer—and such former Coltrane sidemen as Pharoah Sanders and Elvin Jones.

"Maybe it would have been like that if we had stayed in New York," Ravi speculates. "But we were pretty isolated from the jazz scene there in Southern California. My mother used to play a recording of Stravinsky's *The Firebird* that my brothers and sister and I would dance around to as very young kids. But Mom never tried to push any kind of music on us, including my father's or her own. I listened mostly to funk and things like that, like all the other kids I knew."

Even so, all three of Alice Coltrane's boys were playing instruments by high school. Charlie Haden, the bassist and a family friend who was later Ravi's teacher at the California Institute of the Arts, remembers receiving a phone call from Alice during which she held out the receiver to let him hear her three sons improvising a spontaneous blues.

"Both Ravi and John, Jr. were playing tenor by that point, though Ravi had started on clarinet," Haden recalls. "Oran, the youngest son, was playing bass. They sounded good, and Alice was very proud of them."

Ravi says that he temporarily lost interest in music, along with his direction in life, following the death of John, Jr.—older than Ravi by just a year—in a car accident, in 1982. Though she said nothing, he remembers sensing his mother's disappointment when he told her he was thinking of giving up music and applying to the American Film Institute. "That was just a dream, though," he says now. "This was before Spike Lee, when there were no black role models for someone like me to emulate. And I guess everybody who lives in Los Angeles toys with the idea of going to film school at one time or another."

Postponing a decision on college, he drifted through a series of menial jobs. One day when he was working as a supermarket bag boy, the store's manager took him aside and told him he had promise. "He promoted me to frozen foods, or something like that, and said that he knew I would someday make a good manager, because he had started out as a bag boy, too."

Realizing with a shudder that this wasn't the life he wanted, Ravi quickly enrolled in the music program at Cal Arts. He is the first to admit that he was still green in 1992, when he went on the road with Elvin Jones, who had been his father's drummer for five years. "But Elvin had been so close to my father that he considered himself kind of like my uncle. He wanted to give me some exposure and a taste of what it was like to be with a real band, for which I will be eternally grateful to him."

On his first appearance with Jones in Philadelphia—a tribute to John Coltrane, at the Academy of Music in 1993—Ravi improvised mechanically over Jones's polyrhythms and frequently looked as though he would rather be anywhere else. Anyone who has not heard him since that night would have been astonished by the set he played for the Coltrane Society this summer. Though still somewhat shy in addressing an audience, he sliced confidently through the beat provided by the drummer Gerry Gibbs on the set's opening number, a furious interpretation of John Coltrane's "Countdown." (Gibbs, Ravi's downstairs neighbor in Queens, is a son of the vibraphonist Terry Gibbs, the man who introduced John Coltrane to Ravi's mother.)

Complimented on the set, Ravi Coltrane expressed his own misgivings about it. "These last few weeks, I've been so busy doing interviews and lining up gigs that I haven't spent enough time in there," he said, pointing to his small practice room. "You play a gig and as long as it seems to get there and set up and everything, you wind up playing maybe two hours, tops. Whereas, when you're practicing, you can do it for six or eight hours at a stretch, with no responsibilities to an audience or whatever tune you happen to be playing. You can spend two hours practicing nothing but long tones and scales before moving on to something else, if that's where you feel you need work. I'm still at a point where I feel I need to do that. It shows up in my playing when I don't get the chance."

RAVI COLTRANE HAS HIS FATHER'S FACE AND HANDS, BUT DOES HE RESEMBLE him in other ways? The answer is yes and no. In his belief in the value of practice, Ravi might seem a dead ringer for the man who was notorious for running scales in dressing rooms between shows, and for sometimes falling asleep at night with his horn still in his mouth. But what amounted to an obsession for John Coltrane seems mere diligence on the part of his son. John Coltrane's music levitated many listeners into what they believed was a spiritual realm. Lighter in texture and smaller in mass,

Ravi Coltrane's sound is unlikely to inspire anything beyond appreciation for his musicianship. In many ways he's the secular Coltrane.

As he well knows, what makes him so attractive to record companies—along with his name—is his youth. The commercial success first of Wynton and Branford Marsalis (sons of the New Orleans pianist Ellis Marsalis), and then of Joshua Redman (a son of the tenor saxophonist Dewey Redman), has created a vogue for personable, articulate young jazz musicians—and if they're second-generation jazzmen, so much the better. Somebody's buying all those versions of "Autumn Leaves" that Ravi Coltrane so disdains, and it's questionable whether many jazz fans today really want anything else. There are people who will tell you, only half-jokingly, that jazz is a religion; if so, it has something in common with Christianity that some believers probably wish it didn't. The last few centuries have witnessed world wars, earthquakes, famines, the enslavement of one race, and the attempted extermination of another—all of it after the deadline for the Bible. It often seems the book was closed on jazz around the time of John Coltrane's death. Unlike Coltrane's generation of musicians, who were expected to push jazz forward—and did—his son's generation is being asked to save jazz from extinction by keeping the faith, which might prove to be the greater task.

Theology aside, young black man who choose to play jazz, as opposed to embracing the self-destructive nihilism of rap, are regarded in some eyes as potential saviors of their community. The current emphasis on "tradition" in jazz—on symbolic as well as literal fathers and sons—is poignant in light of statistics on the number of African-American children growing up in fatherless homes.

THIS IS TOO MUCH SYMBOLISM FOR A YOUNG MUSICIAN TO SHOULDER AND, given who his father was, Ravi Coltrane may be shouldering the heaviest load of all. His dilemma is that if he were to attempt to avoid John Coltrane's influence, he would be denying himself a legacy that other saxophonists his age accept as a birthright.

But Ravi Coltrane's concert for the Coltrane Society this summer suggested that he's on his way to finding a middle ground. Because the members of his rhythm section had never before played together, and because everyone arrived too late to rehearse, he decided to forego original compositions and to stick with tunes everyone would be sure to know. Just this once, that meant an entire program of numbers composed or recorded by John Coltrane, including "Body and Soul"—a venerable ballad that has been a testing ground for tenor saxophonists since the great Coleman Hawkins daringly reharmonized its melody on his 1939 hit recording. John Coltrane, tackling the song twenty years later, similarly altered its contours, speeding up the melody and substituting his own chords on the bridge.

Surprisingly, Ravi Coltrane played the song more or less straight, in ballad tempo, before fragmenting the melody into a series of artful and logically developed phrases that hung in the summer air like the scent of his grandmother's roses. Even following a completely different path through "Body and Soul" than his father, he sounded so much like him you'd swear that a luminous tone was a family trait. But by the time he took the song out, he had given ample promise of soon becoming his own man.

The Philadelphia *Inquirer* Magazine,
September 22, 1996

MOVING PICTURES (RCA VICTOR 74321 55887-2), RAVI COLTRANE'S FIRST album as a leader, was well worth the wait. If anything, Ravi sounds less like his father than do most of today's young saxophonists. His strongest influence, in terms of both his harmonic ideas and his jagged approach to rhythm, would appear to be Joe Henderson, who's represented here as a composer by "Inner Urge," a donnybrook between Ravi and the alto saxophonist Steve Coleman, the album's producer. A sense of drama and judiciousness in constructing his solos are among Ravi's chief assets as an improviser, and these qualities come to the fore on three tracks that add a hypnotic African percussion trio to the ace rhythm section of the pianist Michael Cain, the bassist Lonnie Plaxico, and the drummer Jeff Watts. The trumpeter Ralph Alessi tussles with Ravi on several numbers, adding to the program's excitement with his bold, assertive lines. One could complain that Ravi Coltrane's soprano is not up to the level of his tenor, and that his interpretation of Horace Silver's "Peace" drags a bit. But these are minor flaws in an album that makes one optimistic about this young musician's future.

Stereo Review's Sound & Vision, October 1998

Leaving Behind a Trail

Meet Dave Douglas

Dave Douglas has suddenly emerged as the most talked-about (not hyped, *talked about*) trumpeter to emerge in jazz since Wynton Marsalis, even though almost nothing is known about him personally. The dedications in his CD booklets, to such cultural theorists as Hannah Arendt, Walter Benjamin, and Noam Chomsky, suggest a very serious fellow. A capsule bio on his debut album, *Parallel Worlds* (recorded in 1993, for Soul Note), tells us only that he has played with an impressive array of musicians (not all of them fellow Lower East Side experimentalists) and that he briefly attended both the Berklee School of Music and the New England Conservatory before earning his undergraduate degree through an independent studies program at NYU. But nowhere is there a clue to so much as his birthplace or exact age.

This lack of biographical information is frustrating, because hardly a month goes by anymore that he doesn't turn up on another CD destined to be counted among this decade's landmarks—*Parallel Worlds* and *In Our Lifetime*, Uri Caine's *Toys*, Myra Melford's *The Same River, Twice*, Ned Rothenberg's *Power Lines*, and John Zorn's *Vav* (the sixth in the alto saxophonist and composer's ongoing series of harmolodic horas, with the quartet he calls Masada). Not counting the cooperative New and Used, Douglas fronts four bands. These include the three-horn sextet featured on *In Our Lifetime,* and the string group, with violin, cello, and double bass, on *Parallel Worlds* and *Five*. There is also his Tiny Bell Trio, whose explorations of music from the former Soviet bloc, and of Douglas's compositions in a similar vein, can be heard to good advantage on an eponymous 1993 CD and the more recent *Constellations*. Sanctuary, an octet that juxtaposes acoustic and amplified instruments, made its recording debut on a CD scheduled for release early next year. All of this is in addition to Douglas's aforementioned work as a sideman and his occasional gigs with the New York–based art/thrash group Dr. Nerve. You'll even find him on the latest release by the Asian-American female pop rappers, Cibo Matto.

The most recent of Douglas's efforts to hit the stores is *Serpentine* (Songlines SGL 1510-2), an album of mostly improvised duets with Han Bennink, a Dutch percussionist and dadaist probably known best in this country as the drummer on Eric Dolphy's *Last Date* (or perhaps for his recent work with the trio Clusone). This new disc hardly ranks with Douglas's best; *Parallel Worlds* and *In Our Lifetime* gave richer evidence of his talent for layering and crisscrossing themes. Too much of *Serpentine* sounds like raw material for music—a common problem with free improvisation. Yet at least seven of the thirteen tracks are fully realized performances whose starkness throws Douglas's virtuosity into bold relief. These include three Douglas compositions, the most fetching of which is the title number, a riff on which he puckishly subverts stock blues figures as Bennink lands hard on the beat and then circles it like a bird of prey. On "Greenleaf," Douglas—following the example of the German trombonist Albert Mangelsdorff—creates multiphonics by humming one note into his mouthpiece while pressing another on his valves (at several points, he also blows into his unattached mouthpiece to great comedic effect, often in response to what sounds like Bennink clog dancing or tumbling down a set of stairs with his entire drum kit). "Delft," a cousin to Monk's "Mysterioso," with its steady loping sixths, is a tiny gem I hope Douglas sees fit to enlarge for one of his regular groups.

Douglas has a perverse streak: He assigns his string group tunes from the jazz canon and Brad Schoeppach, his guitarist in the folkloric Tiny Bell, to layer on the feedback. So it figures that he would choose the unfettered setting of a trumpet-and-drums duet session to interpret a few pop standards. In each instance, he and Bennink successfully apply a free aesthetic to tightly structured material. Douglas climaxes "Cherokee" with a devilish paraphrase of a Dizzy Gillespie lick, after demonstrating a swiftness and ease of articulation that would make any bebop trumpeter envious. He tears into "Too Close for Comfort" with a throaty, swing-era rip that would do Ruby Braff proud. His take on "Young and Foolish," in addition to being simultaneously angular and tender, shows his resourcefulness in widening or constricting his timbre, and in speeding up or slowing down his vibrato in order to lend an element of unpredictability to a fairly straightforward solo. Then there is "Alap," the lengthiest and most cohesive of the free improvisations and the track that puts *Serpentine* on this year's A-list. It starts with trumpet and drums cackling and whispering, then builds to a theme as stabbing as the Booker Little compositions that Douglas reinterpreted on *In Our Lifetime* or the charming pieces by Joseph Kosma (the Bulgarian-born composer of "Autumn Leaves" and the score to Marcel Carné's *Children of Paradise*) that he snatched from obscurity with Tiny Bell.

TO FIND OUT SOMETHING ABOUT DOUGLAS, I PAID HIM A VISIT IN HIS THIRD-floor Brooklyn walkup one afternoon this summer. As you might guess from the literary references in his CD booklets, he is someone for whom music isn't all there is. "I try to leave behind a trail of what I've been thinking," he told me, explaining that he had become interested in Renaissance architecture since hearing the story of a cathedral that he visited on a tour of Europe with one of his bands. "They started work on it in 1294, with the intention of building the highest dome that anyone had ever seen but no idea of how long it might take to do that. They just started putting down rocks, generation after generation, and over a hundred years later, there stood this remarkable structure." The story was on Douglas's mind as he composed an hour-long piece for his octet's forthcoming debut CD. "Although I was also thinking of cyclical works by Schoenberg and Boulez, and Don Cherry's *Symphony for Improvisers*, I began to think that the best thing for me to do might be to provide the basic materials for the improvisers and then get out of the way. To create a work more like Ornette Coleman's *Free Jazz* or Coltrane's *Ascension*— a leap of faith."

Fair and soft-voiced, of average height and build, and with a receding hairline, Douglas was born in Montclair, New Jersey, in 1963—which makes him just two years younger than Wynton Marsalis. One difference between them, besides the latter's greater celebrity, is that Douglas would refuse an offer to record an album of Mozart or Haydn concertos. "First of all, because I know I would suck," he admitted, laughing as though to acknowledge the unlikelihood of even being asked. "I wouldn't presume to be able to do justice to that material unless I took six months to practice those pieces and nothing else, which is something I wouldn't feel inclined to do."

Don't get the wrong idea. An advocate of the Carmine Caruso technique (named for one of his former teachers, a now-deceased "chops doctor" who was credited with saving the lip of many a high-note specialist), Douglas puts in long hours on his horn, and it shows in the loft and consistency of his upper register. (The sense of *voice* in his solos comes from someplace else, possibly from listening so intently as a child to his parents' Billie Holiday records and attempting to play along.) He developed a formidable technique of necessity while playing on Manhattan street corners with the alto saxophonist Vincent Herring and a roving band of other beboppers about ten years ago, when paid gigs indoors were hard to come by. "You had to play loud and fast and exciting all the time, because if you didn't, or if you tried something subtle or esoteric, the crowd moved on and you didn't make any money. Plus, the bass player and guitarist were amplified, through gas generators. The horn players had to carry over them. We use to try to ricochet off the buildings across the street."

Nor does Douglas have anything against classical music. He has recorded Mahler as a member of the pianist Uri Caine's band. The only thing is, in his and Caine's antic interpretations, Mahler often comes out sounding like bebop or hip-hop or klezmer. Less inclined than Marsalis to draw distinctions between different kinds of music—or to set limits about what is or isn't permissible in the name of jazz—Douglas has also recorded Webern and Stravinsky with his own bands. But for him their works are vehicles for improvisation, "because I couldn't imagine playing their music for any other reason."

In fairness to Marsalis, this seems to be an era in which young white players are less weighed down by history than young black players are. "From the very beginning of my career, I didn't fit any of the usual stereotypes of what a jazz musician is supposed to be, so I didn't worry about them," Douglas said in response to a convoluted question about whether he ever felt at an ironic disadvantage in jazz as a result of coming from a relatively privileged background. The son of an IBM systems analyst, Douglas grew up in affluent suburbs and went to prep school at Exeter—

where he must have been quite a challenge to teachers and administrators who saw it as their mission to groom "the next generation of civic and corporate leaders," as Douglas puts it. As out-of-place as he was there (he was once nearly expelled for breaking into the music room to bang on the piano after hours), school policy allowed him to spend his junior year in Barcelona, where he played his first professional engagements in what sounds like a journeyman Spanish hard bop band. "I was the only American, so they thought I knew everything there was to know about jazz," he told me. "But I was also the youngest guy in the band, so the truth is I was learning from them."

Douglas's first record date, in 1987, with the obscure New York–based pianist John Esposito, also paid unexpected dividends—though the album was poorly distributed, a copy somehow wound up in the hands of Horace Silver, the pianist who virtually invented hard bop. Impressed, Silver called Douglas out of the blue with an offer to go on the road. "By coincidence, he also hired Vincent Herring," Douglas recalled. "The main thing that Horace used to tell us, which is still very important to me, is that there's a difference between running the changes and *making* the changes. In other words, the important thing isn't really what you're doing on the chord or over it, but how you move from one chord to the next." Douglas's tour of duty with Silver lasted three months, after which he wasn't rehired. "Which didn't surprise me, in a way, because I was going outside the chords and trying to stretch the boundaries of the rhythm, like Woody Shaw and Joe Henderson had done with Horace in the sixties, and that really wasn't what Horace wanted at that point. He used to tell me I should listen to the earlier records he had made with Blue Mitchell, but I was still young and stubborn and thought that I was going to push jazz forward all by myself, if need be."

Not really cut out for hard bop anyway, Douglas eventually fell in with a circle of like-minded eclectics around the time the Knitting Factory opened its doors on the Lower East Side in 1987. "As a teenager, when I first got serious about jazz and started practicing like mad, I wanted to be a Jazz Messenger and push the tradition forward like Woody Shaw had when he was with Horace Silver and Art Blakey—from within," Douglas told me, implying by his tone of voice that things didn't quite work out that way.

OR MAYBE THEY HAVE, DEPENDING ON WHAT YOU MEAN BY "TRADITION" AND what you consider to be "within" it. A crucial difference between Douglas and Marsalis (who, as music director for Jazz at Lincoln Center, might be seen as Mr. Uptown to Douglas's Mr. Downtown) is their conflicting tastes in literature. Unlike Douglas, with his cultural theorists, Marsalis apparently sticks to the novelists and poets on Albert Murray and Stanley Crouch's approved reading list. But what if Marsalis and Douglas were to swap books? Reading Walter Benjamin's "The Work of Art in the Age of Mechanical Reproduction," Marsalis might be drawn to Benjamin's contention that "the uniqueness of a work of art is imbedded in the fabric of tradition." Douglas, on the other hand, would have already underlined the following sentence: "This tradition is itself thoroughly alive and changeable." Through Murray and Crouch, Marsalis is no doubt already familiar with T.S. Eliot's "Tradition and the Individual Talent," in which Eliot writes "Not only the best, but the most individual parts of [a poet or any artist's] work may be those in which the dead poets, his ancestors, assert their immortality most vigorously." For Douglas, the key concept would be a later passage in which Eliot states "the past should be altered by the present as much as the present is directed by the past."

The two most gifted trumpeters of their generation are on the same page; it's just Douglas's nature to read a little ahead.

Fi. December 1996

Dave Douglas, Continued

Dave Douglas belongs to what I think of as the "protean" school of jazz; its other members include Don Byron, Bill Frisell, and John Zorn, and its founders were Lester Bowie, David Murray, Henry Threadgill, and Arthur Blythe. What these musicians have in common, in addition to their eclecticism and their being more welcome at the Knitting Factory than at Lincoln Center, is their zeal in forming and reforming bands. Twenty years ago, when Blythe fronted both a conventional rhythm section and an outward-bound quintet with tuba, cello, guitar, and drums, he was something of a novelty. Today, for a musician to lead not two but several bands is par for the course—a development as characteristic of the 1990s as the collectivism of groups such as Air and the Art Ensemble of Chicago was of the 1970s. Given the limited market for jazz, especially jazz tar-brushed as "avant-garde," it makes sense for a musician not to limit himself to one format (back when he led a big band, David Murray's response to promoters who couldn't afford an orchestra was likely to be, "What about my octet? No? What about my quartet?"). But economic necessity isn't the only—or even primary—motivation for today's multi-band leaders. No musician now under the age of forty grew up listening exclusively to jazz, or was exposed to jazz by means of an historically linear timeline. By the time musicians of Douglas's age first heard *The Birth of the Cool*, *Kind of Blue*, or *Miles Smiles*, the Miles Davis with whom they were already familiar was quacking like a duck over synthesizer and guitar. If another Miles Davis were to emerge today (and Douglas is as close as anyone has come, in terms of his potential impact), he might simultaneously lead a modal quintet, an electric band, and a nonet as a workshop for himself and other composers—all the while continuing to gig with Charlie Parker (or perhaps John Zorn's Masada) and to cover Stockhausen and Sly and the Family Stone.

What first brought Davis to mind in listening to *Charms of the Night Sky* (Winter & Winter 910 015-2), one of three new Douglas quartet albums, was the title track, a kind of bolero-with-an-extra-beat, with Greg Cohen deftly strumming a bass line vaguely similar to the one Paul Chambers played behind Davis on "Solea," from *Sketches of Spain*. If anything, Douglas's ample technique—matched only by Paul Smoker among avant-garde trumpeters, who generally are a scrappy bunch—gives him more in common with Dizzy Gillespie than with Davis. This Douglas quartet is drummerless and pianoless, but does include, along with Cohen's bass, both Mark Feldman on violin and Guy Klucevsek on accordion; and on "Facing West," a duet with Klucevsek squeezing out sparks, Douglas ladders up to the high register to deliver a series of bends and smears as impressive as Gillespie's in his prime. Yet *Charms of the Night Sky* recalls *Sketches of Spain* both in its dreamlike textures (Klucevsek and Feldman's frequently blend orchestrally, and on his duets with Douglas, Klucevsek is like an orchestra himself—or an organ, at the very least) and in its integration of jazz, "serious" music, and folkloric elements. It includes one of Douglas's classical "covers" (a ringing aria from Francesco Cilea's 1902 *Adriana Lecouvreur*), Herbie Hancock's Miles-era tone poem "Little One," and, in a trilogy of pieces by Klucevsek, examples of contemporary neo-tonalism, high-minded pastiche, and New Music high jinks. Douglas's pieces, of which "Bal Masqué" is the most instantly winning and "Dance in Thy Soul" the most volatile and dramatic, mix and match motifs from all over Europe. Even when their rhythmic infrastructure seems Hungarian or Balkan, as on "Facing West," their melodic content is suggestive of Nino Rota or French chanson. Though dedicated to Charlie Haden, and capturing much of his lyric intensity, "Dance in Thy Soul" is a showcase for Feldman, a tough-minded romantic and Douglas's counterpart on violin—that is, a virtuoso on another instrument whose avant-garde representatives, beginning with Ornette Coleman, have mostly been scrappers. It all adds up to a beguiling album, my choice as this year's best.

Douglas's other new releases are more conventional in instrumentation, but not without twists. On *Magic Triangle* (Arabesque Jazz AJ 0139), he unveils yet another new band, a pianoless quartet with the tenor saxophonist Chris Potter, the bassist James Genus, and the drummer Ben Perowsky. Inevitably, there are echoes of Ornette Coleman, not just in Douglas and Potter's unfettered solos, but in the doubling and halving of tempos that Douglas favors in his compositions, which allow the horns and rhythm section the freedom to movie in opposite directions. What distinguishes this band from other post-Ornette quartets, and identifies it as Douglas's, are the suggestions of Eastern Europe in his compositions and uvular trumpet solos—a trait only slightly less noticeable here than in his work with his Tiny Bell Trio (and isn't it about time for a new release by them?). Douglas and Potter bristle in their improvised exchanges, especially on the jaunty "Coaster" and the patient "Odalisque."

In addition to being a provocative composer, Douglas has a good ear for which material by other writers might be suited to him, no matter how unlikely; the surprise on *Moving Portrait* (DIW 934)—his first album as lone horn with a standard rhythm section—is a trio of songs by Joni Mitchell. Her "My Old Man" is the album's highlight, meditative and suspenseful in Douglas's reinterpretation, with a stinging, flatted trumpet solo. Douglas doesn't make the mistake that Herbie Hancock made on *New Standards*; he doesn't superimpose chord changes on Mitchell's melodies in a foolish attempt to make them into "jazz." He recognizes Mitchell's lyricism and rhythmic quirkiness as not so different from his own, and someone unfamiliar with Mitchell might be unable to tell her three numbers from Douglas's six. What you make of Bill Carrothers's piano solos will depend on your opinion of Keith Jarrett, but when not groaning and succumbing to cheap rapture, the pianist forms a sensitive and propulsive rhythm section with Genus and the veteran drummer Billy Hart. For his part, Douglas once again demonstrates that he might be not just Wynton Marsalis's only serious rival on trumpet but the most intriguing figure in jazz today.

Fi, December 1998

DOUGLAS IS ONE OF A HANDFUL OF MUSICIANS ATTEMPTING TO REPLENISH A depleted jazz repertoire. Jazz has always been as much an interpretive as a creative art; its musicians used to play all manner of borrowed material, including recent pop tunes and adaptations of classics, alongside their own material. Today, most jazz musicians don't know a number unless Miles Davis, John Coltrane, or Bill Evans happened to record it. Douglas is an exception: On his previous CDs he has "covered" (as he and those in his New York circle like to put it) composers ranging from Igor Stravinsky to Rashaan Roland Kirk.

On *Soul on Soul* (RCA Victor 09026 63603-2), his first release for a major label, Douglas turns his attention to Mary Lou Williams, a paragon of Kansas City swing who was also one of the first musicians of her generation to declare her support for the bebop revolution and to absorb elements of bop in her own playing and writing. Rescoring three of Williams's pieces—a conga, a boogie-woogie waltz, and a zippy, Ellington-like tone poem—for a sextet including Uri Caine on piano, Josh Roseman on trombone, and either Chris Speed or Greg Tardy on reeds, Douglas makes a smashing case for her as an unjustly neglected composer. And dispensing with piano and the other horns on her grooving "Play It Mama," he shows himself to be a trumpeter in whose work harmonic investigation and microtonal sound possibilities go hand in hand.

Williams's tunes aren't all there is to *Soul on Soul,* even though the album takes its title from Duke Ellington's encomium to her. The remaining nine numbers are Douglas originals, and the album's title would be just as appropriate to the opener—a funky thing called "Blue Heaven," on which Douglas adds a few twists to the legacy of Art Blakey and Horace Silver. *Leap of Faith* (Arabesque Jazz AJO-145), Douglas's other new CD, featuring his pianoless quartet with Chris Potter, includes only Douglas originals. The highlights are "Another Country," a mournful and angry dirge named after James Baldwin's novel, and "Western Haiku," a puckish waltz that sounds like a secret collaboration between Ornette Coleman and Josef Strauss. With their sulfurous horn voicings and shifting meters and tempos, pieces such as "Mistaken Identity" from *Leap of Faith* and "Ageless" from *Soul on Soul* draw inspiration from Wayne Shorter and from Miles Davis's 1960s rhythm section—the same sources pillaged by most of today's young neo-traditionalists. But in Douglas's case, so much that is surprising is going on in the tunes—and in the improvised solos springing from them—that the results are never derivative. A final word of praise for James Genus, the bassist on both discs: Douglas often writes from the bottom up, building his pieces on strong bass lines, and Genus handles these with admirable skill and sensitivity.

Stereo Review's Sound & Vision, April 2000

Some Recordings

O ne of the strangest recordings I own is *Process and Reality*, by the English saxophonist and free improviser Evan Parker. It ends with a performance called "Lapidary," which consists of Parker tapping the keys of his soprano saxophone in loose counterpoint to a recording by Steve Lacy. Shades of Charlie Parker in a Chicago hotel room in 1943, improvising over 78s by Hazel Scott and Benny Goodman? Not quite, because the practice-recording chosen by this Parker—"The Cryptosphere," from Lacy's 1971 LP *Lapis*—was an overdub to start with, and you'll never guess whose record was on Lacy's turntable.

Lacy's unassenting duet partner was Ruby Braff, a cornetist whose acceptance of swing as holy writ would seem to put him at the opposite end of the musical spectrum from avant-gardists like Lacy and Parker. I like to think their enthusiasm for him is testimony to their ability to spot a fellow original, whatever his stylistic affiliation.

Braff was a rebel of the 1950s, almost a prototype for Wynton Marsalis, minus the latter's celebrity and the race card he takes every opportunity to play. (In the person of John Hammond, Braff even had his own literary champion and propagandist, *à la* Stanley Crouch.) At a time when a young musician was expected to be either a progressive or a moldy fig, Braff shook the status quo by opposing both camps. Though not given to sweeping pronouncements (that was Hammond's job), Braff held that jazz had achieved perfection with swing, and that most of what was being called "modernism" amounted to self-indulgent tweaking. However short-sighted this position was, it worked for Braff—a magnetic soloist who, though hardly an innovator, was nevertheless the first of a recognizable new type: a radical conservative, as opposed to that era's New Orleans reactionaries.

Any resemblance between Braff and Marsalis, beyond a shared ingenuity in expressing their fondness for Armstrong with lower-register smears rather than stratospheric bolts, is strictly coincidental, except that Braff, too, has a stable of "followers"—younger musicians for whom he set the mold, among them Scott Hamilton, Warren Vaché, Ken Peplowski, Loren Schoenberg, Dan Barrett, Randy Sandke, and Howard Alden—most of whom have recorded with him at one point or another. Alden, a guitarist of impressive gifts who, ironically, overcomes his rhythmic inhibitions only when called upon to serve a primarily rhythmic function, was a member of the drummerless and pianoless trio that Braff led for a spell a few years ago. With Frank Tate on bass, this is the group featured on the splendid *As Time Goes By . . .* (Candid CCD 79741), which was recorded at a London concert in 1991 but released only late last year.

Braff's other new release, of more recent vintage and featuring a full rhythm section and four other horns (including a second cornetist) is called *Ruby Braff Remembers Louis Armstrong: Being with You* (Arbors Jazz ARCD 19163), a title that would fit practically any of Braff's albums over the decades—including *As Time Goes By . . .*, whose repertoire explicitly evokes Armstrong with "Shoe Shine Boy," "Jeepers Creepers," and a Cole Porter medley from *High Society*. (For what it's worth, the Braff album used by Lacy was *Ruby Braff Plays Louis Armstrong*, from 1969.) Despite Braff's preference for pop songs with Armstrong's whiskers on them, both of these new discs suggest that Braff is becoming a closet modernist. If that isn't a flatted fifth at the end of his solo on *Being with You*'s "Twelfth Street Rag," it sure sounds like one—a wink in the direction of Dizzy Gillespie. And *As Time Goes By . . .*'s freewheeling version of "Love Me or Leave Me," replete with a riff from Basie's "Dickie's Dream," could pass as the work of a trio of young Lennie Tristano-ites, with Alden sounding like Braff's leaner, rangier echo.

Braff is in snarling good form on both albums, and if the trio disc is a reminder of his savvy as a bandleader, *Being with You* reveals his heretofore unsuspected gifts as an arranger (the credits acknowledge assistance from the trombonist Dan Barrett, without specifying how much) and singer (he winningly croons Cole Porter's "Little One," another song from

High Society—in which it was performed by Bing, not Pops, but never mind). Most of Braff and Barrett's scores are no more than functional, riff-based springboards for solos, but they do their job commendably—especially in the case of the peppy opener, "I Never Knew (That Roses Grew)." Braff's other recent Arbors releases have been duets with pianists, and I have to confess that seeing all those other horns listed among the personnel initially gave me a scare. I feared a blowsy, senior-citizen jazz-party ambiance, with cursory heads and an unending string of solos on each track. But in at least one instance, on "If I Could Be with You," Braff and Barrett put the extra horns to boldly dramatic use—we never hear the full band or even the full rhythm section until the end, a teasing exercise in tension and release. In addition to Braff, the standout soloists include the pianist Johnny Varro, who demonstrates a keen understanding of the subtleties of stride and barrelhouse, and the tenor saxophonist Jerry Jerome, an eighty-five-year-old former Artie Shaw sideman whose booting choruses could pass for those of a man of forty. As for Braff, his introduction to "When Your Lover Has Gone" tugs as deep as any of Ben Webster's ballads—it has the same combination of world-weariness and reawakened ardor.

Braff's philosophy of jazz has always been that the stuff of genius is impervious both to the whims of fashion and to misconceived notions of progress. His own solos are living proof. He's hip enough for Evan Parker and Steve Lacy, and that ought to make him hip enough for anyone.

Fi, June 1998

FOR A DISCERNING FEW, THE SUMMER OF *SGT. PEPPER* WAS ALSO THE SUMMER of *The Far East Suite*, recorded in December 1966 and released the following year. Thirty years on, the greatest of Ellington's later concept albums is an old friend, its grand sweep so familiar that I now listen to it for its small details. Take, for instance, "Blue Pepper," which originally began Side B and seemed an uncharacteristic bid for airplay, what with Rufus Jones's boogaloo drumming. Now it seems to me one of the shrewdest bargains any jazz musician ever struck with rock, and who but Ellington would use Cat Anderson's screech trumpet throughout the piece, instead of as a money shot, à la Stan Kenton or Maynard Ferguson? Has anyone noticed that the brief "Depk" and

"Amad" update "Ko-Ko," employing some of the same harmonic language and massive orchestral effects? The suite is both ambitious composition and a showcase for a stellar group of improvisers: Gonsalves, Hodges, Carney, the unsung Jimmy Hamilton, the inimitable Lawrence Brown (who comes on like the Sheik of Araby on "Amad"), and Ellington himself. By 1967, anything he did risked being thought of as an addendum, but substantial careers have been based on less than he accomplished here.

The Village Voice Jazz Supplement, June 15, 1999

IN THE SAME WAY THAT AVANT-GARDISTS WHO REINTERPRET DUKE ELLINGTON tend to get him mixed up with Charles Mingus, post-bop pianists who attempt stride inevitably filter James P. Johnson through Thelonious Monk, with whom they have more in common. This is what Chick Corea does on "Mediocre," from his CD *Remembering Bud Powell* (Stretch/Concord Jazz SCD 9012-2). The angularity of Corea's left-hand bass and the dissonant ping of his right-hand lines, neither of which would be surprising in another context, raise an eyebrow here only because you don't expect to hear such discernible echoes of Monk on a salute to Bud Powell (whose 1955 recording of "Mediocre" was obsessive rather than playful, with nary a hint of stride). In 1961, during his besotted Parisian exile, Powell recorded an entire album of Monk's compositions. Corea's *Remembering* starts off like it's the "answer record" once removed. The bassist Christian McBride even quotes "Bemsha Swing" on the opening "Bouncing with Bud," after Corea has indulged in his own bit of rhythm-a-ning on the theme. These Monk allusions aren't inappropriate (he and Powell belonged to a mutual admiration society), but I do find them ironic. In the late 1940s, when Powell's influence rivaled Charlie Parker's, Monk was assumed to be a dead end, a pianist and composer whose eccentricities made him both inimitable and minor. Fifty years later, it's Powell whose legacy eludes pianists.

In his youth, Powell's virtuosity arguably exceeded Art Tatum's, but I don't think this was why Powell's contemporaries (and even Powell himself, after 1953 or so) managed to replicate only the most superficial aspects of his style. Powell wasn't Powell without his manic energy, and this was the quality missing from his desultory later recordings. It's also missing here, even though Corea and his "friends" (the billing given McBride, the drummer Roy Haynes, the trumpeter Wallace Roney, and the saxophonists Joshua Redman and Kenny Garrett) play hot and heavy.

Another word for what's lacking might be madness, and maybe it's too much to expect. On its own terms, *Remembering* succeeds on a number of levels, the most welcome of which might be in calling much-needed attention to Powell as a composer. An overlooked gem of the late 1980s, the trumpeter Herb Robertson's *Shades of Bud*, achieved the same result by deconstructing Powell — extricating the elegance of his composed lines from his dazzling pianism. Corea's approach is more conventional but no less useful. In extending Powell's harmonies and spreading out his meters, Corea and his sidemen demonstrate the untapped blowing potential of Powell's tunes. Only Garrett, whose recent Warner Bros. releases have been mighty impressive, is slightly off form here. Redman's upper-register squeals on "Mediocre" are so calculated and tidy they remind me more of Mariah Carey than of Coltrane or Albert Ayler, but his other solos are dark and searching and blessedly free of such pet devices. Roney's solos unfold with such logic and cohesion that for once his tonal resemblance to Miles Davis can be charitably overlooked. And the ageless Haynes, meshing nicely with McBride, adds both contemporary accents and period credibility.

As for Corea, this is his finest showing on disc since . . . well, since his 1981 tribute to Monk. In terms of sensibility alone, Corea and Powell are an odd match (it's difficult to imagine Powell embracing Scientology, for example, or demonstrating the importance of play to an audience by initiating a game of tag with another musician, as I once saw Corea do with Bobby McFerrin). But *Remembering*'s only false touch is Corea's one original, named for Powell: It's so lightweight you almost expect Garrett to switch to flute. Corea pays more meaningful tribute with his crisp unaccompanied variations on Powell's "Celia" to close the album. The combination of fusion and the human-potential movement has been as lethal to the creativity of Corea's generation of musicians as racism and controlled substances were to Powell's, but Corea seemingly has the ability to walk off the casualty list whenever he desires.

THE ALTO SAXOPHONISTS JACKIE MCLEAN AND LEE KONITZ MIGHT APPEAR TO have nothing in common except their instrument, their refusal to coast despite their advancing years, and the debt to Charlie Parker they share with all saxophonists of their generation. McLean, a mighty blower whose new album *Nature Boy* (Blue Note 7243 5 232732 4) is something of a departure for him—a program of standards, most of them ballads— is sixty-eight years old. The prolific Konitz, who has released four new albums in recent months and has recorded in so many different contexts over the years that almost nothing he could do would qualify as a departure, is four years older. As young men, he and McLean were forced to wrestle with Parker's influence or risk being overwhelmed by it. Each met this challenge in his own way, drawn by individual sensibility to a different aspect of Parker's style.

To this day Konitz is often described as the only major alto saxophonist of the late 1940s untouched by Parker in any way—a misconception that Konitz goes on trying to dispel in interviews. The most innovative figures in jazz are frequently those who do the best job of disguising their influences, and this includes Konitz, whose starting point as an improviser is the expanded harmonic possibilities suggested by Parker at the dawn of the bebop revolution in the mid-1940s, but whose timbre and method of phrasing were radically different from Parker's—lighter and more transparent, without noticeable rhythmic accents or blues inflections. At the opposite extreme, Parker's influence on McLean has always been readily evident, because it is almost entirely a matter of sound. Though he too makes use of Parker's harmonic language, McLean was drawn as a young man to the heavier tone and slashing rhythmic attack that Parker adopted in the years just before his death, in 1955.

This talk of timbre and attack borders on musicology, but for most listeners, the difference between McLean and Konitz is as simple as black and white. Konitz, who is white, first attracted notice as a disciple of the pianist Lennie Tristano, a born pedagogue who saw no contradiction in advocating for improvisers both greater spontaneity and greater intellectual awareness. Konitz was also a featured soloist with the Miles Davis Nonet, a short-lived ensemble whose handful of recordings from the late 1940s laid the groundwork for a 1950s offshoot of bebop nicknamed "cool."

In the curious lingo of modern jazz, the opposite of cool isn't "hot," but "hard"—as in hard bop, a late 1950s permutation of bebop whose emotionalism was initially perceived as a reaction to cool's cerebral detachment. The band most identified with hard bop was Art Blakey's Jazz Messengers, one of the best early editions of which featured heated playing by McLean, whose solos continued to epitomize the genre on his own Blue Note albums of the 1960s—even as he began to partake of the freedoms won for jazz by Ornette Coleman and John Coltrane.

So Konitz equals cool and McLean equals hard bop, which—given the way that jazz styles gradually tend to overlap—ought to say nothing more than that one is primarily an abstractionist and the other primarily an expressionist. But in practical usage, "cool" and "hard bop" are as much code words for race as they are musical designations. Race is talked about in jazz (though usually in veiled terms) as if it were a set of artistic traits rather than an ethnic characteristic. White players are branded—sometimes condemned—as introspective and analytical, and black players are assumed to be more intuitive, more volatile, and more in touch with jazz's underlying blues traditions. Exceptions abound, of course, but in a significant number of cases, including those of Konitz and McLean, this isn't necessarily a false dichotomy. It becomes one only when used to argue the superiority (or greater "authenticity") of one style of jazz, or to put a great musician in too small a box.

McLean is a case in point. His best solos can pin your ears back with their crying intensity, but more is generally at stake in them than the unimpeded expression of primal emotions. They are built around sound musical principles, beginning with McLean's careful manipulation of tone and his use of wide intervals for high drama. Cast against type on *Nature Boy*, McLean nevertheless remains true to character, delivering ballads such as "I Can't Get Started" and "You Don't Know What Love Is" as if in one uninterrupted burst; the effect is that of a tough guy suddenly spilling his innermost thoughts. McLean is no stranger to slow tempos, but his own compositions in this vein have generally been dirges rather than ballads—opportunities for him to wail over suspended chords and an insistent vamp. This is something he does here, to mesmerizing end, only on the title track: a quasi-mystical number associated with Nat "King" Cole and John Coltrane.

Despite never successfully keeping a working band together for very long, McLean has showcased an impressive number of young musicians on his recordings over the years, beginning with Tony Williams and Bobby Hutcherson in the 1960s. In recent years, his albums have featured sidemen drawn from the ranks of his students at Hartt College, in Hartford, Connecticut, where he is head of the Jazz Degree program. On *Nature Boy*, McLean is what amounts to a guest soloist with the pianist Cedar Walton's trio, whose other members are the bassist David Williams and the drummer Billy Higgins. On his own, Walton can be bland. But here, his fleet solos provide an effective contrast to McLean's lunging ones.

IN KONITZ'S CASE, ONE OF THE AREAS IN WHICH HE AND OTHER WHITE JAZZ musicians are supposedly deficient is in playing the blues, and in his notes to *Another Shade of Blue* (Blue Note 7243 4 98222–2 1)—like the earlier *Alone Together*, a Los Angeles nightclub recording with the bassist Charlie Haden and the pianist Brad Mehldau—Konitz confesses to being comfortable with the twelve-bar blues form, but not with blues tonality. The title performance here is a blues, and there are moments during a group improvisation on the chord changes of the standard "All of Me" that might as well be. On both of these, Konitz makes an eloquent case for the blues as a form of melodic reflection, rather than the noodling exercise in cliché that it is for many improvisers, black and white. The program's only drawback is its caterpillar tempos, which may be the result of there being no drummer on hand to stir things up.

Konitz's former mentor, Lennie Tristano, was phobic about drummers, preferring steady and unobtrusive timekeeping to any suggestion of direct intervention on their part. His disciples are supposed to share this prejudice, yet Konitz has consistently sought out drummers inclined to give a horn player a tussle; a favorite record of many of his fans is *Motion*, from 1961, which pits him against the super-aggressive Elvin Jones. On each of his other three new releases, Konitz bounces his ideas off an especially active drummer—the coloristic Joey Baron on *Sound of Surprise* (RCA Victor 63909-2), the elliptical and melodic Paul Motian on *Three Guys* (Enja ENJ-9351), and the explosive, Elvin-like Jeff Williams on *Dig-It* (SteepleChase SCCD 31466). All three of these CDs feature Konitz with a pianoless rhythm section, but they are otherwise slightly different. The most spartan of them—the Enja CD, on which the electric bassist Steve Swallow completes the title threesome—is also the most varied in repertoire, featuring knotty compositions by Swallow and Motian plus an Antonio Carlos Jobim ballad (*not* a bossa nova), a swaggering interpretation of Harold Arlen and Johnny Mercer's "Come Rain or Come Shine," a lyrical blues by Konitz, and two other originals by him that are based on the outermost chords of familiar standards.

This last category also describes a good deal of the material on *Sound of Surprise* and *Dig-It*. On both, Konitz is joined on the front line by the tenor saxophonist Ted Brown, another former Tristano cultist, whose transparent tone and zipping phrases trigger memories of Konitz's encounters with the late Warne Marsh. Brown is deservedly billed as co-leader with Konitz on the SteepleChase CD, but plays on only a few tracks of *Sound of Surprise*, where the guitarist John Abercrombie also comes and goes, adding a bit of harmonic shimmer here and there.

What stays the same on these CDs is the spirit of adventure in Konitz's playing; swing is largely a matter of note placement and forward momentum, and Konitz swings with a vengeance—however obliquely. Over the last fifty years, when has he not? In their different ways, he and McLean show that Parker's influence finally amounted to whatever a musician chose to make of it.

The New York Times, February 6, 2000

ZENLIKE IN HIS DISINCLINATION TO JUDGE MOST THINGS, JOHN CAGE COULD BE picky about music. He preferred Mozart to Bach, found Beethoven and Brahms boring, and failed to hear what appealed to intelligent people about jazz—a music whose sequential improvisations and reiterated beat, he supposedly once said, reminded him of a series of dramatic monologues delivered one after another, with a clock ticking in the background.

Jazz fans understandably dismiss such criticisms as nonsense, yet there is often a nugget of truth in them. Given the predictability with which most jazz performances unfold—an opening theme understood to be no more than a clothesline for chord changes, followed by a string of lengthy solos, then a recap of the theme, and then out (cadenzas and "fours" with the drummer are optional)—the potential for boredom is rife. Not even free jazz consistently avoids the problem Cage identified: Liberated rhythm and loosened rules of harmony and pitch frequently yield only longer monologues consisting mostly of screams, and delivered over a louder tick.

Cage's mind probably wouldn't have been changed by *Inspiration* (RCA Victor 74321 64717-2), a new release featuring the seventy-five-year-old saxophonist Sam Rivers with a specially assembled eighteen-piece big band consisting of musicians as much as three or four decades younger and billed as the Rivbea All-Star Orchestra, in honor of the performance space that Rivers and his wife, Beatrice, operated in their Lower Manhattan ground-floor apartment in the 1970s—the birthplace of that decade's loft-jazz phenomenon. Cage disapproved of music with too much of what he called "dialogue," and *Inspiration* is entirely predicated on dialogues of one sort or another—between the band's soloists and the rhythm section, between the soloists and the entire ensemble, between present and past (some of these pieces are from more than thirty years ago, but the orchestra delivers them with blistering immediacy). Besides, it probably takes a greater intimacy with jazz than Cage allowed himself—it takes, that is, an awareness of the music's capacity for transcendence and not just tedium—to appreciate the daring of what Rivers has accomplished here, in sidestepping jazz's overfamiliar routines.

The title track is the album's most accessible number, and one of its most inventive. The sunny melody is doubly familiar: It is based on Dizzy Gillespie's "Tanga," which the forward-leaning Rivers played as an unlikely sideman with Gillespie in the late 1980s, but it is also vaguely reminiscent of Luis Bonfa's "Samba D'Orfeu," from the 1959 film *Black Orpheus.* Gillespie's "Tanga"—already an example of recomposition—began with a lightly syncopated eight-note string bass figure taken directly from Bonfa. Rivers uses the same introductory figure, but scores it for saxophones and brass and has them deliver it almost percussively. The main theme is a variation on Gillespie's; but as delineated by Rivers (on tenor saxophone), who moves through adjoining keys with a dozen or so horns merrily blaring alongside him, it's too dissonant and bruising to be a true samba. After Rivers has finished stating the theme, the band repeats the introductory figure, with the drummer Anthony Cole leaning hard on the beat. Then Rivers returns for a chorus of muscular melodic embellishments.

All of this takes just under three minutes, and it would be a satisfying performance all by itself. But "Inspiration" is just beginning. In its remaining six-and-one-half minutes, there are ten more brief horn solos and three more drum breaks—all of this taking place as either the full band or its various sections unfold a series of elaborate variations on the main theme. Some of these ensemble passages sound collectively improvised, though it is more likely that they were scored by Rivers in such a way as to suggest collective improvisation.

RIVERS WAS A MEMBER OF THE MILES DAVIS QUINTET FOR A BLINK OF AN EYE IN 1964, AFTER establishing a local reputation in Boston. "I was there [in Davis's band], but I was somewhere else, too," he once told an interviewer. Davis objected not just to the exploratory thrust of Rivers's solos, but to their sheer length. With his own band in the 1970s, Rivers frequently played solos that lasted upward of half an hour. By contrast, many of the solos on *Inspiration*, including Rivers's, fly by in under thirty seconds.

In his liner notes, Rivers explains that each of the seven compositions on the album, including the Gillespie-inspired title track, can last as long as fifty minutes in live performance. On his 1983 album *Winds of Manhattan*—one of only two previous albums to feature his writing for large ensemble—Rivers squeezed in more of his compositions by editing out the improvised solos (including his own) after the fact. This, he admits, drained the recording of vitality. His strategy on *Inspiration* is much wiser: He allows composition and improvisation to overlap, while asking his sidemen to keep it brief. The felicitous result is something almost unheard of in jazz: performances that seem both expansive and concise.

Despite the major role that Rivers played in the Blue Note label's synthesis of hard bop and free form in the 1960s with his albums *Fuschia Swing Song* and *Contours*, his precise rank in jazz has always been difficult to gauge. At one point in the late 1970s, his importance seemed as much entrepreneurial as artistic. Studio Rivbea was initially a place for Rivers to rehearse and perform with his own bands, but he soon opened its doors to like-minded experimentalists. Following Rivers's lead, some of them opened lofts of their own, and these informal venues were the crucibles in which the jazz avant-garde of the 1970s tested its ideas in public.

Rivers seems to be the sort of maverick who is better at starting his own scene than he is at fitting into an existing one. After leaving Gillespie in 1990, he moved to Orlando, Florida, and promptly formed a big band whose members were musicians who were gainfully employed at Disney World (talk about Mickey Mouse bands!) and looking for creative moonlighting opportunities. Doug Mathews and Anthony Cole, who are members of Rivers's band in Florida, are the bassist and drummer on *Inspiration;* the studio band's other members include such established New Yorkers as the trombonist Ray Anderson, the baritone saxophonist Hamiet Bluiett, and the alto saxophonists Greg Osby and Steve Coleman (who is also the album's producer). One never gets the feeling that

Mathews and Cole are stepping up in class. Mathews, in fact, playing electric bass, is the ensemble's key man: The stuttering lines that Rivers assigns him frequently recall the period in the late 1970s when Rivers and others gamely, if not always successfully, sought to factor dissonance into funk.

THE CLOSING "REJUVENATION," IN PARTICULAR, HAS SOME OF THE SAME PUSH as Ornette Coleman's first works for Prime Time, though its skidding melody also recalls Thelonious Monk's "Off Minor." Of the seven pieces on *Inspiration*, Rivers has previously recorded only two. Still, the album amounts to a Sam Rivers retrospective: The oldest piece here is the sinuous uptempo ballad "Beatrice," which Rivers recorded on his first album for Blue Note in 1964 but which he dates as belonging to 1968 — presumably the year he finished tinkering with it. But Rivers has apparently never stopped tinkering; "Beatrice" and the pieces from the 1970s sound contemporary rather than vintage, partly because this is music that the jazz mainstream has never quite absorbed, but also because Rivers and the other soloists find so much new to say, and this inevitably changes the character of his compositions.

Despite the abundance of solos, *Inspiration* is no Jam with Sam. Rivers's orchestral writing is high-flying and colorful, and even when he shows his age, it works to his advantage — the unison reed passages near the beginning of the rhumba-like "Solace," with their echoes of Benny Carter (albeit in a more agitated context) could only have been written by someone who remembers the swing era firsthand. Never present merely to goad the soloists on, as happens in most projects of this sort, the orchestra is more like an equal duet partner to them.

The liner notes fail to provide a running list of soloists, and though Rivers and a few of the others are easy to identify (Steve Coleman, for example, with his sideways style of phrasing, and Ray Anderson, with his Snidley Whiplash imprecations), the brevity of most of the solos makes it virtually impossible to tell one trumpeter from another, or to tell which tenor saxophonist is Gary Thomas and which is Chico Freeman. A listener shouldn't be made to guess, especially since *Inspiration* offers so much else to think about.

The New York Times, October 10, 1999

THE CLARINETIST DON BYRON'S *BUG MUSIC* (NONESUCH 79438–2)—NAMED FOR his favorite *Flintstones* episode, one in which Fred's sponging relatives flee in horror at the sound of an insect quartet much like the Beatles— has a surprise ending. Its first fourteen tracks feature ensembles ranging from sextets to an eleven-piece orchestra playing almost note-for-note covers of Duke Ellington's Cotton Club extravaganzas, Raymond Scott's whirligig cartoon symphonies, and John Kirby's gentle send-ups of long-hair composers and early jazz. Byron's approach to this vintage material from the late 1920s, the 1930s, and the early 1940s isn't reverential, exactly; better to say that by following the original arrangements to the letter, he honors their irreverence. Improvised solos are limited mostly to half-chorus solo "breaks" that follow the guidelines laid down by Ellington or Kirby's sidemen (the Scott material allows for no improvisation at all). Which is why tracks fifteen and sixteen—Ellington's "Blue Bubbles," from 1927, and Billy Strayhorn's "Snibor," from 1949—come as such a surprise. We've all been to concerts where the bandleader or conductor rewards the musicians for a job well done by letting them indulge themselves on the encore. Something similar occurs here. Byron and the pianist Uri Caine have "Blue Bubbles" all to themselves and they playfully rip it apart, with Byron exploring his horn's extremes and Caine smashing Ellington's stride figures into atonal clusters. The Strayhorn piece, a winking blues disguised as an unresolved thirty-two-bar pop song, becomes an occasion for tossing, fully contemporary solos by Byron and the guitarist David Gilmore. There's even a snarling bass solo by the agile Kenny Davis, who elsewhere is mostly called upon to do a lot of slapping.

To grumble, as some surely will, that Byron should have taken greater liberties with the rest of the material on *Bug Music* misses the point. (Which isn't to say that he won't eventually open these pieces up: The last time I heard his klezmer band, he and his sideman were going "out" on Mickey Katz's novelty tunes.) Listened to on its own terms, *Bug Music* is simultaneously out-of-the-past and cutting edge—a point best illustrated by Byron's approach to the six Raymond Scott compositions. Scott, whose music will be instantly familiar even to many who have never heard his name, on account of its association with Bugs and Porky and Daffy, attempted in pieces such as the ones here to translate the speed of modern life (it could be the speed of a diesel, a touch typist's fingers, or a tobacco auctioneer's spiel) into pure sound. His music was too dense for improvisation, but Scott borrowed numerous other elements from jazz—its instrumentation, its tonal colorations, its rhythmic snap. No matter that Byron, in a provocative treycard essay, distances himself as well as Scott from jazz; by including Scott on the same album with Kirby and Ellington (and by acknowledging the extent to which Kirby and Ellington's sidemen "routined" their solos), he's implicitly challenging the dogma that improvisation is necessary for a piece of music to be jazz.

It hardly seems a coincidence that the jazz repertory movement got rolling around the same time that the avant-garde shifted its focus from improvisation to composition. Nor does it seem a coincidence that Byron has a foot in both camps. He is the best sort of traditionalist—one who has directed his efforts toward expanding the canon rather than restricting it. Jazz has inherited much from classical music, unfortunately including a snobbery toward music created to serve utilitarian purposes. Just as Scott's works have been devalued for having underscored the antics of mischievous rabbits and ducks, the music of Kirby's sextet may owe its current obscurity to its popularity as dance music in the 1940s. (For that matter, the early Ellington pieces on *Bug Music* were written to accompany lavish floor shows, and Byron's transcriptions retain so much of their swank you can almost hear the click of the chorus girls' heels.) Scott having already become something of a postmodernist passion, *Bug Music*'s major reclamation job may be on Kirby, whose small group was as disciplined as a big band and delighted in swinging Chopin and Tchaikovsky (offhand, the only previous Kirby salute I can think of was by Dave Pell, more than thirty years ago). As demanding as the Scott material is, and as splendid a job as Byron and his men do with it (especially the drummer Joey Baron, with his timely wood blocks and chimes), just finding and keeping the right tempos on the Kirby selections may be the greater accomplishment (the lion's share of the credit for this goes to the terpsichorean rhythm section of Caine, Davis, and drummer Billy Hart). It all adds up to nearly an hour's worth of stellar musicianship and nonstop fun—the best of both worlds.

Fi, March 1997

On Stage and Screen

The Jazzman Bloweth

Resembling one of those cool bop collections Starbucks sells as a side dish to cappuccino and biscotti, *Side Man: Jazz Classics from the Broadway Play* (RCA Victor 0902663444–2) epitomizes everything spurious about a show that epitomizes everything spurious about contemporary live drama. The centerpiece of both this new CD and the second act of Warren Leight's long-running play is Clifford Brown's version of "A Night in Tunisia," recorded at a Philadelphia jam session the night before his fatal 1956 turnpike collision. This electrifying performance wasn't commercially released until 1973, by which point tapes had been making the rounds for years. It's 1967 in the play, and one of Leight's terminally out-of-it white jazz musicians, a former member of Claude Thornhill's trumpet section now scuffling for society dance gigs, has come up with a dub that he can't wait to play for his buddies—fellow ex-Thornhillites on a job with the dreaded Lestin Lanin (and such fuck-ups that their idea of a good time is swapping yarns designed to illustrate what fuck-ups all musicians are). As Brown masterfully elongates a phrase from his first chorus into his second, one of Leight's sidemen lets out a "whew!," only to be told "wait!" by the sideman who's heard the tape before—meaning, it gets even better. Both reactions ring true: This is how such men would listen to music, and this is the monosyllabic way they would talk about it. Then, a few minutes into Brown's solo, one of these guys jumps up and yells "I quit!"—delight giving way to frustration:

the precise reaction of several generations of trumpeters to Brown's unreachable technical prowess and improvisational sorcery.

But the reaction that the staging and lighting draw our attention to is that of Sideman number one, the narrator's father, who scrunches his eyes shut, silently mouths Brown's lines while fingering them on air trumpet, rocks back and forth so hard he looks like he's having convulsions, and breaks into beads of sweat I could see from the fifth row. I once sat next to Bill Evans during a set by Art Blakey's Jazz Messengers, and though I could tell that Evans was listening intently to Blakey's pianist, James Williams, and digging what he heard, he looked like he was waiting for a bus. Whether because they're too cool or just physically inhibited, musicians don't play air instruments or jitterbug in their chairs—this is the behavior of wannabes. But to show us a character listening as musicians actually do would require a subtlety no one in theater trusts audiences to get—an interiority we take for granted in movie close-ups, but nowadays assumed to be impossible on stage.

Today's theater types are hypocrites; they prattle on about Artaud and Stanislavsky, but their actual models seem to be Norman Lear and Garry Marshall. Like so much theater today, *Side Man* is played as broadly as in a TV sitcom, right down to pausing for laughs (the director Michael Mayer seems more to blame for this than his cast, though I swear the sideman with glasses and a lisp is doing Charles Nelson Reilly). A show about underdogs that gets an awful lot right with its in-jokes about Lanin, Tiny Khan, and "Club 92" (the 92nd Street state unemployment office), *Side Man* minus Christian Slater is itself an underdog on Broadway at a time when a hit drama requires both classic status and a bankable star (Brian Dennehy in *Death of a Salesman*, Kevin Spacey in *The Iceman Cometh*, etc.). This is a show with its heart in the right place, and you want to root for it. But it's just one more helping of warmed-over Eugene O'Neill—the semiautobiographical story of a hesitant young man burdened with a demented alcoholic mother and a dreamer artist father. All of theater has become one bickering Irish family in which Mother is to blame for Son but—wait a minute!—Father is to blame for Mother. The irony is that *Side Man* is playing at the Golden, the site of the first New York production of *Waiting for Godot*, the show that supposedly put an end to this sort of overwrought nonsense more than forty years ago.

Side Man's lone flash of originality is in its jazz milieu, but for those of us who know the turf, the very same musical performances that thrill us in other contexts are the show's falsest touch of all. Whenever we hear the music that Leight's sidemen are understood to be playing, what we are actually hearing are classic recordings by Clifford or Miles or Dizzy—the black trumpeters guys like these worshipped and (if wrongly, and only on a musical level) to whom they considered themselves genetically inferior. We should be hearing the likes of Tony Frusella, Doug Mettome, and Don Joseph—and if their names are unfamiliar, that's exactly my point. They were the real-life counterparts of Leight's beautiful losers, white trumpeters of the 1950s who fell casualty to rock and roll, the demise of big bands, and the black nationalism that had been synonymous with jazz since hard bop (and which *Side Man* alludes to only once, in passing). By substituting Brown, Davis, and Gillespie, the show betrays its own characters.

Granted, few Broadway theatergoers will be able to hear the difference. CD shoppers are presumably another story, and *Side Man's* companion album appeals to the most casual of them with a random assortment of great performances by names they're likely to recognize. Who actually buys such anthologies, though, is a mystery to me. Many things are, maybe because I don't drink latte.

The Village Voice, May 4, 1999

The Gypsy in His Soul

In *Sweet and Lowdown,* the new movie written and directed by Woody Allen, Sean Penn plays Emmet Ray, a fictional jazz guitarist of the early 1930s whose neurosis is unlike that of any previous Allen hero. Although self-confident to the point of arrogance, Ray nevertheless knows that he's only the second-best guitarist of his day. No. 1 by consensus and in Ray's own opinion is Django Reinhardt, a real-life figure whose recordings with the Hot Club of France and with such visitors to that country as Benny Carter and Coleman Hawkins made him the first foreign-born player respected as an equal by American musicians. The mere mention of Reinhardt's name infuriates Ray, yet he can't stop himself from jabbering about the Belgian-born Gypsy, even when surrendering to the police after a high-speed chase or reminiscing about his mother's lullabies ("the sweetest music I ever heard," he describes them, before grudgingly adding "except for this Gypsy guitar player in France"). *Sweet and Lowdown* is a mockumentary with Allen and others, including the journalists Nat Hentoff, Dan Okrent, and Sally Placksin (as themselves or fictional jazz authorities), occasionally prodding the narrative along with tales of Emmet Ray's exploits. The point of many of these stories is Ray's sense of inferiority to Reinhardt; the two men have been in the same room only twice, we are told—and Ray fainted both times.

Jazz has always been there on the margins of Allen's films: In the 1979 *Manhattan*, for example, Louis Armstrong's 1927 recording of "Potato Head Blues" makes Allen's character's list of the people and things that make life worthwhile, along with Groucho Marx, Willie Mays, Swedish movies, and Cezanne's apples and pears. But unless one counts *Wild Man Blues*, Barbara Kopple's 1998 documentary account of Allen's tour of Europe with his Dixieland band, this is the avocational clarinetist's first movie with jazz as its subject matter. The movie is a minor work, but Allen's affection for vintage jazz and its colorful characters gives *Sweet and Lowdown* plenty of zing. The stories we hear about Emmet Ray have a shaggy-dog quality reminiscent of the yarns that veteran musicians swap about their departed colleagues on panels at the annual convention sponsored by *JazzTimes* magazine—stories that deliberately beg the question of whether many of the greatest figures in jazz were *truly* larger-than-life or just constitutionally unequipped to deal with it.

This Emmet Ray: Is he merely the latest in what has become a long line of Woody Allen surrogates—self-absorbed artists whose shabby treatment of women supposedly can be excused on the grounds that they have bigger things on their minds? (Really, all they seem to have on their minds are the women they haven't gotten their hands on yet.) Well, yes and no. As played by Penn, who is different from Allen in every way, beginning with being photogenic, Emmet Ray doesn't whine, he doesn't know the language of psychoanalysis, and he is incapable of irony. Accused by one of his many women of locking away his feelings where not even he can find them, he replies in self-defense, "You say that like it's a bad thing"—a comeback worthy of Allen or of Alvy Singer, the character he played in *Annie Hall* (1977), but delivered without a trace of either's winking self-consciousness.

Sweet and Lowdown focuses on Ray's relationships with two women, the society vamp he marries and who betrays him (Blanche, played by Uma Thurman) and a mute New Jersey laundress who loves him unconditionally but whom he betrays (Hattie, played by the talented young English actress Samantha Morton). As a woman incapable of speech, Morton is forced to do most of her acting with her eyes, and she uses them expressively. They're going to remind people of Mia Farrow's eyes, and the character's middy blouses and woolen hats look like things that Annie Hall would have bought in thrift shops four decades later. But the Allen heroine whom Hattie most resembles, in her doting on Emmet Ray, is Soon-Yi Previn, as she was shown in Kopple's *Wild Man Blues*, a film whose real objective seemed to be to undemonize Allen and endear his child bride to movie audiences. In Kopple's film (which seemed as much Allen's, for all intents and purposes), Previn pampers her much-older husband in a way that no woman his own age and with a life of her own would have the time to do, much less the inclination. A similar dynamic is at work between Hattie and Emmet Ray. She's the only person he opens up to, and no wonder—unlike Blanche and his assorted prostitutes and chorus girls, Hattie can't interrupt him with her own two cents.

Yet unlike the celebrity interviewer played by Kenneth Branagh in last year's *Celebrity*, Penn's character never comes across as Woody Allen with more hair and a better face. Allen has always tried to have it both ways—insisting on his right to privacy but making his life the subject of his films. Seeing *Manhattan* twenty years ago, many of us assumed that Allen knew his character was behaving selfishly in trying to persuade a teenager to forego six months of drama school in London so she could continue to warm his bed in New York. Recent events in Allen's personal life now make this reading of *Manhattan* seem naive. With Emmet Ray, however, Allen finally seems to have created a main character from whom he has some emotional distance.

"He had the intelligence of the paysan," the violinist Stephane Grappelli once said of Django Reinhardt, his teammate in the Hot Club of France. "He did not have the intelligence of the poet, except when he [played]," Grappelli told Whitney Balliett. The same could be said of Emmet Ray, who is Allen's first inarticulate hero—an example of typecasting for Penn, who really ought to try playing a character as intelligent as he is, but something of a breakthrough for Allen as a screenwriter and director. Allen seems attracted to the character for much the same reason as Blanche, a would-be novelist curious about what makes jazz musicians tick. When she asks Ray what he thinks about when he's improvising on his guitar, he doesn't have a clue what she's talking about; he finally mumbles that he sometimes thinks about how he's being underpayed. Later on, Blanche asks the affable thug she has been cheating with (Anthony LaPaglia) what goes on in his mind when he's shooting people or beating them up. He can't say either; he just has a knack for the rough stuff, he tells her. Emmet Ray has a knack for what he does too, and that's about as far as his understanding of his art goes. He's an improviser content to let his fingers do the thinking—a self-loathing intellectual's idea of a man of action.

Wild Man Blues revealed Allen to be a rank amateur as a clarinetist, but his film soundtracks have made it obvious that he recognizes good music when he hears it played by someone else. A problem with most jazz films is that the music in them is often inferior or anachronistic: The hero of *Young Man with a Horn*, for example, was a thinly disguised Bix Beiderbecke, the introspective poet laureate of jazz in the late 1920s, but Kirk Douglas's trumpet solos were the work of Harry James, whose robust licks virtually defined a certain kind of big-band jazz of the 1940s.

Sweet and Lowdown's music is right on the money, even if Allen's script never addresses the question of to what extent Emmet Ray's guitar style has been influenced by Reinhardt's (a clue might be that Ray seems to have copied the colorful Gypsy in other ways, including his pool sharking, poker playing, waxed mustache, and lovely pastel shirts). The Ray solos we hear—ghosted by Howard Alden, who also coached Penn on how to finger the strings—sound like those of a swing-era guitarist who has taken as his starting points Reinhardt's tremolo and rhythmic drive, but added his own lyrical streak. In other words, Emmet Ray sounds a lot like Django Reinhardt, but not so much that a knowledgeable listener of the period would have confused them. In a way, Alden is the real star of *Sweet and Lowdown*, along with the pianist Dick Hyman, a longtime Allen associate who wrote the bracing and idiomatically accurate arrangements of the standards we hear Emmet Ray playing with his small group. About the only bone a jazz fan might find to pick with *Sweet and Lowdown* is that it obeys Hollywood convention in having black musicians on hand merely to validate the genius of a white lead. But this shortcoming is forgivable in light of what Allen has accomplished in the name of his favorite musical era.

The last thing we're told about Emmet Ray is that he vanished without a trace after recording his best and most deeply felt performances for RCA Victor in the late 1930s. Django Reinhardt died in 1953, by which point he had begun to incorporate elements of bebop in his solos. Allen, for his part, has never expressed much interest in bop or any other form of modern jazz or pop, and if his nostalgia for the hot jazz of the 1930s gives *Sweet and Lowdown* its glow, it also helps to explain why this newest Woody Allen film ultimately seems as insular as *Celebrity* and the 1997 *Deconstructing Harry*—airless and sour comedies set mostly in Allen's head.

In his early movies, Allen knowingly poked fun at aspects of 1960s and 1970s popular culture, and no director had more to say about the hazards of courtship in the wake of feminism; *Annie Hall*, in particular, affected the way that single or divorced men and women thought about their relationships. (It also started a women's fashion trend.) Twenty years later, Allen's attitude toward popular culture has become openly contemptuous, rather than gently mocking. Except for his casting of younger actors (one imagines him thumbing *Premiere* and *Vanity Fair* and copying down the names of the young actresses he wants to meet), he has allowed himself to become cut off from current trends, and this has robbed his movies of the vitality they once had. In such recent movies as *Dogma*, *Being John Malkovich*, and *Austin Powers: The Spy Who Shagged Me*, there are jokes about pop music and television and other movies that might baffle Allen as much as they would his characters from the 1930s in *Sweet and Lowdown*. This is ironic, because it was Allen's early movies, along with those of Mel Brooks, that opened the floodgates for the sort of irreverent topicality we now expect from movie comedy.

If *Sweet and Lowdown* is more light-hearted than Allen's other recent movies, this could be because he finds much less to dislike about the 1930s than about today. All the same, it would be churlish to criticize him for living in the past—he does his best work there.

The New York Times, December 5, 1999

Scatting Heads

Press releases for *JAZZ*—a ten-part series for public television that the documentary filmmaker and amateur historian Ken Burns has described as the final part of a trilogy including *The Civil War* (1990) and *Baseball* (1994)—give the title in capital letters, and the series practically demands as much, in recognition of its own importance and the comparable importance it attempts to confer on its subject. Having discovered America twice already, at Harper's Ferry and Appomattox, and then in the general vicinity of Yankee Stadium and Ebbets Field, Burns has sighted it yet again—this time in the unsuspecting persons of Louis Armstrong and Bix Beiderbecke, the teenagers who danced to Benny Goodman's big band in the aisles of a Times Square movie theater in 1937, and their black counterparts at the Savoy Ballroom, Harlem's "home of happy feet" years before white kids caught the jitterbug.

Burns put himself on the cultural map with his series on the Civil War, an impressive piece of filmmaking in which nearly every element worked to spellbinding effect: the period stills and illustrations, the elegiac readings of soldiers' letters, the historian Shelby Foote's lyrical commentary, and the chorus of taps implied in every sentence of David McCullough's stately narration. The series wasn't just for buffs, some of whom might have been a little put off by its emphasis on human suffering rather than battlefield strategy. Without undue sermonizing, Burns managed to suggest that this country was still divided over race and questions of states rights. But he next made a gabby series on baseball that was awash in a sentimentality in keeping with what you'd expect from someone who looks like his favorite Beatle was Paul. I was one of the many who stuck with *Baseball* because it was the only game in town in the fall of 1994; the major leagues were on strike, there were no playoffs and World Series, and I needed my annual fix. But I remember wanting to grab a ball myself and bean the next joker Burns coaxed into mugging for the camera and singing "Take Me Out to the Ballgame."

A few seconds into the first episode of JAZZ, the trumpeter Wynton Marsalis—a senior creative consultant to the series who gets so much face time that he might as well have been given star billing—informs us that "jazz music objectifies America" and gives us "a painless way of understanding ourselves." This declaration is followed by a montage of the music's major figures, over which the actor Keith David, reading copy supplied by Geoffrey C. Ward (who also wrote the scripts for Burns's two previous series) solemnly intones that jazz is "an improvisational art making itself up as it goes along, just like the country that gave it birth."

The lecture continues throughout the series, delivered by Marsalis and others. Close to the end, Marsalis restates the theme with a little extra spin, as he might do with a melody to conclude a performance with his band. Jazz "gives us a glimpse into what America is going to be like when it becomes itself," he tells us, talking in the way that presidential candidates are prone to do—as if believing that democracy isn't just a preferable system of government but a form of existentialism.

Marsalis shares Burns's long-standing propensity for overstatement in the service of high ideals. The filmmaker lets Marsalis in particular get away with so much in JAZZ—presenting the character and motivations of long-dead musicians, for example, without distinguishing between legend and actual memory—that his methods as a documentarian are open to question, along with his credentials as a social historian. (At least no one will accuse him of failing to think big. Even his "smaller" films have been examinations of marmoreal Americana: Thomas Jefferson, Lewis and Clark, the Brooklyn Bridge.)

AFTER SOME PRELIMINARY FLAG-WAVING, BURNS'S NEW SERIES BEGINS WITH the hoariest of creation myths: that New Orleans was the single birthplace of jazz, something I doubt that anyone besides Burns and his New Orleans–born senior creative consultant still believes. It ends with the latest in resurrection myths: that Marsalis's arrival on the scene in 1980 saved jazz from death at the hands of self-indulgent avant-gardists and purveyors of jazz-rock fusion (we're even shown snapshots of the baby Wynton).

Marsalis's musicianship is above reproach, and his evolution from Miles Davis sound-alike to composer in the rich vein of Duke Ellington has been as interesting to follow as it was unanticipated. What hasn't changed since 1980 is his scorn for newer forms of jazz he finds deviant and unworthy of the name. As a thinker, Marsalis—like the writer Stanley Crouch, his confidante and associate in the Jazz at Lincoln Center program—is a disciple of Albert Murray, a minor African-American writer usually referred to as a novelist but celebrated more for his non-fiction. Using the terms "jazz" and "blues" interchangeably in books such as *The Omni-Americans* (1970), *The Hero and the Blues* (1973), and *Stomping the Blues* (1976), and rarely stooping to address specific performances, Murray has formulated an aesthetic of jazz that sounds like an ontological creed. "What makes a man human is style," Murray wrote in *The*

Omni-Americans, and "all human effort beyond the lowest level of the struggle for animal subsistence is motivated by the need to live in style."

This effort includes the blues, which Murray and his adherents define as celebration rather than as social protest or an expression of sorrow. Jazz to them represents an extension of the blues: Something either is jazz or it isn't, depending on whether it reveals an obvious blues sensibility. This sensibility is not exclusively black. Marsalis has been accused of practicing reverse racism (or "Crow Jim," as musicians call it) in his role as artistic director for the Lincoln Center jazz program, but this is unfair. His bias isn't against white musicians—he has hired any number of them for the Lincoln Center Jazz Orchestra—but against anyone whose music, improvised or composed, he suspects of being tainted by European influences and vitamin-deficient in the blues. (The problem with this point of view is that it puts the most innovative jazz of the last few decades off-limits.)

Nevertheless, jazz is principally black, coming as it does "from a consciousness of those who are outside of something but in the middle of it," as Marsalis tells us at one point in Burns's opening episode—echoing another of Murray's tenets, which is itself an upbeat variation on W.E.B. DuBois's notion of African-American double consciousness. The black musicians who invented jazz and their original black audiences were denied the full benefits of American democracy, Marsalis explains, "but that doesn't alter the fact that they [were] American, and . . . that they [had] access to all the information that Americans have access to." Such thoughts understandably resonate with Burns, the theme of whose films has been America's ongoing struggle to live up to its democratic ideals. Burns has admitted to knowing little about jazz going into this project, and he seems to have learned most of what he now knows about the subject from Marsalis, who has as much claim as Burns to being the series' auteur. And with Crouch and Murray on the board of advisors and serving as commentators, what we're getting is the party line.

EVEN THOUGH HARDLY ANYONE DANCES TO JAZZ ANYMORE, THE BELIEF THAT dance forms a bond between black performers and their communities remains central to Murray's philosophy—which no doubt explains why Burns keeps dropping into the Savoy Ballroom during the episodes on the Swing Era, even when nothing new seems to be going on there. The series sets out to trace the history of jazz from its birth as a Negro folk music to its present bewilderment of styles, but pretty much gives up after Ornette Coleman's introduction of free improvisation, in 1959. This may be because that was about when jazz ceased to be a sociological phenomenon. In contrast to the dawdling multiple episodes on early jazz and swing, and the single episodes on bebop and its 1950s offshoots, the final episode crams forty years of musical ferment into less than two hours. Although not billed as an epilogue, it resembles one. It also resembles a eulogy, despite repeated assurances that jazz is alive and well, largely thanks to Marsalis. At first I was inclined to be forgiving, because I myself once taught a jazz history course in which we didn't make it much past 1960. As an undergraduate, I took survey literature courses in which we never got around to reading the last few assigned books. The difference, however, is that teaching occurs in real time; I certainly didn't intend to waste an entire two-hour session playing version after version of "Body and Soul" in an attempt to illuminate different improvisational approaches, but it became necessary to do so in order to help my students over a hurdle. Burns could have left himself more room at the end by being more tough-minded at the editing table—and more tough-minded in general. Does it contribute to our understanding of jazz to know that Armstrong didn't find true love until his fourth marriage, or that Benny Goodman used to shoot his sidemen a withering look of disapproval that they called "the ray"? And why on earth did we need to spend quite so much time at the Savoy Ballroom?

Nearly every jazz critic I know has been angrily compiling his own list of current performers who were unfairly omitted from the series—generally speaking, anyone whose music smacks of the avant-garde, which Marsalis apparently convinced Burns was poisoned fruit. Though my list of missing persons includes Albert Ayler, Keith Jarrett, Anthony Braxton, and Sun Ra, it begins long before 1960. JAZZ tells us nothing, or very little, about Mildred Bailey, Red Norvo, Benny Carter, Woody Herman, Stan Kenton, Lennie Tristano, Erroll Garner, Chet Baker, Art Pepper, any of Ellington's sidemen, or—except for Fletcher Henderson—the arrangers, black and white, who gave the big bands of the 1940s their trademark sounds (and who, unlike that era's performers, easily crossed the color line by virtue of being invisible men). For that matter, many of the figures whose names are cited in the final episode fail to receive their full due. Charles Mingus is hailed as "second only to Ellington in the breadth and complexity of his compositions," yet nothing is said about his being a link between Ellington and the contemporary avant-garde. Like the Art Ensemble of Chicago, whose mix of African tribal ritual and post-serialist compositional devices rerouted free jazz in the 1970s, Mingus is here only to illustrate a point about the growing mood of militancy on the part of black musicians in the decades after bebop. Bill Evans was the most influential pianist of the last forty years, but all we really learn about him is that he once played with Miles Davis and was white. You'd think he was significant only as an example of a black trumpeter's enlightened hiring policies.

FOR ALL THAT IS WRONG WITH IT, *JAZZ* IS ENJOYABLE TELEVISION. THERE IS perceptive commentary by the essayist Gerald Early and by the jazz critic Gary Giddins—the latter in the role of Shelby Foote, as it were. (I only wish Giddins had been allowed an opportunity to explicate an Ellington piece chorus by chorus as we hear a recording, the way he does with a piece by Jelly Roll Morton.) A wealth of great music is excerpted, ranging from Morton's "Dead Man Blues" to John Coltrane's *A Love Supreme*, and Burns puts faces on it by drawing on an artful assortment of clips. Much of this footage will be familiar to hard-core jazz fans—Duke Ellington musing at the piano ("dreaming," he calls it) for Edward R. Murrow on *Person to Person*; Charlie Parker and Dizzy Gillespie vengefully ripping through a number after being condescended to by the entertainment columnist Earl Wilson; Billie Holiday and Lester Young ruefully eyeing each other as they perform a blues with an all-star group in 1957, when both of them were staring down death. But it will be new to most viewers, and I dare them to resist it. There are rarer clips here as well, including a surprising one of the trumpeter Clifford Brown on a program hosted by Soupy Sales, and a delightful one of Louis Armstrong spoofing bebop by singing new lyrics to "The Whiffenpoof Song."

The white musicians featured in the series, beginning with Bix Beiderbecke, are invariably depicted as alienated outsiders, but they are treated with respect as bona fide jazzmen. The episodes on the 1920s, which are the most poetic in the series, are essentially the story of Beiderbecke and Louis Armstrong metaphorically calling to each other from steamboats and orchestra pits, though prohibited from playing together except after hours. Along with Ellington, Armstrong is one of two figures whose long careers Burns chronicles from cradle to grave, in what seems as much a bid for human interest as an acknowledgment of their seminal roles in jazz. Ellington, a guarded man who was a master of diversionary chit-chat, eludes Burns at every turn, but Armstrong is captured in all his troubling complexity. My favorite moment in the entire series is a clip of him playing "Tiger Rag," in Copenhagen in 1933. Announcing the tune without looking his audience in the eyes, and appearing to shuffle even though standing still, he really does seem a stereotype of the servile Negro. Then he begins to play, hitting high note after high note with a look of masculine determination. "That horn could kill a man," the actor Ossie Davis, guilty of only slight exaggeration, tells us several episodes later — though you do have to wonder why Ossie Davis in particular qualifies as a commentator. (In choosing commentators, Burns has made an effort to show us as many black faces as possible. Given the subject, this wasn't a bad idea. But they're often the wrong black faces.)

Burns is big on sociological context, so the music unfolds against a backdrop of speakeasies and bread lines, dance crazes and world wars, lynchings and civil-rights marches. The series certainly looks good and it sounds good, too, if you ignore the narrator's overenunciated delivery (he sounds like he was bitten by Maya Angelou) and the melodramatic readings, by a host of other actors, of newspaper editorials, passages from musicians' autobiographies, and texts by F. Scott Fitzgerald, Ralph Ellison, and Langston Hughes. There is a good deal of valuable oral history here too: Mercedes Ellington reminiscing about what a curious fellow her grandfather Duke was; Doc Cheatham recounting subbing for Armstrong and being dressed down by Bessie Smith; Artie Shaw explaining his disenchantment with fame; the writers James Lincoln Collier and James T. Maher and two former Savoy Ballroom regulars describing the excitement of hearing the big bands; Jackie McLean revealing that he once so wanted to sound like Charlie Parker that he was willing to forgo originality; Lester Bowie joking about practicing trumpet as a child with the window open in the hope that Louis Armstrong would pass by and hear him; Charlie Haden talking about breaking the rules of conventional tonality with the alto saxophonist Ornette Coleman.*

---

* I should say here that a few years ago Lynn Novick, who is listed along with Burns as a producer for the series, and Peter Miller, one of two co-producers, took me to lunch to ask my ideas about possible interviewees. I may have suggested some of these people; I honestly don't remember.

But the series features too many other talking heads; some of them don't always know what they're talking about, and talking isn't all they do. With Marsalis as the prime offender, they frequently scat-sing to demonstrate a point about the music under discussion—sometimes getting the rhythm right but never the intervals. It's a relief whenever Marsalis picks up his horn to make his point. As annoying as he can be, though, Marsalis takes a back seat to the preening Matt Glaser, a violinist who played on the soundtracks of *The Civil War* and *Baseball* and who turns up every so often here to share an insight on, say, Armstrong's relationship to the space-time continuum. He sounds like one of those guys you overhear trying to impress their dates in jazz clubs, only now it's us he's trying to score with.

AS MUCH AS JAZZ FANS BICKER AMONG THEMSELVES, THEIR REACTION TO A project aimed at the general public tends not to be to ask if it's any good but to ask whether it's good for jazz. In this case, the answer is yes. The music is exciting, and it is talked about in a way that stirs the imagination. To novices who watch the series and find themselves eager to attend a few concerts or buy a few CDs (even if all that scatting strikes them as the jazzbeau's version of air guitar), the debate among insiders about who and what should not have been left out of the series is going to seem petty. Music isn't baseball; there are no statistics for measuring achievement, and Burns is as entitled to his opinions as I am to mine—even if his seem to have come wholesale from Marsalis and company.

The larger problems with the series stem from the dubious habits Burns has picked up since *The Civil War*. For every person we hear speaking from experience, another comes along to offer information he couldn't possibly know. Talking with certainty about events in the lives of Armstrong and Ellington, Marsalis might as well be a televangelist chatting about his last conversation with Jesus. Of the semi-mythical early-twentieth-century New Orleans cornetist Buddy Bolden, Marsalis says, "[His] innovation was one of personality, so instead of playing all this fast stuff, he would bring you the sound of Buddy Bolden." How could he know? No recording of Bolden survives, and he is said to have last played in public in 1907. As Marsalis speaks, we hear a trumpeter on the soundtrack playing a rollicking blues, with no indication that it's a recent performance by Marsalis. Most viewers will probably assume that it's Bolden, and will surely accept as gospel what Marsalis says about him.

Why do we need to hear from Joshua Redman and the saxophonist Branford Marsalis (Wynton's brother) about the greatness of John Coltrane's "A Love Supreme," when the pianist McCoy Tyner or the drummer Elvin Jones, both of whom were on the recording, are still alive and could have provided an insider's view? As in *Baseball*, Burns shows himself to be susceptible to cockeyed legend, amateur psychoanalysis, and cut-rate sociology. If you swallowed all the fantastic yarns about the old Negro Leagues in *Baseball*, I could probably convince you that Josh Gibson once broke Babe Ruth's record of sixty home runs in a season—then came back and hit another sixty-one in the *second* game of the double-header. In *JAZZ*, it's said that the partially blind pianist Art Tatum had such unerring pitch that he could hear the difference between a penny and a dime being dropped on a table. Who couldn't? We're told that Sidney Bechet as a young man once challenged a pianist to a duel with pistols, after having a disagreement with him over a song's chord changes. Marsalis interprets this as evidence of Bechet's deep commitment to music. Isn't it more likely that at that point in his life Bechet was a hothead, ready to shoot a man or die over anything?

Talking about Bix Beiderbecke, who drank himself to death before he was thirty, Margo Jefferson, a columnist for *The New York Times*, suggests that the trumpeter was psychologically "harmed" by not being allowed to prove himself alongside black musicians who were his equal or better. But Beiderbecke regularly played and recorded with very good white musicians, including Frankie Trumbauer, Eddie Lang, and Tommy Dorsey. And in the 1920s, Armstrong played with no one of his own caliber either, with the exception of Bechet and the pianist Earl Hines (and possibly Johnny and Baby Dodds). He and Beiderbecke were ahead of everybody else, black or white.

We hear as much about Clifford Brown's death in a turnpike accident as we do about the attributes that made him a pacesetter among young musicians of the 1950s. If this were a series on the British romantic poets, which would be more important, Keats's death from tuberculosis at the age of twenty-five (a year younger than Brown) or "Ode to a Grecian Urn"? Everybody dies, as John Garfield said in *Body and Soul*. I also found myself thinking of old movies in listening to the series' account of how Benny Goodman and Artie Shaw—both of whom were sons of Jewish immigrants—embraced music as a way of escaping bleak urban poverty. Wasn't this the same rationale offered for James Cagney's criminal tendencies in those Warner Bros. melodramas of the 1930s? And don't we hear this same old tune every time one rap superstar tries to waste another?

The point of all those return visits to the Savoy Ballroom seems to be to acknowledge the common experience of the instrumentalists on the bandstand and the twirlers on the dance floor. The audience for jazz has changed since then, and a large segment of it is in Europe. A general rule of thumb in the evolution of any musical style is that the people in the audience gradually become the people on stage. For proof, just look at the blues—a style of music that has been largely abandoned by black audiences, and most of whose younger performers now are white. The shift hasn't been as dramatic in jazz, but beginning with the German trombonist Albert Mangelsdorff and the Belgian-born pianist Martial Solal in the 1950s, any number of inventive players have come from outside the United States. You'd think this phenomenon would be of some interest to a filmmaker with pretensions to being a social historian. Yet with the exception of Django Reinhardt in an episode on the early 1940s, not a single foreign-born musician is mentioned. Taking note of the guitarist's Gypsy roots, the French director Bertrand Travernier reasonably argues that "jazz is a music which can incorporate many other kinds of music." As if with this in mind, the last episode features a brief collage showing (among other things) a glimpse of the Cuban-born pianist Gonzalo Rubalcaba and a collaboration between the bassist Ron Carter and the rapper M.C. Solar, as the young tenor saxophonist Joshua Redman talks about the willingness of today's jazz musicians to combine jazz with other kinds of music, including West Indian, hip-hop, and gospel. Absent from his checklist, and presumably from Burns and Marsalis's, are the boldest and most artistically provocative cross-stylistic endeavors of the last decade: the guitarist Bill Frisell's forays into country music, the clarinetist Don Byron's klezmer and John Zorn's Judaica, the pianist Uri Caine's adaptations of Mahler, and the trumpeter Dave Douglas's transfigurations of Eastern European folk melodies.

Loosely drifting through JAZZ are the elements for several smaller and better films Burns might have made, including lovingly detailed ones on Armstrong and the Savoy Ballroom. In taking on the entire history of jazz, he doomed himself to incompleteness and superficiality. Jazz is a melting pot of African and European influences that, as Gary Giddins observes in the opening episode, only Americans could have cooked up.

But does that make it synonymous with America? In Jules Dassin's 1955 movie *Rififi*, which was re-released last year, four thieves rob a jewelry store, with each man contributing his special skill and working in complete trust with the others. Is this, too, an example of democracy in action? Not only are these mugs up to no good; they're French or Italian. And isn't it obscenely self-indulgent for Americans to prattle about still being in the process of defining their national identity, given what is now going on in the Middle East and the former Soviet Union? To insist that jazz bear the weight of its nation's highest ideals at every turn is asking too much of it—or of any art form.

The Atlantic Monthly, January 2001

part three

HERE AND THERE

Tourist Point of View

===

J etlagged scribblings on the initial Matosinhos Jazz Festival, named for and presented this June in a nearby suburb of Oporto, Portugal's second-largest city but its primary trade and industrial center, about 300 kilometers from Lisbon, overlooking both the Atlantic and the Rio Duoro:

Unlike many European festivals, Matosinhos was no grab bag. All of the headliners were pianists. Abdullah Ibrahim played solo. Paul Bley captained an all-star trio featuring the drummer Al Foster and the bassist George Mraz (Tommy Flanagan's teammates not so long ago). Geri Allen co-led a quartet with her husband, the trumpeter Wallace Roney (Buster Williams was on bass, and Lenny White on drums). Muhal Richard Abrams fronted a sextet with Jack Walrath on trumpet, Clark Gaton on trombone, Patience Higgins on tenor saxophone, Brad Jones on bass, and Reggie Nicholson on drums. Representing the locals was Mário Laginha, a talented young pianist whom few Americans have heard of, though he is quite well known in Portugal as music director for the neo-traditional pop singer Maria João.

Not counting two solid hours of abstract hully gully from Abrams on closing night, my favorite moment of the festival occurred as I stood waiting outside a restaurant at dusk with a bunch of Portuguese journalists for the van that would take us to that night's show. Raul Vaz Bernardo, a retired bank employee deeply in love with his record collection who now reviews concerts for *Expresso*, a Lisbon-based weekly, began to sing "Close Your Eyes" in syncopated English and with as much gusto as he had shown talking about obscure sides by Gary McFarland and Eddie Costa over dinner. Most of his fellow journalists, apparently used to his exuberance, paid him no mind. But I laughed aloud in sheer delight, as did Ana Bela Martins da Cruz, a cultural reporter for the Lisbon daily *Diario de Noiticias*, especially when Raul forgot the words to the bridge and resorted to whistling.

Before my departure, an American colleague asked me why—beyond the obvious incentive of an all-expenses-paid trip to the birthplace of port wine—I was willing to cross an ocean to hear musicians I might easily hear in New York, a lot closer to home. The question had been nagging at me, and Raul's spontaneous serenade went a long way toward answering it. I wanted to hear jazz as part of a European audience—to hear how its meaning changed depending on who was listening to it (a perverse desire, perhaps, what with the ongoing dispute over the extent of European content in jazz, and the desirability of such content). Matosinhos was the perfect festival for me; by virtue of being brand new, it wasn't yet on the international jazz vagabonds' map. Except for the musicians and their retinues, I seemed to be the only foreigner in attendance.

One way in which Europe is no different from the United States is that even during a jazz festival, all you hear in the airports and hotel lobbies is Kenny G. Contrary to what Americans have been led to believe, jazz is no more popular with the masses in Europe than it is with the masses back home. On the other hand, could Muhal Richard Abrams or Paul Bley fill a thousand-seat auditorium even in New York, as each came close to doing in Matosinhos? In its own country, jazz offers evidence of the long-standing diversity of American culture, like pizza parlors and Chinese restaurants.

Abroad, along with those same pizzerias and Chinese take-outs, it serves as another example of the Americanization of Europe. Foreign audiences inevitably bring their own references to jazz, and their perceptions can be valuable. Possibly only a European audience like the one I heard Abdullah Ibrahim with would have appreciated how "European" his collage-like performance was in both presentation and hush, for all of Ibrahim's allusions to Ellington, Monk, and Cape Town carnivals. And possibly only a Portuguese-speaking audience would have been aware that Ornette Coleman's "Latin Genetics" (one of three Coleman numbers interpreted by Bley) borrows its opening line from Carmen Miranda's "Mamá, Eu Quero."

Finally, though, for a European an appreciation of jazz is based on the assumption that experience is a function of sensibility. As if to emphasize that the music that fires their passion is theirs by choice, not by birthright, the Portuguese writers and broadcasters I met spent what others might have thought was an absurd amount of time debating among themselves whether the "G" in Gil Evans was hard or soft, and whether a certain American clarinetist pronounces his name Jeuffree, Jeuffray, or Jeuff. I don't find this absurd, any more than I did Raul's rendition of "Close Your Eyes"; I found it endearing, and I hope that doesn't sound condescending.

I'M TOLD THAT GARGANTUAN FESTIVALS LIKE NORTH SEA ARE FUN BECAUSE there's something happening every minute. Matosinhos was fun because there wasn't. There was ample time for sightseeing. José Duarte, who was described to me as his country's Leonard Feather, took me on a tour of Oporto's bookstores and cafés, round winding streets chockablock with modern shops and architecture dating back centuries. In addition to reviewing the festival, Ana Bela Martins da Cruz was writing a piece on the city for her paper's travel section, and she graciously let me trail along as she made the rounds of churches, cemeteries, and Roman bridges.

But enough travel writing—potentially a form of revenge for someone deprived for almost a week of the linguistic skill at which he fancies himself a virtuoso, and forced to keep his most complex thoughts to himself. (You speak, of course, but without subtlety, shadings, circumlocutions, profanity, slang—all of the things that give language its inner meaning, its voltage, its juice. Reduced to a vocabulary of a few dozen English words everyone understands, you spend a lot of time pointing to things and gesturing with your hands.)

The music was top-notch, with only Geri Allen's two sets of modal impressionism counting as a disappointment. Roney's dependence on Miles Davis brought out the Herbie Hancock in Allen, making her sound more derivative than she has in other contexts.

Bley got off to a slow start, with each member of his trio taking a turn unaccompanied. But the music took flight once the three players joined forces, with Bley—expansive now where he once was elliptical—proving himself a master of melodic free association. Ibrahim, as usual, was magnificent (unknown to him, a moth circled his head, as if drawn to his light). Abrams played more piano than he is usually given credit for, and though his pieces featured sequential solos, in the manner of conventional jazz, there was nothing conventional about them (imagine Stockhausen with a sense of rhythm, or Sun Ra with respect for proper intonation). Just when you thought the set couldn't get any better, it did. As for Laginha and his quartet (featuring Julian Argüelles, a Jan Garbarek–like saxophonist who has played with Carla Bley and Django Bates), someone should tell ECM's Manfred Eicher about them—a piece by the leader based on a Portuguese fado was the very definition of Euro-soul, lyrical and resolute.

Adding to the festival atmosphere was the Pin-Stripe Brass Band, from New Orleans, which marched through the streets of Oporto and Matosinhos every afternoon (when I caught up with them, they were doing an infectious version of a Bob Marley song). No jazz festival is complete these days without the blues, and this one featured Carey Bell playing to a packed house in a cellar club every evening beginning at midnight. I caught only a bit of one of Bell's sets, and what I heard sounded so good I wish I could have stayed for more. But coming after the piano concerts, the harmonica player's brand of amplified Chicago blues was like a shot of Thunderbird after a gourmet meal. It kept you going, but you were afraid it was all you'd be able to taste the next morning.

JazzTimes, December 1997

Time Difference

On her after-breakfast walks along West Cliff Drive in Santa Cruz, California, during our August vacations there, my wife, Terry, wears a daisy-yellow gardening hat she says she would be embarrassed to be seen in anyplace else, including a mirror. She bought the hat in a store across from the Santa Cruz boardwalk a few years ago; it has an exaggerated front brim and a girlish bow on the back whose daintiness she defeats by undoing the cotton ribbons and knotting them under her chin, Annie Oakley–style. She wears the hat because it's the only one she's found that effectively shades her face from the sun here on the coast, which even on breezy days can be searing once it burns away the morning fog and begins to reflect off the Monterey Bay.

Except for those mornings when I surprise her by walking with her as far as the Santa Cruz Surfing Museum (a shrine to the sport and the lifestyle squeezed into the ground floor of a lighthouse about three quarters of a mile from our hotel), I protect myself from sunburn by hiding indoors, lying in bed with the remote control and hoping to catch a *Perry Mason* rerun or an episode of VH1's *Behind the Music*. If nothing on television amuses me, or when I become embarrassed for the people on *Jerry Springer* or *Jenny Jones*, I take a book out to the balcony.

One of these years I'll get around to reading a few of the minor contemporaries of D. H. Lawrence whose work Paul Fussell discusses in *Abroad*, his 1980 book on British travel writing between the world wars. "Travel books are a sub-species of memoir," Fussell argues, and then goes on to quote a writer named Norman Douglas that "'the ideal book of this kind' invites the reader to undertake three tours simultaneously: 'abroad, into the author's brain, and into his own.'" A few years ago, another guest at the hotel, a native of this area, gave me a book about the Monterey Peninsula by Robert Louis Stevenson; I should be reading it from cover to cover instead of skimming it for Stevenson's descriptions of "the haunting presence of the ocean," "vast, wet, melancholy fogs," and other natural phenomena right in front of my eyes. But vacation isn't a time for scholarship. Unless John Updike or Scott Spencer has published something new, I end up reading first-person mysteries heavier on observation than action, featuring disillusioned private eyes (Lawrence Block's Matthew Scudder is the best example) who are old-fashioned moralists at heart. This is the sort of novel to which I am addicted and which I harbor vague ambitions of writing myself someday.

All I know for sure about my alter ego is that he's a former cop who tells his clients that he resigned from the force because "I didn't look good in blue." His actual reason, an attempt to do right that played out wrong, he reveals only to the reader (also a paying client, when you think about it, which is why such novels seem to demand the first person). Knowing I'm between assignments, this tough guy shadows me around Santa Cruz, cracking wise. "It makes no sense for young people to quarantine themselves the way they do," he said—a little ruefully, I thought—as Terry and I left a movie theater one Saturday after midnight a couple of years ago, when Pacific Avenue was deserted except for the post-adolescent tribes gathered outside the pizza parlors and clubs. "The last I heard, youth wasn't catching." Maybe if I wrote about him, he would shut up. But no full-time writer wants to spend his vacation writing. Anyway, every writer owes himself at least one imaginary book. My two-fisted novel of sensibility is perfect; if I tried starting it, it wouldn't be.

TO ALL APPEARANCES. WRITERS LIKE ME ARE GENTLEMEN OF LEISURE ANYWAY. "working," in the most literal sense, no more than three or four hours a day. The most time-consuming part of writing is the thinking things over, which I do from morning to night, though it might not look like much to anybody else. I used to have a neighbor who greeted everyone by asking "Working hard, or hardly working?" I never knew which would be the more truthful answer. Being on vacation doesn't make the answer any easier—nor am I convinced that somebody who sneaks out to as many afternoon movies as I do is entitled to the customary few weeks off in the summer.

It probably goes without saying that I am not always fun to travel with. When vacation time comes, I'm either on the run from a deadline or wiped out from having narrowly met one. I begin to experience air rage on the taxi to the airport, thinking of how little leg room I'm going to have (I always seem to wind up behind someone a foot shorter than me, who decides to push his or her seat all the way back. Sometimes it's a child small enough to fit in the overhead compartment, which might be a better place for him). If our plane is delayed, which it almost always is, I have to go to a noisy airport bar to catch a smoke. If the idea is to permit smoking only where alcohol is consumed, why not combine all the vices? Put keno, cockfights, and lap dancing in those airport lounges too. At least if I were smoking, I'd feel like I was getting something done.

My motto when traveling could be the same as Milton's Lucifer: "Whither I fly is Hell." My wife may be the only one who would put up with me. Her workday is longer and more hurried than mine, and she leaves for vacation justifiably exhausted. A good long walk by the bay is usually all the exercise she wants; when she returns to our room, she naps or reads or joins me in gazing out at the horizon—a body in motion the rest of the year now determined to stay put.

By mid-afternoon we're usually ready to hit the book and record stores on Pacific Avenue. Santa Cruz is a beach town, but it's also a college town. With a program in the History of Consciousness, whatever the hell that is, UC Santa Cruz has a reputation as the most radical branch of the University of California. We were there a few years ago, for a production of *Othello*, presented by Shakespeare Santa Cruz. The campus itself was worth the trip. Set amid redwoods on a sprawling former ranch, it looks like a place for lectures on forestry and animal husbandry, not feminism and queer studies. The university seems to draw students who are in no hurry to leave town after they graduate or drop out, and away from the smell of brine and the barking of the sea lions near the bay is a stretch of Pacific Avenue with shops that could be in Berkeley or Harvard Square.

Santa Cruz was near the epicenter of a devastating earthquake in 1989, and on our first trip there, three years later, much of Pacific Avenue was still closed off—but not the blocks where the used book and record stores are. Terry, who might never have been persuaded to go to Santa

Cruz if she had remembered the earthquake, often jokes that nothing short of another one could keep me from my afternoon browsing in Logos Books and Records and Streetlight Records and the Bookshop Santa Cruz. She's probably right. Becoming a critic has allowed me to go on indulging my undergraduate obsession with books and music, and I enjoy being in the company of those similarly obsessed, even though we might not exchange a single word. I am especially fond of Logos, if only because it was the first local store I ever bought a record in (one I had been looking for, by the French pianist Martial Solal), and because the people who work there are such a contrast to the bored kids you find behind the cash registers in most of the big chains, who tend to know nothing about the stock that isn't on their computer inventory display. The clerks at Logos look as if they already have lives, and as if those lives revolve around books and records. They remind me of my days in retail after college, in the 1970s, when everybody I worked with seemed to be the world's foremost unacknowledged authority on some obscure aspect of popular culture, and the only qualification for being hired was being overqualified.

On that first trip to Santa Cruz, a writer friend of ours in from Palo Alto for the day took us to lunch at India Joze (pronounced "Joe's"), which serves ambitious Asian-fusion dishes in an unpretentious setting. We still occasionally go there, though some of the culinary subtleties are wasted on my unsophisticated palate (left to my own devices, I would eat like a college student too). And being so close to the water, we tend to crave fish. A favorite of ours is Carniglia's, where I once had a meal so delicious I occasionally still think about it (North Alaskan halibut with a Sicilian sauce, over risotto), and which has the advantage of being on the Municipal Wharf, a short walk from West Coast Santa Cruz Hotel, where we always stay. (Years ago, when we first started traveling together, we thought nothing of sleeping on a friend's sofa or staying in a bed-and-breakfast without a phone or private bath. But to go on traveling like that once you pass forty doesn't mean you're still romantic and adventurous; it just means you're poor.) When we want something quicker and cheaper, we go to Riva's, which is also on the wharf. Along with the snapper on a kind of chewy sourdough roll found only in northern California, what lures us back there repeatedly is the sight of the large seabirds coming in for a landing, one after another, on the dining room's slanted roof. These include gulls and an almost pterodactyl-like species with fringed wings and an enormous wingspan which it took us East Coast city dwellers years and some amount of research to identify as pelicans (back home, the only large birds you see are pigeons, and they're dirty enough to be rats with wings).

Sunsets are beautiful in Santa Cruz; the fog reappears over the bay, and what we see from our balcony becomes Robinson Jeffers country again, the ocean and cliffs as stark and indifferent as they were in the morning, before the sunbathers and volleyball players filled the beach. The truth is we rarely see the sunset; we're usually at a concert or a movie. Marin Alsop, the conductor of the Cabrillo Music Festival Orchestra and a disciple of Leonard Bernstein's, specializes in contemporary composers whose works might seem hopelessly arcane in any other setting. But most of the concerts are given in the local Civic Auditorium, where you can see the lines of a basketball court drawn on the floor under the folding chairs. And Alsop makes the music accessible by making herself accessible, telling her audience about the character and artistic significance of each piece beforehand, and sometimes having the orchestra play a particularly lovely or rhythmically agitated passage in isolation before performing the piece in full, so we'll have something recognizable to listen for. A few years ago, the festival staged a full production of Bernstein's *Mass*; it was a pastiche that reduced the sections of the orchestra to piecework, but where else were we going to hear it?

When we started going to the West Coast, we used to split our time between Santa Cruz and San Francisco, certain that after a few days of relaxing by the water we would be desperate for the cultural attractions of a city. But Santa Cruz offers many of those cultural attractions, and on a more manageable scale. In one sense, San Francisco comes to us: The name jazz performers scheduled to play there or in Oakland often make a side trip to Santa Cruz, for a Monday-night gig at the Kuumba Jazz Center. (We've heard Lester Bowie, Brad Mehldau, and Dewey Redman there, among others.) The movies we would have to take buses or cabs to see in scattered locations around San Francisco are generally playing at the Riverfront, the Nickelodeon, or the Santa Cruz 9, all within easy distance of one another downtown. One of the joys of being on vacation is going to the movies every night, and so much the better if the movie is any good.

On the drive back to the hotel, there's always something on the car radio we wouldn't be hearing back home—ska, early Dolly Parton, a show hosted by a young woman complaining about her boyfriend between records by Alanis Morissette and Fiona Apple, vintage doo wop and rhythm 'n' blues on a station from Cupertino. This helps me make a list of things to look for in Streetlight and Logos the next day, along with the secondhand jazz albums I passed up that afternoon but subsequently realized ought to be added to the several thousand I already own. If I were home, I would stay up late to watch *Nightline*, *Politically Incorrect with Bill Maher* and *Late Night with Conan O'Brien*. But because I never quite get adjusted to the time difference, I fall asleep soon after Terry does, only half following an episode of *Baywatch* so vintage that David Hasselhoff didn't have to suck in his gut.

THERE ARE PLENTY OF OTHER THINGS WE COULD BE DOING HERE. WE COULD take a trip to Big Sur or to Carmel, to see the Catholic mission church built in 1797. And there is a breeding ground and rookery for sea lions and northern elephant seals just north of Santa Cruz, and a huge redwood forest on the slopes of the mountains. Although the asphalt-covered boardwalk and the amusement rides near our hotel are part of what people from elsewhere in the Monterey Bay area have in mind when they call Santa Cruz "trashy," there are things to marvel at even there, beginning with a wooden Giant Dipper roller coaster from 1924 and a carousel from 1911 with hand-carved ponies and chariots and a genuine pipe organ—certified historic landmarks still in operation. But we made all these trips and looked at all these things on earlier visits, and are in no hurry to see them again. This is the joy of vacationing in the same place year after year: Having fulfilled your obligations as a tourist by doing everything the guidebooks recommend, you're free to do whatever you'd enjoy doing at home if you had the time and the peace of mind.

"Vacations" are an attempt by working stiffs to "summer" like the rich, if only for a week or two. Although many city dwellers don't feel uneasy venturing any closer to nature than beaches and mountain resorts that are as crowded as cities, the growing popularity of supervised "adventure" vacations indicates a desire to return home reborn as a person capable of scaling a cliff or surviving in the woods, if need be.

I experienced such a transformation only once on a vacation, and it required nothing physical of me. More than twenty years ago, on our first vacation together, Terry and I spent three weeks in London. As we dutifully made the rounds of Buckingham Palace and the Tower of London and so on, they became oppressive symbols to me of the rigid class system my British-Irish ancestors had fled. But my feelings about London changed after seeing Keats's house and Henry James's memorial in Westminster Abbey, and after a few days of being asked for directions even by people with British accents, who mistook me for one of their own on account of my pale skin and crooked teeth. It seems no coincidence to me that I began my writing career in earnest after that trip. For better or worse, being in London felt like coming home.

With its movie theaters and concerts and record stores, Santa Cruz has also come to feel like a place where I belong. I can stay who I am in Santa Cruz, even if this means being grumpy and far too self-absorbed. I don't have to pretend to be somebody better—somebody carefree and athletic and curious about nature and ancient ruins. I can spend every day record-shopping and going to the movies and doing all the other things I can do guiltlessly back home only on weekends, if then.

Some of the qualities I love in Santa Cruz are those everybody from the East who goes to this part of northern California loves, beginning with the majestic scenery and the proximity of the ocean. One's relationship to the weather isn't adversarial there, as it is back east, where I guess the temperature only seems to be 90 degrees half the year and 20 degrees the rest (with my fair complexion, I burn like the English Patient in the summer and flake like the Singing Detective in the winter). And although it makes me sound dimwitted to say so, I enjoy being able to sleep a little longer in the mornings without feeling dissolute—I'm as rested as if I slept till noon, but it's only 9 A.M. Pacific Time.

All of this would be true anywhere on the Monterey Peninsula, but only Santa Cruz has Pacific Avenue and the popular culture I crave as much as I did when I was in my twenties. In Philadelphia I live near South Street, a commercial strip that years ago was a bohemian headquarters but now resembles a mosh pit on weekends, when it spills over with suburban teenagers who think they're too cool for the malls. They betray their youthful insecurity, as my generation did, by believing that being hip is a matter of looking the part. Lately a good number of the young white men I see have taken to shaving their heads to the nub, so they look like the comic-strip character Sluggo. Making a pitiful attempt to emulate the black rappers they see in videos, some of these kids wear baggy shirts and jeans, putting me in mind of Negro lawn jockies whose faces have been painted white in a misguided show of racial enlightenment. Their girlfriends have reinstituted the pre-feminist rule of showing lots of skin, exposing their midriffs and the area just below the navel. I'm on South Street on weekends too, but shopping for a Coltrane reissue or something practical like toothpaste, not for an identity. Pacific Avenue is cleaner and less crowded, but it has the same feeling of being a post-adolescent playground, and in an odd and comforting way, the alienation I sometimes feel as I walk from record store to record store is just like being home.

Writers are resigned to being onlookers; some of us actually prefer it that way. I am reasonably comfortable in situations where I am the only white person or the only heterosexual, but I can become irritable and self-conscious when surrounded by the young—maybe because I was never black or gay, but I did used to be young. It's interesting to look back at films by François Truffaut and Jean-Luc Godard from the mid-1960s, just before Woodstock, when these Frenchmen were somehow the directors most in touch with the habits and ideals of American college students. Even as Godard tells us that the young people in *Masculin Féminin* (1966) are "the children of Marx and Coca-Cola," Jean-Pierre Léaud, his lead, is wearing a jacket and tie, like an adult in training. I and most of my forty- or fifty-year-old friends still listen to rock 'n' roll and dress haphazardly, as we did when we were young (here in America, we don't have family crests—just brand names on our T-shirts and caps). This might be why so many adolescents and people in their twenties deface themselves with tattoos and multiple piercings; it's their only hope of looking different from their parents. I haven't seen many Sluggos or lawn jockeys on Pacific Avenue, but I did once see two boys and a girl wearing the combat boots and long black dusters of the Trenchcoat Mafia. And browsing in Streetlight one day, I saw a section for something called "Black Metal," which I realized I didn't know anything about, except for somehow knowing that it wasn't heavy metal performed by African-Americans (about the only thing that really makes me uneasy in Santa Cruz is feeling so at home in a place where just about everyone is white).

Popular culture is hopelessly fragmented today, but its unifying threads are youth and sexual provocation—and these are being marketed as if they were the same thing. I lie in my hotel bed watching a new Britney Spears or Backstreet Boys video and wondering what possible interest, other than a financial interest, an adult could have in these newest pop stars. The answer is a prurient interest. Is someone my age supposed to be turned on by Britney Spears—and what would it say about me if I were? I drift to sleep thinking these thoughts, and in the morning, if I feel up to it, I go with my wife on her walk so that we can continue talking about the movie or concert we saw the night before, even though walking along West Cliff Drive means risking a sunburn and dodging the bicycle riders who prefer the sidewalk to the lane set aside for them in the street.

"I used to have a bike," I muttered one day last year, after narrowly avoiding being run over by a crash-helmeted jerk close to my own age. "I was twelve." Of course, this may have been my tough guy talking. I was working hard, but it felt like I was hardly working.

The Atlantic Monthly, September 2000

part four

UNDERCOVER

Man Lost, Songs Found

I 'm listening to Ted Hawkins sing "There Stands the Glass"—the words torn from his throat, though they were not even his—and remembering the one time I heard him sing it live, at the Bottom Line in New York City, seven or eight months before his death from the effects of a stroke on the first day of 1995. The show, called "In Their Own Words" and hosted by the disc jockey Vin Scelsa, was one of a series presented by the club, the idea being for a bunch of singer-songwriters—in this case Hawkins, Roger McGuinn, Pete Seeger, and Joe South—to sit around swapping songs, yarns, and insights into the creative process. At one point, after South had spoken about his session work and about writing "I Never Promised You a Rose Garden" for Lynn Anderson, after McGuinn had told of collaborating with lyricists by phone or fax, and after Seeger had led the packed house in a sing-along, Scelsa turned to Hawkins, who had been sitting there all evening as though waiting for a bus—stirring himself only when it was his turn to sing.

"How about you, Ted?" Scelsa asked, playing the good host and trying to lure Hawkins into the conversation. "Ever collaborate with anybody on a song? Or write a song with somebody by fax?"

"No," Hawkins replied, giving him the same thousand-yard stare he had been giving the tables all night.

Scelsa must have posed other questions, and Hawkins must have answered them. I honestly can't recall anything he said, and I'm uncertain what else he sang. All I remember for sure, other than that "no," is the sight of him warily sitting there on his stool with his hands draped over his guitar: an imposingly tall, white-whiskered black man in but-toned shirt and pressed jeans, drawing all eyes to his through no appar-ent effort on his part—looking for all the world like someone from Leadbelly's time. My table happened to be next to one occupied by pub-licists from DGC Records, the label that was set to release Hawkins's *The Next Hundred Years*, and I could tell that their enthusiasm for him sur-passed the enthusiasm people in their line of work are able to summon up for any new client. They obviously adored Hawkins, as did the men on stage with him (South, especially, I thought). Hawkins wasn't the odd man out up there; that would have been Seeger, whose generation of folk purists believed that a folk singer couldn't possibly be a songwriter, because folk songs are *collected*, not written by professionals. Even so, Seeger played the crowd like a master, whereas Hawkins seemed as out of place among these music industry insiders as Leadbelly must have seemed that time John Lomax arranged for him to perform before a meeting of the Modern Language Association.

WRITERS USED TO SAY THAT HAWKINS'S VOICE HAD "GRAVEL" IN IT. BUT THAT wasn't gravel they heard; it was the sand that the winds blew into his throat all those years he set up his milk crate seven days a week on the boardwalk in Venice Beach, California. The uvular bends of his vocal style were similar to those of Sam Cooke and Otis Redding, but his soli-tary presentation and vagabond ways gave him more in common with Robert Johnson, Blind Lemon Jefferson, or Blind Willie McTell. Hawkins was a double anomaly: an acoustic soulman and an old-fash-ioned street singer in a day and age when the only remaining street per-formers are gangbangers and the deinstitutionalized homeless—thugs who are their own best audience and crazies who don't require any.

Hawkins was born in Lakeshore, Mississippi, near Biloxi, in 1936, but his life reads like the story of a Delta bluesman born around the turn of the century—one of those misbegotten souls, like Johnson, whose musi-cal talent was either heavenly compensation for hell on earth or some kind of cosmic joke. Hawkins's mother was an alcoholic teenage prosti-tute; his father could have been anyone—one of his mother's tricks. In trouble with the law for minor offenses (shoplifting, and the like) from the time he was eight, he was sent to a reform school in Jackson, Mississippi, and then, while still in his teens, to the notorious state facil-ity in Parchman, where he was subjected to whippings and put to work on road gangs. He became a hobo, riding the rails to various Northern cities before winding up in Southern California in 1966, where he began to earn a living singing on the streets and met and married a woman named Elizabeth, who stuck by him till his death, occasionally singing harmony on his records. Marriage didn't settle him down, nor did it cure him of his dependency on drugs and alcohol. He spent the better part of the next sixteen years in the California Medical Facility at Vacaville. In 1972, he was out long enough to record a session he'd recorded for Bruce Bromberg and Dennis Walker, a production team that would later strike gold with Robert Cray. Bromberg and Walker were unable to sell Hawkins's tapes until ten years later, by which time Hawkins was doing another stretch.

Bromberg and Walker, who did another session with Hawkins after his second release from Vacaville, weren't the first to "discover" Hawkins, and they wouldn't be the last. Somebody would sit him down in a studio every five years or so, and in the last few months of his life, when that someone happened to be a producer for DGC, a subsidiary of Geffen, a mini-major with an ample promotional budget, Hawkins found himself playing clubs in cities he'd once wandered as a hobo. Before that, however, no matter how many records he made, and no matter how many admiring reviews he accumulated, he always seemed to wind up back on the street with nothing but a guitar, a crate to sit on, a wooden board to tap his foot on, and a brass spittoon for the coins and dollars tossed his way.

WE WANT OUR RESPONSE TO MEN WHO HAVE BEEN SCREWED OVER BY LIFE TO be humane, compassionate, uncomplicated. A few years ago, in my hometown of Philadelphia, I played a small part in getting a man released from prison after he had served twenty years of a life sentence for murder. Those of us who worked on this man's behalf believed him to be innocent of the crime for which he was convicted, and since having his sentence commuted, he has done nothing to make us second-guess ourselves. He hasn't wound up back in jail. But he's been a disappointment to us because he can't stop himself from pulling on his well-meaning new friends many of the same hustles that probably helped to keep him alive in jail and, before that, as a junkie on the street. He's been a disappointment to us because we wanted him to be innocent not just of murder, but innocent in every other way—virtuous to an extent that might confirm our faith in our own virtue.

My response to Hawkins was more complicated than I might have wished—but no more complicated than his life, I suppose. The scars from those prison whippings weren't his only disfigurement. In interviews, he claimed to have been raped or otherwise molested more than two dozen times as a child. In light of this, perhaps it isn't surprising that his last stretch at Vacaville was for child molestation. The girl he admitted to "playing around with" was the thirteen-year-old daughter of one of his "side" women; for what it's worth, Hawkins swore till his death that the illegal relationship was never consummated, and this may explain why the charge against him wasn't statutory rape. His rap sheet also included convictions for exposing himself. After a disc jockey in England took up his cause in the late 1980s, he became so popular in that country that he made his home there for a few years, regularly playing the London clubs. But he was deported in 1990, after British authorities searching his flat on a routine passport violation found among his belongings a commercially produced kiddy-porn video, along with tapes he had made himself of neighborhood children at play. He wound up back on the boardwalk at Venice Beach for a while, before trying his luck on an upscale Santa Monica shopping strip, which is where DGC found him in 1993.

Unlike Leadbelly, Hawkins never killed anyone. But I remember thinking, that night at the Bottom Line, that his eyes guarded secrets it might be healthier for us never to know.

SOME OF THE PERFORMANCES HAWKINS MADE FOR BROMBERG AND WALKER featured him with a band, and the slight tentativeness of these works in their favor—they sound like 1950s Sun sessions, with all the energy and freedom of early rock 'n' roll, along with the country twang. Hawkins loved country music, and it seemed not to matter to him if a song was identified as white or black, whether it had originally been a hit for Webb Pierce or Sam Cooke—if he liked it, he sang it. His own songs similarly combined black and white styles, and my biggest complaint with *The Next Hundred Years* (DGC DGCD-24627) is that Tony Berg, Hawkins's last producer, surrounded him with Hawaiian and pedal steel guitars, unnecessarily drawing our attention to the irony of a black man who sounded a little bit like Otis Redding performing songs that sounded a little bit like hillbilly. The other problem with the album is that Hawkins, perhaps as a result of performing unaccompanied on the street, had developed a very unusual approach to tempo, and the sidemen enlisted by Berg prevent him from slowing down and speeding up and letting his moods overtake him as he would when singing and playing by himself — their professionalism holds him in check, and whatever excitement he does manage to generate seems calculated rather than spontaneous.

For all of that, the album includes what I consider to be Hawkins's single most incisive performance of one of his own songs, the stutter-beat "The Good and the Bad," with its warnings to a woman not to get involved with a man who'll "hurt you for the sake of hurting you." Was that man himself? The only other song of Hawkins's that cuts anywhere near as deep as this one is the semi-autobiographical "The Lost Ones," with its images of a mother dying and leaving her young children hungry and on their own, from *Watch Your Step*, his first album, released by Rounder in 1982.

Hawkins was a hypnotic singer and guitarist, but an iffy songwriter. For every "Good and Bad" or "The Lost Ones," he offered five or six numbers full of homilies and melodic riffs borrowed from Sam Cooke's lesser novelty songs. I prefer Hawkins's covers — especially his covers of country-and-western tunes, typified by the harrowing "There Stands the Glass," a hit for Webb Pierce in 1953, when Hawkins was in his teens (if this drinker's lament were a photograph or a painting, the shot glass holding the singer's "first one today" would be in the foreground, dwarfing the loser drinking alone at the bar).

There's a version of "There Stands the Glass" on *The Next Hundred Years*, but it pales before the rougher treatment Hawkins gave the song on the unaccompanied performance he recorded in Nashville in 1985 — one of twenty-eight covers he cut in two long sessions, giving us the best idea we're ever going to have of the sort of material with which he stopped people dead in their tracks on the boardwalk at Venice Beach. Hawkins's Nashville sessions were originally spread over two CDs and released by a Dutch label as *On the Boardwalk*; a tidier single CD available domestically from Evidence Records preserves the fourteen performances that matter most, but denies us the pleasure of hearing Hawkins making as much sense as he can of Johnny Horton's "North to Alaska" and the Mamas and the Papas' "San Francisco." Such performances are valuable to have, for the same reason it would be valuable to have a recording of Robert Johnson doing "Tumbling Tumbleweeds" or Memphis Minnie doing "That's My Desire." Why on earth would

Hawkins do Paul Simon's "59th Street Bridge Song"? Maybe for the same reason Johnson and Memphis Minnie did their homespun versions of songs on the radio in the 1930s and 1940s. Hawkins may have assumed, as they probably did, that people enjoy hearing songs they already know. Or he may have been making cynical assumptions about the taste of the white folks he saw in the crowds that gathered around him. Or maybe he believed that a cheery song like Simon's could provide a counterpoint to his own driven songs, and to his own troubles. Maybe he relied on songs about feeling groovy and wearing flowers in your hair to cheer himself up.

Hawkins's country covers were another story, unambiguous testimony to the greater power of songs, than of people, to cross racial lines. Along with "There Stands the Glass," another of my favorites is Hawkins's version of a song called "Happy Hour," the title track of his second Rounder album. I don't even know who had the original hit, but it hardly matters. The essence of country music is facing defeat with gusto, and in Hawkins's crying interpretation, "Happy Hour" emerges as the quintessential country-and-western loser's anthem—one about drinking too much *and* being cheated on.

We want our response to songs like "Happy Hour" and "There Stands the Glass" to be uncomplicated too, and part of what keeps many otherwise open-minded people from appreciating country as the music of an exploited underclass is their perception of tacit white racism in all those songs about good old boys falling in love with the wrong women and drinking themselves blind. Educated white audiences from other regions have always been a bit unnerved by working-class whites with Southern drawls. And as much as we might like to believe that music transcends its origins, some of us are a lot more comfortable hearing a black man sing such songs, once we overcome our shock. A song familiar almost to the point of contempt to one audience can become another audience's found song.

Pop music, under which rubric I include the blues and most of what's passed for folk music in this century, has always been a vehicle for self-expression. But self-expression has become a concept that we take much too literally. Any number of Hawkins's own songs, beginning with "The Good and the Bad" and "The Lost Ones" can be heard as autobiographical. But self-expression isn't just about words, any more than singing is.

That opening bellow on "There Stands the Glass," with its self-pity and defiance and hint of crazed abandonment to ruinous habits, tells us more about Ted Hawkins than any of his own songs did, even while forcing us to question the part that race or even personal experience plays in determining a man's identity. Singing country songs let Hawkins out of himself. He didn't just transform these songs; he was equally transformed by them.

BY THE TIME I HEARD HAWKINS AT THE BOTTOM LINE, I HAD ALREADY DECIDED to end my book *The History of the Blues* with him, notwithstanding his repeated insistence to interviewers that he didn't want his music called "blues," because that word to him meant being down and out and not seeing things in a positive light (his favorite of his own songs seemed to be a self-delusional ditty called "The Ladder of Success"). By my reckoning, Hawkins was kin to the turn-of-the-century songsters who were the first men to sing the blues, though they also sang all manner of popular and folk songs, both white and black. The difference was that songsters learned numbers from one another; Hawkins learned his off the radio, unself-consciously preserving a folk tradition in a technological age. I ended by predicting that, despite DGC's hopes for him, he was doomed to remain a cult favorite. Sooner or later he was going to find himself back on the street, only to be discovered all over again in a few years' time. When he died, my book was already in production and I could no longer make changes. Given the opportunity, I'm not sure I would have. Music as curious and fierce as Hawkins's speaks to the ages, and my hunch is that he's going to keep right on being rediscovered, posthumously.

The Oxford American, Southern Music Issue, 1997

Country vs. Western

COUNTRY AND WESTERN—WE HAVE BOTH

—A HANDWRITTEN SIGN OVER THE COUNTRY MUSIC
SECTION IN NINTH STREET RECORDS
AND BOOKS, PHILADELPHIA

I got more than I bargained for on a recent visit to a favorite record store when someone behind the counter decided to put on a new release I otherwise might not have given a second glance. I rarely pay attention to the music being played in record stores, most of which I find annoying, trendy, overfamiliar, or combinations thereof (techno, anyone?). But this was something else—something so catchy in its alphabet soup of influences that it defied you to tune it out.

Without being handed a copy of *Pee Wee King's Country Hoedown*, a two-CD collection of performances made for a radio transcription service in the early 1950s, all I would have been able to say for sure was that this was country music of an earlier vintage; it wasn't overproduced, as today's country recordings tend to be, though it resembled them in seeming as much pop as hard-core country. Cowpoke boogies followed honkytonk weepers, and I thought for a moment that what I was hearing might be an anthology from just after the Second World War, when the unhomogenized genre was still called country and western, in recognition of its blend of Southern and Southwestern accents. That era's country and western music seemed a fulfillment of what Jimmie Rodgers, the most influential country recording artist of the late 1920s, had been hinting at in his "Blue Yodel No. 1," where he sang that "T" was for Texas, as well as for Tennessee. Over the decades, the western part of the equation has disappeared, even though Garth Brooks, today's most popular country performer, is from Oklahoma and ten-gallon hats have become standard country issue. But whatever I was listening to was the original mix, and it was heady stuff.

There was even a polka, for heaven's sake, and this was when I finally noticed what turned out to be Pee Wee King's accordion, which had been there all along—trading riffs with the fiddle and pedal steel guitar on the jump tunes, supplying unfussy counterpoint behind the singer on the laments, and giving the band an unmistakable identity on both.

The singer on most of the numbers—Redd Stewart, I later discovered—had a touch of the pop crooner, despite his twang; his delivery was honeyed without being sugary. The band's musicianship was topnotch, and every so often—most jarringly on an otherwise kitschy novelty tune called "Slow Poke" that I dimly remembered from my childhood—there would be an unexpected chord change that would take this supposed hillbilly combo to the doorstep of jazz.

So who was this Pee Wee King? All I really knew about him, before my chance hearing of *Pee Wee King's Country Hoedown* (Soundies 312.222.1707), was that he and Stewart were the composers of "The Tennessee Waltz," a pop standard of sorts—even Sonny Rollins has recorded it—after being a landmark hit for Patti Page, in 1951 (the biggest-selling record of that year by almost two to one, it helped to popularize the use of multitracked vocals).

I was once on a panel with Robert Gottlieb, the editor of *Reading Jazz*, who explained that he had become interested in jazz criticism soon after becoming interested in jazz. "Nothing is ever real to me until I read about it," Gottlieb said; that has always been my philosophy too, though I wouldn't have been able to put it as well. Along with Bill C. Malone's liner notes to *Country Hoedown*, the best source of information on King proved to be Wade Hall's *Hell-Bent for Music*, a 1996 biography in which King—retired from music now and living in Louisville, Kentucky—gets to tell his story in his own words. King was an unlikely candidate to effect a synthesis of bluegrass and western swing; a native of Milwaukee, he was born Julius Frank Kuczynski in 1914, which I reckon explains the polka.

After leading his own bands as Frank King around the Midwest, playing a variety of pop and ethnic material, as well as country music, he took Pee Wee as his new handle when he hit the trail with Gene Autry's Log Cabin Boys, in 1934. He joined the radio cast of the Grand Ole Opry three years later, staying on as a regular for ten years, despite being something of an anomaly in Nashville—and not just because he played the accordion. At a time when most Opry regulars regarded themselves as semiprofessionals and dressed like farmhands to cultivate a homespun image, King made no bones about being in show business and didn't let the fact that he wasn't really a cowboy prevent him from dressing like one. King and his Golden West Cowboys took the stage in Stetsons and flamboyant rodeo wear specially tailored for them by Nudie, a rodeo designer popular with movie cowboys of the 1930s and country rock stars of the 1960s.

King's challenge to Nashville orthodoxy was not merely sartorial. It was his band that dragged the Opry into the modern age with drums, horns, and electric guitar. With "The Tennessee Waltz," which he and Stewart wrote in 1946 and first recorded two years later, hoping only to match the modest success of Bill Monroe's "Kentucky Waltz," King also played a crucial role in demonstrating the crossover potential of country music to pop record producers. Beyond the immediate benefit of spawning other No. 1 hits in the same vein (including Tony Bennett's cover of Hank Williams's "Cold, Cold Heart" and Rosemary Clooney's version of Stuart Hamblin's "This Old House"), Page's success with "The Tennessee Waltz" ultimately made it possible for country singers to put songs on the pop charts themselves (including King's own recording of "Slow Poke" in 1952) and readied the music world for Elvis Presley and rockabilly.

By 1951, when King and Stewart teamed with the lyricist Chilton Price to write "You Belong to Me," which soon became a No. 1 hit by Jo Stafford, they had at least one eye on the pop charts; not many of that era's "hillbilly" songs asked listeners to picture "pyramids along the Nile" and "the sunrise on a tropic isle." Thanks to the 1961 doo-wop version by the Duprees, the song has since become a staple on oldies radio, its country origins long forgotten.

King's own hits and his and Stewart's original recording of "The Tennessee Waltz" were for RCA Victor. Unavailable domestically, these

can be found on an eight-CD boxed set of King's complete RCA recordings, issued by the German label Bear Family. For nonobsessives, the
Soundies set is a splendid introduction to King's work, although there are
a few too many novelty tunes and most of the best material is crowded
together on the first disc. The set helps to answer the question of how a
star of the Grand Ole Opry and the host of his own network television
program in 1955 could have become so utterly forgotten. Over the
course of two hours, King's music occasionally seems a little contrived;
the pop savvy that worked to his advantage in the early 1950s creates
the suspicion of inauthenticity now. King's music is lighthearted in
mood even when the lyrics are about feeling lowdown. Stewart's phrasing is as supple as a jazz singer's, but his vocals never cut to the quick
like those of Hank Williams or Webb Pierce. And only on a nifty, Django
Reinhardt–inspired instrumental do the Golden West Cowboys swing
as hard as Bob Wills and His Texas Playboys did routinely.

Still, it's tough to say no to music this smart and quick on its feet. In
Hell-Bent for Music, King more than once refers to the Golden West
Cowboys as a dance band, and to himself as a performer dedicated to
pleasing his audience—not necessarily a lowly goal. *Pee Wee King's
Country Hoedown* begs to be listened to on its own terms: as extremely
agreeable regional dance music from a period when dancing was still a
national pastime, not the subcultural fetish it is now. This is a music that
is full of surprises, even if you're not as lucky as I was in having it catch
me by surprise.

The New York Times, January 23, 2000

Elvis Presley's
Double Consciousness

In Peter Guralnick's *Last Train to Memphis*, the first half of what will be a two-volume biography, we read that as a teenager Elvis Presley used to sing along with the groups at the all-night gospel meets he took a girl-friend to hear. This embarrassed Presley's girlfriend, particularly his habit of "trying to hit the low notes with the bass singer [and] the high ones with the lead tenor," though we can guess that she also found this irre-pressible urge of his rather endearing. This is just one detail in a book that vibrates with them, but it caught my eye because it reminded me of a similar moment on what's become my favorite of Presley's recordings— one Presley himself probably never heard.

I found a copy of it in a Boston record shop in 1984, seven years after Presley's death. Then available only as a bootleg, it's since been released through legitimate channels, most recently on an RCA compact disc as *The Complete Million Dollar Sessions*. It was recorded on the sly by Sam Phillips, of Sun Records, in his fabled studio on Union Avenue in Memphis on December 4, 1956, during what was supposed to have been a session by Carl Perkins, whose version of "Blue Suede Shoes" (his own song) had preceded Presley's up the charts earlier that year. As luck would have it, Jerry Lee Lewis was also at Sun that afternoon, sit-ting in with Perkins's band on piano. Johnny Cash, yet another of Phillips's contract artists, showed up just long enough to pose with

Perkins, Lewis, and Presley (who had dropped by ostensibly just to say hello) for a picture that ran in the following day's Memphis *Press-Scimitar*, above a paragraph describing a jam session by this "million dollar quartet." In truth, all that made the gathering newsworthy was Presley's part in it. The most Icarus-like of Phillips's discoveries wound up instigating an old-fashioned singalong. And Phillips, though he had sold Presley's contract to RCA Victor a year earlier and could no longer release new product by him, had the foresight to order an engineer to roll the tapes, strictly for posterity.

The music begins with a gospel medley, on which Lewis's boogie-woogie piano and the hepcat yowls during Perkins's guitar solos sound only slightly incongruous. Denounced as heathens by that era's guardians of public morality, Presley and other early Southern rockers tended to view them-selves as God-fearing men—one of the contradictions that gave early rock 'n' roll its tension. At one point, Elvis launches into a version of Ernest Tubb's country gospel tune "I'm with a Crowd, But Oh So Alone," and his hillbilly whine draws a groan from one of the other musicians. This reac-tion is affectionate and a little nervous, not derisive. The music is of a sort that these young men grew up with, and you can tell that this is what the others suspect they must sound like to Northerners.

Presley goes on to sing spirited versions of tunes made popular by Pat Boone, Chuck Berry, Hank Snow, Faron Young, and the Ink Spots, among others. All these are great fun, no matter how off-key both the instrumental backing and the vocal harmonies tend to be. But the moment I love comes about thirty minutes in, when Presley tells the oth-ers about an unnamed singer he heard in Las Vegas, a member of Billy Ward and the Dominoes who did "a thing on me" on "Don't Be Cruel." Noting in passing that the singer was "a colored guy" and praising his interpretation of the song as "much better than that record of mine," Presley explains that "he had it a little slower than me"—and then pro-ceeds to demonstrate. Prefacing each chorus with an explanatory "he said," he halves the tempo and gives the song a big finish, as Lewis gamely pumps away behind him.

But this "Don't Be Cruel" doesn't end there. For the next few minutes, Presley keeps breaking into the song every time there's a lull. He gets laughs with his imitation of the black "Yankee" singer's attempt to give the words of the song what the singer must have thought was a genuine

Southern pronunciation ("*telly*phone!" Perkins—or someone—shouts in amused disbelief). He describes how the singer grabbed the microphone on the last note and slid all the way down to the floor, how on certain lines he shook his head back and forth admonishingly, and how he had his feet turned in "and all the time he's singin', them feet was goin' in and out both ways, slidin' like this." Through all of this, you just know that he's illustrating the story by swooping to the floor himself, shaking his own head and swiveling his own feet. He even duplicates the Dominoes' background chants—along with their choreography.

The unidentified singer who so enthralled Presley (and whom Presley sounded nothing like) was Jackie Wilson, soon to have hits himself. A month later, as if to prove that imitation really is the sincerest form of flattery, Presley concluded his third and final appearance on *The Ed Sullivan Show* with a rendition of "Don't Be Cruel" that Guralnick tells us owed everything to Wilson's, "from finger rolls to his pronunciation of 'tellyphone' to the big pumped-up ending."

"IT SEEMED LIKE HE HAD A PHOTOGRAPHIC MEMORY FOR EVERY DAMNED SONG he ever heard," Phillips tells Guralnick. The venerable music critic Henry Pleasants once characterized Presley as a "naturally assimilative" stylist with a "multiplicity of voices"—that is, a gifted singer with an instinct for mimicry, whose music incorporated gospel, country, rhythm 'n' blues, Neapolitan opera, vaudeville recitation, and sticky early-50s pop of the sort that rock 'n' roll ultimately savaged.

Pop music as it has evolved alongside audio technology has resulted in what I think of as aural culture—similar to, but finally distinct from, the oral traditions on which folk music once depended. Aural culture takes the form of teenagers uninhibitedly singing along with records (if only in the privacy of their bedrooms) and imitating as best they can the sounds on them. Rock 'n' roll has been a form of aural culture from the beginning, and the Elvis who was captured that afternoon at Sun—already famous, already in movies, perched at No. 1 on the pop charts for the fifth time that year, but still only twenty-one—sounds like a kid emulating the vocal mannerisms of his favorite singers, less for the delectation of anyone who might be listening than for the thrill it gives *him* to hear those familiar voices vibrating in his own throat. He's his own juke box.

Although he emulated other singers' styles, Presley was no impersonator. His own personality emerged whether he was singing country, rhythm 'n' blues, or pop. The key to his originality, in something of a paradox, may have been his enthusiasm for so many different kinds of music and his refusal to distinguish between them.

At the time of the "Million Dollar" session, Presley's star was still rising, but the world was already beginning to close in on him. Earlier that year he had made his Las Vegas debut on a bill with the comedian Shecky Greene and the danceband leader Freddy Martin. This unlikely booking had been arranged by Tom Parker, the former carny hustler and honorary Louisiana colonel who had become Presley's manager and who was determined to expose him to adult audiences, which was where everyone assumed the real money was in those days. Most adults of the 1950s didn't know what to make of Presley, except to wish that he would go away. The engagement had been a fiasco, with *Newsweek* crowing that Presley was as out of place in Las Vegas as "a jug of corn liquor at a champagne party" (it being as OK then as it is now to poke fun at Southern white trash). In the stunned silence that greeted Presley's first number on opening night, the guitarist Scotty Moore and the bassist Bill Black realized that for the first time in months they were able to *hear* what they were playing behind him. To their horror, they were badly out of tune.

Presley had reached a point where he was being upstaged by his screaming female fans. In Memphis, his home town, it was becoming virtually impossible for him to leave the house without causing a near-riot. There had been teenage idols before—notably Frank Sinatra, little more than ten years earlier. What made the Presley phenomenon different was the specter of juvenile delinquency. He was being denounced in the editorial pages and (more disturbing to him) from the pulpit for leading youth astray with his voice, his sideburns, and his hips. His ascent had been so swift that it must have seemed like a dream to him, in danger of ending at any moment. In one way he was a creature of the recording studio. Before he cut his first commercial recording, in the Sun studio in the summer of 1954, he had performed in public only twice, singing Red Foley's "Old Shep" at a Mississippi state fair when he was ten, and Teresa Brewer's "Till I Waltz Again with You" at his high school talent show. Returning to Sun must have been like returning to the womb. This would be the last time that he would sing there, and he would never again sound so unguarded.

The reaction of Presley's fellow musicians to his performance is amusing. They go along with him at first, but after a while you can almost hear them wondering why he's making such a fuss about that singer he heard in Las Vegas. They're a little bit like that girlfriend, though not so much embarrassed for him as puzzled.

PRESLEY CONTINUES TO PUZZLE MANY OF US, WHICH MAY BE WHY HE HAS BEEN the subject of so much literature. Books have been published about his relationship with his mother, his army years, his mostly dreadful movies, the final hours of his life, kitsch collectibles bearing his image, and posthumous sightings of him. The books published about him this year alone have included one containing his favorite recipes and one from a Christian press about his untrumpeted philanthropy. Before Guralnick's, there was only one cradle-to-grave biography that I know of: an attempted harpooning by the late Albert Goldman, who went after the latter-day jump-suited pharmaceutical mutant of Graceland as vengefully as Ahab pursued his great white whale.

Nearly five hundred pages long, *Last Train to Memphis* ends with Presley's transport to Germany as a private first class in September 1958, a month after the death of his mother, Gladys, whom he adored and whose loss took some of the life out of him and his already rather passive father, Vernon. Guralnick's edge over the competition isn't simply a matter of his book's greater thoroughness. His previous books, which have included a history of soul music, a meditation on the life of Robert Johnson, and two collections of profiles of country and blues musicians, have won him such credibility that his was assumed to be the definitive Elvis biography the moment it was announced that he was working on it. Guralnick's sources, I think, sensed that this was going to be the last word on Elvis Presley, and opened themselves up accordingly.

Guralnik's first volume isn't a "critical" biography. Despite a wealth of information on Presley's stage shows and recording sessions, and on the role of Memphis disc jockeys in exposing white youths of Presley's generation to black rhythm 'n' blues, there isn't a great deal of musical analysis here. But *Last Train to Memphis* is clearly the work of someone who spent much of his adolescence looking for himself in the records he heard on the radio, just as Presley did. And the empathy that the author feels for his subject permits him to use his research as a springboard.

"He likes the company of women, he loves to be around women, women of all ages," Guralnick writes about Presley at the age of fifteen or sixteen, in an extended passage that conveys something of the book's texture and vibrato:

> His aunt Lillian notices it: "He'd get out there at night with the girls and he just sang his head off. He was different with the girls—I'm embarrassed to tell, but I think he'd rather have a whole bunch of girls around him than the boys—he didn't care a thing about the boys." The women seem to sense something coming out of him, something he himself may not even know he possesses: it is an aching kind of vulnerability, an unspecified yearning; when Sam Phillips meets him just two or three years later, in 1953, he senses much the same quality but calls it insecurity. "He tried not to show it, but he felt so *inferior*. He reminded me of a black man in that way; his insecurity was so *markedly* like that of a black person." Bathed in the soft glow of that streetlight, he appears almost handsome—the acne that embarrasses him doesn't show up so badly, and the adolescent features, which can appear coarse in the cold light of day, take on a kind of delicacy that is almost beautiful. He sings Eddy Arnold's "Molly Darling," Kay Starr's "Harbor Lights," Bing and Gary Crosby's "Moonlight Bay," all soft, sweet songs, in a soft, slightly quavering voice, and then, satisfied, takes his comb out of his back pocket and runs it through his hair in a practiced gesture clearly at odds with his hesitancy of manner.

All of Guralnick's major themes are woven together here: Presley's ability to mimic the singers he heard on the radio, the hint of mother-love and the role his own girlishness played in his attraction and appeal to women, his insecurity as a result of having grown up dirt-poor (the Memphis housing project he lived in as a teenager was a step up for the Presleys, who are described by a former Mississippi neighbor as a family who moved whenever their rent was due), the "blackness" that his first record producer and others sensed in him, and the extent to which the Elvis Presley who exploded on America in 1956 was a teenage misfit's successful attempt to reinvent himself as the most popular boy in class.

Professional musicians sometimes like to give the impression that theirs is the best job of all, in that they're being paid to do what they would be doing just for fun. Stardom is frequently a variation on that theme, and on the idea that the whole world's a stage. You only had to look at Duke Ellington to realize that he was so much the bon vivant he would have found a way to wear finery and hobnob with heads of state even if he hadn't been blessed with prodigious musical talent. To Presley's way of thinking, becoming a star was the only alternative to the role of total nonentity to which his family's low social standing and his own shyness might otherwise have doomed him. ("If you picture him," Guralnick advises us early on, "picture someone you might have missed: a wide-eyed, silent child, scuffling his feet, wearing overalls.") This is someone who acquired what amounted to a stage wardrobe long before setting foot on any stage. Though various classmates remember him as a "loner," "a sad, shy, not especially attractive boy," some also remember him as a peacock who would show up for classes at Humes High School in bolero jackets and dress pants with stripes down the sides that made him look like a carhop (not the effect he intended). Guralnick notes that when Presley started making movies, he eschewed acting lessons because "I want to be me." But in being just Elvis Presley, he was already in character.

PRESLEY BOUGHT THE WILD DUDS THAT GURALNICK IDENTIFIES AS ONE OF THE first manifestations of "his determination to be himself—his determination to be a *different* self" from a clothing store on Beale Street, Memphis's black hub. Presley's debt to black culture is another of the book's recurring themes, as well it should be—it's the aspect of Presley's career that remains controversial.

"Elvis was a hero to most, but he never meant shit to me," ranted Chuck D, the lead singer and chief ideologue of the rap group Public Enemy, on the group's 1989 song "Fight the Power," which was featured over the closing credits of Spike Lee's *Do the Right Thing*. Some people are always going to assume that, because Presley was a white Southerner who rose to fame around the time of the Montgomery bus boycott and the murder of Emmett Till, he was "a straight-up racist . . . simple and plain," as Chuck D put it. Some African-Americans remain convinced that Presley once said "the only thing Negroes can do for me is buy my records and shine my shoes"—a vicious rumor of the late 1950s that Guralnick convincingly demonstrates had no basis in fact.

To some people, white as well as black, Presley is always going to be a sideburned parasite, a white boy who made a bundle by singing like a black man and shaking his hips like one without acknowledging his debt. In fact, he was quite forthcoming about his black influences. "The colored folks have been singing it and playing it just like I'm doin' now, man, for more years than I know," he told an interviewer in 1956. Guralnick cites this and several other interviews in which Presley uttered similar sentiments. Besides, the young Presley listened to, enjoyed, and copied all manner of performers. Among the early influences on him were a white gospel quartet called the Statesmen, whose members included Jake Hess, an emotive lead tenor described by Guralnick as "a spectacular singer with the kind of soaring tenor and controlled vibrato that Elvis would explicitly aspire to," and Jim Wetherington, a bass singer nicknamed the Big Chief who stirred up church audiences with his onstage shaking, which some fundamentalist ministers denounced as lewd.

Presley's early muses were radio and records, and much of his exposure to black music came through them. In that way he was no different from most white youths of his day, regardless of where they happened to live. But as a Southerner during a time when, despite legal segregation, there was probably more daily contact between the races in Mississippi than anywhere in the North, Presley also enjoyed firsthand exposure to black life. Just after the Second World War, his family lived for a brief time in Tupelo, practically across the street from Shake Rag, the city's most densely populated black neighborhood. Within earshot of what Guralnick describes as the quarter's "tumultuous bursts of song," Elvis may also have been drawn to Shake Rag's "sharp flashes of emotion, the bright splashes of color, the feelings so boldly on display." By the time he entered seventh grade, the Presleys were living in an apartment actually in Tupelo's more "respectable" black neighborhood, though in a building understood to be set aside for whites—a distinction that, as Guralnick points out, was perfectly clear to Vernon and Gladys Presley but may have been lost on their twelve-year-old son, who possibly recognized something of his own family's values in those of the neighborhood's black strivers.

Blackness truly does seem to have rubbed off on Elvis Presley, who sang rhythm 'n' blues as unself-consciously as he sang country music, and whose first Sun release, in 1954—a version of Arthur Crudup's 1946 blues hit "That's All Right" backed with Bill Monroe's "Blue Moon of Kentucky"—was about as perfect an expression as you could hope to find of his Southern racial double consciousness. This was just one of the dualities that Elvis embodied. He was a studied natural, a mama's boy with manners who became a role model for a generation of rebellious youth (imagine him playing Brando's role in *The Wild One*: "What are you kids rebelling against?" "Uh, whatta you got . . . sir?"), a kid who could hit both the high notes and the low ones, a biographical subject whose life almost demands to be examined in two parts (when his image was put on a postage stamp, there was a national referendum on whether it should be Young Elvis, the lean progenitor of rock 'n' roll, or Fat Elvis, the camp icon). *Last Train to Memphis* is subtitled "The Rise of Elvis Presley," as if to confirm that volume two will be about the descent—about how the stardom that Presley wished on himself ultimately made him captive, increasing his sense of otherness and cutting him off from his original sources of inspiration. Even with the sympathetic Guralnick telling the story, it figures to make for grim reading.

ELVIS PRESLEY IS ONE OF THE REASONS THAT MEGASTARDOM OF THE SORT THAT he virtually defined has been equated with loneliness, isolation, and mental and physical rot—with tragedy waiting to happen. Stardom of such magnitude inevitably invites the fantasy that the performer in question might have been happier doing something else with his life—or doing the same thing on a smaller, more lifesize scale. Frank Sinatra now usually sings with orchestras in massive sports arenas that make a joke of the implied intimacy with each of his listeners on which his phrasing has always depended, and which is now about all he has left as a singer. Sinatra should be performing with just a pianist in tiny cabarets. But he can't because he's Frank Sinatra, not Bobby Short or even Tony Bennett. Intimacy would be an affront to his fans who were shut out.

The only time I saw Presley live, in 1971, he was essentially imitating Tom Jones, a crude caricature of Presley to begin with and a far cry from Jackie Wilson. I guess he'd caught Jones's act in Vegas and felt both flattered and challenged. It could have been worse. I had the feeling that for years the only music Presley had listened to closely had been "demos" of tunes written in the hope that he would record them, performed in rough fashion by their composers or by anonymous singers chosen for their ability to emulate him. No wonder he became such a self-parody. Maybe he missed his calling. Given his ability to sing practically anything, he might have been the greatest demo singer who ever lived, a record-industry cult figure, a sane and healthy man. But then he wouldn't have been Elvis Presley—at least not in the way his name will forever imply.

According to a slim, pocket-size book of "little-known facts about Elvis" that I recently came across while standing on line at the supermarket, he was offered the role of Joe Buck opposite Dustin Hoffmann in *Midnight Cowboy*—a role for which he would have been a natural: a stud who thinks he's irresistible to women but whose primary appeal is to other men. I doubt Tom Parker informed him of the offer, assuming the story is true. Elvis's last movie was *Change of Habit*, in which he played a ghetto doctor opposite Mary Tyler Moore as a nun who falls in love with him. In the final scene, as she considers breaking her vows, Moore prays for guidance. God or Elvis? Elvis or God? We're not told which one she chooses, just that she faces a difficult choice.

The Atlantic Monthly, October 1994

Beached

<hr>

"Miss Carpenter. Please. I know my own business," the young man said. "You just keep your eyes open for any bananafish. This is a perfect day for bananafish."

"I don't see any," Sybil said.

"That's understandable. Their habits are very peculiar. Very peculiar." He kept pushing the float. The water was not quite up to his chest. "They lead a very tragic life," he said. "You know what they do, Sybil?"

She shook her head.

"Well, they swim into a hole where there's a lot of bananas. They're very ordinary-looking fish when they swim in. But once they get in, they behave like pigs. Why, I've known some bananafish to swim into a banana hole and eat as many as seventy-eight bananas." He edged the float and its passenger a foot closer to the horizon. "Naturally, after that they're so fat they can't get out of the hole again. Can't fit through the door."

—J.D. SALINGER, "A PERFECT DAY FOR BANANAFISH"

Like most solitary activities, reading encourages daydreaming, and this might explain why a book can call up memories of another to which it bears absolutely no resemblance. I hadn't thought of J.D. Salinger's short stories for years, until starting *Wouldn't It Be Nice?*, the autobiography of Brian Wilson, the former Beach Boy whose songs for his group— about little deuce coupes, California girls, and the warmth of the sun— are themselves part of my generation's collective memory. (Wilson wrote the book with Todd Gold, a reporter for *People* magazine.) "A Perfect

Day for Bananafish" sentimentalizes childhood, ends with a suicide, and takes place, for the most part, on the beach. I first read it, in Salinger's *Nine Stories*, in the summer of 1963, when its author was still fashionable and the Beach Boys were on the radio with Wilson's "Surfer Girl."

When not lost in a book, I spent that summer fine-tuning my transistor with the skill of a safe-cracker, listening to my local Philadelphia stations but pulling in signals from cities as far away as Chicago and Indianapolis on clear nights. It was on a station from Buffalo, of all places, that I first heard "Surfer Girl," a ballad so tender in its evocation of beaches and blondes that it sounded sunburned. Its intricate and shapely vocal harmonies, which I later found out were inspired by those of the Four Freshmen, a 1950s jazz vocal group, gave me goosebumps, even through the static.

But my reason for dragging Salinger into this is that Wilson is pop music's biggest bananafish—bigger than even Elvis Presley, who, in his own way, rewrote the book on the artist as social invalid, substituting gluttonous overindulgence in fats and pharmaceuticals for the asceticism of a Dickinson or Proust (or the asceticism of Salinger and his tiresome Seymour Glass, bananafish of a leaner, more sensitive school). In an amusing anecdote in *Wouldn't It Be Nice?*, Wilson tells us that his only meeting with Presley, in a Los Angeles recording studio in 1969, ended with The King shaking his head in disbelief and saying to his entourage, "Let's go, boys. This guy's crazy."

CELEBRITY-COMEBACK SAGAS, THE GENRE INTO WHICH WILSON'S BOOK FALLS, usually begin with the narrator's having hit rock-bottom and then backtrack in an effort to explain what precipitated the fall. *Wouldn't It Be Nice?* starts off in 1982, as Wilson—"a zonked-out zombie, a star-crossed sixties head who took a drug trip and never returned," "a grown man [then forty] who functioned with the emotional capacity of a deeply disturbed six-year-old"—is told of his expulsion from the Beach Boys. Wilson had formed the group in 1961. The other original members were his younger brothers Dennis and Carl, their cousin Mike Love, and Al Jardine, a football teammate of Brian's in high school in Hawthorne, California, a working-class suburb of Los Angeles. In the beginning, record buyers probably had trouble figuring out which striped-shirted Beach Boy was which, but the group began as an extension of Wilson's vision as a songwriter and record producer. Although he generally didn't write the Beach Boys' lyrics, he did practically everything else.

"The songs might have sounded simple," Wilson observes later in the book, presumably meaning the Beach Boys' early string of hits beginning with "Surfin' Safari" in 1962,

> but the complex weave and backgrounds and textures were all thoroughly thought out before I ever got into the studio. Only after I heard the finished song in my head did I begin building the tracks in the studio. I knew exactly what instruments I wanted, the arrangements, and the vocals. Everyone learned his part individually, a process that made perfect sense to me because I knew how the final version would sound. But it left the other guys in the dark till the end, infuriated.

By 1982 what infuriated the rest of the Beach Boys was that Wilson's songs were never leaving his head, and perhaps not going on even there. "Back in those days, I was content to live inside myself, a mass of misery and confusion," writes Wilson, who, in addition to smoking five or six packs of Marlboros a day, was "consuming unthinkable quantities of junk food, booze, and cocaine," not to mention untold cups of "megacoffee," each made with as many as six scoops of instant-coffee crystals and "sugar—lots of it." Then carrying 340 pounds on his once athletic six-foot-two-inch frame, Wilson also neglected personal hygiene out of fear that the faucets in his bathroom would run blood, snakes, or fire. "In the past two years, I'd been sponged in the hospital and taken the rare dip in the pool, but I hadn't showered or bathed once."

Divorced from his wife, Marilyn, and discouraged by her from seeing their daughters, Carnie and Wendie (now members of the pop group Wilson Phillips), he was then living with Carolyn Williams, ostensibly his nurse but "more like a wife or girlfriend," and her three children. Williams "stocked the house with food and booze, masturbated me when I wanted, but otherwise left me alone." Indeed, Wilson writes, she left him alone to the point of not bothering to phone for help when he passed out on the floor after inhaling four full grams of cocaine. When he came to, the next morning, she blithely asked Wilson to call his accountant to ask for money.

The call was to no avail. Wilson was "broke and in arrears to the IRS"—or so he was led to believe by the Beach Boys and their management, who were attempting to force him back into the care of Dr. Eugene Landy, an unorthodox California psychotherapist whom they had fired as Wilson's keeper five years earlier.

Wilson had ceased touring full time with the Beach Boys in 1965, needing solitude to write the group's songs and produce its records. But along with drugs and the emotional wounds inflicted on him by a physically abusive father and an indifferent alcoholic mother, Wilson blames his nearly fatal tailspin on the strain of being both his group's *auteur* and its cash-cow. In the early 1960s, he writes, Capitol Records pressured him into delivering enough material for as many as four albums a year, and a contract the Beach Boys signed with Columbia Records in 1977 stipulated that Wilson—by then deep in his funk—had to supply at least eighty percent of the group's new songs. Considering that Wilson's output had been decreasing since 1967 or so, when he had withdrawn into himself to work on *Smile,* his unfinished "teenage symphony to God," some might argue that his dementia resulted from his having taken to absurd extremes the hedonistic consumership extolled in some of his most famous songs.

This, however, strikes me as an uncharitable way of looking at Wilson's plight, even though it's true that the Beach Boys have become synonymous with summer and mindless fun on the beach, much as Guy Lombardo once was synonymous with New Year's Eve and hypocritical Auld Lang Synes. Along with "Fun, Fun, Fun" and the other joyrides most people think of when they hear the Beach Boys mentioned, Wilson has written songs that illuminate—as Mark Moses, who wrote about pop music for *The New Yorker* until his death, in 1989, eloquently put it— "the melancholy longing that hides just behind those songs' easy good times."

Moses cited Wilson's "In My Room," a song whose anthem-like melody and lyrics (by Gary Usher, one of Wilson's numerous songwriting partners) delineate the fine line an emotionally isolated teenager is likely to draw between privacy and loneliness, as quite possibly "the saddest song in all of rock." Wilson himself refers to "In My Room" frequently in *Wouldn't It Be Nice?,* recalling either pianos in empty recording studios or the one in the music room of his parents' house (the room he moved his bed into as a teenager). But even among Wilson's own songs, "In My Room" faces stiff competition from the two that open and close the 1966 album *Pet Sounds,* his masterpiece.

"Caroline, No," the final number on *Pet Sounds*, is the ultimate breakup song, but it's also about "growing up and the loss of innocence," as Wilson describes it. Graced by one of his most harmonically sinuous melodies, it ends with the sound of his dog (named Banana, of all things) barking at a speeding train. ("Can't you just see me on the back of that train?" Wilson asks his wife, without waiting for an answer. "I can. Just going away.")

What's heartbreaking about "Wouldn't It Be Nice?," the surging, uptempo song that opens *Pet Sounds*, is its virginal ebullience: It's a teenager's idyllic vision of what married life will be like, which urges you to forget that things seldom work out that way. Songs such as these (and "The Warmth of the Sun," "Don't Worry, Baby," and "I Just Wasn't Made for These Times") enable us to overlook the adolescent specificity of their lyrics. Divorced men and women who hear "Wouldn't It Be Nice?" probably find themselves thinking of their ex-spouses and wondering what went wrong.

Wilson's sad songs can also affect the way we hear his odes to joy. Written by a young man who spent far more time on the piano bench than on the beach (and whose ocean phobia prevented him from ever mounting a surfboard), Wilson's songs turn out to be less about fun than about the unfulfilled desire for it. I think that's why they struck a chord with me as a teenager who had no access to a car, much less to surf, and I know that's why they still strike a chord with me as an adult.

ASIDE FROM WILSON HIMSELF, THE CENTRAL FIGURES IN HIS AUTOBIOGRAPHY are his late father, Murry Wilson, and his shrink. Wilson says that his father terrorized him as a child, savagely beating him and once even throwing a newspaper on the kitchen floor and ordering him to defecate on it. A second-rate songwriter himself (a group called the Bachelors recorded his "Two Step Side Step" in 1952, and Lawrence Welk once played it on TV), the elder Wilson appointed himself the Beach Boys' manager. After badgering Brian into signing over the publishing rights to his songs, Murry sold the catalogue for a quick $700,000 in 1969—petty cash, given the millions that Wilson's songs have earned for their new copyright holders in the years since.

Eugene Landy is the man Wilson credits with springing him from his bananahole. A strict behaviorist, Landy put Wilson under round-the-clock team surveillance, believing that (in Wilson's words) "if a patient's behavior was changed, his feelings and emotions would change accordingly." Regaining control of Wilson in 1982 and immediately weaning him from drugs and empty calories, Landy brought his weight down to a fit 186 pounds within three years, Wilson says. To teach Wilson self-dependence, he enrolled him in a wilderness-survival program. He retaught him such everyday skills as shopping for groceries and making small talk at the dinner table. (At one moment in *Wouldn't It Be Nice?*, Wilson, obeying Landy's instructions to look people in the eye and introduce himself in a firm but friendly tone, says before a concert, "Hello, I'm Brian Wilson," to his daughter, Carnie, whom he's failed to recognize.)

"The only person I'd ever really listened to before was my dad," Wilson writes.

> I listened to him solely because he made me. He beat me. He threatened me with pain. He tortured me psychologically. . . .
> Lo and behold, Landy comes into my life and he has the same power. He beat me too—but not physically, like my dad. He beat me at my own Scrabble game in my head. It was dumbfounding how he got inside my head, knew my thoughts.

But Landy—whom Wilson credits with teaching him how to live, though it sounds more like Wilson is imitating life—had more in common with Murry Wilson than Brian indicates: The Good Doctor fancies himself a songwriter too. With Landy's encouragement, Wilson started writing songs again and resumed his recording career with an uncertain-sounding solo album called *Brian Wilson*, released in 1989. Landy's name appears alongside Wilson's as co-composer (presumably lyricist) of two of that album's eleven songs, and on two others Wilson shares credit with Landy and Alexandra Morgan, Landy's longtime fiancée.

In 1988, shortly before California's Board of Medical Quality Assurance challenged Landy's credentials on the basis of a complaint filed in 1984 by Carolyn Williams, Landy released Wilson from his care, referring him to a colleague and becoming his (as Wilson explains it) "friend, partner, and manager," rather than his analyst. Citing the stress that court proceedings would put on Wilson's fragile psyche, Landy agreed to a two-year suspension of his practice in California, although he remained licensed in New Mexico and Hawaii.

On last April Fool's Day, Landy agreed to dissolve his business partnership with Wilson and to have no contact at all with him for a period of ninety days, in exchange for which Carl Wilson, of the Beach Boys, agreed to postpone what amounts to a custody suit for his brother.

Wouldn't It Be Nice? thus ends like a cliffhanger, with Brian Wilson's fate still uncertain even at press time. Aside from these recent developments, the book reveals little that anyone who's followed Wilson's and the Beach Boys' fortunes over the years doesn't already know. The old news includes Wilson's sexual relationship with his wife's older sister, Diane, and his unconsummated desire for her younger sister, Barbara; the drowning death, in 1983, of Wilson's brother and fellow drug abuser Dennis; and the musical disagreements between Wilson and his cousin Mike Love, who from the beginning opposed Wilson's moodier and more experimental songs and under whose de facto leadership the Beach Boys have become balding, paunchy teenagers, an enjoyable-to-hear but painful-to-watch oldies act. All of this and more has been detailed in other books, most notably Steven Gaines's exemplary *Heroes and Villains: The True Story of the Beach Boys* (1986).

Even so, Wilson's unironic first-person telling of his own sad and often sordid story can break your heart, just like the idealistic optimism of the song from which *Wouldn't It Be Nice?* borrows its name—and just like that dog barking at the train at the end of "Caroline, No."

The Atlantic Monthly, November 1991

Everybody's Composer

The Man from Heaven

B urt Bacharach, the composer with the lyricist Hal David of "The Look of Love," "(They Long to Be) Close to You," and "Do You Know the Way to San Jose," was once the subject of an article in an academic quarterly, though the larger social significance of those and his other pop hits of the 1960s and early 1970s would seem to be nil. Almost two years after Bacharach won a pair of Oscars for his work on the movie *Butch Cassady and the Sundance Kid*, one for best original score and the other for "Raindrops Keep Fallin' on My Head," Bruce A. Lohof's "The Bacharach Phenomenon: A Study in Popular Heroism" appeared in the Winter 1972 issue of *Popular Music and Society*, a journal at Bowling Green State University. Lohof discussed Bacharach's music in some detail, acknowledging its melodic sophistication and metrical complexity, but what most interested him was Bacharach's emergence as a "national idol"—a celebrity songwriter who was to his day what Stephen Foster, Irving Berlin, George Gershwin, and Cole Porter had been to theirs.

According to Lohof, Bacharach met several of the criteria of popular (as opposed to classical) heroism that had been outlined by a sociologist named Orrin E. Klapp some twenty years earlier. Bacharach's two Oscars, along with a pair of 1970 Grammys, qualified as "formal recognition and honor." As for "the building up of an idealized image or legend of the hero," two television specials devoted to Bacharach and a series of best-selling albums that featured him conducting orchestral versions of his hits had gained for him a degree of visibility almost unheard of for a songwriter not primarily identified as a singer. He had even appeared on the cover of *Newsweek*. And though Lohof discreetly downplayed the point, it didn't hurt that Bacharach was married to the actress Angie Dickenson, a thinking man's trophy blonde who had been John Wayne's love interest in *Rio Bravo*, Frank Sinatra's in *Oceans Eleven*, and, according to rumor, one of John F. Kennedy's in real life.

Lohof's thesis appeared to be that a modern-day hero like Bacharach, as much image as flesh and blood, was made of flimsier stuff than the mythological heroes of antiquity; finding an opportunity for analogy in the fact that Bacharach was then renting a mansion in Beverly Hills because he was too impatient to have one built, Lohof concluded that Bacharach was himself a "rented" hero who filled the needs of a technological society that was in too much of a hurry to pay more than lip service to the enduring virtues of an Achilles or Odysseus. On what seems to have been intended as a lighter note, the author observed that Bacharach's "total" heroism—his fulfillment of Klapp's final two criteria, "commemoration" and "the establishment of a cult"—might depend on his death in an automobile accident or plane crash.

Yet a quarter century later, after dying only in the metaphorical, show-business sense—nothing new on the pop charts for a seven-year stretch beginning in 1974, and then no new hits after Patti LaBelle and Michael McDonald's No. 1 recording of "On My Own" in 1986—Bacharach has seen his name become synonymous with the craft of songwriting at its most elegant and imperiled. He is a cultural signifier—far more meaningful than being the face on a posthumous postage stamp. Just as John Coltrane's name is dropped by black essayists and novelists to signify artistic commitment and racial pride, Bacharach's is pressed into service by pop reviewers to commend groups that at least recognize the value of good songs, even if they haven't figured out how to write any yet.

OLDIES RADIO, WHERE DIONNE WARWICK AND DUSTY SPRINGFIELD'S RECORD-ings of Bacharach's songs are staples, has inherited the role once played by cabaret singers and jazz instrumentalists in determining which songs will survive from one generation to the next. But Bacharach's hits of nearly thirty years ago are among the very few of their era to be cherished not just as "oldies" (that is, as period songs by specific performers), but as "standards" comparable in quality to the best-known songs of Irving Berlin, George Gershwin, Cole Porter, Jerome Kern, Harold Arlen, Frank Loessor, and Rodgers and Hart. By this point, more people know Bacharach and David's "(They Long to Be) Close to You" than know Kern's "Long Ago and Far Away"; more people know their "I'll Never Fall in Love Again," from *Promises, Promises*, than know Loessor's "I've Never Been in Love Before," from *Guys and Dolls*.

Bacharach and David's hits, because they were pop rather than rock, were anomalies in their own day—bridges across the generational divide, built by men born in the late 1920s, whose musical sensibilities were formed before the onslaught of rock 'n' roll. While competing for a rung on the Top 40 with Lennon and McCartney and with the Motown songwriting and producing team of Holland-Dozier-Holland, Bacharach and David were also competing for movie assignments with such older writers as Dimitri Tiomkin, Johnny Mercer, and Jimmy Van Heusen. ("Raindrops Keep Fallin' on My Head" was Bacharach and David's fourth song to be nominated for an Oscar, following their title songs for *A House Is Not a Home* and *Alfie*, and "The Look of Love," from *Casino Royale*).

Bacharach and David were also, however fleetingly, men of the theater. On her 1995 album *The Story Goes On*, the cabaret singer Liz Callaway includes a medley of "Promises, Promises" and "Knowing When to Leave," from Bacharach and David's only Broadway score, alongside songs from *Annie Get Your Gun*, *South Pacific*, and *Merrily We Roll Along*. The two Bacharach and David songs sound out of place in this company only because Callaway, with the overearnestness typical of so many younger cabaret performers, sounds as if she's mentally counting beats on them. Her rendition of "Promises, Promises"—a song that starts off in a 3/4 time too fast and diabolically syncopated to be called a waltz and then changes meter twenty times, often after just one bar— makes one yearn for Warwick, Bacharach and David's premier interpreter. On her hit 1968 recording of the song Warwick refused to be thrown by any of this rhythmic trickery, let alone by the many notes she was required to hold for an entire measure while the chords and instrumentation behind her shifted along with the rhythm.

Warwick appeared with Bacharach on cable television last New Year's Eve. American Movie Classics promoted their gala concert at the Rainbow Room (which had been taped several weeks earlier) as an attempt to restore "elegance" and "glamour" to a New York New Year's Eve—that is, as an alternative to the hubbub of Dick Clark and rock 'n' roll in Times Square. Thus Bacharach was positioned as the new Guy Lombardo.

Yet Bacharach, in the language of marketing demographics, also "skews" young, and this is what I find surprising—that with no apparent effort on his part he has become a figure of cult adulation among the young. A tip-off that Bacharach was again becoming at least a mini-phenomenon was the color poster of him as he looked thirty years ago, plainly visible on the lower left-hand corner of *Definitely Maybe* (1994), the first CD by Oasis, a British group that has since become a favorite on college and alternative-rock stations. Noel Gallagher, the group's primary songwriter and lead guitarist, joined Bacharach on stage to sing "This Guy's in Love with You" during one of Bacharach's concerts in London last year.

Gallagher's own songs sound nothing like those of his reputed idol's: They have too much guitar, and too much adolescent snarl. But his admiration for Bacharach seems genuine, in contrast to those younger musicians whose admiration for Bacharach takes the form of a postmodern smirk. In San Francisco, for example, a band called Burt plays nothing but Bacharach songs, though before making too much of this, you should know that yet another Bay Area band, called Herb, plays nothing but old hits by Herb Alpert and the Tijuana Brass. Rumor has it that Green Day will record a version of "Do You Know the Way to San Jose" for a Hollywood Records collection called *Loungapalooza*, and no one will be surprised if the thunderous grunge band gives this catchiest of Bacharach's numbers a nose ring and a few unsightly tattoos.

Not all of the younger performers playing Bacharach's songs are having sly fun at his expense. The most awkwardly sincere of recent Bacharach tributes, and also the most ambitious, is *Great Jewish Music: Burt Bacharach* (Tzadik TZ 7114-20), a two-disc set produced by the avant-garde composer John Zorn for his own label, on which instrumentalists and singers from Zorn's orbit of noisemakers and deconstructionists give what perhaps only they would consider to be reasonably faithful interpretations of Bacharach classics. "More than great pop songs," Zorn writes in his liner notes, "[these songs] are deep explorations of the materials of music and should be studied and treated with as much diligence as we accord any great work of art." He might have added that it seems the peculiar fate of major artists to attract disciples they might be hard put to recognize as theirs.

THE TITLE *GREAT JEWISH MUSIC* TELLS US MORE ABOUT ZORN, WHO NOW GIVES interviews only to the Jewish press, than it does about Bacharach, who has never made an issue of his religion or ethnicity. Still, the title serves to remind us that songwriting was a quick way up the ladder for the Jewish songwriters of Irving Berlin's generation—Eastern-European immigrants and their sons. Popular songwriting in the first few decades of this century was as much a business as an art, often less dependent on inspiration than on salesmanship. Berlin, if asked the secret of his success as he made the rounds of publishers along Tin Pan Alley in the 1920s, might have given the same reply as a man in dry goods or the rag trade: *"Volume!"* The true secret was writing all manner of songs and peddling them to all manner of singers, in the hope that a few tunes would capture the public's fancy.

Berlin wrote more great songs than any other American songwriter, but he also wrote hundreds that no one remembers. Bacharach and David, too, wrote their share of forgotten songs, beginning with two that actually made the Top 40 in 1957 and 1958—"Magic Moments," recorded by Perry Como, and "The Story of My Life," recorded by the country singer Marty Robbins. (As journeymen, Bacharach and David also contributed title songs to movies that didn't particularly need any, including *The Blob*, a Jerry Lewis vehicle called *The Sad Sack*, and John Ford's *The Man Who Shot Liberty Valance*.) Whatever else had changed about the music business, songwriting was still a hustle. Writers were the first workers on an assembly line that included music publishers, independent record producers, record-company directors of artists-and-repertoire, arrangers, singers, promotion men, and disc jockeys. A good way to persuade a singer like Gene Pitney to record your latest song was to model it on one of his earlier hits. But what if Pitney or his label rejected the song? It had to be something that another singer could hear himself doing without appearing to be feeding off Pitney's leavings (Bacharach and David's "Blue on Blue," a Top 10 hit for the insipid Bobby Vinton in 1963, sounds like it was written with Pitney in mind, as a sound-alike follow-up to his hit of the team's "Only Love Can Break a Heart" from the previous year).

Singers were considered interchangeable during this period, and so were songwriters. Without consulting a reference book, I can never remember that it was Gerry Goffin and Carole King who wrote "Point of No Return" for Gene McDaniels, and Bacharach and Bob Hilliard who wrote "Tower of Strength," instead of the other way around (both of these songs from the early 1960s stuck to the bouncy formula devised by Bob Elgin, Luther Dixon, and Kay Roger on "A Hundred Pounds of Clay," McDaniels's first huge hit). This system of making music hardly encouraged experimentation or originality, but it somehow produced a steady stream of songs that still sound great when you hear them on the radio today.

Common wisdom has it that nothing of lasting value occurred in pop between Elvis Presley's induction into the Army in 1958 and the Beatles' arrival in the United States in 1964. In conspiracy with other manic rockabilly and renegade rhythm 'n' blues acts like Little Richard and Chuck Berry, Presley is supposed to have "blackened" pop—to have loosened both its beat and its restraints, giving voice to rude emotions pop had never before been allowed to express. A few years later, the story goes, the Beatles and Bob Dylan came along and shut down the assembly line for good, reshaping pop into a vehicle for self-expression by performing their own songs. The period in between is supposed to have been dominated by innocuous pop idols mouthing (to the best of their limited abilities) words and melodies provided by hacks whose only incentive was a fat royalty check.

Of course, this isn't the way it seemed if, like me, you were a teenager with an ear glued to a transistor radio. Nor is it the way that pop of the early 1960s sounds to me now, as a middle-aged adult. It isn't nostalgia that makes me think of the Shirelles' 1961 recording of Goffin and King's "Will You Still Love Me Tomorrow" as a great record. It could be the way the song combines the identities of the young white woman who co-wrote it, the young black women who sang it, and that era's teenage girls, who fretted over the consequences of surrendering their virginity and for whom "Will You Still Love Me Tomorrow" became a tremulous anthem (an example of the consumer putting the finishing touches to the product).

During the first several years of their partnership, Bacharach and David each continued to work with other collaborators, aiming songs at both the adult and the teen market with occasional commercial success but little artistic distinction. They seemed an unlikely bet to surpass not just Goffin and King, but Lennon and McCartney, to become the lead-ing songwriting team of their era. The song that is usually pointed to as their breakthrough is "Don't Make Me Over," the first of their numbers to be recorded by Dionne Warwick, in 1962. To that day's teenagers it was simply another "slow" song: a dreamy record of the sort that a TV dance show host might designate a ladies' choice. In retrospect it seems one of the most innovative songs of the early 1960s, if only for the way its meter vacillated between 12/8 and 6/8 (each an uncommon time sig-nature in pop) and for the way Bacharach's orchestration spaces Warwick and the background singers so far apart. It was followed the next year by "Anyone Who Had a Heart," an erotic chant with passages in 5/4 (a signature only then becoming popular in jazz, as a result of its use by Dave Brubeck and Paul Desmond), and the majestic "Walk On By," with its driving woodblocks, flügelhorns, and strings. These proved to be the earliest in a long string of hits by Warwick of Bacharach and David songs which lasted into 1970, spanning what are usually defined as two pop eras.

Warwick has since become a figure of fun, because of her infomercials for the Psychic Friends Network. As singers frequently do when age robs them of breath and plays havoc with their pitch, she cheated quite a bit in the Rainbow Room show with Bacharach. She changed the legato connecting phrase she sang to such thrilling effect on her record of "Do You Know the Way to San Jose" (the *oooh* before "L.A. is a great big free-way") into a bumpy legato *A-oh, A-oh*; she didn't even chance "Promises, Promises." In her prime, though, Warwick was Aretha Franklin's only rival as the finest female pop singer of the 1960s, and she surpassed Franklin in versatility. Atypically for singers of that period, Warwick was a trained musician—a music student who was part of a gospel group that was doing studio backup vocals when Bacharach and David happened upon her. She sounded as though she could sing anything put in front of her, and when Bacharach started writing for her, he began sprinkling his melodies with accidentals and descending intervals greater than a fifth.

Bacharach and David never worked exclusively with Warwick, and the series of hits they wrote for Gene Pitney in the early 1960s demon-strate the ingenuity they brought to assignments that might just as easily have resulted in confectionery ballads and corny novelty tunes. The Bacharach and David song for Pitney that most people are likely to remember is "Only Love Can Break a Heart," a tearjerker in keeping with Pitney's image as the most sensitive of that day's male pinups—the one in whose voice the ache seemed most genuine. A song more worth remembering is the follow-up: "True Love Never Runs Smooth," a full-blown chanson disguised as a cha-cha, with what sounds like an accordion and a zither (but could be a concertina and a bouzouki) lending an exotic air to the instrumentation. The title song from *The Man Who Shot Liberty Valance* may have represented an attempt by Pitney's managers to put some hair on his chest. Instead of dashing off a vague cowpoke narrative in the tradition of Frankie Laine's recording of the theme from *High Noon*—all that was really called for—David encapsulated practically the entire movie in his lyric. Bacharach matched him in ambition, juxtaposing a country fiddler against a full string section and using rhythms evocative of square dances and horse clops to capture more than just the required hint of the Old West.

"Twenty Four Hours from Tulsa," my choice as Bacharach and David's masterpiece for Pitney, was an attempt to give the singer another hit in the same vein. This time, in the absence of an actual movie, David had to invent a plot—a southwestern noir about a man who succumbs to the charms of a beautiful stranger on his way home to his sweetheart. But it's Bacharach's double-timed, out-of-phase mariachi trumpets that give the song its nightmarish momentum: You half expect the singer and his new flame to go on a killing spree south of the border after the final diminuendo.

THE VARIETY OF BACHARACH'S SONGS JUST FOR PITNEY SHOULD INDICATE THAT there is no such thing as a typical Bacharach song, despite the composer's many identifiable melodic traits. Bacharach has probably written more songs in triple meter than any other popular songwriter since Berlin: "What's New Pussycat?" is a waltz, and so is "What the World Needs Now Is Love." Bacharach's melodies are deceptively simple. Despite what the ear thinks it's hearing, they rarely change key; what often accounts for their oddity is Bacharach's refusal to modulate into an easier key where another songwriter might, in order to give the singer a break. Meter does change constantly in Bacharach's songs, and they gain even greater rhythmic complexity as a result of his fetish for a kind of syncopation more common in Stravinsky than in jazz and pop, and for eccentric note groupings like the sixteenth-note triplets that begin "Anyone

Who Had a Heart." Writers of early feature stories on Bacharach marveled that his songs had achieved great popularity despite offering nothing that the man on the street could easily whistle. (This is the same poor fellow who is said to have problems with Stephen Sondheim.) A more justifiable complaint would have been about Bacharach's failure to give dancers much of a toehold: That teenagers of the early 1960s found a way to push each other across the floor to "Anyone Who Had a Heart" is a tribute to their youthful insouciance.

Many of the flourishes that one might think characterize Bacharach as a songwriter turn out on closer inspection to be evidence of his skills as an orchestrator. Bacharach himself might not see the point of such a distinction; he explained in a recent interview that writing a melody and determining which combinations of instruments go where is a one-step process for him. This may also explain why he has never seemed very interested in orchestrating other composers' songs. Early in his career Bacharach had a reputation for showing up in the studio when one of his songs was to be recorded and gradually taking over every detail of the production, regardless of who was nominally in control. When he and David began producing Warwick's albums, he sometimes entrusted to others the task of orchestrating and conducting those songs he hadn't written.

Tone color and voicing are as important to Bacharach as they were to Debussy and Ellington. He hears bells: triangle and chimes on "You'll Never Get to Heaven," vibes on "Alfie" and "Make It Easy on Yourself," glockenspiel on "A House Is Not a Home." We hear a poky trumpet or flügelhorn in many of his songs, where in others of the era we would hear a honking tenor saxophone. Even when a tenor saxophone is featured, as on Dusty Springfield's hit recording of "The Look of Love," from 1967, it is light and airy—consciously evocative of Stan Getz rather than of King Curtis, and set atop rhythms borrowed from Brazilian samba and bossa nova.

The best evidence of Bacharach's genius as an orchestrator might come from comparing Jonathan Tunick's orchestrations for *Promises, Promises* with Bacharach's own orchestrations for Warwick of three songs from the show: "Knowing When to Leave," "I'll Never Fall in Love Again," and the title song. Tunick's orchestrations of Stephen Sondheim's scores have been of such high quality that often it's difficult to tell where one man's contribution ends and the other's begins. But Tunick's orchestrations for *Promises, Promises* on the original-cast album are drab and colorless compared with Bacharach's for Warwick.

As a young man Bacharach studied with Darius Milhaud—a fact duly noted in most early articles about him, as if to suggest that what gave him an edge over other pop songwriters of the 1960s was his greater technical sophistication. I find it of greater relevance that before establishing a clear identity as a songwriter Bacharach served as music director for a number of singers and big-time entertainers, including Marlene Dietrich. "He's my accompanist, he's my arranger, and I wish I could say he's my composer, but that isn't true," Dietrich said about Bacharach, introducing him to her live audience on the album *Dietrich in Rio*. "He's everybody's composer." In addition to his formal training, Bacharach's wealth of practical experience set him apart from most of the other pop songwriters of the early 1960s; he was also slightly older than most of his competitors. Like them, he was writing songs calculated to appeal to teenagers, which were usually recorded by singers not much older; unlike them, however, he knew what it took to put a song across to adult nightclub audiences. Once given the opportunity to produce his own songs, he made dramatic use of this knowledge in the recording studio.

Phil Spector, the first record producer to be written about as an artist in his own right, was also the first to recognize the operatic scale of adolescent emotions, on such early-1960s records as the Ronettes' "Be My Baby" and the Righteous Brothers' "You've Lost That Lovin' Feeling," which featured Wagnerian orchestrations by Jack Nitzsche and Gene Page, respectively. The record producer Jerry Wexler and the songwriters Jerry Lieber and Mike Stoller usually receive credit for being the first to make organic use of a string section on a rhythm 'n' blues record—the Drifters' "There Goes My Baby," in 1959. The record's unsung hero was the string arranger Stan Applebaum. Bacharach's writing for strings was more sophisticated than Nitzsche's, Page's, or Applebaum's; he took Spector's big sound and slowed it to an adult pace. The first Bacharach song to *sound* vaguely like a Bacharach song was "Make It Easy on Yourself," a 1962 hit for Jerry Butler, a Billy Eckstine–like baritone. All these years later what's remarkable about the song is how grown-up it sounds—as much a reflection of Bacharach's elegant melodic line as of the stoicism conveyed by Butler's vocal and David's lyrics.

The unassuming David played an even greater role than Warwick in Bacharach's success. Bacharach and David complemented each other; Bacharach's melodic phrases often extended across several bar lines, and David often wrote uncommonly long, complex sentences. The team's movie title songs provide the best evidence of David's resourcefulness. It's no easy trick to craft an affecting lyric about love and separation around a song called "A House Is Not a Home," from a movie about an aging madam and her stable. Frank Loessor sold his broken heart to the junkman, in a song from 1934; thirty-two years later David, in a characteristically witty line from "Alfie," inquired what a pawnbroker would "lend on an old Golden Rule." In 1966, the year that *Time* devoted a cover to the New Theology and the question of whether God was dead, David put secular humanism on the hit parade:

> As sure as I believe there's a heaven above, Alfie,
> I know there's something much more,
> Something even non-believers can believe in. . . .

David's lyrics were forever gazing heavenward; on "You'll Never Get to Heaven If You Break My Heart," Bacharach's beatific arpeggios created the impression that the melody was written by a man who called heaven home.

Not surprisingly, Bacharach's fellow professionals were the first to recognize his genius. Early "cover" versions of his songs—for example, Sandie Shaw's 1964 remake of "(There's) Always Something There to Remind Me," a song written and produced by Bacharach for Lou Johnson earlier the same year—tended to copy his arrangements practically note for note, amounting to acts of homage. And when a performer would take great liberties with a Bacharach song, as Aretha Franklin did in bringing gospel fervor to her 1968 interpretation of "I Say a Little Prayer" (produced by Jerry Wexler), it usually had the effect of drawing attention to a detail Bacharach had written into the song but chosen not to emphasize. The song remained identifiably his.

BACHARACH SOON WENT FROM BEING A BEHIND-THE-SCENES FAVORITE TO BEING A STAR— an astonishing transformation at precisely the moment when assembly-line songwriters were being told that their services were no longer required. For a time Bacharach was as famous as any of the singers who put his songs on the charts. When *Promises, Promises* opened on Broadway, he eclipsed not only his nearly invisible lyricist but also the show's producer, David Merrick, and the author of its book, Neil Simon, neither of whom was ever accused of being a shrinking violet. People who would have been unable to say for sure who wrote "Raindrops Keep Fallin' on My Head" or "What the World Needs Now Is Love" knew Burt Bacharach by name, just as they would have known the name of Irving Berlin without being able to identify him as the composer of "White Christmas" and "Easter Parade." After a television commercial for a brand of vermouth in which Bacharach and Dickenson (by then Sergeant Pepper Anderson in the TV series *Police Woman*) appeared together as themselves, people knew what Bacharach looked like—more than could be said of Berlin even at the height of his fame. In show business the people behind the scenes are often there for a good reason: Berlin looked like a wholesaler and the joke about Mickey Rooney as Lorenz Hart in the movie *Words and Music* was that this was the only role Rooney ever played for which he was too good-looking. Bacharach was handsome in a tousled-haired, sleepy-eyed, long-jawed, blissed-out-genius sort of way. In the vermouth commercial Dickenson gazed at him as though ready to serenade him with the opening lines to "(They Long to Be) Close to You" about the angels getting together to create a dream come true.

Why Bacharach's moment ended so abruptly is difficult to explain, beyond observing that mass taste is unpredictable. Of possible significance is that he and David acrimoniously terminated their partnership after writing the songs for *Lost Horizon*, a lavish and unrelievedly sappy 1973 movie musical that brought them nothing but embarrassment. Much as Richard Rodgers's music changed for the worse when, after the death of the clever Hart, he began writing with the platitudinous Oscar Hammerstein, Bacharach's suffered when he began working with his third wife, the singer and lyricist Carol Bayer Sager. Three of their collaborations reached No. 1 during the 1980s, but of these, only the poignant "That's What Friends Are For," recorded by Dionne and Friends in 1985, was instantly recognizable as Bacharach's. Originally sung by Rod Stewart in the 1982 movie *Night Shift* as just a song about friendship, it has since become a fundraising tool in the fight against AIDS, with the proceeds from Warwick's recording going to the

American Foundation for AIDS Research. A stirring anthem, the song cemented Bacharach's reputation as our day's Irving Berlin.

More typical of the songs that Bacharach wrote with Sager before they parted were "Arthur's Theme (The Best That You Can Do)," from 1981 (written with Peter Allen and Christopher Cross, and performed by Cross), and "On My Own," from 1986—plush, sorry-for-itself, gold-card soul. Better Bacharach should have married Hal David, who never again reached the heights he scaled with Bacharach; one of his few hits of the 1980s was the maudlin "To All the Girls I've Loved Before," recorded by Willie Nelson and Julio Iglesias.

MANY OF BACHARACH'S LATER SONGS MIGHT HAVE SOUNDED LIVELIER IF HE had been allowed to produce them. His resurgence has been as unexpected as his disappearance from the charts after *Lost Horizons*. Despite his not having written a new Top 40 song in over a decade, his name and his music are suddenly everywhere. (Ironically, a new hit might endanger his cult status.) Earlier this spring *Promises, Promises* was performed in concert five times as part of the Encores! series at City Center in New York. The series is the same one that was responsible for the full-scale Broadway revival of *Chicago*, and there has been speculation that similar plans are in store for Bacharach's musical, especially given that the cast for the modest concert presentation included name actors in Martin Short and Christine Baranski. (A breakthrough show in its own time, for merging traditional Broadway song forms with contemporary pop rhythms, *Promises, Promises* has always seemed to me to have been the secret inspiration for Sondheim's *Company*.) One of last year's offerings off-Broadway was Tim Pinckney's *Message to Michael*, a show about New York's gay dating scene that, although "laced with references to Barbra Streisand and [Stephen Sondheim]," according to *The New York Times*, took its title from a Bacharach and David hit for Dionne Warwick. Also last year Warwick's recording of Bacharach and David's "Wives and Lovers" was featured in the hit movie *The First Wives' Club*, and Harry Connick, Jr. sang "This Guy's in Love with You" on the soundtrack of *One Fine Day*, a romantic comedy starring Michelle Pfeiffer and George Clooney. *Grace of My Heart*, a movie set largely in the pop-music world of the early 1960s, featured as its take-home song—the number heard over the closing credits and leading off the soundtrack album—a gorgeous new song called "God Give Me Strength," written by Bacharach and Elvis Costello.

The pianist McCoy Tyner and the arranger John Clayton turned nine of Bacharach's classics into gauzy mood music on Tyner's recent *What the World Needs Now Is . . . the Music of Burt Bacharach* (Impulse); this disc is significant only for being, to the best of my knowledge, the first album of jazz interpretations of Bacharach songs since one by Stan Getz, in 1967. *The Look of Love*, a British compilation of hit versions of Bacharach songs, last year entered the UK charts at No. 6, selling 60,000 copies within two months of its release. (I'm told that Bacharach's soundtrack for the 1967 movie *Casino Royale* is one of the out-of-print LPs most sought after by audiophiles, even though it has been reissued on CD; vinyl is said to better capture the sensuality of Dusty Springfield's rendition of "The Look of Love.") Early next year Rhino Records plans to release a far more ambitious three-disc Bacharach retrospective, featuring obscurities as well as classics. And just last month, as part of its Great Performances series, PBS broadcast a British-produced documentary called *Burt Bacharach: This Is Now.**

Popular heroes can have their Achilles' heels; Bacharach's is his inability to carry a tune. But many songwriters are awful singers; it's why they become songwriters, and why we find it so charming when they sit at a piano and modestly deliver their own songs. Bacharach's own albums have been anything but modest, yet even his own pompous long-form instrumental versions of his songs have found their champions, not just among the musicians who participated on Zorn's tribute album but also among fans of what is variously called "cocktail," "bachelor pad," or "E-Z listening"—those strange young men with an overdeveloped (or underdeveloped?) sense of kitsch, wardrobes of Rat Pack leisurewear like Kramer's on *Seinfeld*, no girlfriends, and too many good albums in their collections already.

---

*Bacharach's songs have been featured in numerous other films since this was written, including *My Best Friend's Wedding* and both *Austin Powers* movies. The 1998 Rhino collection is also called *The Look of Love* (Rhino R2 75339). Despite good reviews, the revival of *Promises, Promises* ended with the five performances at City Center. It was said that Bacharach was working on a new show, a musical adaptation of *Snow White*, with lyrics by B.A. Robertson, formerly of the group Mike and the Mechanics. But this was never staged. My wish is that somebody would write a new show around two dozen or so of Bacharach and David's classic songs. Like *Sophisticated Ladies* or *Cole*, it would be a show whose score audiences would already be humming on the way to their seats.

Bacharach now enjoys a hip cachet denied him back when a new song of his was practically guaranteed a spot in the Top 10. In its own day, a song like "(They Long to Be) Close to You"—best remembered as a No. 1 hit by the Carpenters in 1970, though it was first recorded by Richard Chamberlain, TV's Dr. Kildare, seven years earlier—could be dismissed as the sticky candy of slightly out-of-it young people who grew their hair long but continued to have it styled—young people who were more sexually active than their parents, but who continued to date and have traditional weddings. Bacharach's songs gave off a whiff of Cashmere Bouquet at a time when most songs on the radio, including those sung as well as written by Carole King, smelled of patchouli. Amid the political protest and guitar sputter of that day's music, crafts-manship of the sort that Bacharach epitomized was taken as a sign of inauthenticity.

POP SONGS THAT ENDURE FOR DECADES OFTEN DO SO BY DISCARDING THEIR original meanings, or by acquiring new ones. Karen Carpenter's voice means something very different to us now than it did in 1970, in light of her death from anorexia. We can now appreciate her for exactly what she was—a pretty young woman from a working-class California suburb who had a poor self-image and a better sense of rhythm than the white women singers of her day who foolishly thought that growling lyrics and pushing hard on the beat would make them sound black.

Bacharach's songs now mean something different too, as a result of belonging to the past without seeming to belong to a specific era. People in their twenties or early thirties, for whom Gershwin and Porter must seem as ancient and remote as the Greek gods, might not be old enough to have heard "The Look of Love" and "This Guy's in Love with You" on radio the first time around, but it means something to them that these are songs in the classic manner that were written in their own lifetime, or close enough. (A friend of mine who just turned thirty says that one of her earliest memories is of her divorced mother singing her and her brother to sleep at night with "I'll Never Fall in Love Again.") Unlike the hits of Motown and the Beatles, which will forever conjure up images of the 1960s, Bacharach's hit songs of twenty-five or thirty years ago strike younger people as having always been there—like "Star Dust" and "Body and Soul," and unlike "Light My Fire" and "Purple Haze."

I Didn't Know He Was Jewish

All of the best stories are apocryphal, probably including the one about how Burt Bacharach came to write "I'll Never Fall in Love Again," in 1968. Hospitalized with pneumonia after finishing the score to *Promises, Promises*, Bacharach was told by the show's producers that the second act needed another song and that he had roughly twenty-four hours to supply it. The usually painstaking Bacharach dashed off what proved to be one of his best-selling numbers when it was recorded by Dionne Warwick two years later; as an in-joke, the always resourceful Hal David rhymed "pneumonia" with "they never phone ya."

Cute story, but what most interests me about it, on the chance it's true, is that Bacharach, working with uncharacteristic haste and swooning with fever, fell back on his early influences for one of the few times in his career. Early magazine stories on Bacharach invariably attempted to legitimize his music (shades of Dave Brubeck) by dropping the information that he briefly studied with Darius Milhaud, but one listens in vain to Bacharach for even a hint of Milhaud's cranky wit. The same articles usually mentioned that Bacharach had spent long nights on 52nd Street as a teenager, learning from Charlie Parker and Dizzy Gillespie the many ways to flatten a fifth. Yet the influence of bebop is hardly discernible in songs like "The Look of Love" and "A House Is Not a Home." This doesn't mean that Bacharach was deaf to jazz. One of the most notable features of "I'll Never Fall in Love Again" is its odd, practically on-the-beat syncopation—a possible source for which was Gerry Mulligan's 1953 "Sextet" with Chet Baker and Lee Konitz.

Bacharach's obsession with timbre and counterpoint gave him a natural affinity with 1950s cool. His peak years as a hit maker dovetailed the bossa-nova craze, and no other North American tunesmith so successfully adapted bossa's rhythms, which one could argue were themselves Brazilian adaptations of 1950s West Coast jazz. All of this makes it surprising that so few jazz musicians have chosen to interpret Bacharach's songs—commercially tainted collections by Stan Getz and Cal Tjader, Bill Evans's numerous recordings of "Alfie," Sonny Rollins's "A House Is Not a Home," a few items by Stanley Turrentine, and that's pretty much it. Or maybe it isn't surprising at all. By the mid-1960s, jazz improvisers had long ceased looking to the Top 40 for new material, except for occasional misguided attempts to cash in. Then, too, Bacharach's songs aren't very good blowing vehicles; their richness generally lies in their harmonic palate, not in their chord changes.

As springboards for contemporary reinterpretation of any sort, Bacharach's songs face a serious image problem. Both he and his LP *Burt Bacharach Plays His Hits* make cameo appearances in the recent *Austin Powers, International Man of Mystery*—camp relics of the 1960s, as seen through the eyes of the adult's delusional adult swingers. The grown-up sensibility of Bacharach and David's songs is now counted among their virtues, but they initially had the misfortune of appealing mostly to adults at precisely the moment when the young became sole arbiters of what was hip. Bacharach's influence was enormous, but it manifested itself in black pop (Philadelphia International, in particular), not in rock 'n' roll.

Now, though, as the pop critic Milo Miles recently bemoaned of the inexplicable vogue for "lounge" or "cocktail," something can become hip simply because it didn't use to be. My Aunt Lillian adored Dean Martin, and apparently so do the tattooed youngsters behind the counter of my local Tower Records (a taste for Dino must skip generations, like certain hereditary diseases). On the plus side, it's now OK to collect klezmer, organ combos, and film scores, and Bacharach is suddenly all the rage.

One sign of his newfound cachet is *Great Jewish Music: Burt Bacharach*, whose very title sounds like a spoof, though Judaism is apparently among the few subjects that John Zorn—present here only as auteur—is disinclined to joke about. Bacharach, whose marriage to Angie Dickenson in the 1960s should be proof enough of his assimilation, figures to be dumbfounded by the treatment he receives from Zorn's postmod crowd. Yet notwithstanding that some of the set's musicians are incapable of expressing even admiration unironically, the set as a whole comes across as a valentine. As with most various-artists anthologies, *Great Jewish Music* begs to be judged on a track-by-track basis. Only Shelly Hirsch delivers a deconstructionist trashing, and her uneasy mix of vocalese and performance art on "What's New Pussycat" is so preposterously avant-gardsy that the joke is on her ("Pussy, pussy," indeed). Kramer's "Walk On By" is driven but essentially rhythmless, and Joey

Baron's unaccompanied drum solo on "Alfie" amounts to a pointless stunt. But the good stuff is terrific, beginning with Mark Ribot's pulp fictionalization of "Don't Go Breaking My Heart" and Elliott Sharp's translation of "The Man Who Shot Liberty Valance" into Ennio Morricone. Lloyd Cole and Robert Quine reimagine "I Just Don't Know What to Do with Myself" as it might sound if written by Lou Reed for the Velvet Underground's third LP (the one that revealed the band's dreamier side). The cellist Erik Friedlander rearranges "Promises, Promises" as a Schoenberg chamber piece, but with a melody and a beat. Yuka Honda and Sean Lennon comically transform the leisurely sensual "The Look of Love" into a panting adolescent premature ejaculation. Ironically, the trumpeter Dave Douglas's arrangement of "Wives and Lovers"—though the most faithful and immediately winning of these performances—might seem the most transgressive to anyone unfamiliar with the composer's own extended instrumental version.

Is any of this jazz? The Douglas track certainly is, as are two performances I'm saving until the end, in order to contrast them to McCoy Tyner's dire *What the World Needs Now Is . . . the Music of Burt Bacharach*, with its overlush John Clayton string arrangements. "Sometimes it's good to do something different," Tyner says in a press release. "[Coltrane] did that with 'My Favorite Things,' and you'd be surprised how many people thought it was a compromise." But that's where the comparison ends. This is nothing more than a mood album; when Tyner occasionally wakes from his slumber to voice a block chord, he sounds less like McCoy Tyner than like Ferrante and Tyner. Aside from a ponderous attempt to modalize "(There's) Always Something There to Remind Me," Clayton dares nothing novel with these tunes—unlike Marie McAuliffe and Bill Frisell, who, in their different ways, illustrate Bacharach's full jazz potential on the Tzadik set.

Leading a sextet with a three-horn front line, McAuliffe, a pianist whose name is new to me, treats "I Say a Little Prayer" to a series of harmonic and rhythmic variations reminiscent of early George Russell. And Frisell's lovely, unaccompanied "What the World Needs Now Is Love" demonstrates, as Sonny Rollins did with Al Jolson forty years ago, that practically any tune can serve as a vehicle for improvisation. The secret is in realizing that just as a song is more than its chord changes, improvisation involves more than systematically blowing on them.

The Best Years of Our Lives

===

Napoleon in Rags and the
Language That He'd Use

"**W**ish I was Bob Dylan," Robert Creeley wrote in the late 1960s, a time when this seemed to be nearly everybody's wish—apparently including anthologized poets whose confinement to print gave them good reason to envy Dylan's greater immediacy and perceived social relevance. In the same poem ("In London," not one of the epigrammatic poems for which Creeley is famous but a series of notebook jottings whose loose tongue seems the result of Dylan's influence coupled with Allen Ginsberg's, drugs, and a dilly of a midlife crisis), Creeley also wished he could hear Dylan's "Tears of Rage" sung by the sweeter-voiced Joan Baez. This could be taken to mean that Creeley was one of many who admired Dylan, even during his greatest period of influence and popularity, more as a songwriter than as a performer—more as a *voice* than as a singer. If so, it hardly amounted to a slight. "He's got a subtle mind," Creeley decided in the poem, for all intents and purposes embracing Dylan as a fellow wordsmith, perhaps even a fellow poet.

I happened upon "In London" while paging through Creeley in search of another poem I recalled reading years ago, which darted to mind as I listened last fall to Dylan's *Live 1966* (Columbia/Legacy C2K 65759), a concert recording from a period when he stood accused of betraying folk music—and of jeopardizing such folkie ideals as nuclear disarmament and Negro voter registration for the sin of cupping his

281

hands to his mouth and shouting his lyrics above the big bang of a rock and roll band at the 1965 Newport Folk Festival. Not exactly a new release and not exactly a reissue, *Live 1966* is the first authorized edition of a performance in Manchester, England, that has been obtainable on one bootleg or another almost continuously since 1971. The recording location is so frequently misidentified as London's Royal Albert Hall that Columbia/Legacy has given its two-disc set the subtitle "The 'Royal Albert Hall' Concert," in an effort to assure potential customers that this is the one they've heard so much about over the years. Like many rock bootlegs of the 1970s, the various pirate editions of Dylan's "Albert Hall" concert were often packaged in plain white sleeves; you knew you had the right show if, below the hum of the amplifiers and the snarl of Dylan and Robbie Robertson tuning their electric guitars in preparation for "Like a Rolling Stone," you heard an outraged audience member cry "Judas!"

I FOUND THE LINES FROM CREELEY I WAS LOOKING FOR IN "AFTER":

> *I'll not write again*
> *things a young man*
> *thinks, not the words*
> *of that feeling.*

The fourth line should be read as "of *that* feeling," because Creeley tends to accent the second word or syllable of a line, like a jazz musician accenting the second and fourth beats of a measure. *That* feeling of what a young man thinks—what I felt in listening to Dylan as a young man—was something I found difficult to recapture in listening to *Live 1966*. To throw one of Dylan's most famous aphorisms back at him, he was so much older then—older than I was, at any rate. He's younger than that now; that is, his recorded voice of thirty-odd years ago sounds almost younger than I can remember ever being.

As a college student I was one of those who stayed up late debating the meaning of Dylan's lyrics, as though arguing fine points of Christian theology or of hexagrams from the *I Ching*. In the absence of printed lyric sheets the subject of the debate would sometimes be what his lyrics actually were. I remember that when *John Wesley Harding* was released, an agitated fellow English major spotted me in a classroom and barged right in, interrupting the lecture to ask me what symbolism I found in the trees behind Dylan on the cover. (This same friend was the only person I knew who fell for the hoax that smoking banana peels was a cheap, legal high. The last I heard, he was translating French poetry and teaching English at a Midwestern university.) I also remember thinking even then that the claims for Dylan as not just a poet but *the* poet of the second half of the twentieth century were both greatly exaggerated, and that they ignored the true nature of his impact on American culture as a singer and songwriter—not necessarily lesser crafts.

Dylan obviously saw himself as a poet. He was steeped in poetry, even if when he burst onto the Greenwich Village folk scene in 1961 as a University of Minnesota dropout he tried to give the impression that he was a guitar-slinging Tom Joad whose lyrics spoke the wisdom of the common man and whose book-learning was limited to the tattered King James on whose inside cover his grandmother dutifully entered family births and annual grain prices. Dylan's early topical songs—the ones that got him published in *Sing Out!* and signed to Columbia Records— were diligently modeled on those of Woody Guthrie. But the wordier songs he soon became identified with, such as "Gates of Eden" and "Desolation Row," with their breath-length measures and apocalyptic imagery, owed more to Allen Ginsberg than to Guthrie or any folk singer. With these songs—and with "Like a Rolling Stone" and "Subterranean Homesick Blues," in 1965—Dylan put folk music, and then pop, in touch with the bardic strain of one branch of American literature. This strain is usually traced to Walt Whitman, though its actual origins may lie in the sermons of Jonathan Edwards and Cotton Mather, who took it verbatim from the Old Testament. To judge from striking images such as the one of an orphan "crying like a fire in the sun" in "It's All Over Now, Baby Blue," Dylan also knew his French symbolists. As Robert Sheldon—the *New York Times* music writer who gave Dylan his first rave review and later became his biographer—has pointed out, the otherwise inexplicable song title "Just Like Tom Thumb's Blues" may be a reference to a line in Wallace Fowlie's translation of Rimbaud's "My Bohemian Life (Fantasy)." In his 1967 novel *Tarantula* as well as in his song lyrics Dylan often aspired to surrealism—though something about the English language, or perhaps about the American character, must be unconducive to dreaming aloud, because like most American writers who have taken a stab at automatic writing, Dylan fell victim to a word virus.

His most glaring weakness as a poet or songwriter, however, was his imperiousness, even after he stopped issuing political broadsides. I admit that certain of Dylan's lines have stuck with me over the years, but these tend not to be his most messianic ones; frustrated by work or unfinished business in my personal life, I go to bed at night thinking, "Let me forget about today until tomorrow"—Dylan's prayer for oblivion in "Mr. Tambourine Man." But powerful as they remain, such accusatory songs as "Positively Fourth Street," "Ballad of a Thin Man," and "Like a Rolling Stone" might sting more and have greater emotional complexity if one suspected even for a moment that Dylan's putdowns were aimed at himself as well as at his unnamed foes—if, for example, in telling an overly demanding woman that he isn't the man for her in "It Ain't Me, Babe," he sounded as if he wished the opposite was true. "We make out of the quarrel with others, rhetoric, but of the quarrel with ourselves, poetry," William Butler Yeats wrote in *Per Amica Silentia Lunae*. Dylan has never been able to tell the difference, and this is his greatest failure both as a songwriter and as a performer.

Just as in the late 1940s some jazz listeners thought Thelonious Monk wasn't a facile enough pianist to do justice to his own compositions, in the 1960s many preferred their Dylan sung by Joan Baez, the Byrds, or even Peter, Paul & Mary. These people were taken aback by Dylan's unmellifluous voice. But countless singers, including some great ones, have gotten by with less. The problem, I think, was something more subjective—something perhaps best illustrated by example. One of Dylan's very best songs, and one of only a handful you can whistle, is "Just Like a Woman," from his 1966 album *Blonde on Blonde*. Its stop-and-start melody is a perfect match for its speechlike lyrics about an ex-lover who "takes just like a woman," "makes love just like a woman," and "fakes just like a woman" (orgasms?), but "breaks just like a little girl." Predictably, these lyrics earned Dylan a reputation as a misogynist; he delivers them almost too convincingly, his voice dripping disdain for the woman in question, with "her fog, her amphetamine, and her pearls." Sexual politics aside, it's a great performance. Yet the singer who really did "Just Like a Woman" justice was Van Morrison, who never recorded it for commercial release but frequently performed it in the early 1970s, including as part of the live show captured on the bootleg *Van the Man* (good luck finding a copy).*

Morrison, an Irishman whose version of "It's All Over Now, Baby Blue," recorded while he was still a member of the group Them, also trumped Dylan's, is a "blacker" singer than Dylan, whose only noticeable debt to black music is a harmonica style derived from Sonny Terry. With his better sense of time and wider expressive range, Morrison transforms "Just Like a Woman" into a soul ballad worthy of Al Green or James Brown; all that's missing is a horn section. More to the point, Morrison evinces a thwarted need—a hurt and an anger—unavailable to the self-satisfied Dylan, whether on his version with Nashville session men on *Blonde on Blonde* or on the version with just his own guitar and harmonica on disc one of *Live 1966*. "My weariness amazes me," Dylan tells us in "Mr. Tambourine Man," another of the songs that he performs during his solo acoustic set. Everything about himself does, and this has always been to his detriment as an artist.

IT'S DIFFICULT NOT TO TALK ABOUT DYLAN MOSTLY IN THE PAST TENSE. IN THE same way that the blues is black music, rock 'n' roll is youth music— music about *being* young. Our relationship to what used to be our favorite rock songs changes as we get older, and a rock performer's relationship to his own material also changes. A subtext of Muddy Waters's early records for Chess was what it felt like to be black and poor and a recent arrival in Chicago from Mississippi. Decades later, Waters could still perform those songs and similar ones with gusto; the South was far behind him, and he was no longer poor, but he was still black. Dylan and the other pop deities who fashioned a modern sensibility for rock 'n' roll in the 1960s, often by striving for a wisdom beyond their years, are no

---

*Morrison's version became notorious for a liberty he takes with Dylan's lyrics. Dylan calls it quits because he can't stand "this pain in here"—"here" possibly meaning the bed they share or maybe his heart. Morrison says he's leaving because he can't stand "this queer in here." The alteration makes sense only if Morrison believed Dylan was singing about a transsexual or a transvestite—or if, as many Dylan watchers have claimed, the song was about his brief affair with Edie Sedgwick, the most famous (and ultimately the most tragic) of Andy Warhol's drug-deluded "superstars," in which case Morrison might be taking a dig at Warhol.

longer young (Dylan is fifty-eight), and the shock of this realization has thrown most of them for a loop.

Middle age has been kinder to Dylan than to, say, Mick Jagger, who should think twice these days before singing "Sympathy for the Devil": Younger fans might take him literally when he boasts of having been on hand for the Crucifixion. But Dylan no longer means to people what he once did, and his last dozen or so albums lack intensity, partly because not even his most loyal fans have much invested in him anymore.

Despite his identification with the insurrections of the 1960s, Dylan's appeal cut across ideological lines. In 1997, when he was honored at the Kennedy Center, the only politician who made a bigger fuss over Dylan than Bill Clinton was Newt Gingrich, whose pop futurism and delusions of grandeur as speaker of the House made him seem every bit as much a child of the 1960s as Clinton—the confessed adulterer and accused moral relativist whom Pat Robertson once condemned as that decade's "poster boy." Gingrich told reporters, "The sheer magic, I think, for everyone in my generation, is to finally have our nation recognize Bob Dylan."

I doubt either Clinton or Gingrich or other fans still ponder Dylan's supposed meanings. For the last twenty years the only puzzle with each new Dylan album has been whether this serial monotheist is now a Christian or a Jew, and most people I know stopped caring long ago. His 1997 album *Time Out of Mind* was a decent piece of work, but hardly worthy of the nearly unanimous praise it received from rock critics; the notion that it recaptured the Dylan of the 1960s was itself a Golden Oldie—a tune we'd heard countless times, beginning in 1974 with the release of *Planet Waves. Time Out of Mind* won a Grammy as album of the year, but the honor seemed more a lifetime-achievement award, especially since it followed Dylan's hospitalization for a potentially fatal heart infection.

DYLAN'S CREATIVE PEAK LASTED ONLY THREE YEARS, ROUGHLY FROM Mississippi Freedom Summer to the Summer of Love, or from *Bringin' It All Back Home* to *John Wesley Harding*—a period during which rock 'n' roll gained intellectual credibility and folk music suffered an irreversible decline, largely as a result of his strapping on an electric guitar and rejecting the role of pamphleteer. Three years is nothing, yet in this brief span Dylan altered the course of popular music more fundamentally than even Frank Sinatra, Elvis Presley, or the Beatles. As songwriters, John Lennon and Paul McCartney were surprisingly traditional; they brought a youthful cheekiness to pop, but in terms of lyrical sentiment and melodic structure their songs of the 1960s merely updated Tin Pan Alley conventions. Dylan shifted the focus of lyric writing from crafts-manship to self-expression—a concept once as alien to pop as it was to folk, whose modern-day practitioners were encouraged to speak their minds only about pressing social issues.

Folk purists had begun voicing displeasure with Dylan even before he plugged in. At issue was the increasingly personal nature of his lyrics and their diminished social relevance. Irwin Silber, the editor of *Sing Out!* and an early Dylan champion, spoke for many in Greenwich Village folk circles in 1964 when he published an open letter to Dylan in which he argued that whereas "any songwriter who tries to deal honestly with real-ity in this world is bound to write 'protest' songs," Dylan's were becom-ing "all inner-directed now, inner-probing, self-conscious—maybe even a little maudlin or a little cruel on occasion."

Dylan issued no rebuttals, except in the form of "Positively Fourth Street," a song from 1965 that begins "You've got a lot of nerve to say you are my friend" and that Dylanologists have always believed targeted Silber. Nevertheless, the victor in this dispute was the songwriter Silber believed wasn't living up to his responsibilities as a people's troubadour. By 1964 "folk" music, as Silber and other veterans of political struggles of the 1930s and 1940s understood it, was a dying form—a casualty of mass technology that had been only briefly revitalized by young per-formers who, like Dylan, embraced folk less out of any abiding interest in it than out of a commitment to a progressive social agenda. These were people in their early twenties, Dylan included, who had spent their teenage years singing along to Elvis Presley and Buddy Holly records; for many of them folk music amounted to a way of demonstrating to leftist elders like Silber and Pete Seeger how grown up they were—and what good little leftists. Once the Beatles made it respectable for adults to like rock 'n' roll, it was inevitable that Dylan would change his tune, having been a member of teenage rock bands in his native Minnesota and (as "Elston Gunnn," with three "n"s) having once talked his way into a job as piano player and backup singer in the Shadows, the backup band for the Holly-influenced teen idol Bobby Vee.

Dylan was the one playing "people's" music—music that the masses listened to. Some thirty years after his defection, "folk" no longer means traditional ballads and workers' songs. If it is still understood to mean anything, it means a sensitive young guy or girl with a guitar performing his or her own introspective songs. Folk music has become a pop sub-genre, a style appropriated by unlikely advertisers. Dow Chemical, once a target of protests for manufacturing napalm and now a sponsor of *This Week with Sam Donaldson and Cokie Roberts*, airs spots featuring a woman singing about "what good thinking can do" as though leading a hootenanny; you half expect Sam and Cokie, William Kristol, and the two Georges to come back from the break singing along.

Folk would probably have undergone this transformation even without Dylan. But rock 'n' roll would not be the same had he not transformed it into a vehicle for creative writing. In a way, rock's evolution in the 1960s was similar to that of swing twenty years earlier. Some of the youngsters of the 1940s who did the lindy to the big bands eventually stopped dancing and began to crowd the bandstand—the boys to concentrate on the virtuoso instrumentalists, the girls to get a closer look at the dreamy singers. In the 1960s the boys still moved close to the stage to watch the soloists (likely to be guitarists rather than saxophonists or trumpeters), but now girls and boys alike paid rapt attention not just to the singers but to the lyrics.

Songwriters everywhere sought to emulate this "Napoleon in rags and the language that he'd use," to quote a line from "Like a Rolling Stone" in which I'm reasonably sure Dylan was describing himself (one thing he has never been accused of is being tall). The first of pop's major figures to try doing it Dylan's way was John Lennon, who started opening himself up more in his lyrics (far more than the guarded Dylan ever did) around the time the Beatles recorded the songs for the movie *Help!*. With typical candor Lennon admitted Dylan's influence in a *Rolling Stone* interview in which he dismissed his own early lyrics as those of "a stylized songwriter" who saved his literary and most personal thoughts for "me books"—*In His Own Write* and *A Spaniard in the Works*. Lennon briefly even took to wearing a railroad cap, like the one Dylan had worn on the cover of his first album. Though black audiences showed little interest in Dylan, black performers fell under his influence: In addition to recording the definitive interpretation of Dylan's "All Along the Watchtower," Jimi Hendrix wore his hair like Dylan's, in a cumulus of tendrils that was only incidentally an Afro. Even Mick Jagger began to cultivate a hitherto unsuspected poetic streak.

By 1967 the lead singers in anonymous bar bands had begun to imitate Dylan as slavishly as they had copied Jagger only a year or so
before — only this time under the delusion of creativity, rather than in a
parasitic bid for sex appeal. Well into the 1970s, despite Dylan's waning
cultural significance, record companies continued to position any new
discovery whose songs were literate (or just wordy) as the new Dylan;
among the performers who were initially burdened with this label were
John Prine, Loudon Wainwright III, and Bruce Springsteen. Each eventually asserted his individuality, though audiences might not have known
what to make of them without Dylan's prior example; Springsteen
became famous for reasserting the element of social protest that Dylan
had abandoned. Dylan's success also opened the door to a recording
career for Leonard Cohen, a published poet whose prior credentials
included several books of verse and two inscrutable novels. We have
Dylan to thank for Patti Smith and Neil Young, and to blame for Janis
Ian and Billy Joel.

There was no rock style of the late 1960s or early 1970s that Dylan
didn't touch in some way, no matter how alien its aesthetic might have
seemed to him. This even includes "glam" rock: On his 1971 breakthrough album *Hunky Dory*, David Bowie dedicated a song to Dylan,
and Ian Hunter, the lead singer of Mott the Hoople, added his British
accent to Dylan's hip sneer. Dylan's influence on pop has been so fun-
damental that it has never really diminished, just become indirect. It
extends to countless performers who might not recognize him as an
inspiration, and who might believe his music to be irrelevant to theirs for
reasons of age, race, or gender. The late Kurt Cobain and Tupac Shakur
were among his offspring, and so are Jewel, Fiona Apple, and Alanis
Morissette.

ON *LIVE 1966* (COLUMBIA/LEGACY C2K 6J759), AS ON DYLAN'S STUDIO ALBUMS
from the same period, the excitement is in hearing him bend the rules of
pop to his own will. In effect, the original bootleg of Dylan's "Albert
Hall" concert was a follow-up to *Great White Wonder*, a bootleg double
LP from 1969 that had caused a stir by allowing Dylan's fans to judge for
themselves the merits of his 1966 "basement tapes" — a collection of new
songs he had recorded informally while recovering from a motorcycle
accident but had decided not to release. By 1969, the songs themselves
were well known through cover versions by other artists; Manfred Mann

had a hit with "Mighty Quinn (Quinn the Eskimo)," for example, and Julie Driscoll and Brian Auger's version of "This Wheel's on Fire" was an FM favorite. But Dylan's fans wanted to hear *his* interpretations. This desire intensified in 1968, following the release of *Music from Big Pink*, the first album by the Band, a quintet of formerly anonymous rock 'n' roll journeymen—the guitarist Robbie Robertson, the pianist Richard Manuel, the organist Garth Hudson, the bassist Rick Danko, and the drummer Levon Helm—who had forged an identity while serving as Dylan's backup band and had collaborated with him on the basement tapes (which were actually recorded in the Band's communal home near Woodstock, New York). *Music from Big Pink* included three of the basement Dylan songs, further whetting the appetite for Dylan and the Band's original versions.

Great White Wonder was hardly the first bootleg: Sub rosa LPs of Metropolitan Opera broadcasts and Charlie Parker's nightclub appearances preceded it by more than a decade. But GWW, as it was often referred to, was the first bootleg aimed at rock fans, a demographic which to that point had been passive consumers, content with whatever record companies offered them. The ready market for GWW, and then for *Royal Albert Hall* (or whatever your copy happened to be called), was a by-product of disenchantment with Dylan's often banal "official" releases of the period, which seemed to bear little more than his name and likeness—the only things missing from the bootlegs. The sales of these other rock bootlegs also reflected the simplistic belief, carried over from the 1960s, that "the music belongs to the people," and an unwillingness on the part of that era's catered-to youth to leave anything to legend. "Albert Hall" was desirable contraband because it included, in addition to Dylan's solo set, what was then his only "live" recording with the Band, who were still billing themselves as the Hawks when they accompanied Dylan on his British tour in 1966, with the drummer Mickey Jones subbing for Helm.

The music was worth bootlegging. It was the finest of Dylan's career. Dylan had performed solo on his British tour of 1965, the subject of—or at least the setting for—D.A. Pennebaker's cinema-verité style portrait of Dylan, *Don't Look Back*. One of my favorite scenes from Pennebaker's movie shows a British journalist dictating his review of a Dylan concert into a pay phone and concluding with what he clearly thinks is a poetic flourish of his own: "'The times, they are a-changing,' sings Dylan. They are, when a poet and not a pop singer fills a hall."

Dylan may still have fancied himself a poet in 1966, but he was by then also unambiguously a rock 'n' roller, thanks in no small measure to the company he kept. These were musicians with an encyclopedic repertoire of riffs, veterans of countless one-nighters backing singers far less "poetic" than Dylan. They roughed him up, and he gave back as good as he got, sounding as though he might sing himself hoarse. On some of Dylan's earlier "folk" songs, like "One Too Many Mornings" and "I Don't Believe You (She Acts Like We Never Have Met)," his bandmates frequently sound two notes away from breaking into Chuck Berry's "Memphis" or Tommy Tucker's "Hi-Heel Sneakers," and this is all to the good. Playing the role of barroom rocker and functioning as one musician among six discouraged Dylan from indulging in the sort of self-conscious preening he does far too much of on his opening solo set, in which the main point of interest (for me, anyway) is his atmospheric and doggedly idiosyncratic harmonica. He was at his most playful on "Leopard Skin Pill Box Hat," essentially a talking blues whose leering non sequiturs, delivered over a shuffle beat, free him from the requirements of narrative, and also from his usual pretensions to larger social significance.

Dylan was smart enough to realize that the verbal complexity of his lyrics was best offset by a comparable sonic density, which only a rock 'n' roll band could provide. But not all of the credit for the success of this music *as* music belongs to his sidemen. As the Band, these same men demonstrated the limits of utilitarian musicianship. The brand of roots-rock Americana they introduced on *Music from Big Pink* amounted to an artistic vision, but as singers and even as instrumental soloists, they lacked personality—a quality Dylan has always possessed in abundance, whatever one thought of it. On *Live 1966* his overweening pride becomes a virtue: This is a young man meeting rock 'n' roll head on, confident that rock 'n' roll stands to gain from the encounter. "It used t' be like that, and now it goes like this," he says, introducing a revved-up version of "I Don't Believe You." He might as well have been talking about rock 'n' roll, which had never before been so raw and open and unregimented.

DYLAN WAS A NEW BREED OF POP STAR. ELVIS PRESLEY LOVED SHOW business, and so did the Beatles—though their affection was for British music hall and *The Goon Show*, not Las Vegas and 1950s television variety shows. Dylan, who was as much a product of 1960s Greenwich

Village as of his native Hibbing, Minnesota, saw rock 'n' roll less as an extension of show business than as a form of absurdist theater. *Live 1966* documents the mutual hostility between Dylan and a segment of his audience at a turning point in his career. The British folkies dramatize their displeasure with him by stomping their feet between songs. When someone yells "Judas!," Dylan, in his best halting James Dean, retorts "I don't *believe* you," and then "You're a *liar*," before telling his sidemen (off-mike but clearly audible, and clearly meant to be overheard) to "play fuckin' loud."

To me, what is remarkable about this exchange is that we hear Dylan's speaking voice and it sounds like someone else's (and actually might have been someone else's, according to Dylanologists). This ambiguity is one of the reasons the former Robert Zimmerman has been an enigma even to his most obsessive fans. It's been said over and over that Dylan is the guy who made it okay for any songwriter to sing his own songs, no matter how unlovely or technically restricted his voice might be. This is true as far as it goes, but the irony is that Dylan himself has never been a naturalistic singer; he has never even settled on one voice. Early on, a reviewer described him as "Marlon Brando imitating [a] Southern farm-hand." On going electric he became, in the words of another writer, "a Rolling Stone singing Immanuel Kant." On *Time Out of Mind*, as on most of his recent albums, he frequently sounds like Gabby Hayes doing Bob Dylan for the amusement of the other cowpokes around the camp-fire. In this respect John Lennon was Dylan's exact opposite: No matter how often he attempted to reinvent himself, through transcendental meditation or primal-scream therapy or political consciousness raising, Lennon was always identifiably Lennon. Singing for him was a form of self-revelation; for Dylan, it has always been an act of self-concealment that apparently doesn't end when the show does. In *Eat the Document*, a film of Dylan's 1966 European tour made for American television but rejected (it was shown last year at the Museum of Television & Radio in New York), an interviewer who has had enough of Dylan's put-ons and put-downs asks him "Don't you ever come offstage? Are you ever yourself at any time?" Dylan has no answer for the interviewer—at least not that we hear. (The Museum's print of *Eat the Document* includes the com-mercials that would have been seen by viewers had the film been aired as part of ABC's *Sound Stage 67*, as originally planned. The movie ends with Dylan in freeze-frame, and the next thing we see is the full-screen legend THE GREAT IMPOSTER. It takes a moment to realize this is a spot for Welch's Grape Juice, a drink that supposedly tasted so good kids didn't realize it was good for them.)

To many of Dylan's most ardent fans his profanity at the Manchester concert (assuming that he was the one who instructed the musicians to crank up the volume and not Robbie Robertson, as many people, including me, suspect) is the stuff of high drama—the beginning of an era in pop music when performers would, just like real artists, refuse to let themselves be defined by their audiences. Those fans hear the version of "Like a Rolling Stone" that ends *Live 1966* as an act of brave retaliation: In the words of Corey Greenberg, reviewing *Live 1966* in *Stereo Review*, what follows the instruction to Dylan's sidemen to turn up their amps is "either Lee Harvey Oswald's bolt-action rifle cracking across Dealey Plaza or drummer Mickey Jones's apocalyptic rim shot that kicks off the loudest, meanest, most awe-inspiring version of 'Like a Rolling Stone' Dylan or anyone else has ever laid down."

The allusion to Oswald is tasteless, the hyperbole may be adolescent, and anyone who thinks Dylan or Robertson needed to be provoked into uttering a swear-word hasn't spent much time around young musicians. But reading Greenberg underscores how very 1960s this music, and the controversy that once surrounded it, now seems. I don't mean that Dylan's early music has become dated, merely that hearing Dylan being called a Judas restores it to its original context.

Eighty-One Questions, "96 Tears"

Live 1966 was released early last fall; I caught up with it a few months later, listening to it during the House impeachment hearings—a backdrop against which the unresolved issues of the 1960s seemed eerily relevant. In an October issue of *Rolling Stone* in which rock stars and other celebrities weighed in on the Lewinsky scandal, Patti Smith called Starr's investigation a "crucifixion" of her and the president's generation. "They are finally nailing us for introducing new ideas about sexual mores, sexual freedom, personal freedom," she said. Liberal paranoia? Two months later Cal Thomas, the nationally syndicated conservative columnist, lampooned the president and first lady as grown-up "flower children" from "the Age of Aquarius," representatives of a "pampered" generation that "thought abortion on demand was an answered prayer to their pagan hedonistic god." Huffed Thomas, "They forgot venereal disease, broken homes, abandoned children and a general decline in civility for which they are mostly responsible."

The wackiest argument I read in favor of impeachment was an unsigned article in *The American Conservative* that concluded Clinton was already guilty of treason on taking office, for having "organized and led demonstrations against American servicemen on foreign soil" during the Vietnam war. You might have thought that Clinton's real crime was polluting the mind of the young intern at his knee with stories of a time when people her age built bonfires from their bras and draft cards, and lit reefers as fat as cigars off the flames.

Much as diehard segregationists despised John F. Kennedy for his identification with civil rights, today's evangelical conservatives ("theo-conservatives," as Andrew Sullivan calls them) loathe Clinton for his administration's liberal policies on abortion and gay rights. Though they were the ones gagging at the mention of oral sex, the president's Republican character assassins (including Bill McCullough, a chipmunk-cheeked Florida representative who looked sickened every time he referred to Lewinsky's genitalia, which he mispronounced as "genitilia") repeatedly said that their case against Clinton wasn't about sex. It wasn't— it was about contested forms of sexual behavior. With the Cold War over, the new enemy within is the libido. In the 1950s God-fearing Americans looked under their beds for Communists; now they look in the bed for subversion.

At year's end Clinton and Kenneth Starr, our Arthur Dimmesdale and Roger Chillingworth, shared the cover of *Time* as the magazine's Men of the Year ("the leader of the Democratic party and the leader of the Republican party," Joe Lockhart, the White House press secretary, quipped). The *Time* cover that caught my eye, though, was the one from the week before which showed Clinton in silhouetted profile, his hair illuminated as if on fire—it vaguely resembled the cover of *Bob Dylan's Greatest Hits*, a popular 1960s poster.

NO OTHER STYLE OF POPULAR MUSIC HAS EVER BEEN AS CLOSELY IDENTIFIED with a particular generation's coming of age as 1960s rock was. In the absence of a just war or a cataclysmic domestic event like the Great Depression, the only things that those of us doomed to hearing ourselves described as "baby boomers" into old age ever had in common were sex and drugs and rock 'n' roll—and for many of us the sex and drugs were proverbial, or something we'd be ashamed to admit to now. Newt Gingrich isn't the only conservative with a lingering affection for 1960s pop. Ann Coulter, the author of *High Crimes and Misdemeanors* and one of a new breed of blonde, right-wing Republican pundettes (she's as thin as Ally McBeal, and wears her skirts as short), supposedly used to be a Deadhead—one of those dedicated fans who follow the Grateful Dead from city to city, rarely getting high on the music alone. Maybe Coulter didn't inhale.

In condemning the excesses of the 1960s, the right conveniently over-looks its own roots in the struggles of that decade. The anti-abortion movement would not exist in its present form without the example of the civil-rights and anti-war movements, which legitimized both civil dis-obedience and the involvement of clergy in political issues that were also matters of individual conscience. Before feminism, the personal was impolitic: Clinton would have been given a pass on his sexual misad-ventures in the Kennedy era, when willing women were considered to be among the spoils of high office. A frequent conservative lament is the decline of civility in our social discourse, which the right traces to the protest movements of the 1960s. But conservatives are now more likely to be the ones spewing invective and the ones willing to resort to any means necessary to effect their agendas—apparently including the weak-ening of the administrative branch by legislative fiat. One look at Dick "You and What" Armey should be enough to tell you which side, Democrat or Republican, left or right, is spoiling for a fight.

The current vogue for everything pertaining to the Second World War—from swing dancing to *Saving Private Ryan* to Tom Brokaw's *The Greatest Generation*—has, in addition to mythologizing our dying par-ents, been interpreted as a rebuke to a generation that supposedly took democracy for granted and chose in large numbers to protest a war rather than fight in it. But democracy as we define it today is as much the result of battles fought in America's classrooms and streets in the 1960s as of battles fought overseas twenty years earlier. The sixteen House Judiciary Committee Democrats who voted as a block against impeaching Bill Clinton included three women, five African-Americans, and one openly gay man—a representation of minorities that would have been unthink-able at the time of Iwo Jima or Normandy. Another box set I was listening to around the time of the impeachment—and John Glenn's reorbit of the earth—was *Nuggets* (Rhino R2 75466), an anthology of 1960s proto-punk and -psychedelic bands with no redeeming social value but abundant sociological importance. The best stuff on *Nuggets* is wonderfully adolescent; "These are your zits," you can imagine a television announcer intoning over the Farfisa-organ solos, "and these are your zits on drugs." The goofiest song of all might be the Barbarians' "Moulty," in which the band's drummer tells of soldiering on despite the loss of a hand. The Barbarians, who better caught the spirit of the time with a song called "Are You a Boy or Are You a Girl," were from Boston; I couldn't hear their drummer's New England deadpan on "Moulty" without thinking of the scenes involving a handless ex-sailor in *The Best Years of Our Lives*, William Wyler's 1946 movie about the difficulty many of the men who fought in the Second World War had in readjusting to civilian life (the role was played by Harold Russell, a real-life ex-sailor—and non-actor—who lost both hands in a submarine explosion). And I somehow couldn't hear talk of the eighty-one questions with which the House Republicans hoped to entrap Clinton without flashing back to ? and the Mysterians' "96 Tears," a hit from 1966 that wasn't included on *Nuggets* but should have been.

Perhaps none of this has anything directly to do with Dylan, yet it goes a long way toward explaining why his music and that of others in the 1960s holds greater than nostalgic meaning for those of us who grew up with it (and in some ways long ago outgrew it). Whatever seemed at stake in the music for its original fans remains at stake today, however irrelevant Dylan himself has become.

The Atlantic Monthly, May 1999

Infamous

You couldn't have paid me to see the Rolling Stones on their concert tour last fall, even though I still like their old records. It's just *them* I can't stand—the blown-out satyrs. But I wouldn't have missed *Songs for 'Drella—A Fiction*, a collaboration between Lou Reed and John Cale, two of the four original members of the Velvet Underground, at the Brooklyn Academy of Music last fall.*

Songs for 'Drella was presented as part of BAM's Next Wave Festival, an annual interdisciplinary performing-arts series that last year also staged new works by Laurie Anderson and the choreographers Bebe Miller and Christine Brunel, among others. The performance consisted of fifteen new songs written and sung by Reed or Cale, about the late Andy Warhol, the Velvet Underground's early benefactor—in addition to everything else he was. ("'Drella," compounded from "Dracula" and "Cinderella," was a nickname for Warhol, of which he was not supposed to have been especially fond.)

This wasn't a Velvet Underground reunion concert, nor could it have been without the rhythm guitarist Sterling Morrison and the drummer Maureen Tucker. Hardly more than an hour in length and over before 9:30 P.M., it wasn't even a rock concert. It was more of a

---

*Sire Records eventually released a studio recording of *Songs for 'Drella*. All four original members of the Velvet Underground, including Tucker and Morrison, were reunited for a European tour in 1992.

small-scale performance piece, with Reed and Cale seated reading music in front of (and sometimes behind) Jerome Sirlin's riveting slide projections, which included Warhol's famous electric chairs, stills from his movies, and tabloid headlines—"POP GOES THE POP ARTIST!"— about Valerie Solanis's 1968 attempt on his life. There was no stomping or cheering until the end, when some audience members began to yell out titles of old Velvets songs ("I'm Waiting for the Man," about a white boy scoring drugs in Harlem, was the consensus choice). Reed and Cale ignored these requests for a familiar encore, at least at the show I attended. Still, the sight of them both on stage, in one of their few performances together since Cale left the group, in 1968, brought back memories of how lonely it was rooting for the Velvet Underground in the late 1960s.

As an undergraduate, I bought *White Light, White Heat*, the Velvets' second album and the last with Cale, on the day it was released, early in 1968. I took it with me that night, still in its shrink wrap, to the apartment of friends, where about six people were already gathered in that era's equivalent of a poker game or coffee klatch—passing around a hash pipe, with Jimi Hendrix blaring on the stereo. Aside from Hendrix's *Are You Experienced?*, the only other record our hosts owned was Cream's *Disraeli Gears*. When I offered to relieve the monotony by breaking open *White Light, White Heat*, everybody groaned. So we sat there and listened to Hendrix and Cream over and over, for what seemed like hours (or was it just the hash?).

IT'S PROBABLY JUST AS WELL THAT I DIDN'T GET TO PLAY THE ALBUM THAT night, because of the seventeen-minute track "Sister Ray." If the lyrics about transvestites and their sailor boyfriends mainlining heroin at an orgy hadn't bummed everybody out, what might have was Cale's overloaded organ crescendos and Reed's guitar feedback, which was different from Hendrix's—shrill and intentionally grating, with not a touch of the blues. More extreme than anything else the Velvet Underground ever recorded, "Sister Ray" nevertheless typifies what made the 1960s counterculture uneasy about them: Lou Reed's perverse identification with junkies, speedfreaks, drag queens, sadomasochists, and other subspecies crossbred from the drug culture and the sexual revolution. Reed's songs (the titles "Heroin" and "Venus in Furs" give an idea of their content) graphically detailed the darkness and depravity that no one wanted to admit might be on the other side of the walls that were then coming down. Because he wrote from the point of view of his characters, avoiding the autobiographical moralizing favored by most of the era's rock bards, some people just didn't know what to make of him. His detachment gave his lyrics something approaching literary complexity, but also left him open to charges of amorality and exploitation.

Though the melodies to ballads like "I'll Be Your Mirror" and "Femme Fatale" were surprisingly lovely, their lyrics described emotional isolation—especially as delivered by Nico, the toneless German-born blonde whom Warhol teamed with the Velvets on their first LP. But Reed's prickly pose as a sick-of-flower-power *fleur du mal* wasn't the Velvet Underground's only shortcoming, as far as most record buyers were concerned. The essayist and longtime Velvets chronicler Ellen Willis once aptly described the band's music as "prophetic of a leaner, meaner time." In an era in which countless rock bands convinced themselves that they were upgrading rock 'n' roll into an art form with raga rhythms, jazz harmonies, and learned classical allusions, the Velvets seemed bent on demonstrating that rock's proverbial three chords would suffice, providing you stretched them to the breaking point. Even on their quieter and more playful songs, the band's sound was so spare and unadorned that their musicianship was inevitably called into question.

IN FACT, THE GROUP'S MINIMALISTIC APPROACH TO ROCK 'N' ROLL WAS A MATTER of choice. The Welsh-born John Cale, whose droning patterns on bass and electric viola contributed as much as Reed's lyrics to making the Velvet Underground's music the antithesis of good vibes, had studied composition at Goldsmiths' College, in London, and—on the recommendation of Aaron Copland—had been awarded a scholarship to study with Iannis Xenakis at the Eastwood Conservatory. A disciple of the prototypical minimalist composer La Monte Young, Cale had been one of a relay team of pianists (including John Cage) that played Erik Satie's "Vexations," an eighty-second passage of music repeated 840 times, without interruption, over eighteen-and-a-half hours in 1963. The band's only completely intuitive musician was Maureen Tucker, whose unflagging drive made up for her lack of conventional technique. (Of course, the very fact that the Velvets would let a woman do their drumming was all the proof some needed that they couldn't be serious.)

For a band like the Velvet Underground, to be scorned wasn't as ignoble a fate as not to be taken seriously—which they initially weren't, as a result of Warhol's sponsorship. The popular assumption was that Reed and his bandmates were four more of Warhol's talentless, strung-out "superstars," destined to be infamous for fifteen minutes, like International Velvet or Baby Jane Holzer. Warhol had recruited the Velvets to supply the music for his Exploding Plastic Inevitable shows, in 1966. He briefly served as the band's manager, designing the cover of their first LP (a peelable banana). (The album was produced, if only in the entrepreneurial sense, by Warhol and his aide-de-camp Paul Morrissey.) Soon afterward the band disassociated itself from him, but it was too late.

Before finding the Velvet Underground, Warhol had considered starting a rock band of his own with several fellow visual artists. Nothing if not shrewd, he realized that his competition as a pop deity was Bob Dylan and the Beatles, not Claes Oldenburg and Jasper Johns. Did Warhol hope to experience rock stardom vicariously through the Velvets, as he vicariously experienced sin and degradation through his Factory-line of Bike Boys and Chelsea Girls? If so, he chose the wrong band, for the Velvets never achieved commercial success (though Reed later did, on his own).

But Warhol had the last laugh, because, as the British critics Simon Frith and Howard Horne succinctly put it in their recent book, *Art into Pop*, the Velvet Underground "became the model for an avant-garde *within* rock and roll, the source of a self-conscious, intellectual, trash aesthetic." So did Warhol, as British glam rockers like David Bowie emulated his modern-day Oscar Wilde act of making himself his most famous piece of art. (In 1973, Bowie produced "Walk on the Wild Side," Reed's only hit single.) Warhol also inspired Malcolm McLaren, the proprietor of a London boutique called Sex, who ultimately went him one better by creating practically from scratch both a rock band (the Sex Pistols) and a pop look (late-1960s punk). On their own turf the Velvet Underground's immediate successors were the New York Dolls, five heterosexual men in drag who looked as though they had just stepped out of a Lou Reed song, and who first gained notoriety with their performances at New York's Mercer Art Center (significantly, also the first location for the Kitchen, the performance space that nurtured the minimalist composer Philip Glass).

A critic once remarked that "the Velvet Underground didn't sell many records, but everyone who bought one formed their own band." Virtually every New York punk, new-wave, or no-wave band of the late 1970s, including Talking Heads, masterminded by art-school dropout David Byrne, incorporated some aspect of either the band's music or its alienated stance. More recently, popular bands like REM and the Cowboy Junkies have paid homage to the Velvets by covering Reed's more tuneful songs ("Pale Blue Eyes" and "Sweet Jane," respectively); the bohemian art band Sonic Youth has based its sound on the all-out assault of "Sister Ray." A recent photograph of Perfect, described as Poland's most popular rock band, showed the leader wearing a T-shirt with a photograph of the cover of *The Velvet Underground*, the paperback book about sadomasochism from which Reed's band took its name.

According to what I read, the Velvet Underground's influence now dominates alternative college radio. Their latest generation of progeny is said to include such emerging bands as 11th Dream Day, Stone Roses, Thelonious Monster, Field Trip, Das Damen, Died Pretty, Galaxie 500, and the Buck Pets. I admit I haven't heard any of these new bands. Like most people my age, I no longer listen to much new rock.

In my case, I at least like to think that middle age isn't the only reason. Twenty years ago, regardless of which bands you preferred or what else you listened to, it was possible to believe that rock 'n' roll wasn't *just music*. That's why the question of how your favorite rockers compared as musicians to their jazz or classical counterparts was irrelevant. Rock still isn't just music, but in light of what else it's become, the difference you can't help noticing is that jazz and classical musicians never have to worry about what to do next. They sing, compose, or play their instruments: Artistically, they are what they do. Every time a rock star makes a new record, he needs to decide on a unified motif for his videos, his carefully orchestrated press interviews, and his promotional tour. It has become impossible to tell the performer from his sales pitch.

WHAT MADE *SONGS FOR 'DRELLA* EXCITING EVEN BEFORE REED AND CALE appeared on stage was the anticipation of hearing new songs unaccompanied by stage maneuvers already audience-tested on MTV. (There had been just one previous performance, at St. Ann's Church in Brooklyn, earlier in the year—a dry run of sorts, minus Sirlin's visuals and minus one song. The new item was a "dream" monologue, written by Reed but delivered by Cale, in the style of Warhol's diaries.) These new songs, although jauntier and softer-edged, recalled in their spare textures and straightforward imagery the ones that Reed and Cale had performed with the Velvet Underground. The majority of them were first-person songs from Warhol's point of view, tracing his life from his childhood as the "gay and fatty ... pinkeyed, painting albino" son of working-class Czechoslovakian immigrants near Pittsburgh to his death from complications following routine gallbladder surgery in 1987—an event foreshadowed, in this subjective telling of the story, by the wounds inflicted by Solanis nineteen years earlier: "The bullet split my spleen and lung/The doctors said I was gone. ... " (The quotation is from Reed's "Nobody But You.")

Although Cale was generally more successful in capturing Warhol's affectless "wow," Reed filled his songs with rich observations about Warhol's arch naturalism as a filmmaker ("What you get is what you see"), his aversion to physical contact ("I like lots of people around me, but don't kiss hello and please don't touch"), and his anger at being blamed by some for the drug-related deaths of so many of his acolytes ("I'm no father to you all. ... I never said give up control"). But despite having Warhol admit that "if you're looking for deep meaning, I'm as deep as this high ceiling," Reed seemed to be trying, unsuccessfully for the most part, to persuade you that there was more to Warhol than met the eye. He was sentimentalizing Warhol, ascribing to him gut feelings that he consciously avoided in both his life and work.

Even so, I think I know what Ellen Willis was talking about, in her review of *Songs for 'Drella* in *The Village Voice*, when she said the songs nearly moved her to tears. My reaction wasn't quite as emotional, but I felt something. I didn't know exactly what it was until I went back and listened to Reed's 1989 album *New York* (Sire). In "Halloween Parade," Reed is amused by some of the getups at the annual Greenwich Village dragfest, but saddened by the absence of some familiar faces. He doesn't need to mention AIDS for you to realize that's what the song is about, nor do you need to have lost a friend to the epidemic to be moved. In "Dime Store Mystery," he sees *The Last Temptation of Christ*, muses that "the duality of nature, Godly nature, human nature, splits the soul," wonders what went through Warhol's mind "when you realized that the end had come for you," and wishes that he himself "hadn't thrown away my time on so much human and so much less divine." What makes Reed one of the few rock performers of the 1960s still worth listening to (out of more than sheer habit) is that he continues to deliver messages that the rest of us wish to ignore—in this case, that nobody lives forever, and that none of us including him is getting any younger.

The Atlantic Monthly, April 1990

Victim Kitsch

The American theater chases after a new musical sensation with all the messianic fervor of a religious sect pursuing redemption. And when the composer/librettist dies the day before his show begins previews, we have all the conditions required for cultural myth-making—a martyred redeemer, a new gospel, hordes of passionate young believers and canonization by The New York Times, *which devoted virtually all the theater columns of a recent Arts and Leisure section to* Rent, *the "rock opera for our time."*

—ROBERT BRUSTEIN, *THE NEW REPUBLIC*, APRIL 22, 1996

As everyone has surely heard by now, Jonathan Larson's *Rent*—the seventh musical ever to win a Pulitzer Prize for drama and the first to do so in advance of its Broadway premiere—is a rock musical in the tradition of *Hair* but with even grander pretensions to opera, "sung through" by an energetic cast that plays contemporary East Village versions of the artists and paupers in Puccini's *La Bohème*. The painter Marcello and the poet Rudolfo have been transformed into Mark, a documentary film-maker, and his roommate Roger, a rock singer and songwriter and a former junkie. Their friend, Tom Collins, a computer whiz fired from MIT and now homeless, is based on Puccini's philosopher, Colline. Musetta, Marcello's former lover, is Maureen, a performance artist who has decided she's a lesbian. The seamstress Mimi, Rudolfo's tubercular inamorata, is still Mimi, but now she's an exotic dancer trying her best to stay off the needle. She's also HIV-positive, as are Collins, Roger, and a Latino street drummer and drag queen named Angel, who corresponds to Puccini's Schaunard.

This Mimi doesn't die—or not exactly. She's brought back from a near-death experience by her self-absorbed Roger, who in effect tells her, "Hey, babe, don't die—you ain't heard my song yet." The one who does die is the drag queen, who, like so many fatally ill people on stage and screen nowadays, is a Life Force whose role in the grand scheme of things is to instill in others the courage to live (no petty, vain, hormonally fractured Candy Darling, s/he).

A rock opera isn't exactly a new idea. Whether we're talking concept albums or actual Broadway productions (*Tommy*, you'll recall, was both), there have been too many of them to count, none of them very good. Andrew Lloyd Webber's scores borrow the volume and aerobicized pulse of disco, and twenty-six years ago Stephen Sondheim built his score for *Company* around brass figures and bass lines that would not have sounded out of place on a Dionne Warwick record (almost nobody noticed, because he did this without saying so in *Playbill*). Staging *La Bohème* in modern dress isn't exactly unprecedented either, although one has to wonder if those who have tried it realize that Puccini's opera was a period piece to begin with (first presented in 1896, it was set sixty years earlier, in keeping with the Henri Murger serial novel on which it was based). Legend has it that operagoers were initially scandalized by Puccini's glorification of people they regarded as lowlifes. The truth seems to be that *La Bohème* was given a lukewarm reception because its Turin premiere closely followed that of Wagner's *Götterdämmerung*; despite Puccini's artful synthesis of traditional Italian and modern French elements *La Bohème* must have sounded positively quaint by comparison. So might *Rent* to anyone passingly familiar with current trends in performance art or rock 'n' roll. Except for a few bars of "Musetta's Waltz" played twice to comic effect on electric guitar (if you're like me, you first heard it as "Don't You Know," a hit by Della Reese in 1959), *Rent* borrows none of Puccini's music, just his characters and stray narrative details. Using the story of a great opera for a new musical might be as pointless as watching a Fred Astaire and Ginger Rogers movie for the plot. But this is something that could be charitably overlooked if it were *Rent*'s only problem.

I'VE SEEN THE SHOW TWICE NOW, THE FIRST TIME LAST WINTER, AT A CLOSE friend's urging, when—already a hot ticket—it was still being presented off-Broadway, at a downtown performance space blocks from Larson's grimy Alphabet City setting. There and on Broadway, where remarkably little about the show had changed, the first act ended with a bouncy song called "La Vie Bohème," Larson and the director Michael Greif's one stab at a big production number. This finds the entire fifteen-member cast at a banquet table following an offstage demonstration against a landlord (Mark and Roger's former roommate, turned yuppie) who's trying to evict them from their apartments and to remove an encampment of the homeless from the vacant lot next door. The scene corresponds to one in which Puccini's bohemians feast in a Latin Quarter café and then flee into the crowd when presented with the bill. "La Vie Bohème" is nothing if not catchy, but having it buzz around my head all through intermission allowed me to place exactly where I had heard that sporty, nonstop bass riff before—in "Cool Jerk," a 1966 dance hit by the Capitols, which I suspect is also where Larson first heard it. Todd Rundgren's remake from seven years later is another possibility, given that almost every number in *Rent* sounds vaguely like a tune that Larson would have heard on the radio as a teenager in the 1970s. (A tail-end Baby Boomer, he died in January, just short of his thirty-sixth birthday, after attending the final dress rehearsal for his show. So much has been made of his death in conjunction with his creation of characters facing imminent death from AIDS that many assume he was a casualty of the disease. But the aortic aneurysm that killed Larson isn't part of his show's zeitgeist.)

A story endlessly retold in the reams of copy devoted to Larson following *Rent*'s debut has it that he broke up with a girlfriend who doubted his ability to write an authentic gospel tune—the implication always being that "Seasons of Love," Larson's second-act opener, proves that he was right to ditch a woman of so little faith. But "Seasons of Love" is just Curtis Mayfield's "People Get Ready" stripped to the bone and reharmonized into something bland and blue-eyed enough to serve as a jingle for Hallmark or the friendly skies.

I don't think that Larson was guilty of plagiarism; he was just being derivative in much the same way I was when, in my younger and more vulnerable years, I unwittingly wrote *The Great Gatsby*. Like the books we love, our favorite songs won't let go. *Superbia, tick, tick ... BOOM!*, and *J.P. Morgan Saves the Nation*, Larson's previous shows, opened and closed quickly, in out-of-the-way venues. I haven't heard their scores, so I don't know if *Rent* marked a departure for Larson. Given his worship of Stephen Sondheim (another recurring theme in the articles on him), my guess is that he was a songwriter working more or less within the conventions of Broadway who, having decided to write a rock musical, wound up imitating the rock songs he remembered from his adolescence, which was probably the last time he had paid much attention to rock. Because I had read over and over that Larson waited tables for ten years at the Moondance Diner, near the foot of Sixth Avenue, while waiting for his big break, another of my hunches was that the Golden Oldies on the diner's jukebox had permeated his consciousness. A hike to the Moondance hours before I saw *Rent* on Broadway disproved this theory, because the place doesn't have a jukebox. Even so, in the theater that night, I felt as if I were listening to one stocked with hits from the 1970s.

With its echoes of Meat Loaf, Bruce Springsteen, David Bowie, Billy Joel, Gamble and Huff, *Flashdance*, and *The Rocky Horror Picture Show*, *Rent* is a musical in which the hits keep coming, but not ones we haven't heard before. The first time I saw *Rent*, I overheard a fellow intermission-smoker exclaim to a companion, "To think that out of the death of theater, *this* can grow." It just goes to prove that everyone is a critic these days, though perhaps only when the licensed critics have been unanimous.

ABOUT *RENT* THEY WERE ALMOST UNANIMOUSLY ECSTATIC, PAYING IT THE ultimate compliment of pinning their hopes for the survival of music theater on it. Their logic went something like this: By virtue of being so up-to-the-minute musically and in its depiction of characters for whom race, sexual orientation, and T-count present no barriers to friendship, *Rent* would sell tickets to young adults unlikely to pay to see Julie Andrews in *Victor/Victoria*, Carol Channing in *Hello, Dolly*, or anyone in *The King and I* (true of most young adults, I would think).

Another show making the transition from downtown to Broadway which was supposed to help get the fabulous invalid up and boogying was *Bring in 'da Noise, Bring in 'da Funk*, the latest offering from George C. Wolfe, who, in his capacity as producer for the Joseph Papp Public Theater/New York Shakespeare Festival, is emerging as the David Merrick of identity politics. Fast on its feet if somewhat soft in the head, *Bring* in 'da Noise is a dance musical in praise of rhythm—rhythm as a survival tactic, as a moral principle, as the secret ingredient in black life—with very few songs as such. Still running on Broadway as I write, it was assumed by critics to be of special interest to younger black audiences on account of having captured not just the sound of hip hop but a good deal of hip hop's combative street posture. Reviewers were enthusiastic about Bring in 'da Noise, and especially about the hoofing and choreography of its star, Savion Glover—the spoonful of sugar that helps the medicine go down in what's essentially a series of brilliantly staged but preachy vignettes on four centuries of pain and degradation inflicted upon African-Americans, beginning with slavery.

Rent was praised to a degree that would have seemed unrealistic even for The Threepenny Opera. In the opinion of Time, Rent was only "the most exuberant and original American musical to come along this decade." In the eyes of The Wall Street Journal, it was "the best new musical since the 1950s, the time of Leonard Bernstein's Candide and Jean Latoúche's The Golden Apple." (So much for West Side Story, How to Succeed in Business Without Really Trying, Cabaret, Company, and Sweeney Todd.) Michael Sommers, of the Newark Star-Ledger, enjoyed himself so much that he forgot to take notes, and Michael Feingold, of the Village Voice, was reduced to tears, presumably by Angel's death scene and its bitter reminder of Larson's own death hours away from triumph. The Voice was one of several papers to devote team coverage to Rent, with both the classical critic Leighton Kerner and the rock critic Evelyn McDonnell giving it their blessings. (McDonnell did complain that because "two of the main characters [Roger, the romantic hero, and Mark, who serves as the narrator] are straight white guys . . . for the umpteenth time, the stories of 'others' are made palatable by a dominant-voice narration." That Larson was a straight white guy himself is apparently no excuse, and he should have known better than to try to slip that dominant-voice narration past the Village Voice.)

The greatness of Rent is one of very few issues on which the Voice and The Wall Street Journal have ever seen eye to eye. Not that the opinion of either paper counts for very much when it comes to theater. Only The New York Times can make or break a show, and the smitten paper of record began blowing kisses Rent's way even before the show's official downtown opening, on February 13. A lengthy advance feature on Larson and Ben Brantley's rave review were only the beginning. A

Sunday Arts & Leisure section preceding the Broadway opening looked like a *Rent* supplement; in addition to yet another feature tracing the show's birth from the moment of conception on, the section included head shots and thumbnail biographies of each cast member and a large front-page color photo of them in costume, performing "La Vie Bohème." The whole thing was reminiscent of those team photos that lesser newspapers tuck into the Sunday funnies to celebrate a victory in the World Series or Super Bowl.

Rent emerged as a legitimate source of news when it became the prize in a bidding war between Broadway's two largest theatrical organizations, and then when it won four Tony Awards, including one as the season's best new musical and two others for Larson's book and score. (It was such a shoo-in that the producers of *Charlie Rose* and *The Late Show with David Letterman* didn't wait for the awards ceremony to book the show's principal cast members for post-Tony appearances.) But hardly a day seemed to go by early last spring without some mention of *Rent* in the *Times*, whether it was Margo Jefferson telling us how much like genuine Lower East Siders the cast looked in their "grunge-meets-salsa-meets-B-Boy-meets-Riot Grrl clothes," or Frank Rich arguing, on the Op-Ed page, that even though

> some of the turn-of-the-millennium fears given powerful voice by the dis-possessed bohemians of "Rent" resemble those of what we now call Pat Buchanan voters . . . [Mr. Larson] takes the very people whom politicians now turn into scapegoats for our woes—the multicultural, the multisexual, the homeless, the sick—and, without sentimentalizing them or turning them into ideological symbols or victims, lets them revel in their joy, their capacity for love and, most important, their tenacity, all in a ceaseless out-pouring of melody.

With the *Times* having spoken, *Rent* was soon everywhere, including the cover of *Newsweek*. Just over a week after the show's April 29 Broadway premiere the cast—already the most overexposed group of fic-tional young people since the cast of *Friends*—turned up in the *Times* once again, this time striking poses in a full-page Bloomingdale's ad announcing the opening of a *Rent* boutique. It was less a case of life imi-tating art or of couture imitating thrift-shop dishabille than of advertising imitating editorial.

I'VE BEEN TELLING FRIENDS THAT *RENT* ISN'T AS GOOD AS THE *TIMES* SAYS IT
is, but probably not as bad as I make it sound. A number that almost
everyone but me finds especially moving, "One Song Glory," has Roger,
the HIV-positive songwriter, whom we're told used to sing with a punk
rock band, expressing his desire to write one great song in the little time
he may have left. "One Song Glory," like the song Roger ultimately
writes, is a preening, melodramatic rock ballad of the sort that punk was
supposed to smash to smithereens. Still, this is one of those instances in
which good theater doesn't necessarily require a good song. Tim Weil,
the show's music director, has provided a starkly effective orchestration,
with guitar reverb suggesting the steady drip of an IV. Blake Burba's lighting increases the chill by dwarfing Roger in his own shadow—the
shadow of death. Frank Rich wasn't the only theatergoer to equate
Roger's desire for one final blaze of glory with what might have been
Larson's, had the composer known that this would be his final triumph
as well as his first.

The problem is that Roger could be *Rent* the show, and his bigger-
than-life shadow *Rent* the phenomenon. So much has been written
about *Rent* that future audiences may already be a little sick and tired of
it on their way into the theater. The show could fall victim to the media's
tendency to follow each binge with a purge. Already some of *Rent*'s most
ardent early champions, including Brantley and Jefferson, have begun to
question whether the show lost some of its purity or charm or social relevance in its transfer to Broadway. (The answer is no: It's a Broadway
musical that happened to have its debut off-Broadway.)

I find it significant that the only *Times* writers to express strong reser-
vations to begin with were two who know something about music—the
pop critic Jon Parales and the classical columnist Bernard Holland. I
once heard a pop critic argue that rock 'n' roll was impervious to satire;
Weird Al Yankovic was hardly the first to disprove this. What rock may be
impervious to, however, is emulation. *Rent* may look like rock 'n' roll,
with its spandex- and flannel-clad cast wearing head mikes and shouting
lyrics into one another's faces above a live band, but, like *Hair* almost
thirty years ago, it sounds more like Broadway.

Judged as Broadway, Larson's score does not lack simple virtues.
Stephen Sondheim praised his late disciple's music as "generous," a word
that strikes me as particularly apt, though Sondheim probably meant
something different by it than I would. Larson's melodies give themselves

up very easily. Even someone who isn't especially taken with the songs might find himself humming them on the way out, and this is all that many theatergoers ask of a musical. Larson's songs stick in your head, and not all of them are unwelcome there. (That they're also extremely easy to sing probably means that *Rent* will eventually become a favorite of college music and theater departments.) But this generosity is achieved at a cost. Larson's melodies are too close to the surface. Nothing harmonically complicated of the sort that goes on in Sondheim's songs goes on in Larson's. Although his lyrics are occasionally clever (when he's not making lists or settling for easy rhymes), his meanings are very close to the surface too. Unlike Sondheim's songs, Larson's are never shaded by the context in which they're sung. His lyrics are never revealed to be delusional; they mean exactly what they say. These may be faults common to all young composers, however talented; still, Larson seems not to have learned very much from his mentor, although this doesn't seem to bother reviewers and audiences distrustful of what they perceive to be Sondheim's frosty intellectualism.

In *Rent*'s book, Larson's generosity takes the form of bigheartedness toward his characters. Only two are beyond redemption, both of them peripheral and, in this context, stock villains: a drug dealer who tempts Mimi back on junk and a pastor who refuses to bury Angel and condemns Collins as a "faggot." Even Benny, the nouveau-yuppie landlord, does a good deed or two by the end, and the casting complicates our response to him by giving the part to an extremely affable black actor named Taye Diggs. If nothing else, *Rent* is laudably unstereotypical in its characterization. Collins, the homeless MIT hacker, is black, and one of the other black characters (Maureen, the performance artist's lesbian lover) is an attorney. The show's music is another story: As soon as we hear the opening bars of "Seasons of Love," we just know that one of the black actresses is going to step forth to supply a few gratuitous melismatic flourishes. This has become such a cliché that it even turned up in the 1995 Broadway revival of *How to Succeed in Business Without Really Trying*, in the song "Brotherhood of Man."

Larson's bigheartedness, which I imagine was a joy to those who knew him, works to his disadvantage as a playwright. In *Rent*, he indulged in a sentimentality of the sort that has always gone over big on Broadway, regardless of what social ills are being addressed (it's the same sort of sentimentality that keeps some of us from enjoying *La Bohème*). The show's title comes from an early song in which Larson's would-be artists defiantly refuse to pay their back rent. That they identify with their neighborhood's teeming homeless population is a given, yet the issue of social class is virtually ignored. Typical of *Rent*'s lack of political sophistication, Larson's bohemians—the voluntarily, and probably only temporarily, poor—oppose gentrification without realizing that aspiring artists such as themselves are inevitably gentrification's advance guard.

This is a show in which the observation that "the filmmaker cannot see, the songwriter cannot hear" passes for a profound insight. It's as though Larson believed that his characters faced no problems they couldn't solve by getting in touch with their feelings. Angel, the drag queen envied by artists for being his own canvas, is a character we've met countless times, and so is Mark, the filmmaker who wishes to document life but is afraid to participate in it. Mark, the show's narrator, is a stand-in of sorts for Larson and a surrogate for the audience. He's also the one principal character who isn't some combination of gay, HIV-positive, a woman, or a member of a racial minority. It's a difficult role, in that it asks the actor to be as self-effacing as a person in such company might be, for fear of being denounced as "privileged." Anthony Rapp, an energetic blur of an actor who's the best thing about *Rent*, may have succeeded too well in conveying his character's desire for inconspicuousness. The Tony nominating board overlooked him in favor of four others in *Rent*'s ensemble who sang louder and did a showier job of emoting: Adam Pascal, as Roger; Daphne Rubin-Vega, as Mimi; Idina Menzel, as Maureen; and Wilson Jermaine-Heredia, the only one of the four nominees who won (in the featured-actor category), as Angel.

Unlike Pascal, who, according to his program bio, used to sing and play guitar with a rock band called Mute, and Rubin-Vega, who once reached No. 1 on Billboard's dance chart, Rapp is a child of the theater and not pop music. Yet he's the only performer in *Rent* who looks comfortable singing rock on stage—maybe because he's the only one with sufficient stage experience to realize that behaving naturally while singing material of any kind in a theatrical context requires a great deal of acting technique. He obviously glanced at rock videos; with his hunched shoulders and slightly pigeon-toed gait, he has exactly the right look. Rapp is called on to deliver Larson's attempts at recitative, and displays a real knack for this style of singing. He makes even "La Vie Bohème" satisfying, which is no easy trick, given its endless and dated roll call of artists who were evidently favorites of Larson's but who have little resonance for today's young adults (Bertolucci? Kurosawa? Stephen Sondheim? Susan Sontag?).

Music and contemporary youth culture aren't the only areas in which *Rent* seems hopelessly out of touch. The character of Maureen, the performance artist, epitomizes everything that rings false about the show, even though it's fun watching Idina Menzel perform Maureen's act at the demonstration against Benny, the landlord. Maureen was Larson's chance to poke fun at the excesses of performance artists like Annie Sprinkle, who puts her feet in stirrups and invites her audiences to conduct a gynecological examination, and Karen Finley, infamous for supposedly committing unnatural acts with yams. But Maureen's act is annoyingly tame: She doesn't scream obscenities, smear anything on herself, or bleed on anyone. And since performance artists are exhibitionists practically by definition, wouldn't one who has only recently come out make her newly acknowledged lesbianism the focus of her piece?

LARSON COULD HAVE DEMONSTRATED WITH THE CHARACTER OF MAUREEN HOW well he knew his way around the Lower East Side, but he seems to have been too genuinely nice a person to take much glee in wicked satire. Besides, it's tough to be a satirist when you're always going for the goo. In a song called "Will I," an unnamed AIDS victim who is eventually joined by the entire company wonders if he'll lose his dignity along with control of his body. The song is meant to be moving, but finally it's only embarrassing. The friends I've lost to the epidemic, no matter how needy they were at the end, had too much dignity to make such a naked appeal for pity (or perhaps I just prefer to think so). Larson wanted to blast audiences out of their apathy, with the help of rock 'n' roll. But his show comes dangerously close to romancing the virus—to downgrading it to one more symptom of post-adolescent disengagement. In the 1960s, *Hair*, while inviting theater groups to cluck in wonder at that era's young people, with their free love, their psychedelics, and their loud music, reduced all of the world's evils, including the carnage in Vietnam, to the musical question, "How can people be so heartless?" *Rent*, for all that's supposed to be new about it, similarly invites theater groups to cluck in wonder at today's young people, with their bisexuality, their compromised immune systems, and their performance art.

Say what you will about *Hair* (and I'll say worse), that prototypical rock opera was transgressive in ways that *Rent* only imagines itself to be. In its own day *Hair* was as notorious for its nudity and its quasi-tribalism—elements borrowed from experimental theater, notably Julian Beck's Living Theater—as it was for its facsimile of the big beat. In some ways *Hair* was nothing more (but also nothing less) than an amplified, optimistic, mainstream version of the Living Theater's *Paradise Now*.

Rent serves a similar function in regard to today's experimental forms of performance art, but does so far less obviously and in a manner that promises to be far less liberating for mainstream theater. Two years ago Arlene Croce, the dance critic for *The New Yorker*, created a tempest by condemning as an example of an unfortunate trend a work by the HIV-positive dancer and choreographer Bill T. Jones that she admitted not having seen. This was *Still/Here*, a performance in which Jones's choreography was interspersed with videotapes of people with fatal illnesses talking about their impending deaths. I think Croce misjudged *Still/Here*, which I found to be moving largely for the videotaped interviews to which she categorically objected (the dancing itself struck me as mannered and earthbound). But I think that Croce was right to complain of being "*forced* to feel sorry for . . . performers, in short, who make of victimhood victim art" and to define this art as "a politicized version" of the "blackmail" practiced by even as great an artist as Charlie Chaplin when he asked audiences to share in his self-pity. Like *Noise/Funk*, with its pep talks on black pride and calculated appeal to a peculiar sort of pleasure that disguises itself as outrage at injustice, *Rent* neutralizes and mainstreams avant-garde victim art by sentimentalizing it into what I'm tempted to call victim kitsch.

Will *Rent* revitalize Broadway by persuading young adults who have grown up with rock 'n' roll that music theater has something to offer them? I doubt it, because rock is itself a form of theater for such young adults, just as street is a form of theater for the B-boys and gangbangers whose moves are emulated in *Noise/Funk*. Thirty-nine years ago did teen hoods flock to see their likenesses sing and dance in *West Side Story?*

Shows like *Rent* and *Noise/Funk* represent Broadway's attempt to colonize off-Broadway—to plunder its perceived riches. A relic of art before the age of mechanical reproduction, the theater has been dying for as long as anyone can remember, though despite Broadway's constant state of peril it contributes greatly to New York's tourism industry and the city's sense of itself as an artistic mecca. Music theater now seems in genuine peril, in large part because of the staggering cost of staging a new show and the consequent high cost of tickets (for $67.50, the price of a good ticket to *Rent*, you can see ten movies or buy five CDs). Originating shows downtown and then moving the most successful of them to Broadway appeals to producers as a sensible means of cutting down on start-up costs.

But this doesn't explain why *Rent* has sparked such enthusiasm among reviewers and others with no direct stake in its box office. The only explanation I can think of is that they love music theater so much they wish it to have what Larson's Roger wishes for himself—one great song to go out on. Either that or both they and Broadway are so out of touch that they mistake attempted social relevance for genius, and the slightest twitch for resurrection.

The Atlantic Monthly, September 1996

The Moral of the Story
from the Guy Who Knows

The original plan called for me to be in the studio last fall when Dion, now going by his full name, Dion DiMucci, recorded *Yo Frankie*—his first rock 'n' roll album after a decade of recording only Jesus songs. But Zach Glickman, Dion's manager, thought better of the idea. "He doesn't even want *me* there," Glickman said. "You have to realize this is the toughest record of his career. He's not a nineteen-year-old kid anymore. He's a fifty-year-old man and this could be his last shot."

Glickman mentioned, however, that Dion would be returning to his old neighborhood in the Bronx to present a signed copy of his autobiography, *The Wanderer*, to the branch library there. A crew from *Entertainment Tonight* would be tailing him, and there would also be a photographer from *People* magazine. So one more putz with a notebook wasn't going to make a difference.

"You can see where he grew up," Glickman said, shrugging.

The photographer on assignment from *People* turned out to be David Gahr, an old pal of Dion's. We piled into the hired car, with Dion sitting between me and Glickman in back, Gahr up front with the driver, and the TV crew following us over the Major Deegan Expressway in their van.

"You're looking good," Gahr told Dion, turning round to face him.

"A little heavier, though?" Dion asked.

"Maybe in the face," Gahr admitted. "But it looks good on you."

"Susan's pasta," Dion said, patting his belly.

"You still in Miami?" Gahr asked.

"No, we moved to Boca. Last month. All of Susan's friends were moving up there, so they convinced her and she convinced me. She was right. Miami was beginning to look like here," Dion said, gesturing toward the window. "Like the Bronx."

As we neared Dion's old block—Belmont and 188th Street—he began to point out remembered sights. "Dick Gidron Cadillac!" he said as we raced up Fordham Road. "That's where I bought my first car. A white T-Bird. We'd load in it and go for hamburgers at the White Castle.

"This library we're going to used to be the local movie house, and it was really a little dump," he explained to me, donning the checkered tweed cap he wears on stage and for photographs, though it never quite goes with the rest of him. (He wears it for the reason you think he does. But his hair is thin only at the temples, not on top.) Typically, he was otherwise outfitted almost entirely in black: jacket, shirts, slacks, boots, shades. "The nice movies was the Paradise. It was on the Grand Concourse, a little ways from here. It was called the Paradise because the ceiling was painted with clouds and twinkling stars. I took Susan there on our first date."

Dion had the driver stop on Belmont Avenue and 188th, across from a concrete lot. He struck a pose under the street sign.

"The standard Belmont Avenue shot, right?" he asked the *ET* producer.

"Did you guys actually used to sing on this corner?" the producer asked, after getting his footage.

Dion grinned. "We sang in church halls and recreation centers, not on street corners. But people say we did—even some of the people who still live around here."

We walked over to 187th Street—"the main drag," Dion told us. "And that was the hub," he added, pointing to Our Lady of Mount Carmel, the Roman Catholic church on the corner. "There's three choir lofts in back, and in the third loft there was this guy named Hugo, who played the organ. My father loved the organ, and he used to take me in there every day when I was small. We'd climb up the steps, and the bell tower was the next tier. Hugo died. The funny thing is I remember them holding the service for him up in the organ loft and carrying the casket down.

That was the last time my father ever took me to church. I must have been eight years old."

Trailed by Gahr and the umbilically linked *ET* camera and sound men, Dion spent the next half hour exchanging handshakes and hugs with store owners and shoppers, strutting up 187th Street in his big, slow, hitchy, bad-motherfucker Bronx walk.

"Tremont north of Crotona is still Italian," he explained, giving us the lay of the land. "But if you wander just a few blocks, you're in another part of the Bronx—another world. The people up on this end don't leave the neighborhood much. They go to their jobs, they spend the weekends wallpapering their kitchens, and they never notice that the world is changing all around them."

Along with a Foto Quick, the block we were on included a bakery, a pork store, a bridal shop, a Catholic bookstore, a sub shop, a shop that appeared to sell nothing but egg noodles, and another whose window displayed nothing but olive oil in gallon tins. Most of the shops had terrazzo flooring outside their entrances and basement doors that opened on the sidewalk. There were cars double-parked in the middle of the street, as there always seem to be in solidly Italian neighborhoods. Some of the people who passed by spoke in Italian. They either recognized Dion or asked one of us, in English, who he was.

"Don't waste this trip up here," Dion kept telling us, playing the civic booster. "Buy some food. People come here from all over New York for the bread."

As we left the library after the book presentation, there was a white Chrysler New Yorker stopped at the red light, with Dion's "The Wanderer," from 1961, playing on the radio. Everybody laughed.

"You have good taste, my man," Dion said, leaning into the driver's window.

"*Dion!*" shouted the driver, who'd been oblivious to him to that point. "I been to hear you all over."

"When 'I Wonder Why' became a hit and the guys and I still lived here, this whole neighborhood was like one giant speaker," Dion said after the fan drove off. "People would have their windows up, yelling to my father, 'Hey, Pat—Hey, *Pasquale*. Your boy is on the radio.'"

Dion asked if anyone besides him was hungry.

"Then let's go see David," he said, leading us to the deli counter of a meat and produce market on Arthur Avenue, where a young man named

David made him a hero stuffed with salami, caparole, prosciutto, smoked mozzarella, and sweet and hot peppers, naming each ingredient for the camera.

"David, what *the* fuck!" Dion yelled, turning to me and showing me the bulging sandwich. "You expect me to eat this?"

It was comforting to hear him swear—he was no ordinary born-again Christian, that was for sure.

"This is how they show love around here," he said, emphatically, slicing the hero into sections and passing them around. "They feed you. Even when you're not hungry."

On the way back to the car, he stopped to talk with several well-wishers, including an intense young man carrying a book on reincarnation by Edgar Cayce who talked with me about the neighborhood's drug problem, after Dion gave him the brush. He said his name was Geno and that he was in his early thirties (I would have guessed him to be in his early twenties). He was on his way to the Botanical Gardens, he told me, and he'd asked Dion to join him. "I just wanted him to know what an inspiration he's been to some of us who are trying to stay clean, and to encourage him in his faith," Geno said. "He said maybe another time."

Dion beckoned to me from up the block as I dawdled along with Geno, who apparently wasn't in the script. "I'm gonna get a cream ice," Dion yelled. "Come on and walk me."

As we watched the woman in the store scoop the flavored ice into two paper cups, it occurred to me that although Dion had given us the grand tour, he hadn't shown us his old apartment building. I asked him where it was.

"Around here," he said, dismissing the question with a shrug. "But let me ask *you* something. What were you talking about with that wiggy kid?"

I told him that Geno had said that drugs in this neighborhood were worse than I could imagine, and that his own brother was hooked. He'd also told me that the basements of all of the buildings on one block of 187th were interconnected, and that it was like a subterranean drug supermarket under there.

"Uh huh," Dion said dismissively. "Can you imagine, if you were a kid growing up around here, walking around with a book on reincarnation and saying to people"—he imitated blissed-out—" 'It's such a beautiful day. Let's go to the park and meditate.' "

On the ride back to Manhattan, Dion talked animatedly about the new record and his hopes for it. But as we passed under a bridge that cast his face in shadows, his mood changed in a New York minute. Suddenly looking very tired, he again raised the question of "the wiggy kid."

"What I don't understand," he said, staring straight ahead but addressing himself to me, "is why if you're writing about me, you want to talk to a kid who doesn't even know me, who I never even laid eyes on before today."

I reminded him that I had questioned a lot of the people we saw in the Bronx, including a young woman with a baby and a stroller who had timidly approached him in the market. She'd told me that Dion had been a friend of her late brother.

"Her brother and I used to shoot smack together on her mother's roof," he said, grimacing slightly as he turned to confront me through his shades. "Did she tell you that?"

She hadn't, but I said nothing, sensing that no answer I could give would be the right one.

"I don't know," he said in response to my silence, waving his arms around comically, which was no easy trick in that crowded backseat. "I just don't know about this."

We had arrived at the hotel.

"I'm sorry, man," he said as he climbed out of the car.

As we shook hands, I instinctively gripped his a little tighter and a little longer than was necessary, and to our mutual embarrassment, we wound up going through all the positions of a soul handshake.

"Take your nap, Guido, and I'll be by for you around six," Glickman called after him.

"Give the guy a break, will you?" Glickman then said to me. "You'd be depressed, too, if somebody took you back to the neighborhood you grew up in every time you had a new record. He'll talk to you when he's ready to talk to you. He liked you all right."

He did?

"Hey, if he didn't, he wouldn't've said he was sorry."

DION'S FIRST HITS WERE AS LEAD SINGER OF DION & THE BELMONTS (THE singsong "A Teenager in Love" is the one everybody remembers, although "I Wonder Why," with its rocketing harmonies and faster-than-the-speed-of-song intro, is the one worth remembering). His solo hits included "Runaround Sue," "The Wanderer," and a belated cover version of the Drifters' "Ruby Baby" that was even grittier than the original — something you could say of no other white cover version of a black rhythm 'n' blues hit before the Beatles covered Barrett Strong's "Money." Alone, or with the Belmonts, Dion had twenty records on the Top 40 between 1958 and 1963. After the British invasion, he had nothing on the charts until "Abraham, Martin and John," in 1968, a hymn to its era's martyrs that didn't reverse his slide, only halted it temporarily. Although he continued to release albums into the late 1970s, none of them sold.

A born-again Christian since the late 1960s, Dion performed mostly church-sponsored concerts after 1979. He rarely sang his old hits for the faithful, even though "the congregation would go wild whenever he did," says Glickman. "Some of them weren't always Christian, you know."

Though one of Dion's six Christian albums was nominated for a Grammy in that category, few outside the evangelical subculture knew about the born-again Dion. After not having given him a thought in years, many people confused him with Fabian or Frankie Avalon, or any of the other Italian-American singers who helped teenagers to pass the time between Elvis's induction into the Army and the Beatles' first appearance on *Ed Sullivan*. The question most frequently asked about Dion wasn't "Whatever happened to him?" but "Which one was he?"

HE WAS THE ONE THAT BOYS LIKED—PERHAPS EVEN MORE THAN GIRLS DID. He was especially popular with white boys who imagined themselves tougher, darker, Italian (a way of being black while still being white). "Here's the moral of the story from the guy who knows," Dion sang in "Runaround Sue," and the moral of the story was essentially the same in all of his songs: "'This chick's a tease, this chick's a bitch, this chick's a real cunt,'" says the novelist and screenwriter Richard Price, who grew up a decade after Dion in a multiethnic housing project on the other side of the Botanical Gardens from Dion's predominantly Italian neighborhood. Price, a self-described "sharkskin bar mitzvah boy, a Myron who wanted to be a Vinny" as a teenager, called his first novel, about a fictional Italian-American street gang, *The Wanderers*.

"Runaround Sue, what was her big crime?" Price asks. "She goes out with other guys."

In my neighborhood, we used to sing "goes down" on other guys and assume that's what Dion meant.

"So?" Price asked. "I mean, big deal. If I think back on it, now that I have a three-digit IQ, his songs all had one message: Pussy can kill. It was all macho woe-is-me, sort of like a guinea version of country and western. But you didn't think about music then, except to react to it."

"I grew up in the Bronx in the early 1960s, so Dion was it for me," says Mitchell Cohen, of Arista Records, who signed Dion after hearing him do his old hits at Radio City Music Hall, in 1987. "It's hard to define, but I think that his music served the same function for male adolescents of that time that rap and heavy metal do now. That kind of swagger—'Hey, hey, I'm a man, and that chick who just put me down is nothin', you know?'"

Richard Price: "It was sharkskin music, white working-class music, before working-class street music became self-conscious, with Bruce Springsteen. I never got into the girl group thing because I didn't particularly want to be Diana Ross or the Shangri-Las. Dion and, I would say, the Four Seasons were the ultimate in teenage macho, before macho became a concept. It was music that you could posture with in your mind. Pretend that you were tough and *coool*. The music you like when you start having hard-ons is the music you remember for life. It becomes your war song."

A FRIEND OF MINE WHO GREW UP IN THE NORTH BRONX AND WAS IN ELEMEN-
tary school when Dion was riding high remembers another kid pointing to a group of neighborhood toughs loitering outside P.S. 14, and whispering "Dion & the Belmonts"—facetiously, my friend thinks. Dion, in his autobiography (co-written by Davin Seay), remembers himself and the group (Carlo Mastrangello, Angelo D'Aleo, and Freddie Milano) decked out in greaser finery: "shiny nylon shirts, pegged pants with thin black belts, and low, Cuban-heeled shoes—what we called pimp boots." But album jackets and teen magazines of the period showed Dion & the Belmonts conservatively dressed in sports coats or cardigans, with white dress shirts. Dion retained the collegiate look after parting with the group in 1961.

"The young people who were recording in those days had to be well-groomed and well-dressed, because the press thought that rock 'n' roll was the lowest form of life, and that the people who sang it had just crawled out from under a rock," says Connie DeNavé, whose press agency, Image Makers, represented Dion, Fabian, Frankie Avalon, and Connie Francis.

"We had to let them know that this music wasn't garbage, which is what we were being told morning, noon, and night by the newspaper columnists and *Time* magazine. There was a limited amount of acceptable fashion for a young man at that time. We had to pay attention to color and cut, because any deviation from the norm might have had hoodlum or even homosexual connotations. We couldn't allow the Guido look, but we were walking a fine line, because we didn't want to dress these young boys like their fathers.

"The trick was for them to look comfortable in nice clothes. Young people in the music business were very unsophisticated then. They had to be trained never to smoke in public and never to have a glass in front of them, even a glass of water, when they were photographed, because it might look like they were drinking and they would be finished overnight.

"They had to be taught how to enter a restaurant and take their seats in gentlemanly fashion. Did Dion tell you the story of how I locked him and the Belmonts in my office and taught them how to eat with the right fork? I had hundreds of menus for them to look over and tell me what items they didn't know, because like most kids, they were used to ordering hamburgers and french fries when they ate out. My biggest problem was with Carlo, who wouldn't put a napkin across his lap because he thought it would make him look gay.

"They got even with me, though. We were in Sardi's once, practicing for a press conference, and I kept asking them, 'Isn't this nice? Isn't this comfortable?' And they'd mumble, 'Aw, we dunno.' Either Freddie or Carlo, I forget which, ordered a lamb chop, and when it came, he picked it up and said, 'Hey, this is a nice piece of meat.' They passed it around the table, saying, 'Yeah, it really is good meat,' until it was back on Freddie or Carlo's plate. That was just to shake me up, but when I saw whichever one of the boys it was begin to eat, he proceeded to cut a piece of the lamb chop, put his vegetables and a little bit of the mashed potatoes on the fork, put the whole thing in his mouth, which was extended out to here, and then begin to chew. God forbid if a reporter asked him a question—he would have spit food on him trying to answer."

The perception of Dion as an archetypal street-corner "hitter" was based on something we *heard*, not on anything we saw in his glossies. But it was the pictures that lied. He was expelled from seven different high schools, dropping out altogether after recording the pre-Belmonts "The Chosen Few," in 1957. He was, he admits, the kind of punk who would "punch somebody in the face to show them you exist. I was always being thrown out of school for fighting in the lunchroom, picking up chairs and hitting people—just crazy, you know? Carlo remembers first meeting me in a pool room. He says we talked about music, then the next thing he knew, I punched somebody and walked out.

"I was even kicked out of a *town* once." The town was Bergenfield, New Jersey, where Dion was sent to live with an uncle who was supposed to rehabilitate him.

"I was accused of being a bad influence on these kids from the suburbs because I did the grind with the girls at the parish dance. We used to go to the shopping mall, my cousin Tommy and I and a bunch of other kids, and make like we were in a James Dean movie. We'd come screeching into the parking lot, park our cars in a circle, and everybody'd put their lights on and make as much noise as we could. A guy named Ronnie would set his drums up right there in the center of the cars, and he'd be hitting his fucking drums, and I'd be standing on the hood of a car singing and everybody else would be banging on the cars or whatever else they could find, until the cops would come and bust us up."

He was a Fordham Baldy, a Bronx street gang that many who've seen the film version of Price's *The Wanderers* assume were so-named because they shaved off their hair on joining.

"Nah!" Dion says. "It was after the American Eagle, the insignia on the jackets. Just like the Diggers, their insignia was a dagger with a snake around it. But a lot of people really did think the Baldies shaved their heads to be in the gang. You know how stories get around a neighborhood.

"But some of those stories from my time were *true*. Like Shorty Neely, an Irish guy. He and a bunch of his friends took on a whole gang one night, and they wiped up the street with Shorty. He had stab wounds from the top of his neck to the bottom of his spine. He would show you his stitches. He had a hundred-and-fourteen stitches down his back. A local legend, whew! I mean, I wanted to be tough, and I was in the gang fights. But nothing like that. Some of those guys were animals. They would put their fist through a refrigerator!

"It was so senseless. South of us were the Sinners, a black gang, and the Harlem Redwings, who were Hispanic. To the east of us were the Italian Barettas and another Italian gang that called themselves the Golden Guineas, believe it or not. But it wasn't just the Italians against the blacks or Spanish. We'd fight one another, if we had to."

DION WAS ALSO A JUNKIE. "THE THING I GREW UP WITH WAS THAT GENE KRUPA smoked pot. He was on the front page of all the newspapers, and he was supposed to be a drug addict. I started smokin' pot when I was about thirteen, and I tried heroin real young, too. I did it and I liked it, and I wanted to do more of it. I thought I had control of it. I thought it *gave* me control. I really did.

"I remember I was in a basement on 187th Street, where you were with me that day. We were in there, a bunch of guys, with baby carriages and all the other stuff that people stored down there, and we opened up this little bag, and took the ends of two matches, and you hold it between them and snort.

"Man, I came out of that basement and I walked up Crotona Avenue and I remember I was on the white line in the middle of the street with the tenement buildings on either side of me, and it was like the world was in the palm of my hand. The kid has arrived: The fucking *kid* has arrived! All my doubts and insecurities were gone. The second-guessing. What to say to Susan, who I had a crush on, when I saw her. I walked up to her in the corner candy store and started talkin' some shit and I couldn't say anything wrong. I had self-confidence up the kazoo."

He made no attempt to keep his habit secret from his girlfriend or his parents. "I used to grub money off Susan for drugs. After a while, I didn't even try to hide it from my mom and dad, because I had no respect for them. In my eyes, my father was a wimp and a pain in the ass. If he told me to do something, I'd do the opposite."

By 1964 the need to stay high—preferably on heroin, but on amphetamines or alcohol in a pinch—governed Dion's life, almost to the exclusion of his career. He remembers once driving nonstop to New York from Boston to score, missing his opening night at a Boston supperclub as a result, and being threatened with baseball bats by the irate, mob-connected promoters. In 1965, when he and Susan (who, surprisingly, never left him or became a user herself) were living in a house overlooking the Hudson River, in Nyack, New York, he decided to take his own life. A voice within him, which he says he recognized as his own voice, said "God, please help me." When he opened his door, he discovered that his car had been stolen and this was all that prevented him from driving off the Tappan Zee Bridge. He now recognizes this moment as a prelude to his spiritual rebirth. Although a previous attempt at supervised rehabilitation had failed, he finally weaned himself from heroin with a long and difficult treatment at a private New York hospital in 1966. But he admits in his autobiography that he drank so heavily in compensation over the next two years that "I might just as well have been mainlining scotch, the way I let booze take me over."

Dion finally straightened out his personal life with help from his father-in-law, the late Jack Butterfield, himself a recovering alcoholic who exchanged the bottle for the Bible. "Drugs were never my real problem," he says now. "My problem was that I couldn't handle my emotions. Plus, both of my parents had alcoholic fathers. The way I understand it, if somebody has an addictive personality, they're different. Saying 'just say no' to them is like telling somebody with diarrhea to use their willpower, to *just cut it out!*"

DION CAME ALONG AT A TIME WHEN TEENAGERS' ALLOWANCES WEREN'T sufficient to sustain a young performer's career. This was why he donned a tuxedo when he first went solo in the early 1960s, for a nightclub act as "The Last of the First-Name Singers," and why his early albums included, along with his own hits and cover versions of recent hits by other young singers, knock-'em-dead Vegas showstoppers like "My Mammy," "One for My Baby," and "You're Nobody 'til Somebody Loves You." "I want to learn more about my profession. I want to be in Broadway musicals. I want to do a nightclub act. . . . I want to know how I, too, can become a truly great entertainer," he said in a piece written by DeNavé that appeared under his byline in the fan magazine *Dig* in 1961, a year before he signed with Columbia, a label then more identified with Mitch Miller, Andy Williams, Johnny Mathis, and Broadway cast albums than with rock 'n' roll. "I was forced to record songs for my parents, not my friends," Dion admits in his autobiography. "When it came down to it, the role they were grooming me for was already more than adequately filled by Bobby Darin," he adds in a chapter that ends with him tossing "$25,000 worth of show business schmaltz"—including his tuxedo, scripted patter, and arrangements—into the incinerator.

That was in 1963, when, along with his substance abuse, Dion was going through an intense period of musical self-examination, trying to rediscover what had made singing pleasurable for him in the first place. His style had always been a hybrid of black and white influences. There were difficult-to-place rural echoes on "A Teenager in Love"—they're what makes the song palatable. You can hear Hank Williams in Dion's phrasing. Williams was Dion's first musical passion, when he was ten years old. He began to collect the country singer's records after hearing him sing "Honky Tonk Blues" on a New Jersey station's hillbilly show. To this day, he can't tell the story without bursting into the song, and you can imagine what a revelation it must have been for him to stumble on something so raw and vigorous—something so close to what became rock 'n' roll —when pop music still meant "Papa Loves Mambo" and "The Song from *Moulin Rouge*."

Imitating Williams, Dion appeared on a local TV show wearing a straw hat and standing next to a haystack—a preteen Bronx country boy, and before he balked at the notion, his parents envisioned him becoming a child star. "I used to sing Hank's songs, like 'Cold, Cold Heart,' in those little neighborhood bars where everybody else sang dirty Italian drinking songs. Who knows? I might eventually record an album of Hank Williams songs, because I still like them. They're still inside of me."

Dion grew up in one of those white, working-class neighborhoods in which blacks are regarded as invaders. Yet kids in these neighborhoods tend to walk black, talk black, and especially *sing* black. This is true of Bensonhurst today, and it was true of Crotona Avenue in the late 1950s. Dion & the Belmonts emulated black harmony groups such as the Paragons, the Cadillacs, and the Jesters: Dion describes the group's background riffing as "vocal percussion," likening the voices to r&b honkers, saxophonists like Red Prysock and Big Al Sears. (There was once even a black Belmont. When Angelo D'Aleo joined the Navy, soon after the release of "A Teenager in Love," in 1959, a black studio singer named Prentice—no one remembers his last name—took his place on the group's recordings.)

But before that, Dion used to sit on his front stoop parroting the blues songs he heard the building's black superintendent singing. "Willie would be doing his work, singing, 'The ol' jack rabbit is a-jumpin' in the grass/Wait 'til he hear that shotgun blast,'" Dion told me, singing with a Mississippi slur. "If Willie was alive today, I'd be asking him a million questions about how he learned those songs. He might have been from Mississippi, but I don't really know, because who the hell wondered, in those days, where anybody was from before they were from the Bronx?"

He'd forgotten all about Willie when one day he was in his producer Robert Mersey's office at Columbia Records and overheard a Robert Johnson record through the wall. The next office belonged to John Hammond, the well-born record producer who had been instrumental in the careers of Bessie Smith, Billie Holiday, Count Basie, Benny Goodman, Aretha Franklin, and Bob Dylan. Hammond introduced Dion to the work of other country blues singers, including Lightnin' Hopkins, Furry Lewis, and Mississippi John Hurt.

Dion had moved to Greenwich Village by then, within proximity of the coffeehouses that were the temples of the blues revival of the early 1960s, and he became obsessed with the blues. He found out that Reverend Gary Davis was living in the Bronx, and showed up at Davis's door for a slide guitar lesson. "He didn't know how to teach. But he did know how to play, and he would say 'Watch me do this.' All he knew about me was that I was on Columbia Records, making a hundred thousand dollars a year. That was unreal to him."

Dion's attempts to sing the blues fell on unsympathetic ears at Columbia. "I would play something on the guitar that Robert Mersey liked, and he would want to bring horns in to play that lick," Dion recalls in disgust. He agrees that Hammond would have been a perfect choice to become his producer, given their mutual interest in the blues. "But you have to realize that Columbia had signed me for mucho dollars, and I was supposed to be making that money back for them with hit singles. Hammond wasn't there to produce hits, just to bring prestige to the company, sort of like the classical division, but in his own way. So it never occurred to anyone, including me, that we should work together. Plus, I got the feeling that he thought the blues were something only blacks had any business singing."

In other words, Dion probably wasn't "authentic" enough for a purist like Hammond. Nor, as it turned out, was he authentic enough for most of the white youths who discovered the blues around the same time he did. As an acoustic solo act on the coffeehouse circuit in the late 1960s and early 1970s, he was in a no-win situation. Because he was Dion, there were die-hard fans in his audiences who wanted to hear "The Wanderer" and "Ruby Baby" but were likely to be mystified by Dion's blues and original folk songs. But if he did his old numbers, even as talking blues, which he sometimes did, he risked being thought of as desperate and opportunistic, a greaser who had tie-dyed his muscle shirts and grown his hair. "Abraham, Martin and John" was a fluke pop hit, not a rock hit. It was played on AM radio, with Motown and Tommy James, not on FM with Ten Years After and Canned Heat.

None of us thought about whether Dion was a great singer in the late 1950s and early 1960s. Like Richard Price says, you didn't think about music then, except to react to it. I liked Dion, and that was enough. As an adult, I enjoyed hearing "The Wanderer" or "Runaround Sue" by surprise on oldies programs.

But if that was all there had been to it, Dion wouldn't have moved me so deeply keening the words to "No One Knows" on the 1972 Dion & the Belmonts reunion album from Madison Square Garden. I didn't know then that he'd been influenced by Hank Williams, but I might have guessed from the pang of his blue notes and the way he shivered his vowels—the sharp emotions he channeled into the song. There was an ironic subtext to the performance: Dion was singing better than ever—as expressively as John Lennon, but with better technical equipment—and he was probably never going to have another hit.

I VISITED DION AT HOME IN BOCA RATON LAST YEAR, A FEW DAYS AFTER Christmas. He picked me up at my hotel in his steel-gray Volvo after calling to ask if it would be all right if he squeezed in his morning run first. I don't know what sort of rock 'n' roll mobile I was expecting, but the Volvo surprised me—a car for a parent concerned with quality, economy, and safety. Dion was wearing a black T-shirt and denim shorts—no hat. As he drove, he kept reaching his right hand up to a wooden crucifix hanging from the rear-view mirror, obviously uneasy at the prospect of a formal interview.

He pulled the Volvo into his driveway, behind his wife's Nissan. The house was a modest stucco suburban one-story, with a wreath on the door and a tree in the living room.

"What's August call that tree?" Dion asked his wife, referring to the youngest of their three daughters as we walked into the kitchen.

"Your Charlie Brown tree, because it's so scrawny and sad-looking," said Susan, a lightly freckled woman with startling green eyes and her red hair in a shoulder-length shag.

We sat at the kitchen table, looking out at the enclosed swimming pool and the man-made lake behind it.

"I hope you don't mind being indoors today, but when it's this hot in Florida, no one goes outside until around five o'clock or six, when it lets up a little bit," Dion said.

Susan set three napkins and saucers on the table and brought us coffee and crisp, knotty, powdered, orange-flavored pastries that Dion said were traditional Italian Christmas *dadal*. His grandmother taught Susan the recipe.

We small-talked, the three of us. Susan asked me about my flight, and we all agreed that flying during the holidays was a chore.

"I remember the first time I got on an airplane," said Dion, who, if he had been willing to chip in $25, might have been on the private charter that crash-landed on an icy Minnesota field in 1959, killing Buddy Holly, Richie Vallens, and the Big Bopper—the most famous airplane crash in rock 'n' roll history. "It could have been the *very* first tour I was ever on, me and the Belmonts with Bobby Darin and some other people. I was probably eighteen. I got a window seat, and Carlo is sittin' there beside me, sweatin' it out, because he doesn't like to fly. We got above New York, and I look down and see all those little squares and cars that looked the size of ants. I looked down at what I thought could be my neighborhood, and all the stuff I thought was so important, the gangs, the fighting for turf, the things that seemed so important that you were willing to kill for them—get zip guns and brass knuckles and smash each other's heads in. 'The shit is on,' we used to say. You ever hear that? 'The shit is on.' It all seemed so senseless to me and insignificant from that airplane window. I had an awakening of sorts. I mean, I always knew that the world was bigger than the Bronx, but I needed to physically *see* that it was. Does that make any sense?

"I mean, I was always in fights, but there was somethin' in me sayin', 'What am I doin'?' My sister Joanie tells a funny story, about going to see *Rock Around the Clock* at the Paradise Theater. The gang down there was the Imperial Hoods, and one of the members was a guy named Richie. A *bad* guy. Joanie and her friend, Arlene, are in their seats, tryin' to watch the movie, and Richie and his whole gang gather around them. 'Hey, honey, what's your name?'—that whole bit. She said, like, 'Hands off and cool it, or you'll be sorry. My brother is with the Baldies.' And they said, 'Oh, yeah? What's his name?' She said, real tough, 'His name is Dion DiMucci, and just maybe you heard of him.' And they just laughed! But they left her and Arlene alone after that, because those guys knew me and respected me as, like, the neighborhood singer. But crazy as I was, they weren't afraid of me."

Lark, the middle of Dion and Susan's three daughters, on winter break from the Academy of the Dramatic Arts, in New York City, wandered into the kitchen. I recognized her because I'd seen her onstage with Dion over the summer, at Pier 84; wearing a flared red dress, she'd sung "Maybe" and "The Boy from New York City," two songs from her father's era.

"This is Lark!" Dion announced in a comically loud voice. "The famous actress! Home from acting school! And sleeping very late! Lark, this man saw you! Your famous red dress."

Lark nodded hello, then fled, embarrassed by her father's teasing.

"Tane, our oldest, who's real smart, wants to be a teacher when she gets out of college, but Lark wants to be in Broadway musicals," Dion said. "I took her on the road with me this summer mostly to give her some idea of what it's like to be in front of an audience, but also because I wanted to be able to spend some time with her before she left home— although don't tell her that. I had to teach her those two songs you heard her sing. She just knows *Cats*, Andrew Lloyd Webber, things like that.

"You know, the other morning, Lark was telling us about school, and she was amazed when she found out that Susan once went to acting school, too. She couldn't even imagine that! Could she, Sue?"

"I told her I'm playing the part of a wife and mother now," Susan replied, clearing the table.

"I'll tell you a story about one of my kids," Dion said. "A few years ago, I was in Town Center with August. She must have been around ten. It was Valentine's Day. *PM Magazine*, a local TV show, was there taking pictures of valentines: boyfriends and girlfriends, husbands and wives, mothers and fathers and their kids. They recognized me and asked me to be in it—the local celebrity, you know? So they set up the cameras, and I took August in my arms and said, 'Give Daddy a kiss for Valentine's Day.' She turned her head away from me. I said, 'No, come on, gimme a kiss.' She said, 'I don't want to.' And everybody from the show is saying,

'Whatsa matter? You don't love your Daddy?' I let her go and said forget about it. No big deal. Later we're in the car, pulling out of the parking lot, and August starts crying: 'Oh, Daddy, I feel so bad I didn't do what you wanted.' I said, 'Sweetheart, listen to me. You didn't have to do anything you didn't wanna do. They were just doin' their thing for the TV show, and when they asked me to be in it, I felt obligated because they know who I am and they've been very nice to me. But it's no big deal. We had a ball today, right, just walkin' around the mall?' But I could tell that she still felt bad.

"So, later on, I was in the living room closet, down on the floor going through some files I keep in there. I forget what I was looking for, but I looked up and saw August standing there, watching me. I asked her what she wanted, and she got down on her knees and threw her arms around me and says, 'Oh, Daddy, I love you so much!' Then she runs right out. And all of a sudden, I remembered the scripture where Jesus says when you pray, go into your prayer closet and pray to your Father in private. Don't be like the hypocrites who make a big public display with the beads and shawls. It would have been nice if August had kissed me on TV, and we were all sitting around watching it later that night. But what she did came right from her heart, with the honesty of a ten-year-old kid. She was being more honest than any of us."

DION WASN'T ON; HE WAS JUST TALKING. SO IT SEEMED LIKE A GOOD TIME TO ask about his own parents. In consenting to my snooping, he'd made one request: that I not attempt to speak with his father, Pasquale, or his mother, Frances, who were apparently unhappy with the way Dion had characterized them in his book. Although he's closer to his parents than most middle-aged men (they even live nearby, in the house he bought for them in Miami), Dion's childhood grievances against them remain. According to Dion, Pasquale was the neighborhood jerk, a small-time puppeteer and failed all-around entertainer who never earned enough money in one year to have to file an income tax. In contrast, his mother was an overwrought scold: "Always looking for the next thing to be done while my dad was in the attic making puppets or down in the basement lifting weights."

"Here were two people that I had to wake up to each day and hear them at each other's throats," Dion said when I asked what it had been like for him growing up in such a house. "So I found music. I found something of my own. And my father decided he knew about show business and was going to coach me. When he would try to tell me what to do, I would just shut off. I wanted to say, 'Get the fuck away from me. This is mine. You can't have this. *You*—you can't even control your own shit.'

"But even then, I sensed that my father maybe knew some things I could pick up on. He could paint a little bit. He could sculpt. He knew a little bit about music. I admired him for what I knew he did have on the ball. But I'd watch him from a distance, very careful not to get too close, because I didn't want to *be* like him."

I said that a lot of people I knew would have loved to have a father like Pasquale (who taught his son to shoplift, for example), instead of nine-to-fivers hidden behind newspapers at breakfast and dinner. Pasquale sounded pretty cool to me. I guess he was the sort of free spirit that any kid would want for a father, except the kid who's actually stuck with him.

"You hit it on the head, my friend," Dion said. "Ricky Guilliano, my oldest friend from the Bronx, who I'm still in touch with, *loves* my dad. He still talks about how my father used to take us to the park when we were kids and take his shirt and pants off and dive into the lake. Ricky loved that, and I guess I did, too. There were things about my father I thought were great. He was everybody's buddy, including mine."

But Dion didn't want a buddy?

"Exactly. I needed a father. Especially with the dynamics between him and my mom, you know? If we were going someplace in the car, to visit relatives or something, my mother would be telling my father, 'Now, don't talk so much, and when they mention *this*'—it didn't matter what it was—'don't you start up again.' She's directing him, and he's taking it. For a kid, it was a very aggravating thing to watch. They've been married over fifty years now, and they're still at it. My parents walk into this house, and we *know* that my mother read him the riot act in the car. Told him how to act, where to sit, what to say and what not to say. You can see it as soon as they walk in. It didn't use to be funny, but now that they're older, it's become a joke with us. We figure it must turn them on. We tease them about it every time they start to fight, and it stops them for a little while."

I asked Dion if he recognized anything about his father in himself— beyond artistic temperament.

"My father gave me his love for nature and a kind of different perspective on things," Dion said, drumming his fingers on the kitchen table and speaking very slowly, with long, expressive pauses. "It was very frustrating for me as a kid that he wasn't more respected, because in many ways I liked where he was coming from. I still do. He's seventy-six years old, and he's never been sick a day in his life. The only time he was sick was when my mother left him for a year. That totally wiped him out. But the reason he can brag about never having needed so much as an aspirin is that he's never had a worry or a responsibility that he recognized as his. He's never worked seriously at anything in his life. Work to him is a novelty. Emotionally, he's still a teenager. He plays at life. And seeing a man, a grown man, with his whimsy and his loose outlook on life—it's wonderful to watch. People love my father. You would love him. I look at him and think that we should all have a part of us that is like that. He's given me a childlike perspective. But I know that only goes so far.

"In a lot of ways I'm *just* like him. Which is funny. I tried to be just the opposite, because the message I got as a kid from my mother was 'Don't be like your father. He is why we never have enough money. He is why I'm a very unhappy woman. He is the reason for all our problems.' So my feeling was that I'm not going to be like him. When I get married, I'm gonna make my wife happy. But first, I'm going to make up for all of his mistakes. I'm going to make it up to my mother. I tried to be a surrogate husband to her, not in a physical way but in an emotional sense. I was going to be responsible for her feelings. Then, you grow up and you realize you have a terrible resentment toward this woman, because you're *not* responsible for her feelings. That's crazy, to think that you are.

"And you know, if a mother looks at her son and says, 'Son, I love you,' who is that person she loves? You have to let her know who you are. I got to a point where I had to say to her, 'This is me,' and who I was hurt her at first, I think, because she would have preferred to deal with a son who was strong and silent and made her proud without ever making a mistake or showing what he was feeling. Honor thy father and mother—in my family, that meant don't rock the boat. My mother's belief was that if you ever expressed what you were really feeling inside, your feelings could kill.

"What I'm trying to do is open her up, and she's coming along. But maybe not this week, if you see what I mean. She read the book—my book—and I talk about wanting to drive off a bridge and shooting up and cheating on Susan and putting myself and her through hell, and my mother's response was, 'What about your Uncle Mike? He was good to you.' What about Uncle Mike! She was worried that some of the relatives would be offended because I didn't mention them. I gave up. I said, 'Ma! Write your own damn book!'"

SUSAN CURLED UP TO READ ON THE L-SHAPED SECTIONAL, AND DION AND I went into the study so he could play me some of the tapes from Yo Frankie, the album he and Arista Records hoped would land him back on the charts.* Except for framed, still-in-their-sleeves 45s of "Where or When" and "Runaround Sue," and a blowup of Dion and Zach Glickman dressed as Doc Holliday and Zapata (a joke on Phil Spector, who, when he was producing Dion's Born to Be with You in 1976, would show up in the studio every day dressed as a different historical or fictional character), all of the memorabilia on the walls of Dion's study was from the most recent phase of his career. There was a poster announcing his 1987 comeback concert at Radio City Music Hall, with a diagonal SOLD OUT superimposed over it, and a photograph of him on stage with Paul Simon, Lou Reed, Bruce Springsteen, and Billy Joel at a 1987 Madison Square Garden benefit for homeless preschool children.

Dion warned me that he wasn't completely happy with his producer Dave Edmunds's mixes. "I'm gonna have to go into a studio down here and do some remixing," he said, handing me a lead sheet for a song called "King of the New York Streets," which he'd written with his frequent collaborator, the lyricist Bill Tuohy.

> People call me the scandalizer
> The world was my appetizer
> I turned gangs into fertilizer
> The king of the New York streets

---

*Yo Frankie, which was released in April 1989, stayed on the charts for eighteen weeks, though it never climbed higher than Number 132—not good enough to satisfy Arista, which dropped Dion. But he's still doing secular material and still writing new songs. He has recorded for Vision Records and Collectibles Records, independent labels based in Florida and Pennsylvania, respectively.

The fucking kid has rearrived! The beat was tough, but apparently not tough enough to satisfy Dion, who sat soundlessly strumming a black acoustic guitar as he listened to himself. "The backbeat has too much echo on it," he shouted over his recorded voice. "It slows down the strut."

> I didn't need no bodyguard
> I just ruled in my backyard
> Livin' fast, livin' hard
> King of the New York streets
> Well, I was wise in my own eyes
> I woke one day to realize
> You know, this attitude came from cocaine lies.

The myth-deflating last stanza wasn't on the lead sheet. "I added that," Dion said. "I mean, the guy in the song is *sincerely* deluded. But he has his pride, and the beat should reflect that. You know, that *attitude* you have walkin' down the street with your gang when you're young. I wanna hear the bass drum like a *thud* through the whole song."

Turning off the music, Dion suggested lunch at a nearby restaurant, where he likes the ziti with broccoli. Waiting with Susan while he changed upstairs, I asked her what her first impression of Dion had been when they were both teenagers in the Bronx (where she and her family had moved from Vermont).

"I was afraid of him, because he was two years older than me and had a pretty bad reputation," she said. "But I thought he was cute, and that can overcome a lot when you're that age. I used to take the bus home from school, and I would pass him every day. He'd be on the corner, outside the candy store where my bus stopped, and we just would look at each other. That went on for a long time, because he was too shy to ask me out. Then he went away for a year, to New Jersey. After that, the church had a St. Paddy's Day dance and talent show that I sang in with a couple of my girlfriends. He was in it, too, and I guess that's how we started to talk, during the rehearsals. Anyway, some more time went by without him asking me out. I belonged to a church sodality, and I finally asked *him* to one of our dances."

"Is that the one I came to in my Chinese shirt?" Dion asked, jingling his car keys.

"Yeah, he and his friend, Ricky, went to Harlem and bought these awful shirts with Chinese collars, black with gold polka dots," Susan explained, laughing.

"Black with gold polka dots!" Dion said. "We were *bad!*"

Like most commercial establishments in Boca Raton, the Italian restaurant was in a shopping center. In terms of atmosphere and "authenticity," it wasn't much different from the chain pizzeria that my Jewish in-laws had taken me to in Del Ray Beach the night before, which at least had checkered tablecloths. After we were served and Dion said grace, we chatted about Italian cuisine. "My mother's family comes from *Bari*," Dion said, giving it a Mediterranean pronunciation, "which is right above the heel of the boot. My father's parents were from *Abruzzi*, in the center, and *Calabria*, in the southeast. No Northern Italian or Sicilian," he said, gesturing toward Susan. "When we traveled through Italy by car a few years ago, starting at the top, from Switzerland, it was an education for me. At the top, the food is very light, lots of delicate wine sauces. But as you go south, the sauces get heavier and heavier, and redder and redder. By the time you get to Sicily, they're like tar."

Two men who were casual acquaintances of Dion and Susan stopped at our table on their way to the cashier. One of the men told Dion that he'd heard him in concert in Miami in June. But the conversation soon drifted to girls' soccer (August had just made varsity) and the subject of most of the conversations I'd overheard since arriving in Boca: who was thinking of moving "down here" (to Florida from New York, New Jersey, or Connecticut) and who was thinking of moving from "down there" (from Miami to Boca).

I took care of the bill, while Dion and Susan waited for me in the parking lot. Holding hands, they could have been anybody's middle-aged suburban neighbors, except that they were talking about Mississippi John Hurt.

"Susan wanted to adopt him, I think," Dion said.

"He looked at everybody in the audience in those coffeehouses as though they were entertaining *him*," Susan said.

On the road, I asked Dion if he used to slowly cruise the narrow streets of the Bronx in that white T-Bird of his with the radio blasting rock 'n' roll.

"Like this?" he asked, turning up the John Hiatt cassette we'd been listening to. "Remember, Sue?" he asked, squeezing her knee, as we sped along the six-lane highway in a steel-gray Volvo with the air conditioner on and the windows rolled up and John Hiatt singing about marital relationships at ear-splitting volume.

The Village Voice Rock & Roll Quarterly, Fall 1989

Index